Astrology for the Aquarian Age

Astrology for

the Aquarian Age

Alexandra Mark

An Essandess Special Edition New York

ACKNOWLEDGMENTS

Ever mindful that God helps those who help themselves, I have tried to be as scrupulously painstaking as possible in the preparation of this book: in the long hours spent in studying subjects which were so alien in the beginning and in the systematic organization of data accumulated from the great number of interviews with people who have sought my help over the years. In return for my labor, I have been very much aware of the Help that I have received every step of the way.

Words will have to do to express my gratitude to my husband, Vernon, whose knowledge and experience I drew upon heavily. His patience and loving counsel were a never-ending source of strength. No wife could ask for greater devotion.

In addition, I wish to express my thanks to the following individuals: to Mary Glidden, who introduced me to the world of astrology many years ago; to Dorothea Lynde, for those stimulating sessions of astrological give-and-take, whose common-sense approach to the subject encouraged me to delve deeper; to Jeff Mayo, whose more scientific approach served as a model for an orderly accumulation of data; to Ruth Montgomery, whose "Search for the Truth" led me to my own; to Mrs. Beatrice Moore, for her editorial assistance and perception which enabled her to see the deeper significance of this book; and to Jane Plimpton, for all her help whenever it was needed. And finally, my thanks to my children: Jeffrey, for his help in testing the charts; Daniel, for his helpful criticism; David, whose interest and enthusiasm were contagious; and my daughter, Valerie, for relieving me of some very tedious chores.

Brookline, 1970

ASTROLOGY FOR THE AQUARIAN AGE
SBN: 671–10397–0
Copyright, ©, 1970, by Alexandra Mark.
All rights reserved.
Published by ESSANDESS SPECIAL EDITIONS,
a division of Simon & Schuster, Inc.,
630 Fifth Avenue, New York, N.Y. 10020,
and on the same day in Canada by
Simon & Schuster of Canada, Ltd.,
Richmond Hill, Ontario.
Printed in the U.S.A.
Designed by The Etheredges

Contents

Introduction

The purpose of this book is to acquaint the reader with a nonmathematical approach to astrology whereby he can construct his own chart and test for himself, in his own life and in the lives of his family and friends, the validity of this fascinating subject. This will be accomplished not just with Sun signs or a table of ascendants, but with a detailed astrological profile of you, the reader.

In addition, I want to introduce an approach which utilizes the fourth dimension, time. I shall try to redefine the basis of astrology in a way that will be acceptable not only to the scientific community, but also to those talented young people who have it within their power to restore astrology to an acceptable position in the academic world.

One of the most common failings of contemporary astrologers is their chronic insistence on evoking such names as Galileo, Kepler, Tycho Brahe, Newton and Hippocrates to show what good company they're in. The logic of this reasoning is that if these brilliant men were sympathetic to astrology, then obviously there must be something to it. It is important to remember, however, that these great men whose names are still revered by us today were not astrologers, and whether these men believed in astrology is not known. But what is important to remember is that as educated men, who were ahead

1

of their times in many respects, they were curious about the art of prediction. That they were acquainted with some of these techniques does not make them astrologers. It does not even guarantee that they necessarily approved. They simply investigated the subject and became aware of its logic and, in some cases, for the sake of financial remuneration, were forced to cast horoscopes.

Isn't it significant that astrologers must go back several hundred years to find a favorable reference? Why has no contemporary scientist of world repute stepped forward to defend the art? Why is Jung the only psychiatrist of note to be used as a reference by astrologers? Can it be that present-day astrologers have not refined their theories or techniques to meet the critical requirements of modern scientific logic?

This question unfortunately strikes at the most vulnerable aspect of contemporary astrology. The entire body of astrological knowledge, handed down from generation to generation, has been accepted by many contemporary astrologers without a critical reappraisal and, in fact, without a true understanding of what astrology really is.

What is astrology? What is the significance of this term? How can we define it in relation to our new technological Aquarian age? How can we give it a meaning that has relevance to our everyday lives?

Astrology is the science of time. It is the synchronization of astronomical time with biological time, and the scientific facts which allow this correlation form the basis of every astrological chart. I will describe these facts in detail in the chapter entitled "Nature's Clock."

Today, some accredited astrologers place emphatic significance on Nature's clock. However, at the dawn of human civilization all of astrology was nurtured and kindled by superstition, magic and witchcraft. As you can understand, this was a reflection of the mental processes of the men who used and created it. Then as primitive man sharpened his powers of observation and learned to organize his ideas, he discovered the relationship and correlation between the movement of the planets and human behavior, and this discovery added to the development of the astrological craft. These correlations were organized into a systematic body of knowledge. They served astrology well and led to its acceptance by the priest-scientists and early scholars of Babylon, Egypt, Greece, and Rome as one of the basic scientific disciplines. Astrology ascended to undreamed-of heights of power and influence during the Middle Ages, but fell from scientific favor after the Renaissance. Now, centuries later, its real value is unrecognized, and it is considered by most people to be either an occult amusement or an exercise in character analysis.

However, the fact that this subject is not presently accepted by the entire scientific community is not a reflection on the intrinsic worth of astrology. Scientists are reluctant to accept anything that cannot be demonstrated repeatedly under specific laboratory test conditions. But because of an inherent prejudice, few scientists have bothered to subject astrological findings to the rigid statistical analysis that is necessary before a subject can gain acceptance. This is not the fault of astrology. Rather it is the fault of the scientist, for up until now he has not taken the time to learn what is happening. Instead, he has branded astrology as "hogwash," "nonsense," "a tool of the addle-brained." Is it? Is astrology simply for amusement? Is it to be thrown into the same category as tea-leaf and card reading? Is it superstitious nonsense? Why is the word of an academician any more acceptable than the word of educated men and women who have known how to use astrology and have demonstrated repeatedly through the centuries that it works? History shows us that scientists have often been slow to accept new theories of their colleagues who, in some instances, have had the unhappy fate of being ahead of their times.

Considering the tremendous skepticism and the negative viewpoints of many scientists, you might ask, "Why has astrology endured so long?" How has it happened that, in spite of the scorn and ridicule that have been heaped upon this subject, no one has yet completely succeeded in laying astrology to its final rest? Not only have the scholars tried, but so have kings and popes and emperors. Still, it remains stubbornly alive. The survival of astrology, generation after generation, century after century, is dependent on human acceptance and based upon human need. The fact is, a void exists in the lives of many people that needs to be filled. Despite the strides we have made that permit us to land humans on the moon, or to transplant human hearts, modern technology does not provide us with answers or reassurance for the many difficult problems we endure during our short and precarious existence on earth. In a similar fashion, traditional organized religions have proved inadequate to cope with all the problems produced by our technological society. As life has grown more and more complex, pure science or pure faith have not provided the answers that we need. So we can assume that astrology has remained alive because it fills a void and because it brings a promise: the promise that somewhere, somehow, life is meaningful and worthwhile.

But the fact that astrology has survived is not enough. The subject should no longer have to live in the shadows of superstition, witchcraft, magic and fortunetelling. The stigma of being a lonely, unwanted, and unloved stepchild of science must be erased once and for all.

Astrology is a subject which can be as complex or as simple as you make it. Some people are highly skilled in the field while others only dabble in it. But this is as it should be. Not all of us can do differential or integral calculus, but most of us can do simple addition and subtraction. Not all of us are proficient in chemistry or languages, but most of us can discuss these subjects generally. My purpose is to give the reader a very simple astrological education so that he may decide for himself whether or not he wants to pursue the subject further.

All of us have been exposed to astrology of the Sun signs through newspaper columns and small paperback books. "Taurus and Virgo make the best marriage combinations," we are told. We are warned to "beware of the Aries and Cancer combination." "Nonsense," I say. This book will explain just how meaningless these statements are. Sun signs have formed the basis for much astrological amusement. However, the Sun sign alone does not provide anything but the most general picture. It must be supplemented by other factors from your natal chart to provide you with meaningful information.

People are always asking me, "Do you really believe in astrology?" To be honest, I don't know whether or not I "believe" in it—I *use* it, and I have learned to use it successfully. It is neither my religion nor my faith, but it is my clock. I know how to tell *time*, and astrology has provided limitless help.

"It is a science," say some astrologers, yet the scientific aspects have never been proven. "It is an occult art," say others, yet these practitioners will spare no effort to withhold their secrets of "divination" from the public. "It is of the Divine Will," say the esoteric astrologers, so they make astrology a veritable religion. Is astrology any of these things, or is it none of them? We can only answer these questions through a study of the subject.

Much is being written about the new sexual revolution among the young. Is it a revolution or is it the same problem that has always existed? Books abound on the subject of sex, how-to-do-it manuals that explain techniques in detail—as simple to follow as a recipe book. Eroticism flourishes in books and in movies. The emphasis is on erotic love rather than romantic love. But an individual who understands himself astrologically is far less likely to blunder sexually than one who is uneducated in this subject, and the satisfaction that will come with understanding will certainly be worthwhile.

Help and direction from a competent astrologer can be invaluable, not because the astrologer is an "oracle," but because he can encourage you to focus your talents and energies in the right direction at the proper time. You see, the astrologer is a specialist in *time*. There is no area in our lives that is not related to or influenced by time—we live by it, we die by it. Time is the key to your life and your success, whether that be in politics, science, religion, art, or even marriage. The historical roots of astrology are not only tied to both religion and politics, but also to the origins of science. Indeed, the astrology of the future may provide the link between what we believe (religion) and what we know (science).

Finally, this book is dedicated to the young scientific student of astrology on whom the mantle of knowledge now falls. It is my fervent hope that he will wear it with courage, dignity and wisdom, for he will have in his hands a gift of God.

1

Astrology—Mystic Cult or Science?

This book was written to explain astrology and to teach you how to work out your own destiny with the aid of astrological tools. These tools have been surrounded by mystery and superstition, resulting in a great deal of misinformation and misunderstanding. The mystery, initiated by ancient Babylonian priests to keep the secrets of "divination" in the hands of a select few, has become a part of contemporary astrology. Let us then strip away the mystery and the misconceptions that have plagued astrology so that you can learn to use this valuable subject for your own purposes without having to rely upon complicated mathematics or astronomical processes.

Astrology has been in the doldrums for the last three hundred years because some of its early theories were found to be inaccurate. For example, the Copernican revolution established that the Sun, not the Earth, occupied the central position in the solar system. Also, physicists explained the principles of the Moon's effects on the tides on a physical basis which could have no effect on brain function, and meteorologists explained the weather cycles without evoking a metaphysical relationship between each individual and the Sun.

Because of these discrepancies in early astrological dogma, society has not unanimously embraced astrology, and the subject has been downgraded by scientists as having no fixed rational basis. The condemnation of astrology by scientists was partially valid, but their criticisms revealed in the "Zodiac debate" were unjust: When the Zodiac was first discovered, the sign Aries was seen against the background of the constellation Aries. Then, due to the Precession of the Equinoxes, the signs of the Zodiac no longer lined up with the constellations of the same name. This fact was responsible for considerable confusion and astrology, because of this, was believed to be unreliable. There is no real significance, however, in the relationships of the signs of the Zodiac to the constellations in terms of astrological usefulness to the individual. We are, in fact, using the astrological clock to help you tell your own time. This is an individual time scale and not a universal one. There is no absolute time on an astrological clock (or any other clock, for that matter), and this ancient criticism of astrology is meaningless.

The chief criticism of astrology by scientists is that they cannot see why there should be a cause-and-effect relationship between astronomical events and human events. The contemporary astrologers were not able to help. Modern astrologers, while they have made a sincere effort to promote the subject, are not, for the most part, scientifically oriented. They have tried to graft popular new scientific concepts onto old fallacies—and it will not work. They confuse the scientists, they confuse and disillusion the public, and they confuse themselves. If we want to study and understand astrology, we must discard the old theories related to untenable Moon "forces" and Sun "forces" that supposedly affect us and look to a rational explanation of how and why astrology works. This new explanation must be consistent with scientific facts and useful to the new astrology student, for if he understands the theory, the practice will be easier and the results more accurate. And when you learn to map your own future with regard to your career, love, sex, and marriage (to name just a few areas where astrology can be most helpful), you will discover for yourself that there is validity to this subject and astrology will work for you, even in the absence of advanced complicated techniques.

Let's begin by describing a workable basis for modern astrology. In order to do this, we must first know the true meaning of our subject. What are we talking about when we use the word "astrology"? In essence, we are talking about *time*. And to tell time, we must have a clock. Here, then, is the real meaning of astrology. It is the study of Nature's clock—a clock of such gigantic proportions that few people have the imagination to comprehend its scope. The reason that the study of astrology has been so difficult is that the workings of Nature's timepiece are not yet fully understood. The machinery of this vast and wonderful celestial object is as intricate and complicated as the most precise watch; however, there are few competent "jewelers" to explain the mechanism. But you need not be a "jeweler" to use astrology, any more than you need be a watchmaker to tell time. A general knowledge of how a timepiece works does, however, give you confidence that the readings from the face of the clock are valid. In a similar way it is important to know the theory and facts which form the basis of astrology, for they provide the understanding that is necessary to tell astrological time accurately.

②

Nature's Clock

We have defined astrology as Nature's clock, a timepiece of unprecedented scope and accuracy, but a timepiece that has never been subjected to scientific verification. Until now, there has been no valid scientific theory to explain how astrology works. No one has been able to tell why there is a correlation between what we see in the heavens and what we know to be true in the pattern of human events.

It has been maintained that the Moon, Sun, and other planets and stars exert a direct physical, gravitational, or electromagnetic force that influences human behavior. Some astrologers contend that since the Moon can exert powerful forces on the ocean's tides, it can exert powerful electromagnetic or gravitational forces that alter and guide human behavior.

Unfortunately, there is no solid scientific evidence to back up these theories. Brain scientists have shown that electromagnetic currents have to be applied to the brain itself in order to produce statistically reliable responses. Attempts to explain the lunar effect on the tides have been based on physical laws which separate this effect from the physical forces that could change human behavior. Gravity (or lack of it) does not significantly alter human behavior or human brain waves. The astronauts, for example, have not only escaped the Earth's gravitational pull, but have traveled to the surface of the Moon without any noticeable change in behavior or personality.

In this chapter, we will examine new scientific evidence that could form a theoretical basis that will relate astronomy to human affairs. This correlation is based on a measure of time. Let us, as a first step, take a look at the celestial vault to see if we can sketch in our minds the timepiece used by astrologers.

The heavens as we see them are not a complete unit. From our vantage point on Earth, we are limited to those portions of the heavens that we can see either with the naked eye or with the complex instruments that astronomers use. For the purpose of defining Nature's clock, however, we should be more selective than the astronomer. We should consider only that section of the celestial vault known as the "ecliptic," and this, in fact, is the face of the clock you will be studying.

What is the ecliptic? It is the circular path that the Sun seems to follow in its yearly journey around the Earth. In reality, however, the ecliptic is that great circular path defined by the Earth as it revolves on its own axis around the Sun. As we all know, the Earth requires a little over 365 days to complete this orbit. The Sun is the spatial center of gravity for the Earth and for the other planets of the solar system. The ecliptic, then, is not only the actual path taken by the Earth as it orbits around the Sun, but it also corresponds rather closely to the plane of the orbits of the other major planets. The ecliptic derives its name from the fact that an eclipse can occur only when the Moon is very near or in the path of this orbit. The Sun can never be out of the ecliptic. Thus, the ecliptic becomes a reference point for the entire solar system.

Now that we have defined the face of Nature's clock as the ecliptic, we should learn the other parts that are required to tell time. Of course, we need two hands. Since Nature's clock in the heavens is not formed like a man-made timepiece, the symbols for the various parts, such as the hands, will obviously not look like the mechanical hands to which we are accustomed, but they will serve our purpose every bit as effectively. Let us, therefore, use the "luminaries"—the Sun and the Moon—to serve as the primary hands on the face of our clock and the eight planets as the secondary hands. The Sun and the Moon help us to tell time very accurately here on Earth, yet if we were in outer space, we might find the cycles of other orbiting planets more useful. But you and I are Earth people, interested in what happens from our Earth observation platform.

We already know that the Earth's orbit has traced out the face of the clock, the ecliptic. Now let us examine the face of the clock in more detail by considering that belt of the heavens which has the ecliptic as its center. This belt, which extends about 8° on either side of the ecliptic, is known as the Zodiac, a word which is derived from the Greek, meaning "small figure" or "image." The Zodiac, an ellipse containing 360°, is divided into twelve equal segments of 30° each. These segments were not only given names by the early astrologers-astronomers, but they were assigned numbers which correspond to the segments which we will start calling "houses." This will be discussed fully in Chapter 4. The twelve segments, like an evenly sectioned pie, form a relatively stationary background by which we can measure the apparent movement of the Sun, the Moon, and the other planets of the solar system. In other words, these segments become the numerals of our clock.

Now you should have a clear picture of the face of our clock: the ecliptic, with its two primary hands, the luminaries; its secondary hands, the planets; and its twelve numerals, the Zodiac. What is still missing? We must look for the works, the part that contains the jeweled movement responsible for keeping the clock running. What makes our celestial clock tick? Does it need winding? Will it ever stop? At this moment we do not have all the answers. But let us assume that the Earth's gravitational and magnetic field is the jeweled movement of our clock. Our clock, then, is a gravitational and magnetic one, and the forces which keep the planets and luminaries moving in spacial orbits are the same forces that keep our celestial timepiece ticking.

Now we have a reasonably complete picture of Nature's clock as it appears to the astrologer. It is not a conventional clock in that the numerals move. That is because we are not looking at the moving parts of the clock from a fixed position, since the Earth is constantly moving in a patterned orbit. A skeptic would ask if this clock is accurate. I can only answer that the measure of time is relative, and that since the hands of our clock—the Sun and the Moon—fix the measure of time we use on Earth, we can assume it is accurate. Moreover, the movement of the other planets in the solar system is not only rhythmic in relation to the Sun, but predictable according to our own measurement of time on Earth. However, one part of Nature's clock is not more accurate than another—the different parts are susceptible to different uses.

While all of us have a need to tell time, the need is not for the same purpose. The astronomer needs to read the clock for one set of values, the doctor needs it for another. The farmer, the minister, and the housewife all require the knowledge of time, but not necessarily for the same reasons.

Let us first look at Nature's clock from the point of view of the physicist and see how he tells time. He knows that the entire Universe is in constant motion. Motion is present not only in the constellations of the stars, but in our familiar earthly environment and in the tiny invisible atoms and subatomic particles of energy that make up all living and nonliving things. Scientists have been amazed at the constantly recurring cycles in our universe. This has been true not only in the astronomer's observations of the stars and planets in interstellar space, but in the physicist's and chemist's determination of the structure of submicroscopic molecules and atoms that are the building blocks of nature. Since we are convinced that the cycles are orderly, it isn't likely that the motion of these particles is disorderly. What are the facts that we can measure and observe to prove this point to ourselves? First, we can measure the characteristics of certain forms of energy, such as light, sound, and electricity. We find that these forms of energy not only move, but they move with a definite speed and wave length. Modern physics teaches us that the waves of energy are made up of particles, but no one has denied that there is a characteristic and basic rhythmicity that is part and parcel of every known form of energy. In other words, the movement of these energy particles in light waves or sound waves is not random; it is precise and rhythmic and predictable. This movement, in fact, forms one of the basic rhythms of Nature.

At one time, scientists thought the atom was constructed like our solar system. They postulated that the nucleus was like our Sun and that the electrons were like the planets—each revolving in its own orbit around the nucleus. This theory is no longer accepted by the physicist, but this does not mean that electrons are in random motion around the nucleus. A new science called "quantum mechanics" has predicted that atomic electrons form a pattern of waves that is restricted (because of the attracting force of the nucleus) to a very small region around the nucleus. Although these waves are not confined, as in older atomic models, to a definite boundary, they are limited to a very precise series of patterns. These patterns are rhythmic and predictable. Thus, even the smallest particles we know of take part in Nature's time sequence.

This rhythmicity of subatomic particles can be demonstrated in another way, and that is by the study of radioactive substances.

These radioactive elements, or isotopes, have, as we know, a very unstable nucleus that stabilizes itself by emitting radiation. The *rate* at which this radiation is emitted is constant for each element and is measured as the "half life" of a given radioactive element or isotope. Now some isotopes, such as carbon 14, decay (i.e., emit radiation) very slowly over thousands of years. Yet this decay occurs at an absolutely constant rate. It is so constant, in fact, that the decay of isotopes like carbon 14 can be used as an *atomic clock**, and this clock can actually measure the antiquity of prehistoric civilizations or the age of any organic material. The atomic clock is one way by which the physicist tells time, and it represents another of Nature's basic rhythms.

From the physicist's point of view, elementary particles as well as the basic elements of energy have a movement which is both rhythmic and predictable. Indeed it must be so, for if our moving Universe were not both patterned and rhythmic, the world would be a nightmare of unaccountable disorder and life would be impossible. The bridge formed by astrology, relating the order of the Universe to the order of life, is based on a measure of time. However, as I previously pointed out, some ancient and even contemporary astrologers believed that the planets and luminaries exerted direct physical forces that controlled human behavior just as they controlled the tides and seasons. But as classical physics advanced and the relationships between the Moon and the tides and the Sun and the seasons were explained, scientists concluded that the physical basis of astrology had been disproved. They then discarded as worthless the mass of information which had been set down by intelligent men over thousands of years relating the rhythms of human activity to the celestial clock of our solar system. You can question whether this action was justified or whether it was another gigantic blunder of partially informed people blindly searching for "immediate truth" with dull and inadequate instruments. Then you can answer yourself. Just look for the relationship between the physical world of the astronomer and the biological world of human activity. If a relationship exists, it must be a temporal one; yet time is the one dimension that was ignored by those scientists who felt that astrology had no theoretical foundation. We have learned that there is an atomic clock used by physicists to tell time, but how does the biolo-

---

* *The physicist also uses the transitions and inversion frequencies in the spectrum of certain elements, such as cesium and hydrogen, to tell time. These frequencies are so rapid that they cannot be used directly, but they can be modulated to regulate an electric clock. This system is also sometimes known as the "atomic clock."*

gist tell time? Is there also a biological clock? Do living things exhibit an orderly rhythm that could be related to our celestial clock? The evidence here is clear-cut in both plant and animal life.

Biologists have discovered that all plants have a diurnal twenty-four-hour cycle. To this they have attached the name "circadian rhythm." The word "circadian" is derived from the Latin *circa,* meaning "about," and *dies,* meaning "day." Some types of plants, for example, spread their leaves during the day and raise them to stem at night. Biologists noted that this rhythm continued on a twenty-four-hour cycle even when the plants were kept in total darkness. Moreover, in some simple plants luminescence, photosynthesis, and cell division were shown to have separate circadian rhythms unrelated to environment. There is in these plants a compensating mechanism that keeps the circadian rhythm unchanged. In other words, these plants have an internal biological clock that protects and preserves their natural rhythm in spite of changes in their environment. This has been proven by experiments carried out in botanical laboratories.

Animals also exhibit this rhythmic phenomenon. Think about it. From the wake-sleep cycle (which is a reflection of our rhythmic brain waves) , to our heartbeat, to our unconscious rhythmic breathing, to the recurring menstrual cycle of the reproductive human female, rhythmicity abounds in everyday life. Before discussing the human biological clock, however, it may be well to describe the ubiquitous evidence of the cyclical phenomena in lower animal forms.

The seasonal changes in the behavior of birds and mammals is of a definite cyclic nature and has been repeatedly described. Some of these changes, such as the migration of birds, are said to be an adaptation to climate, and many of them are related to the behavior of reproduction.

The palolo worm, an inhabitant of the South Pacific, is a spectacular example of this kind of behavior. This marine worm spawns only on special days in October and November as the Moon reaches its last quarter. Similar spawning habits are seen in a certain marine worm which inhabits the Atlantic coast of America. This worm is called the nereid worm, and it spawns at a different, although equally regular, time of the year.

It is often difficult to subject the rhythms of wild animals to the rigid conditions of the laboratory, but we must do so in an effort to test for the existence of circadian rhythms and the presence of a biological clock. There is one group of animals that can be readily tested; this group includes the "social insects," such as ants, termites, wasps, and bees. It is with this last group, the bees, that we shall demonstrate the existence of the circadian rhythm, for there has been a significant amount of research done on them. One of the very best descriptive studies on bees was carried out by Dr. Karl von Frisch in his book entitled *The Dance Language and Orientation of the Bee.* He reviewed the evidence that bees have an internal clock and that this clock is attuned to a twenty-four-hour cycle. It was discovered by biologists that they could regulate the time of feeding and collecting of pollen in the honey bee, but they could only accomplish this training on a twenty-four-hour cycle. They tried training the bees to a nineteen-hour cycle and a forty-eight-hour cycle, but they were not successful in rearranging the natural time clock of the bees. They even tried to regulate the larval period to a nineteen-hour day in the hope that they could ultimately change the bees' rhythms, but this too failed. The bees remained irrevocably on their own circadian cycle. It is my guess that this cycle has been firmly imprinted on their primitive nervous systems, and it cannot be altered except by very drastic measures which might ultimately destroy bee life.

Biological clocks and circadian rhythms exist extensively in the entire animal world. Hamsters, rats and other nocturnal animals, for example, show regular periods of night activity even when they are not given any environmental clues as to whether it is day or night. For reasons which we do not completely understand, the time of day also affects the susceptibility of certain animals to poisons. A dose of poison that will kill 10% of a beetle population at dawn will kill 90% of them three hours later. Furthermore, rats are more susceptible to radiation poison at night than in the daytime.

Reports on the daily fluctuations in the human being are even more unique. For example, humans are more apt to be born or to die between the hours of three and four in the morning. There is a two-degree fluctuation of body temperature during a twenty-four-hour period, and this fluctuation has a reproducible and characteristic pattern for each human being in good health. In addition, blood pressure, pulse rate, hormone secretion, blood electrolyte levels and sedimentation rate all vary according to a diurnal or circadian rhythm. Some surgeons who have studied these rhythms feel that the variation is so important that the optimal time for surgical procedures ought to be calculated according to the circadian rhythm of each individual patient who needs an operation. As in the case of the bee, the circadian rhythm is undoubtedly controlled in the brain. This fact is strongly substantiated by the results of investigations by West Coast brain surgeons which show that the circadian cycles are disturbed by the existence of brain abnormalities, such as Parkinson's Disease. In these instances, the daily cycle is shortened and time appears to pass more rapidly for these brain-diseased victims. It has been established, too, that patients afflicted with brain fever (encephalitis) may actually have a reversal of their day–night patterns.

Thus, we can conclude that rhythmic movement does exist in all living things and that the biological clock has as important a function as the atomic or astronomical clock. Furthermore, we know that the biological clock is a part of every human being.

Now, how can we relate the human biological clock to the great celestial clock of the astrologer? There is a great deal of evidence to demonstrate that the moment of birth will, to a very large extent, influence the course of an individual's life. (See Chapter 3 for a more detailed discussion.)

Since the human biological clock is regulated by the brain, it is not surprising that the neurological milestones such as sitting, standing, walking, and talking are roughly similar in children born on the same day. Furthermore, the reproductive cycle (a striking example of the biological clock) is intimately related to the celestial clock. The human menstrual cycle bears a close relation to the phases of the Moon, and, indeed, it has an ultimate relation to the natal day. Moreover, the period of gestation (that period between conception and birth of a human child) bears a fixed relationship to the celestial clock, and this time is almost always precise in the development of every human fetus.

The circadian rhythms controlled by the human biological clock have a definite relationship to the time cycles described by the Sun and the Moon. Consider this point: At one time, the limitations on travel made it impossible for a human being to get his biological clock out of step with his environment. The Jet Age, however, has brought the inherent rhythmicity of man in conflict with his environmental changes. An individual flying four thousand miles from West to East will experience a derangement of his biological clock. This is recognized by physicians. For example, diplomats are allowed to rest after a long flight to allow their circadian rhythms to adjust to a new time pattern, because a man in such tired condition might be subject to faulty judgment. Now, note that a four-thousand-mile flight from North to South produces no derangements of the biological clock. The reason is that when a man travels from West to East, his own clock must race the celestial clock to catch up with local time, and his body must overwork to make the adjustment in a hurry.

You may ask how we can verify the more detailed predictions of astrology concerning complex facets of human behavior. The answer is that it is not easy to verify any causal relationships to human behavior, and this is true whether you approach the topic from the point of view of a psychologist, psychiatrist or sociologist, or from an astrological point of view. Biological phenomena are not as easy to define with mathematical certainty as physical phenomena, and behavioral data are more complex than most other forms of biological information. A forward step was introduced with the advent of the mathematics of chance (originally related to the mathematics of gambling), which provided a valid basis for deciding whether the relation between two phenomena is genuine or factitious. This kind of mathematics will tell us whether two occurrences are related by some causal link (even if the mechanism is unknown), or whether the relationship is a vagary of chance. Sometimes there is an apparent correlation, because two things occur in a time sequence that makes us believe they are related. But only repeated and controlled observations will show us whether or not the relation is real.

Chance and chance alone may bring unrelated occurrences together and confuse a casual observer into believing they are related. These correlations have crept into many fields of science. However, the intelligent application of the mathematics of chance, called statistical analysis, has enabled us to keep and to build on those correlations which are valid, and to discard those which are the results of chance alone.

Unfortunately, the statistical method has never been effectively applied to the science of astrology. Astrologers, for the most part, have not been trained in the scientific method, and those few scientists who have tried to test the subject have not been sufficiently trained in astrology. Moreover, physical scientists and mathematicians have not been interested enough to test astrological hypotheses. Many "pure" scientists have taken an unscientific attitude toward astrology and rejected its tenets without giving it the statistical tests that they use for many less worthy ideas.

We are at present in an era where the complex relationships between planetary movements and human events are open to mathematical scrutiny through the use of statistical methods, Experiments could be performed using the same statistical methods employed by physicians to see if a new treatment is effective, or by biological scientists to see if an observation is valid. Criteria could be established by comparing fifty or one hundred subjects whose exact natal charts were available and from whom an accurate history could be taken by a neutral scientific observer. Then the correlation or lack of correlation between the events indicated by their natal charts and the actual events that take place at a particular time in their lives could be computed by mathematical processes. By the use of control groups and the mathematics of statistics, we could find out whether these relations are valid (i.e., have some causal link) or whether they occur by chance alone. This, hopefully, will be the task of the new generation of astrologers trained in the latest techniques of statistics. My task, I feel, is to point the way.

3

You and Your Biological Clock

You have learned thus far that astrology is essentially the art and practice of reading Nature's clock. You have learned that Nature's clock is composed of the luminaries, the planets, the Zodiac, and the ecliptic—and that these elements are part and parcel of our physical environment. Scientists have agreed that man cannot be separated from his environment without serious consequences; therefore, it is imperative that we look at every aspect of our environment without bias.

It also has been established that animals and mankind possess a biological clock. Since man is a unique animal, it is not surprising to find that his clock is unique—unlike that of the palolo worm, or the bee, for example. Let us now look at the human biological clock from the point of view of astrology.

To begin with, the most important organ in the human body is the brain. Without the brain there can be neither life nor meaningful behavior. If, for instance, the brain is damaged at birth, depending upon the extent of the injury, we have a corresponding alteration or aberration in the human body or in its behavior. With severe brain damage, life may be extinguished. Even though the heart may continue to beat, doctors now define death as the moment at which brain waves cease to register. Why should this be so? What is there about the brain that sustains life? We cannot answer this question any more scientifically than we can answer the question, "How does the sun support the life of our solar system?" In a general way, the principle function of these two bodies is similar. That is, the sun of Nature's clock performs the same function as the brain of the human biological clock. The fact is that humans are all timepieces, ticking away at differing speeds, mounted in a variety of "cases," but all with essentially the same equipment.

The first thing that a jeweler does to a new clock is to set it. In other words, he *synchronizes* the timepiece to the local time in the area to harmonize with the rest of the clocks and watches. If this were not done, the new timepiece would be absolutely worthless— that is, as an indicator of the correct diurnal time.

So it is at birth that we humans—all of us miniature timepieces of the Universe—are synchronized with the clock in the heavens. This carries absolutely no implication that the planets and luminaries which compose Nature's clock *affect us directly*. It only means that at the precise moment you enter this world and take your first breath, the "machinery" of your clock has been set in motion. For it is now that the tiny lungs have filled with air and the brain has begun to receive its first messages from an independent environment. You are now "ticking" away on your own, but remember, the key here is synchronization. You may be on your own, but your biological clock has been "set" by nature according to the time registered on the celestial clock at the moment of your birth.

If, then, the relationship of your human clock to that of the astrological clock is one of synchronization, it should be possible to show how, by the movement of the hands of the celestial clock, you can tell what astrological time it is for you. Isn't that the purpose of any clock? The important step now is to learn the process of determining astrological time.

4

The ABC's of Astrology

First, you must know how to recognize the symbols and to learn the meanings of the planets and luminaries (the hands of your clock), as well as the houses and numerals (the face of your clock).

Let us look at the signs of the Zodiac which are the numerals. There are twelve signs: Aries, Taurus, Gemini, Cancer, Leo, Virgo, Libra, Scorpio, Sagittarius, Capricorn, Aquarius, and Pisces. This order is not random or haphazard, but is based on the position of the Sun as it travels through the various signs of the Zodiac. In reality, the Sun hardly moves at all, but each month of the year, because our Earth is revolving on its axis around the Sun, it is seen against the background of a different sign of the Zodiac. The approximate dates of the Sun's "entrance" into these signs are as follows:

ARIES	*March 21 to April 20*	Vernal Equinox
TAURUS	*April 21 to May 20*	
GEMINI	*May 21 to June 20*	
CANCER	*June 21 to July 22*	Summer Solstice
LEO	*July 23 to August 22*	
VIRGO	*August 23 to September 23*	
LIBRA	*September 24 to October 23*	Autumnal Equinox

SCORPIO	*October 24 to November 21*	
SAGITTARIUS	*November 22 to December 21*	
CAPRICORN	*December 22 to January 19*	Winter Solstice
AQUARIUS	*January 20 to February 18*	
PISCES	*February 19 to March 20*	

These dates can vary by a day or so in times of sign changes.

Each of these signs represents either a human figure, a living thing or an image, and has a corresponding symbol. It is important to learn them:

ARIES	♈	The ram
TAURUS	♉	The bull
GEMINI	♊	The twins
CANCER	♋	The crab
LEO	♌	The lion
VIRGO	♍	The virgin
LIBRA	♎	The scales
SCORPIO	♏	The scorpion
SAGITTARIUS	♐	The archer
CAPRICORN	♑	The goat
AQUARIUS	♒	The water bearer
PISCES	♓	The fish

Each of these signs has a planetary "ruler." This ruling planet expresses many of the same qualities as the sign it rules. These rulerships are based on long standing empirical observations and correlations. The signs and their ruling planets are as follows:

ARIES is ruled by Mars
TAURUS is ruled by Venus
GEMINI is ruled by Mercury
CANCER is ruled by the Moon
LEO is ruled by the Sun
VIRGO is ruled by Mercury
LIBRA is ruled by Venus
SCORPIO is ruled by Mars and Pluto
SAGITTARIUS is ruled by Jupiter
CAPRICORN is ruled by Saturn
AQUARIUS is ruled by Saturn and Uranus
PISCES is ruled by Neptune and Jupiter

You must learn that each of these signs is associated with a particular house. This means that there is a similarity between the principle of the sign and the nature of the house:

ARIES	The first house
TAURUS	The second house
GEMINI	The third house
CANCER	The fourth house
LEO	The fifth house
VIRGO	The sixth house
LIBRA	The seventh house
SCORPIO	The eighth house
SAGITTARIUS	The ninth house
CAPRICORN	The tenth house
AQUARIUS	The eleventh house
PISCES	The twelfth house

Each of these signs is correlated with certain characteristics or qualities, and these qualities can be divided into both positive and negative aspects. Let us look at some of them:

ARIES
(*pioneers*)
+ outgoing, original, dynamic
− foolhardy, low self-sufficiency, deceitful

TAURUS
(*builds*)
+ loyal, dependable, patient
− excessive pride, self-indulgent, greedy

GEMINI
(*communicates*)
+ versatile, genial, creative
− two-faced, superficial, unstable

CANCER
(*nourishes*)
+ retentive, maternal, protective
− possessive, retiring, moody

LEO
(*dramatizes*)
+ regal, entertaining, commanding
− pompous, domineering, conceited

VIRGO
(*analyzes*)
+ practical, analytical, intellectual
− critical, hypochondriacal, prim

LIBRA
(*conciliates*)
+ romantic, aesthetic, judicial
− lazy, temperamental, superficial

SCORPIO
(*investigates*)
+ scientific, passionate, dedicated
− secretive, revengeful, cold-blooded

SAGITTARIUS	+ jovial, prophetic, logical
(*philosophizes*)	− blunt, fanatical, intolerant
CAPRICORN	+ executive, conservative, persevering
(*directs*)	− depressive, miserly, pessimistic
AQUARIUS	+ diplomatic, altruistic, inventive
(*humanizes*)	− selfish, eccentric, impulsive
PISCES	+ intuitive, sympathetic, artistic
(*harmonizes*)	− martyr, indecisive, melancholy

Let us now consider the planets and their symbols. (In astrological parlance, the luminaries—i.e., the Sun and the Moon—are considered planets since they are all moving hands of Nature's clock. The Sun and the Moon are the "primary hands" of Nature's clock; the other eight planets are "secondary hands," but very useful, nonetheless.)

The Sun	☉	Jupiter	♃
The Moon	☽	Saturn	♄
Mercury	☿	Uranus	♅
Venus	♀	Neptune	♆
Mars	♂	Pluto	♇

The principle of each planet can be expressed in a single key word:

The Sun	vitality
The Moon	moods
Mercury	communications
Venus	emotions
Mars	energy
Jupiter	expansion
Saturn	lessons
Uranus	opportunities
Neptune	idealism
Pluto	change

The face of Nature's clock, the ecliptic, is an ellipse of 360° and is divided into twelve equal, pie-shaped segments, or "houses," of 30° each (see Figure 1). Study these houses carefully in terms of characteristics and activities, for they make up the face of our clock.

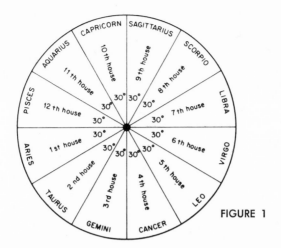

FIGURE 1

DIVISION OF SIGNS OF THE ZODIAC INTO TWELVE HOUSES

FIRST HOUSE	outlook on life, physical body
SECOND HOUSE	possessions, income earned
THIRD HOUSE	short journeys, neighbors, brothers and sisters, letters, writing and communications, early education
FOURTH HOUSE	early environment, real estate, home and family, parents
FIFTH HOUSE	romances, children, speculations, pleasures, school functions, talents and hobbies, "brain" children
SIXTH HOUSE	health, service to others, employees, small pets, work and employment
SEVENTH HOUSE	business partners, marriage partner, close friends, open enemies, public activities, contracts, doctors, lawyers, dentists
EIGHTH HOUSE	partnership finances, legacies, wills, sex, birth, occult subjects, insurance
NINTH HOUSE	long-distance or overseas travel, reasoning, higher learning, philosophy, attorneys, mental outlook, judges, clergymen, professors

TENTH HOUSE	prestige, career, social recognition, administrators, politicians
ELEVENTH HOUSE	acquaintances, clubs and organizations, aspirations, casual friendships, get-togethers, altruism
TWELFTH HOUSE	subconscious, institutions, universities, prisons, banks, hospitals, libraries, hidden enemies, intuition, inspiration, dream and sleep patterns, solitary pursuits, large pets

In summary, we have covered the symbols of Nature's clock. It is important to commit these to memory. Not only will this enable you to read the ephemeris in the back of the book, but it will serve as a solid first step in helping you to construct your own natal chart. Before you can accomplish this, however, you must learn how to put these symbols together to form a natal chart, or what could be called *a single setting of Nature's clock.*

In the next two chapters, you will learn not only how to construct a horoscope (natal chart), but how to use it. In other words, you are going to learn to tell time from Nature's clock.

⑤

Clock Watching

Learning to recognize and to read the astrological clock (Nature's clock) is vastly different from reading the timepiece we all know from early childhood. We cannot study Nature's clock by picking it up, for this clock is in the heavens. Let us, therefore, use diagrams which represent the celestial timepiece and compare this to an ordinary clock.

Look at Figure 2. The face of the clock represents the ecliptic. (In reality this would be more elliptical than circular.) In the center of the clock we have placed the Earth, because it is from this vantage point that we measure the distances and calculate the speeds of the orbiting planets as they travel through the ecliptic. (In reality, the Earth, too, is moving in the ecliptic.) Now look at Figure 3, which is a diagram of an ordinary clock, and you will notice one very big difference between the two: The celestial clock is numbered *counterclockwise*. Also, our regular clock shows twelve o'clock to be the highest point, while the celestial clock shows the Zodiacal sign Capricorn* in this position. Thus, when the hands of the regular clock are in the noon position, the Sun is in the same position (i.e., at the top) in the celestial clock. It occupies the tenth house.

* *This sign is said to "rule" the tenth house and occupies the most elevated position of the Zodiac.*

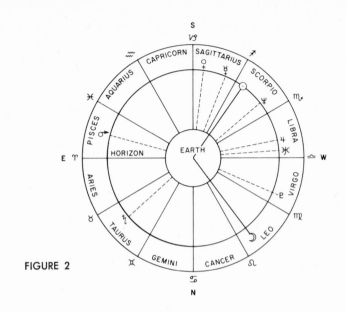

FIGURE 2

NATURE'S CLOCK AS IT APPEARS FROM EARTH

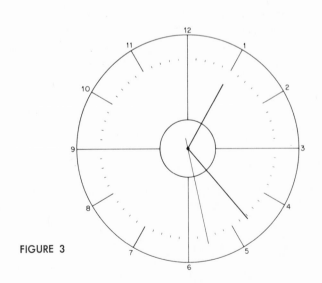

FIGURE 3

REGULAR CLOCK

You will note, too, that the regular clock has numbers, Roman numerals, or some other kind of marking to indicate the separations of the twelve hours, while Nature's clock uses the Zodiacal signs. Each of the twelve segments in Nature's clock is composed of 30°, and each segment is referred to as a "house." At the point where one house ends and another one begins, we have what is called a "cusp," and to make it easier to read, the symbol for the sign is usually placed at the cusp.

As the table in Chapter 4 indicates, the sign Aries correlates with the first house, and Figure 2 shows our clock at a time when this is the case. But as there is a constant movement of the signs in a clockwise direction at the rate of one degree every four minutes, a new sign appears on the cusp of the first house approximately every two hours. In a twenty-four-hour period there is one complete rotation of every sign over this first house cusp.

Each of these clocks has two primary hands. These are the hour and minute hands for a regular clock and the Sun and the Moon for an astrological clock. While the regular clock has one secondary hand (the second hand), Nature's clock has many. These are the eight planets: Mercury, Venus, Mars, Jupiter, Saturn, Uranus, Neptune, and Pluto. They move at different speeds and are used to tell not only present time, but future time as well.

You can see, then, that every part of Nature's clock is instructive, and in the next chapter you will learn how it applies to you.

6

How to Construct Your Natal Chart

Now you are ready to set up your own natal chart, or horoscope, as it is often called. The natal chart is nothing more than a diagram relating the time that was registered on Nature's clock at the moment of your birth. For those of you who do not know the true time of your birth, this chart will be based on the time shown on Nature's clock on the *day* of your birth. I want to make it clear that a horoscope is simply a diagrammatic representation of a moment of time, based on the astronomical calculations of the positions of the luminaries and the planets, showing their particular relationships to each other at a given longitude and latitude on the day of your birth. It is much simpler than it sounds.

To the beginner, the mathematics of astrology seem hopelessly complicated, and many people become discouraged by the endless adjustments and conversions that must be made to their birth time before it can be used to erect a chart. We are going to do away with all the complicated mathematics. My purpose is to get this useful tool into your hands as soon as possible. If astrology is valid, you must be shown that it will work even in the absence of advanced techniques; if you can demonstrate for yourself that it "works," you very likely will decide to study the more advanced procedures at a later date.

For our purposes, we will use two kinds of charts: the Solar chart and the Equal House chart. A Solar chart is one in which the Zodiacal sign and degree of the Sun are placed on the cusp of the first house and the rest of the signs are placed on each of the eleven remaining cusps in their natural sequence—counterclockwise.* An Equal House chart is one in which the sign and approximate degree of your *ascendant* is placed on the cusp of the first house.** This ascendant is determined by finding the approximate time of your birth in the table of ascendants in the back of the book. Your Sun is then placed in the appropriate *house* that contains the same sign that your Sun is in.

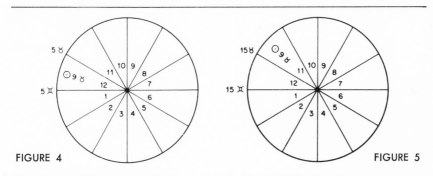

FIGURE 4   FIGURE 5

For example, if you were born on April 30th, your Sun will be in approximately 9 degrees of Taurus. If on that same day your birth occurred at 6:30 A.M., the sign Gemini will be rising and is placed on the cusp of the first house and is then referred to as your ascendant. According to the natural sequence of Zodiacal signs, Taurus will be on the cusp of the twelfth house (for it is the sign that precedes Gemini) and your Sun will "fall in" either the eleventh or the twelfth house—depending on the number of degrees of the Sun with relation to the number of degrees on your ascendant. If five degrees of Gemini are rising, placing five degrees of Taurus on the twelfth house cusp, your Sun will be in the twelfth house (Figure 4). If more than nine degrees are rising, your Sun will be in the eleventh house (Figure 5).

* There are 30 degrees to each sign, and when you refer to the ephemeris in the back of the book you will notice that the Sun, on the day you were born, will be found in a particular "degree," which may be anywhere from zero to 29 degrees of a sign. This number, then, becomes significant for you, for it will be repeated at all the house cusps on your Solar chart.
** The sign and degree that was rising at the precise moment of your birth. Astronomically, this is the place where the East point of the horizon (of your locality) and the ecliptic intersect.

On the other hand, a Solar chart places the Sun on the cusp of the first house and assumes that the birth occurred sometime around sunrise.

The following table shows the approximate positions of the Sun at various times of the day.* You can use this table to check your accuracy in setting up your own chart, for if you were born around 4:00 A.M. and find that you have placed your Sun in the twelfth house, you will know that you have made an error in placement.

For a birth between 4:00 A.M. and 6:00 A.M., the Sun is in the first house.

For a birth between 6:00 A.M. and 8:00 A.M., the Sun is in the twelfth house.

For a birth between 8:00 A.M. and 10:00 A.M., the Sun is in the eleventh house.

For a birth between 10:00 A.M. and noon, the Sun is in the tenth house.

For a birth between noon and 2:00 P.M., the Sun is in the ninth house.

For a birth between 2:00 P.M. and 4:00 P.M., the Sun is in the eighth house.

For a birth between 4:00 P.M. and 6:00 P.M., the Sun is in the seventh house.

For a birth between 6:00 P.M. and 8:00 P.M., the Sun is in the sixth house.

For a birth between 8:00 P.M. and 10:00 P.M., the Sun is in the fifth house.

For a birth between 10:00 P.M. and midnight, the Sun is in the fourth house.

For a birth between midnight and 2:00 A.M., the Sun is in the third house.

For a birth between 2:00 A.M. and 4:00 A.M., the Sun is in the second house.

Since the signs move in a clockwise direction, if you move your own chart in a clockwise direction you will notice that the Sun is found in a different house each time you bring a new sign to the ascendant, or East point, of the chart. You will notice, too, that as you turn your chart the planets seem to either *rise* or *fall*. This means that all planets (or luminaries) from the fourth to the tenth

* *If you were born during daylight saving time, subtract one hour.*

houses are said to be rising, or ascending, and those that leave the tenth house are said to be falling, or descending. The fourth house, then, is the lowest point of the chart, and the tenth house is the highest point.

Let us now proceed to erect a Solar chart for your own birth date. Turn to the back of the book and find the year in which you were born. Then find the month in which you were born. Look at the left-hand column and find the day on which you were born. Draw a line under this day to make it easier for your inspection. This will prevent your eye from wandering to the wrong line, and you will be assured of greater accuracy. Now that you can recognize the signs and planets by their symbols, you can easily transfer this information to a piece of paper. List the planets in the order in which you find them, one on top of the other. Next, draw a large circle and divide it into twelve equal parts. Look at the sign in which your Sun was found and notice the number of degrees it contains. Transfer this sign and number to the East point of the chart. Notice that the cardinal points, E, S, W, N, are not in the same position that you are accustomed to seeing them in. There are astrological reasons for this, but they are not pertinent to our work. Astrologers are accustomed to these reversed orders, but the beginner might be confused. Next, working in a counterclockwise direction, place the rest of the signs at each cusp in their natural sequence, repeating the same number of degrees that you found the Sun to be in. Let us set up a chart for a birth on November 7, 1935, to illustrate how this is done (Figure 6).

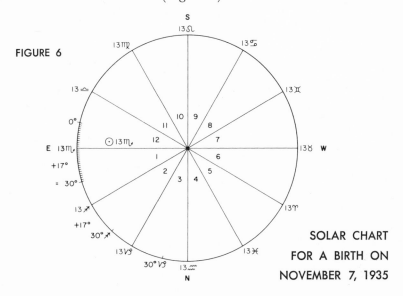

FIGURE 6

SOLAR CHART
FOR A BIRTH ON
NOVEMBER 7, 1935

Our sample chart has 13° of Scorpio on the cusp of the first house. Since there are 30° to every sign, that means that there are 17° more of Scorpio in the first house, plus 13° of Sagittarius. So you can see that although each house contains equal segments of 30° each, it can also contain parts of two signs. It is particularly important to pay attention to this point when you put in the planets, for it is extremely easy to forget that we are working in a counterclockwise direction. If you remember that each sign *increases* in a counter-clockwise direction and *decreases* in a clockwise direction, you are not likely to make any mistakes.

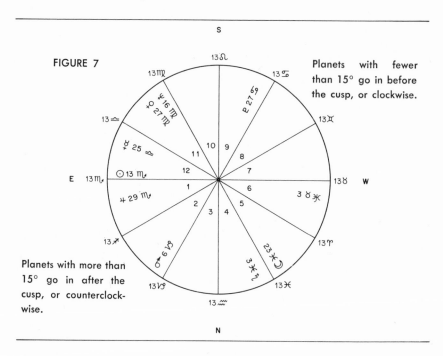

FIGURE 7

Planets with fewer than 15° go in before the cusp, or clockwise.

Planets with more than 15° go in after the cusp, or counterclock-wise.

Now you are ready to put in the rest of the planets. Look at Figure 7 to see how this is done. Remember to leave enough room if you find that you have many planets in the same sign.

That's all there is to erecting a Solar chart. Understanding what is indicated by the chart is only partially explained in this book. However, there are numerous volumes available to equip you in that area.

Now, for the Equal House chart, look at the table of ascendants. Find the table nearest to your birth date. Since we are using November 7 as our example, let us continue to use this date; but we will assume that the birth occurred at 8:22 A.M. Before we take the next step, we must determine whether or not the birth occurred during daylight saving time. If so, we must subtract one hour from the birth time. Consider, too, that during the years 1942 through 1945, war time was in effect in many states. It began on February 9, 1942, at 2:00 A.M., and ended on September 30, 1945, at 2:00 A.M. War time was the same as daylight saving time but was in effect all year long. You must make the correction by subtracting one hour if you were born during these years. In the case of our example, no adjustment is necessary.

Refer to the table of ascendants in the back of the book; you will find that November 6 is the closest date to the birth date we are using. Since the ascending signs are calculated for the hour, we must make a slight adjustment to find the ascending sign for our birth time of 8:22 A.M. We find that 29° of Scorpio are rising at 8:00 A.M. and that at 9:00 A.M., 12° of Sagittarius are rising. Therefore we must determine the number of degrees rising halfway between these two points. This is how we make the calculation: If 29° of Scorpio are rising at 8:00, there is one more degree of Scorpio left. In addition, there are 12° degrees of Sagittarius rising at 9:00. Adding these together, we have 13° of movement in one hour. In half an hour there are approximately 6°. Add 6° to 29° of Scorpio, which gives us an ascendant of 5° of Sagittarius. It is that simple. Since there are only 30° to each sign, we must add 1° to the 29° of Scorpio; now we are in the next sign, Sagittarius. Adding 5° more brings us to 5° of Sagittarius rising at 8:30 A.M. on November 6. The date of our sample chart is November 7, but this is close enough for our work.

Now you must do the same with your birth time. Do not worry about precision; we are more concerned with the sign for now. Precision is for advanced students. Draw a circle as before and divide it into twelve equal sections. Put the sign and number of degrees of your ascendant at the cusp of the first house. Then add the rest of the signs in their natural sequence around the cusps of the other eleven houses. Remember to do this in a counterclockwise direction. Repeat the same number at each of these cusps as we have done in our example (Figure 8) .

Under ordinary circumstances, the ascendant would be calculated by a series of mathematical steps. Several books of reference are used to find the data relative to this procedure. There are also many ways to divide the chart, one of which is the Placidean method. This would show an unequal distribution of the signs and would bring the Sun into the eleventh house. We are not concerned

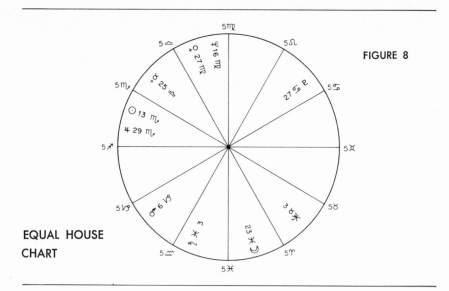

FIGURE 8

EQUAL HOUSE
CHART

with the slight discrepancy produced by the different methods of procedure. We are primarily interested in finding the sign on the ascendant and the signs in which your planets are found. For our purposes, however, a Solar chart is just as effective, even when the correct birth time is known. Therefore, do not feel you have to use the Equal House system alone even if you know your birth hour; work with the Solar chart as well.

For simplified and detailed instructions on how to construct Solar and Equal House charts, refer to the Appendix in the back of the book.

Now that you have set up these charts—the Solar chart and the Equal House chart—what does it mean to you? As a beginning, by applying the proper key words of the sign, the planet and the house, you will have some indication of your general planetary makeup and your orientation towards life; and by noting the particular houses that hold the planets, you can see where you may have the most strength. Some houses, you will note, have no planets in them at all, and others may hold as many as five or six. As you become acquainted with your own chart, experience will tell you the significance of the chart distribution. But we will approach the chart from a different point of view. The following chapters will enable you to use your chart in a number of different ways. This will be based, for the most part, on the signs in which the planets are found. Let us now proceed to learn about the kinds of help and direction this new tool will provide you. Let us go to the problem areas of your life.

⑦ Romance and Sex

The first six chapters of this book were written to give you the tools of astrology along with sufficient facts to enable you to make these tools work for you. Now let us apply this information to one of the basic problem areas of your life: sex. You may say, "I don't have a problem with sex. It's a natural part of life—just like eating—and, depending on whether I'm sexually hungry or not sexually hungry, I adjust."

Is that philosophy good enough? Is that really a satisfactory answer? Does sex require just an appetite, like eating? Or is there something more to it: a certain chemistry, a certain emotion, a spiritual union that makes the sexual act complete? And how can you keep from getting hurt or from hurting someone else? Will your relationship be a lasting one or simply a passing fancy? Will it be important or will it be one of a long string of inconsequential or sordid affairs that you look back upon with regret or disgust? The answers to these questions are within your reach, for you now have, with your new astrological knowledge, a method of finding a pathway to genuine satisfaction and sexual harmony. In addition, you will learn how to avoid the pitfalls and heartaches that often accompany chance sexual encounters.

For the sake of making my point, let us assume that you are

currently dating someone steadily, and you are wondering what is to become of this relationship. Nowadays it seems quite acceptable for two people to make love from the moment of their first date. But men and women do not always see eye to eye on what the sexual experience signifies. Perhaps *he* enjoys the novelty of the chase and conquest. Perhaps *she* hopes to win him in marriage by her "outstanding performance." Very often she pretends enjoyment, yet feels disappointment.

How can you protect yourself from heartache and disillusionment? The sex act, after all, means different things to different people. To some, it requires a total emotional commitment; to others, it is simply an appetite that must be satisfied. How can you tell whether or not you are a victim of circumstance or whether your relationship is genuine and meaningful? The answer lies in a comparison of your natal chart with the chart of the other person involved.

Astrologically speaking, certain planetary contacts produce certain kinds of attractions and relationships. The most compelling of these attractions is produced by Uranus. Uranian contacts can inject incredible amounts of "chemistry" into a relationship between two people, but, sad to say, these relationships are nearly always short-lived or disastrous. Not that there is anything inherently evil about Uranus, it is just that this planet is no respecter of age, position or circumstances, and often brings people together who were not meant to become sexually involved.

Interestingly enough, Uranus, the Great Awakener, is most effective during the teen-age and early dating years. Uranian action is meant to acquaint the male and the female—to draw them together, to let them enjoy the excitement of being close; it is meant to awaken them to *romance*. This is what young people are meant to do: to enjoy each other, to be free and independent, to learn to get along as friends, to play together, to romance—but *not to make love*. Does it seem strange that a planet that produces so much chemistry should place such severe limits on a thriving romance? Not at all. For these are the years in which you are meant to enjoy the search— to discover the opposite sex; to experience the tremendous exhilaration that is apparent when two people are attracted. However, as soon as this relationship takes physical form, that is, becomes a sexual affair, Uranus often shows the other side of its nature and becomes the disrupter. Eventually one partner or the other becomes tired or ashamed of the relationship and then wants out. Consequently, the abandoned one usually ends up brokenhearted because of the abrupt and unexpected turn of events. It takes a very mature young woman to enter into a "Uranian affair," knowing full well it is of fleeting duration and that she runs the risk of being rejected soon after its physical consummation. Sad to say, a broken Uranian romance can cause long-term heartache, because the rejected partner usually feels that he (or she) must have done something terribly wrong. The torment continues needlessly with grieving for what was imagined to be a great love!

Uranian attractions are not only evanescent but can be dangerous if one of the involved persons is married. He or she might feel, "If only I could be free to marry my new love. . . . I must get a divorce." Fate can have a cruel reward for an individual who lives with this fantasy. By the time the divorce is granted the romance may have ended, and both individuals will have succeeded only in breaking their own family ties and setting themselves adrift in a life of emptiness. Often an even worse fate awaits the individual who succeeds in marrying the new love, for he (or she) may find that romance has flown and that both partners are now victims of a new arrangement that is more odious than the old one.

Uranian attractions are common in middle-aged men and middle-aged women who become involved with younger and shallower partners. And when the attraction is gone, they very often end up asking themselves, "How could I have been such a fool?"

Let us now put this information to use. You have learned how to set up a chart for yourself. Set up a similar one for your current romantic interest. Then we will look for Uranian contacts between the two charts:

Find the planet Uranus in your chart and note the sign in which it appears. Let us say that it is in 21° of Gemini.

Now look at the chart of your friend and note the sign and degree of the Sun, Moon, Venus, and Mars. If any of these four planets are found in the sign of Gemini within a range of about 10° of being in conjunction—i.e., the same degree and sign—you have what is called a Uranian contact. An exact conjunction would be one in which any of the four planets were also in 21° of Gemini. We cannot predict to the exact degree when we are dealing with the problem of "orbs"—i.e., the allowable range between planetary contacts—for if 10° is valid, then, without doubt, 11° will work, too. You will be able to decide for yourself when you have become familiar with the various kinds of contacts. In general, the closer the contact, the stronger the relationship. But do not discount the wider orbs.

The next step is this: Look at your friend's Uranus and note the sign and degree in which it is found. Examine it in relation to *your* Sun, Moon, Venus, and Mars. If it is found in the same sign and reasonably near the same degree, this, too, is a Uranian contact. These are the conjunctions. Now let us look for the oppositions, for they are equally valid.

If, for example, your Uranus is found in 12° of Scorpio and your friend has a Sun, Moon, Venus, or Mars in the sign opposite to Scorpio, which is Taurus, within the same 10° range, they are in opposition. Now, examine your friend's Uranus in relationship to your Sun, Moon, Venus, and Mars. If his Uranus is in 16° of Libra and if any of your four planets are in the sign Aries within the allowable range, then it will be in opposition to his Uranus.

You might question what to do if you find that you have Uranian contacts between you. That is entirely up to you, but the message is "beware." Don't get carried away by the moment. Don't do anything you might regret later. These Uranian contacts are "romantic" contacts; they are not meant to take sexual form except to the very mature personality. Pass at your own risk, but don't count on a lasting romance on the basis of just these contacts.

Let us review: Uranus is the planet of romance and excitement, and while this planet in your chart may lead to a sexual encounter, the results over a long period of time are usually extremely unsatisfying, particularly to teen-agers. Nature has built-in safeguards that will permit you to protect yourself, but first you must learn to recognize them.

The planets of true romance are Venus and Mars. The interaction of the principles of these two planets produces the most satisfaction from a sexual point of view. Nature intended sex to be satisfying but, strange as it may seem, even in this era of freedom whereby a person can select unlimited numbers of sexual partners, sex is often a disappointment.

Unsatisfactory sex usually stems from the wrong two people getting together. That is why mismatched couples rely to such a great extent on the how-to-do-it sex manuals, erotic movies and literature, and require endless counseling.

Do you want to avoid the frustration? Learn astrology, but learn it well.

Astrologically speaking, the planet Mars is the symbol of sexual energy or drive; it is also the symbol of masculinity. Venus, on the other hand, is the planet of emotions and romantic desire. It is the symbol of femininity and the natural complement to Mars. It is by the fusion or opposition of the principles of these two planets (found by comparing these two planets in your respective charts) that you can achieve satisfaction not only physically, but emotionally. For it is through the emotions that true sexual happiness is achieved.

It stands to reason, then, that to achieve harmony you must select a partner who answers your requirements.

Now let us see how the planets function in the various signs in your chart and that of your current interest. First of all, examine the Venus in the woman's chart for a good indication of her emotional needs and her approach to love:

VENUS IN ARIES:
Very ardent, but fussy. Can be easily turned off by an insecure man. Has a need to be dominated. Is a stickler for form and detail.

VENUS IN TAURUS:
Very practical; knows instinctively how to use her body to get what she wants; extremely natural about sex. Needs a man who can give her financial security. Love in a rustic setting would appeal.

VENUS IN GEMINI:
Very fickle. Needs a man who is her superior intellectually before she can love unreservedly.

VENUS IN CANCER:
Very maternal—she needs a man she can take care of and who will take care of her; needs the security of a home and family. If you won't let her fuss over you, stay away; she's not for you.

VENUS IN LEO:
Very enthusiastic; loves to show off and be appreciated. She needs a man who knows how to express his emotions. You must at least *play* the role of lover.

VENUS IN VIRGO:
Very selective; has a desire to serve. Her emotional response will be in direct proportion to how much she senses you need her.

VENUS IN LIBRA:
Very romantic; in love with love. Candlelight and flowers appeal. Likes a man who is well groomed. Would like to be "swept off her feet." To keep her in love, don't keep her guessing.

VENUS IN SCORPIO:
Very sensual. Needs a strong man who knows what he's doing; has a

need to feel possessed, but with a skillful hand; feelings are very intense.

VENUS IN SAGITTARIUS:

Very playful; love burns brightly but can go out just as quickly. She wants to be where the action is. Be sure to communicate with her—she wants to hear it said. Keep her "fires" burning by a change of pace.

VENUS IN CAPRICORN:

Very conventional; will not show her emotions too openly. Love is for keeps with her; appears reserved but is waiting for you to make the approach. She prefers to know where she stands early in the game.

VENUS IN AQUARIUS:

Very bohemian; she is everybody's friend. Can be quite independent; to keep her interested, keep her guessing. Loves the unusual and the dramatic. Don't try to monopolize her.

VENUS IN PISCES:

Very devoted; put her on a pedestal and she will adore you; very receptive and vulnerable. Don't ask her where she would like to go—tell her. Help her make decisions.

The complement to Venus is Mars, and in a man's chart Mars represents how he will express his physical drives. Let us then look at Mars in the various signs in a man's chart:

MARS IN ARIES:

Forceful, aggressive, and enthusiastic; loves the chase as much as the prize.

MARS IN TAURUS:

Earthy; sex urge develops slowly, but once it blooms it is very strong. Can be very self-indulgent; loves to eat and drink with a date.

MARS IN GEMINI:

Flirtatious, but very intellectual about love; not likely to lose his head too easily. Likes to talk about love; very changeable—may forget you one hour after he has made the conquest.

MARS IN CANCER:

Protective; loves to be comfortable while making love—preferably at your home. Is quite considerate and responds to mothering; possessive. Likes "older" women.

MARS IN LEO:

Dramatic; appears very warmhearted and passionate, but watch out —it may be all show. He may not let you know his real feelings, but don't be afraid to express yours.

MARS IN VIRGO:

Analytic; is a bit cool about getting involved; may need quite a bit of help getting started. Needs consistent encouragement; somewhat shy or puritanical.

MARS IN LIBRA:

Aesthetic; loves the poetic side of love; will observe the niceties. Generally prefers companionship to indiscriminate sex.

MARS IN SCORPIO:

Intense; very passionate; demanding. Can appear cold-blooded, but emotions are very deep when finally committed. Likes variety.

MARS IN SAGITTARIUS:

Idealistic. Master of the brief encounter; not good for the long haul —loves his freedom too much. Keep him guessing.

MARS IN CAPRICORN:

Inhibited; easily offended if rejected; deep sensual nature responds to real affection.

MARS IN AQUARIUS:

Experimental; willing to try anything. Attracts friendships easily; to hold him, give him plenty of freedom and trust him completely.

MARS IN PISCES:

Intuitive; is a real romantic; takes sex seriously and loves it with a little mystery thrown in! Idealistic.

These are only key words to give you some indication of how the planet Mars projects itself in each of these signs. Now you should check your chart and your partner's chart to determine whether there is a Venus–Mars tie between you, because here is where real satisfaction can be found. If you are a woman, find the planet Venus and notice the sign and degree in which it is found. Next, examine the chart of the man in whom you are interested and find his Mars. For example, if his Mars is in Taurus and your Venus is in Taurus reasonably close together, this will be a strong indication of sexual and emotional harmony between you. The difference between the action of the close conjunction, i.e., when they are in the same sign and near the same degree, and just being in the same sign is this:

The conjunction draws two people together very swiftly, for they instinctively feel one another's presence. When they are both in the same sign but widely apart, this means that if they find one another on the basis of some other planetary tie, they will instinctively know how the other partner will respond and what his needs will be.

This is true also of the opposition of the Venus and Mars principle. If your Venus is in Taurus and his Mars is in Scorpio (the opposite sign) within a radius of about 10° or 11°, there will be an opposition of the two planets. This, too, is a very strong tie because one partner acts as a catalyst to the other partner: The Scorpio Mars is very intense and passionate; the earthy Venus is instinctive and natural about sex. One provides what the other one needs.

As we have seen, Venus in a woman's chart indicates to some extent what she is searching for in romance, but in a man's chart Venus gives us a clue to the kind of woman to whom he is attracted. The following will provide a short description of how Venus behaves in a man's chart:

VENUS IN ARIES:
He is attracted to women who are outgoing, athletic, or adventuresome. He would like you to be self-confident and independent. Female executives do not put him off.

VENUS IN TAURUS:
Soft and pliable is the way he likes you. Women who are domestic, attractive, and don't make too many demands upon him will appeal. He admires loyalty above all. Let him know he can depend upon you.

VENUS IN GEMINI:
He likes you to be witty and amusing. Don't be afraid to show him your Phi Beta Kappa key! He is rather dualistic in love affairs, but if you are a good storyteller, love to travel on a moment's notice, and do not become alarmed at his mood changes, you stand a good chance of qualifying.

VENUS IN CANCER:
Older women often appeal to him. He is attracted to the maternal qualities as well as your physical attributes. Invite him home for dinner only if you are a good cook, otherwise, suggest a good restaurant.

VENUS IN LEO:
Better keep up with the latest fashions. He loves someone he can

show off. He expects you to be dramatic, elegant, and won't mind if you are the center of attention—provided you have eyes only for him. He does not mind your being madly in love with him and letting him know it. But do keep up appearances at the same time!

VENUS IN VIRGO:

Service and dedication to a cause are qualities that he admires in a woman. He would like to feel that you have saved yourself for him alone. Nurses are particularly attractive to him. Here is a man who does not wear his heart on his sleeve. He may seem maddeningly aloof to you in the beginning. He loves a rational woman.

VENUS IN LIBRA:

He is a romantic and will want to maintain his illusions about romance. Try not to rock his boat. Don't come on too "strong." He will be perfectly content to have you as a companion. Don't create a scene if you don't hear from him for a while; just send him a poem or some other subtle reminder.

VENUS IN SCORPIO:

Don't think you can play with this man's affections. He is attracted to intense, passionate women. He approaches a love affair like a clinician—intense, thorough, and probing.

VENUS IN SAGITTARIUS:

If you want to impress him, be a little hard to get. He appreciates someone who doesn't try to close in on him. His passion may seem short-lived to you, but when the fires seem to burn low be a pal to him until he is "fired up" again! He is often attracted to outdoor types or women from other countries.

VENUS IN CAPRICORN:

He is challenged by a woman who is in a higher social strata than his. He does not in the least mind learning from you. He admires a woman who is confident of her own worth and competent in her own field. He is enchanted with a woman who appears to be ladylike, serene or even businesslike in public, but who is completely feminine and passionate in private.

VENUS IN AQUARIUS:

He likes his women to be different from the ordinary run-of-the-mill types. The more unpredictable or unusual you are, the more he will like it. Do something different, try something new. He will expect you to be independent, so don't be possessive for more than a few hours!

VENUS IN PISCES:

He dreams of a gentle, sensitive creature whom he can protect and adore. Artistic women attract him. Don't be afraid to express your feelings for him. If you can create an aura of mystery around yourself, well and good.

For the male reader: Now that you have some clue to a woman's emotional needs (Venus), you must next learn what she will need to keep her happy if you have any desire for longevity and harmony in your relationship. Her Mars will provide you with some helpful hints:

MARS IN ARIES:

She admires athletic and masculine men. Even if you aren't an outstanding athlete, you can at least behave in a forceful way. She won't mind if you show off a bit. This girl needs a man she can look up to. Even if you are no expert, at least act self-confident.

MARS IN TAURUS:

It doesn't matter how sexy you are if you can't provide this girl with financial security. She loves a nice home and nice things, and although she may not necessarily want to spend all your money, she likes to know that it is nonetheless there. However, if you show indications of becoming a good provider, she will be satisfied.

MARS IN GEMINI:

This girl admires versatility in a man. If you can play the piano, speak at least three languages, and know all the latest dance steps, you may succeed in keeping her interest. But keep learning—she is inclined to be a bit restless. Don't count on taking her for granted, as you will be in for a surprise.

MARS IN CANCER:

This girl will expect you to settle down. Be prepared to provide her with a home of her own, and be prepared to spend quite a bit of time in it, for she expects to see you there often! She needs a strong man to play the role of protector. As long as you don't demand it, she will adore mothering you. Her feelings are easily hurt, so don't criticize her.

MARS IN LEO:

She will expect you to show your feelings quite overtly. In addition, she likes her man to be well groomed, stylishly dressed and upwardly mobile! She likes her romance with a great deal of flamboyance. She wants to feel proud of you and to show you off to her friends. She may tolerate quiet evenings at home while you are still courting, but she will be most forceful about insisting upon her "rights" once you are married to her!

MARS IN VIRGO:

This girl may get swept off her feet momentarily, but ultimately it will be her head that dictates her course of action, not her heart. She wants to be important to you and will work unselfishly in your behalf—if you let her know how much you need her. Don't be put off by her seemingly overrational approach to love. She responds best when you show a genuine concern for her, have an intellectual grasp of her needs, and in addition are clean-cut, conventional and smarter than she is.

MARS IN LIBRA:

Outward appearances count for much with this girl. She wants a man who appreciates the romance in life—who appreciates the effort she has taken to make her surroundings more artistic. Disorder and untidiness have a disturbing effect upon her, so even if you are no fashion plate, at least be immaculate.

MARS IN SCORPIO:

Women with Mars here very often outdistance their men sexually at an early stage. Be prepared to offer her warmth and passion for the long haul, because if she doesn't find it at home she will eventually feel compelled to seek it elsewhere. Exert your superior physical strength over her, for she expects you to be that way. Physicians and scientists are particularly attractive to this girl.

MARS IN SAGITTARIUS:

"Fly me to the moon" is the theme song for this girl. She aims high and she likes to keep soaring. She is attracted to outdoor men and sportsmen. Even if you can't measure up athletically, talk a good game!

MARS IN CAPRICORN:

She will not object if you aspire to become Chairman of the Board. She shares your enthusiasm for climbing to the top, whether it is in business, sports, or wherever. Her own organizing talents might assist you. If you are somewhat aloof on the surface, she will not mind, but do unbend when you are alone. She admires the qualities of experience and dependability.

MARS IN AQUARIUS:

Don't be too possessive of this girl. She likes the idea that she may have to work at it to get you involved. She enjoys the unexpected gesture, the complete change of pace. Artistic or inventive men appeal to her.

MARS IN PISCES:

Here is the real romantic. She is looking for the ideal man, and you will be constantly tested against those qualities she has decided constitute her "ideal." She wants gentleness in love, but great strength of character. Sing to her, proclaim your great love, tell her she's indispensable to you, but above all don't let her take advantage of your good nature. She won't admire you for it.

As we have seen, the female needs to be awakened through her emotions. Her Venus searches for fulfillment through the expression of the man's physical passion—his Mars. Therefore, if two people are matched on the basis of the Venus–Mars fusion or complement, the chances of their needing a variety of partners will be very slim indeed. Sex, astrologically speaking, is meant to be far more selective than anyone has imagined. It has always seemed logical and reasonable that two attractive people, given the freedom and having "that feeling" between them, could easily find satisfaction in a sexual encounter. But this is not so. Nature has arranged it so that not everyone can answer your needs. Too many people are disappointed and bewildered by sex. What seems to be such a natural and easy function is far more complicated than young people realize. It is extremely difficult to achieve long-term satisfaction when you are mismatched. When the Venus–Mars tie between two charts is satisfied, this not only brings a natural and easy expression to the sexual life, but it involves an emotional commitment on the part of both partners. They share a mutual feeling of responsibility without which no really satisfying sexual union can exist.

⑧

Love and Marriage

Why do so many marriages end in divorce? Can it be that marriage is no longer a useful institution? Do people today need a variety of mates, or do they need greater self-discipline, that old-fashioned quality which enabled their grandparents to endure a lifetime marriage, with or without romance? Are modern couples more courageous, or more confused?

Even the steadily climbing divorce rate does not offer a true picture of the marriage crisis. There are many couples who do not resort to divorce but whose marriages survive without love. One cannot help but wonder why the marriage picture looks so grim; why the passing years take such a formidable toll of romance, despite the fact that most couples believe themselves to be in love when they marry. Psychologists, psychiatrists, and sociologists are trying to define the problems in an effort to reverse the trend. Thus far, however, they have not had any noticeable success, for the divorce rate continues to rise alarmingly. Perhaps astrology may point the way to the solution of this pressing problem. As a beginning, let us compare the role of astrology to the role the computer is playing in the realm of romance, love, and marriage.

Computer dating appears to be having great success. New agencies are springing up all over the country. Little if anything, however, is heard of astrological dating except perhaps in the Orient. There is no question that the computer is a welcome addition to our technological age, but this machine should not be expected to perform miracles. When dealing with intangibles such as romantic love, we are on unscientific footing. Psychologists and psychiatrists cannot measure love; in fact, they have a difficult time defining the emotion. What is that unexplainable something that creates an attraction between two people? Is it chemical? Or do two human beings upon meeting radiate certain electrical impulses that attract or repel? Obviously, the computer cannot provide us with answers to these questions unless we feed it absolutely accurate information.

One would naturally assume that an individual participating in computer dating would provide accurate data about himself, but it is not always easy to know what is accurate without the help of astrology. For example, a young woman might answer a computer question such as "Are you a sexually responsive individual?" with an unequivocal "No"—only to have an astrologer tell her "Nonsense!" The astrologer would then be able to explain that her apparent lack of sexual drive was, perhaps, the product of faulty conditioning. There is an important difference, then, between computer matching and a similar service based on astrological dicta; that difference is that facts gleaned by the astrologer from the birth chart enable him to penetrate the conditioning that often passes for the genuine personality. At best, the personal data fed into the computer represents only a scanty picture of each individual's development and his momentary needs. I have not yet learned of a computer geared to predict future potential for a couple matched this way. Once the machine has performed its function of getting two people together, it is hit-and-miss once they marry as to whether they'll live happily ever after. This fact in no way reflects upon the function of the computer. It does the job it was intended to do.

Although computer matchmaking is highly entertaining, it is far too recent an innovation for any reliable statistical results to have been accumulated. It will have to withstand the test of time. Astrology, on the other hand, has withstood the test of time, but the findings of the astrologers have not been subjected to the verification scientific methods demand.

Astrology can match people more successfully than the computer; moreover, it can teach two people how to avoid the inevitable pitfalls that often lead to divorce.

We mentioned earlier that some people appear to require a variety of partners. There is very little indication, astrologically speaking, that this is a characteristic of any mature person. The need for variety exists in the early dating years, and this is when an individual should freely indulge in variety. Going steady before maturity is an unnecessary obstacle to marital happiness, because it inhibits the natural search that is vital before selecting a life partner.

The astrological correlates in the typical teen-age relationship usually reflect a purely physical attraction, although a steady-dating couple might insist that they are genuinely "in love." It is not until the post-teen years that the real solar personality emerges in most individuals, and sometimes it is as late as the early thirties. Naturally each case is unique, but it is certainly possible to trace an individual's development with surprising accuracy by using astrological tools.

What often happens is that an early steady-dating pattern leads to an early marriage, and this may be satisfying for only a few years, or until the novelty wears off. The fact is that the planetary picture changes (dramatically in many cases) with the passing years; and by the time the couple has been subjected to the stressful test conditions of a transiting Saturn, the taskmaster of the Zodiac, or Uranus, the disrupter, the marriage may be in serious trouble. It is under the transits of these two planets that most marriages either fall apart or end in divorce. In many cases, subsequent marriages are no happier because the same mistakes are apt to be repeated. If more couples were aware of the potentially disruptive nature of these planets, much heartache could be avoided. What often seems like a very valid reason for divorce when Saturn and Uranus are transiting will not seem as important several years or even several months later.

Let us consider the ingredients for a happy and satisfying marriage. To begin with, a couple contemplating marriage should have as a starting point a solid sexual attraction. This, as we noted in Chapter 7, should be based on the Venus–Mars fusion or complement. If you are planning to marry someone with whom you have no such ties, then you must learn how to give what the other partner expects, or you may soon find yourself in difficulty. If, for example, your fiancée has a Venus in Aries and your Mars is in Virgo, there is no natural complement. You must provide her with the warmth, ardor and strength that she craves by making a special effort. Mars in Virgo can be very "cool," and if changing your natural mode of expression is too tall an order for you, you would be wise to think twice about such a union. For as soon as the newness of the relationship wears off, your ardor may have lessened considerably and your wife may prove too demanding for you, unless you are determined to meet her needs.

From an astrological viewpoint in relation to sexual attractions, the Venus–Mars tie produces the most harmonious and natural satisfaction. When this occurs, each partner is instinctively aware of the other's needs, and this mutual understanding creates gratifying results. There are, however, several other ties that produce physical attraction or "chemistry," so that when these are found to exist between a couple there is a basis upon which to build a happy future. These ties are Sun–Mars or Moon–Venus—that is, when the Sun of one partner conjuncts the Mars of the other partner, and when the Moon of one partner conjuncts the Venus of the other partner. For example, if your Sun is in Aquarius and your fiancé has a Mars in Aquarius very near to the degree, there will be a strong physical tie between you. The same will be true if the Moon of the man's chart conjuncts the Venus of the girl's chart. These are the ties that bring the "chemistry" to the union; they do not guarantee sexual harmony as in the case of the Venus–Mars combinations. The couple must still build this principle into their relationship—but they have a very good starting point. The marriage can endure a great deal of trial and error, unlike the case of Uranian ties (or where there are *no* ties at all) where one partner or the other gets tired of trying or simply "turns off."

These, then, are the planets which deal with the physical side of a marriage. But there is more to a good marriage than sex, and one of the most important elements is friendship. Two people who are sexually suited to one another and who, in addition, are friends, will never have to fear that their marriage will deteriorate into the boring relationship that we find too often. What planetary ties produce marital friendship? They are the Sun and the Moon ties. These can occur in several ways: first, if the Sun of the woman's chart conjuncts or is in opposition to the Moon of the man's chart— for example, if your Sun is in Taurus and your partner's Moon is in Taurus *or* Scorpio (the opposite sign to Taurus) ; second, if the Sun of the man's chart is in conjunction or opposition to the Moon of the woman's chart.

So you see that when there is an interchange of the principle of the luminaries we have a solid basis for friendship. This friendship may, of course, exist outside the bounds of marriage, but two people contemplating a legal marriage with permanence as well as har- mony in mind would do well to satisfy this Sun–Moon complement. This is the single, most important tie between two people in terms of a real marriage. There are also several other ties which are valid, but these ties require more of an adjustment to achieve perfect harmony. For instance, if your ascendant sign is known to you, and the Sun or the Moon of your partner rests upon this sign in exact or slightly greater number of degrees (for example, your ascendant is 22° of Capricorn and your partner's Sun or Moon is no less than 19° nor greater than 27° of Capricorn), then this is a harmonious tie. We cannot always predict with accuracy the exact number of degrees of orb to allow, but in general, the closer they are, the better. This tie, however, is better for the partner whose ascendant receives the conjuncting Sun or Moon because he will benefit the most. There is no such guarantee for the partner whose Sun or Moon participates in the tie.

There is still another kind of tie that keeps marriages together, one that can be every bit as satisfying to those who are emotionally responsible. This is the tie brought about through Saturn, the planet responsible for introducing duty and responsibility into the relationship of two mature people. To the immature, this tie brings restrictions, obligations, and severe trials. In spite of the limitations imposed upon each partner as a result of this tie, the couple's obligations may hold them together. For some people, this is a rewarding relationship. For others, it is not. Let us, then, look at the various ways in which Saturn can work—forewarned is forearmed.

If the Saturn in one chart conjuncts or opposes the Sun or Moon of the other chart, the results can be difficult to live with, unless the aspects are fully understood. This stems from the fact that the partner who "holds" the Saturn will try to limit or restrict the partner who has the Sun or the Moon. If both individuals comprehend the nature of the tie, they can learn to use it more harmoniously.

In order to simplify the comparison of chart factors, I have prepared a concise table. Look at your planets and then compare your partner's planets on the basis of the following information:

VENUS CONJUNCT MARS MARS CONJUNCT VENUS	Excellent for sexual harmony, easily and naturally achieved.
VENUS OPPOSE MARS MARS OPPOSE VENUS	Same as above, but with more combativeness; i.e., the couple will enjoy a playful struggle in their lovemaking.

URANUS CONJUNCT OR
OPPOSE THE MOON

URANUS CONJUNCT OR
OPPOSE MARS

URANUS CONJUNCT OR
OPPOSE VENUS

URANUS CONJUNCT OR
OPPOSE THE SUN

Strong physical attraction, very magnetic and compelling. Very romantic. Not good for longevity of relationship; abrupt breaks; not good for sexual fulfillment.

VENUS CONJUNCT THE MOON

VENUS CONJUNCT THE SUN

MARS CONJUNCT THE MOON

MARS CONJUNCT THE SUN

Romantic attractions often occur between people who are unable or unwilling to be married. Best for mature relationships. Attraction is based on physical presence, an urgent need to be with one another—not necessarily sexual, but very stimulating.

SATURN CONJUNCT OR
OPPOSE THE MOON

SATURN CONJUNCT OR
OPPOSE THE SUN

Duty or responsibility holds partners together. Can be very restricting. Feelings are hurt by constant nagging or criticism; sense of oppression can result. Shared responsibilities can provide mutual satisfaction for those who are emotionally mature.

SATURN CONJUNCT OR
OPPOSE VENUS

Inability to achieve emotional harmony. Very poor tie for marriage. Severely limiting and difficult to overcome. Faultfinding, critical.

There is one more tie of Saturn that is also very difficult to overcome and occurs when Saturn *squares*, that is, is 90° away from your Sun, Moon, or Venus. We have not mentioned square relationships for the simple reason that they are usually so limiting that people with these ties never get close enough to think of marriage. If, however, there are many other close ties between you in addition to a Saturn square, you may go along for a long time without any problems. Usually, however, it will make its presence known.

NEPTUNE CONJUNCT
THE SUN
NEPTUNE CONJUNCT
THE MOON
NEPTUNE CONJUNCT VENUS

These are the spiritual ties. They can be very deceiving unless both partners are morally "in tune" or developed. They are also idealistic ties and can bring two people together on the basis of mutual suffering or mutual understanding. Love of this kind can be the purest and the most inspiring.

Now that you have checked your planets with those of your fiancé (or fiancée), you will have some indication of what one might expect from the other. Suppose you find there are no important ties between you, yet you still insist that you are "in love." What then? In this case, you must proceed with utmost caution. Astrological ties were meant to be observed, but unfortunately too few people have been aware of their own astrological makeup. On the basis of Sun signs alone, you cannot tell what you are facing in a marriage partner, and your chart is your protection against getting involved in a disastrous or boring marriage. If you make certain early that you and your partner share some of the important ties, you need never worry about the problem of divorce. The absence of ties is a good indication that there may be something wrong with the union. I know this sounds ominous, but there is a sound basis for this reasoning. Where no astrological ties exist you should ask yourself a variety of pertinent questions. If you are a man, you might ask: "Am I being married for my money, my family name, my social position, or to satisfy her desire for children? Am I a means of escape from her tyrannical parents? Does she want a husband to relieve her of her responsibilities?" If you are a woman, you might ask: "Does he want someone to take the place of his mother? Does he want a maid and a housekeeper? Does he want easily available sex? Is it my social position, money, or particular talent that he needs?"

If you can answer these questions unflinchingly and you still want to marry, your chances of a successful relationship are good—provided you both understand the truth and are willing to expend the time and effort that it takes to tolerate and appreciate each other's emotional, physical, and spiritual needs. You must build into your character the qualities you are lacking, as indicated by your chart comparison. You must each provide what the other is seeking in order to achieve enduring happiness.

Let us, as an example, look at the astrological makeup of two people who were contemplating marriage and who had no significant ties between them.

HERS	HIS
Sun 17° Taurus	Sun 29° Sagittarius
Moon 28° Leo	Moon 24° Capricorn
Mercury 11° Taurus	Mercury 14° Capricorn
Venus 24° Aries	Venus 1° 1° Aquarius
Mars 4° Cancer	Mars 20° Gemini
Jupiter 19° Taurus	Jupiter 7° Taurus

Just by using simple key words to describe each planet we can get an indication of potential difficulty:

HIS CHART INDICATES:		HER CHART INDICATES:	
♐ ☉	Freedom-loving, travel-minded, philosophical.	♉ ☉	Home-loving, domestic, loyal.
♑ ☽	Compulsive, organizing, serious.	♌ ☽	Love of ease, luxuries and good times; dramatic.
♑ ☿	Responsible, ambitious, moody.	♉ ☿	Dependable, constructive thinker.
♒ ♀	Independent, friendly.	♈ ♀	Warm-hearted, enthusiastic; needs strong show of affection.
♊ ♂	Fickle, restless, love of change.	♋ ♂	Maternal, compassionate, sensitive.

You can see from this comparison that each person expresses definite qualities and requires compatible responses. These two people look at life quite differently, and each of them may at some time wonder why the other one doesn't think, act, or respond compatibly. When there is nothing to go on except what people tell each other, it makes the way hazardous. The comparison of charts reduces the risks immeasurably.

The chances of meeting your "true love," astrologically speaking, are very good if you do not become impatient. The tendency is to marry too soon and without sufficient knowledge of each other. Just because a couple sleeps together or lives together before marriage does not guarantee success in marriage. The newness of the relationship and youth alone will provide sufficient attraction, but there has to be a foundation to hold a marriage. A computer may match you on the basis of compatibility of interests, religion, desire for children, and your need for a partner with a sense of humor. But even these elements are not enough to keep a relationship vital and meaningful over a long period of time. On the other hand, the outward signs of compatibility may be lacking, but the marriage will be successful if it is astrologically harmonious.

There are other questions you might ask yourself with regard to your future marriage partner: "Where will we meet and what will that person be like?" I cannot personally answer these questions for each of you, but by now you should have your own chart from which to work. Look at that chart now and let us see if we can work out the age-old problem of finding the best marriage partner.

The seventh house of your chart holds the key to these questions and you can use it to help with the quest. For best results, you should work from an Equal House chart based on the correct or approximate time of your birth, for it is important to know the sign on your ascendant. However, if it is impossible to get this information, use your Solar chart as though it were an Equal House chart. Now look at your chart. You will notice that the sign opposite your ascendant is placed on the cusp of the seventh house, the house of your marriage partner (among other things). This sign is a clue to the kind of partner who would best suit your needs. For example, if you have Cancer on your ascendant, you will have the sign Capricorn on the cusp of your seventh house. This indicates that your lifetime mate should to a large extent answer the description based on this sign. He or she may be older, serious, reliable, hardworking, ambitious, determined, or have other qualities indicative of the sign Capricorn. He or she may even be a Capricornian.

This is the first test that you must put to anyone you are considering for marriage. There is a very good reason for this. If you have Cancer on the ascendant, this suggests that your outlook or approach to life is intuitive, sensitive, and dependent. You need someone to lean on. This is particularly true of a Cancer woman. Capricorn will provide the strength and dependability. He will not mind protecting you. This does not mean that the partner must be a

Capricorn, but he should have all the qualities of Capricorn. In other words, there is a natural balance between the first house sign, which represents you, and the seventh house sign, which represents your marriage partner.

Each sign has certain definite qualities; the sign opposite contains those qualities which are lacking. So the two signs together make a natural and harmonious whole. This is what a marriage partner should provide among other things: a balance and a contrast. The following table will help you to make the proper selection based on your ascendant sign. Find your own ascendant sign and read the description based on the opposite sign—that of the seventh house:

Ascendant Sign	*Description of Marriage Partner*
ARIES NEEDS:	An attractive, peace-loving, romantic partner; someone to provide balance and stability. Aries requires a harmonious and well-run home in an attractive setting.
TAURUS NEEDS:	Someone to take the initiative, to provide direction and force; someone who will be intense, passionate. May be foreign-born. May be a scientist, in the medical profession, in research.
GEMINI NEEDS:	A fun-loving, athletic, outdoor type who loves to travel and enjoys change. A deep thinker. He or she may be younger, from a different country, or previously married. May be born under the sign Sagittarius.
CANCER NEEDS:	Someone to lean on. A strong, steady, reliable person, with a dependable job and security; an older partner who takes his (or her) responsibilities seriously. May be someone born under the sign Capricorn: executives, presidents of corporations or associations.
LEO NEEDS:	An independent partner who will not be overawed by the show that Leo loves to put on. A partner who is stronger; who will show appreciation and admiration. Someone spontaneous, creative. May be born under the sign Aquarius: engineers, radio and T.V. personnel.
VIRGO NEEDS:	A gentle, sympathetic and idealistic partner.

Someone to care for and direct. A romantic and easy-going nature who will know how to give of his or her time. May be born under the sign Pisces: artist, doctor, or actor.

LIBRA NEEDS: An energetic, forceful, outgoing partner. Someone who is ardent, ambitious, and enthusiastic. May be born under the sign Aries or Scorpio.

SCORPIO NEEDS: A tranquil, domestic, attractive partner. Someone who loves home and family life and is affectionate and reliable. May be a banker, in real estate, or in nursery work (flowers, etc.) .

SAGITTARIUS NEEDS: Someone who will share his or her desire for travel, who loves change, and can be an intellectual companion. Should be versatile, witty, and a good conversationalist. May be found among secretarial or business groups, artists, linguists, or writers.

CAPRICORN NEEDS: A paternal (or maternal) and protective partner; someone who will soothe and reassure him (or her) . Should be home-loving and family-oriented, and share his need for success no matter how long it takes. May be found in the nursing or medical profession; historians, antique dealers, or food industry.

AQUARIUS NEEDS: A forceful, attractive, and regal partner. Someone who knows how to entertain on the spur of the moment and how to cope with the unpredictability and independence of Aquarius. Should be a person who can play a variety of roles to keep life interesting. A partner may be found in the theater, modeling, and advertising fields; also lecturers or public speakers.

PISCES NEEDS: A down-to-earth, practical, methodical partner; one who will give force and direction to his or her life. Should be someone kindly but firmly in command. May be found in the social-work field; in teaching; among medical technicians, or in service of some kind. May be born under the sign Virgo.

These are merely sketches of some of the characteristics that should be part of your consideration when you are choosing a partner. They are meant to serve only as a guideline so that you may eliminate those who do not in some way answer the needs of your opposite sign. To consistently ignore a signpost is to find yourself on a wrong-way street. Look to the seventh house and then examine the person. Let us say you have a Leo ascendant and that you have not chosen your partner with extreme care; the sign on your seventh house cusp, Aquarius, can work against you. It might even bring about a divorce. The reason is clear. The sign Aquarius (which is opposite to the sign Leo) on your seventh house cusp can become very independent, abrupt, brusque, or tactless. If you were not careful in examining all your partner's characteristics and you are not well-matched, arguments, normal marital obligations, etc., might cause you to display your very volatile temper. This, in turn, may disturb your mate, who will probably absent himself from home on every possible occasion, turn to other friends, and draw farther apart from you. Aquarius then becomes the disrupter. This is true of every sign, for if you have not selected someone who represents the best qualities of your seventh house sign, you will very likely attract into your life someone who exhibits the worst qualities. Capricorn on the seventh cusp, instead of being reliable, hard-working, and trustworthy, becomes cold, aloof, miserly, indifferent, restrictive, and inhibiting.

Keep in mind at all times that this seventh house sign only indicates in a general way some of those qualities which are lacking in your own makeup. If you find those positive qualities in your potential partner's makeup, you have taken the first step in securing a rewarding marriage for yourself. The next step is to look for those ties which we described earlier in this chapter.

We have covered some of the likely professions or occupations in which you might find your prospective mate. There are, of course, many others; when you become familiar with the signs, you will be able to see for yourself what they are.

Now let us see if we can answer, at least in part, the other question: "Where will we meet?" Again we must work from a time chart so that we may know the sign on the cusp of the seventh house. This sign has a ruler, and if you will refer back to page 22, you will see the ruler of your ascendant sign. For example, if you have Aries on the ascendant, Libra will be on the cusp of the seventh house. The ruler of Libra is Venus. Now look at your chart and see in which house you find Venus. Suppose you find this planet in the ninth house; the indications are that you will find your true mate overseas, or at a long distance from your own home. For someone who lives in a small town and travels very little, the ninth house can mean a big city a few hundred miles away. Therefore, these people would do well to take a long trip every now and then to keep the channels open! Also, Venus in the ninth house could mean that your partner was born in a foreign country, even though he is living close to you.

The following table is meant to give you some clue to the whereabouts of your real love. Look at your Equal House chart, then look to see what sign is on the cusp of the seventh house. Find the ruler of that sign on page 22. Now look to see in which house on your chart that planet appears:

RULER OF THE SEVENTH IN THE FIRST HOUSE:
This could be someone with whom you grew up, or with whom you spent considerable time as a child. It should be a person who is very well known to you over a long period of time.

RULER OF THE SEVENTH IN THE SECOND HOUSE:
May be found in the stock exchange, at the teller's window, or in any occupation in which money is handled. May be in the decorating field or in the furniture business.

RULER OF THE SEVENTH IN THE THIRD HOUSE:
May be found on short trips, at your neighbor's, through your brother or sister, or through correspondence. Also in a book shop or at your local travel bureau.

RULER OF THE SEVENTH IN THE FOURTH HOUSE:
May be found on a farm; through your parents; in the real estate business; in mining, agricultural pursuits, or in the archeology field; or in the restaurant or food industry.

RULER OF THE SEVENTH IN THE FIFTH HOUSE:
May be found at school functions or dances; at the races, sporting events, or at camp; at movies, theaters, or other places of amusement.

RULER OF THE SEVENTH IN THE SIXTH HOUSE:
May be found at your place of work; in the armed services, the civil services, the Peace Corps, or in other serving organizations. Also in the teaching profession.

RULER OF THE SEVENTH IN THE SEVENTH HOUSE:
May be your business partner or someone you meet through your

business partner or close friends. May be found at a public function, rally, press conference, or at a public speaking event; also a medical, dental, or legal conference.

RULER OF THE SEVENTH IN THE EIGHTH HOUSE:
May be found at a séance or through astrology; in the field of pathology; in the laboratory; through investment counseling, or through some connection with a legacy. Also in the insurance business or with fund-raising groups.

RULER OF THE SEVENTH IN THE NINTH HOUSE:
May be found overseas or on a long journey; at college or at a gathering of foreign students or groups which cater to the needs of foreigners; at law school or at a religious gathering.

RULER OF THE SEVENTH IN THE TENTH HOUSE:
May be found at the home of or through the influence of important people or executives; at socially prominent gatherings; with politicians or at a political rally.

RULER OF THE SEVENTH IN THE ELEVENTH HOUSE:
May be found at organizations or at a charitable party; through a casual acquaintance or on a blind date; through some unusual encounter. May be in the electronics or engineering field. May be in astrological or psychic research associations.

RULER OF THE SEVENTH IN THE TWELFTH HOUSE:
May be found in a hospital; at a university; in a bank, library, charitable association, or some institution.

Now we have some slight indication as to where you might find your life mate, if that is your desire. This does not mean that he or she will not be found elsewhere, but these signs and rulers of the seventh house were intended to serve as guidelines. The ultimate test in any marriage partner is whether that person shares with you those planetary ties which were discussed earlier in this chapter and which form the basis for all lasting and satisfying marriages.

9

Astrology of the Sun Signs

When the average person thinks of astrology, he thinks of Sun signs. Sun signs are the most obvious and most well-exploited factor in astrology. However, you must not assume that with only the knowledge of the Sun sign you hold the key to your own behavior or the behavior of someone else. When you consider that there are approximately three billion people on earth and that there are only twelve signs, it is beyond belief to think that anybody could accurately categorize all these people into twelve types. How useful is it then, to know *only* your Sun sign? The answer is, not very!

It is quite true that all Aries people have something in common, and so do all Taureans. The same is true for those individuals born under all the other signs. The reason is that there are certain specific traits which distinguish one sign from another. These traits, which were correlated with human behavior over thousands of years by empirical observations, have basic validity even today.

Let us take a look at some of the characteristics that are attributed to each of these signs. To begin with, they are based on the theory that each of the twelve signs has a natural affinity for each of the twelve houses. Aries is the natural ruler of the first house and "comes first" in the Zodiac. Its symbol is the ram's horns. Therefore, the correlate in human behavior of those born when the Sun was in

Aries (March 21 to April 21) is that they like to "come first," or break down the barriers. They are the trail blazers of the Zodiac. In addition, they have been observed to be:

Innovators, impulsive, exploring, gregarious, enterprising, and energetic.

Taurus is the natural ruler of the second house, which deals with money. The symbol of Taurus is the bull. By virtue of coming after the pioneering Aries, who has cleared out the "underbrush," the Taurean is supposed to build; therefore, the correlate in the behavior of people born when the Sun was in Taurus (April 21 to May 20) is that they like to build for their security. They are the "financiers" of the Zodiac. In addition, they have been observed to be:

Domestic, strong in will power, proud, reliable, plodding, philanthropic, and determined.

Gemini is the natural ruler of the third house, which deals with communication—by word of mouth or by writing. Its symbol is the "twins." Therefore, Gemini is supposed to spread the word about what the other two signs, Aries and Taurus, did. The correlate in the behavior of people born when the Sun was in Gemini (May 21 to June 20) is that they like to reach people either by writing or talking—and they are willing to travel to do so. They are the "transporters" of the Zodiac. In addition, they have been observed to be:

Restless, changeable, quick-thinking in emergencies, versatile, able to do two things at once, and high-strung.

Cancer is the natural ruler of the fourth house, which deals with home and family. The symbol of Cancer is the crab. It is Cancer, therefore, who is supposed to nurture and sustain the others. The correlate in human behavior of those born when the Sun was in Cancer (June 21 to July 22) is that they are protective and that they act with all the tenacity of the crab. They are the "parents" of the Zodiac. In addition, they have been observed to be:

Retentive, homebodies, ancestor-conscious, lovers of history, sensitive, acquisitive.

Leo is the natural ruler of the fifth house, which deals with children and pleasures. Its symbol is the lion. Therefore, as the lion is *supposed* to be king of the jungle, Leo is *supposed* to be the ruler of the people. More often, however, he is the figurehead monarch; he would rather *pretend* to be in authority. The correlate in the behavior of people born when the Sun was in Leo (July 23 to August 22) is that they like to "rule their own roost"—at least, they like it to appear that they do. But they would sooner have fun. They are the entertainers of the Zodiac. In addition, they have been observed to be:

> *Dramatic, commanding, lovers of pomp and ceremony, impulsive, organizing, and self-assured.*

Virgo is the natural ruler of the sixth house, which deals with service to others and to health. Its symbol is the virgin. Virgo is assigned the task of doing the "chores" for the others. The correlate in the behavior of those born when the Sun was in Virgo (August 23 to September 23) is that they understand the value of hard work and are glad to be of genuine service to others. They know that health is determined by habits and products which are pure and unadulterated. They are the "intellectuals" of the Zodiac. In addition, they have been observed to be:

> *Practical, resourceful, shy, reasoning, level-headed, methodical, and discerning.*

Libra is the natural ruler of the seventh house, which deals with partnerships—marriage as well as business. Its symbol is the scales. By virtue of its being placed opposite the first house, it deals with struggles or with those who oppose. It struggles to stay in "balance." The correlate in the behavior of people who were born when the Sun was in Libra (September 24 to October 23) is that they do not like to live alone; they are happiest when in the company of other people. They are the "romantics" of the Zodiac. In addition, they have been observed to be:

> *Easygoing, aesthetic, peace-loving, lovers of beauty (surroundings, art, jewels), impartial, and orderly.*

Scorpio is the natural ruler of the eighth house, which deals with birth, sex, and regeneration. Its symbols are the scorpion and the eagle. The Scorpio was meant to "dig" for the facts. It was Scorpio, too, who brought the dimension of ecstasy to the sex act. The correlate in the behavior of those people who were born when the Sun was in Scorpio (October 24 to November 24) is that they will search for the facts, no matter how "dirty" the job—and they will do it with dignity. They are the "researchers" of the Zodiac. In addition, they have been observed to be:

Intense, dignified, enigmatic, exacting, mysterious, and probing.

Sagittarius is the natural ruler of the ninth house, which deals with philosophy. Its symbol is the archer. By virtue of coming after Scorpio, who has "dug" for the facts, Sagittarius puts them into logical form and expounds them—or has them published. The correlate in the behavior of those who were born when the Sun was in Sagittarius (November 22 to December 21) is that they philosophize —and they will travel far and wide in search of the truth. They are the "prophets" of the Zodiac. In addition, they have been observed to be:

Quick-witted, truthful, freedom-loving, profound, farsighted, and penetrating.

Capricorn is the natural ruler of the tenth house, which deals with prestige and recognition. Its symbol is the mountain goat. Therefore, it is Capricorn who makes his way to the top, inch by inch, utilizing the work contributed by all the others and making sure that it receives the recognition it deserves. The observable correlate in the behavior of those born when the Sun was in the sign Capricorn (December 22 to January 19) is that they are intent upon success, no matter how many setbacks they receive. The Capricornian goes at it little by little, never giving up. They are the "executives" of the Zodiac. In addition, they have been observed to be:

Authoritarian, dignified, cautious, disciplined, reserved, persistent, and enduring.

Aquarius is the natural ruler of the eleventh house, which deals with organizations and friendships. Its symbol is the water bearer or waves of electricity. It is the Aquarian who is supposed to share without discrimination. His "flashes" of genius enable him to be ahead of his time. The correlate observed in the behavior of those born when the Sun was in Aquarius (January 20 to February 18) is that these people love the unusual, the original or the scientific. They are usually found to be working for some cause or organization. They are the "inventors" of the Zodiac. In addition, they have been observed to be:

Impersonal, independent, "everybody's friend," the "organization man," creative.

Pisces is the natural ruler of the twelfth house, which deals with institutions, the subconscious and the occult. It is Pisces, therefore, who is the natural healer of the Zodiac. And it is Pisces who inspires Aries who sets Taurus in motion! The correlate in the behavior of those born when the Sun was in Pisces (February 19 to March 20) is that Pisceans work quietly behind the scenes, ministering to the sick and disabled. They are the "healers" of the Zodiac. In addition, they have been observed to be:

Gentle, sympathetic, intuitive, altruistic, fair-minded, and perceptive.

You can see, then, that the Zodiac embraces most human behavior, and that together the twelve signs form a complete circle. Each sign is dependent on the next. These brief descriptions of characteristics created by the Sun passing through the various signs fall short of the lengthy character analyses based on Sun signs that are found in many astrology books. The reason for this variance is quite simply that the lengthy and detailed delineations are not based on the Sun signs alone, but on the reading of an "empty" Solar chart; i.e., a chart without the Moon or any of the other planets placed in their proper positions in the chart. This is a chart which positions the Sun sign on the first house and places the rest of the signs in their natural sequence around the other eleven houses. Each of these houses, then, takes on a meaning according to the nature of the sign on each of the house cusps. These meanings can be enlarged and embellished *ad infinitum*. Interestingly enough, however, even when you have considered every possible variation based on these empty Solar charts, you still do not have a complete picture of an individual, for it is the Moon and the rest of the planets—in addition to the Sun—that distinguish one individual from another in a truly personal way when properly placed in a natal chart.

You will notice that none of the key word descriptions that we have used to describe your Sun sign take into consideration the negative qualities attributed to each of the signs. That is because it is not the sign itself that is accountable for evil—there is no such thing as a "bad" sign—there are only certain human characteristics which, when overstressed or abused, result in negative or "undeveloped" behavior. For example, Capricorn is naturally thrifty. Capricornians know how to conserve; but the abuse of this characteristic in terms of behavior becomes miserliness. Virgo can exert excellent critical judgment; but the abuse of this characteristic becomes shrewishness or nagging.

Let us look at some of the more serious forms of negative human responses as they relate to the Sun signs. Since the Sun projects a person's individuality, the very essence of his being, let us see how these signs express themselves when people turn to crime and murder. If an Aries turns to a life of crime, he will do it in a characteristically Arien way. He may devise a new plan for robbing a bank, something that has never been tried before. Moreover, he may do it for the thrill of it rather than for any monetary gain. Taurus, on the other hand, would kill for the love of money and the things it can buy. Gemini would turn his versatility to forgery or blackmail. This is the sign that would consider kidnapping. Cancer, the mother of the Zodiac, would never surrender what he believes belongs to him. If he killed, he would probably do so because someone stole his wife or girl friend from him. Here we have the "wronged lover" who manages to make everyone feel sorry for him rather than for the victim!

Leo is flamboyant. If he turned to a life of crime, he would do it with "class." But the Leo wants to be noticed and appreciated; thus his crimes are usually devised so that they make headlines. He plans the spectacular robbery dressed in some form of disguise.

Virgo is very fastidious. If he turned to a life of crime, he would probably do it quite neatly. He cannot bear the sight of blood—neither his nor anyone else's. Therefore, if he were to commit murder, he would probably poison his victim.

Libra, the sign of beauty and harmony, would have to approach a crime from the aesthetic point of view. He could not bear to see another suffer, so he would have to make his victim happy while following the wayward path. Here is the embezzler—from his employer or from a little old lady. He always has some poetic story that makes his victim surrender his life's savings willingly. Here, too, is the gigolo!

When Scorpio turns to murder, you can be sure that sex is implicated somewhere along the way. This is the sign of a person who commits crimes of passion; he has no hesitancy in plunging the knife into his victim's back or heart. He might even cut him up!

Sagittarius is quick and to the point. He would administer the blow swiftly. He would no doubt plan a crime that involved the use of his marksmanship skills—a high-powered rifle that uses special sights. Then, too, if he were true to form, he would murder because of some religious or philosophical fanaticism.

Capricorn is ambitious for success. If he turned to a life of crime the Capricornian way, it would have to bring him into a position of authority. Here is the boss of the syndicate. He will hire others to go out and do the dirty work. He prefers to run the show—and he will demand allegiance from his underlings.

Aquarius, ordinarily inventive, would use scientific techniques. Perhaps he would devise a way to program the computer to pay him huge dividends. If he killed, it would be impulsively—on the spur of the moment and with much remorse afterwards!

Even gentle Pisces is capable of being a killer. But if Pisces turned to murder, it would be because of some imagined ideal. He would dream of it for weeks or months in advance, and once the foul deed was a *fait accompli,* he would feel justified, vindicated. The reasons would always seem high-minded to him.

Now that we have seen how extreme character disorders correlate with the various Sun signs, let us consider the positive or attracting qualities of the Sun signs as they apply to relationships between two people. Can you love or hate an individual on the basis of his Sun sign alone? The answer is an unequivocal "no"!

Many astrology books claim that people can be matched successfully on the basis of Sun signs. Nothing could be farther from the truth, for the simple reason that no matter how entertaining or enlightening Sun sign delineations seem to be, they may not apply exclusively to you except out of sheer coincidence. As we have seen, there are certain characteristics associated with each of the signs, but beyond that Sun sign delineations are not specific.

How could you possibly pick a mate on the basis of his or her Sun sign? Let us see just how little or how much they provide in matters of love and marriage. Let me cite as an illustration two young people considering marriage who come to me for astrological counseling. He is an Aquarian and she is a Piscean. What could I, as a competent astrologer, tell these people from the Sun signs alone? I might be able to tell her that he is independent, that he may appear to be quite detached at times, or that he is unemotional and not particularly family-oriented. I might mention that he possesses a scientific mind, is very experimental about sex, that he might develop a few pet eccentricities through the years, and that his friends would be a big part of their lives.

To him I might say: "Your fiancée is gentle, sympathetic, and will make a good mother. She is very good-natured and her friends would no doubt take advantage of her because she is willing to listen to their tales of woe. She may have difficulty making up her mind, because she can always see another person's point of view. She is very artistic or musical, and she's an idealist and a dreamer."

I have not told these two people anything that would serve as a certain guide to their marital happiness, because these Sun sign characteristics can be grossly modified by other factors in their charts. For example, what if his Saturn was "sitting on" or conjucts her Sun? Could she cope with the restriction that this relationship implies? What if their Mars and Venus had no relation to one another or indicated incompatibility? Would their marriage survive without a satisfactory sexual adjustment? What if either of them had Moon–Mercury stresses, so that one or the other was in a constant state of emotional turmoil? What if Pluto was aspected in his chart to accentuate volatile behavior? Could the bride adjust to his temperament if she didn't know about it in advance? And, of course, she couldn't know about it if she had only the information gleaned from a Sun sign delineation. From this example, I think you can see how unpredictable and even misleading it would be to choose your marriage partner on the basis of Sun signs alone.

Sun signs have been used to popularize astrology, and they have formed the basis for continuing astrological entertainment. They are easy to find and it's always fun to read about yourself—even though the descriptions are quite general. Sun signs do have value, but if your astrological needs go beyond amusement, if you have a personal problem in the field of friendship, sex, love, romance, marriage, career, or a problem of emotional turmoil, then you need to look at your natal chart as a whole. Even the Sun sign will take on a new dimension when it is properly read in relation to your Moon and other planets. And then, for the first time, you can begin to look at your chart for personal answers to your very personal problems.

10

Astrological Predictions and How They Are Made

Most people, at one time or another, make predictions. Scientists, on the basis of mathematical probabilities, make them all the time. The geneticist predicts what man will look like hundreds of years from now; and architects tell us about the style and form of the cities of the twenty-first century. Even the astro-physicists make long-range predictions, such as the year in which the Sun will burn out and life will cease to exist on Earth. But one doesn't have to be a scientist to make predictions. Many people make them on the basis of hunches or intuitive flashes that seem to come in mysterious ways. Everyone is accustomed to these kinds of predictions, and no one would discredit the people who make them. This penchant for making predictions is nowhere more prevalent than in the field of astrology. Some astrologers feel that their reputations as skillful practitioners rest upon the number of their successful prophecies. And since a number of these prophecies find their way into print, many people have confused astrology with fortune-telling. Some of the most spectacular predictions deal with death, illness, and a variety of other disasters. Most often, the victim in the story is a public figure; and one cannot help wondering how these people feel upon learning from a book or newspaper that they are facing death or disgrace! Should the astrologer's predictions prove accurate, his reputation as a seer may be considerably enhanced. From the professional point of view, however, his reputation as a reliable or competent astrologer is questionable.

To begin with, no responsible practitioner would ever make an unequivocal statement regarding death because he knows that on the basis of pure astrology this is impossible to do. And for him to predict any other kind of calamity for a public figure is not only unethical but unreliable. While it is true that an astrologer can know the times when a particular person is subject to intense stresses based upon planetary correlations, he is never absolutely certain how these conditions will materialize or how a given individual will react. Therefore, while these public "prophecies" make spectacular reading and serve to reassure the public that even the famous have problems, they do nothing to enhance the reputation of astrology as a serious study. It is important not to confuse astrology with the talents of a "psychic" or "clairvoyant." Occasionally, an astrologer possesses these gifts, but then his predictions are on the basis of his clairvoyance rather than on his practice of astrology.

Let us consider, too, the predictions that appear in most daily newspapers. Many individuals are fanatically devoted to these astrological columns and follow their horoscopes religiously every day. Some go so far as to predicate their daily activities upon what they read. These readings, however, have almost no chance of being applicable to an individual except on the basis of coincidence. But the power of suggestion cannot be overlooked. Suppose your horoscope one morning cautions: "Trouble where you work can mean worry that will leave you apprehensive over future prospects." This is the day you have an important interview planned concerning a possible promotion. If the promotion doesn't materialize, you might feel that the turndown was inevitable: it was the fault of the stars. It was foreordained, you might tell yourself, and there was nothing you could have done to change the course of events. Your preoccupation with what you read in the newspaper that morning may have caused you to project yourself in an unsatisfactory manner. Thus, inadvertently, you made the prediction come true.

In the chapter dealing with Sun signs, it was pointed out that newspaper and magazine "horoscopes" have only a general application to any given person; they should not be seriously considered as a source of reliable information. For that matter, even a complete and accurate natal chart is not an infallible guide to the future.

What if astrology really could predict your future accurately? What would be the point in trying to work out your own destiny? Wouldn't it happen anyway? Would you really want to know if you were facing certain disaster? The answers to these questions lie in a complete understanding of the nature of astrology.

Realizing that there is an astrological "clock" in the heavens, we should be able to tell astrological time. Telling time affords us a schedule for tackling specific activities. Some of us literally live by the clock, but even those whose lives are less rigidly controlled are subject to time cycles. It is these clock cycles, whether used on an hourly or daily basis, that keep our lives orderly. So it is with telling future time. By the movement of the luminaries and planets, we are given clues to what we should do, what we could do, and even what we should not do at specified times. This is invaluable information to those who are seeking to establish order and meaning in their daily lives and to achieve success in a chosen field. For example, it would be foolhardy to invest a fortune in a new business when astrological indications specify that this is not the time to expand. It would be fruitless to spend money on a costly European vacation when it appears that you will likely meet with serious delays, losses, or added responsibilities. It would be advisable to wait until the "hands of the clock" tell you that the time is more favorable. This is not fatalism, nor is it fortune-telling. Astrology cannot predict your future, but it can predict, with precision, those planetary correlations that act upon you at any moment of time. It can predict the trends that test your endurance or strength, or that teach you the lessons of patience, or that give you the opportunity to forge ahead toward your own goal. Astrology cannot guarantee that you will make the most of your opportunities, or that you will learn from your mistakes. That's up to you! Therefore, even though you can become aware of your prospects in advance, your future will largely depend on your actions. This is the major advantage to be gleaned from a knowledge of astrological time. You can learn to make better progress when the tide is running with you and you can learn to suffer the least when Nature's clock is adverse to your interests and goals. I would like you to understand how all astrological predictions are made, but please do this on the basis of your own chart. In other words, it will be to your advantage to learn how to tell astrological time, present and future, starting with yourself.

STEP I.

Draw a circle and divide it into twelve equal sections. These sections will be called "houses." Number the houses from one to twelve starting at the left side, or East point, and working in a counter-clockwise direction (Figure 9).

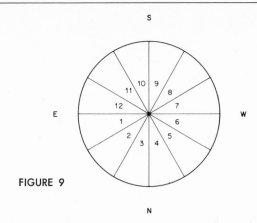

S

E   W

FIGURE 9

N

KEY TO HOUSE MEANINGS:

FIRST HOUSE	Physical body, appearance, outlook on life.
SECOND HOUSE	Possessions (household goods, clothing, jewelry), cash expenditures, income earned, money.
THIRD HOUSE	Short trips, neighbors, brothers and sisters, correspondence, writing skills, communications, early education, or elementary school.
FOURTH HOUSE	Place of residence (dormitory, apartment, etc.), parents, real-estate holdings.
FIFTH HOUSE	Romances, children, hobbies or avocations, amusements, speculations, school functions, high school.
SIXTH HOUSE	Service to others, work, place of employment, job opportunities, health, employees, small pets.
SEVENTH HOUSE	Marriage partner, business partner, close friends, open enemies, general public, contracts, doctor, dentist, trials.
EIGHTH HOUSE	Legacies, wills, insurance, sex, birth, partnership finances, occult subjects.
NINTH HOUSE	Long-distance travel, philosophy, college education, overseas communications, attorney, clergyman, professors, judges, lawsuits, marriage vows.
TENTH HOUSE	Prestige from career, social recognition, promo-

tions, type of career attraction, profession, administrators, politicians.

ELEVENTH HOUSE   Acquaintances, casual friendships, clubs and organizations, get-togethers, services from others, aspirations.

TWELFTH HOUSE   Universities, banks, hospitals, libraries, specialized education or advanced degrees, subconscious mind, intuition, dream and sleep patterns, solitary pursuits, hidden enemies, large pets.

You will notice that each house has several meanings. Each meaning is significant in the context of your own life and circumstances. For example, perhaps you are not a college graduate but have given yourself the equivalent of a college education. Or, although your circumstances prevent your touring overseas, you are an "armchair traveler." These meanings would still be entirely within the limits of the ninth house. Similarly, a bachelor does not have children of his own but he may have much to do with other people's children. Or he could choose from any of the other meanings of the fifth house which seem most suitable for a particular time. You can see then that you will be the best judge as to which meanings are most applicable to you.

STEP II.

Place the sign of your Sun and the number of degrees in which it is found at the East point of your chart. Add the rest of the signs in their natural sequence—always working in a *counterclockwise direction* (Figure 10).

FIGURE 10

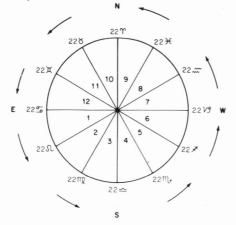

SOLAR CHART
FOR A CANCER
SUN AT 22°

If you know your birth time, calculate your rising sign as shown in Chapter 6. Place the sign and degree number at the East point, or ascendant, as it is now called. Add the rest of the signs in their natural sequence in a *counterclockwise* direction (Figure 11).

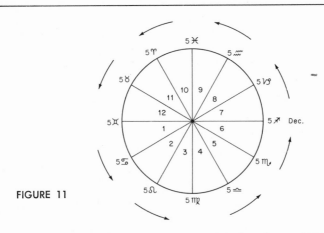

FIGURE 11

TIME CHART WITH ASCENDANT AT 5° OF GEMINI

STEP III.

Look at the ephemeris chart below (Figure 12) and select the day you wish to examine. Suppose you have chosen November 4, 1970.

NOVEMBER

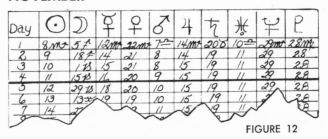

FIGURE 12

KEY				KEY			
Aries	♈	Libra	♎	Sun	☉	Jupiter	♃
Taurus	♉	Scorpio	♏	Moon	☽	Saturn	♄
Gemini	♊	Sagittarius	♐	Mercury	☿	Uranus	♅
Cancer	♋	Capricorn	♑	Venus	♀	Neptune	♆
Leo	♌	Aquarius	♒	Mars	♂	Pluto	♇
Virgo	♍	Pisces	♓				

Draw a line under this day for easy reading. Copy this line down on a separate sheet of paper. Convert it to the proper symbols for easy placement in your chart. (After you have placed a planet on your chart, check it off your list.)

Sun	11 SCORPIO	= ⊙ 11 ♏ √	Jupiter	15 SCORPIO	= ♃ 15 ♏ √
Moon	15 CAPRICORN	= ☽ 15 ♑ √	Saturn	19 TAURUS	= ♄ 19 ♉ √
Mercury	16 SCORPIO	= ☿ 16 ♏ √	Uranus	11 LIBRA	= ♅ 11 ♎ √
Venus	20 SCORPIO	= ♀ 20 ♏ √	Neptune	29 SCORPIO	= ♆ 29 ♏ √
Mars	9 LIBRA	= ♂ 9 ♎ √	Pluto	28 VIRGO	= ♇ 28 ♍ √

STEP IV.

Starting with the Sun, place each of the planets with their proper sign and degree around the outer rim of your chart (Figure 13). Remember that there are only 30° to each sign; therefore if a planet is at 29° of one sign, the next degree changes it into the next sign. The numbers *increase* in a *counterclockwise* direction, and they *decrease* in a *clockwise* direction. If there are many planets in one sign you will have to crowd them together slightly, but these positions are approximate and you only have to place them in such a way that you can see what house they belong in.

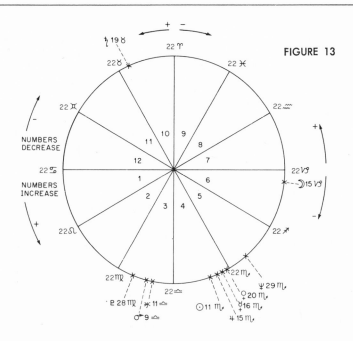

FIGURE 13

When you have placed the transiting planets in their proper places around your natal chart, you will notice that they fall in different houses. You have already covered the meanings of the various houses; now you must learn the nature of each of the planets. In addition, it is helpful to know that each planet correlates with certain kinds of individuals. The following list will enable you to see some of the things these planets stand for, without reference to the particular house in which they may be found.

MOON — Focuses on your moods and may bring minor changes; represents women, servants, nurses, children.
(negative: irritability)

SUN — Illuminates, warms, intensifies; represents men, important people, superiors, honors.
(negative: loss of prestige, disappointment)

MERCURY — Communicates, brings messages, letters, short trips, or information; represents students, businessmen, linguists, dealers, teachers.
(negative: gossip, bad news)

VENUS — Focuses on the emotions, brings pleasures, gifts, fleeting romances or flirtations; represents young girls, sisters, beauticians.
(negative: overindulgence, sloth)

MARS — Stimulates, energizes, hastens; represents young men, servicemen, athletes, policemen.
(negative: impulsive behavior, threats, burns)

JUPITER — Brings expansion, increase, optimism; represents middle-aged people, philanthropists, sportsmen, publishers, clergymen, trial lawyers.
(negative: overextension, overspending)

SATURN — Teaches, steadies, controls, brings added responsibilities; represents old people, administrators, civil lawyers, people in authority.
(negative: deprives, limits, depresses)

URANUS — Opens doors, creates opportunities, brings the unexpected, invents; represents artisans and craftsmen, engineers, physical scientists, astrologers, mechanics and electricians.

(negative: ruptures ties, such as in broken romances or marriages, eccentric behavior)

NEPTUNE   Creates yearning, seeks to inspire, searches for the ideal; represents artists, actors and actresses, biological scientists, psychics and parapsychologists.
(negative: dissolves, deceives, hides, defrauds)

PLUTO   Regenerates, rejuvenates, changes, transforms; represents researchers, plumbers, technicians, surgeons, morticians, detectives.
(negative: brings upheaval, revolution, violence and anarchy, destroys, represents gangsters and the underworld)

Here, then, in capsule form, is a description of the kinds of energy inherent in the principle of each of the transiting planets, the kinds of conditions they are likely to bring, and the various types of people or professions that could come into your life as a result of the transits. Now look at your chart and the planets that you have placed around it. You will notice that some planets are about to leave one house and enter a new one, while others have been in a particular house for a long period of time. If you apply the key word meanings of each of the planets to the house in which it is found, you will begin to comprehend its personal significance. You may also test the validity of the transits by applying the planetary meanings to those houses which the planets have recently left. In this way, by testing "past" time, you will have some indication as to the accuracy of the planetary correlations insofar as future time is concerned. You will also have some understanding of why certain events have happened and how you should respond.

As a guideline, let us illustrate how these transits could work out in the various houses. Remember, once you are familiar with the meanings of the planets and the houses, you will know which interpretations are most applicable.

Let us start with the slowest of the planets and work backwards to the swiftest, for it is the slower planets that require the most understanding and adjustments.

PLUTO
Pluto remains in one sign approximately twenty years. It is therefore important to understand the significance of this long transit as it applies to the house in which it is found or about to enter. For the

most part, it correlates with restless energy. It seeks to change exist-ing conditions, to transform, to regenerate. For some the desire for change is so strong that they refuse to go through proper channels—Pluto can then bring upheaval, revolution, or chaos. In order to make the best use of this long transit, think of the house involved in terms of needed changes—the place to apply your missionary-like spirit or your crusading zeal.

FIRST HOUSE

Pluto could transform you completely. You may decide on a whole new look for yourself by changing your hair color, undergoing plastic or cosmetic surgery, going on a very rigid diet, or changing your entire outlook on life. You may experience feelings of intense restlessness and discontent due to lack of proper outlets for energies.

SECOND HOUSE

Either your source of income will change or the ways in which you have been saving or spending it will. Some of you may get rid of all your old furniture, or have it refurbished and reupholstered. If you are too impatient, the urge to increase income may encourage you to become involved with associates of questionable reputation.

THIRD HOUSE

You may change your name, adopt a *nom de plume,* change schools, become restless, and travel frequently; your handwriting may be-come more artistic or unusual. Some of you will study journalism or become professional writers or reporters. Your brother or sister could change locales.

FOURTH HOUSE

Renovations of all kinds can come with Pluto here. You may go into the business of buying old houses, renovating them, and selling them at a profit. You may change your residence several times due to restlessness. Some of you will find that you must make needed repairs on the foundations of your houses or the plumbing may have to be changed completely. Check heating systems periodically to avoid explosions or breakdowns.

FIFTH HOUSE

You might be in a position to influence a large group of young people as a result of some revolutionary new concept. Some of you may change your ideas about fun and pastimes, be willing to try something new. Others may turn a hobby into a specialized talent. Changes in your investment portfolio can come.

SIXTH HOUSE

You will have a chance to change jobs if you wish to. You may become interested in health foods or dietetics. Small pets may be added to the household or may be gotten rid of. Employees become restless to leave. Some will enter the Peace Corps or other such service organizations. A complete new line of work attracts many, while others of the older generation think of retiring.

SEVENTH HOUSE

Certain individuals will grow restless with Pluto here and will think of discarding their old mates for "newer models." Business partners may be changed. A talent for public speaking may be developed into a rewarding outlet. Close friends come in for a "weeding out."

EIGHTH HOUSE

Students may decide to enter the field of medical research or medicine. Some make changes in their wills. Married men may find their wives want to return to work in order to augment family finances.

NINTH HOUSE

Restlessness and dissatisfaction could cause students to drop out of college. Others become involved in school disorders and protests. Some move to a foreign country. Old religions could be discarded in favor of something else or another religion. Many of you feel an intense need to educate yourselves.

TENTH HOUSE

Some will consider returning to a former profession. Some may take an administrative job, or change places with a superior who may have to work under them. Some may change careers or professions completely. Some experience an intense need for recognition. Others may have deserved notoriety.

ELEVENTH HOUSE

Some of you take a hand in transforming a group or organization. Clubs and societies could bring out your sense of pioneering. You may take up an altruistic crusade. Casual friends may assist greatly with your plans for reforms. You could be in a position to "transform" others.

TWELFTH HOUSE

Those who work in a bank, library, or hospital may change from one institution to another. Some are involved in renovating or transforming a school or institution, or building it into something new. Sleep patterns could change, requiring much less under this transit. Many become active in the concerns of museums, or in prison reform.

NEPTUNE

Look at your chart and notice where the planet Neptune is stationed. Neptune's stay in one sign is approximately fourteen years. Neptune seeks to inspire, to make dreams come true, to search for the ideal. This transit is a test of your faith and morality. The houses transited are significant in the sense that they are the areas in which you may learn your spiritual lessons or rewards. Unfortunately, too many people find deception, intrigue, and losses either in terms of goods, money, reputation, vitality, or any number of other things applicable to the house being transited. Faith, integrity, and straightforward dealings are required under a Neptune transit. The unwary are often caught off-guard. Take off your "rose-colored glasses." Have faith and trust in others, but take every practical precaution to protect yourself from fraudulent dealings.

FIRST HOUSE

You are inclined to be your own worst enemy when Neptune transits your first house because vague fears and phobias can interfere with the development of any innate artistic talent. Minor ailments are magnified out of proportion; sometimes there is a preoccupation with one's appearance. Some become a source of inspiration to others through their faith or particular talents.

SECOND HOUSE

Money may seem to drift through your fingers if you are not careful. Here is the chance to improve your earnings substantially if you use your creativity. Household furnishings—the luxuries, not the necessities—may be acquired. Some of you find that you have been deceived in your purchase of articles which turn out to be not of genuine quality. Examine fine paintings or antiques carefully.

THIRD HOUSE

Neighbors drift out of your life or seem mysterious. A talent for writing can be developed. Short trips may be a source of inspiration; for others, carelessness on trips results in losses or accidents. You may have a desire to write love letters or other emotional or inspirational forms of correspondence.

FOURTH HOUSE

The house of your dreams may come within your grasp now. If you live with your parents, they might try to induce you to remain indefinitely by catering to your comforts. Do not allow too much ease to rob you of your independence. Big real-estate or property deals can come up, but be sure they are based on firm foundations before you become involved.

FIFTH HOUSE

A search for an "ideal love" could set you on a wild goose chase; particularly vulnerable are the already married! Your yearnings for children can be satisfied now. For the unmarried, working with young people is a source of pleasure. Here is the chance to develop the hobby of a lifetime. Some take up the study of music or the piano. Fraudulent investment deals can result in losses for the unwary.

SIXTH HOUSE

You may imagine that you have every ailment in the books under this transit. Too much emotional expenditure in the wrong direction may leave you feeling absolutely "drained." You may find that you have a chance to be of service in an altruistic way. Servants, tradesmen, or employees may be quietly robbing you. The ideal job could come your way at this time; just be sure to have all the facts before you accept. Sloppy workmanship is possible from workers. Ask for references before work is done for you.

SEVENTH HOUSE

Public appearances and much publicity are possible for some of you; be certain to look your best, for you will be in the spotlight. Your marriage partner may deceive you at this time because of an illusion that things seem better elsewhere. Take care that your own indifference does not precipitate such action. Close friends may disappoint you because of their duplicity. They may use you for their own ends. Some find the ideal business partner; others may be deceived by a business partner. Contracts should be examined closely. Certain married couples could become more spiritually "in tune" and draw closer together.

EIGHTH HOUSE

Be careful that you don't dissipate an inheritance. If you are in business, pay close attention to company funds. Some of you may embark upon a series of sexual unions only to have them fall short of expectations. An interest in research, ESP, or the occult can develop now. Some find their marriage partner's income substantially increased.

NINTH HOUSE

A yearning for overseas or long-distance travel can be satisfied now. Ocean voyages or cruises will be appealing. A new spiritual approach to life becomes apparent to some. Others give way to "fuzzy thinking" and unreasonable fears. Lawsuits may result because of deception. Students will find their major subjects in college curricula.

TENTH HOUSE

This transit could bring you much publicity, recognition, and prestige if you have earned it. Otherwise it could bring scandal and notoriety. Social affairs offer the background for your talents and desire to "shine." Promotions are possible now; it is your chance to show what you can do. If you are unprepared, you may be overlooked completely when openings arise—almost as though you were invisible!

ELEVENTH HOUSE

The years during which Neptune transits the eleventh house are exceptionally rewarding to the idealistic. The chance could come to put your philosophy to work for some cause or organization. People of high principles may enter your life and inspire you. Dreams you have nurtured and cherished may come true if you have laid solid foundations. You may find that acquaintances prove to be unrealistic and even dishonest. Dreams seem to turn sour, and hair-brained schemes may divert your real purpose into illusory channels.

TWELFTH HOUSE

Inspiration comes with dreams or during periods of solitude. Prayers seem to be answered as though you had a direct line to heaven! Some of you will find your life's work in a hospital or some other institution. To the academician, the university may be a place of much intrigue. Disillusionment and disappointment could cause some to turn to alcohol and drugs. For the weak, the need to escape from the consequences of not having attended to their responsibilities might induce them to try suicide as a way out. These people rarely succeed in completing the job, but they may do untold damage to themselves in their attempt. Mediumistic tendencies can be developed, as can an interest in psychic phenomena; however, these are rewarding only for the spiritually and morally awakened. Avoid those with "Messianic complexes"; they will not be a source of real inspiration, and you may only attract the enmity of these people. Some of you will share a secret part of your life with a very idealistic and compassionate person.

URANUS

This is the planet that opens up doors and creates opportunities, often in unexpected ways. Some of you are propelled precipitously into situations for which you are poorly prepared—and will either sink or swim. The houses transited by Uranus are important to you in that they indicate where you may apply your creative genius or talent and where you may make progress rather sensationally. If you have not given any thought to what you want and where you are going, you could easily seize the wrong moment. Uranus opens the way for crackpots, eccentrics, and other unreliable characters to enter your life. Uranus' action seems to correlate with waywardness and discontinuity. The rewards are long lasting only to the discriminating and to those who know how to stick to it, for not only does Uranus encourage one along new and unusual avenues, but there is a decided tendency to break off too soon—to leave tasks unfinished, to become impatient. In this case, Uranus can take away opportunities as swiftly as it brings them.

FIRST HOUSE

Your energy quotient may be higher now. Your appearance can be dramatically improved. New fads and current eccentricities of fashion will perhaps be appealing at this time. Some of you will become more bohemian in outlook, others more creative.

SECOND HOUSE

Opportunities to earn added income appear. Get-rich-quick schemes will appeal to some, but rarely work out for the impatient. Expenditures could be heavy, but money seems to come in as abruptly as it goes out. Electrical equipment and gadgets for the house may be acquired. Some will be tempted to borrow money.

THIRD HOUSE

Expect to travel on short notice. You may have unusual incidents on these trips. Interesting neighbors might come into your life. Young students seem exceptionally restless due to lack of challenging educational opportunities. It is a good time to try your hand at short-story writing or some other unusual project. Opportunities arise to acquire a car or to get rid of one.

FOURTH HOUSE

You may leave your parents' home and set up housekeeping for yourself. Others may acquire an unusual or unique piece of property. Some of you give up your houses in favor of an apartment.

Others leave town for a new start in some other part of the country. These opportunities can arise very suddenly. Decide in advance whether such a move would be advantageous in the long run.

FIFTH HOUSE

An unusual romance could enter your life at this time; even the married are vulnerable, and home life could be disrupted badly. Do not lose your head as well as your heart, because this new "love" will undoubtedly leave your life as unexpectedly as he (or she) entered it. For the eligible, this is a time of marvelous opportunities for new and interesting romances. Some will take up an unusual hobby which could open doors for future security. Some will perfect a unique talent. Try the unusual. It is the time for vacationing and fun. Unexpected babies could come along. Some will try their hand at the stock market or other investments; others will have a desire to gamble. The wise can profit greatly during this transit; the impulsive will lose heavily. There is a tendency to buy quickly (stocks, etc.) and sell quickly.

SIXTH HOUSE

Household help may suddenly "fall into your lap," or you may decide to get rid of unsuitable help. Here is the opportunity to find a new and more exciting job. You may have a chance to be of genuine service to others. Even the young student will be able to be helpful in performing odd jobs for others. Openings could arise at work enabling you to advance. Decorators, architects or other artisans may play a part in your life now. You may find that ailments come on suddenly but respond readily to treatment—and leave just as suddenly. Your pet may require medical attention at this time. Some of you develop an interest in hygiene. Some may find that they have been unexpectedly fired or laid off from work. Others may quit their jobs as a result of temporary flare-ups. This planet also enables you to make mistakes, so you must think carefully rather than leave on the spur of the moment.

SEVENTH HOUSE

After a lengthy engagement, some may finally decide to get married. Others will marry on an impulse with no previous thought to their future. Some of you will divorce your husband (or wife) , and live to regret it. You may find yourself the center of attention by making an impromptu speech or by performing at some public function. The professional will find opportunities to be in the public eye. Business and business partnerships can be started now. Contracts of all kinds come up for consideration. Older people may sell their businesses.

EIGHTH HOUSE

An unexpected legacy might come your way. Some of you may now decide to take out insurance or make out your wills. Some will be initiated into a sexual experience that will probably be disappointing. Others keep flitting from one to another, searching. Partnership funds are subject to fluctuation. An interest in the occult or astrology might develop. There is a chance to work on some research project.

NINTH HOUSE

Here is the opportunity to go back to college, or to go to college if you have not done so. Some will start on a safari or some other unusual adventure, for long-distance travel beckons. The unwary may find themselves involved in divorce proceedings or lawsuits. Impulsiveness leads to mishaps on long journeys. Your mind seems more open to new ideas or unusual philosophies. Creativity demands an outlet, otherwise excessive energy turns to extreme nervousness and irritability.

TENTH HOUSE

This can be one of the high points of your career if you are ready. Recognition can come your way rather sensationally. Opportunities abound to meet important people. You may achieve a high promotion on the executive or managerial level. Doors can open to you socially—and close just as fast if you are not prepared to accept prescribed requirements. The world or circle in which you travel will broaden considerably, and people will have a chance to assess you. You may decide to return to an old career or switch to an entirely new field. Administration shake-ups might place you in a different situation. Some of you may even be forced out of your jobs because of scandal.

ELEVENTH HOUSE

Clubs, societies, and organizations may hold great appeal for you now. Here is your opportunity to meet unusual individuals. You may work hard for a charitable cause. Help from an unexpected source could bring you closer to your goals. You may be turned down for club membership. Unusual friendships will be formed, but they will not be long lasting as a rule. Long separations are possible.

TWELFTH HOUSE

A new receptivity to unusual ideas will now be noticed. Flashes of genius may seem to come from out of the blue. Unexpected trips to the hospital are possible. Opportunities open up with regard to some institution. Medical personnel may change hospitals. Some will be introduced to the study of astrology or related subjects. For those who work in schools or banks or libraries, new opportunities open up. Some may acquire large pets.

SATURN

This is the planet that correlates with lessons, teachings, self-control, responsibility, and maturity. Saturn tests your patience and endurance; without these qualities life becomes very "chancy" indeed, for you are soon broken by every little adversity that comes along. You are not meant to run from the hardships of a Saturn transit—you are supposed to learn the lessons intended. Saturn rewards those who endure and conquer, who learn from their hardships but do not become martyrs. To the immature, Saturn indeed seems to be ruthless, for it can bring restrictions, limitations, depression, and seemingly insurmountable problems. But often it is your own attitude toward these tests of life rather than the test itself that is important. Saturn's gains are for the long term, and they are the most enduring. It remains approximately two and one-half years in each sign.

FIRST HOUSE

Saturn in the first house generally brings a renewed sense of responsibility and well-being only to those who have done their "homework." You may seem more purposeful now and feel that you know your life's direction. For the unprepared, there is a feeling of frustration due to one's own inadequacies. Some may appear more somber and reflective.

SECOND HOUSE

Your income may increase very consistently during Saturn's stay in this house. Some of you may sell your household goods. You may find that your income is limited or that your salary is cut. Others have difficulty in collecting bills owed to them. It is a time when people in small business think of giving up because the restrictions and limitations in immediate earning power seem great. Much patience and hard work is needed.

THIRD HOUSE

Less running around means that you can now settle down and accomplish something. Delays, cancellations, and assorted problems take the pleasure out of travel. Young people in grade school may begin to have difficulties in reading, writing, or comprehension. It is frequently a temporary problem and is often due to an unsympathetic teacher. Some will find it very difficult to settle down and write letters. Others will assume more responsibilities for their brothers or sisters. There is sometimes a temporary estrangement between family members.

FOURTH HOUSE

Some may dispose of a piece of property. Some sell the old family homestead. Students or young people may feel disenchanted with family life or parents. Some will find that home life tests their patience severely. This is a poor time generally to build a new home, for there are often costly delays and problems. Some will acquire real estate as a future investment. Mother or father may be an added responsibility or need help.

FIFTH HOUSE

Investments should be made with the idea that they are for long-term gains. A romance entered upon now may not be too satisfying. The already married could become involved with another partner because of a feeling that romance is passing them by, but chances of satisfaction are slim. Children seem to be a bit of a burden. This transit seems to delay some in starting a family. Some will find a much older love.

SIXTH HOUSE

Feelings of fatigue can be due to emotional frustration. Employees could leave you shorthanded, and there may be delays or difficulties in replacing them. Any change of job at this time may not prove immediately satisfying. Be cautious about leaving your old job unless you are sure of getting something better. It is usually a difficult task to get a better job at this time. It is a good time to have that medical checkup.

SEVENTH HOUSE

An old friend may come back into your life at this time. Some of you will lose the friendship of someone to whom you were very close because of your own irresponsible or offhand behavior. Some will have more responsibility in making public appearances. Some may not appear too magnetic under this transit—be sure to be prepared rather than rely on your charm. Your old doctor or dentist may retire. Men often marry at this time, but not necessarily for love. It is more often with the feeling that "it's time to settle down." Marriages are subject to testing and some emerge more united than ever.

Old enmities are patched up. Some experience delays in negotiating contracts.

EIGHTH HOUSE
Partnership funds may be rather limited for a period of time. There may be delays in distributing cash or goods from a legacy. Some may go into the insurance business. Life insurance or bonds could come to maturity at this time. Some will go into the investment or counseling business. Others will find that they have been appointed executors or trustees.

NINTH HOUSE
Saturn's transit here sends many people off to their attorney in search of a divorce. It is usually a mistake to divorce at this time because what seems like a valid grievance now will not seem so important at a later date. Lawsuits often give cause for concern. Things are maddeningly slow, but the delays can work to your ultimate benefit. Those of you who take an overseas trip at this time usually find that you have difficulties and responsibilities to cope with that you had not planned on. Some will marry an older or very responsible partner. The college student may experience difficulties. The urge to drop out will be very strong, but the rewards come to those who stick with it.

TENTH HOUSE
If you have prepared the way by your previous actions, you can now achieve remarkable prestige and honors in your career. For many it is a time of testing. You may find that the boss has placed some obstacle in the way, or seems to restrict you, or asks you to take on extra obligations. If you are prepared to be patient and "eat humble pie" for a while, you will emerge triumphant. False pride may cause others to quit, and they may have to start the long climb to build up seniority again. Do not be upset if you seem to be slighted socially— you are simply being tested. Do not overreact.

ELEVENTH HOUSE
Decide in advance how much work you want to do for your club or organization before you get involved. This is a time when all the responsibility could fall on your shoulders. Be prepared to do it yourself. Old friends may need your help, and you could find yourself involved in their problems much of the time. Do not expect help from the old established members of your club if you have just joined; you must prove yourself first. Some of you will have your

requests for membership turned down or subject to much delay. Try again when Saturn leaves here.

TWELFTH HOUSE

Students may find that much time is taken up in solitary pursuits, such as research. You could spend many hours in a library. Older people could seem antagonistic or unreliable at this time. Old friends may temporarily become your antagonists. Don't be disappointed by estrangements—consider what these people really mean to you. Some of you will learn your greatest lessons while you're alone. The receptive will discover their true purpose in life; the weak and immature will bog down in self-pity and depression. Some will become prey to unreasonable fears. Stimulants will be resorted to in an attempt to avoid having to think. Others will sequester themselves and refuse to face up to the facts of life. Extraordinary psychic experiences could occur at this time. This is the transit that will determine your future actions and is one of the hardest lessons to learn because you must face it alone for the most part; others will be unaware of your difficulties. For those who pass their tests, the benefits are the most rewarding of all.

JUPITER

This planet spends approximately one year in each sign and tries to make life very rewarding in terms of the house it is transiting. Jupiter is supposed to be the "greater benefic," and while this is possible, it is not necessarily better in the long run than Saturn, which has been called a "malefic." One usually feels very expansive and optimistic under this transit. It is a time to put out your best effort. Rewards can come to you if you make an effort to put yourself in the right place at the right time. Jupiter can bring failure if you allow your optimism to blind you to the practical realities. Enthusiasm is no substitute for preparation. There is always the tendency to overextend with this planet; with Jupiter "the sky is the limit," and people often forget that lean days may follow. For example, if Jupiter brings a windfall financially, some will spend it just as fast as it comes in and even go into debt. They can emerge from this transit worse off than they were before. Others will invest part of the money and allow themselves the pleasure of spending up to a certain limit.

FIRST HOUSE

Feelings of optimism predominate. You may put on weight because of a more relaxed mood. Life seems more hopeful now. Some feel more independent and may want to be free of unpleasant responsibilities. Some indulge in rich foods which can produce unhealthy side effects.

SECOND HOUSE

Great sums of money (relative to your own circumstances, of course) could be spent now. Money seems more plentiful and easier to come by. Some will have a tendency to overextend themselves and get into debt. Extravagant gifts could come your way.

THIRD HOUSE

You may find that you are constantly writing letters and enjoying it immensely. Short trips could be most rewarding. Children seem happier at grade school now. You might have more to do with brothers or sisters at this time. If you have always wanted to write a book or story, now is the time to start.

FOURTH HOUSE

If you have been wanting to move to a bigger house, this is the time to look. Some of you will add a new room or make major improvements on your present dwellings. Don't be surprised if you have to spend more money than you had anticipated. Real-estate opportunities should be investigated at this time. Many will find genuine pleasure in entertaining at home.

FIFTH HOUSE

A marvelous time can be had for those who are looking for romance. Go where the action is—don't wait for the "right one" to just drop into your lap. Get out and meet people. Accept that blind date—it may be a steppingstone to something very important. Some will meet the person who will eventually become their marriage partner. Investigate the stock market for "blue chips." Some will have a lucky streak, but should not count on its duration. The married could increase their family at this time. Others may give birth to their "brain child." If you can take a vacation, plan to go somewhere special. Some will try their hand at ranching, polo, horseback riding, or archery.

SIXTH HOUSE

If you have been wanting to hire help, this is a good time to try. You may have better luck with workmen or employees. It's a time when many job offers can come your way. Some will find just what they have been looking for. Now you can take steps to remedy old conditions which you have been neglecting. Some enter the nursing profession or other fields of service.

SEVENTH HOUSE

The marriage-minded could have great success in finding true love if they have paved the way. Partnerships may be started now. Business contracts and negotiations may be entered upon. You will have great appeal with the public. It's a good time to develop your public speaking talents, even if only at the P.T.A. Some will have a great deal of publicity. Politicians will be favorably received by the public. This is the time to increase your circle of friends.

EIGHTH HOUSE

Inspiration may seem to come from some occult or psychic source. Some will receive an inheritance now. Your marriage partner may receive an increase in salary. Some will receive news of a birth. Some will take out additional insurance policies. The research-minded will be able to make much progress.

NINTH HOUSE

Now is the time to take that trip abroad. Some will take their first jet ride. The adventuresome will travel around the world, or investigate new philosophies or religions. College students will find their fields of major interest. Marriages can be successfully entered upon now. This is a good time to settle a lawsuit. Some will have a short story or book published. Foreign investments can be negotiated successfully. Your attorney can be most helpful to you.

TENTH HOUSE

When Jupiter reaches the top of your chart, you will receive the rewards of your previous efforts. It is a good idea to begin to pave the way long before it gets there so that you may take the fullest advantage of this transit. Honors, promotions, and social recognition could come at this time. If you are not a professional or do not have a career, you might achieve status and esteem from your social peers. You will be in the limelight—make the most of it. It's a good time to contact executives or those in authority who could assist you. The student may be attracted to politics as a possible career.

ELEVENTH HOUSE

If you know what you want and you have laid the groundwork, you could have your desires materialize. Friends and acquaintances are very helpful now. Clubs and organizations may be a source of pleasure. Some of you will be asked to join the club of your choice. It's a good time to ask someone to put you up for membership if they have not already asked you. A casual acquaintance could prove to be a benefactor. You may have much to do with people from foreign countries.

TWELFTH HOUSE

There is a tendency to want to be alone. For some, these moments will be the most relaxing, but there are likely to be many demands made upon you when you try to get off by yourself. It's a good time for research. The medical student or nurse could find the perfect hospital to be associated with. Banks play a prominent role for some. A love affair could be carried on quietly, unknown to anyone. Some are in love with someone who seems very elusive. Large pets will be acquired or need attention. Ranching and cattle business attract some.

MARS

Mars hastens and stimulates. Where you find Mars, you generally find action. The particular house that is being transited seems to come to life. Mars is like a catalyst, for it can set others in your life into action. Mars can remain in one sign for as little as six weeks or as long as eight months. In the course of one year and 322 days, it makes one entire revolution around your natal chart and, in so doing, forms every conceivable aspect to all your natal planets. The lesson of this transit is to take your time.

FIRST HOUSE

You will seem to be much more energetic now. You will have the initiative to put all those self-improvement plans you've made into action.

SECOND HOUSE

If you have accumulated any money, Mars will try to stir you into spending it. Some will overspend and find the bills accumulating. In some cases, bills come due for purchases made much earlier. It is a poor time to get involved in installment-plan payments unless you have planned ahead.

THIRD HOUSE

In your hurry to get to your destination, you might throw caution to the wind and bring about some mishap by speeding, running, etc. This is no time to write that nasty letter. Some will take up neglected correspondence.

FOURTH HOUSE

Fires, burns, and accidents are possible if you are careless. Don't smoke in bed. Others will accomplish a lot of work around the house or property. If you have been wanting to move, you may do so at this time.

FIFTH HOUSE

If you're not in shape, don't take up skiing at this time. There is always the tendency to live dangerously with Mars here. Use this time to perfect skills which have lain dormant. Accent is on romance and fun.

SIXTH HOUSE

Your work load increases tremendously and you have the energy to handle it. If you are unemployed or between jobs, this is a good time to look for work. Some may find employees or fellow workers very aggressive or outspoken.

SEVENTH HOUSE

There is much activity with close friends. If contracts have been pending, this is the time that they will be signed or that you will come to an agreement about a partnership. Public functions put you in the spotlight.

EIGHTH HOUSE

Money from your partnership or as a result of a contract comes into your hands. Your friends could introduce you to the novelty of a séance, or you might attend a function relating to the occult. You might be tempted to cash in an insurance policy.

NINTH HOUSE

Lawsuits come to judgment at this time. Foreign communications are accentuated. College students may find they are involved in some campus turmoil. The urge to travel is strong. Some will call upon their ministers.

TENTH HOUSE

If you have been hoping to come to the attention of your boss, now is the time it could come to pass. Superiors or politicians or executives could assist in getting you a promotion or recognition. Others may tell the boss off in a fit of anger. Do not be upset at any social slight that you may receive now—do not overreact. Some may have reason to gossip about you.

ELEVENTH HOUSE

It may seem that all the clubs and organizations that you belong to will be having some function that claims your time and energy. Some will feel enthusiastic about entertaining friends. New acquaintances will be made. It is a time to take the initiative and "get about." Some will raise funds for some charity.

TWELFTH HOUSE

Those who have put off elective surgery will now have the courage to go through with it. Some will have difficulty in finding a moment to themselves. It's a good time to visit museums, libraries. Students may contemplate starting graduate studies.

VENUS

Venus may spend as little as twenty-six days or as much as four months in one sign. This planet does not correlate with any particularly difficult lesson except that of overindulgence, and if this can be tolerated by your financial condition and your physique, all well and good. Venus strives for peace and harmony and pleasure through our emotions. Sometimes, however, it brings disappointment.

FIRST HOUSE

You may view the world through rose-colored glasses with Venus here. You are very receptive to music and art appreciation, and you will try to look your best. Your friends may remark that you seem more lighthearted and amiable.

SECOND HOUSE

The feeling that you want to look your best could inspire you to spend rather lavishly for a new wardrobe or replenish your old one. You may receive a bonus or a gift. The homemaker will splurge for new and exciting food items.

THIRD HOUSE

Some pleasant experience in connection with neighbors is possible. The mail may bring a pleasant invitation. A call could come from someone special to please you. This is a good time to write a love letter. Those of you who are careless will lose a piece of jewelry while on a short trip.

FOURTH HOUSE

Your home can be a real source of pleasure. Even bachelors may decide to entertain in their apartments. This is a good time to look at property with an eye to making a change at some future date.

FIFTH HOUSE

This is a time for fun and good times. Romance is in the air for the eligible. Accept invitations with Venus here—even the most uninspiring date could be a prelude to meeting someone more attractive. A lucky win at the races is possible for some. Others will enjoy a special outing with their children or other young people. Investments dealing with luxury items can be made.

SIXTH HOUSE

Any vacancies in your work force can be filled to advantage. Overindulgence in rich foods might cause an upset. Some happy social event at your place of business is possible. Now is the time to acquire a pet.

SEVENTH HOUSE

Some may receive a lovely gift from their marriage partner or a close friend. It's a good time to entertain close friends or your business partner. Husbands and wives may share some happy experience. There's popularity with the press for those in the limelight. Some may attend a rally or other public function.

EIGHTH HOUSE

A gift of money could arrive at this time. Romance with a "sweet young thing" could be tempting now. Some will find themselves clipping coupons and cashing them in. This is the time to insure jewels or furs.

NINTH HOUSE

Foreign communications bring much pleasure. News could be received from a sister living at a great distance from you. Books will provide mental pleasure for those unable to travel.

TENTH HOUSE

People you have been trying to impress may be most receptive to your advances now. You may find a young woman most helpful to you. Social affairs are a source of pleasure and helpful contacts for the future.

ELEVENTH HOUSE

Now is the time to visit clubs and societies with an eye to becoming a future member. You may be the guest of a young woman who could put you up for membership in the future. Some will attend testimonial dinners. Invitations will arrive from casual friends.

TWELFTH HOUSE

Reconciliation with a girl friend is now possible. Some will find pleasure in solitary pursuits. Others will open a savings account or put their jewelry in a vault.

THE SUN

Since the Sun illuminates, we can think of that particular house being transited with its lights on! It's a time to take a look at those affairs governed by the house in which the Sun is found. The Sun also correlates with important people or superiors, and it is possible that you might see where your potential source of help can come from ahead of time.

FIRST HOUSE

The spotlight is on you. Your vitality seems lower, but it is only because it is a time to revitalize yourself with rest and health-giving foods. Some appear to be more self-assured. Now is the time to start becoming the person you want to be, even if it means that you must play a role in the beginning.

SECOND HOUSE

Take a look at your wardrobe or personal belongings to see what needs to be done to improve matters. Some will find the boss very receptive to a raise at this time. Household items are now being scrutinized.

THIRD HOUSE

It's a good time for that short trip. Important contacts can be made for the future. You may be aware that your correspondence is piling up and is in need of your attention. Family reunions are possible.

FOURTH HOUSE

Some find that they now have a house guest. You might entertain the boss or some other important person at home. Some of you will see your houses in a different way. Property matters come to light.

FIFTH HOUSE

You may feel like playing now. Some of you will find much pleasure at the theater or other places of entertainment. Take the children to some special event. Some will look over their investment portfolios.

SIXTH HOUSE

Now is the time to go on that diet to achieve a new sense of well-being. Some man could assist dramatically at work. Others of you realize that you are not in the right job and could find a more sympathetic person to work for. It's a good time to hire temporary help.

SEVENTH HOUSE

Public speeches and appearances may be in the offing. Your audience will really warm up to you now. Affairs of friends may keep you involved. Important people could assist in your business. You and your marriage partner may spend time alone.

EIGHTH HOUSE

Some of you will take a new look at the amount of insurance you are carrying. Others find their partnership finances are in need of auditing. Young women could find a man intent on playing the role of their lover. Some will attend a christening.

NINTH HOUSE

A holiday trip could take you a long distance. Others may stay at home with travel magazines. Some will have dealings with a lawyer or judge. For those contemplating marriage, it is a time to select a minister or to consult with your family minister.

TENTH HOUSE

Contact people who can help you get ahead. Some man in an influential position may assist. Social engagements bring recognition or allow you to shine. People may notice you more now.

ELEVENTH HOUSE

If you want to get into that special club, use your most important reference. Some will feel particularly charitable now. You may be asked to volunteer for some cause. The emphasis is on your aspirations for the future. Get to work and find out the best way to make your dreams come true.

TWELFTH HOUSE

If your work requires research, now is the time to take care of it. Visits to the library can yield rewards. Secret consultations are possible. Romance may be blooming behind the scenes. Some are in love with a dream man who is unaware of their devotion.

MERCURY

Mercury correlates with correspondence, communications, transportation, and salesmen, to name just a few things. Mercury passes swiftly through the signs. It may spend as few as fifteen days in one sign or as long as two months. In negative aspects, it correlates with petty thievery, forgery, plagiarism, and gossip.

FIRST HOUSE

Thoughts turn to how to project a more important or attractive public image. Some will get in touch with those who can advise them about self-improvement or personal problems.

SECOND HOUSE

Some will make financial gains by signing some form of agreement. Some must make calls or take trips to collect money or goods. Bills will come in which need to be attended to. Students purchase or sell books.

THIRD HOUSE

Your mind turns to thoughts of travel. Some of you will find that you seem to be doing a lot of running around. You may get news of your brothers or sisters. Feelings of restlessness may stimulate you to put your thoughts down on paper. Be sure to have all the facts before writing any important letters.

FOURTH HOUSE

Agreements concerning property or real-estate matters can be reached. Some will now consider the possibility of a future move. Others will find that their homes are a temporary haven for young people or students. Traveling salesmen may call upon you at home. Your child's teacher may visit.

FIFTH HOUSE

Invitations to a dance or a school social could arrive. Others think about taking up a new hobby. Thoughts turn to fun and romance. Some check up on their investments. Some may even make a trip to the races.

SIXTH HOUSE

Communications concerning interviews or job opportunities can reach you. Some think about getting help with their medical problems. Others decide to go on a health diet. Thoughts turn to getting a new pet, or you may be concerned about your present one. Some will receive notice that their help is leaving.

SEVENTH HOUSE

Contracts of all kinds may be signed now. You may reach an agreement about going into business. Thoughts turn to close friends or marriage partner's concerns. A visit to your doctor or dentist is possible. Some will appear in court.

EIGHTH HOUSE

Word may reach you of an inheritance. Some may experiment with drugs or sex indiscriminately. Trips to your insurance broker are a possibility. Partnership funds may be of temporary concern.

NINTH HOUSE

Letters or other forms of communication may be received from those who live at a great distance from you—perhaps overseas. You may make plans for your next vacation. College students could have some concern with their grades or exams. Writers may be waiting for word from their publishers.

TENTH HOUSE

There may be visits to potential employers. Someone in authority may have an important message or idea for you. An invitation from or to your boss is possible. You may have some temporary concern about your chosen field or career. Many send out résumés.

ELEVENTH HOUSE

Invitations are received to attend a banquet or a charitable party. Casual acquaintances might contact you for a favor. Young people may need your help. Consider carefully before signing any agreements for a friend.

TWELFTH HOUSE

If your work requires some research, now is the time to take care of it. Visits to the library are more productive for those who cannot be free of interruptions at home. Some will have secret consultations. Some will be concerned about clandestine romance.

THE MOON

The Moon makes one complete revolution around your natal chart in one month and spends approximately two and one-half days in each house. The following list will give you some indication as to the nature of this transit.

FIRST HOUSE

Some female acquaintance may give cause for a slight or hurt feelings. This transit may act as a catalyst for deciding on a particular course of action.

SECOND HOUSE

Purchases made previously may arrive now. Some may buy a present for a nurse or a child. Checks may arrive.

THIRD HOUSE

There may be a call from a woman friend; there may be a short trip or chance encounter with a woman while on a trip. Visits to the neighbors are possible.

FOURTH HOUSE

Some will have an urge to rearrange the house or change a furniture grouping. Some woman might call on you at home.

FIFTH HOUSE

A night out on the town, or a visit to a special restaurant or movie is likely. Some woman plays an important role temporarily. Some feel the urge to gamble. Dividends from a stock might arrive.

SIXTH HOUSE

A chance to be of service to someone is possible. Some may feel the concerns of a woman employee. Your pet may go off to the kennel or pet "beauty shop."

SEVENTH HOUSE

You may have a chance to shine in the eyes of the public for a brief moment. You may make an impromptu speech. An occasion arises to be with an old girl friend. Some of you will attend graduation exercises or a P.T.A. meeting. You may need to see your dentist.

EIGHTH HOUSE

Some may feel particularly amorous with the Moon here. A question of taxes may arise now. Some might attend a meeting on something to do with astrology or the occult.

NINTH HOUSE

You may receive a letter from a foreign friend. An occasion to be with the minister's wife or daughter could arise. You might meet a publisher, or your lawyer. You may be required to testify.

TENTH HOUSE

Recognition from the boss's wife could come your way. There may be a chance to be with someone who might hold the key to future advancement. Invitations to a debutante cotillion might arrive.

ELEVENTH HOUSE

The occasion to attend a testimonial dinner could arise. Others attend a function relative to fund-raising or other charitable or club work.

TWELFTH HOUSE

The Moon here usually marks the day when one makes a trip to the bank or visits a friend in the hospital. Some may take their child to the library. Others find that they sleep very fitfully during a twelfth house transit.

The Moon can be compared with the second hand on a clock. In addition, it seems to correlate with feelings of temporary restlessness or irritability. The Moon is the significator of fertility and cyclical activity—not only physiological, but psychological as well.

Its transits explain why one seems to be up one day and down the next. Most of the activity connected with the Moon as it makes its way around your chart is of no lasting consequence, but it is interesting to note how accurately it brings the particular house transited into focus. For the beginner, this is a good test of the astrological hypotheses. The Moon, being so swift, allows one to notice results and accumulate data in a relatively short time. Learn to observe the sign in which the Moon is found as it transits your chart so that you can be aware of a corresponding attitude on the part of the people who come into your life at that time. For example, an Aries Moon is swift, and if you are at the hairdresser's or the barber shop, you will notice that the operator seems to get you in and out of there in a hurry. A Taurus Moon is much slower, and people are inclined to take their time. If you are thinking of hiring an employee with the idea that he or she will stay with you a long time, do so in a Taurus Moon, but by the same token, you may have trouble getting rid of this person if you are not satisfied with his work! A Gemini Moon is talkative, and you may notice that people in the supermarket or at other stores where you do your shopping are anxious to make conversation. Also, you may accomplish tasks swiftly at this time. A Cancer Moon is sensitive. Your digestion, for better or worse, may be the topic on your mind. Or you may be in the mood to prepare some special dish or to putter around the house. Leo wants to play, so you may find that people are more friendly and amusing during a Leo Moon. When the Moon is in Virgo, you will notice that some people seem more fussy or critical. Things that had not bothered your marriage partner before may suddenly become irritating, and you will hear about it.

If you have planned some public function, dinner party, or other get-together, you might notice that things look more beautiful or that the affair runs very smoothly under a Libra Moon. The women seem more charming and the men more considerate or romantic. A Scorpio Moon often seems to correlate with an intensity of feeling. People are generally interested in probing; some may seem more secretive or reserved. Sagittarius brings out the philosophy in others. Your milkman may suddenly expound his particular viewpoint at this time. Workers may make a brilliant start, but fizzle out before the work is done. Capricorn correlates with caution, and you may notice that people seem more reserved or melancholy. Workers will be more painstaking. Expect the unexpected in an Aquarius Moon; things never seem to work out as you think. Moods, however, are much brighter and friendlier.

People seem kinder and more humane when the Moon is in Pisces. If you happen to be a patient in a hospital, you could notice that the medical personnel really seem to care about your welfare.

In summation, all bonafide astrological predictions are made on the basis of Nature's clock (i.e., the movement of the luminaries and the planets) . An accurate reading of this clock not only makes it possible for you to be able to tell present time, but also to anticipate likely avenues for expansion, pleasure, and so forth, well into the future. There is, of course, always more than one way in which these transits can work. For this reason, it is impossible for the astrological practitioner to state unequivocally that an event will materialize. That is not his function in any case. At best, he is able to help you to plot your own course of action over a period of time by explaining the nature of the transiting planet, its relation to the house in which it is found, and the dates on which you might expect action precipitated by the planet under consideration. Now you will be able to do this for yourself. Remember, though, that no matter what planet or aspect you may find in plotting future time, you are not allowed to see disaster or, for that matter, success. What the transits indicate, however, is what you must do either to avoid unnecessary hardships or to take advantage of favorable aspects. Many individuals wonder why all the "bad" aspects seem to bring trouble right on time, and that so often they are shortchanged or even by-passed by the good. This imbalance stems from the fact that it is necessary to know *beforehand* the nature and timing of the various transits. It is important to prepare the way long before the easy aspects arrive in order to derive the maximum benefit. Similarly, when an individual knows that a difficult aspect from Saturn, for example, will be in his sixth house, he must take steps beforehand to protect himself by having a thorough physical examination and by paying special attention to good health habits.

Once you have firmly mastered the art of telling time, life will take on a new meaning for you. You will feel more secure knowing that the game of life need not be left to chance. The smile of fortune is not solely for a few lucky individuals—it is meant for each and every one of you. Though you may not have been born rich, or of famous parents, or even good-looking, each of you can be successful if you are willing to do the work of plotting future time from your own chart—and the more difficult work that prepares you to take maximum advantage of favorable aspects and develop the patience to persevere during the times of stress.

Of Good . . . and Evil!

Those of you who are familiar with astrological lingo are aware that astrologers often speak of, or refer to, "afflicted charts" or "afflicted planets." This term sounds ominous, particularly if it refers to you. In terms of modern astrology the reference to affliction is completely invalid, having been based on an antiquated concept. There is no such thing as a true astrological affliction. The word itself is defeating because it seems to represent an insurmountable weakness or obstacle, and if this were true, astrology would be a tool for the morbid. It is not!

It is important to remember that at one point in history life was extremely precarious. Plagues and infections carried people off at an alarming rate and often at an early age. The diseases of childhood which we can so easily cope with today took a formidable toll on young lives. Modern surgical techniques were unknown. It was no wonder, then, that ancient astrologers were prognosticators of gloom. However, astrological interpretations have not taken into consideration the important new developments in so many fields. These interpretations still carry the old references, and people have been needlessly frightened by them. It is up to the new generation to define these so-called afflictions in a modern context. Let us now take a new look at the old problem.

A chart is said to be afflicted when it contains many planets in square relationships or when planets are in opposition to other planets. Another form of affliction purportedly occurs when any of the "malefic"* planets, such as Mars, Saturn, Uranus, Neptune, or Pluto, are in conjunction with any of the other planets or luminaries. While it is quite true that the malefics are usually implicated in cases of disaster, it is quite untrue that the planets or the aspects themselves are in any way evil. It is simply a matter of correlation. Mars, for example, correlates with energy. This energy might pursue undesirable avenues, however, resulting in unpleasant consequences.

Another example is the planet Uranus. This planet correlates with opportunities. Uranus opens doors, often in an unexpected way. If, however, you were to choose a course of action without giving it intelligent consideration, Uranus could just as easily open the door to chaos instead of opportunity. It is not the planets that are to blame, nor is it your "afflicted" chart—rather it is a question of what you have done previously to prepare the way, or what you intend to do when a specific planetary aspect occurs, that becomes of paramount importance.

Let us consider three aspects which are supposed to cause the afflictions: the square, the opposition, and the conjunction. The first of these, the square, has always had the reputation of being the worst possible aspect because the square correlates with endings and beginnings, stops and starts. This aspect has a way of ending conditions which have either just begun or which you'd hoped to continue. A chain is no stronger than its weakest link, and the square is the test that will find that weakness. The square has commonly been held as an energizing aspect. This can be true, but more often it is just the opposite. It slows things down considerably. Look at a square. It has four sharp angles or corners. Before you can go around a corner, you must make a very sharp turn. Try to walk in a square and you will understand some of the difficulty implied. If you turn the corner too fast, you are in danger of being thrown off balance. And so it is in life. If you have set out upon a particular plan of action, under a transiting square aspect you may be in danger of being thrown off course as you try to "turn your corner." Under the square aspect you are being tested. If you are temporarily derailed by certain diffi-

---

* Ancient astrologers considered Mars and Saturn to be the only malefics, since Uranus, Neptune, and Pluto were all discovered within relatively modern times. Modern astrologers however, have classified the last three as malefic for the most part.

culties, you might become discouraged and break off. This is precisely what happens in so many cases. For this reason, astrologers
find it easy to predict difficulties for many people, because it is
human nature to follow the path of least resistance. Instead of
persevering, the normal inclination is to become despondent and
then to lose self-confidence because of a temporary defeat. There
are, of course, many effects of the square. It is important to learn
how to calculate and how to recognize a square, for if you are aware
of it in advance, you will be able to anticipate the nature and timing
of your own tests. Then you are not so likely to be caught off guard
nor to be thrown into a state of despondency when situations do not
materialize as expected.

How to Calculate a Square

First, draw a circle and divide it into twelve equal parts. For a
Solar chart, place the Sun sign and the number of degrees it is found

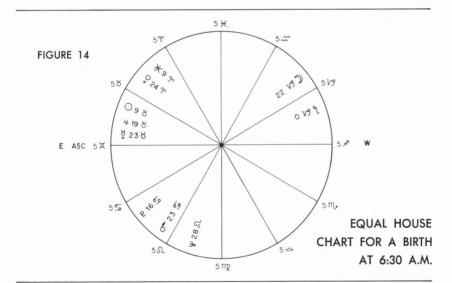

FIGURE 14

EQUAL HOUSE
CHART FOR A BIRTH
AT 6:30 A.M.

in at the East point (left side) ; or, for a Time chart, place the sign
of your ascendant and the number of degrees at the East point
(Figure 14). Place your natal planets in the chart as you learned to
do in Chapter 6. For example:

Next, choose a particular month or day that you wish to examine for potential or current square aspects. Suppose it is the month
of September, 1970. Consult the ephemeris in the back of the book
and find September, 1970. Start with the slowest moving planet,

HOW TO RECOGNIZE AND CALCULATE A SQUARE

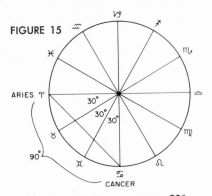

FIGURE 15

The sign Aries is square to or 90°
away from Cancer.

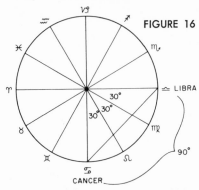

FIGURE 16

The sign Cancer is square to or 90°
away from Libra.

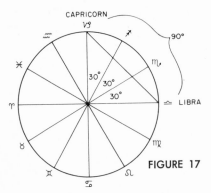

FIGURE 17

The sign Libra is square to or 90°
away from Capricorn.

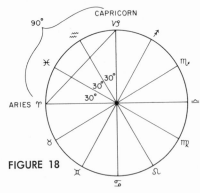

FIGURE 18

The sign Capricorn is square to or 90°
away from Aries.

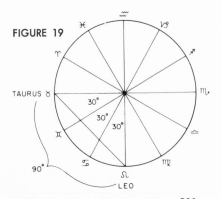

FIGURE 19

The sign Taurus is square to or 90°
away from Leo.

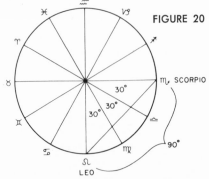

FIGURE 20

The sign Leo is square to or 90°
away from Scorpio.

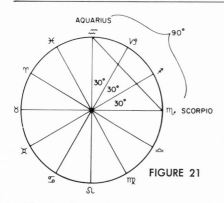

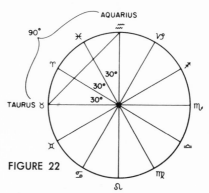

The sign Scorpio is square to or 90°
away from Aquarius.

The sign Aquarius is square to or 90°
away from Taurus.

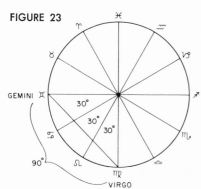

FIGURE 23

FIGURE 24

The sign Gemini is square to or 90°
away from Virgo.

The sign Virgo is square to or 90°
away from Sagittarius.

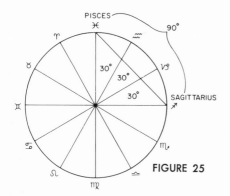

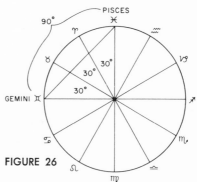

The sign Sagittarius is square to or 90°
away from Pisces.

The sign Pisces is square to or 90°
away from Gemini.

which is Pluto. Pluto, during the month of September, goes from 26° of Virgo to 27° of Virgo. Before you can determine whether or not it is in square aspect to any of your natal planets, you must know how to quickly reckon those signs which are square to one another. Figures 15–30 will help you.

Now look at Neptune. Note that during September it is at 28° of Scorpio. The signs Aquarius and Leo are both square to Scorpio. Our sample chart shows no planets in Aquarius, but it does show

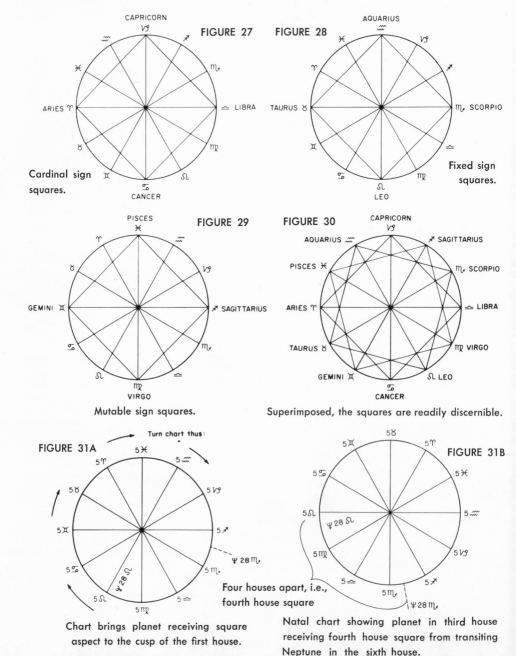

FIGURE 27

Cardinal sign squares.

FIGURE 28

Fixed sign squares.

FIGURE 29

Mutable sign squares.

FIGURE 30

Superimposed, the squares are readily discernible.

FIGURE 31A

Turn chart thus:

Four houses apart, i.e., fourth house square

Chart brings planet receiving square aspect to the cusp of the first house.

FIGURE 31B

Natal chart showing planet in third house receiving fourth house square from transiting Neptune in the sixth house.

Neptune in Leo at 28°—exactly 90° away from or square to transiting Neptune. Continue to examine each of the transiting planets for square formations in a similar fashion, jotting them down on a piece of paper when you find they exist.

There are two kinds of square relationships, and it is important that you learn to differentiate between them. The first is a tenth house square (Figures 32a and 32b) and correlates with beginnings, a chance for constructive action, and new responsibilities which relate to your career or job or to social areas. The second kind is a fourth house square (Figures 31a and 31b) and correlates with endings or conditions which are finished or broken off. These may often correlate with situations concerning home and family or health. How can you tell the difference between them? In this way: Turn your chart around so that the planet in your chart receiving the square aspect from the transiting planet is at the left side, or East point. Now examine the positions of the planets. If they are ten houses apart, it is a tenth house square and would indicate that this is the time to expand, to take on new responsibilities, or to make changes even though difficulties might be involved. The tenth house square can be a steppingstone to something better, but it does require a major effort on your part. If, on the other hand, the natal planet and the transiting planet are four houses apart, it is a fourth house square and will correlate with some condition that is about to come to an end or to be discarded. This would be no time to push ahead or to start anything new. Since the transiting planet is found in the sixth house of our sample chart and is making a fourth house square to a natal planet in the third house, the indications suggest that this would not be the time to look for a new job, but that some old work should be finished. It is also no time to hire new employees. There might also be the possibility that an employee is about to leave.

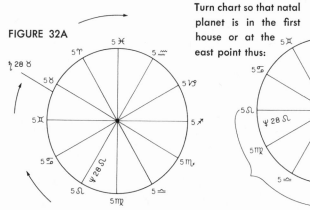

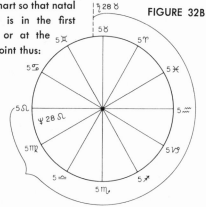

Chart showing planet in third house receiving tenth house square from transiting Saturn in twelfth house.

Now count the houses that separate them and you will note that there are ten. Therefore the transiting Saturn is making a tenth house square to the natal Neptune.

The next form of so-called affliction is the opposition. Oppositions are easy to calculate because they are directly across from each other. For example, when you consult the ephemeris for October, 1970, you will note Uranus to be at 9° of Libra and directly opposite (180°) from Uranus in the natal chart (at 9° of Aries). The behavioral correlate of an opposition is a struggle, an awareness of conditions, or a fulfillment, depending on what has gone on before in this particular area. The opposition lets us know that there is an open channel which can bring two opposing forces into harmony or conflict. In other words, it is something that has to be resolved through your awareness of certain conditions.

The last of the so-called afflictions is the conjunction. This is the easiest of the three to calculate. When the transiting planet is in the same sign and degree as a planet on your own chart, it is said to be in *conjunction*. The principle of the conjunction is that there is a "fusing" of qualities. It is as though the nature of the transiting planet is stamped upon the natal planet. If the transiting planet happens to be Saturn and is making a conjunction to Mercury, this indicates among other things a steadying influence added to Mercury, or more responsibility in terms of the house in which the conjunction is found. Some people, when they are faced with added responsibilities, become depressed. Consequently, there is the possibility of depressing results with the conjunction. But more often than not, it is the way you respond to the situation that makes the difference. Whether or not you forge ahead under a conjunction depends on the nature of the planets involved. When Uranus goes over a natal planet it can open up opportunities in terms of the planet and the house involved. It is up to you, however, to recognize whether the opportunity is genuine. If Jupiter goes over a natal planet, it brings expansion or optimism with regard to the planet and house in which you find it; but there is always the chance of being overconfident and underprepared. Pluto in conjunction to a natal planet can bring intense restlessness, feelings of discontent, or frustration which you may or may not do something about. Some people are incited to violence under this transit, others make needed changes, and others simply take it out on themselves by worrying and make no progress at all.

To get an idea of the nature and possibilities of the transit of the major planets as they "afflict" your natal planets, you may consult the list that follows. However, this is intended only as a guideline. These transits have a very personal meaning in the context of your own life and cannot be completely "isolated."

Transits of the Major Planets

JUPITER FOURTH HOUSE SQUARE THE SUN:

A period of lowered vitality. A tendency to overindulge in rich foods or alcohol. Financial losses possible. This is no time to speculate. Do not expect your boss, superiors, or important social contacts to be too helpful. The "man" in your life, or a man, may disappoint you.

JUPITER OPPOSE THE SUN:

A time in which you may be considering certain investment possibilities. For some, trying to raise capital will be a "tug-of-war." Your boyfriend may appear maddeningly aloof, or there may be a temporary separation.

JUPITER CONJUNCT THE SUN:

An element of luck seems to enter your life. Last-minute decisions bring success when you had all but given up. A pleasant time for dealing with men, especially your boss, or for studying some new philosophy. Feelings of intense optimism and a desire to "branch out." Good time to go on a self-improvement course, entertain, travel, or contact important people. Girls and eligible women may meet a romantic interest. It's a good time to marry.

JUPITER TENTH HOUSE SQUARE THE SUN:

Put on your best "image" and tackle the impossible! Try all the contacts in all the places you like. Good for those in the entertainment field to talk contracts. Some will take on added financial responsibilities.

JUPITER FOURTH HOUSE SQUARE THE MOON:

This can be a period of wild extravagance. Your wife may embark on a trip. A woman friend may cause you a great deal of expense or anxiety. This is no time to take your case to the public. Domestic affairs may temporarily trouble you.

JUPITER TENTH HOUSE SQUARE THE MOON:

A fortunate time for dealing with or hiring servants or employees. Your mood may seem more buoyant, more hopeful, and expansive. Some men will marry under this aspect. Others take on responsibilities which put them in the public eye.

JUPITER OPPOSE THE MOON:

Something comes to fulfillment. You could be aware of a struggle within you in trying to decide whether or not to expand. Some find they have come up against parental disapproval.

JUPITER CONJUNCT THE MOON:

Feelings are particularly expansive. A good time to go on vacation or travel. You may meet a very important woman. A married man could experience much happiness through his wife. Will bring out the oratorical power of some.

JUPITER FOURTH HOUSE SQUARE MERCURY:

Disappointments are likely with regard to correspondence. Students will be dismayed because of their marks. Poor time to sign contracts or to make future commitments that bind you. Feelings of pessimism prevail. Judgment is not as sharp as usual.

JUPITER TENTH HOUSE SQUARE MERCURY:

Brings a desire to improve one's mind or to take up some new study. It's a good time to seek legal or financial advice. You might be feeling more confident now.

JUPITER OPPOSE MERCURY:

Optimism seems to be at war with common sense; there seems to be a need to select from several opportunities. Some consider making a charitable donation. Travel may cause financial struggle for some.

JUPITER CONJUNCT MERCURY:

Feelings of contentment prevail. The mind is more confident and optimistic. Very receptive to religious concepts. Good time to travel, or go into business. Good time for traveling salesmen to make contacts. Teachers may sign up for refresher courses.

JUPITER FOURTH HOUSE SQUARE VENUS:

This is a disappointing period for love and romance. One has to work at having fun. Some will spend for a costly gift, but it's a poor time to do so. Generally an emotionally frustrating time—expectations are high, but reality is dismally bleak.

JUPITER TENTH HOUSE SQUARE VENUS:

A good time to pick out a ring for your girl friend. There is usually the desire to spend for the luxuries of life. Some will find that they have more social obligations to attend to. Many invitations come in that must be accepted. It is a good time to improve your wardrobe.

JUPITER OPPOSE VENUS:

Your past excesses may catch up with you at this time. Some will decide to lose weight, but not without an emotional struggle. Good time to polish latent talents. Performers may be held up temporarily in getting an agreeable contract. You may be aware of a new popularity.

JUPITER CONJUNCT VENUS:

Excellent time for fun, romance, entertainments. Good time for performers or people who must deal with or please the public. Fine time to start a business, relationship, or marriage if you have the right partner. Some will receive a very special gift. You will find that you feel receptive to love; even that bachelor might give up his preferential status. Invitations to weddings are likely.

JUPITER FOURTH HOUSE SQUARE MARS:

Broken promises, disappointments, and extravagances of all kinds can come with this transit. Loss of money through carelessness. Courage may seem to leave you temporarily. Feelings of impatience may compel you to quit before you complete your tasks. Writers may receive rejection slips.

JUPITER TENTH HOUSE SQUARE MARS:

Feelings of daring and courage may propel some into trying their hand at a sport which requires skill and athletic prowess. Some may give a rather impassioned speech or become involved in a religious organization. Good time for working with young men, promotional work.

JUPITER OPPOSE MARS:

Good time to take up sports to work off excess "steam," or to engage in debates. Some will be sustained by faith. An element of combativeness might be temporarily apparent in your makeup.

JUPITER CONJUNCT MARS:

A tendency to spread yourself too thin. Leads to excesses of all kinds. An intense need for action propels some into foolhardy or daring missions. A good time to discipline yourself financially. Some become missionaries or attempt reforms in their fields of work.

JUPITER FOURTH HOUSE SQUARE JUPITER:

A major completion cycle in life—usually brings a finishing condition or an ending. Do not expect favorable response from publishers. Some may finish paying off the mortgage.

JUPITER TENTH HOUSE SQUARE JUPITER:

A time to make a new beginning, to take on financial commitments, or to start a new job.

JUPITER OPPOSE JUPITER:

Some will make tremendous progress at this time. Finances may be more plentiful. A good time to consider making investments for future security. Money that has been withheld may finally arrive.

Others will notice that they must really "sell" themselves before they can make progress.

JUPITER CONJUNCT JUPITER:

When Jupiter returns to its place it is time to assess the benefits that have arrived as a result of its transit. It's time to begin anew and to try to accomplish your unfinished business. Generally, it is a time of renewed faith and optimism.

JUPITER FOURTH HOUSE SQUARE SATURN:

A depressing time financially. Some will have dental problems. It is a poor time to have cosmetic surgery.

JUPITER TENTH HOUSE SQUARE SATURN:

A time to make inquiries into matters of future security. Some will take trips in connection with their work or as a means of income, with an element of obligation attached.

JUPITER OPPOSE SATURN:

A time to exert all your self-control. Things may seem to go maddeningly slow. Some will seemingly be pulled in two directions, for there will be contrasting possibilities from which to choose. Some will be aware of their fathers' need for them.

JUPITER CONJUNCT SATURN:

This is a rather good time to approach those in authority. Some find a very sympathetic teacher to turn to. Others will dip into savings for something they have always wanted or needed.

JUPITER FOURTH HOUSE SQUARE URANUS:

A nasty time for accident-prone or careless people. Some will gamble —and lose. Others find they must spend for something on which they hadn't planned. Tendency toward discontinuity of action. It is a time to change direction, not to give up.

JUPITER TENTH HOUSE SQUARE URANUS:

An unusual opportunity might arise in connection with travel, investments, or a legacy. It is a time to be rapidly discriminating.

JUPITER OPPOSE URANUS:

You may feel as though you have been maneuvered into a very uncomfortable position concerning a particular course of action that has been presented for your consideration. You may feel a new creativity that seeks an outlet. A time to be very selective.

JUPITER CONJUNCT URANUS:

You may experience a sudden desire for freedom. The creative will find this a time of discovery. Others may appear temporarily bohemian.

JUPITER FOURTH HOUSE SQUARE NEPTUNE:

A time when you are likely to be imposed upon. Financial losses will cause some to lose faith. A time to avoid religious cults or fanatics, for this aspect tends toward deception and misplaced devotion.

JUPITER TENTH HOUSE SQUARE NEPTUNE:

A time to recharge your faith. Some experience feelings of altruism and compassion. There is a need for working with the underprivileged and helpless in other parts of the world or country.

JUPITER OPPOSE NEPTUNE:

Many will be aware of a need to question old values, morality or religious beliefs. The direction seems unclear and many will experience a struggle. Some will resort to alcohol or tranquilizers rather than try to resolve their problems.

JUPITER CONJUNCT NEPTUNE:

The artistic will benefit greatly from this transit. A time of heightened sensitivity. A good time to take up the study of music in some form. Others will experience unusual dreams.

JUPITER FOURTH HOUSE SQUARE PLUTO:

Accidents occur on trips; some will find that they have had an unpleasant experience in a mob or with the police, or that they have been victimized. A tendency toward violence for those who are immature or who are attracted to the macabre. Those in the ranching business or those who deal with animals may experience hardship. A good time to get rid of the untenable, to pay off debts and to start anew.

JUPITER TENTH HOUSE SQUARE PLUTO:

A time to be very selective in terms of new financial commitments or investments. Avoid any entanglements with those whose reputations are questionable. Some take constructive steps to put their financial situation on a sure footing.

JUPITER OPPOSE PLUTO:

Feelings of optimism are at war with reality. Many will take a considered risk and emerge triumphant. Others merely experience temporary feelings of rebelliousness, but may not take steps to remedy what they know needs to be done.

JUPITER CONJUNCT PLUTO:

Don't put up with anything that has been causing you discontent—

do something about it, but remember to go through proper channels. Good time for those who engage in missionary work, in religious crusades, in hospitals or welfare.

SATURN FOURTH HOUSE SQUARE THE SUN:

A time when vitality is lowered and hidden structural defects may come to light. A good time to have a thorough physical checkup. Everything may seem impossibly depressing now, but it is good to remember that it is only temporary. This is no time to apply for a new job, accept a new job, apply for favors, or expect help from those in supervisory or executive positions. Avoid arguments, accept the fact that your pride may suffer for a short time, and think positive! Don't be surprised if you and your current beau have a falling-out. Fathers may be a source of concern or interference.

SATURN TENTH HOUSE SQUARE THE SUN:

Those changes you had hoped to make may be subject to much delay. It is a time to persevere, even though the going seems impossibly difficult. Some take on more responsibility on the administrative level. It may be harder to convince those in upper echelons to help, but the rewards come through the struggle. Some wives find that their husbands are undergoing a period of stress.

SATURN OPPOSE THE SUN:

Delays seem to be most annoying to your plans, but there could be a deeper significance. Decide what you really want and if it's worth going after. Some are aware of a struggle between their desire for fun and their intense involvement in responsibility. You may not feel particularly magnetic at this time—you'll just have to work harder at it.

SATURN CONJUNCT THE SUN:

If you seem to be blamed for everything that happens, do not be alarmed—it will pass. Nothing seems to go right for those who are unprepared for this transit, for the tendency is to take everything too seriously. This is a time to consciously relax and "ride with the tide"! Those who swallow their pride and do not let feelings get in the way will emerge triumphant. The responsible and the emotionally mature will fare quite well. Others may give in to self-doubt and torment themselves needlessly.

SATURN FOURTH HOUSE SQUARE THE MOON:

Functional disorders come to light. It is a time when women can miscarry, for Saturn tests the growing fetus for defects. The affairs of your wife or mother may cause concern. There may be extra burdens or responsibilities at home. Your feelings may be "supersensitive" at this time. Do not wallow in self-pity. This is no time to play the martyr. Some end a long-standing condition. Relatively poor time for public performers; be prepared to work harder. Saturn may delay or slow down those affairs of the particular houses involved.

SATURN TENTH HOUSE SQUARE THE MOON:

This is no time to be maneuvered into an engagement even if pressure is applied. Some men will find that they have to marry. People in the public eye may find that their responsibilities increase. A time when business people tend to be cautious. New products can be tested successfully.

SATURN OPPOSE THE MOON:

An old girl friend may come back into your life. Actors are unable to give their best performances. A decided tendency to feel sorry for yourself. Mother and father may seem to be temporarily at odds or enmeshed in a struggle. Others become aware that their own feelings are holding them back. Do not be disappointed if you do not "sway the crowds" under this aspect.

SATURN CONJUNCT THE MOON:

A very steadying influence for those who tend to be extroverted. Others may feel slightly depressed or restricted. Feelings are easily hurt, crying spells may occur. You may feel intensely discontented with your image. This is a test of your stamina. Some will receive an inheritance from a woman. Others find that they are needed to fill a vacancy.

SATURN FOURTH HOUSE SQUARE MERCURY:

A time when the susceptible experience intense depressions. Some succumb to mental breakdowns rather than seek professional help. Many suffer in silence, feeling that their judgment is impaired or that they are "slipping" mentally. Memory may seem poorer temporarily. It is no time to write creatively. Studying may seem more of an effort, and marks may not be up to usual standards. This is no time to resort to stimulants or alcohol—the need is for more constructive effort. This is no time to sign important documents unless it is your divorce decree, for this aspect favors endings rather than new starts. Travel will be rather disappointing if the purpose is for pleasure only. Salesmen will have a difficult time selling.

SATURN TENTH HOUSE SQUARE MERCURY:

Good time to think about adult education courses, going back to school, or educating yourself. Some find that they have added obligations with regard to correspondence. The impulsive will tend to be more conservative. Good time to get your affairs in order, for this aspect tends to be methodical. Some find that they must travel. Business affairs need reorganizing or must be attended to.

SATURN OPPOSE MERCURY:

You may have trouble making up your mind at this time. Reason things through slowly. Those in authority or your teachers may seem to be against you; don't hesitate to let them know your side of the situation. This is a good time to at least act cheerful even if you don't feel it.

SATURN CONJUNCT MERCURY:

If you are naturally pessimistic it may be tough going for a while, but things are not as bad as they seem at first. This transit is meant to teach self-control, not to oppress you. Some may be called upon to make a very difficult decision. Letter writing may be more of a chore. You may have to travel more. Some may feel mentally fatigued, but outgoing types will feel like settling down to hard work.

SATURN FOURTH HOUSE SQUARE VENUS:

Love affairs may come to an unhappy ending. It is generally a poor time to plan entertainments, meet interesting people, or go on vacation—unless it is for a rest only. Entertainers are denied the roles they want or seem not to give their best performances. It is no time to play the role of goodwill ambassador or intermediary in any important dispute or arbitration. You may feel emotionally "dead" because of some disappointment. Loss of jewelry possible.

SATURN TENTH HOUSE SQUARE VENUS:

Some will make a marriage of convenience or marry for money or security. Some may find that they have to make compromises which may not be emotionally satisfying but which will be spiritually rewarding. Some will take on more responsibility because of a sister. Some in the promotional field will take on a protégé.

SATURN OPPOSE VENUS:

You may experience frustration in your romantic life. The object of your love seems hard to pin down. This is not a particularly good time to buy jewelry. You seem to be aware of your social limitations. Good time to make improvements in your appearance or wardrobe.

SATURN CONJUNCT VENUS:

Some will experience much happiness because they have fulfilled their obligations honorably. This is not a time of lighthearted gaiety, but those who do not run from responsibility will be relatively unaffected. Teachers may seem exacting. Actors will have a difficult time in bringing warmth to their roles. But many will be "discovered."

SATURN FOURTH HOUSE SQUARE MARS:

Falls and accidents are possible. This is no time to take up skiing or other strenuous or hazardous sports. The urge for discontinuity is very great. Some feel abused or become abusive to others. Some men feel sexually impotent under this aspect.

SATURN TENTH HOUSE SQUARE MARS:

You may set off on an exploring trip or undertake a mission which is attended by hazards. You are able to put up with physical discomforts at this time. Good time to start physical training or improve your physique. Work load increases but endurance is good. You may experience feelings of physical lethargy but at the same time feel mentally alert.

SATURN OPPOSE MARS:

You may feel stymied by those in authority. You may have to work twice as hard to get results. Energy quotient can run erratically—periods of fatigue followed by periods of exhilaration.

SATURN CONJUNCT MARS:

A rather restraining aspect. Enthusiasm may be at a low pitch. Tendency to physical lethargy. Muscle cramps or sprains can occur. An older person may try to curb your youthful exuberance. Some may be temporarily squelched by the cutting remarks of a thoughtless person.

SATURN FOURTH HOUSE SQUARE JUPITER:

Poor time for financial gains. Poor time to think of asking for a raise. Do not make any important long-term investments under this aspect. Some feel real financial deprivation. Expenses could be very high. Notes come due, savings may be used up to cover debts. Revenue from some published work may be disappointingly small.

SATURN TENTH HOUSE SQUARE JUPITER:

A time to make necessary economies. Try to work out a budget or come to terms with your financial situation. Be exceptionally discriminating about making investments, as returns will be for the long run. Some have more responsibility with the law, legal affairs, or church work. Some set up trust funds, buy tax-exempt bonds, or start a savings account.

SATURN OPPOSE JUPITER:

If you have difficulty getting a loan, this may be the reason why. Delays may cause temporary hardships and disappointments if you are trying to start your own business. Some get what they want after much litigation, dispute or delay. Others become aware that they have been too extravagant in the past.

SATURN CONJUNCT JUPITER:

For some, the financial picture looks brighter because there seems to be an end in sight to outlays of cash. Feelings of optimism may temporarily leave you. You may learn an important lesson about faith. Others become more mature about spending money, or their source of income seems to have run dry.

SATURN FOURTH HOUSE SQUARE SATURN:

This is no time to start important dental work. Youngsters will find that their braces can be taken off now. Your skin may need the attention of a specialist. A time to tidy up long-standing conditions.

SATURN TENTH HOUSE SQUARE SATURN:

This is a good time to attend to those dental problems or to seek medical help for a specific problem. Some will undergo plastic surgery to correct a deformity. Others take on more responsibility.

SATURN OPPOSE SATURN:

Something of a long-standing nature comes to fruition; it is the culmination of many years of hard work. This is the time that you will receive your just rewards if you have earned them. Some find that structural problems come to light.

SATURN CONJUNCT SATURN:

Some may find this a terribly restricting time of life according to the house in which this conjunction is found. It is a good time to start something that can be built up slowly. Do not expect immediate results. Some will find their most important role in life. Others feel that they are getting old and that youth is over—which is rarely the case, since this aspect occurs for the first time around twenty-nine years of age.

SATURN FOURTH HOUSE SQUARE URANUS:

A restraining influence to the impulsive—they may find themselves held in check by someone in authority or bogged down by responsibilities. Many receive their divorce decrees at this time. Some seem to act in a manner that is contrary to their own better judgment. A time of impatience for some. Your attempt at reforming others may fall flat on its face. Organization work may not be too rewarding. Some will lose a job because of poor performance. Avoid tangling with those in authority—you may tend to be too abrupt or inadvertently tactless.

SATURN TENTH HOUSE SQUARE URANUS:

You may feel like breaking loose from all responsibilities, but most will end up by accepting more responsibilities rather than fewer. Some will entertain a group of acquaintances of long-standing duration. Others become involved in politics or charitable organizations. You may at long last find yourself in a position of authority, or even power, if that has been your aim and you have prepared yourself.

SATURN OPPOSE URANUS:

You may think that your creative talent is lower. Others are aware that they have not made use of their own particular talents. It is a good time to think of lending your efforts to some organization or welfare project. The extroverted have a moment of reflection in which to assess the direction they seem to be going in. The introverted may make an effort to be more individualistic.

SATURN CONJUNCT URANUS:

Opportunities may come that test your powers of adaptability. You could be called upon to give a speech, make a report or head a committee. Some may balk at more responsibility and refuse to make an effort. Others rise to the occasion magnificently.

SATURN FOURTH HOUSE SQUARE NEPTUNE:

Not the best time for the executive. Things may suddenly seem to get away from you. Some will be taken up with the notion of retirement. Others have a great need to withdraw from something which seems to be too much for them. This is a poor time for those who rely on publicity, for they might be overlooked for a while. Others come in for scandal or notoriety—if they have earned it. The artist is rarely satisfied with his work at this time. Do not lose faith.

SATURN TENTH HOUSE SQUARE NEPTUNE:

A good time for hard work and faith. For projects that require organization, this is a good aspect under which to tackle them. Be certain to pay close attention to details, and do not sign contracts unless they have been gone over in fine detail. The "old guard" may place obstacles in your path, but it is a time to persevere even though the way is difficult.

SATURN OPPOSE NEPTUNE:

It may seem as though those in authority have no idea of your high intentions. The desire for reform is strong, but there is usually a struggle from those who would resist new ideas. You must be extremely persistent and have a strong idea of the direction in which you are trying to proceed. The clearheaded may achieve results by traditional means.

SATURN CONJUNCT NEPTUNE:

The dream you have achieved may turn out to be something quite different from that which you had anticipated. Generally, it is a good time to tackle organizational and promotional work. Some will get more publicity or get their pictures in the paper. Students who start college under this aspect should make an extra effort to begin properly and stay with it, for sometimes there is a tendency to early disillusionment. It simply calls for an adjustment. Some are troubled by a recurring dream.

SATURN FOURTH HOUSE SQUARE PLUTO:

A decidedly violent aspect for the revolutionary. Some do not take kindly to being thwarted and resort to antisocial behavior. Others find that their crusade has failed to ignite a movement. This is a poor time to make changes, yet some will find that change has been forced upon them. This aspect may test your patience and tenacity and your ability to make a comeback. The more temperamentally placid will not be unduly aware of this transit.

SATURN TENTH HOUSE SQUARE PLUTO:

The scientifically oriented will make great strides under this aspect. Tendency to perseverence, self-control, and deliberation. A time for exploration for some. Some will become involved in rallies or crusades or a constructive "revolution." The path to success may be full of obstacles, but self-discipline will enable the patient to proceed. More work involved for those who counsel others.

SATURN OPPOSE PLUTO:

Some feel rebellious under what they consider the unfair restraints of the "establishment." Some feel hesitant about making needed changes.

SATURN CONJUNCT PLUTO:

You may feel very discontented with the status quo. Those who seek to make changes under this transit may find that they are subject to delays and difficulties. Those who deal in investigative work may find that they have temporary restrictions placed upon them.

URANUS FOURTH HOUSE SQUARE THE SUN:

A time of extreme nervousness and irritability. It is no time to attempt to put into action any new plans or schemes in which you hope to succeed. Most feel a new surge of energy or creativity, but the tendency is to do something foolhardy rather than constructive. It is a time to be most discriminating about any partnerships. Your boyfriend may suddenly leave you. Husbands seem to act unpredictably. Married women may think that they want a divorce, but it is a very poor aspect under which to make this decision. This is a better aspect for the "observer" rather than the "participator." Do not be surprised by developments, particularly if you have been promised great expectations. Some seem very antagonistic and short-tempered under this aspect. Indecisiveness and anxiety may also be apparent.

URANUS TENTH HOUSE SQUARE THE SUN:

Now is the time to experiment—you may meet very unusual people under this aspect. Do not hesitate to approach someone who is in a position to help; the results are not always as planned, but they are usually very interesting. Try to curb any feelings of invincibility. Avoid the eccentric at this time. It is a good time for creative people. Unusual ideas come to those in promotional work. Some will meet a very compelling man. Can be a very romantic time, but don't count on longevity—just fun!

URANUS OPPOSE THE SUN:

Some seem torn between two choices they must make. The urge to try the uncharted will have to be weighed against more traditional approaches. Young women may be considering an engagement to a man who is contrary to family expectations. Those who are well matched will find it a time of fulfillment. For those who have no creative outlets it may be a time of nervousness.

URANUS CONJUNCT THE SUN:

Many youngsters are separated from their fathers through divorce. Others find that their fathers or husbands leave suddenly or unexpectedly. It is a poor time to become engaged, but it is a fine time to meet unusual people. Do not take new acquaintances too seriously and you will not be disappointed. Some suffer from intense feelings of anxiety. It is a good time to channel excess energy into something constructive. It is a poor aspect under which to attempt anything athletic if you are not in condition.

URANUS FOURTH HOUSE SQUARE THE MOON:

This is an accident-prone time. Some notice that their mothers seem very nervous or irritable. Men sometimes leave their wives under this aspect. It is no time to trust your intuition or your "hunches"— you could be badly misled. Functional disorders come to light. Indigestion, stomach disorders, and other related nervous disorders occur. If your girl friend breaks her engagement, or doesn't want to go steady any more, don't be upset; it usually works out for the best in the long run. Poor time for those who must perform in public or court the public's favor. Politicians may suffer temporary defeat; performers may have a temperamental outburst. Feelings are super-sensitive.

URANUS TENTH HOUSE SQUARE THE MOON:
Some may be propelled into the limelight. This aspect does not always guarantee that you will reach the "top," but you will have a chance to show what you can do, and it may become a steppingstone to your future chances. Some women may be particularly inspiring and possibly helpful, but most likely in an unusual way. You may become interested in astrology as a profession. Men sometimes find themselves engaged—much to their own surprise. The decision often comes on an impulse.

URANUS OPPOSE THE MOON:
You may be considering a change of environment at this time. Some become aware of a woman's unusual circumstances. Some may receive unexpected news or a visit from their mothers or some other women.

URANUS CONJUNCT THE MOON:
Bachelors often become involved with married women at this time. And married men become infatuated with a single woman. It tends to contrariness. Things are never the way you wish they would be. Do not divorce an old mate with the hope that your new love will be available. For the emotionally steady, it may lead to a time of creativity or productivity along new and unusual lines.

URANUS FOURTH HOUSE SQUARE MERCURY:
A nasty aspect from the point of view of mental tranquility. Feelings of anxiety can be so intense that breakdowns sometimes occur. Uranus seeks to "liberate" Mercury, but the unprepared are unable to cope with the thoughts that come to them. Many turn to tranquilizers. It is a poor time to sign agreements or contracts. Studies may suffer temporarily. Some drop out of school. It is a time when one is one's own worst enemy: unpredictable, irascible, temperamental. This is no time to plan an important trip.

URANUS TENTH HOUSE SQUARE MERCURY:

Creativity is stimulated. Some are offered an unusual opportunity to travel or to write. There is a tendency to be unconventional, to "shoot from the hip." Some get the notion to sue—it is a poor time to do so. Those who deal in selling, sales promotion, or advertising should make the most of this aspect by widening their circle or horizon.

URANUS OPPOSE MERCURY:

There is a strong urge for the conservative type to throw caution to the winds. Some will spend much time worrying about their urge to try something new rather than actually making the effort and doing it. The naturally rebellious may be swayed to "sound off" at the wrong time and to the wrong person. It should be a time of creative awareness—to try something new, but still to be selective. This aspect can attract very unusual people into your life.

URANUS CONJUNCT MERCURY:

Can be an extremely trying time for the unprepared. Some will wonder why they seem to be so nervous and temperamental. The transit is meant to allow you to broaden your horizons, to expand mentally, to be more original. Many are unable to cope with the feeling. Some receive a great deal of publicity. Salesmen take up new lines; students may change their fields of concentration. Opportunities open up unexpectedly.

URANUS FOURTH HOUSE SQUARE VENUS:

Don't despair if your lovelife seems hopelessly bleak. Many have an unhappy love affair, are jilted, or grow tired of a current attraction. Some will lose money or goods through carelessness. Any love affair started under these aspects will no doubt lead to unhappiness or disillusionment. Unusual people enter your life with a "slick" story; they may take advantage of you and depart just as suddenly. Some have an extraordinary desire to do something unusual or bohemian. It is a very poor time to do so.

URANUS TENTH HOUSE SQUARE VENUS:

Have fun under this aspect, but do not take everything you hear as the "last word." This tends to be disruptive socially. Try not to abandon all your old standards at this time, although it is a good time to loosen up a bit. This is the aspect that makes people rise to the challenge when they hear someone say: "I dare you!" Some take on entertaining that they had not planned. Many feel more alive emotionally.

URANUS OPPOSE VENUS:

The long-married may have a bit of a struggle keeping on the "straight and narrow path." The urge is to have that last fling, but the odds are that you will be discovered or jilted. If you do not expect too much in return for your investment of time, you will not be disappointed. Some are smoothtalked into parting with a great deal of their cash or other tangible assets. The level-headed and emotionally secure will find this a most interesting time. They will not be carried away by romantic notions, but they will be able to enjoy an unusually interesting time.

URANUS CONJUNCT VENUS:

The urge to be unconventional may land you in unhappy straits. This aspect seems to draw very attractive and compelling people into your life, but they are rarely the kind that want to stay around for long. Young people are often sold a bill of goods—they believe what they hear no matter how preposterous. You may get rid of all your old clothes and start wearing unconventional outfits. Sometimes common sense departs temporarily. Be prepared. The sensible will find this a most entertaining period.

URANUS FOURTH HOUSE SQUARE MARS:

This is an accident-prone time. People are often hasty, reckless, or foolhardy. It's a very poor time to take a chance, gamble, or engage in dangerous sports. No time to go hunting—you may end up being the hunted! Your temper may be very uncertain; be careful who you "tell off" at this time.

URANUS TENTH HOUSE SQUARE MARS:

Some unusual opportunity may come up to test your endurance. You may meet servicemen, athletes, or surgeons. Some go on camping trips, climb mountains, or go to athletic games.

URANUS OPPOSE MARS:

Men often become aware that they are getting soft or flabby muscularly and go on a course of athletic improvement. Others are aware of their condition and do nothing about it. Good time to take up dancing or go to a gymnasium for a workout under supervision.

URANUS CONJUNCT MARS:

Energy may seem unusually high now. Some men feel rejuvenated sexually. Others express more physical or moral courage. Some have a chance to perform some unusual service with an element of heroism involved. Some achieve much recognition. Those who are in poor shape physically ought to refrain from "instant athletics."

Many are tempted to try something they have never done before, but the consequences can be unhappy for those who are unprepared.

URANUS FOURTH HOUSE SQUARE JUPITER:
Financial losses are possible now. It is no time to invest in new business, lend money, or sign notes for others. Your income may suddenly be cut in half or considerably diminished. Some will go into bankruptcy. It is a good time to pay off your debts if your reserves permit. Avoid any get-rich-quick schemes. It's a poor time to approach a publisher. Some may have legal problems.

URANUS TENTH HOUSE SQUARE JUPITER:
A time to consider selective investments. Some will take on more responsibility for foreign friends or acquaintances. The urge to travel overseas could come at this time. You may have a "winning streak"—do not count on it to last. Quit while you are ahead. You may hear good news from a publisher now.

URANUS OPPOSE JUPITER:
You may feel as though your money is burning a hole in your pocket. Some are anxious to make money but are uncertain of the direction. Unusual people may come to you with compelling schemes. One needs all the best advice he can get to decide. An excellent time for foreign ministers, philosophers, clergymen—it's a mentally and morally stimulating time.

URANUS CONJUNCT JUPITER:
Sudden expenditures could place you in an uncomfortable position financially. Do not make long-term commitments unless you know where the money will come from. Some feel exceptionally philanthropic now. You might have surprise visits from your minister, a "sportsman," or someone from another country.

URANUS FOURTH HOUSE SQUARE SATURN:
No time to approach politicians, executives, or people who have authority over you. This aspect has accident potential. There is a tendency to break bones that are weakened. No time to have any dental bridgework done, even if it is necessary—wait until this aspect passes.

URANUS TENTH HOUSE SQUARE SATURN:
If you have been invited to a party or gathering, by all means go. You could meet some very important people who might be influential to your career or advancement. Some will meet politicians, government officials, administrators. A time to be less conservative.

URANUS OPPOSE SATURN:
You may feel a lessening of responsibility, or you may become aware that you are too tense or stodgy. It is a time to consider new methods. Some are aware of a restraining hand temporarily withdrawn.

URANUS CONJUNCT SATURN:
Some unique individual may show you a new way to do something. Others are aware that they have been martyred and will seek to free themselves from their oppressors. Some are aware of their fathers' unusual behavior.

URANUS FOURTH HOUSE SQUARE URANUS:
This occurs to the twenty-one- to twenty-seven-year-old age group. Usually brings an ending, such as a graduation from college or graduate school. It completes a major cycle in life. It tends to be disruptive and revolutionary for some who become fed up with conditions. They seek to disrupt, to challenge established ways, but it is a very poor time to achieve anything more than temporary notoriety. It is best to concentrate on completing work rather than attempting anything new.

URANUS TENTH HOUSE SQUARE URANUS:
This occurs to those in the fifty-seven- to sixty-five-year-old age bracket, and often correlates with starting a new career unexpectedly. New surge of creative opportunities arise to the prepared.

URANUS OPPOSE URANUS:
This brings opportunities for fulfillment in terms of the houses that are involved. One can achieve one's goals at this time. It marks a major cycle in life, but not everyone will take advantage of it.

URANUS FOURTH HOUSE SQUARE NEPTUNE:
Some may lose faith or feel that there is nobody to turn to. This is a poor time for those who are in the entertainment field or who depend upon publicity. This is an aspect of middle age and the elderly; it often brings retirement or seclusion.

URANUS TENTH HOUSE SQUARE NEPTUNE:
Not valid for this generation.

URANUS OPPOSE NEPTUNE:
Not valid for this generation.

URANUS CONJUNCT NEPTUNE:
A most troublesome aspect to the generation as well as to the

individual. It is a test of one's faith. This is what causes one to rebel against phony and hypocritical religious practices and beliefs. One searches for the tenable, for something to believe in. This aspect is rather agnostic and upsets traditional values. There is a need to be free from dogma and meaningless rituals. In another sense it brings about publicity, often in an unexpected way. Some young people can be promoted to stardom if they have prepared the way.

URANUS FOURTH HOUSE SQUARE PLUTO:
This aspect causes major changes in life due to retirement, resettling, selling the old home, and so forth. Unexpected endings.

NEPTUNE FOURTH HOUSE SQUARE THE SUN:
Do not be disappointed if your hopes for advancement seem to be stymied. Some are disillusioned by those in authority. Actors and actresses do not seem to be able to present their best image or bring their best efforts to a role. Some will be deceived and become morose as a result. This aspect can induce one to try hallucinogenic drugs, but with very poor consequences. It is a test of your moral fiber and faith. Avoid cults, strange individuals. Stay conventional. Do not allow yourself to be "seduced."

NEPTUNE TENTH HOUSE SQUARE THE SUN:
You may be offered what seems to be the chance of a lifetime, only to have it snatched from your hands at the last minute. Things are not usually what they seem under this aspect. But for the discriminating it may be a dream come true if they are prepared to move quickly. It is a time to set out and see if you can make headway by using your artistry. It is a good time for the writer and the painter, or those who are intuitive. Some experience temporary "psychic experiences." Some man may be masquerading as your savior; be exceptionally wary of accepting advice.

NEPTUNE OPPOSE THE SUN:
Some experience vague feelings of anxiety. Neptune seeks to bring your dreams to fulfillment. For those who have no idea of where they are going, this transit may leave them feeling intensely uneasy. The others will feel refreshed spiritually.

NEPTUNE CONJUNCT THE SUN:
Some may feel that they have found their ideal man, but it could easily be an illusion. You must put any relationship entered into under this aspect to very realistic tests. There may be an interest in spiritualism, the occult, and mysticism. Others make great strides in

their music or art. This transit is relevant only to those who were born under the signs Scorpio and Sagittarius at this time.

NEPTUNE FOURTH HOUSE SQUARE THE MOON:
Many will find that they have psychic experiences or strange dreams. This is no time to try to promote any new products or expect to be magnetic with the public. You may be deceived by some woman. It is a poor time to become engaged. Take care that you are not drawn into some degrading situation through another person. You cannot be too selective about the company you keep at this time. Nervous disorders may turn some to drugs or alcohol.

NEPTUNE TENTH HOUSE SQUARE THE MOON:
You may feel intuitive flashes to which you should give serious consideration. It is a good time for marketing new products and for favorable publicity. You could find that you are on the radio or that your picture appears in the newspapers. Some woman may be very idealistic and give you an assist.

NEPTUNE OPPOSE THE MOON:
Your feelings might be imposed upon now, for Neptune brings a certain receptivity. It is a time when one responds intuitively rather than intellectually. A good time for those who work in hospitals. Some may become aware of a woman or child who needs help or attention.

NEPTUNE CONJUNCT THE MOON:
Functional disorders sometimes come to light at this time or have to be taken care of. If you are a woman, you may have very idealistic feelings about motherhood. Some might find the ideal housekeeper or nurse. Good time for the artistic. Possibility of spiritual illumination or clairvoyant experiences.

NEPTUNE FOURTH HOUSE SQUARE MERCURY:
A most disturbing time of it will be had by those who tend to be nervous to begin with. Many become phobic, morose, despondent, and even irrational, because they are not able to cope with certain recurring thoughts or fears. It is a time when one is subject to deceptions of all kinds. One cannot be too careful about those whom one must trust. This is no time to take stimulants or drugs—you must deal with your fears openly. It is a good time to seek professional help and to try to develop your faith, even though you may have been badly "burned." Your ideas may be most unsound at this time even though you may not think so. Do wait until this aspect has passed before initiating any important undertakings. You may be

surrounded by intrigue. Poor time for sales promotion and publicity. Accidents can occur due to carelessness, an inattention to detail.

NEPTUNE TENTH HOUSE SQUARE MERCURY:
This is a good time to try to find the ideal agent if you are in need of one. Some become more contemplative, receptive to humanitarian occupations. Others will find that they have added responsibilities because of someone's failure to complete his allotted tasks. Do not make any "gentleman's agreement." Everything ought to be down in black and white and be very specific. You ought not to take at face value anyone coming into your life who promises to do you a favor, no matter how "evolved" he seems to be. Some experience disappointment at the hands of someone who seemed sympathetic. Do not part with any money under this aspect unless you know exactly what you are paying for. Take necessary precautions while traveling. Tendency to confusion.

NEPTUNE OPPOSE MERCURY:
Here is the perfect time to test your faith and find out what life is all about. For those who believe in a "spirit world," the answers will come in almost mysterious ways. A time to exert your faith and integrity. This aspect can introduce the morally awakened to another dimension. Many will discover that they are aware of their past transgressions. Some become slightly paranoid and begin to think that their phones are being tapped or that their mail is being tampered with or that something terrible is about to befall them.

NEPTUNE CONJUNCT MERCURY:
You might feel exceptionally creative at this time. Those who perform may find that they bring a new dimension to their performances. The artistic are inspired. Those who are not ordinarily intuitive may become so during this transit. Those people who have never believed in such things are likely to become emotionally disturbed. Listen to the "inner stirrings" within you and have faith; you might find the answer to your prayers. Be careful of all documents that must be signed—read all the fine print.

NEPTUNE FOURTH HOUSE SQUARE VENUS:
Love affairs can only turn out badly at this time. You must be very careful not to enter into a union in which you have any doubts about your partner's integrity. Unfortunately, most people do not exercise their powers of discrimination—they want to believe, and they are often deceived. Do not agree to conduct a romance in secret, no matter what excuses you are given. There is always an element of

seduction and subversion. Some will find that their "love" is married. Some experience theft of jewelry.

NEPTUNE TENTH HOUSE SQUARE VENUS:

A time when you might meet very unusual people, idealistic, artistic, and talented, who may become very devoted to you. Favors spiritual ties. Emotions are very vulnerable.

NEPTUNE OPPOSE VENUS:

A very spiritually uplifting time. Some are aware that they seem to have a heightened sensitivity to art, music, decorating, and so on. It is a time to develop talents that require good taste, such as decorating. Some may be aware of a growing love that is idealistic—someone they may worship from afar. Others become aware that their "true love" was nothing but an illusion.

NEPTUNE CONJUNCT VENUS:

Some seek a love which is totally unable to be fulfilled. They search in terms of an ideal that they have held in their minds, devoid of the practical realities. It often forces a sort of sublimation, good for those who paint or play an instrument. There is an element of ecstasy in it which may materialize in any number of ways—rarely in a physical sense.

NEPTUNE FOURTH HOUSE SQUARE MARS:

Your hopes to succeed as a dancer may be disappointed. On the emotional level, you may feel frightened and insecure. Some take to alcohol to give themselves the courage they seem to lack. This is a poor time to go swimming by yourself; it's also a poor time to take a boat trip.

NEPTUNE TENTH HOUSE SQUARE MARS:

Some may go into the pharmaceutical business. A tendency to take on more responsibility with regard to sports or athletes. Some become trainers or managers of sports figures.

NEPTUNE OPPOSE MARS:

Some feel a renewed sense of moral obligation. Others feel the need to "go on the wagon," or become aware of their tendency to overindulge. Preconceived notions of morality may be put to the test.

NEPTUNE CONJUNCT MARS:

Some will feel the need to go off on a romantic adventure, to explore exotic countries. Others become involved in some nefarious scheme. It is an aspect of morality and courage, but not everyone responds in a positive way.

NEPTUNE FOURTH HOUSE SQUARE JUPITER:

The gullible will find that they have been defrauded. Financial losses, vague schemes, dishonest deals may be apparent at this time. One ought not to make any financial commitments other than those that are absolute necessities. This is no time to travel or to become involved with the law or legal affairs. Some will be deceived by a foreign friend. Avoid religious fanatics.

NEPTUNE TENTH HOUSE SQUARE JUPITER:

Be ultracautious about accepting responsibility for other people's money. It is the rare individual who knows how to use Neptune to the best advantage; it requires absolute honesty and straightforward dealings. One must avoid vague schemes for making money. It is a good time to evolve one's philosophy, to study and investigate religious philosophies.

NEPTUNE OPPOSE JUPITER:

A poor aspect under which to gamble. Some may find a "good Samaritan" who comes to their rescue. Others may try to impose upon your philanthropic sense; be wary of those who come to you with some great tale of financial woe.

NEPTUNE CONJUNCT JUPITER:

You may be introduced to the world of the occult under this aspect. It is a time to think of things other than worldly goods. There are mysteries of life which will be revealed to those who are morally evolved. Others find financial losses and are often taken advantage of. Some become veterinarians.

NEPTUNE FOURTH HOUSE SQUARE SATURN:

A very poor time for administrators or those who hope to become administrators. Some will discontinue present lines of work because of impatience. Avoid questionable activities which could cause you to become involved in scandal or bring about your downfall. Some will have trouble with skin lesions or eruptions. Others may have trouble with their teeth. Some may have problems with their fathers.

NEPTUNE TENTH HOUSE SQUARE SATURN:

Excellent for starting out in business, organizing a business, and organizing in general. It is a good aspect for those who produce and direct and who are extremely hardworking and responsible. One is able to plan his strategy and put his affairs in order. One can work hard for an ideal or a dream which may come to fruition in the future. It favors the long term.

NEPTUNE OPPOSE SATURN:

An awareness that dreams cannot come true unless you are willing to pave the way by hard work. Some find that they dream of success but do not really wish to succeed if it means extra exertion.

NEPTUNE CONJUNCT SATURN:

Some take on work that is so spiritually rewarding that they are unaware of the hardships they must endure; it is a labor of love. Others feel that a source of inspiration has become available to them. This is a time when very idealistic and high-minded people could assist.

NEPTUNE FOURTH HOUSE SQUARE URANUS:

This is no time to dabble in strange cults. This is an aspect of religious fanaticism, and you may be led to excesses of every kind.

NEPTUNE TENTH HOUSE SQUARE URANUS:

You often become interested in mysticism, engineering, or extrasensory perception and related fields. You are often imbued with high ideals and seek to persuade others of the "truth." Some seek adventure in the unusual. Others take on more responsibility with a cause or movement or organization. There is a tendency to play the "Pied Piper."

NEPTUNE OPPOSE URANUS:

Many are aware of a need for a more tangible form of religion. They have questioned the old values and rejected them. They have not found anything to replace them, but the search goes on. Some have turned to sex and drugs, and others have joined unusual groups or organizations dedicated to certain ideals which often fall far short of meeting practical requirements. One feels invincible.

NEPTUNE FOURTH HOUSE SQUARE NEPTUNE:

A major cycle denoting an end to some long-standing condition. The artist may complete a major work, but it is not likely to arouse enthusiasm in the beginning. Doctors may have an urge to change the direction of their interests. Some experience a loss which eventually turns out to be a blessing in disguise. Others can be badly deceived if they initiate any new starts without having all the facts.

NEPTUNE FOURTH HOUSE SQUARE PLUTO:

Some are incited to violence under the guise of altruism. This transit has stirred up those born between 1940 and 1956. The young teen-agers have been feeling the brunt of this aspect of late. It tends to restlessness, a desire to try the unusual. Also tends to illusions, disillusion, immoral behavior, experimentation with drugs and alcohol.

PLUTO FOURTH HOUSE SQUARE THE SUN:

A terribly disturbing period, with feelings of intense restlessness, a desire to force the issues, and an impatience that often leads to rash acts. This is no time to seek honors or promotion. It is a time to tidy up old business. Some will be fired or laid off or retired against their wishes. It causes some to become very morose and even violent, if that is their natural inclination to begin with. Some become self-destructive because they feel that they have failed or that there is nothing left.

PLUTO TENTH HOUSE SQUARE THE SUN:

A good time to think of making changes in your job or career, provided you have something else waiting. Sometimes one forces changes only to find that he is left in "limbo" for a long period of time. It's a time when many become impatient for recognition.

PLUTO OPPOSE THE SUN:

You will no doubt be aware that it is a time to make some sort of change in your life. This can be in terms of your agent, your publisher, or your business partner. It leads to vacillation and dissatisfaction, but it is always best to have a "second string to your bow" before forcing the issue.

PLUTO CONJUNCT THE SUN:

Restless feelings, discontent, and nervous irritability are sometimes felt under this transit. Some women will want to change their marriage partner. If there are any structural weaknesses in the body, this transit may aggravate them. It is a good time to have a checkup.

PLUTO FOURTH HOUSE SQUARE THE MOON:

Functional weaknesses are aggravated. Some may notice a tendency to indigestion or other stomach problems. Moods may feel "black" for a while. Do not initiate any changes. It is a poor time for those who must perform in public. Some may become alarmed at the intensity of their destructive feelings—one needs an outlet under this transit. Losses can occur. One ought not to initiate changes under this aspect, just respond to the inevitable. Feelings may be easily hurt. Some have crying spells.

PLUTO TENTH HOUSE SQUARE THE MOON:

Rebelliousness and need for change can be channeled into constructive outlets. It is a time to initiate changes, to find a physical activity for excessive emotionalism. Some may take on responsibility for a parent or young child.

PLUTO OPPOSE THE MOON:

Don't lose your self-control. Your feelings may be very volatile, and there is a tendency to "sound off"—sometimes at the wrong time. Some feel frustrated, but there is a need to be patient.

PLUTO CONJUNCT THE MOON:

Your need to bring about necessary reforms or changes in your work may cause you to become impatient about your tactics. Some become very argumentative. Feelings become intensely self-centered. It is a good time to bend over backwards to be objective about another's viewpoint.

PLUTO FOURTH HOUSE SQUARE MERCURY:

This aspect has been known to correlate with nervous breakdowns. There is an intense self-destructive tendency. It is often difficult for people to cope with their own thoughts, for Pluto forces people to face up to things that they would rather not think about. There is therefore a desire to run away—but there is no place to run. This is no time to travel for amusement. There are sometimes difficulties with one's automobile. Agreements and contracts often get broken under this aspect. Jobs that were promised do not materialize. Swindles can occur. It is a poor time for studies. Children may have difficulties at school but may be unable to express them.

PLUTO TENTH HOUSE SQUARE MERCURY:

Some develop a talent for mystery writing. Your handwriting may become more artistic or unusual. Some may be befriended by a person of questionable reputation. One must be careful to choose the proper associates. This is a fine aspect under which to develop "magic" talents. Some consider entering the fields of surgery, research, deep-sea diving, or excavating. Many have to travel for business.

PLUTO OPPOSE MERCURY:

You may feel an intense desire to travel due to restlessness. You may be aware of your lack of specialized education or of a lack of knowledge in general. Some think of making changes in their school curricula. Salesmen, writers, or teachers may experience inner struggles about leaving their fields.

PLUTO CONJUNCT MERCURY:

The purpose of this transit is to introduce you to new ideas and new ways of expressing yourself. Some are unable to cope with this feeling. They become restless, nervous. There is a reforming tendency about this aspect. It seeks to renovate, but not everyone wants to do what has to be done. Some become the victims of gossip or blackmail. The advanced thinker and research-oriented are aware of a new freedom to expand mentally. They are able to begin new lines, to explore uncharted areas.

PLUTO FOURTH HOUSE SQUARE VENUS:
Love affairs may end rather violently. This aspect tends toward sadism or masochism. A decidedly perverse attitude is exhibited. Some seem to feel the need to suffer. Many are the victims of another's viciousness. It is no time to form any unions. Feelings are easily hurt.

PLUTO TENTH HOUSE SQUARE VENUS:
This is a far better aspect for perfecting an art form or struggling with artistic concepts than entering into any love affairs. Pluto enjoys the struggle, and for those of you who like your love affairs to have a touch of brutality, this may be your dish. You'll attract a rather rough or unpolished type into your life at this time.

PLUTO OPPOSE VENUS:
You might be contemplating making a change in your love life. Some will consider the idea of getting out of an "arrangement" or taking on someone new. Others seem troubled by a struggle with their emotions—erotic fancies can temporarily take hold.

PLUTO CONJUNCT VENUS:
For those who can rise to the true spirit of Pluto, it may mean adventure into the world of art, color, and creativity. There is an element of the sublime for those who are receptive. Others find that they are drawn into the world of the erotic and the sensuous—generally, there is an aftersense of degradation. One ought to be most cautious about one's direction under this aspect. Pluto appears to lead the weak astray. Many experience an intense desire to free themselves from their inhibitions.

PLUTO FOURTH HOUSE SQUARE MARS:
This is a rather hazardous aspect, for you are inclined to be careless and overconfident. The results are often disastrous. Others feel emotionally volatile. Ugly displays of temper may be noticed; poor impulses and a general lack of humility are also typical. This is no time to travel or to be involved in any mob scenes. You can become the victim of violence. This aspect favors activities which use your

energies constructively, such as digging in the garden, getting rid of the old to make way for the new, and so on.

PLUTO TENTH HOUSE SQUARE MARS:
Some feel imbued with a desire to get ahead—and fast. You can easily become your own worst enemy under this aspect, for there is a tendency to "sound off," to feel that you are absolutely in the right, and there is an unfortunate tendency to be completely undiscriminating. Your target could even be your boss! Some find that they have forced themselves into a position where they must consider changes. Others may be demoted or transferred. This is no time to decide on elective surgery, but the surgeon may perform some particularly difficult operation during this time.

PLUTO OPPOSE MARS:
The need for activity is often felt. Many become intensely restless. Some consider the field of pathology. Others are aware that they are the victims of extortion or that someone seems to be trying to manipulate them. It favors those whose work is in the field of sports, archeology, research, or detection.

PLUTO CONJUNCT MARS:
Can be very disturbing to the hot-tempered. There is an element of perversity and unrestrained extravagance at every level. Your passions are aroused, often to a white-hot intensity. Be extremely selective about stirring up others—you could easily become brutalized. Stay away from controversy during this aspect; you may feel like fighting your way through!

PLUTO FOURTH HOUSE SQUARE JUPITER:
Some find themselves in a financial jam. You may even be fired or laid off your job. This is no time to feel sorry for yourself; it is a good time to think of whether or not you are really in the right line of work. Don't apply for a loan or take out a mortgage or go into debt. Some find that previous excesses have put them into an unpleasant situation.

PLUTO TENTH HOUSE SQUARE JUPITER:
There is a tendency to want to gamble or take a chance on some financial deal that you might not have ordinarily considered. You often feel invincible at this time. Some become involved with loan sharks or gamblers. The responsible may find that they are making selective investments. Some tackle a problem in the field of social reform.

PLUTO OPPOSE JUPITER:

You may become aware of a tendency to "psychism," or something in related areas. Many experience a growing awareness that there is something more than meets the eye! It is a time of discovery for the "evolved." Some become restless with their present financial conditions and consider changing them. This may be a time of fulfillment for some who have tried to raise money.

PLUTO CONJUNCT JUPITER:

This aspect can be very revitalizing or rejuvenating. Some experience a moral awakening. Others become imbued with the feeling that they can become emancipators. It is a good time for those whose work leads them into the field of reconstruction: builders, psychologists, explorers, and so on. This may free capital for others, or help them consider a major expenditure with judgment.

PLUTO FOURTH HOUSE SQUARE SATURN:

If you feel like becoming involved in a "revolution," don't! Some experience feelings of intense hostility; a desire for revenge, for instant action. Many become involved with those in authority. Some are misled into situations into which their better judgment would ordinarily not tempt them. One becomes so unhappy or restless or impatient with the existing order of things that there is a tendency to strike out in whichever way seems most opportune at the moment. A tendency toward violence and unconstructive moods! The best way to use this transit is to punch a punching bag, work for a road gang, dig out the weeds in your garden, and bide your time. Students are often tempted to take up some weird cult and proclaim that they have founded a religion.

PLUTO TENTH HOUSE SQUARE SATURN:

This aspect is relevant only to those around the ages of forty-one to forty-three, and to the eleven to thirteen-year-olds. The older age group will cope with new responsibilities and will find themselves in positions of authority or control—if they have worked in that direction. This endows them with tenacity and self-discipline through perserverance. The younger generation may become interested in "black magic," "vampirism," weird fads, cults, or violent movies, etc. The responsible ones will take on extra responsibilities for their fathers or older people.

PLUTO OPPOSE SATURN:

Some might become tempted to argue with those in authority.

Others feel the need to throw their weight around, to test their strength. Just be sure you have some alternative plan if things don't work out. This is an aspect that pits strength against strength. It is the voice of reconstruction against those who prefer the status quo. Neither is necessarily right, but judge carefully if you would avoid making the wrong choice. Some are aware of the concerns of a parent or an older person.

PLUTO CONJUNCT SATURN:
It may be difficult to hold on to your old sense of tradition. Pluto forces a re-evaluation of old established ways. Some will respond to the challenge in a constructive way—they will only discard the old to make way for something more progressive or productive. Others will be bewildered by the choice and may succeed in doing nothing more than stirring up trouble. Good aspect for the scientific researcher—it seems to force a new look at old perspectives.

PLUTO FOURTH HOUSE SQUARE URANUS:
This aspect has correlated with much of the unrest felt by those born between the years 1942 and 1949. It is one of the most perverse, for it tends toward violence, gang wars, strange cults, immorality, wanton destruction, and every manner of sexual perversion. There is an impatience to change the old ways that will not brook interference or reason. Those who cope with this aspect want it now and in their way. They feel that theirs is the only way; they are often unreasonable and unwilling to suggest alternate methods; they want to destroy. Here we find the orgies, the crimes of passion, the thrill seekers. Under this aspect one wants freedom—immediately. On other levels, this correlates with divorce, nervous breakdowns, and a need for tranquilizers or drugs. Some leave home, school, or work.

PLUTO TENTH HOUSE SQUARE URANUS:
Not valid for this generation.

PLUTO OPPOSE URANUS:
Forces changes, often in an abrupt and unexpected manner. Many become aware that it is time to get rid of the old to make way for the new. Opportunities may come in a rather unusual way. For some it is the culmination of a long wait.

These capsule interpretations of the aspects are intended to suggest possible events which could materialize as a result of the transiting planets. Naturally, each of these aspects must be applied to the individual's own chart and circumstances. While it has often been said that the aspects or the planets cause the unhappy circumstances in one's life, this is not true. It is a matter of timing and astrological correlations with human behavior. People often unwittingly choose the wrong paths when their astrological clocks show that it is time to pass a "test." Because many people consistently choose the path of least resistance, an astrologer often makes seemingly miraculous predictions. For reliable results, however, an astrologer has to know the circumstances of a client's life to make an accurate appraisal of how these transits will work out. And, of course, you can do this best yourself.

These aspects that we have just described can also be used to determine whether or not your natal chart is "afflicted"; that is, your natal squares, oppositions, and conjunctions can be calculated in the same way—but with a wider orb or distance between them. It is on the basis of these so-called afflictions that many astrologers claim they can determine not only an individual's character, but his moral qualities and his destiny. This is absolute nonsense. To begin with, these aspects are present in the horoscopes of saints as well as sinners. They do nothing more than indicate where one must endure and conquer—or be conquered. Therefore, a murderer may hold an aspect such as Pluto square Mars, or Uranus conjunct the Moon, in his natal chart, but not everyone who has these aspects will be a murderer or even necessarily violent. He will have his corresponding tests to pass as they relate to his life's circumstances, but he could just as easily turn out to be a world-famous explorer.

The point to remember, then, about these aspects, whether they are found in the natal chart or formed by the transits, is that they must be judged individually, not only on the basis of your chart, but within your own particular circumstances. They do not operate in an independent manner. Nor do they represent a fixed pattern to which you are irrevocably bound. Since the natal chart is nothing more than a moment of time to which you are synchronized, you must learn to work in harmony with that moment. Astrology would be absolutely meaningless as a useful tool if you were held to be a thief, a moral degenerate, or even a famous figure because of your chart. Your destiny is what you make it; astrology can help to point the way.

How to Calculate a Trine

Earlier in this chapter you learned about square aspects and how to calculate them. Whether they are formed by the transiting planets or are in the natal chart, they carry with them a particular message. Sometimes difficulties are implied, or obstacles to overcome, or more responsibilities. The trine, on the other hand, implies "ease" and is supposed to be the most beneficial aspect of all. In essence, it is your reward for a job well done. Often, people are discouraged because they fail to note an improvement or good fortune in their lives under a transiting trine aspect. The reason for this is that many people do not know that what they have done before becomes of paramount importance. Suppose, for example, transiting Jupiter is going to make a trine to your natal Sun. If you sit at home and expect good fortune to find you under this aspect, you may discover that your hopes will not materialize as expected.

What you must do is anticipate well in advance when an important trine can be expected; then put yourself in a position to reap the benefits of having done your "homework"! If you have hopes of meeting a person who could be important to your life, and you notice that Jupiter is going to make a trine aspect to your natal Sun, put yourself in circulation well in advance. Get yourself into shape. Don't go out looking less than your very best. Accept invitations to all events where you might meet other people. Even someone you consider dull might provide the link to your dreams. Then eventually, when the clock shows that the time is right, that is, when your trine comes due, you may be rewarded handsomely. In addition it is also the correct time to initiate some activity in terms of the houses involved. Now let us learn how to calculate a trine.

When two planets are approximately 120° apart, they are said to be in trine aspect. On the basis of the signs of the Zodiac, any sign which is four signs away from its neighbor is in trine relationship to it, thus:

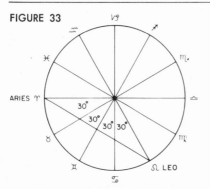

FIGURE 33

Aries is 120° from or trine to Leo.

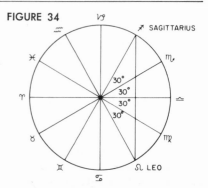

FIGURE 34

Leo is 120° from or trine to Sagittarius.

FIGURE 35

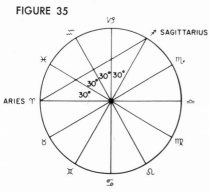

Sagittarius is 120° from or trine to Aries.

FIGURE 36

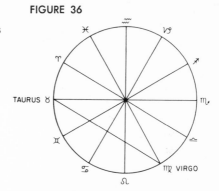

Taurus is 120° from or trine to Virgo.

FIGURE 37

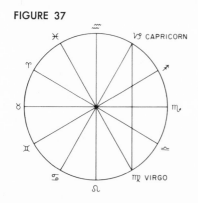

Virgo is 120° from or trine to Capricorn.

FIGURE 38

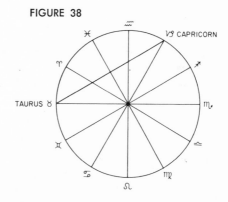

Capricorn is 120° from or trine to Taurus.

FIGURE 39

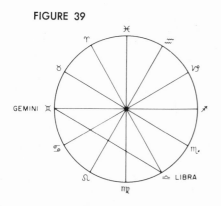

Gemini is 120° from or trine to Libra

FIGURE 40

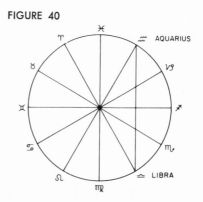

Libra is 120° from or trine to Aquarius.

FIGURE 41

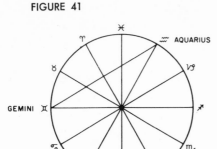

Aquarius is 120° from or trine to Gemini.

FIGURE 42

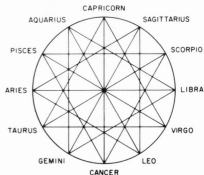

Aries, Leo, and Sagittarius are called fire signs and are trine to one another.

Taurus, Virgo, and Capricorn are called earth signs and are trine to one another.

Gemini, Libra, and Aquarius are called air signs and are trine to one another.

Cancer, Scorpio, and Pisces are called water signs and are trine to one another.

These are the *signs* which are in trine relationship to one another. You will notice that the signs are classified as belonging to one of the elements, such as fire, air, and water. Keeping this in mind, it becomes easier to calculate a trine since, as you have seen by the diagrams, all fire signs are trine to one another, as are all earth, air, and water signs.

In order to calculate trine relationships between *planets,* first note the sign in which the planets are found and then the number of degrees. Suppose one planet is in 2° of Taurus and another is in 2° of Virgo—they are in perfect trine relationship to one another. But in a natal chart planets are rarely found to be in the same degree. Therefore, we must allow for orbs, or acceptable distances between them. In the case of a trine, allow an 8° orb. If either the Sun or the Moon is involved, you may allow 10°. This is by no means a hard and fast rule, but it is generally acceptable. Therefore, if Mars is in 17° of Sagittarius and the Sun is in 7° of Aries, they are still in trine to one another. You may wonder if any two planets which are between 110° and 120° away from each other are in trine? The answer is that they are. In this case, it is called a dissociate trine and is a bit more difficult to calculate, since you must actually count the degrees between the planets, for they involve signs which are not technically in trine. For example, if Venus is in 24° of Aries and Saturn is in 0° of Capricorn, they are 6° short of the required 120°, but still close enough to be in trine, although Aries and Capricorn are not of the same element. This is a technicality that you should keep in mind only if you wish to calculate your own natal trines. However, for purposes of calculating transiting trines, consider only a perfect trine. In other words, the two planets must be in the exact same degree. If your natal Sun is at 29° of Pisces and Jupiter is in the sign Cancer (trine, by sign), Jupiter will be in perfect trine to your Sun when it reaches 29° of Cancer. This is when you may expect to see results if you have prepared the way.

⑫

Be Your Own Psychiatrist

Most of us at one time or another suffer from some form of mental or emotional disturbance. These disturbances can range from mild depressions, minor phobias, compulsions, and other states that fall within the normal range of behavior, to the more complex, limiting, and debilitating neuroses. The search for emotional happiness has led people into every conceivable avenue: cigarettes, tranquilizers, stimulants, drugs, sleeping pills, and liquor, to name but a few of the obvious ones. In the same vein, people have searched for mental solace via religion, yoga, psychiatry, meditation, and sex. Why do people find themselves in such an unhappy predicament? It is fruitless, sometimes perilous, to search for mental health via the drug and pill circuit! In addition to masking the symptoms that cause the anxiety, these remedies often become habit-forming and produce painful withdrawal symptoms when the user tries to stop. This in turn gives rise to more anxiety, hence more pills, and the vicious cycle continues.

The goal of mental health need not prove so elusive. The key to peace of mind lies in understanding your emotional makeup in terms of astrological significance.

Many people are convinced that in dealing with mental or emotional problems, the organ at fault is the brain. Indirectly, this may be true, for all behavior—meaningful or otherwise—is "sifted" through the brain. But a perfectly normal brain-wave test result is possible, even though an individual may be suffering from some form of emotional disturbance, such as depression. Astrology, however, shows us that the problem may have begun long ago in early childhood—in the way that you were conditioned. And what is the astrological correlate of conditioning? The answer is your *Moon*. Here is the first clue to finding the path to emotional health, for you respond according to the way you have been conditioned. And when you respond, you do so in the manner in which you think, speak, and write. Now we come to the planet Mercury, which also correlates with your mental outlook (as well as your motor function). Mercury is the outlet for conditioned responses.

Refer to your own chart now and take an astrological look at your Moon and Mercury, for these two form the "package" that is correlated with mental conditioning. If you understand the natural inclination of your Moon and Mercury, you will understand why you respond as you do. Who hasn't wondered, at some time or other, why he was so depressed for no apparent reason, or why his feelings are so easily bruised while others seem to slough off the hurt or rebuff swiftly? And who hasn't wondered why he becomes nervous or anxious when there seems to be no obvious cause for such a response? In order to find the answers to these questions, you must understand your own astrological "package," for it is the key to your peace of mind.

First, let us consider the Moon. The following table will give you an idea of how the Moon correlates with the sign in which it is found in your chart.

MOON IN ARIES:

Feelings are intense (combative at times). There's a need for independence. Restrictions are not tolerated too well. May bite off more than he can chew, but experience is the best teacher. Should be encouraged to work off steam in athletics. Tends to be "mother's pet."

MOON IN TAURUS:

Emotionally placid. Able to accept responsibility at an early age. Responds to tact rather than force. Outwardly not too responsive. Very proud. Mother may have been oversolicitous. Can find emotional solace in pastoral environment.

MOON IN GEMINI:

Feelings are easily bruised, but bounces back easily. Very impatient. Will accept discipline if the reasons are understood, otherwise will argue endlessly. Feels best when involved in a project. Mother may have been too busy with outside interests to supervise.

MOON IN CANCER:

Feelings are easily hurt, but may never let the "offender" know what he has done. Tends to be too closemouthed about problems. Loves to be "babied." Needs firm but unemotional discipline; cannot bear to be shouted at. Mother may have been overprotective. Outlet in water sports at the seaside, or in antique shops or archeology.

MOON IN LEO:

Emotionally expressive—tends to dramatize everything. Pleasing personality attracts others. As a child, lives in a make-believe world. Overconfidence makes up for lack of training. Mother may have inadvertently encouraged vanity. Relaxes at the theater.

MOON IN VIRGO:

Very practical nature; may appear impatient to others. Emotional response is controlled. Self-confidence is sometimes slow to develop due to mother's nagging or lack of warmth. Usually assumes an emotional burden for other members of the family at an early age. Willingness to please often gives added responsibility. Disillusionment sometimes turns to criticism or intolerance in later years. Predilection for acquiring mother's prejudices. Solace in books— browsing, reading, or arranging.

MOON IN LIBRA:

Very sociable. Mood is often dependent upon surroundings. Does not tolerate disharmony. Emotionally easygoing. An intense need to be accepted by others. Will put up a "front" rather than expose any weakness. Will go to great lengths to avoid taking part in a controversy. Expresses feelings of concern for another's welfare but does not usually do anything about it. Mother inadvertently fosters superficial behavior because of her insistence upon worrying about what others will say. Very susceptible to flattery. Loves to entertain. Solace in companionship or camaraderie of others.

MOON IN SCORPIO:

Feelings are intense and need an outlet. Very inquiring nature. Early interest in research or science. Once committed to a project, becomes passionately involved. Can be very self-sacrificing and may try to please parents or others at the expense of own true nature. Mother may have taken a singlehanded missionarylike approach to his or her career. Emotional outlet in the occult, transforming others, working with charitable groups.

MOON IN SAGITTARIUS:

Generally happy-go-lucky attitude. Very perceptive. Prefers to search for truth on his own. Sometimes conflict between his views and established family traditions. Very tolerant of other's viewpoint. Respects discipline, but will always test the limits which have been set. Must be able to think freely. Mother may have been more of a pal. Emotional solace found in travel, riding, or literary pursuits.

MOON IN CAPRICORN:

Appears very standoffish or aloof, but is more likely shy. Needs love and affection, but rarely gets it as a child. Usually assumes many responsibilities early in life. Much is expected of these children, they may have learned that to excel is the only way to earn admiration. Therefore, much effort is usually expended to insure success in chosen field. Mothers sometimes have a hard time warming up to these children, or else they are very ambitious for them. Outlet in organizing activities or groups.

MOON IN AQUARIUS:

Feelings are controlled. Appears to be quite mature at an early age. There is a tendency to lead "crusades." Unusual causes may attract his or her attention. Occasional outbursts of emotion may be a surprise to others because of intensity and infrequency. Very independent. Very faithful about honoring alliances. Mother may have been ahead of her times or very unusual in some way.

MOON IN PISCES:

Extremely sensitive and intuitive. Very receptive nature may result in being subject to imagined fears or phobias. Need for strong direction in early years. Ability to receive impressions easily allows him or her to take on the moods of others—fine for actors and actresses, but otherwise may be imposed on by others. Very good-natured and loving. As a child, may have been very quiet and unobtrusive. Very creative in writing. Mother may have been too easygoing.

These few descriptive phrases describe the general characteristics or tendencies associated with the Moon in each of the signs. One is not better than another as far as emotional health is concerned;

rather, each sign has its own particular response, and while we are youngsters our response is intuitive (Moon) rather than intellectual (Mercury). The problem arises when parents try to "remove" or redirect the natural inclination of your Moon sign in a way which is emotionally unacceptable to you. For example, children with the Moon in Capricorn are very eager for loving expression, but they rarely get it because they appear to be so self-sufficient and cold that even their parents can be misled. These children want to be told how much they are loved. Instead, parents often try to "loosen" them up by scolding or criticizing—exactly the opposite of what they really want. Knowing your Moon sign, then, indicates to you the fundamental principle of your natural response. It is entirely possible that you may alter your own manner of response, but this is more often done as an adult, when you rely on your intelligence or reasoning (Mercury).

The next clue to your emotional conditioning lies in knowing the relationship of your Moon to certain planets. Earlier, you learned to calculate the square aspects and the oppositions and conjunctions, find your own Moon in your chart, and calculate the various planets in the aforementioned relationships. These "stressful" relationships may be inadvertently responsible for some of your emotional problems. They do not alter the natural inclination of the sign, but they may correlate with some of your seemingly unpredictable behavior. For example, the planets Mars, Saturn, Uranus, Neptune, and Pluto correlate with a particular type of activity. When they are in "stress" relationship to your Moon, your form of response will be correlated with the nature of the aspecting planet. Let us look at the following table to note the various responses possible as a result of the added stress:

MOON CONJUNCT, SQUARE, OR OPPOSE MARS:
Mars stimulates or correlates with energy; therefore, this may produce sporadic outbursts of temper. Feelings are easily hurt. The tendency is to respond in anger and to lose control. Exceptionally thin-skinned.

MOON CONJUNCT, SQUARE, OR OPPOSE SATURN:
Saturn steadies or correlates with restrictions; therefore, this may induce intense feelings of self-pity. Feelings of paranoia result from accepting abuses without striving to eliminate the causes. Learn to put up with difficult conditions for only a limited period of time; do not play the role of martyr. Emotionally inhibiting.

MOON CONJUNCT, SQUARE, OR OPPOSE URANUS:
There's a tendency to take up very unusual causes or lead a crusade; emotionally unreliable; exceptionally independent. Can be misled by eccentric characters. Very violent temper, but quickly spends itself.

MOON CONJUNCT, SQUARE, OR OPPOSE NEPTUNE:
Imagined fears can cause hysterical outbursts or a retreat into unreality. Very phobic. Difficulty in distinguishing between the real and the imagined. Tendency to hypochondria. Learn to have faith. Emotional inertia sometimes results from not facing up to reality.

MOON CONJUNCT, SQUARE, OR OPPOSE PLUTO:
Extremely restless. Inability to complete tasks. Extremely volatile emotionally. There's a tendency to seek a change of pace as soon as the going gets tough. Very argumentative; tends to be unforgiving. Feelings of intense frustration.

The main point to remember about the Moon is that it is the signpost of your early conditioning. In spite of faulty conditioning, you alone are responsible for your own emotional behavior. If you take the easy path and give in to the moods suggested by the stressful planetary aspects, you are choosing the path of least resistance. Sometimes the problem is compounded by other people who serve to reinforce your weaknesses; for these square, conjunction, or opposition aspects can attract individuals into your life who are characteristically weak (Neptune), impulsive (Uranus), brutal (Pluto), or selfish (Saturn), etc., and unless you understand why this is so astrologically, and make some attempt to eliminate the potential damage these people can do, you will find yourself in chronic emotional hot water. These individuals might even be your parents. The point is not to succumb to drawbacks. You must know your own chart and compensate for, or overcome, your weakness. For example, a person with a Moon squared by Saturn might never outgrow the tendency toward self-pity. Although that person might have a splendidly aspected Mercury, he would never really use it—it would simply be the instrument through which he expressed his phobias, fears, or delusions. If, however, that individual were aware of his astrological makeup, he could take steps to rectify these adverse responses. Strength, of course, lies in knowledge. That is why I stress the importance of studying astrology rather than reading it.

Mercury is the other half of your emotional package. The following table will give you an idea of how Mercury performs in the various signs:

MERCURY IN ARIES:

Enterprising and dynamic. The planner of great schemes. Enjoys overcoming obstacles. Has a need to be heard.

MERCURY IN TAURUS:

Slower, less brilliant, but dependable over the long haul. Very practical; reasons slowly but carefully. Can bring to fruition that which has been started by others. Very constructive.

MERCURY IN GEMINI:

Quick and witty. Talkative, creative and artistic. Ability to excel at many things. Talent for languages. Needs change.

MERCURY IN CANCER:

Retentive and intuitive. Sympathetic. Master of many moods. Very imaginative. History and antiquity have great appeal.

MERCURY IN LEO:

Forceful. Desire to lead. Has the ability to sway the crowd by using power of oratory. Dramatic.

MERCURY IN VIRGO:

Very rational. Has the ability to analyze a situation in a cool and impersonal way. Desire to impart knowledge often leads to social work or teaching.

MERCURY IN LIBRA:

Gives balanced judgment even in the absence of formal education. Aesthetic. Usually very pleasing way of speaking. Ability to appreciate art and poetry. Likes to arbitrate.

MERCURY IN SCORPIO:

Ability to probe deeply. Mind is sharp and penetrating. Very intuitive. Aptitude for science and research. Intense.

MERCURY IN SAGITTARIUS:

Mind is quick and prophetic. Has ability to make rapid judgments. Has a need to speak the truth—can be quite blunt. Loves travel and the outdoor life.

MERCURY IN CAPRICORN:

Serious and responsible. Can be counted on to pay close attention to detail. Stickler for formality. Conservative. Thrifty.

MERCURY IN AQUARIUS:

Very artistic and original. Judgment is impartial, reasoning is clever. Ideas are often in advance of the times. Inventive.

MERCURY IN PISCES:

Impressionistic. Artistic, flexible. Makes an excellent diagnostician. Gentle. Sympathetic. Visionary.

These brief descriptions serve to illustrate the natural mode of expression of Mercury in each of the signs. As you can see, Mercury in each sign has individual identification. This is neither an advantage nor a disadvantage; it is simply a question of "inclination." Some astrologers have held to the old-fashioned notion that planets perform better in some signs than in others. This old concept is no longer valid in modern astrological interpretation and should be discarded.

As in the case of the Moon, it is important to check to see whether there are "stressful" aspects to your Mercury. These planets in no way alter the intelligence. Actually, an astrologer cannot determine your I.Q. from the chart on the basis of planetary aspects, but he can very often determine your characteristic intellectual response. This is one of the reasons it is so easy for astrologers to make "predictions." Many people invariably choose a path of least resistance instead of making the necessary struggle for adjustment. Again, consider only the square, conjunction, and opposition aspects, for these hold the greatest threat of mental instability unless they are fully understood. Also consider Mercury only with relation to Mars, Saturn, Uranus, Neptune, and Pluto.

First, consider Mars. Mars is the planet that correlates with dynamic action. When Mars is found in square, conjunction, or opposition to Mercury, the natural tendencies of the sign in which Mercury is found are subject to stimulation. Mars adds the combative element, and in reasonable quantities this is good. But if Mars is allowed to go unchecked, it will alter Mercury's performance to the extent that it becomes argumentative, faultfinding, sharp-tongued, opinionated, or rude. Moreover, unless there is some channel for this energy, the result is usually extreme mental irritability under stress. The stress aspects of Mars harmonize with some signs more than with others. If your Mercury is found in Taurus, Cancer, Pisces, or Capricorn, these aspects are less likely to be troublesome because Taurus is very solid and can stand the extra energy from Mars. Cancer is very sensitive and needs the self-assurance that Mars provides. Capricorn is so conservative that Mars is almost therapeutic, and Pisces can be so indecisive that Mars provides some direction.

When Mars is square, conjunct, or opposite to Mercury and Mercury is in the signs Aries, Leo, Virgo, or Scorpio, the action of the stressful aspects synchronize less harmoniously because of the inherent qualities of these signs. Aries could become a liar and a cheat. Leo might become bombastic, arrogant, and selfish. Virgo might possibly be supercritical, backbiting, and intolerant. And Scorpio could be downright vicious or tyrannical.

Mercury in Gemini holds the possibility of being unstable with a stress from Mars. The natural talents of Gemini could turn into such paths as shoplifting or forgery, for Mars adds more impatience to an already restless Mercury, and for some individuals, stealing could be the most expedient way of earning a living.

Mercury in Sagittarius when in square, conjunction, or opposition to Mars could become expectionally unreliable. There could be a tendency to speak as an "oracle." Every word uttered would purportedly be gospel truth, but unfortunately this is not usually the case. Here is the talebearer *par excellence!*

Mercury in Libra in stress relationship to Mars becomes intensely insecure. Libra ordinarily prefers peace and harmony, but Mars can tip the "balance," which is upsetting to some individuals, so that they will occasionally give way to impulsive behavior, with much remorse afterwards. In addition, they find it hard to complete work which requires an extended effort.

In Aquarius, Mercury could become erratic because the extra energy of Mars might prod an already impulsive Mercury into violent "crusades." In other words, one could possibly take up a cause and fight for it without any particular emotional commitment.

As you can see, there is nothing evil about these squares. They simply provide added impetus. How it works in your case is up to you.

Let us now look at another of the so-called "malefics"—the planet Saturn. Saturn correlates with that which is slow, ponderous, gloomy, obsessive–compulsive, and depressive at its worst. At best it provides stability, control, and reason. Again, this planet in no way correlates with intelligence; it simply gives a person the ability to stick with something—to work long and hard under difficult conditions. In stress condition to Mercury, Saturn's lessons become too hard for some individuals. They become depressed, obsessed with deep fears about their security, and generally have a difficult time in carrying any long-term projects to completion. They turn to alcohol or stimulants to provide relief from the sense of oppression that can result. They become indecisive, overcautious, or inhibited. They are afraid to express an opinion for fear of rebuff. On the other hand, they may become narrow-minded tyrants as a result of their own personal feelings of inadequacy. Mercury in Aries, Gemini, Leo, Libra, Sagittarius, and Aquarius are less affected by Saturn only because these signs are generally outgoing and can tolerate restrictions more readily; whereas Mercury in Taurus, Cancer, Virgo, Capricorn, Scorpio, and Pisces (signs which tend to be more conservative, impressionistic and moody to begin with) are more sensitive to the ponderousness of Saturn. Therefore, an aspect of Saturn is more difficult for these individuals, and depressions of varying degrees often result.

Next, let us look at Mercury in relation to Uranus. Here is the planet of genius, inventiveness, originality, and eccentricity. Mercury in square, conjunction, or opposition to Uranus becomes abrupt, indiscreet, exceptionally restless, bohemian, or exceedingly intolerant. The negative response to Uranian stress produces cyclothymic behavior or manic disorders. In spite of the difficulty of coping with the excessive nervous energy with which this planet correlates, it is a distinct advantage to have Mercury in contact with Uranus, for the planet is so original and creative. Under this influence, however, there is a tendency to break off a task before completion. So if you are unable to curb the restlessness of this contact, it may become self-defeating only because the necessary stick-to-itiveness essential for success in any field will be lacking. When the going gets tough, your tendency will be to give up or change direction abruptly. Uranus correlates with unusual opportunities and creativity. However, you must learn to work with it. This is the planet that induces people to turn to tranquilizers.

Now let us consider the planet Neptune with relationship to your Mercury. Here is the planet correlation that sends more people off to the psychiatrist, causes more near-nervous breakdowns, and produces more panic and neurosis than any other planet. Why should this be so? Neptune's action correlates with the subtle, the diffuse, intrigue, mystery, or deception. It is the planet of mysticism, fanaticism, and idealism. It correlates with phobias as well as with ecstasy. It is the planet of the visionary or the planet of the crackpot. When Neptune is in square, conjunction, or opposition to Mercury, the correlate in your mental response will be a tendency to suffer from unreasonable fears, phobic behavior, paranoia, or delusions. The imagination produces hysterical ailments. Because Neptune is so spiritual and sublime, it is more difficult to be aware of the message it brings. Neptune is intuitive, altruistic, and artistic. But the artistry of Neptune is far more subtle than that of a draftsman. It is the artistry produced by a blending of factors—in knowing instinctively the proper proportions for putting anything together in words, in colors, in any phase of daily living. It is the planet of faith —and faith is the antidote for coping with stressful aspects. You must learn to differentiate between what is real and what is imagined. Neptune is often implicated when a person has the desire to escape from unpleasantness via hallucinatory drugs, believing new worlds will open up or that impressions and responses will be heightened. But most people will find inner turmoil, because anxiety is the usual outcome of chemical tampering for those whose Mercury is in stressful relationship to Neptune. Some take to deep meditation sessions in search of a "lovely world." People invariably search inward under these aspects, yet the real lesson of Neptune is to reach outward; that is, to become involved in reality, not the illusory.

Finally, let us look at the planet Pluto. Pluto's action correlates with destruction, renovation, regeneration, transformation, or revolution. It is violent only for those who are lacking in self-control or discipline. It sometimes destroys, but only to make way for the new. It reforms. When Pluto is found in square, conjunction, or opposition to Mercury, the usual response is intense restlessness—a desire to change conditions and an inability to "go through channels"! In other words, these people sometimes take the law into their own hands or will participate in their own personal revolution. In addition, these contacts correlate with sadistic or masochistic behavior. Often there is a deep sense of personal unworthiness. The inability to cope with existing conditions that seem unfavorable or intolerable correlates with self-destructive behavior. This may take the form of attempted suicide or mental flagellation. Pluto wants to transform, but it sometimes takes time—more time than the afflicted individual wants to wait. Therefore the action of this planet is subverted into underworld activities or anarchy. Mercury and Pluto make an excellent combination if it is understood that it represents transformation—the ability to work for a real cause, to bring about necessary social and political reforms under due process of law. It is the true missionary. But it has to be understood to be used properly.

These then are the brief descriptions of the planets and stresses that can cause us so much mental and emotional anguish. All of them may cause nervous breakdowns, but for different reasons. An emotional breakdown usually occurs when you are no longer able to cope with your problems, when they seem to be either insurmountable or unaccountable—and when you can see no hope for the future. Of course, your hope is in your own natal chart. It indicates the path that you must take to alleviate these unpleasant symptoms. But the path is sometimes difficult, and in order to gain the strength to tread this path you must understand your own particular astrological problem and what you can do to change or overcome it. This understanding, in turn, can come to you by a thorough study of the Moon and Mercury in your own chart and their aspects to Mars, Saturn, Uranus, Neptune, and Pluto. This study will give you the knowledge and the remedy—it only remains for you to use it.

⑬

Astrology and the Generation Gap

Many young people today feel isolated from their parents. They find parental ideas inappropriate and antiquated, not applicable to the challenges of today. At the same time, many parents cannot understand their children. Every mode and mannerism seems to be a repudiation of the ideals our traditional past held dear. The modern idiom in music and art has no obvious relationship to the conventional values of yesteryear.

Although the present generation gap is obvious and pronounced, it is not something new. There has always been a gap between generations, and there always will be, for this is a phenomenon correlated with Nature's clock, and it has a perfectly rational astrological explanation.

Astrologically speaking, the generation gap is defined by the astronomical–behavioral correlations of certain slow-moving planets which cast their shadows upon a whole generation. Each group of young people on the threshold of maturity under these planetary correlates is caught in their spell. Each person, of course, responds to these transits in his own way. But the algebraic summation of all the personal responses makes it possible to trace the general response of the many people who make up a generation.

See for yourself. Examine the transits of some of the planets to see how they correlate with the atmosphere and changes in our present society. Look for their indications for the future. The three slow-moving planets that influence a generation are Pluto, Neptune, and, to a certain extent, Uranus. Uranus spends approximately seven years in one sign and is correlated with unusual opportunities, the sensational, the unconventional, emancipation, and fads in general. Its stay of only seven years is too swift to color an entire generation, but it does present opportunities for the trial of new trends. For example, in 1968, Uranus had been in the sign Virgo for six years. Virgo is the natural ruler of the sixth house, and you will remember we discussed some of the possible interpretations in the natal chart. On a mundane level, however, Virgo deals with such things as public health, the armed forces, warships, unions, teachers, and the working class. By combining the meaning of the sign with the nature of the planet, it is easy to pinpoint some of the corresponding conditions that have occurred in our society: an unprecedented number of strikes called by unions, new medical health care plans for the working man, and unusual new advances in the field of preventive medicine. There were spectacular tragedies as well, such as those produced by the use of the drug thalidomide. The "Pill" typifies, and may yet prove itself, another Uranian fad.

Young people began staging marches for racial equality, and much attention was aroused concerning equal opportunities in employment. The sporadic outbreak of draft card burnings and the attack on a United States ship under odd circumstances were characteristic of this transit. In addition, unusual clothing fads were initiated by the young, and pop art came into being. In 1968, Uranus entered the sign of Libra, where it will remain until 1975. Since this sign correlates with the expression of beauty, justice, and romance, and since Libra is also the natural ruler of the seventh house, which deals with open enemies, arbitration, marriages, and international relationships, we would expect to see unusual events and opportunities in these areas. New fads will be adopted in fashion—perhaps a return to the romantic look. There will be an effort to restore balance to our society; divorce rulings may be broadened, old laws may be overturned or reversed, experimental marriages outside the bounds of legality may be promoted; opportunities may occur to make peace with former enemies and, conversely, a chance to make enemies of former friends! People will demand better quality in products instead of the slipshod varieties that have flooded the market. Peace through arbitration could easily be the keynote. In general then, the seven years or so that Uranus takes to travel through a sign are those years that see new and unusual customs, fads, and eccentricities take hold of the population. Each country, according to its own natal chart, finds that the house in which this transit occurs is the area that will be subject to the most "emancipation," rupture, or opportunity. These are some of the potentialities for the future. These are not predictions.

Next, consider the planet Neptune. This planet correlates with extreme receptivity, and it readily takes on the qualities of the sign in which it is found. Neptune has pronounced spiritual and moral qualities, but for some reason many people have not responded to this side of the planet.

Neptune has spent fourteen years in the sign Scorpio. We must therefore look at the qualities correlated with Scorpio to see just how this transit has worked out in our society. Remember that although we may talk as though the planet itself were causing the problems or creating the situations, it is not the planet—it is those who react to the correlate of its transit who set the stage. Nations react, and countries react, and generations react. It is on an individual basis, however, that these planetary correlates operate. One individual can act as a catalyst for many others if he is in a position to influence public opinion. This in turn produces a chain reaction. Whether this is for better or for worse has to be decided ultimately by society as a whole, but it usually takes many years before the value or damage that has occurred as a result of a transit can be determined.

The influence of Neptune in Scorpio has been heavily accented in our society. Unfortunately, for the most part it has been the influence from the negative sides of both the planet and the sign that has attracted the most attention. Like the other signs, Scorpio has both positive and negative attributes. Moreover, Scorpio has two symbols which are quite explicit: the eagle and the serpent! Scorpio, designated by the eagle, can reach the heights of nobility and compassion; or it can sink to the depths of degradation when symbolized by the serpent. There is nothing inherently evil about the sign or the planet; it is the individual's response that makes the difference.

In order to further define the scope of a Neptune transit, we must take another look at this planet. It has been known negatively as the planet of escape because it correlates with dissolution. Neptune also rules such things as alcohol, sleeping pills, drugs, anesthesia, and hallucinatory agents. Neptune is the natural ruler of the twelfth house, which in a negative sense can be called the house of "self-undoing" or suicide, incarceration in jail or a mental institution, and long illnesses. Realizing this, it is easy to understand how people try to escape via the Neptune way: by an overdose of sleeping pills, by alcohol, by a retreat into insanity, or by drug addiction and hallucinatory agents. Any of these escape routes can lead to an institution of one kind or another.

Now consider the sign Scorpio. At worst, it represents the sex act removed from its natural environment—not used for procreation, not performed in love, but an act that is compassionless and sordid. In addition, Scorpio seems to bring out the brutality of certain individuals in a society. The natural intensity and ardor of Scorpio may be corrupted; it then becomes vicious, violent, and depraved. Putting these two factors, Neptune and Scorpio, together, we find the potential set-up for some characteristically "undeveloped" or irresponsible behavior on the parts of many individuals. By their actions, it may seem as though every form of evil has crept from its secret (twelfth house) hiding place and has come out into the open to test the moral fiber of a generation. And how does this generation respond? The evidence has been obvious. The need of many young people to escape via drugs and alcohol, the emphasis on sex without love, the crime and murder rates, the exploitation of young people through simulated copulation on the stage and screen, the almost compulsive need of many individuals to expose their nude bodies, the sanctioning of lesbianism, male homosexuality, and other acts of immoral behavior in our movies (also Neptune-ruled), the obsessive trend in fiction to pander to the erotic, and the recurrent theme of "God is dead." This is all unmistakable evidence of a negative Neptune in Scorpio.

You might wonder if all these negative trends are based on the sign. They are not. The fact is that some of the individuals who have been in the vanguard of the so-called "new morality" were born when Neptune was in the sign Leo. The transiting Neptune in Scorpio has been forming a fourth house square aspect to their own natal planet. Since the square does not always produce the most constructive results, some of these individuals have made a characteristically tortuous or irritable response, which then causes others to respond similarly. This has been evident in literature, art, medicine, religion, and the theater. Not all the results, of course, have been immoral or disruptive. But those people who have responded to the positive side of this transit—those who are morally and spiritually "in tune"—have been productive, even though they perhaps have not earned headlines. Many have been patient, have been weighing the evidence and measuring the benefits that have resulted from this atmosphere. New voices, impatient to be heard, will speak out. The real purpose of a Neptune transit is to give each generation a chance to test its moral fiber and to search for the ideal along lines suggested by the sign.

Neptune is on the threshold of a new sign, and a new generation of young people will rise to the challenge. Neptune entered Sagittarius in 1970. Sagittarius, among other things, correlates with philosophy, religion, metaphysics, prophecy, sportsmanship and sporting games, foreign affairs, and large animals. It is fortunate that, even at its worst, Sagittarius does not correlate with behavior or activity that is as potentially evil as that of a negative Scorpio.

The last of the planets that influence a generation is Pluto. Pluto's orbit is extremely erratic and as a result this planet may remain for as few as fifteen years and as many as thirty-odd years in one sign. For this reason, people are given an opportunity to test certain theories and practices over a longer period of time before the results become a part of the framework of society. Uranus might correlate with an insurrection, a new style, fad, or eccentricity, but after seven years or so, people are tired of it and are ready to try something new. Neptune brings the faith and moral fiber of a society into focus along lines peculiar to the sign. But Pluto is the ultimate test. The unfit will not survive the Pluto transit. That which is found to be unworkable, untenable, or unacceptable to the oncoming generation is swept away to make way for a whole new philosophy. Various facets of government are abandoned and new policies and agencies are introduced. Revolutions occur, new social theories gain acceptance, an era is ushered in or ushered out. New theories are applied and, ultimately, either they work and are incorporated into the structure of our lives and society, or they are discarded.

At the present time, Pluto is in the sign Virgo, and we have already discussed some of the various meanings of Virgo. On the other hand, Pluto correlates with change, regeneration, rejuvenation, life forces (birth, sex, death, and rebirth). In a negative sense, Pluto correlates with revolutions, willful destruction, gangsterism, and violence. We can see some of the more obvious correlations of this transit in our society by combining the meaning of the sign and the planet: Great changes have been made over the past several years in the practice of medicine with an emphasis on specialization and with a more socialized approach to medicine. Human organ transplants have been successfully carried out; there is a revolution in our universities with a destruction of the sterile, academic ivory tower and a rise in humanism. The servant class has virtually disappeared, and the blacks who made up much of this class are rapidly entering the artisan and business strata of society. On the other hand, we have seen the growth and infiltration of the gangster elements into unions and business. Unions have grown big and powerful, with the ability to make far-reaching decisions for the masses of people they represent. The working man has made great strides in benefits and wages, and attention has been diverted from the moneyed aristocracy to the working class. We have also seen Virgo at its worst: a gradual poisoning of our atmosphere and natural resources by the careless use of chemical agents and pollutants. Chemical preservatives have been added to our food. Workers have generally lacked a sense of pride in their work. Goods of inferior quality with planned obsolescence built into them have been foisted onto the consumer, and gangster elements have cheated the public and propagated violence. These, then, are some of the phenomena we have witnessed that correlate with the transit of Pluto in Virgo.

In 1971, Pluto enters the sign Libra. Here again we may see the emphasis slowly shift to more tranquil times. People will demand law and order and will grow impatient with laws that protect the lawless. Reforms will be made in our divorce laws. Marriages may take on a new meaning with less emphasis on security for the woman and more on romance. Women will perhaps assume more responsibility for the financial support of a husband who may prefer to remain at home. But even though Libra is usually peace-loving and tranquil, this sign does have the potential for being exceptionally violent if "thrown off balance." Thus, with the stress of a negative Pluto, society could have some very difficult tests to pass. In general, though, we should expect that the forces encouraging revolution by violence will subside, leaving a more stable social structure. There will be some very serious attempts to put into practice what Mrs. Lyndon Johnson strove so hard to encourage—more beauty on the American scene.

These then are the planets that produce the generation gap. They color our lives to the extent that they are incorporated into our society. Each nation, state, city, and town has a natal chart. To the extent that new laws are adopted or new forms of government are embraced under a Pluto transit or a Neptune transit, there will be a reflection of the prevailing mood of the generation of citizens that make up the population. Knowing the meaning of the slow-moving planetary transits can be of significant help. Political leaders will have some idea of the potential responses of their constituents. By knowing both the positive and negative aspects of the planets and their signs, psychologists and sociologists will have some guidelines as to what might otherwise seem like unpredictable behavior among certain groups of individuals. But most of all, this knowledge can minimize the generation gap between parents and children. And by understanding the various aspects of a particular transit, it might be possible for parents to encourage the more constructive expression of these transits in their children.

There will always be a generation gap. But it is the nature of the transiting planets that defines the degree of stress between each generation. An understanding of astrology can help to bridge the gap.

A Job...or a Career?

Next to affairs of the heart, the problems of career most frequently cause individuals to seek the advice of an astrologer. A young college student considers dropping out; the attractive graduate tries to balance her future professional career against the prospects of becoming a wife and mother; the elderly man flounders between keeping his own business or working for someone as a manager; the hair stylist is torn between the choice of earning more money or doing something more intellectually challenging. These are the kinds of problems that worried clients present to an astrologer for solution. Except for those lucky individuals who have expressed a certain predilection for a career early in life, or those who have some unusual talent, most people toss about helplessly, hoping to find the job or career that will propel them into the path of fame or fortune.

The question of fame has always interested astrologers and their critics who have tried to determine whether horoscopes have forecast fame for the now famous. From the astrological point of view, this kind of search for the clue to fame leads to a blind alley. There is no such thing as a natal chart that is typical of the famous. And once a person becomes famous, there are innumerable astrological reasons that can be used to "prove" the basis of such a person's fame. It would seem hopelessly fatalistic to assume that your chart is the sole indication of whether you will reach the "top" or whether you will be forever consigned to a life of humdrum obscurity.

What can astrology do about your career? If it cannot guarantee that you will be famous, can it help you choose your life's work or your job? Can it indicate whether you will become rich? Can astrology offer you assurance that you will achieve satisfaction in your chosen field? I can tell you assuredly that astrology cannot do this by itself. There is no easy road to fame or fortune, to which many of the successful will attest, and there is rarely achievement without effort. But astrology very definitely can guide you to the areas in which you are likely to enjoy the smoothest sailing and to those areas in which you must swim upstream. In either of these circumstances you might find fame or fortune or both, but there are certain factors you must take into consideration. For one thing, career satisfaction may not be compatible with financial remuneration or even security, and neither of these may be compatible with fame or recognition. It is important to remember, too, that the circumstances of your birth may play a significant part in determining whether or not you select the proper career or vocation. Suppose two people were born at the same moment at the same place, but one was the product of educated parents who were responsible people while the other child was born of impoverished parents who were alcoholics. On the basis of their natal charts, each child would have equal opportunity for success, but there is no question that the first child would have a far easier time of it. Both could ultimately achieve money, recognition, and even satisfaction, but each would likely do it within the framework of his own life. Many people rise far above their early environment, and family background should not be used as an excuse for failure—at least not for the individual who is hard-working and responsible. In fact, on the basis of a natal chart there is no excuse for anyone not achieving his goal, if his goal is realistic. Sometimes, however, an individual works hard at a job for which he has little aptitude and then wonders why he never seems to make progress. He could remedy this with a knowledge of his natal chart, learning from it where his natural talents or inclination lie, and where he might apply his best efforts to move in the right direction. You can consider taking the first step from a study of your own chart.

One of the most important indications of job and career potentialities is the sign on the ascendant—that sign that was "rising" at the exact moment of your birth. (Even if you do not have this information, it is often possible to arrive at a successful guess once

you are familiar with the characteristics of all the signs.) * Therefore, as you learned to do in Chapter 6, draw a chart using the time
of your birth and find your ascendant sign from the Table of
Ascendants on page 193. Very often, the sign on the ascendant is
different from that of the sign in which the Sun is found. In terms of
aptitude and career interests, each sign orients in a particular way.
Therefore, you can narrow down your search by studying your
ascending sign, for it indicates your natural mode of expression. The
following list will enable you to understand the key to your career
individuality.

ARIES:

Generally speaking, this sign is very outgoing, very much the go-get-
ter, and in need of being in a position of authority. It seeks to open
new territories, to pioneer. One of the characteristics assigned to
Aries is a penchant for saying "me first." This is not always reflected
in a negative way, but Aries ascendant people do like to be ahead of
everyone else. These people can tread where angels fear—but this in
no way makes them "fools." They are often fearless and are willing
to tackle a task or commission that would cause another to retreat.
For the most part, they would rather initiate and leave the details
for others to clean up. Therefore, Aries ascendant people often work
well in partnership; one initiates and the other brings to completion.
They are the "tycoons" in whatever is their field. The work they do
must have a challenge to it, obstacles to overcome, and an element of
risk, and they must be able to see results in a relatively short time.
Some of the fields Aries is attracted to are: professional sports, such as
baseball, swimming, or track, that do not involve animals (such as
polo) , exploring, police work, stockbroking, surgery, small businesses,
manufacturing, or any field that calls for daring, enterprise, and
pioneering.

TAURUS:

A security-oriented sign. It is often called upon to straighten out the
confusion created by others, because Taurus ascendant people are
patient, thorough and plodding and will stay with a task no matter
how hopeless it may seem to others. In some there is an element of
sluggishness because they seem to deliberate endlessly before making
a decision. Taurus ascendant people work for the long haul. They

* If there is no way of knowing your correct birth time, use your Solar chart as though
it were a Time chart.

enjoy a situation as long as they can continue to build it up and see it grow. They move slowly and they need to be in positions that do not threaten them with constant change. They like to know how much money they are going to get in advance and are therefore not happy with jobs or careers in which their income is subject to much fluctuation—unless it fluctuates along a very healthy wage scale! They are good in positions of trust and security. They can be relied upon to complete a job and are generally intensely loyal to anyone or anything to which they have made a firm commitment. They have a very down-to-earth manner and a common-sense approach to a problem. They do not like to have to divide their time. They prefer to do one thing at a time and to have enough time to do it. These people are attracted to anything that "grows" and are therefore often drawn to such fields as gardening, building, real estate, banking, and securities.

GEMINI:

A very restless, versatile, and quick sign. Gemini people have a talent for doing two things at once. They thrive on change. They cannot stand to be chained to routine. They love anything that does not commit them to a regular time schedule unless there is much flexibility within that routine. They are witty, artistic, and very often musical. There is sometimes an aptitude for drawing, languages, or selling. They seem to thrive on situations which others might classify as "chaotic." They are therefore very good in emergency situations, as they rise to the challenge immediately and will have it well in hand before some of the other signs have even defined the problem. They do not particularly enjoy deep, sophisticated, or esoteric philosophies; they usually see the underlying simplicity. For this reason they have been accused of being superficially clever. Gemini is often manually dexterous, and this talent often expresses itself through some musical instrument. This sign is the one that enjoys communicating—either by traveling, talking with other people, performing, or writing. These people are also found as traveling salesmen, railroad workers, writers, broadcasters and announcers, artists, dancers and other performers, typists, secretaries, linotype operators, cashiers, pilots, or in any profession where versatility, quick thinking, and constant change predominate.

CANCER:

Basically a home-loving sign. Very much conscious of family and traditions. Cancerians are interested in history and antiquity and love to surround themselves with memorabilia of the past. They are collectors of antiques and anything else that relates to the past—old books, coins, etc. This sign is very protective and has a need to care for others, and for this reason Cancer ascendant people are very often attracted to the profession of nursing or medicine. Cancer has an affinity to nourishment and is therefore associated with the food industry, restaurant business, cooking, and child care. Although basically very ambitious, Cancer people are rather thin-skinned and will be best in positions where they do not have to be subject to constant supervision or harassment from those in authority. They seem to retreat under these conditions and are not able to produce. They love to mother people and are happiest when they have someone or something in their complete charge. A job or profession that is best suited for the Cancerian should bring out any of the aforementioned qualities. They are also drawn to the following professions or fields: food serving, used and rare books, history, the restaurant business, medicine, food-production, either on the management level or at the farm level, movie production, heraldry, antiques, and archeology.

LEO:

Essentially a sign of showmanship. Leo ascendant people love to pretend and have a keen sense of the dramatic. Quite forceful in their presentation and very commanding, they are often the center of attraction. They have an innate sense of power and love to be in a position where they can "throw their weight around." They need recognition and admiration, and are not content as a rule to work quietly behind the scenes. Leo loves to be in the public eye and very often attracts attention by behavior that is calculated to bring publicity. Many have a regal bearing or are attracted to the trappings of royalty and ceremony. Although Leo is known as the sign of the organizer, it is not generally known for its attention to detail. Leo people prefer to let others take care of such things, and they are wonderful at directing others. Their love of the make-believe often draws them to such professions as acting, entertaining, publicity, or working as stagehands. Other Leo ascendants can be found as maîtres d'hôtel, corporation heads, beauty consultants, fashion designers, school administrators or working in any capacity that allows them to "rule" others—even if it is more illusory than real!

VIRGO:

A sign of dedication and service to others. This is a rather unemotional, practical, and reserved sign. Virgo people often exhibit a talent for analyzing and are able to extract the significant details from a morass of information. Their faculty for criticism is usually well developed, and they are not always aware that they have the habit of informing others of their weaknesses or of always finding fault. Their sharp intellects and analytic minds penetrate deftly, and they will see a weakness and try to ferret it out. Their lack of emotion will not allow them to dwell on the fact that someone's feelings might get hurt. They have a real desire to be of use to others, and they make dedicated teachers and academicians. Since this sign is connected with the sixth house of health, Virgo people are often found in the field of hygiene and preventive medicine. Their analytic qualities find an outlet in such fields as psychology, physical science, microbiology, bookkeeping, and accounting. In addition, they make good efficiency experts, veterinarians, editors, and writers. These people can be found in positions where they are able to make a contribution to the welfare of others, and they will work long and hard for some cause in which they believe. However, this is basically a shy and retiring sign, and those with a Virgo ascendant must learn to project a warmer image if they wish to get ahead in any job that requires public approval or acceptance.

LIBRA:

Generally speaking, a sign of peace and harmony. Librans may plan a battle, but they rarely care to take part in one. More than anything, there is a love of the beautiful in the nature of this sign. The Libran approach to life is essentially romantic and, while they can be quite sentimental, they are rarely "gushy." Art, literature, and poetry often play significant parts in the lives of educated Librans. They are basically orderly and they like their surroundings to be tranquil and aesthetically appealing. Those who rise to the top usually rule others with smoothness—theirs is the "iron hand in the velvet glove." Because of their love of beauty, they are drawn to vocations that utilize this faculty—such as ownership of a boutique shop, clothing design, jewelry appraisal or buying, hair styling, and copy and layout designing. The ability to exert the quality of balanced judgment makes them well suited to the field of marriage counseling, arbitration, civil law, and military strategy. Librans have a special ability to put others at their ease, and they would do well in the capacity of professional host such as one sees on television talk shows. A Libran would be most productive wherever there is an opportunity to express the poetic side of life, to enjoy the beautiful or to create it, or to arbitrate.

SCORPIO:

This sign is associated with an intensity and passion for digging, whether this be in the ground or after the facts, such as in research. Scorpio people are generally very reserved and secretive. One is rarely allowed fully into their private world—they withhold much of themselves until a person has had a chance to merit such consideration. There is usually an innate love of the mysterious and/or the macabre. They are not particularly easy to be with at times because their sharp, penetrating wit has a way of reaching you where it hurts! There is nothing they like more than a debate, for they enjoy tearing the other fellow's arguments apart. This ability to probe deeply leads to such fields or professions as surgery, psychiatry, research of all kinds, newspaper reporting, and statistics. Scorpio is also associated with such vocations as undertaking, plumbing, pathology, chemistry, insurance, sanitation, excavation, and renovation. In addition, Scorpio people are also drawn to the field of birth control and reproduction.

SAGITTARIUS:

The need for freedom is the most characteristic quality of this sign. Sagittarians exhibit an early predilection for travel. On an intellectual level, they love nothing more than a discussion of profound subjects, and they are often given to philosophizing. Foreign lands have great appeal for the Sagittarian, and there is a pronounced interest in horses and, to a certain extent, other animals. This sign is not noted for its continuity and grows weary after the initial outburst of energy and enthusiasm is over. Sagittarians are best suited for those professions that allow them much flexibility not only of movement but of thought. They make good college professors, trial lawyers, and travel agents. There is another quality of Sagittarius that is often quite evident, and that is its insistence on delivering the "truth"—and usually quite bluntly. People born under this sign have a way of wounding people who would prefer a little less "honesty." For this reason they ought not to work in those professions where people need reassurance and want to cling to their illusions—but unfortunately this is where too many of them end up. Sagittarius is very effective in the fields of religion, ranching, publishing and big-game hunting. This sign is sometimes said to endow the quality of prophecy; although very few individuals possess anything close to the gift of prophecy, many of them do indeed have the ability to grasp the right direction intuitively, which they can apply very successfully to business. Polo players, jockeys, zoo keepers, and boxers are also associated with Sagittarius.

CAPRICORN:

Basically a conservative sign. These people have the capacity to endure and conquer, and very early exhibit a penchant for hard work. Naturally thrifty, the tendency to save is often carried over into other areas and they are reluctant to part with anything that might eventually be useful. This sign usually comes into its own later in life, and the early years are not always as productive, which may cause the parents of Capricornians some anxiety. They have an ability to achieve their goals by dint of persistence and perseverance. They usually have a need to rise to the top no matter how difficult the path, even though they may temporarily retreat. This sign correlates with leadership and executive ability, and for this reason many are found in positions of authority because they are able to assume responsibility for others. People born under Capricorn have a rather serious approach to their goals and life in general and, although they have as good a sense of humor as anyone born under any other sign, they often appear aloof or even unfriendly—but this is not usually the case. Since Capricornians like to have real power, they are drawn to fields such as politics where they can make far-reaching decisions. In addition, they make good executives, managers, and foremen. Skin specialists, dermatologists, dentists, industrial real estate people, orthopedic surgeons, and osteopaths are also suitable to the indications of a Capricorn. As a general rule, those professions that allow one to assume command, that present a challenge, and that have some social esteem attached will be attractive to Capricorn people.

AQUARIUS:

One of the most characteristic qualities of this sign is the need for independence. Aquarians are often ahead of their times, for they seem to sense the coming trends and are able to apply this talent to their particular job. Originality and inventiveness are customarily part of their makeup; however, occasionally they are seized with the urge to go bohemian. When this talent is applied to art and decorating, Aquarians are able to break with tradition and establish themselves as "originals." They are able to think up new ways to present old facts and are therefore good in the fields of sales promotion and advertising. Fields that provide inventive scope and that allow freedom and originality are compatible with the Aquarian nature. Many will also consider space exploration, engineering, architecture, electronics, and theoretical science. They are also astrologers, electricians, radio announcers, interior decorators, fund raisers, co-ordinators for charitable programs, and designers. Because of the duo-rulership of Saturn (as well as Uranus), many are found in politics.

PISCES:

The exceptional receptivity of this sign makes Pisceans accessible to information a less perceptive person would miss. They are instinctively able to know the right thing to do, and this gives them an awareness intuitively before they arrive at the conclusion intellectually. They are the true humanitarians, for they are very much aware of the sorrows and sufferings of others. They will often be found at work in hospitals or other institutions that care for people's health or welfare. Extremely sympathetic, they have the ability to empathize with others and almost to "put themselves in the other fellow's shoes"; for this reason they can be very effective in portraying a dramatic role—or even appealing to the crowds through their emotions. Many Pisceans are attracted to parapsychology, for they seem to sense more of the mystery of life than do others. Problems of air pollution and water pollution are of paramount interest to many of this sign. They are also attracted to marine biology, sailing, fishing, oil refining, anesthesiology, biology, publishing, and social service. Painters and artists are also found strongly represented in this sign, for they have an intuitive ability to work with colors.

As you can see, each of the signs as they are found on the ascendant provides a natural inclination that must be considered initially. Consequently, any job or profession is expressed through this sign. For example, suppose you are wondering if you should go into medicine and the sign on your ascendant is Libra. As an initial step, read the Libran characteristics, then decide if your love of beauty and order, etc., is harmonious with the medical profession, or some part of it. You may decide to enter the field in an administrative capacity, or go into cosmetic surgery, or legal medicine. In other words, whatever you decide to do should be in keeping with your ascending sign.

The problem of selecting a career is very difficult for many people because many contrasting emotions lie within their own nature. Some people have a compelling desire to rule over others—even to push them around. So we find some very disgruntled individuals in positions of authority where their underlings feel subservient. And instead of being kind or helpful, these individuals are rude and patronizing. But if these same individuals were sincere about learning natural inclinations, they would consider the requirements of their ascending signs, and this would provide the first step toward job satisfaction for themselves—and tranquility for those who work with them!

Now consider the sign in which your Sun is found. Try to synthesize the meaning of these two factors (i.e., your Sun sign and your ascendant sign). The basic qualities of your Sun will be expressed in conjunction with your ascendant. Suppose your Sun sign is Taurus, making you very reliable and security-conscious with a desire to see things grow. Your ascendant sign is Scorpio, which is intense, penetrating and research-oriented. Combining these two factors, we get a picture of someone who may like to manage other people's money. The investment or brokerage fields may beckon. It is important, of course, to consider a particular predisposition to a profession. But it is easier to narrow down the job possibilities by using astrological techniques.

Each of these signs has a ruling planet. The next step is to determine the ruling planet of your ascending sign. The following table will simplify this for you:

Ascending sign	Ruling Planet
ARIES	Mars
TAURUS	Venus
GEMINI	Mercury
CANCER	Moon
LEO	Sun
VIRGO	Mercury
LIBRA	Venus
* SCORPIO	Pluto (Mars)
SAGITTARIUS	Jupiter
CAPRICORN	Saturn
AQUARIUS	Uranus (Saturn)
PISCES	Neptune (Jupiter)

When you have determined your ruling planet, you must discover in which house in your own chart your ascendant "ruler" is found. Jot this down on a piece of paper for handy reference. Next, note the house in which your Sun is found in your natal chart. If both the Sun and the ruling planet are found in the same house, refer to pages 79–102 and apply the meaning of that house in terms of possible career or job interests. In addition, the following list simpli-

* In the case of duo-rulership, you may use either ruler according to your natural preference or whichever planet is better aspected, i.e., in trine relationship to another planet.

fies the clue to possible professions or fields of concentration according to houses.

FIRST HOUSE

Mountaineering, police work, professional sports such as baseball, football, swimming, track and field, boxing, exploring, entrepreneurship, advertising, barbering, millinery, anthropology.

SECOND HOUSE

Banking, gardening, stocks and bonds, clothing, jewelry, dry goods and notions, furniture, any money concerns, buying, laundering and dry cleaning, building.

THIRD HOUSE

Writing, secretarial work, post office work, selling, railroad industry, truck driving, chauffeuring, selling, illustrating, sales promotion and advertising, transportation industry in general, elementary schools.

FOURTH HOUSE

Antiques, heraldry, history, restaurant industry, food business, nursing and nursing homes, foster parent or adoption agencies, real estate.

FIFTH HOUSE

High schools, camp counseling, gambling casinos, dramatics field, entertaining, theaters, playgrounds, sporting event promotion, speculating, stockbroking.

SIXTH HOUSE

Armed forces, Red Cross, hygiene, dietetics, employment agencies, pet shops, domestic service, missionaries, Peace Corps, nursing.

SEVENTH HOUSE

Partnerships, wedding experts, public events, law, performing, diplomacy, military strategists, agencies (theatrical, etc.) .

EIGHTH HOUSE

Insurance agencies, sex research, paleontology, mining, undersea exploration, laboratories.

NINTH HOUSE

College administration, college teaching, sociology, law, foreign affairs, colonial administration, metaphysical work.

TENTH HOUSE

Politics, executive-level work, social arbitration, mining, society column writing, prestige jobs—("ruler" here shows an innate need for recognition).

ELEVENTH HOUSE
Clubs, organizations, guidance counseling, professional fund-raising, charitable work.

TWELFTH HOUSE
Medicine, hospital personnel, astrology, institution personnel, banking, library work, cloisters, universities.

If you find that your Sun and the ruler of your ascendant both fall in the same house, this is favorable verification for following the lines suggested by the house interpretation. If, however, they are not both in the same house, choose the house in which your ascendant ruler is found first; then refer to the house in which your Sun is found for additional potentialities.

Not everyone wants to be a professional, or have a career, or even to go to college, but everyone should do something worthwhile that is suitable to his interests or natural inclination. If you want job satisfaction, it is far better to know where your strength lies —but what you choose to do about it is up to you.

⑮

Astrology and the Aquarian Age

Society is poised on the threshold of a new era. This era was brought into focus by a Broadway hit song entitled "Aquarius." What is most significant about this song is that it comes from a show featuring nude players as part of the scenario. Whether or not this production would have achieved such notoriety in the world of the theater without nudity and on the basis of the songs alone is a matter of opinion. There is some reason to wonder, however, whether this type of presentation is an omen of the future. Drama in the raw seems to have triggered off a series of theatrical ventures into the realm of nudity and sex; and each one vies with the other to see how far they can go and still remain "legitimate." Is this what the Age of Aquarius holds for us? Must we revise all our moral and ethical values? Astrology can help us answer these questions, but first we must appreciate the astrological perspective. Remember, the Age of Aquarius will encompass a very long period of time, and changes during this age will be slow and long-lasting. Because history is more clearly understood in retrospect, and not always recognized when it is being made, the full impact of this new age may not be apparent to individuals of the generations that will comprise the Aquarian Age.

To appreciate the astrological concept, let us first consider an age. An age is a span of time—approximately two thousand years—and it is measured by the Precession of the Equinoxes. When priest–astronomers first plotted the skies, the first point of Aries was seen against the background of the constellation Aries. In the course of time, the sign Aries was eventually seen against the constellation Pisces. The signs appear to be going backward through the constellations; soon the first point of Aries will be seen against the constellation Aquarius. And we will remain in the Aquarian Age until the first point of Aries is seen against the background of the constellation Capricorn—some two thousand years hence.

It is impossible to be living in this new age and not be affected by it. All of us are caught between the old and the new. You might reason that most people do not live long enough to comprehend the overall significance of an age, but as we shall see, there may be reason for the next generation to dispute this theory. For now, let us consider the present emphasis on sex. Are we witnessing something portentous? Will nudity and public fornication become the newest form of freedom? Is there a correlation between this kind of behavior and the sign Aquarius?

To answer these questions, we must remember that Aquarius is an independent and freedom-loving sign. Thus, only to the extent that nudity is a bold stroke against restraint does it have some correlation with Aquarius. Let us look then at what we might expect in the area of human sexual expression as it pertains to the Aquarian Age. There is no doubt that the old traditional sexual patterns are being subjected to profound stress. We, who are on the brink of this new era, are witnessing the painful demise of an old concept of morality (the concept that sex is for procreation only). However, the present surge toward uninhibited freedom is still, in many ways, an overreaction to the Piscean, Judeo-Christian theology with its strict moral overtones. But this sex revolution will not change sexual mores in one clear or continuous wave. Rather, there will be a series of surges and counterreactions which will result in a number of uneven changes in our sexual attitudes and practices. Many of the people who are in the forefront of the new sexual ethics will fall victim to society's reaction and its everpresent Puritan morality—the trappings of the Piscean Age.

It would be a mistake to predict that the Aquarian Age might introduce unrestrained promiscuity. On the contrary, although there are expected changes in sexual practices and attitudes, there will not be a profound change in moral standards, because Aquarius is far too honest and enlightened a sign to countenance such behavior. But it may take a long time before we achieve complete freedom and honesty in sexual matters. Our society is still the conditioned product of past history and traditions—some of which have been fraudulently emotional and flagrantly dishonest.

What is the Aquarian approach to sex? How does it contrast with the views and practices of the Piscean Age? For one thing, sexual relations will ultimately become more honest. Once sex is unshackled from commercial exploitation, it will assume its normal function of being a very important *personal* experience. It would be hopelessly naïve to think that everyone is going to be satisfied with such a wholesome approach. Each person must decide for himself what avenue he wishes to take. In general, however, Aquarian sex will be unfettered, discriminating, and removed from overtones of guilt. Many individuals now experimenting with complete sexual freedom will eventually learn that sex must involve a deep emotional bond and a spiritual and physical commitment to one's chosen partner; a commitment with no limits, rules, or regulations, but one that is the natural expression of an individual's capacity to love —and to be loved. The rest is fornication!

Scientists and lay people alike are beginning to speculate on the future of our civilization. They foresee an end to the institutions of marriage and family life. They predict that advances in the field of reproductive biology are likely to produce vast changes in these institutions and our way of life, and in the human form as well. Let us consider some of these problems from the astrological point of view, keeping in mind that the clue to future development can be found, to some extent, in the nature of the sign Aquarius. What about marriage? Considering the present divorce rate, the number of disillusioned partners who are "sticking it out," and the prevailing mood of the younger generation, it would seem that legal marriage will be judged as an impediment to the happiness and welfare of individuals; and marriage as we know it today might eventually succumb to some other looser arrangement. This is certainly the view of some self-proclaimed experts but it is not confirmed by astrology.

Looking into the past, we are aware that marriage used to be an arrangement which, for the most part, provided for the financial protection of the woman and the security of the children. Women were prohibited from many forms of employment, so that the majority of them entered marriage knowing that their welfare and comfort depended upon the husband. If they also found love, that was ideal; but mutual respect, a sharing of the burdens and the rearing of children were the primary responsibilities. Each partner knew his role, a role rigidly prescribed by society. History and literature abound with stories of romantic lovers who agonized over the conventions that refused to acknowledge that love alone was sufficient basis for a marriage. Suitors had to conform to the parents' idea of acceptability, and young women were often bartered and married off to the highest bidder. Although it would be unfair to state categorically that marital happiness did not exist, marriage for the most part was a covenant between two people who gave up something to get something. Men gave up their freedom in return for regular sex, for heirs to carry on the family name. Women gave up their virginity in return for children to love, for financial security and protection.

But little by little, profound and far-reaching changes have taken place in our marriage customs. Parents no longer have a voice about whom their sons and daughters will marry. Women are no longer content to be just housewives; many have full-time jobs. Young women are being accepted into fields and professions that once belonged exclusively to men. Many women no longer need to marry for financial reasons, nor for mental stimulation; and if they can have an active sex life outside the bonds of marriage, would these not appear to be good reasons why legal marriage might become obsolete?

But what about children? Surely women still need the security of marriage to bring up well-adjusted and productive children? Even this line of reasoning, however, is being challenged by sociologists, and a new question arises. If women are relieved of the burden of having and caring for babies through any number of new techniques now being considered, what will happen to the institution of marriage? Is there any reason to suppose that it will survive on its own merit? Will we not completely abandon our old morality and unite freely with whomever we please, whenever we please? The astrological answer is "no."

At the present time, the concept of indiscriminate mating has a great deal of appeal to some individuals—particularly to those whose marriages are emotionally and physically unsatisfying. Certainly there is a great deal of it going on, both among the unmarried and the married. New living arrangements have been tried out among groups, e.g., the communal living approach where, theoretically, no one belongs to anyone. Each shares the privileges and companionship of any individual involved in the "tribe." This approach to marriage and family life, presented as an alternative to our present form of legal marriage, is not new. It has been going on for centuries among certain primitive tribes and cultures, cultures which remain far less complex and undeveloped technologically. Indeed, these cultures, with their simple and open approach to sex and marriage, appear as the ideal to which we might direct our efforts. But this direction—that of developing temporary alliances without too much responsibility—is more in keeping with the negative expression of Aquarius. We must remember that it is individual behavior that makes the difference; the signs and planets merely present the timing of opportunities. And, to the extent that people rise to the challenge of the sign Aquarius, our society will progress. Keep in mind that there is a side to Aquarius that correlates with less developed behavior, and therein lie the qualities of eccentricity, extreme impatience, erratic and disruptive conduct, and a desire to break loose from ties which threaten to bind closely. It is quite conceivable, therefore, that a non-legal, non-binding approach to marriage, with the possibility of a rapid turnover of partners, will appeal to some. But this is not the best that Aquarius can offer and it will not be the dominant theme of the future.

There is a new avenue available to the new generation which promises to remove much of the guesswork and hazards from marriage partner selection. This avenue will utilize astrological techniques (see Chapter 8). Within the not too distant future, improvements will be apparent in the quality of relationships. There will be a strengthening of the marriage bonds. Many individuals will find partners who will satisfy them far beyond their wildest expectations. People will conclude that sex is not simply intercourse, that intercourse is not necessarily romantic, and that romance is not necessarily love. People will know that these three ingredients are the vital components of a total experience which finds its best and most harmonious outlet in an arrangement called marriage—an institution that man will be hard-pressed to improve upon. Unfortunately, this kind of complete experience in marriage has been too rare in our society. Even some of those who believed they were a part of such a union are dismayed to find that, with the passing years, there is a lessening of the bonds; that there is a general decline in the vitality of the marriage. This has all too commonly been held as a perfectly natural sequence. It most assuredly is not.

Once people begin to unite selectively, they will become non-adulterous (to use a Piscean reference), not because they are forced to, but because they want it that way (see Chapters 7 and 8). Aquarius, although he may like to flirt and to befriend all kinds of people, is incapable of being unfaithful once his heart is firmly committed. The point to remember is that his faithfulness does not depend upon his living up to someone else's idea of his responsibilities; it is not based upon fear of disapproval by the members of his community or by his friends; and it is not dependent upon his fear of God's wrath. It is simply the expression of his being in complete and total harmony with his partner—an individual who brings to the union, and receives from it, a sense of completion as a human being, a total fulfillment: a perfect Unity.

What about babies in the Aquarian Age? Scientists are beginning to talk about projects which could conceivably place childbearing outside the body and outside the domain of the woman. Specialists have concluded that sex and reproduction are not necessarily a part of marriage and have projected the premise that marriages in the future might be solely for the pleasure of the individuals. When and if a couple decide to have a child, it might involve nothing more than a consultation with a human engineering scientist to arrange for a particular kind of infant. According to the recent breakthroughs in the field of genetics and reproduction, scientists predict that there will be several potential arrangements that a couple of the future could consider. One of them is the "in vitro" arrangement, whereby the child is developed in a glasslike apparatus in the laboratory which allows the scientist and the parents to observe the growing infant from fertilization to, presumably, birth. In this way the mother is relieved of the tiresome burden of giving birth. There are some very practical applications to this method. For one thing, it would make the developing fetus easily accessible to medical intervention. Anomalies would be readily apparent and, if it should prove necessary, the technician could terminate the entire process. And since this process was begun outside the mother's body and without any moral, spiritual, or emotional entanglements, it could, theoretically, be terminated with about the same amount of emotion, and without any trauma to either parent.

There are quite naturally many fine technicalities that need to be ironed out. However, there are some other important considerations beyond the realm of the scientist, and it is worthwhile to mention these. What is human life? Is it different from animal life? This is not an easy question, nor is it a new one. We do know that up to a certain point the developing human fetus shares an almost identical evolutionary process with many lower forms of animals. It is the human brain, however, that ultimately sets the human child apart. But is this all that separates man from the animal kingdom?

Is the life that the scientist creates in the laboratory synonymous to or part of what philosophers have called the Spirit of Life? At what point does the fetus become "alive" so that both the scientist and the philosopher are satisfied? Is it alive simply because certain sequential events occur beginning with cell division? Or does life perhaps begin at the moment of quickening, which could be the time that the human form becomes "occupied"? Or does this correlate only with a certain stage of brain maturity? Without evoking the old Aristotelian dichotomy of the soul and the body, it is time to begin to look at this picture anew—and this is precisely what is going to happen in the Aquarian Age.

Many well-intentioned and intelligent people have considered childbirth a form of bondage for the female, and it is quite true that to a tiny minority of women, it is bondage. Pregnancy is a rather lengthy process, debilitating to some, restricting to others, and in rare cases it is a dangerous one. But for the vast majority of women, it is the highest form of creativity. It is the very essence of her femininity. While there are always individuals in a society who are willing to do anything or try anything, there is no doubt that most women would not want to have this vital function taken from them. Woman was designed with childbearing as part of the plan.

This concept of producing babies in vitro is just one of many startling new concepts being advanced by scientists and specialists in the field of reproduction and genetics. There is another process which is receiving serious consideration, and that is the technique of reproduction by tissue culture—or "cloning," as it is called technically. In theory this means that human life should be able to be reproduced without uniting the sperm and the egg. Rather, we ought to be able to grow life by the process of planting tissue cultures in the laboratory. By extracting a cell from anywhere in an individual's body, it should be possible to grow the individual all over again. This theory has gained credence because of great advances using this method in the laboratory with lower animal forms, and it has some very exciting implications. For one thing, by removing a cell or cells from some of the world's most talented and brilliant individuals, we could reproduce them on demand. This line of deduction has been advanced by some very reputable scientists. Why not, they reason, establish cell banks where these extraordinary individuals could deposit their cells for present or future demands? But even assuming that one managed to produce an apparent physical double, would this technique be able to guarantee that the talent and uniqueness of such an individual would also be

reproduced? Would they necessarily become doctors, writers, states-
men, etc., all over again? The astrological answer is obviously "no,"
and for the reason that this approach has not taken into consideration the relationship of Nature's clock to an individual. We have
seen that our moment of birth, which represents a single setting on
this clock, predisposes us to a particular conditioning potential as it
relates to environment—not heredity. There are, it seems, certain
times which are more favorable for following along specialized lines.
Therefore, even though an individual may be an exact physical
replica of a world figure, there is absolutely no chance at all that his
talent, outlook on life, personality, etc., will be anything close to the
"original." Moreover, astrologers know and philosophers suspect
that the human body is the vehicle for the very specialized life
within. It is quite unlike any other animal form. Quite naturally,
however, the scientist approaches life from a characteristically different viewpoint, attributing this term to anything which satisfies
the basic minimum requirements for its particular species or genre.
For instance, one-celled organisms are technically living, but are far
removed from what we recognize as a human being with his very
unique brain.

From the standpoint of science, then, there are many new and
interesting techniques being experimented with in the hope that
man will some day be the designer, as well as the master, of his own
ship. Some of these new developments in the field of sex, reproduction, and genetics will yield invaluable information; and couples of
the future with problems will have access to help that is not possible
at this time. But in general, the Age of Aquarius will not see an end
to marriage, it will not bring communal living as a way of life;
children will not be born routinely outside the family group as
wards of the state or in a laboratory. Women's sexual appetites are
not going to grow to the point where they threaten to literally
devour the weak and helpless male. Indiscriminate mating is not the
rage of the future. There is a change, however, that may occur in
family life, for the sign Aquarius is not supposed to be particularly
family oriented. This negative characteristic is not completely accurate, for the Aquarian is as much taken with family life as any other
astrological sign. The difference is that the ties of blood are unim-
portant to him. His family ties will be based on friendship, need,
love, and mutual respect, rather than on an accident of birth. He
will not feel compelled to hold together a group of dissimilar and
hostile relatives simply because they are related by blood, because

the Aquarian can very easily "adopt" a family. In addition, families will grow characteristically smaller and huge families will be a rarity.

What about religion in the Aquarian Age? No one can deny that there has been a lessening of the church's influence in everyday life. Churchmen themselves are the first to admit that a real dilemma exists. People no longer fear the wrath of God as they once did. This seems apparent from the great number of people who have not let the fear of God deter them from any behavior or activity they want to embrace. Even the clergy has been forced to re-examine its positions in matters which were once so neatly compartmentalized as to allow little room for interpretation. Will God no longer be a part of the Aquarian Age? Have we outgrown Him? Will science replace religion? The old Piscean ways have already begun to crumble, and with them the twelfth house orientation. But what will replace it? A general disbelief—an atheistic society without any reference to God? In our desire to placate every minority—and in the spirit of tolerance—will the new age abandon religious references? Will we worship each other, or a particular person in our society? Or will we pray to the scientist?

Fortunately, a cataclysmic end of all organized religion is not consistent with the positive expression of the sign Aquarius. Religion, in fact, will begin to take on new meaning. There will be an emphasis on the individual and his needs. Since Aquarius is known as the sign of universal brotherhood, the church in this new age will strive to make religion more meaningful in terms of man's relationship to man.

Who among us has not prayed? Even the hard-nosed atheist has likely been known to utter an exhortation to the Almighty in times of severe stress. It would not be unreasonable to suppose that people pray because they have hope that their prayers will be heard—and answered. And why not? In order for religion to be a vital and meaningful force in our lives, there should be evidence that it works. But how can we determine whether it works? The real test of a workable religion is how well it teaches us to function, how it teaches us to extract the goodness, the pleasure and the meaning out of ordinary everyday life. The Aquarian Age, then, will see a new dimension added to man's comprehension of God, and with it a new ability to practice a workable religion that has a genuine significance in this changing world. It will be a religion that not only recognizes man's responsibility to his fellow beings, but a religion that has a more personal relation to God and provides a more reasonable explanation of the continuity of life's spark than does the genetic tree of inheritance.

In the beginning of this chapter, we mentioned the fact that people do not live long enough to comprehend the overall meaning of an age. This is true, but if we think of human life as more than a biological phenomenon, then death will eventually be understood to mean not the end of human life, but an end to one physical segment. This theory, the theory of reincarnation, long believed by Eastern philosophers, will eventually establish firm roots in our culture. Events, both startling and inspiring, will elevate this theory beyond the realm of science fiction or romantic superstition. Individuals of unquestioned integrity, some of them scientists, will act as catalysts for this revelation, and a whole new chapter in the theory of religion will be written for the Aquarian Age.

In summary, the pertinent fact to remember about this new age is that it will color the next two thousand years. However, while there will be the same kinds of human activities that we know today within that span of time, the difference will be that these activities will be expressed through the sign Aquarius. It is as though our world has a natal chart and Aquarius has come to the ascendant! We can be sure then that religion, science, philosophy, etc., will over a period of time begin to shed the Piscean characteristics, and that these fields will begin to unfold more in keeping with Aquarius. And this is true too of astrology. For too long astrologers have held to the reasoning that we must not tamper with astrological interpretation. Because of this, astrology has not kept pace with the other sciences and an information gap has occurred. Now new interpretations must be added to keep astrology abreast of modern life. Those of us who bring the gift of perception to astrology know that the time is right for this accomplishment. Those of us with a modern concept of astrology must point the way. It remains for the new student of astrology with a scientific background to fill in the details.

Astrology is our link with the future. It is the key to a "brave new world," and it will play a major role in all walks of life. But this ancient art is about to undergo a transformation; and one day, in the not-too-distant future, astrology will be picked up by the scientist, and it will be re-evaluated, redesigned, renamed, and incorporated into the framework of the Aquarian Age.

Bibliography

ADAMS, EVANGELINE. *Astrology: Your Place in the Sun.* New York: Dodd, Mead and Company, 1927.

—— *Astrology: Your Place Among the Stars.* New York: Dodd, Mead and Company, 1965.

ARMITAGE, ANGUS. *The World of Copernicus.* New York: The New American Library, Signet Science Library, 1951.

ASIMOV, ISAAC. *The Universe.* New York: Avon Books, 1966.

BATES, GRACE E. *Probability.* Reading, Mass.: Addison-Wesley Publishing Company, 1965.

BRUNHUBNER, FRITZ. *Pluto.* Washington: National Astrological Library, 1934.

CARDANO, GEROLAMO. *The Book on Games of Chance.* New York: Holt, Rinehart and Winston, 1961.

CARTER, CHARLES E. O. *Symbolic Directions in Modern Astrology.* New York: Macoy Publishing Company, 1947.

—— *The Principles of Astrology.* 5th ed. London: The Theosophical Publishing House, 1963.

CURTIS, HELENA. *Biology.* New York: Worth Publishers, 1968.

FRASER, J. T., ed. *The Voices of Time.* New York: George Braziller, 1966.

FRAZER, WILLIAM R. *Elementary Particles.* Englewood Cliffs, N.J.: Prentice-Hall, 1966.

VON FRISCH, KARL. *The Dance Language and Orientation of Bees.* Cambridge, Mass.: Harvard University Press, Belknap Press, 1967.

GAUQUELIN, MICHEL. *The Scientific Basis of Astrology.* New York: Stein and Day, 1969.

—— *The Cosmic Clocks.* Chicago: Henry Regnery Company, 1967.

GEORGE, LLEWELLYN. *A to Z Horoscope Maker and Delineater*. St. Paul, Minn.: Llewellyn Publications, 1966.

GOOD, I. J. *The Estimation of Probabilities*. Cambridge, Mass.: M.I.T. Press, 1965.

GNEDENKE, B. V. and KHINCHIN, A. YA. *An Elementary Introduction to the Theory of Probability*. New York: Dover Publications, 1962.

GUILLEMIN, VICTOR. *The Story of Quantum Mechanics*. New York: Charles Scribner's Sons, 1968.

HALBERG, FRANZ VON; ENGEL, RUDOLF; SWANK, ROY; SEAMAN, GEOFFREY; und HISSEN, WOLFGANG; JORES, HERRN PROF. A. *Cosiner-Auswertung circadianer Rhythmen mit niedriger Amplitude im menschlichen Blut*. Physikalische Medizin und Rehabilitation, May 1966.

HALL, MANLY PALMER. *Astrological Keywords*. Los Angeles: The Philosophical Research Society, 1966.

HASTINGS, J. WOODLAND. "The Biology of Circadian Rhythms from Man to Microorganism." *New England Journal of Medicine* 282 (1970) :435.

HELLIWELL, T. M. *Introduction to Special Relativity*. Boston: Allyn and Bacon, 1966.

HONE, MARGARET. *The Modern Textbook of Astrology*. London: L. N. Fowler & Company, 1951.

JONES, MARC EDMUND. *Essentials of Astrological Analysis*. New York: Sabian Publishing, 1960.

JUNG, C. G. *Psyche & Symbol: A selection from the writings of C. G. Jung*, edited by Violet S. de Laszlo, New York: Doubleday & Company, Anchor Books, 1958.

KUHN, THOMAS S. *The Copernican Revolution*. New York: Random House, Vintage Books, 1957.

LANGNER, LAWRENCE. *The Importance of Wearing Clothes*. New York: Hastings House, 1959.

LEO, ALAN. *Practical Astrology*. Edinburgh: Edinburgh International Publishing, 1953.

LEWI, GRANT. *Heaven Knows What*. St. Paul, Minn.: Llewellyn Publications, 1969.

MACNEICE, LOUIS. *Astrology*. New York: Doubleday, 1964.

MAURY, L. F. *Le Magie et L'Astrologie*. Paris: Didier et Cie., 1860.

MAYO, JEFF. *The Astrologer's Astronomical Handbook*. London: L. N. Fowler & Company, 1965.

MEDAWAR, P. B. *The Future of Man*. New York: The New American Library, Mentor Books, 1961.

MEEHL, PAUL E. *Clinical versus Statistical Prediction*. Minneapolis: University of Minnesota Press, 1954.

MILBURN, LEIGH HOPE. *The Progressed Horoscope Simplified*. Washington: National Astrological Library, 1959.

PAGAN, ISABELLE M. *From Pioneer to Poet*. Wheaton, Ill.: The Theosophical Publishing House, 1954.

PARCHMENT, S. R. *Astrology: Mundane and Spiritual*. San Francisco: Rosicrucian Anthroposophic League, 1933.

"Raphael." *Private Instructions in Genethliacal Astrology*. Chicago: The Aries Press, 1946.

ROSENFELD, ALBERT. *The Second Genesis*. Englewood Cliffs, N.J.: Prentice-Hall, 1969.

RUDHYAR, DANE. *An Astrological Study of Psychological Complexes and Emotional Problems.* San Jacinto, Calif.: Dane Rudyar, 1966.

——— *The Astrology of Personality.* The Hague: Servire, 1963.

SAGGS, H. W. F. *The Greatness That Was Babylon.* New York: The New American Library, Mentor Books, 1968.

SAXON, DAVID S. *Elementary Quantum Mechanics.* San Francisco: Holden-Day, 1968.

SKINNER, B. F. *Science and Human Behavior.* New York: The Free Press, 1953.

SMITH, DR. HEBER J. *Transits.* Washington: American Federation of Astrologers.

SMYTHIES, J. R., ed. *Brain and Mind.* London: Routledge & Kegan, Paul, 1965.

STRUCE, OTTO. *The Universe.* Cambridge, Mass.: The M.I.T. Press, 1962.

TOULMIN, STEPHEN and GOODFIELD, JUNE. *The Fabric of the Heavens.* New York: Harper & Row, Torchbooks, 1961.

TUCKER, WILLIAM J. *Astrology and the Abnormal Mind.* Kent, England: Pythagorean Publications, 1960.

Simplified Table of Ascendants

JANUARY 1

A.M.			P.M.		
1	20	Libra	1	12	Taurus
2	1	Scorpio	2	2	Gemini
3	13	Scorpio	3	18	Gemini
4	25	Scorpio	4	3	Cancer
5	7	Sagittarius	5	16	Cancer
6	20	Sagittarius	6	27	Cancer
7	3	Capricorn	7	9	Leo
8	18	Capricorn	8	21	Leo
9	6	Aquarius	9	2	Virgo
10	27	Aquarius	10	15	Virgo
11	22	Pisces	11	27	Virgo
12 *noon*	18	Aries	12 *midnight*	9	Libra

JANUARY 4

A.M.			P.M.		
1	22	Libra	1	16	Taurus
2	4	Scorpio	2	5	Gemini
3	15	Scorpio	3	21	Gemini
4	27	Scorpio	4	5	Cancer
5	10	Sagittarius	5	18	Cancer
6	22	Sagittarius	6	0	Leo
7	6	Capricorn	7	12	Leo
8	21	Capricorn	8	23	Leo
9	10	Aquarius	9	5	Virgo
10	2	Pisces	10	17	Virgo
11	28	Pisces	11	29	Virgo
12 *noon*	24	Aries	12 *midnight*	11	Libra

JANUARY 7

A.M.			P.M.		
1	24	Libra	1	21	Taurus
2	6	Scorpio	2	8	Gemini
3	17	Scorpio	3	24	Gemini
4	29	Scorpio	4	8	Cancer
5	11	Sagittarius	5	20	Cancer
6	25	Sagittarius	6	2	Leo
7	9	Capricorn	7	14	Leo
8	24	Capricorn	8	25	Leo
9	14	Aquarius	9	7	Virgo
10	6	Pisces	10	19	Virgo
11	3	Aries	11	1	Libra
12 *noon*	29	Aries	12 *midnight*	13	Libra

JANUARY 10

A.M.			P.M.		
1	27	Libra	1	24	Taurus
2	8	Scorpio	2	11	Gemini
3	20	Scorpio	3	27	Gemini
4	2	Sagittarius	4	10	Cancer
5	14	Sagittarius	5	22	Cancer
6	27	Sagittarius	6	4	Leo
7	12	Capricorn	7	16	Leo
8	28	Capricorn	8	28	Leo
9	19	Aquarius	9	10	Virgo
10	13	Pisces	10	22	Virgo
11	8	Aries	11	3	Libra
12 *noon*	2	Taurus	12 *midnight*	15	Libra

JANUARY 13

	A.M.			P.M.	
1	29	Libra	1	28	Taurus
2	11	Scorpio	2	14	Gemini
3	23	Scorpio	3	29	Gemini
4	4	Sagittarius	4	12	Cancer
5	17	Sagittarius	5	25	Cancer
6	0	Capricorn	6	7	Leo
7	15	Capricorn	7	18	Leo
8	2	Aquarius	8	0	Virgo
9	22	Aquarius	9	12	Virgo
10	17	Pisces	10	23	Virgo
11	13	Aries	11	6	Libra
12 *noon*	7	Taurus	12 *midnight*	17	Libra

JANUARY 16

	A.M.			P.M.	
1	1	Scorpio	1	1	Gemini
2	13	Scorpio	2	17	Gemini
3	25	Scorpio	3	2	Cancer
4	7	Sagittarius	4	15	Cancer
5	19	Sagittarius	5	27	Cancer
6	2	Capricorn	6	9	Leo
7	18	Capricorn	7	21	Leo
8	6	Aquarius	8	2	Virgo
9	27	Aquarius	9	14	Virgo
10	22	Pisces	10	26	Virgo
11	18	Aries	11	8	Libra
12 *noon*	12	Taurus	12 *midnight*	20	Libra

JANUARY 19

A.M.			P.M.		
1	4	Scorpio	1	5	Gemini
2	15	Scorpio	2	20	Gemini
3	27	Scorpio	3	5	Cancer
4	9	Sagittarius	4	17	Cancer
5	22	Sagittarius	5	0	Leo
6	6	Capricorn	6	12	Leo
7	21	Capricorn	7	23	Leo
8	10	Aquarius	8	5	Virgo
9	2	Pisces	9	17	Virgo
10	28	Pisces	10	29	Virgo
11	23	Aries	11	11	Libra
12 *noon*	16	Taurus	12 *midnight*	22	Libra

JANUARY 22

A.M.			P.M.		
1	6	Scorpio	1	8	Gemini
2	18	Scorpio	2	23	Gemini
3	29	Scorpio	3	7	Cancer
4	12	Sagittarius	4	20	Cancer
5	25	Sagittarius	5	2	Leo
6	9	Capricorn	6	14	Leo
7	24	Capricorn	7	25	Leo
8	14	Aquarius	8	7	Virgo
9	7	Pisces	9	19	Virgo
10	3	Aries	10	0	Libra
11	27	Aries	11	12	Libra
12 *noon*	19	Taurus	12 *midnight*	24	Libra

JANUARY 25

A.M.		P.M.	
1	8 Scorpio	1	11 Gemini
2	20 Scorpio	2	27 Gemini
3	2 Sagittarius	3	10 Cancer
4	14 Sagittarius	4	22 Cancer
5	27 Sagittarius	5	4 Leo
6	12 Capricorn	6	16 Leo
7	28 Capricorn	7	28 Leo
8	18 Aquarius	8	9 Virgo
9	12 Pisces	9	21 Virgo
10	7 Aries	10	3 Libra
11	2 Taurus	11	15 Libra
12 *noon*	23 Taurus	12 *midnight*	27 Libra

JANUARY 28

A.M.		P.M.	
1	11 Scorpio	1	14 Gemini
2	23 Scorpio	2	29 Gemini
3	4 Sagittarius	3	12 Cancer
4	17 Sagittarius	4	25 Cancer
5	0 Capricorn	5	6 Leo
6	15 Capricorn	6	18 Leo
7	2 Aquarius	7	0 Virgo
8	22 Aquarius	8	12 Virgo
9	16 Pisces	9	23 Virgo
10	13 Aries	10	6 Libra
11	7 Taurus	11	17 Libra
12 *noon*	27 Taurus	12 *midnight*	29 Libra

JANUARY 31

A.M.		P.M.	
1	13 Scorpio	1	17 Gemini
2	25 Scorpio	2	2 Cancer
3	7 Sagittarius	3	15 Cancer
4	19 Sagittarius	4	27 Cancer
5	2 Capricorn	5	9 Leo
6	18 Capricorn	6	21 Leo
7	6 Aquarius	7	2 Virgo
8	27 Aquarius	8	14 Virgo
9	22 Pisces	9	26 Virgo
10	18 Aries	10	8 Libra
11	12 Taurus	11	20 Libra
12 *noon*	1 Gemini	12 *midnight*	1 Scorpio

FEBRUARY 3

A.M.		P.M.	
1	15 Scorpio	1	20 Gemini
2	27 Scorpio	2	5 Cancer
3	9 Sagittarius	3	17 Cancer
4	21 Sagittarius	4	0 Leo
5	5 Capricorn	5	12 Leo
6	21 Capricorn	6	23 Leo
7	10 Aquarius	7	5 Virgo
8	2 Pisces	8	17 Virgo
9	28 Pisces	9	29 Virgo
10	22 Aries	10	11 Libra
11	15 Taurus	11	22 Libra
12 *noon*	5 Gemini	12 *midnight*	4 Scorpio

FEBRUARY 6

A.M.		P.M.	
1	17 Scorpio	1	23 Gemini
2	29 Scorpio	2	7 Cancer
3	11 Sagittarius	3	20 Cancer
4	25 Sagittarius	4	2 Leo
5	8 Capricorn	5	14 Leo
6	24 Capricorn	6	25 Leo
7	13 Aquarius	7	7 Virgo
8	5 Pisces	8	19 Virgo
9	1 Aries	9	1 Libra
10	27 Aries	10	13 Libra
11	19 Taurus	11	25 Libra
12 *noon*	8 Gemini	12 *midnight*	6 Scorpio

FEBRUARY 9

A.M.		P.M.	
1	20 Scorpio	1	26 Gemini
2	2 Sagittarius	2	9 Cancer
3	13 Sagittarius	3	22 Cancer
4	27 Sagittarius	4	4 Leo
5	11 Capricorn	5	16 Leo
6	28 Capricorn	6	28 Leo
7	17 Aquarius	7	10 Virgo
8	11 Pisces	8	22 Virgo
9	7 Aries	9	3 Libra
10	2 Taurus	10	15 Libra
11	23 Taurus	11	27 Libra
12 *noon*	11 Gemini	12 *midnight*	8 Scorpio

FEBRUARY 12

	A.M.			P.M.	
1	22	Scorpio	1	29	Gemini
2	4	Sagittarius	2	12	Cancer
3	16	Sagittarius	3	25	Cancer
4	0	Capricorn	4	7	Leo
5	14	Capricorn	5	18	Leo
6	1	Aquarius	6	0	Virgo
7	22	Aquarius	7	12	Virgo
8	16	Pisces	8	23	Virgo
9	13	Aries	9	6	Libra
10	7	Taurus	10	17	Libra
11	27	Taurus	11	29	Libra
12 *noon*	14	Gemini	12 *midnight*	11	Scorpio

FEBRUARY 15

	A.M.			P.M.	
1	24	Scorpio	1	2	Cancer
2	6	Sagittarius	2	15	Cancer
3	19	Sagittarius	3	27	Cancer
4	2	Capricorn	4	9	Leo
5	17	Capricorn	5	21	Leo
6	4	Aquarius	6	2	Virgo
7	27	Aquarius	7	14	Virgo
8	22	Pisces	8	26	Virgo
9	16	Aries	9	8	Libra
10	10	Taurus	10	20	Libra
11	1	Gemini	11	1	Scorpio
12 *noon*	17	Gemini	12 *midnight*	13	Scorpio

FEBRUARY 18

A.M.		P.M.	
1	26 Scorpio	1	5 Cancer
2	9 Sagittarius	2	17 Cancer
3	21 Sagittarius	3	0 Leo
4	5 Capricorn	4	12 Leo
5	20 Capricorn	5	23 Leo
6	8 Aquarius	6	5 Virgo
7	0 Pisces	7	17 Virgo
8	26 Pisces	8	29 Virgo
9	22 Aries	9	11 Libra
10	15 Taurus	10	22 Libra
11	5 Gemini	11	4 Scorpio
12 *noon*	20 Gemini	12 *midnight*	16 Scorpio

FEBRUARY 21

A.M.		P.M.	
1	29 Scorpio	1	7 Cancer
2	11 Sagittarius	2	21 Cancer
3	24 Sagittarius	3	1 Leo
4	8 Capricorn	4	12 Leo
5	23 Capricorn	5	25 Leo
6	13 Aquarius	6	7 Virgo
7	5 Pisces	7	19 Virgo
8	1 Aries	8	0 Libra
9	27 Aries	9	12 Libra
10	19 Taurus	10	23 Libra
11	8 Gemini	11	5 Scorpio
12 *noon*	23 Gemini	12 *midnight*	17 Scorpio

FEBRUARY 24

A.M.		P.M.	
1	2 Sagittarius	1	9 Cancer
2	13 Sagittarius	2	22 Cancer
3	26 Sagittarius	3	4 Leo
4	11 Capricorn	4	16 Leo
5	27 Capricorn	5	28 Leo
6	15 Aquarius	6	9 Virgo
7	9 Pisces	7	21 Virgo
8	8 Aries	8	3 Libra
9	4 Taurus	9	15 Libra
10	26 Taurus	10	27 Libra
11	11 Gemini	11	8 Scorpio
12 *noon*	26 Gemini	12 *midnight*	20 Scorpio

FEBRUARY 27

A.M.		P.M.	
1	4 Sagittarius	1	12 Cancer
2	16 Sagittarius	2	25 Cancer
3	0 Capricorn	3	6 Leo
4	14 Capricorn	4	18 Leo
5	1 Aquarius	5	0 Virgo
6	21 Aquarius	6	12 Virgo
7	15 Pisces	7	23 Virgo
8	11 Aries	8	6 Libra
9	6 Taurus	9	17 Libra
10	27 Taurus	10	29 Libra
11	14 Gemini	11	11 Scorpio
12 *noon*	29 Gemini	12 *midnight*	23 Scorpio

MARCH 2

	A.M.			P.M.	
1	6	Sagittarius	1	15	Cancer
2	19	Sagittarius	2	27	Cancer
3	2	Capricorn	3	9	Leo
4	17	Capricorn	4	21	Leo
5	4	Aquarius	5	2	Virgo
6	25	Aquarius	6	14	Virgo
7	20	Pisces	7	26	Virgo
8	16	Aries	8	8	Libra
9	10	Taurus	9	20	Libra
10	1	Gemini	10	1	Scorpio
11	17	Gemini	11	13	Scorpio
12 *noon*	1	Cancer	12 *midnight*	25	Scorpio

MARCH 5

	A.M.			P.M.	
1	8	Sagittarius	1	17	Cancer
2	21	Sagittarius	2	29	Cancer
3	5	Capricorn	3	11	Leo
4	20	Capricorn	4	23	Leo
5	8	Aquarius	5	4	Virgo
6	0	Pisces	6	17	Virgo
7	26	Pisces	7	28	Virgo
8	22	Aries	8	10	Libra
9	15	Taurus	9	22	Libra
10	3	Gemini	10	4	Scorpio
11	20	Gemini	11	15	Scorpio
12 *noon*	5	Cancer	12 *midnight*	27	Scorpio

MARCH 8

A.M.			P.M.		
1	11	Sagittarius	1	19	Cancer
2	24	Sagittarius	2	1	Leo
3	8	Capricorn	3	13	Leo
4	23	Capricorn	4	25	Leo
5	13	Aquarius	5	7	Virgo
6	5	Pisces	6	18	Virgo
7	1	Aries	7	0	Libra
8	27	Aries	8	12	Libra
9	19	Taurus	9	24	Libra
10	7	Gemini	10	6	Scorpio
11	23	Gemini	11	17	Scorpio
12 *noon*	7	Cancer	12 *midnight*	29	Scorpio

MARCH 11

A.M.			P.M.		
1	13	Sagittarius	1	22	Cancer
2	26	Sagittarius	2	4	Leo
3	11	Capricorn	3	15	Leo
4	27	Capricorn	4	28	Leo
5	17	Aquarius	5	9	Virgo
6	11	Pisces	6	21	Virgo
7	5	Aries	7	3	Libra
8	1	Taurus	8	15	Libra
9	23	Taurus	9	27	Libra
10	10	Gemini	10	8	Scorpio
11	26	Gemini	11	20	Scorpio
12 *noon*	9	Cancer	12 *midnight*	2	Sagittarius

MARCH 14

	A.M.			P.M.	
1	16 Sagittarius		1	24 Cancer	
2	29 Sagittarius		2	6 Leo	
3	14 Capricorn		3	18 Leo	
4	1 Aquarius		4	29 Leo	
5	20 Aquarius		5	12 Virgo	
6	14 Pisces		6	23 Virgo	
7	11 Aries		7	6 Libra	
8	6 Taurus		8	17 Libra	
9	26 Taurus		9	29 Libra	
10	13 Gemini		10	11 Scorpio	
11	29 Gemini		11	23 Scorpio	
12 *noon*	12 Cancer		12 *midnight*	4 Sagittarius	

MARCH 17

	A.M.			P.M.	
1	18 Sagittarius		1	27 Cancer	
2	1 Capricorn		2	9 Leo	
3	17 Capricorn		3	20 Leo	
4	4 Aquarius		4	2 Virgo	
5	25 Aquarius		5	14 Virgo	
6	20 Pisces		6	25 Virgo	
7	16 Aries		7	7 Libra	
8	10 Taurus		8	19 Libra	
9	0 Gemini		9	1 Scorpio	
10	16 Gemini		10	13 Scorpio	
11	1 Cancer		11	25 Scorpio	
12 *noon*	14 Cancer		12 *midnight*	7 Sagittarius	

MARCH 20

A.M.		P.M.	
1	20 Sagittarius	1	29 Cancer
2	4 Capricorn	2	11 Leo
3	20 Capricorn	3	22 Leo
4	7 Aquarius	4	4 Virgo
5	0 Pisces	5	16 Virgo
6	26 Pisces	6	28 Virgo
7	21 Aries	7	10 Libra
8	15 Taurus	8	22 Libra
9	3 Gemini	9	4 Scorpio
10	19 Gemini	10	15 Scorpio
11	4 Cancer	11	27 Scorpio
12 *noon*	17 Cancer	12 *midnight*	9 Sagittarius

MARCH 23

A.M.		P.M.	
1	23 Sagittarius	1	1 Leo
2	7 Capricorn	2	13 Leo
3	23 Capricorn	3	25 Leo
4	11 Aquarius	4	7 Virgo
5	4 Pisces	5	18 Virgo
6	0 Aries	6	0 Libra
7	25 Aries	7	12 Libra
8	18 Taurus	8	23 Libra
9	7 Gemini	9	6 Scorpio
10	22 Gemini	10	17 Scorpio
11	6 Cancer	11	29 Scorpio
12 *noon*	19 Cancer	12 *midnight*	11 Sagittarius

MARCH 26

	A.M.			P.M.	
1	26	Sagittarius	1	3	Leo
2	11	Capricorn	2	15	Leo
3	27	Capricorn	3	27	Leo
4	16	Aquarius	4	9	Virgo
5	9	Pisces	5	21	Virgo
6	5	Aries	6	3	Libra
7	1	Taurus	7	15	Libra
8	22	Taurus	8	27	Libra
9	10	Gemini	9	8	Scorpio
10	25	Gemini	10	20	Scorpio
11	9	Cancer	11	2	Sagittarius
12 *noon*	22	Cancer	12 *midnight*	14	Sagittarius

MARCH 29

	A.M.			P.M.	
1	29	Sagittarius	1	6	Leo
2	14	Capricorn	2	18	Leo
3	1	Aquarius	3	29	Leo
4	20	Aquarius	4	12	Virgo
5	14	Pisces	5	23	Virgo
6	11	Aries	6	5	Libra
7	6	Taurus	7	17	Libra
8	26	Taurus	8	29	Libra
9	13	Gemini	9	11	Scorpio
10	29	Gemini	10	22	Scorpio
11	12	Cancer	11	4	Sagittarius
12 *noon*	24	Cancer	12 *midnight*	17	Sagittarius

APRIL 1

A.M.		P.M.	
1	1 Capricorn	1	9 Leo
2	17 Capricorn	2	20 Leo
3	4 Aquarius	3	2 Virgo
4	25 Aquarius	4	13 Virgo
5	20 Pisces	5	25 Virgo
6	16 Aries	6	7 Libra
7	10 Taurus	7	19 Libra
8	0 Gemini	8	1 Scorpio
9	16 Gemini	9	13 Scorpio
10	1 Cancer	10	24 Scorpio
11	14 Cancer	11	7 Sagittarius
12 *noon*	26 Cancer	12 *midnight*	19 Sagittarius

APRIL 4

A.M.		P.M.	
1	4 Capricorn	1	11 Leo
2	20 Capricorn	2	22 Leo
3	8 Aquarius	3	4 Virgo
4	0 Pisces	4	16 Virgo
5	25 Pisces	5	28 Virgo
6	20 Aries	6	10 Libra
7	13 Taurus	7	22 Libra
8	3 Gemini	8	3 Scorpio
9	19 Gemini	9	14 Scorpio
10	4 Cancer	10	27 Scorpio
11	16 Cancer	11	9 Sagittarius
12 *noon*	29 Cancer	12 *midnight*	21 Sagittarius

APRIL 7

A.M.		P.M.	
1	7 Capricorn	1	13 Leo
2	23 Capricorn	2	25 Leo
3	11 Aquarius	3	7 Virgo
4	4 Pisces	4	18 Virgo
5	0 Aries	5	0 Libra
6	25 Aries	6	12 Libra
7	18 Taurus	7	24 Libra
8	7 Gemini	8	5 Scorpio
9	22 Gemini	9	17 Scorpio
10	6 Cancer	10	29 Scorpio
11	19 Cancer	11	11 Sagittarius
12 *noon*	1 Leo	12 *midnight*	24 Sagittarius

APRIL 10

A.M.		P.M.	
1	10 Capricorn	1	15 Leo
2	27 Capricorn	2	27 Leo
3	16 Aquarius	3	8 Virgo
4	9 Pisces	4	21 Virgo
5	5 Aries	5	2 Libra
6	1 Taurus	6	14 Libra
7	22 Taurus	7	26 Libra
8	10 Gemini	8	8 Scorpio
9	25 Gemini	9	20 Scorpio
10	9 Cancer	10	2 Sagittarius
11	22 Cancer	11	13 Sagittarius
12 *noon*	3 Leo	12 *midnight*	26 Sagittarius

APRIL 13

A.M.		P.M.	
1	13 Capricorn	1	18 Leo
2	29 Capricorn	2	29 Leo
3	20 Aquarius	3	11 Virgo
4	14 Pisces	4	23 Virgo
5	11 Aries	5	5 Libra
6	6 Taurus	6	17 Libra
7	26 Taurus	7	28 Libra
8	13 Gemini	8	11 Scorpio
9	28 Gemini	9	22 Scorpio
10	12 Cancer	10	4 Sagittarius
11	24 Cancer	11	16 Sagittarius
12 *noon*	6 Leo	12 *midnight*	0 Capricorn

APRIL 16

A.M.		P.M.	
1	16 Capricorn	1	20 Leo
2	3 Aquarius	2	2 Virgo
3	25 Aquarius	3	13 Virgo
4	19 Pisces	4	25 Virgo
5	15 Aries	5	7 Libra
6	9 Taurus	6	19 Libra
7	0 Gemini	7	1 Scorpio
8	16 Gemini	8	12 Scorpio
9	0 Cancer	9	24 Scorpio
10	14 Cancer	10	6 Sagittarius
11	26 Cancer	11	19 Sagittarius
12 *noon*	8 Leo	12 *midnight*	2 Capricorn

APRIL 19

A.M.			P.M.		
1	19	Capricorn	1	22	Leo
2	7	Aquarius	2	4	Virgo
3	28	Aquarius	3	16	Virgo
4	24	Pisces	4	28	Virgo
5	20	Aries	5	10	Libra
6	13	Taurus	6	22	Libra
7	3	Gemini	7	3	Scorpio
8	19	Gemini	8	14	Scorpio
9	4	Cancer	9	27	Scorpio
10	16	Cancer	10	9	Sagittarius
11	28	Cancer	11	21	Sagittarius
12 *noon*	10	Leo	12 *midnight*	9	Capricorn

APRIL 22

A.M.			P.M.		
1	23	Capricorn	1	25	Leo
2	13	Aquarius	2	6	Virgo
3	4	Pisces	3	18	Virgo
4	0	Aries	4	0	Libra
5	25	Aries	5	12	Libra
6	18	Taurus	6	23	Libra
7	7	Gemini	7	5	Scorpio
8	22	Gemini	8	17	Scorpio
9	6	Cancer	9	29	Scorpio
10	19	Cancer	10	12	Sagittarius
11	1	Leo	11	24	Sagittarius
12 *noon*	13	Leo	12 *midnight*	8	Capricorn

APRIL 25

A.M.		P.M.	
1	26 Capricorn	1	27 Leo
2	16 Aquarius	2	8 Virgo
3	9 Pisces	3	20 Virgo
4	5 Aries	4	2 Libra
5	1 Taurus	5	14 Libra
6	22 Taurus	6	26 Libra
7	10 Gemini	7	8 Scorpio
8	25 Gemini	8	19 Scorpio
9	9 Cancer	9	2 Sagittarius
10	21 Cancer	10	13 Sagittarius
11	3 Leo	11	26 Sagittarius
12 *noon*	15 Leo	12 *midnight*	11 Capricorn

APRIL 28

A.M.		P.M.	
1	1 Aquarius	1	29 Leo
2	20 Aquarius	2	11 Virgo
3	14 Pisces	3	23 Virgo
4	9 Aries	4	5 Libra
5	4 Taurus	5	17 Libra
6	26 Taurus	6	28 Libra
7	13 Gemini	7	10 Scorpio
8	28 Gemini	8	22 Scorpio
9	11 Cancer	9	4 Sagittarius
10	24 Cancer	10	16 Sagittarius
11	6 Leo	11	29 Sagittarius
12 *noon*	18 Leo	12 *midnight*	14 Capricorn

MAY 1

A.M.		P.M.	
1	3 Aquarius	1	2 Virgo
2	23 Aquarius	2	13 Virgo
3	18 Pisces	3	25 Virgo
4	15 Aries	4	7 Libra
5	9 Taurus	5	19 Libra
6	29 Taurus	6	1 Scorpio
7	16 Gemini	7	12 Scorpio
8	0 Cancer	8	24 Scorpio
9	14 Cancer	9	6 Sagittarius
10	26 Cancer	10	18 Sagittarius
11	8 Leo	11	2 Capricorn
12 *noon*	20 Leo	12 *midnight*	17 Capricorn

MAY 4

A.M.		P.M.	
1	7 Aquarius	1	3 Virgo
2	28 Aquarius	2	16 Virgo
3	24 Pisces	3	27 Virgo
4	20 Aries	4	9 Libra
5	13 Taurus	5	21 Libra
6	2 Gemini	6	3 Scorpio
7	19 Gemini	7	14 Scorpio
8	4 Cancer	8	26 Scorpio
9	16 Cancer	9	8 Sagittarius
10	28 Cancer	10	20 Sagittarius
11	10 Leo	11	4 Capricorn
12 *noon*	22 Leo	12 *midnight*	20 Capricorn

MAY 7

A.M.			P.M.		
1	11	Aquarius	1	6	Virgo
2	4	Pisces	2	17	Virgo
3	0	Aries	3	0	Libra
4	25	Aries	4	12	Libra
5	18	Taurus	5	23	Libra
6	6	Gemini	6	5	Scorpio
7	22	Gemini	7	17	Scorpio
8	6	Cancer	8	29	Scorpio
9	19	Cancer	9	11	Sagittarius
10	0	Leo	10	24	Sagittarius
11	12	Leo	11	8	Capricorn
12 *noon*	24	Leo	12 *midnight*	23	Capricorn

MAY 10

A.M.			P.M.		
1	15	Aquarius	1	8	Virgo
2	8	Pisces	2	20	Virgo
3	3	Aries	3	2	Libra
4	29	Aries	4	14	Libra
5	22	Taurus	5	26	Libra
6	9	Gemini	6	8	Scorpio
7	25	Gemini	7	19	Scorpio
8	9	Cancer	8	1	Sagittarius
9	21	Cancer	9	13	Sagittarius
10	3	Leo	10	26	Sagittarius
11	15	Leo	11	10	Capricorn
12 *noon*	26	Leo	12 *midnight*	27	Capricorn

MAY 13

A.M.		P.M.	
1	19 Aquarius	1	11 Virgo
2	13 Pisces	2	23 Virgo
3	9 Aries	3	5 Libra
4	4 Taurus	4	17 Libra
5	25 Taurus	5	28 Libra
6	12 Gemini	6	10 Scorpio
7	28 Gemini	7	21 Scorpio
8	11 Cancer	8	4 Sagittarius
9	24 Cancer	9	16 Sagittarius
10	6 Leo	10	29 Sagittarius
11	17 Leo	11	14 Capricorn
12 *noon*	28 Leo	12 *midnight*	1 Aquarius

MAY 16

A.M.		P.M.	
1	23 Aquarius	1	13 Virgo
2	18 Pisces	2	24 Virgo
3	15 Aries	3	6 Libra
4	9 Taurus	4	18 Libra
5	29 Taurus	5	1 Scorpio
6	15 Gemini	6	12 Scorpio
7	0 Cancer	7	24 Scorpio
8	13 Cancer	8	6 Sagittarius
9	26 Cancer	9	18 Sagittarius
10	8 Leo	10	1 Capricorn
11	19 Leo	11	17 Capricorn
12 *noon*	1 Virgo	12 *midnight*	4 Aquarius

MAY 19

A.M.		P.M.	
1	28 Aquarius	1	15 Virgo
2	24 Pisces	2	27 Virgo
3	20 Aries	3	9 Libra
4	13 Taurus	4	21 Libra
5	2 Gemini	5	3 Scorpio
6	18 Gemini	6	14 Scorpio
7	3 Cancer	7	26 Scorpio
8	16 Cancer	8	8 Sagittarius
9	28 Cancer	9	20 Sagittarius
10	10 Leo	10	4 Capricorn
11	21 Leo	11	20 Capricorn
12 *noon*	3 Virgo	12 *midnight*	8 Aquarius

MAY 22

A.M.		P.M.	
1	4 Pisces	1	17 Virgo
2	28 Pisces	2	0 Libra
3	24 Aries	3	12 Libra
4	17 Taurus	4	23 Libra
5	6 Gemini	5	4 Scorpio
6	21 Gemini	6	17 Scorpio
7	5 Cancer	7	29 Scorpio
8	19 Cancer	8	11 Sagittarius
9	0 Leo	9	24 Sagittarius
10	12 Leo	10	8 Capricorn
11	24 Leo	11	23 Capricorn
12 *noon*	6 Virgo	12 *midnight*	13 Aquarius

MAY 25

A.M.			P.M.		
1	7	Pisces	1	20	Virgo
2	3	Aries	2	2	Libra
3	29	Aries	3	14	Libra
4	21	Taurus	4	26	Libra
5	9	Gemini	5	8	Scorpio
6	24	Gemini	6	19	Scorpio
7	8	Cancer	7	1	Sagittarius
8	21	Cancer	8	13	Sagittarius
9	3	Leo	9	26	Sagittarius
10	15	Leo	10	10	Capricorn
11	26	Leo	11	27	Capricorn
12 *noon*	8	Virgo	12 *midnight*	16	Aquarius

MAY 28

A.M.			P.M.		
1	13	Pisces	1	22	Virgo
2	9	Aries	2	5	Libra
3	4	Taurus	3	16	Libra
4	25	Taurus	4	28	Libra
5	12	Gemini	5	9	Scorpio
6	28	Gemini	6	21	Scorpio
7	10	Cancer	7	3	Sagittarius
8	23	Cancer	8	16	Sagittarius
9	5	Leo	9	29	Sagittarius
10	17	Leo	10	13	Capricorn
11	28	Leo	11	1	Aquarius
12 *noon*	11	Virgo	12 *midnight*	20	Aquarius

MAY 31

A.M.			P.M.		
1	18	Pisces	1	24	Virgo
2	15	Aries	2	6	Libra
3	9	Taurus	3	18	Libra
4	29	Taurus	4	1	Scorpio
5	15	Gemini	5	12	Scorpio
6	0	Cancer	6	23	Scorpio
7	13	Cancer	7	6	Sagittarius
8	26	Cancer	8	18	Sagittarius
9	7	Leo	9	1	Capricorn
10	19	Leo	10	17	Capricorn
11	1	Virgo	11	4	Aquarius
12 *noon*	12	Virgo	12 *midnight*	25	Aquarius

JUNE 3

A.M.			P.M.		
1	24	Pisces	1	27	Virgo
2	18	Aries	2	9	Libra
3	12	Taurus	3	21	Libra
4	2	Gemini	4	2	Scorpio
5	18	Gemini	5	14	Scorpio
6	3	Cancer	6	26	Scorpio
7	16	Cancer	7	8	Sagittarius
8	28	Cancer	8	20	Sagittarius
9	10	Leo	9	4	Capricorn
10	21	Leo	10	20	Capricorn
11	3	Virgo	11	7	Aquarius
12 *noon*	15	Virgo	12 *midnight*	0	Pisces

JUNE 6

A.M.			P.M.		
1	28	Pisces	1	0	Libra
2	24	Aries	2	12	Libra
3	16	Taurus	3	23	Libra
4	6	Gemini	4	4	Scorpio
5	21	Gemini	5	17	Scorpio
6	5	Cancer	6	28	Scorpio
7	18	Cancer	7	10	Sagittarius
8	0	Leo	8	23	Sagittarius
9	12	Leo	9	7	Capricorn
10	24	Leo	10	22	Capricorn
11	6	Virgo	11	11	Aquarius
12 *noon*	17	Virgo	12 *midnight*	4	Pisces

JUNE 9

A.M.			P.M.		
1	3	Aries	1	2	Libra
2	29	Aries	2	13	Libra
3	21	Taurus	3	26	Libra
4	9	Gemini	4	7	Scorpio
5	24	Gemini	5	19	Scorpio
6	8	Cancer	6	1	Sagittarius
7	20	Cancer	7	13	Sagittarius
8	3	Leo	8	26	Sagittarius
9	15	Leo	9	10	Capricorn
10	26	Leo	10	27	Capricorn
11	8	Virgo	11	16	Aquarius
12 *noon*	20	Virgo	12 *midnight*	9	Pisces

JUNE 12

A.M.			P.M.		
1	9	Aries	1	4	Libra
2	2	Taurus	2	16	Libra
3	25	Taurus	3	28	Libra
4	12	Gemini	4	9	Scorpio
5	27	Gemini	5	21	Scorpio
6	10	Cancer	6	3	Sagittarius
7	23	Cancer	7	15	Sagittarius
8	5	Leo	8	28	Sagittarius
9	17	Leo	9	13	Capricorn
10	28	Leo	10	29	Capricorn
11	10	Virgo	11	20	Aquarius
12 *noon*	22	Virgo	12 *midnight*	14	Pisces

JUNE 15

A.M.			P.M.		
1	13	Aries	1	6	Libra
2	7	Taurus	2	18	Libra
3	29	Taurus	3	0	Scorpio
4	15	Gemini	4	11	Scorpio
5	29	Gemini	5	23	Scorpio
6	12	Cancer	6	5	Sagittarius
7	25	Cancer	7	18	Sagittarius
8	7	Leo	8	1	Capricorn
9	19	Leo	9	16	Capricorn
10	1	Virgo	10	3	Aquarius
11	12	Virgo	11	25	Aquarius
12 *noon*	24	Virgo	12 *midnight*	19	Pisces

JUNE 18

A.M.			P.M.		
1	18	Aries	1	9	Libra
2	12	Taurus	2	21	Libra
3	2	Gemini	3	2	Scorpio
4	18	Gemini	4	14	Scorpio
5	2	Cancer	5	26	Scorpio
6	16	Cancer	6	7	Sagittarius
7	27	Cancer	7	20	Sagittarius
8	9	Leo	8	4	Capricorn
9	21	Leo	9	19	Capricorn
10	3	Virgo	10	7	Aquarius
11	15	Virgo	11	28	Aquarius
12 *noon*	27	Virgo	12 *midnight*	24	Pisces

JUNE 21

A.M.			P.M.		
1	24	Aries	1	11	Libra
2	16	Taurus	2	23	Libra
3	6	Gemini	3	4	Scorpio
4	21	Gemini	4	17	Scorpio
5	5	Cancer	5	28	Scorpio
6	18	Cancer	6	10	Sagittarius
7	0	Leo	7	23	Sagittarius
8	12	Leo	8	7	Capricorn
9	24	Leo	9	22	Capricorn
10	5	Virgo	10	11	Aquarius
11	17	Virgo	11	4	Pisces
12 *noon*	0	Libra	12 *midnight*	0	Aries

JUNE 24

A.M.			P.M.		
1	29	Aries	1	13	Libra
2	21	Taurus	2	25	Libra
3	9	Gemini	3	7	Scorpio
4	24	Gemini	4	18	Scorpio
5	8	Cancer	5	0	Sagittarius
6	20	Cancer	6	13	Sagittarius
7	3	Leo	7	25	Sagittarius
8	15	Leo	8	10	Capricorn
9	26	Leo	9	26	Capricorn
10	7	Virgo	10	15	Aquarius
11	19	Virgo	11	9	Pisces
12 *noon*	1	Libra	12 *midnight*	4	Aries

JUNE 27

A.M.			P.M.		
1	2	Taurus	1	16	Libra
2	24	Taurus	2	27	Libra
3	11	Gemini	3	9	Scorpio
4	27	Gemini	4	21	Scorpio
5	10	Cancer	5	3	Sagittarius
6	23	Cancer	6	15	Sagittarius
7	5	Leo	7	28	Sagittarius
8	17	Leo	8	13	Capricorn
9	28	Leo	9	29	Capricorn
10	10	Virgo	10	20	Aquarius
11	22	Virgo	11	13	Pisces
12 *noon*	4	Libra	12 *midnight*	9	Aries

JUNE 30

A.M.			P.M.		
1	7	Taurus	1	18	Libra
2	29	Taurus	2	0	Scorpio
3	15	Gemini	3	11	Scorpio
4	29	Gemini	4	23	Scorpio
5	12	Cancer	5	5	Sagittarius
6	25	Cancer	6	17	Sagittarius
7	7	Leo	7	0	Capricorn
8	19	Leo	8	16	Capricorn
9	1	Virgo	9	3	Aquarius
10	12	Virgo	10	23	Aquarius
11	24	Virgo	11	18	Pisces
12 *noon*	6	Libra	12 *midnight*	15	Aries

JULY 3

A.M.			P.M.		
1	12	Taurus	1	21	Libra
2	1	Gemini	2	2	Scorpio
3	17	Gemini	3	14	Scorpio
4	2	Cancer	4	26	Scorpio
5	16	Cancer	5	7	Sagittarius
6	27	Cancer	6	20	Sagittarius
7	9	Leo	7	4	Capricorn
8	21	Leo	8	19	Capricorn
9	2	Virgo	9	7	Aquarius
10	15	Virgo	10	28	Aquarius
11	27	Virgo	11	24	Pisces
12 *noon*	8	Libra	12 *midnight*	20	Aries

JULY 6

A.M.			P.M.		
1	16	Taurus	1	23	Libra
2	5	Gemini	2	4	Scorpio
3	21	Gemini	3	16	Scorpio
4	5	Cancer	4	28	Scorpio
5	18	Cancer	5	10	Sagittarius
6	0	Leo	6	23	Sagittarius
7	12	Leo	7	7	Capricorn
8	24	Leo	8	22	Capricorn
9	5	Virgo	9	11	Aquarius
10	17	Virgo	10	4	Pisces
11	29	Virgo	11	0	Aries
12 *noon*	11	Libra	12 *midnight*	25	Aries

JULY 9

A.M.			P.M.		
1	21	Taurus	1	25	Libra
2	8	Gemini	2	7	Scorpio
3	24	Gemini	3	18	Scorpio
4	8	Cancer	4	1	Sagittarius
5	20	Cancer	5	13	Sagittarius
6	2	Leo	6	25	Sagittarius
7	14	Leo	7	10	Capricorn
8	25	Leo	8	26	Capricorn
9	7	Virgo	9	16	Aquarius
10	19	Virgo	10	7	Pisces
11	1	Libra	11	4	Aries
12 *noon*	13	Libra	12 *midnight*	29	Aries

JULY 12

A.M.			P.M.		
1	23	Taurus	1	27	Libra
2	11	Gemini	2	9	Scorpio
3	27	Gemini	3	20	Scorpio
4	10	Cancer	4	2	Sagittarius
5	22	Cancer	5	15	Sagittarius
6	5	Leo	6	28	Sagittarius
7	16	Leo	7	13	Capricorn
8	28	Leo	8	29	Capricorn
9	10	Virgo	9	19	Aquarius
10	22	Virgo	10	.13	Pisces
11	4	Libra	11	9	Aries
12 *noon*	16	Libra	12 *midnight*	4	Taurus

JULY 15

A.M.			P.M.		
1	27	Taurus	1	0	Scorpio
2	14	Gemini	2	11	Scorpio
3	29	Gemini	3	23	Scorpio
4	12	Cancer	4	5	Sagittarius
5	25	Cancer	5	17	Sagittarius
6	7	Leo	6	0	Capricorn
7	19	Leo	7	15	Capricorn
8	0	Virgo	8	3	Aquarius
9	12	Virgo	9	23	Aquarius
10	24	Virgo	10	18	Pisces
11	6	Libra	11	15	Aries
12 *noon*	18	Libra	12 *midnight*	9	Taurus

JULY 18

A.M.			P.M.		
1	1	Gemini	1	2	Scorpio
2	17	Gemini	2	14	Scorpio
3	2	Cancer	3	26	Scorpio
4	15	Cancer	4	7	Sagittarius
5	27	Cancer	5	20	Sagittarius
6	9	Leo	6	3	Capricorn
7	21	Leo	7	19	Capricorn
8	2	Virgo	8	7	Aquarius
9	14	Virgo	9	28	Aquarius
10	26	Virgo	10	24	Pisces
11	9	Libra	11	18	Aries
12 *noon*	20	Libra	12 *midnight*	12	Taurus

JULY 21

A.M.			P.M.		
1	5	Gemini	1	4	Scorpio
2	20	Gemini	2	16	Scorpio
3	5	Cancer	3	28	Scorpio
4	17	Cancer	4	10	Sagittarius
5	0	Leo	5	23	Sagittarius
6	12	Leo	6	6	Capricorn
7	23	Leo	7	22	Capricorn
8	5	Virgo	8	11	Aquarius
9	17	Virgo	9	2	Pisces
10	29	Virgo	10	28	Pisces
11	11	Libra	11	24	Aries
12 *noon*	22	Libra	12 *midnight*	16	Taurus

JULY 24

	A.M.			P.M.	
1	8	Gemini	1	7	Scorpio
2	23	Gemini	2	18	Scorpio
3	7	Cancer	3	0	Sagittarius
4	20	Cancer	4	12	Sagittarius
5	2	Leo	5	25	Sagittarius
6	14	Leo	6	10	Capricorn
7	25	Leo	7	26	Capricorn
8	7	Virgo	8	15	Aquarius
9	19	Virgo	9	7	Pisces
10	1	Libra	10	3	Aries
11	13	Libra	11	29	Aries
12 *noon*	25	Libra	12 *midnight*	21	Taurus

JULY 27

	A.M.			P.M.	
1	11	Gemini	1	8	Scorpio
2	26	Gemini	2	20	Scorpio
3	10	Cancer	3	2	Sagittarius
4	22	Cancer	4	15	Sagittarius
5	4	Leo	5	28	Sagittarius
6	16	Leo	6	12	Capricorn
7	28	Leo	7	29	Capricorn
8	10	Virgo	8	19	Aquarius
9	22	Virgo	9	13	Pisces
10	4	Libra	10	9	Aries
11	15	Libra	11	4	Taurus
12 *noon*	27	Libra	12 *midnight*	25	Taurus

JULY 30

A.M.		P.M.	
1	14 Gemini	1	11 Scorpio
2	29 Gemini	2	23 Scorpio
3	12 Cancer	3	4 Sagittarius
4	25 Cancer	4	17 Sagittarius
5	6 Leo	5	0 Capricorn
6	18 Leo	6	15 Capricorn
7	0 Virgo	7	2 Aquarius
8	12 Virgo	8	23 Aquarius
9	23 Virgo	9	18 Pisces
10	6 Libra	10	14 Aries
11	17 Libra	11	7 Taurus
12 *noon*	0 Scorpio	12 *midnight*	28 Taurus

AUGUST 2

A.M.		P.M.	
1	17 Gemini	1	14 Scorpio
2	2 Cancer	2	25 Scorpio
3	15 Cancer	3	7 Sagittarius
4	27 Cancer	4	20 Sagittarius
5	9 Leo	5	3 Capricorn
6	21 Leo	6	19 Capricorn
7	2 Virgo	7	6 Aquarius
8	14 Virgo	8	28 Aquarius
9	26 Virgo	9	24 Pisces
10	8 Libra	10	18 Aries
11	20 Libra	11	12 Taurus
12 *noon*	2 Scorpio	12 *midnight*	2 Gemini

AUGUST 5

	A.M.			P.M.	
1	20	Gemini	1	16	Scorpio
2	5	Cancer	2	27	Scorpio
3	17	Cancer	3	10	Sagittarius
4	0	Leo	4	22	Sagittarius
5	12	Leo	5	6	Capricorn
6	23	Leo	6	21	Capricorn
7	5	Virgo	7	10	Aquarius
8	17	Virgo	8	2	Pisces
9	29	Virgo	9	28	Pisces
10	11	Libra	10	24	Aries
11	22	Libra	11	16	Taurus
12 *noon*	4	Scorpio	12 *midnight*	6	Gemini

AUGUST 8

	A.M.			P.M.	
1	23	Gemini	1	18	Scorpio
2	7	Cancer	2	0	Sagittarius
3	19	Cancer	3	12	Sagittarius
4	2	Leo	4	25	Sagittarius
5	14	Leo	5	9	Capricorn
6	25	Leo	6	25	Capricorn
7	7	Virgo	7	14	Aquarius
8	19	Virgo	8	7	Pisces
9	1	Libra	9	3	Aries
10	13	Libra	10	29	Aries
11	25	Libra	11	21	Taurus
12 *noon*	6	Scorpio	12 *midnight*	9	Gemini

AUGUST 11

A.M.			P.M.		
1	26	Gemini	1	20	Scorpio
2	9	Cancer	2	2	Sagittarius
3	22	Cancer	3	14	Sagittarius
4	4	Leo	4	27	Sagittarius
5	16	Leo	5	12	Capricorn
6	28	Leo	6	28	Capricorn
7	10	Virgo	7	19	Aquarius
8	21	Virgo	8	13	Pisces
9	3	Libra	9	9	Aries
10	15	Libra	10	3	Taurus
11	27	Libra	11	25	Taurus
12 *noon*	9	Scorpio	12 *midnight*	12	Gemini

AUGUST 14

A.M.			P.M.		
1	29	Gemini	1	23	Scorpio
2	12	Cancer	2	4	Sagittarius
3	25	Cancer	3	17	Sagittarius
4	6	Leo	4	0	Capricorn
5	18	Leo	5	15	Capricorn
6	0	Virgo	6	2	Aquarius
7	12	Virgo	7	23	Aquarius
8	23	Virgo	8	18	Pisces
9	6	Libra	9	14	Aries
10	17	Libra	10	7	Taurus
11	29	Libra	11	27	Taurus
12 *noon*	11	Scorpio	12 *midnight*	15	Gemini

AUGUST 17

A.M.		P.M.	
1	1 Cancer	1	25 Scorpio
2	15 Cancer	2	7 Sagittarius
3	27 Cancer	3	20 Sagittarius
4	9 Leo	4	3 Capricorn
5	21 Leo	5	18 Capricorn
6	2 Virgo	6	6 Aquarius
7	14 Virgo	7	27 Aquarius
8	26 Virgo	8	22 Pisces
9	8 Libra	9	18 Aries
10	20 Libra	10	12 Taurus
11	1 Scorpio	11	1 Gemini
12 *noon*	13 Scorpio	12 *midnight*	18 Gemini

AUGUST 20

A.M.		P.M.	
1	5 Cancer	1	27 Scorpio
2	17 Cancer	2	10 Sagittarius
3	29 Cancer	3	22 Sagittarius
4	11 Leo	4	6 Capricorn
5	23 Leo	5	21 Capricorn
6	5 Virgo	6	10 Aquarius
7	17 Virgo	7	2 Pisces
8	28 Virgo	8	28 Pisces
9	10 Libra	9	24 Aries
10	22 Libra	10	16 Taurus
11	4 Scorpio	11	6 Gemini
12 *noon*	15 Scorpio	12 *midnight*	21 Gemini

AUGUST 23

	A.M.			P.M.	
1	7	Cancer	1	0	Sagittarius
2	19	Cancer	2	12	Sagittarius
3	1	Leo	3	25	Sagittarius
4	14	Leo	4	9	Capricorn
5	25	Leo	5	24	Capricorn
6	7	Virgo	6	14	Aquarius
7	19	Virgo	7	7	Pisces
8	0	Libra	8	3	Aries
9	12	Libra	9	28	Aries
10	24	Libra	10	21	Taurus
11	6	Scorpio	11	8	Gemini
12 *noon*	17	Scorpio	12 *midnight*	24	Gemini

AUGUST 26

	A.M.			P.M.	
1	9	Cancer	1	2	Sagittarius
2	22	Cancer	2	14	Sagittarius
3	4	Leo	3	27	Sagittarius
4	15	Leo	4	12	Capricorn
5	28	Leo	5	28	Capricorn
6	9	Virgo	6	19	Aquarius
7	21	Virgo	7	13	Pisces
8	3	Libra	8	8	Aries
9	15	Libra	9	2	Taurus
10	27	Libra	10	25	Taurus
11	8	Scorpio	11	11	Gemini
12 *noon*	20	Scorpio	12 *midnight*	27	Gemini

AUGUST 29

A.M.		P.M.	
1	12 Cancer	1	4 Sagittarius
2	25 Cancer	2	17 Sagittarius
3	6 Leo	3	0 Capricorn
4	18 Leo	4	15 Capricorn
5	0 Virgo	5	2 Aquarius
6	12 Virgo	6	22 Aquarius
7	23 Virgo	7	16 Pisces
8	6 Libra	8	13 Aries
9	17 Libra	9	7 Taurus
10	29 Libra	10	29 Taurus
11	11 Scorpio	11	15 Gemini
12 *noon*	23 Scorpio	12 *midnight*	29 Gemini

SEPTEMBER 1

A.M.		P.M.	
1	15 Cancer	1	7 Sagittarius
2	27 Cancer	2	20 Sagittarius
3	9 Leo	3	3 Capricorn
4	20 Leo	4	18 Capricorn
5	2 Virgo	5	6 Aquarius
6	14 Virgo	6	27 Aquarius
7	26 Virgo	7	22 Pisces
8	7 Libra	8	18 Aries
9	20 Libra	9	12 Taurus
10	1 Scorpio	10	1 Gemini
11	13 Scorpio	11	18 Gemini
12 *noon*	25 Scorpio	12 *midnight*	2 Cancer

SEPTEMBER 4

A.M.			P.M.		
1	17	Cancer	1	9	Sagittarius
2	29	Cancer	2	22	Sagittarius
3	11	Leo	3	5	Capricorn
4	23	Leo	4	21	Capricorn
5	4	Virgo	5	10	Aquarius
6	16	Virgo	6	2	Pisces
7	28	Virgo	7	28	Pisces
8	10	Libra	8	23	Aries
9	22	Libra	9	16	Taurus
10	4	Scorpio	10	5	Gemini
11	15	Scorpio	11	21	Gemini
12 *noon*	27	Scorpio	12 *midnight*	5	Cancer

SEPTEMBER 7

A.M.			P.M.		
1	19	Cancer	1	11	Sagittarius
2	2	Leo	2	25	Sagittarius
3	14	Leo	3	9	Capricorn
4	25	Leo	4	24	Capricorn
5	7	Virgo	5	14	Aquarius
6	18	Virgo	6	7	Pisces
7	0	Libra	7	3	Aries
8	12	Libra	8	27	Aries
9	24	Libra	9	19	Taurus
10	6	Scorpio	10	8	Gemini
11	17	Scorpio	11	24	Gemini
12 *noon*	29	Scorpio	12 *midnight*	8	Cancer

SEPTEMBER 10

A.M.			P.M.		
1	22	Cancer	1	14	Sagittarius
2	4	Leo	2	27	Sagittarius
3	15	Leo	3	12	Capricorn
4	27	Leo	4	28	Capricorn
5	9	Virgo	5	18	Aquarius
6	21	Virgo	6	12	Pisces
7	3	Libra	7	7	Aries
8	15	Libra	8	2	Taurus
9	27	Libra	9	23	Taurus
10	8	Scorpio	10	11	Gemini
11	20	Scorpio	11	27	Gemini
12 *noon*	2	Sagittarius	12 *midnight*	10	Cancer

SEPTEMBER 13

A.M.			P.M.		
1	25	Cancer	1	17	Sagittarius
2	6	Leo	2	0	Capricorn
3	18	Leo	3	15	Capricorn
4	29	Leo	4	2	Aquarius
5	12	Virgo	5	22	Aquarius
6	23	Virgo	6	16	Pisces
7	5	Libra	7	13	Aries
8	17	Libra	8	7	Taurus
9	29	Libra	9	27	Taurus
10	11	Scorpio	10	14	Gemini
11	22	Scorpio	11	29	Gemini
12 *noon*	4	Sagittarius	12 *midnight*	12	Cancer

SEPTEMBER 16

A.M.			P.M.		
1	27	Cancer	1	19	Sagittarius
2	9	Leo	2	2	Capricorn
3	20	Leo	3	18	Capricorn
4	2	Virgo	4	6	Aquarius
5	13	Virgo	5	27	Aquarius
6	25	Virgo	6	22	Pisces
7	7	Libra	7	17	Aries
8	19	Libra	8	12	Taurus
9	1	Scorpio	9	1	Gemini
10	13	Scorpio	10	17	Gemini
11	24	Scorpio	11	2	Cancer
12 *noon*	7	Sagittarius	12 *midnight*	15	Cancer

SEPTEMBER 19

A.M.			P.M.		
1	29	Cancer	1	21	Sagittarius
2	11	Leo	2	5	Capricorn
3	22	Leo	3	21	Capricorn
4	4	Virgo	4	10	Aquarius
5	16	Virgo	5	2	Pisces
6	28	Virgo	6	28	Pisces
7	10	Libra	7	22	Aries
8	22	Libra	8	15	Taurus
9	3	Scorpio	9	5	Gemini
10	15	Scorpio	10	20	Gemini
11	26	Scorpio	11	5	Cancer
12 *noon*	9	Sagittarius	12 *midnight*	17	Cancer

SEPTEMBER 22

A.M.			P.M.		
1	1	Leo	1	25	Sagittarius
2	13	Leo	2	8	Capricorn
3	25	Leo	3	24	Capricorn
4	7	Virgo	4	13	Aquarius
5	18	Virgo	5	6	Pisces
6	0	Libra	6	1	Aries
7	13	Libra	7	27	Aries
8	24	Libra	8	19	Taurus
9	6	Scorpio	9	8	Gemini
10	17	Scorpio	10	23	Gemini
11	29	Scorpio	11	7	Cancer
12 *noon*	11	Sagittarius	12 *midnight*	20	Cancer

SEPTEMBER 25

A.M.			P.M.		
1	3	Leo	1	27	Sagittarius
2	15	Leo	2	12	Capricorn
3	27	Leo	3	28	Capricorn
4	9	Virgo	4	17	Aquarius
5	21	Virgo	5	11	Pisces
6	2	Libra	6	7	Aries
7	14	Libra	7	2	Taurus
8	26	Libra	8	23	Taurus
9	8	Scorpio	9	11	Gemini
10	20	Scorpio	10	27	Gemini
11	2	Sagittarius	11	10	Cancer
12 *noon*	14	Sagittarius	12 *midnight*	22	Cancer

SEPTEMBER 28

A.M.		P.M.	
1	6 Leo	1	0 Capricorn
2	18 Leo	2	15 Capricorn
3	29 Leo	3	2 Aquarius
4	11 Virgo	4	22 Aquarius
5	23 Virgo	5	16 Pisces
6	5 Libra	6	13 Aries
7	17 Libra	7	7 Taurus
8	28 Libra	8	27 Taurus
9	11 Scorpio	9	14 Gemini
10	22 Scorpio	10	29 Gemini
11	4 Sagittarius	11	12 Cancer
12 *noon*	17 Sagittarius	12 *midnight*	25 Cancer

OCTOBER 1

A.M.		P.M.	
1	8 Leo	1	2 Capricorn
2	20 Leo	2	17 Capricorn
3	2 Virgo	3	4 Aquarius
4	13 Virgo	4	26 Aquarius
5	25 Virgo	5	22 Pisces
6	7 Libra	6	16 Aries
7	19 Libra	7	10 Taurus
8	1 Scorpio	8	1 Gemini
9	12 Scorpio	9	17 Gemini
10	24 Scorpio	10	2 Cancer
11	6 Sagittarius	11	15 Cancer
12 *noon*	19 Sagittarius	12 *midnight*	27 Cancer

OCTOBER 4

A.M.		P.M.	
1	10 Leo	1	5 Capricorn
2	22 Leo	2	20 Capricorn
3	4 Virgo	3	8 Aquarius
4	16 Virgo	4	0 Pisces
5	28 Virgo	5	26 Pisces
6	10 Libra	6	22 Aries
7	22 Libra	7	15 Taurus
8	3 Scorpio	8	5 Gemini
9	15 Scorpio	9	20 Gemini
10	26 Scorpio	10	5 Cancer
11	9 Sagittarius	11	17 Cancer
12 *noon*	21 Sagittarius	12 *midnight*	0 Leo

OCTOBER 7

A.M.		P.M.	
1	13 Leo	1	8 Capricorn
2	25 Leo	2	23 Capricorn
3	7 Virgo	3	13 Aquarius
4	18 Virgo	4	5 Pisces
5	0 Libra	5	1 Aries
6	12 Libra	6	27 Aries
7	24 Libra	7	19 Taurus
8	5 Scorpio	8	8 Gemini
9	17 Scorpio	9	23 Gemini
10	29 Scorpio	10	7 Cancer
11	11 Sagittarius	11	19 Cancer
12 *noon*	24 Sagittarius	12 *midnight*	2 Leo

OCTOBER 10

A.M.		P.M.	
1	15 Leo	1	11 Capricorn
2	27 Leo	2	27 Capricorn
3	9 Virgo	3	17 Aquarius
4	20 Virgo	4	11 Pisces
5	2 Libra	5	7 Aries
6	14 Libra	6	2 Taurus
7	26 Libra	7	23 Taurus
8	8 Scorpio	8	11 Gemini
9	20 Scorpio	9	26 Gemini
10	2 Sagittarius	10	9 Cancer
11	13 Sagittarius	11	22 Cancer
12 *noon*	26 Sagittarius	12 *midnight*	4 Leo

OCTOBER 13

A.M.		P.M.	
1	18 Leo	1	14 Capricorn
2	29 Leo	2	1 Aquarius
3	11 Virgo	3	22 Aquarius
4	23 Virgo	4	16 Pisces
5	5 Libra	5	11 Aries
6	17 Libra	6	7 Taurus
7	28 Libra	7	27 Taurus
8	10 Scorpio	8	14 Gemini
9	22 Scorpio	9	29 Gemini
10	4 Sagittarius	10	12 Cancer
11	16 Sagittarius	11	25 Cancer
12 *noon*	0 Capricorn	12 *midnight*	6 Leo

OCTOBER 16

A.M.		P.M.	
1	20 Leo	1	17 Capricorn
2	2 Virgo	2	4 Aquarius
3	13 Virgo	3	25 Aquarius
4	25 Virgo	4	21 Pisces
5	7 Libra	5	16 Aries
6	19 Libra	6	10 Taurus
7	1 Scorpio	7	1 Gemini
8	12 Scorpio	8	17 Gemini
9	24 Scorpio	9	1 Cancer
10	6 Sagittarius	10	15 Cancer
11	18 Sagittarius	11	27 Cancer
12 *noon*	2 Capricorn	12 *midnight*	9 Leo

OCTOBER 19

A.M.		P.M.	
1	22 Leo	1	20 Capricorn
2	4 Virgo	2	8 Aquarius
3	16 Virgo	3	0 Pisces
4	28 Virgo	4	26 Pisces
5	10 Libra	5	22 Aries
6	21 Libra	6	15 Taurus
7	3 Scorpio	7	5 Gemini
8	14 Scorpio	8	20 Gemini
9	26 Scorpio	9	5 Cancer
10	8 Sagittarius	10	17 Cancer
11	21 Sagittarius	11	29 Cancer
12 *noon*	5 Capricorn	12 *midnight*	11 Leo

OCTOBER 22

A.M.		P.M.	
1	25 Leo	1	23 Capricorn
2	6 Virgo	2	13 Aquarius
3	18 Virgo	3	5 Pisces
4	0 Libra	4	1 Aries
5	12 Libra	5	27 Aries
6	23 Libra	6	19 Taurus
7	5 Scorpio	7	7 Gemini
8	17 Scorpio	8	23 Gemini
9	29 Scorpio	9	7 Cancer
10	10 Sagittarius	10	19 Cancer
11	24 Sagittarius	11	1 Leo
12 *noon*	8 Capricorn	12 *midnight*	13 Leo

OCTOBER 25

A.M.		P.M.	
1	27 Leo	1	27 Capricorn
2	8 Virgo	2	17 Aquarius
3	20 Virgo	3	11 Pisces
4	2 Libra	4	6 Aries
5	14 Libra	5	14 Taurus
6	26 Libra	6	23 Taurus
7	8 Scorpio	7	11 Gemini
8	19 Scorpio	8	26 Gemini
9	1 Sagittarius	9	9 Cancer
10	13 Sagittarius	10	22 Cancer
11	26 Sagittarius	11	3 Leo
12 *noon*	11 Capricorn	12 *midnight*	15 Leo

OCTOBER 28

A.M.			P.M.		
1	29	Leo	1	1	Aquarius
2	11	Virgo	2	20	Aquarius
3	23	Virgo	3	15	Pisces
4	5	Libra	4	11	Aries
5	17	Libra	5	6	Taurus
6	28	Libra	6	26	Taurus
7	10	Scorpio	7	13	Gemini
8	21	Scorpio	8	29	Gemini
9	4	Sagittarius	9	12	Cancer
10	16	Sagittarius	10	24	Cancer
11	29	Sagittarius	11	6	Leo
12 *noon*	14	Capricorn	12 *midnight*	18	Leo

OCTOBER 31

A.M.			P.M.		
1	1	Virgo	1	4	Aquarius
2	13	Virgo	2	25	Aquarius
3	24	Virgo	3	20	Pisces
4	6	Libra	4	16	Aries
5	18	Libra	5	10	Taurus
6	1	Scorpio	6	0	Gemini
7	12	Scorpio	7	17	Gemini
8	24	Scorpio	8	1	Cancer
9	6	Sagittarius	9	14	Cancer
10	18	Sagittarius	10	26	Cancer
11	1	Capricorn	11	9	Leo
12 *noon*	17	Capricorn	12 *midnight*	21	Leo

NOVEMBER 3

A.M.		P.M.	
1	3 Virgo	1	8 Aquarius
2	16 Virgo	2	0 Pisces
3	28 Virgo	3	26 Pisces
4	9 Libra	4	21 Aries
5	21 Libra	5	15 Taurus
6	3 Scorpio	6	3 Gemini
7	14 Scorpio	7	19 Gemini
8	26 Scorpio	8	4 Cancer
9	8 Sagittarius	9	16 Cancer
10	20 Sagittarius	10	29 Cancer
11	4 Capricorn	11	11 Leo
12 *noon*	20 Capricorn	12 *midnight*	22 Leo

NOVEMBER 6

A.M.		P.M.	
1	6 Virgo	1	13 Aquarius
2	18 Virgo	2	5 Pisces
3	0 Libra	3	0 Aries
4	12 Libra	4	26 Aries
5	23 Libra	5	19 Taurus
6	5 Scorpio	6	7 Gemini
7	17 Scorpio	7	23 Gemini
8	29 Scorpio	8	7 Cancer
9	11 Sagittarius	9	19 Cancer
10	24 Sagittarius	10	1 Leo
11	7 Capricorn	11	13 Leo
12 *noon*	23 Capricorn	12 *midnight*	25 Leo

NOVEMBER 9

A.M.			P.M.		
1	8	Virgo	1	16	Aquarius
2	20	Virgo	2	9	Pisces
3	2	Libra	3	5	Aries
4	14	Libra	4	1	Taurus
5	26	Libra	5	22	Taurus
6	8	Scorpio	6	0	Gemini
7	19	Scorpio	7	25	Gemini
8	1	Sagittarius	8	9	Cancer
9	13	Sagittarius	9	22	Cancer
10	26	Sagittarius	10	3	Leo
11	10	Capricorn	11	15	Leo
12 *noon*	27	Capricorn	12 *midnight*	27	Leo

NOVEMBER 12

A.M.			P.M.		
1	11	Virgo	1	20	Aquarius
2	23	Virgo	2	14	Pisces
3	4	Libra	3	11	Aries
4	16	Libra	4	6	Taurus
5	28	Libra	5	26	Taurus
6	10	Scorpio	6	13	Gemini
7	21	Scorpio	7	29	Gemini
8	4	Sagittarius	8	12	Cancer
9	16	Sagittarius	9	24	Cancer
10	29	Sagittarius	10	6	Leo
11	14	Capricorn	11	18	Leo
12 *noon*	1	Aquarius	12 *midnight*	29	Leo

NOVEMBER 15

A.M.		P.M.	
1	13 Virgo	1	25 Aquarius
2	25 Virgo	2	20 Pisces
3	6 Libra	3	16 Aries
4	18 Libra	4	10 Taurus
5	1 Scorpio	5	0 Gemini
6	12 Scorpio	6	16 Gemini
7	23 Scorpio	7	1 Cancer
8	6 Sagittarius	8	14 Cancer
9	18 Sagittarius	9	26 Cancer
10	1 Capricorn	10	8 Leo
11	17 Capricorn	11	20 Leo
12 *noon*	4 Aquarius	12 *midnight*	2 Virgo

NOVEMBER 18

A.M.		P.M.	
1	15 Virgo	1	0 Pisces
2	27 Virgo	2	26 Pisces
3	9 Libra	3	21 Aries
4	21 Libra	4	14 Taurus
5	3 Scorpio	5	3 Gemini
6	14 Scorpio	6	19 Gemini
7	26 Scorpio	7	4 Cancer
8	8 Sagittarius	8	16 Cancer
9	20 Sagittarius	9	28 Cancer
10	4 Capricorn	10	11 Leo
11	19 Capricorn	11	22 Leo
12 *noon*	8 Aquarius	12 *midnight*	4 Virgo

NOVEMBER 21

	A.M.		P.M.
1	17 Virgo	1	4 Pisces
2	0 Libra	2	0 Aries
3	12 Libra	3	25 Aries
4	23 Libra	4	18 Taurus
5	5 Scorpio	5	7 Gemini
6	17 Scorpio	6	22 Gemini
7	29 Scorpio	7	6 Cancer
8	10 Sagittarius	8	19 Cancer
9	23 Sagittarius	9	1 Leo
10	7 Capricorn	10	13 Leo
11	23 Capricorn	11	25 Leo
12 *noon*	11 Aquarius	12 *midnight*	7 Virgo

NOVEMBER 24

	A.M.		P.M.
1	20 Virgo	1	9 Pisces
2	2 Libra	2	5 Aries
3	14 Libra	3	1 Taurus
4	26 Libra	4	22 Taurus
5	8 Scorpio	5	10 Gemini
6	19 Scorpio	6	26 Gemini
7	1 Sagittarius	7	9 Cancer
8	13 Sagittarius	8	22 Cancer
9	26 Sagittarius	9	3 Leo
10	10 Capricorn	10	15 Leo
11	26 Capricorn	11	27 Leo
12 *noon*	16 Aquarius	12 *midnight*	9 Virgo

NOVEMBER 27

A.M.		P.M.	
1	22 Virgo	1	14 Pisces
2	4 Libra	2	11 Aries
3	16 Libra	3	6 Taurus
4	28 Libra	4	26 Taurus
5	9 Scorpio	5	13 Gemini
6	21 Scorpio	6	28 Gemini
7	3 Sagittarius	7	12 Cancer
8	15 Sagittarius	8	24 Cancer
9	28 Sagittarius	9	6 Leo
10	13 Capricorn	10	18 Leo
11	29 Capricorn	11	29 Leo
12 *noon*	20 Aquarius	12 *midnight*	11 Virgo

NOVEMBER 30

A.M.		P.M.	
1	24 Virgo	1	20 Pisces
2	6 Libra	2	16 Aries
3	18 Libra	3	10 Taurus
4	0 Scorpio	4	0 Gemini
5	11 Scorpio	5	16 Gemini
6	23 Scorpio	6	1 Cancer
7	5 Sagittarius	7	14 Cancer
8	18 Sagittarius	8	26 Cancer
9	1 Capricorn	9	8 Leo
10	16 Capricorn	10	20 Leo
11	3 Aquarius	11	2 Virgo
12 *noon*	25 Aquarius	12 *midnight*	13 Virgo

DECEMBER 3

A.M.		P.M.	
1	27 Virgo	1	24 Pisces
2	9 Libra	2	20 Aries
3	21 Libra	3	13 Taurus
4	2 Scorpio	4	3 Gemini
5	14 Scorpio	5	19 Gemini
6	26 Scorpio	6	4 Cancer
7	8 Sagittarius	7	16 Cancer
8	20 Sagittarius	8	28 Cancer
9	4 Capricorn	9	10 Leo
10	19 Capricorn	10	22 Leo
11	7 Aquarius	11	4 Virgo
12 *noon*	0 Pisces	12 *midnight*	16 Virgo

DECEMBER 6

A.M.		P.M.	
1	0 Libra	1	0 Aries
2	11 Libra	2	25 Aries
3	23 Libra	3	18 Taurus
4	4 Scorpio	4	7 Gemini
5	16 Scorpio	5	22 Gemini
6	28 Scorpio	6	6 Cancer
7	10 Sagittarius	7	19 Cancer
8	23 Sagittarius	8	1 Leo
9	7 Capricorn	9	13 Leo
10	22 Capricorn	10	25 Leo
11	11 Aquarius	11	6 Virgo
12 *noon*	4 Pisces	12 *midnight*	18 Virgo

DECEMBER 9

	A.M.			P.M.	
1	1	Libra	1	5	Aries
2	13	Libra	2	1	Taurus
3	25	Libra	3	22	Taurus
4	7	Scorpio	4	10	Gemini
5	19	Scorpio	5	25	Gemini
6	0	Sagittarius	6	9	Cancer
7	13	Sagittarius	7	22	Cancer
8	25	Sagittarius	8	3	Leo
9	10	Capricorn	9	15	Leo
10	26	Capricorn	10	27	Leo
11	15	Aquarius	11	8	Virgo
12 *noon*	9	Pisces	12 *midnight*	20	Virgo

DECEMBER 12

	A.M.			P.M.	
1	4	Libra	1	10	Aries
2	16	Libra	2	5	Taurus
3	27	Libra	3	26	Taurus
4	9	Scorpio	4	13	Gemini
5	21	Scorpio	5	28	Gemini
6	3	Sagittarius	6	12	Cancer
7	15	Sagittarius	7	24	Cancer
8	29	Sagittarius	8	6	Leo
9	13	Capricorn	9	18	Leo
10	29	Capricorn	10	29	Leo
11	20	Aquarius	11	11	Virgo
12 *noon*	14	Pisces	12 *midnight*	23	Virgo

DECEMBER 15

A.M.		P.M.	
1	6 Libra	1	15 Aries
2	18 Libra	2	9 Taurus
3	0 Scorpio	3	0 Gemini
4	11 Scorpio	4	16 Gemini
5	23 Scorpio	5	0 Cancer
6	5 Sagittarius	6	14 Cancer
7	17 Sagittarius	7	26 Cancer
8	0 Capricorn	8	8 Leo
9	16 Capricorn	9	20 Leo
10	3 Aquarius	10	2 Virgo
11	23 Aquarius	11	13 Virgo
12 *noon*	18 Pisces	12 *midnight*	25 Virgo

DECEMBER 18

A.M.		P.M.	
1	8 Libra	1	20 Aries
2	20 Libra	2	13 Taurus
3	2 Scorpio	3	3 Gemini
4	14 Scorpio	4	19 Gemini
5	26 Scorpio	5	4 Cancer
6	7 Sagittarius	6	16 Cancer
7	20 Sagittarius	7	28 Cancer
8	4 Capricorn	8	10 Leo
9	19 Capricorn	9	22 Leo
10	7 Aquarius	10	3 Virgo
11	28 Aquarius	11	16 Virgo
12 *noon*	24 Pisces	12 *midnight*	28 Virgo

DECEMBER 21

A.M.		P.M.	
1	11 Libra	1	25 Aries
2	22 Libra	2	18 Taurus
3	4 Scorpio	3	6 Gemini
4	16 Scorpio	4	22 Gemini
5	28 Scorpio	5	6 Cancer
6	10 Sagittarius	6	19 Cancer
7	23 Sagittarius	7	1 Leo
8	7 Capricorn	8	12 Leo
9	22 Capricorn	9	24 Leo
10	11 Aquarius	10	6 Virgo
11	4 Pisces	11	18 Virgo
12 *noon*	0 Aries	12 *midnight*	0 Libra

DECEMBER 24

A.M.		P.M.	
1	13 Libra	1	1 Taurus
2	25 Libra	2	22 Taurus
3	7 Scorpio	3	9 Gemini
4	18 Scorpio	4	25 Gemini
5	0 Sagittarius	5	9 Cancer
6	13 Sagittarius	6	21 Cancer
7	25 Sagittarius	7	3 Leo
8	10 Capricorn	8	15 Leo
9	26 Capricorn	9	27 Leo
10	15 Aquarius	10	8 Virgo
11	8 Pisces	11	20 Virgo
12 *noon*	4 Aries	12 *midnight*	2 Libra

DECEMBER 27

A.M.		P.M.	
1	16 Libra	1	4 Taurus
2	27 Libra	2	25 Taurus
3	9 Scorpio	3	12 Gemini
4	21 Scorpio	4	28 Gemini
5	3 Sagittarius	5	11 Cancer
6	15 Sagittarius	6	24 Cancer
7	28 Sagittarius	7	5 Leo
8	13 Capricorn	8	17 Leo
9	29 Capricorn	9	28 Leo
10	19 Aquarius	10	11 Virgo
11	13 Pisces	11	23 Virgo
12 *noon*	9 Aries	12 *midnight*	5 Libra

DECEMBER 30

A.M.		P.M.	
1	18 Libra	1	9 Taurus
2	0 Scorpio	2	29 Taurus
3	11 Scorpio	3	15 Gemini
4	23 Scorpio	4	0 Cancer
5	5 Sagittarius	5	13 Cancer
6	18 Sagittarius	6	26 Cancer
7	0 Capricorn	7	8 Leo
8	16 Capricorn	8	19 Leo
9	3 Aquarius	9	1 Virgo
10	23 Aquarius	10	12 Virgo
11	18 Pisces	11	25 Virgo
12 *noon*	15 Aries	12 *midnight*	6 Libra

Simplified Ephemerides from 1931 to 1953

These Ephemerides have been calculated for 0 hours Greenwich Mean Time. For those of you wishing to make a correction to your Moon, which is the swiftest-moving body, the following directions will be helpful:

Determine the number of hours between 0 hours and your birth time. For every two hours of difference add 1 degree* to the number shown in the ephemeris on the date of your birth. For some of you, this may put your Moon into a new sign.

* The Moon moves approximately one degree, or sixty minutes, every two hours, or thirty minutes every hour.

1931

JANUARY

Day	☉	☽	☿	♀	♂	♃	♄	♅	♆
	° ′	° ′	° ′	° ′	° ′	° ′	° ′	° ′	° ′
1	9♑36	23♉35	20♑42	28♏13	15♌36	16♋14	13♑43	11♈29	5♍38
2	10 37	7♊ 1	19 R 50	28 49	15 R 24	16 R 6	13 50	11 30	5 R 37
3	11 38	20 54	18 48	29 27	15 12	15 58	13 57	11 31	5 37
4	12 40	5♋12	17 38	0♐ 7	14 59	15 50	14 5	11 31	5 36
5	13 41	19 49	16 21	0 47	14 45	15 42	14 12	11 32	5 35
6	14 42	4♌37	15 1	1 29	14 31	15 34	14 18	11 33	5 34
7	15 43	19 28	13 40	2 11	14 16	15 26	14 25	11 34	5 33
8	16 44	4♍14	12 21	2 55	13 59	15 17	14 32	11 35	5 32
9	17 45	18 47	11 6	3 40	13 43	15 9	14 39	11 36	5 31
10	18 46	3♎ 4	9 57	4 26	13 25	15 1	14 46	11 36	5 30
11	19 48	17 3	8 56	5 13	13 7	14 53	14 53	11 38	5 29
12	20 49	0♏45	8 3	6 1	12 48	14 45	15 1	11 39	5 28
13	21 50	14 11	7 20	6 49	12 29	14 37	15 8	11 40	5 27
14	22 51	27 22	6 46	7 39	12 9	14 29	15 15	11 41	5 26
15	23 52	10♐21	6 22	8 29	11 49	14 21	15 22	11 42	5 25
16	24 53	23 8	6 8	9 20	11 28	14 13	15 29	11 44	5 23
17	25 54	5♑45	6 D 3	10 12	11 6	14 5	15 36	11 45	5 22
18	26 55	18 12	6 6	11 4	10 44	13 58	15 43	11 46	5 21
19	27 57	0♒28	6 17	11 58	10 22	13 50	15 50	11 48	5 20
20	28 58	12 36	6 35	12 52	9 59	13 43	15 57	11 49	5 19
21	29 59	24 35	7 0	13 46	9 36	13 35	16 4	11 51	5 17
22	1♒ 0	6♓28	7 31	14 41	9 13	13 28	16 11	11 52	5 16
23	2 1	18 16	8 8	15 37	8 49	13 21	16 18	11 54	5 15
24	3 2	0♈ 3	8 49	16 33	8 25	13 13	16 25	11 55	5 14
25	4 3	11 53	9 35	17 30	8 1	13 6	16 32	11 57	5 12
26	5 4	23 51	10 25	18 28	7 37	12 59	16 39	11 59	5 11
27	6 5	6♉ 3	11 18	19 26	7 13	12 52	16 46	12 1	5 9
28	7 6	18 34	12 14	20 24	6 49	12 45	16 53	12 2	5 8
29	8 7	1♊28	13 14	21 23	6 25	12 38	16 59	12 4	5 6
30	9 8	14 51	14 17	22 22	6 1	12 32	17 6	12 6	5 5
31	10 9	28 44	15 22	23 22	5 38	12 26	17 13	12 8	5 3

Pluto 19 Cancer all month

FEBRUARY

Day	☉	☽	☿	♀	♂	♃	♄	♅	♆
	° ′	° ′	° ′	° ′	° ′	° ′	° ′	° ′	° ′
1	11♒10	13♋ 6	16♑29	24♐22	5♌14	12♋20	17♑20	12♈10	5♍ 2
2	12 10	27 52	17 39	25 22	4 R 51	12 R 13	17 26	12 12	5 R 1
3	13 11	12♌57	18 51	26 23	4 28	12 7	17 33	12 14	4 59
4	14 12	28 8	20 4	27 24	4 5	12 2	17 40	12 16	4 58
5	15 13	13♍17	21 18	28 26	3 42	11 56	17 46	12 19	4 56
6	16 14	28 13	22 34	29 28	3 20	11 51	17 53	12 21	4 54
7	17 15	12♎49	23 52	0♑30	2 58	11 45	17 59	12 23	4 53
8	18 15	27 3	25 11	1 33	2 37	11 40	18 6	12 25	4 51
9	19 16	10♏52	26 32	2 36	2 17	11 35	18 12	12 28	4 50
10	20 17	24 19	27 54	3 39	1 57	11 30	18 19	12 30	4 48
11	21 18	7♐25	29 17	4 43	1 38	11 25	18 25	12 32	4 46
12	22 18	20 13	0♒41	5 47	1 19	11 20	18 31	12 35	4 45
13	23 19	2♑47	2 6	6 51	1 0	11 16	18 38	12 37	4 43
14	24 20	15 9	3 32	7 55	0 42	11 11	18 44	12 40	4 41
15	25 20	27 21	5 0	9 0	0 25	11 7	18 50	12 42	4 40
16	26 21	9♒25	6 28	10 5	0 9	11 4	18 56	12 45	4 38
17	27 21	21 23	7 57	11 10	29♋53	11 0	19 2	12 47	4 36
18	28 22	3♓16	9 27	12 15	29 39	10 57	19 8	12 50	4 35
19	29 22	15 5	10 59	13 21	29 25	10 53	19 14	12 53	4 33
20	0♓23	26 53	12 31	14 27	29 11	10 50	19 20	12 56	4 31
21	1 23	8♈41	14 4	15 33	28 58	10 47	19 26	12 58	4 30
22	2 24	20 34	15 38	16 39	28 46	10 45	19 32	13 1	4 28
23	3 24	2♉34	17 13	17 45	28 36	10 42	19 38	13 4	4 26
24	4 25	14 46	18 49	18 52	28 26	10 40	19 44	13 7	4 25
25	5 25	27 15	20 26	19 58	28 17	10 38	19 49	13 9	4 23
26	6 25	10♊ 4	22 4	21 5	28 8	10 36	19 55	13 12	4 21
27	7 26	23 19	23 43	22 12	28 0	10 34	20 0	13 15	4 20
28	8 26	7♋ 3	25 23	23 20	27 53	10 32	20 6	13 18	4 18

Pluto 19 Cancer all month

1931

MARCH

DAY	☉	☽	☿	♀	♂	♃	♄	♅	♆
	° ′	° ′	° ′	° ′	° ′	° ′	° ′	° ′	° ′
1	9♓26	21♋15	27♒ 4	24♑27	27♋47	10♋31	20♑11	13♈21	4♍16
2	10 26	5♌54	28 46	25 35	27 R 42	10 R 30	20 17	13 24	4 R 15
3	11 27	20 55	0♓29	26 43	27 37	10 29	20 22	13 27	4 13
4	12 27	6♍ 8	2 13	27 51	27 33	10 28	20 27	13 30	4 11
5	13 27	21 25	3 58	28 59	27 30	10 28	20 33	13 33	4 10
6	14 27	6♎35	5 44	0♒ 7	27 28	10 27	20 38	13 36	4 8
7	15 27	21 28	7 32	1 15	27 27	10 27	20 43	13 39	4 6
8	16 27	5♏58	9 20	2 23	27 26	10D 27	20 48	13 43	4 5
9	17 27	20 2	11 10	3 32	27D 26	10 27	20 53	13 46	4 3
10	18 27	3♐39	13 0	4 40	27 27	10 28	20 57	13 49	4 1
11	19 27	16 50	14 52	5 49	27 28	10 28	21 2	13 52	4 0
12	20 27	29 39	16 45	6 58	27 30	10 29	21 7	13 55	3 58
13	21 27	12♑10	18 39	8 7	27 33	10 30	21 12	13 58	3 57
14	22 26	24 25	20 34	9 16	27 37	10 31	21 16	14 2	3 55
15	23 26	6♒29	22 30	10 25	27 41	10 33	21 21	14 5	3 53
16	24 26	18 25	24 27	11 35	27 45	10 34	21 25	14 8	3 52
17	25 26	0♓17	26 25	12 44	27 51	10 36	21 30	14 12	3 50
18	26 25	12 5	28 23	13 54	27 57	10 38	21 34	14 15	3 49
19	27 25	23 53	0♈22	15 3	28 4	10 40	21 38	14 18	3 47
20	28 25	5♈44	2 23	16 13	28 12	10 43	21 42	14 21	3 46
21	29 24	17 38	4 24	17 23	28 20	10 45	21 46	14 25	3 45
22	0♈24	29 38	6 24	18 33	28 28	10 48	21 50	14 28	3 43
23	1 24	11♉46	8 25	19 43	28 37	10 51	21 54	14 32	3 42
24	2 23	24 6	10 26	20 53	28 47	10 54	21 58	14 35	3 40
25	3 23	6♊40	12 26	22 3	28 57	10 57	22 2	14 38	3 39
26	4 22	19 32	14 26	23 13	29 8	11 0	22 5	14 42	3 37
27	5 21	2♋44	16 24	24 23	29 20	11 4	22 9	14 45	3 36
28	6 21	16 19	18 20	25 33	29 32	11 8	22 12	14 49	3 35
29	7 20	0♌18	20 15	26 43	29 45	11 12	22 16	14 52	3 33
30	8 19	14 41	22 7	27 54	29 58	11 16	22 19	14 55	3 32
31	9 19	29 24	23 57	29 4	0♌12	11 20	22 22	14 59	3 31

Pluto 18 Cancer all month

APRIL

DAY	☉	☽	☿	♀	♂	♃	♄	♅	♆
	° ′	° ′	° ′	° ′	° ′	° ′	° ′	° ′	° ′
1	10♈18	14♍23	25♈44	0♓15	0♌26	11♋25	22♑25	15♈ 2	3♍29
2	11 17	29 29	27 26	1 25	0 41	11 29	22 28	15 6	3 R 28
3	12 16	14♎34	29 5	2 36	0 56	11 34	22 31	15 9	3 27
4	13 15	29 29	0♉41	3 47	1 11	11 39	22 34	15 12	3 26
5	14 14	14♏ 6	2 12	4 57	1 27	11 44	22 37	15 16	3 25
6	15 13	28 20	3 37	6 8	1 43	11 50	22 40	15 19	3 23
7	16 12	12♐ 7	4 58	7 19	2 0	11 55	22 42	15 23	3 22
8	17 11	25 28	6 13	8 30	2 17	12 1	22 45	15 26	3 21
9	18 10	8♑23	7 22	9 41	2 35	12 6	22 47	15 29	3 20
10	19 9	20 57	8 25	10 52	2 53	12 12	22 50	15 33	3 19
11	20 8	3♒13	9 23	12 3	3 11	12 18	22 52	15 36	3 18
12	21 7	15 15	10 15	13 14	3 30	12 25	22 54	15 40	3 17
13	22 6	27 8	11 1	14 25	3 49	12 31	22 56	15 43	3 16
14	23 5	8♓57	11 40	15 36	4 9	12 38	22 58	15 47	3 15
15	24 3	20 44	12 13	16 48	4 29	12 44	23 0	15 50	3 14
16	25 2	2♈34	12 40	17 59	4 49	12 51	23 2	15 53	3 13
17	26 1	14 29	13 0	19 10	5 10	12 58	23 4	15 57	3 12
18	27 0	26 32	13 14	20 22	5 30	13 5	23 5	16 0	3 12
19	27 58	8♉45	13 22	21 33	5 51	13 13	23 7	16 4	3 11
20	28 57	21 8	13 R 24	22 45	6 13	13 20	23 8	16 7	3 10
21	29 55	3♊44	13 20	23 56	6 35	13 28	23 9	16 10	3 9
22	0♉54	16 33	13 11	25 8	6 57	13 35	23 10	16 14	3 8
23	1 53	29 37	12 57	26 19	7 20	13 43	23 11	16 17	3 8
24	2 51	12♋56	12 37	27 31	7 43	13 51	23 12	16 20	3 7
25	3 49	26 31	12 12	28 42	8 6	13 59	23 13	16 24	3 6
26	4 48	10♌23	11 43	29 54	8 29	14 7	23 14	16 27	3 6
27	5 46	24 32	11 11	1♈ 6	8 53	14 16	23 14	16 30	3 5
28	6 45	8♍55	10 37	2 17	9 17	14 24	23 15	16 34	3 5
29	7 43	23 31	10 1	3 29	9 41	14 33	23 16	16 37	3 4
30	8 41	8♎14	9 23	4 41	10 5	14 41	23 16	16 40	3 4

Pluto 18 Cancer all month

1931

MAY

DAY	☉	☽	☿	♀	♂	♃	♄	♅	♆
1	9 ♉ 39	23 ♎ 0	8 ♉ 44	5 ♈ 52	10 ♌ 30	14 ♋ 50	23 ♑ 17	16 ♈ 43	3 ♍ 3
2	10 38	7 ♏ 40	8 ℞ 5	7 4	10 55	14 59	23 17	16 47	3 ℞ 2
3	11 36	22 8	7 26	8 16	11 20	15 8	23 ℞ 17	16 50	3 2
4	12 34	6 ♐ 19	6 49	9 28	11 46	15 17	23 17	16 53	3 2
5	13 32	20 8	6 14	10 40	12 12	15 26	23 16	16 56	3 1
6	14 30	3 ♑ 32	5 41	11 52	12 38	15 36	23 16	16 59	3 1
7	15 28	16 32	5 11	13 3	13 4	15 45	23 16	17 3	3 1
8	16 26	29 10	4 45	14 15	13 30	15 55	23 16	17 6	3 1
9	17 24	11 ♒ 28	4 23	15 27	13 56	16 4	23 15	17 9	3 0
10	18 22	23 32	4 4	16 39	14 23	16 14	23 15	17 12	3 0
11	19 20	5 ♓ 25	3 50	17 51	14 50	16 24	23 14	17 15	3 0
12	20 18	17 14	3 41	19 3	15 17	16 34	23 13	17 18	3 0
13	21 16	29 2	3 36	20 15	15 45	16 44	23 12	17 21	3 0
14	22 14	10 ♈ 56	3 D 35	21 28	16 13	16 54	23 11	17 24	3 0
15	23 12	22 57	3 39	22 40	16 40	17 4	23 10	17 27	3 0
16	24 10	5 ♉ 10	3 48	23 52	17 8	17 15	23 9	17 30	3 D 0
17	25 8	17 36	4 2	25 4	17 36	17 25	23 7	17 33	3 0
18	26 5	0 ♊ 18	4 20	26 16	18 5	17 36	23 6	17 35	3 0
19	27 3	13 14	4 42	27 28	18 33	17 47	23 4	17 38	3 0
20	28 1	26 26	5 8	28 40	19 2	17 57	23 3	17 41	3 0
21	28 59	9 ♋ 50	39	29 53	19 31	18 8	23 1	17 44	3 0
22	29 56	23 27	6 13	1 ♉ 5	20 0	18 19	23 0	17 47	3 0
23	0 ♊ 54	7 ♌ 13	6 51	2 17	20 29	18 30	22 58	17 49	3 1
24	1 52	21 9	7 34	3 29	20 58	18 41	22 56	17 52	3 1
25	2 49	5 ♍ 13	8 21	4 41	21 28	18 52	22 54	17 55	3 1
26	3 47	19 24	9 10	5 54	21 58	19 3	22 52	17 57	3 2
27	4 45	3 ♎ 40	10 3	7 6	22 28	19 14	22 50	18 0	3 2
28	5 42	17 59	11 0	8 18	22 58	19 25	22 48	18 2	3 2
29	6 40	2 ♏ 19	12 0	9 31	23 28	19 37	22 46	18 5	3 3
30	7 37	16 34	13 3	10 43	23 58	19 48	22 43	18 7	3 3
31	8 35	0 ♐ 42	14 9	11 55	24 29	20 0	22 40	18 10	3 4

Pluto 18 Cancer all month

JUNE

DAY	☉	☽	☿	♀	♂	♃	♄	♅	♆
1	9 ♊ 32	14 ♐ 37	15 ♉ 18	13 ♉ 8	25 ♌ 0	20 ♋ 11	22 ♑ 38	18 ♈ 12	3 ♍ 4
2	10 30	28 15	16 31	14 20	25 30	20 23	22 ℞ 35	18 15	3 5
3	11 27	11 ♑ 33	17 46	15 33	26 1	20 35	22 33	18 17	3 5
4	12 25	24 30	19 4	16 45	26 32	20 47	22 30	18 19	3 6
5	13 22	7 ♒ 7	20 25	17 57	27 3	20 59	22 27	18 22	3 7
6	14 20	19 25	21 49	19 10	27 34	21 11	22 25	18 24	3 7
7	15 17	1 ♓ 29	23 16	20 22	28 5	21 23	22 22	18 26	3 8
8	16 14	13 23	24 45	21 35	28 37	21 35	22 19	18 28	3 9
9	17 12	25 13	26 17	22 47	29 9	21 47	22 16	18 31	3 10
10	18 9	7 ♈ 2	27 52	24 0	29 41	21 59	22 13	18 33	3 11
11	19 6	18 58	29 30	25 12	0 ♍ 12	22 11	22 9	18 35	3 12
12	20 4	1 ♉ 4	1 ♊ 10	26 25	0 44	22 23	22 5	18 37	3 13
13	21 1	13 25	2 53	27 38	1 16	22 36	22 2	18 39	3 13
14	21 59	26 3	4 39	28 50	1 49	22 48	21 58	18 41	3 14
15	22 56	9 ♊ 1	6 28	0 ♊ 3	2 21	23 1	21 55	18 43	3 15
16	23 53	22 19	8 19	1 16	2 53	23 13	21 51	18 45	3 16
17	24 51	5 ♋ 54	10 12	2 29	3 26	23 26	21 47	18 46	3 17
18	25 48	19 44	12 8	3 41	3 59	23 38	21 44	18 48	3 18
19	26 45	3 ♌ 45	14 6	4 54	4 32	23 51	21 40	18 50	3 19
20	27 42	17 52	16 6	6 7	5 4	24 3	21 36	18 52	3 20
21	28 40	2 ♍ 3	18 8	7 19	5 37	24 16	21 32	18 53	3 22
22	29 37	16 13	20 13	8 32	6 11	24 28	21 29	18 55	3 23
23	0 ♋ 34	0 ♎ 22	22 19	9 45	6 44	24 41	21 25	18 56	3 24
24	1 31	14 28	24 27	10 58	7 17	24 54	21 21	18 58	3 25
25	2 29	28 30	26 36	12 11	7 51	25 7	21 17	18 59	3 26
26	3 26	12 ♏ 27	28 46	13 24	8 25	25 20	21 13	19 1	3 28
27	4 23	26 18	0 ♋ 56	14 36	8 59	25 33	21 8	19 2	3 29
28	5 20	10 ♐ 1	3 7	15 49	9 32	25 46	21 4	19 4	3 30
29	6 17	23 33	5 18	17 2	10 6	25 59	21 0	19 5	3 32
30	7 15	6 ♑ 51	7 29	18 15	10 40	26 12	20 56	19 6	3 33

Pluto 19 Cancer all month

1931

JULY

DAY	☉	☽	☿	♀	♂	♃	♄	♅	♆
1	8♋12	19♑54	9♋40	19♊29	11♍14	26♋25	20♑52	19♈ 7	3♍34
2	9 9	2♒40	11 50	20 42	11 58	26 38	20℞48	19 9	3 36
3	10 6	15 10	13 59	21 55	12 23	26 51	20 43	19 10	3 37
4	11 3	27 24	16 7	23 8	12 57	27 4	20 39	19 11	3 39
5	12 1	9♓26	18 13	24 21	13 31	27 17	20 34	19 12	3 40
6	12 58	21 18	20 19	25 34	14 6	27 30	20 30	19 13	3 42
7	13 55	3♈ 7	22 23	26 47	14 40	27 43	20 26	19 14	3 43
8	14 52	14 56	24 25	28 0	15 15	27 57	20 21	19 15	3 45
9	15 49	26 52	26 25	29 13	15 50	28 10	20 17	19 16	3 47
10	16 47	9♉ 0	28 23	0♋27	16 25	28 23	20 13	19 16	3 48
11	17 44	21 25	0♌20	1 40	17 0	28 36	20 8	19 17	3 50
12	18 41	4♊10	2 15	2 53	17 35	28 49	20 4	19 18	3 52
13	19 38	17 19	4 8	4 6	18 10	29 2	19 59	19 19	3 53
14	20 35	0♋51	6 0	5 20	18 45	29 15	19 55	19 19	4 55
15	21 33	14 46	7 49	6 33	19 21	29 29	19 50	19 20	3 57
16	22 30	28 59	9 36	7 46	19 56	29 42	19 46	19 20	3 58
17	23 27	13♌25	11 22	9 0	20 32	29 56	19 41	19 21	4 0
18	24 25	27 58	13 6	10 13	21 8	0♌ 9	19 37	19 21	4 2
19	25 22	12♍30	14 48	11 26	21 43	0 23	19 33	19 22	4 4
20	26 19	26 57	16 27	12 39	22 19	0 36	19 28	19 22	4 6
21	27 16	11♎15	18 5	13 52	22 55	0 49	19 24	19 22	4 8
22	28 14	25 22	19 42	15 6	23 31	1 2	19 20	19 22	4 9
23	29 11	9♏18	21 17	16 20	24 7	1 16	19 16	19 22	4 11
24	0♌ 8	23 2	22 49	17 34	24 43	1 29	19 11	19 22	4 13
25	1 5	6♐34	24 19	18 47	25 19	1 42	19 7	19 23	4 15
26	2 3	19 55	25 48	20 1	25 55	1 56	19 3	19℞23	4 17
27	3 0	3♑ 4	27 15	21 14	26 31	2 9	18 59	19 23	4 19
28	3 57	16 0	28 39	22 28	27 8	2 23	18 54	19 22	4 21
29	4 55	28 44	0♍ 2	23 42	27 44	2 36	18 50	19 22	4 23
30	5 52	11♒15	1 23	24 55	28 21	2 49	18 46	19 22	4 25
31	6 49	23 33	2 42	26 9	28 57	3 3	18 42	19 22	4 27

Pluto 20 Cancer all month

AUGUST

DAY	☉	☽	☿	♀	♂	♃	♄	♅	♆
1	7♌47	5♓39	3♍59	27♋23	29♍34	3♌16	18♑37	19♈22	4♍29
2	8 44	17 35	5 13	28 36	0♎11	3 29	18℞33	19℞21	4 31
3	9 42	29 26	6 25	29 50	0 48	3 42	18 29	19 21	4 33
4	10 39	11♈13	7 35	1♌ 4	1 25	3 56	18 25	19 20	4 35
5	11 36	23 [illegible]	8 43	2 18	2 2	4 9	18 21	19 20	4 37
6	12 34	4♉57	9 48	3 32	2 39	4 22	18 18	19 20	4 39
7	13 31	17 4	10 51	4 45	3 16	4 35	18 14	19 19	4 41
8	14 29	29 28	11 50	5 59	3 54	4 49	18 10	19 18	4 43
9	15 26	12♊14	12 47	7 13	4 31	5 2	18 6	19 18	4 46
10	16 24	25 24	13 42	8 27	5 9	5 15	18 3	19 17	4 48
11	17 22	9♋ 2	14 33	9 41	5 46	5 28	18 0	19 16	4 50
12	18 19	23 6	15 21	10 55	6 24	5 42	17 56	19 16	4 52
13	19 17	7♌34	16 6	12 9	7 1	5 55	17 53	19 15	4 54
14	20 14	22 18	16 47	13 23	7 39	6 8	17 49	19 15	4 56
15	21 12	7♍12	17 24	14 37	8 17	6 21	17 46	19 13	4 58
16	22 10	22 7	17 57	15 51	8 55	6 34	17 43	19 13	5 1
17	23 7	6♎55	18 26	17 5	9 33	6 47	17 39	19 11	5 3
18	24 5	21 31	18 51	18 20	10 11	7 0	17 36	19 10	5 5
19	25 3	5♏49	19 11	19 34	10 49	7 13	17 33	19 9	5 7
20	26 1	19 50	19 26	20 48	11 27	7 26	17 30	19 8	5 9
21	26 58	3♐31	19 36	22 2	12 6	7 39	17 27	19 6	5 12
22	27 56	16 54	19 41	23 16	12 44	7 52	17 24	19 5	5 14
23	28 54	0♑ 1	19℞40	24 31	13 22	8 5	17 22	19 4	5 16
24	29 52	12 52	19 34	25 45	14 1	8 18	17 19	19 2	5 18
25	0♍50	25 30	19 21	26 59	14 39	8 30	17 17	19 1	5 20
26	1 48	7♒56	19 3	28 13	15 18	8 43	17 14	19 0	5 23
27	2 45	20 11	18 38	29 28	15 57	8 56	17 12	18 58	5 25
28	3 43	2♓17	18 8	0♍42	16 35	9 9	17 9	18 57	5 27
29	4 41	14 14	17 32	1 56	17 14	9 21	17 7	18 55	5 29
30	5 39	26 6	16 51	3 10	17 53	9 34	17 4	18 54	5 32
31	6 37	7♈53	16 5	4 25	18 32	9 47	17 2	18 52	5 34

Pluto 20 Cancer all month

1931

SEPTEMBER

DAY	☉	☽	☿	♀	♂	♃	♄	♅	♆
1	7♍35	19♈40	15♍15	5♍39	19♎11	9♌59	17♑ 0	18♈51	5♍36
2	8 33	1♉29	14R21	6 54	19 51	10 12	16R58	18R49	5 38
3	9 31	13 25	13 25	8 8	20 30	10 24	16 56	18 47	5 41
4	10 30	25 32	12 27	9 23	21 9	10 36	16 55	18 45	5 43
5	11 28	7♊55	11 29	10 37	21 49	10 49	16 53	18 44	5 45
6	12 26	20 37	10 32	11 51	22 28	11 1	16 52	18 42	5 47
7	13 24	3♋44	9 37	13 6	23 7	11 13	16 50	18 40	5 49
8	14 22	17 17	8 46	14 21	23 47	11 25	16 49	18 38	5 52
9	15 21	1♌18	7 59	15 35	24 26	11 37	16 48	18 36	5 54
10	16 19	15 46	7 19	16 50	25 6	11 49	16 46	18 34	5 56
11	17 17	0♍35	6 45	18 4	25 46	12 1	16 45	18 33	5 58
12	18 16	15 39	6 19	19 19	26 26	12 13	16 44	18 31	6 0
13	19 14	0♎49	6 2	20 34	27 6	12 25	16 43	18 29	6 3
14	20 13	15 55	5 54	21 48	27 46	12 37	16 42	18 27	6 5
15	21 11	0♏49	5 D55	23 3	28 26	12 49	16 41	18 24	6 7
16	22 10	15 24	6 5	24 18	29 6	13 1	16 41	18 22	6 9
17	23 8	29 37	6 25	25 32	29 46	13 12	16 40	18 20	6 11
18	24 7	13♐25	6 54	26 47	0♏26	13 24	16 40	18 18	6 13
19	25 5	26 49	7 31	28 2	1 6	13 35	16 39	18 16	6 16
20	26 4	9♑51	8 18	29 17	1 46	13 47	16 39	18 14	6 18
21	27 2	22 34	9 13	0♎31	2 27	13 58	16 39	18 12	6 20
22	28 1	5♒ 0	10 15	1 46	3 7	14 9	16 39	18 9	6 22
23	29 0	17 13	11 23	3 1	3 48	14 20	16 D39	18 7	6 24
24	29 59	29 16	12 38	4 16	4 29	14 31	16 39	18 5	6 26
25	0♎57	11♓12	13 59	5 30	5 10	14 42	16 39	18 3	6 28
26	1 56	23 2	15 25	6 45	5 51	14 53	16 40	18 0	6 30
27	2 55	4♈50	16 55	8 0	6 32	15 4	16 40	17 58	6 32
28	3 54	16 38	18 29	9 15	7 13	15 15	16 41	17 56	6 34
29	4 53	28 28	20 6	10 29	7 54	15 26	16 41	17 53	6 36
30	5 52	10♉22	21 45	11 44	8 35	15 36	16 42	17 51	6 38

Pluto 21 Cancer all month

OCTOBER

DAY	☉	☽	☿	♀	♂	♃	♄	♅	♆
1	6♎51	22♉23	23♍26	12♎58	9♏16	15♌47	16♑43	17♈49	6♍40
2	7 50	4♊34	25 10	14 13	9 57	15 57	16 44	17R46	6 42
3	8 49	16 58	26 54	15 28	10 38	16 8	16 45	17 44	6 44
4	9 48	29 40	28 39	16 43	11 20	16 18	16 46	17 42	6 46
5	10 47	12♋42	0♎25	17 57	12 1	16 28	16 47	17 39	6 48
6	11 46	26 7	2 12	19 12	12 42	16 38	16 48	17 37	6 50
7	12 45	9♌57	3 59	20 27	13 24	16 48	16 50	17 34	6 52
8	13 44	24 12	5 45	21 42	14 5	16 57	16 51	17 32	6 54
9	14 44	8♍51	7 31	22 56	14 47	17 7	16 53	17 29	6 56
10	15 43	23 48	9 18	24 12	15 29	17 17	16 55	17 27	6 57
11	16 42	8♎57	11 4	25 27	16 10	17 26	16 57	17 25	6 59
12	17 42	24 9	12 50	26 41	16 52	17 36	16 59	17 22	7 1
13	18 41	9♏13	14 35	27 56	17 34	17 45	17 1	17 20	7 3
14	19 40	24 2	16 19	29 11	18 16	17 54	17 3	17 17	7 5
15	20 40	8♐27	18 3	0♏26	18 58	18 4	17 5	17 15	7 6
16	21 39	22 27	19 46	1 41	19 41	18 13	17 8	17 12	7 8
17	22 39	5♑58	21 28	2 56	20 23	18 22	17 10	17 10	7 10
18	23 38	19 3	23 10	4 11	21 5	18 31	17 13	17 8	7 12
19	24 38	1♒45	24 52	5 26	21 47	18 39	17 15	17 5	7 13
20	25 38	14 7	26 33	6 41	22 30	18 48	17 18	17 3	7 15
21	26 37	26 14	28 13	7 55	23 12	18 56	17 21	17 0	7 17
22	27 37	8♓10	29 52	9 10	23 55	19 4	17 24	16 58	7 18
23	28 37	20 0	1♏31	10 25	24 37	19 12	17 27	16 56	7 20
24	29 36	1♈47	3 9	11 40	25 20	19 20	17 30	16 53	7 21
25	0♏36	13 35	4 47	12 55	26 3	19 28	17 33	16 51	7 23
26	1 36	25 26	6 24	14 10	26 46	19 36	17 36	16 49	7 24
27	2 36	7♉23	8 1	15 25	27 28	19 43	17 39	16 46	7 26
28	3 36	19 26	9 37	16 40	28 11	19 51	17 43	16 44	7 27
29	4 36	1♊38	11 12	17 55	28 54	19 58	17 46	16 42	7 29
30	5 36	14 1	12 47	19 9	29 37	20 5	17 50	16 39	7 30
31	6 35	26 35	14 21	20 24	0♐20	20 12	17 53	16 37	7 31

Pluto 22 Cancer all month

1931

NOVEMBER

DAY	☉	☽	☿	♀	♂	♃	♄	♅	♆
1	7♏35	9♋23	15♏56	21♏39	1♐4	20♌19	17♑57	16♈35	7♍33
2	8 36	22 27	17 30	22 54	1 47	20 26	18 1	16℞33	7 34
3	9 36	5♌47	19 3	24 9	2 30	20 33	18 5	16 31	7 35
4	10 36	19 27	20 36	25 24	3 13	20 39	18 9	16 29	7 36
5	11 36	3♍27	22 8	26 39	3 57	20 46	18 13	16 26	7 38
6	12 36	17 48	23 40	27 54	4 40	20 52	18 17	16 24	7 39
7	13 36	2♎26	25 12	29 9	5 24	20 58	18 21	16 22	7 40
8	14 36	17 18	26 43	0♐24	6 7	21 4	18 25	16 20	7 41
9	15 37	2♏17	28 14	1 38	6 51	21 9	18 30	16 18	7 42
10	16 37	17 15	29 44	2 53	7 35	21 15	18 34	16 16	7 43
11	17 37	2♐3	1♐14	4 8	8 19	21 20	18 39	16 14	7 44
12	18 38	16 33	2 44	5 23	9 3	21 25	18 43	16 12	7 45
13	19 38	0♑39	4 13	6 38	9 47	21 30	18 48	16 10	7 46
14	20 39	14 18	5 42	7 53	10 31	21 35	18 53	16 8	7 47
15	21 39	27 29	7 10	9 8	11 15	21 40	18 58	16 6	7 48
16	22 39	10♒15	8 38	10 23	11 59	21 44	19 3	16 4	7 49
17	23 40	22 38	10 5	11 38	12 43	21 49	19 8	16 3	7 49
18	24 40	4♓45	11 32	12 52	13 27	21 53	19 13	16 1	7 50
19	25 41	16 39	12 59	14 7	14 11	21 57	19 18	15 59	7 51
20	26 42	28 27	14 25	15 22	14 56	22 1	19 23	15 57	7 51
21	27 42	10♈14	15 50	16 37	15 40	22 4	19 28	15 56	7 52
22	28 43	22 4	17 14	17 52	16 25	22 8	19 33	15 54	7 53
23	29 43	4♉0	18 38	19 7	17 9	22 11	19 38	15 53	7 53
24	0♐44	16 5	20 0	20 22	17 54	22 14	19 44	15 51	7 54
25	1 45	28 21	21 21	21 37	18 38	22 17	19 49	15 50	7 55
26	2 45	10♊49	22 41	22 52	19 23	22 20	19 55	15 48	7 55
27	3 46	23 30	23 59	24 6	20 8	22 22	20 1	15 47	7 55
28	4 47	6♋23	25 16	25 21	20 52	22 25	20 6	15 45	7 56
29	5 47	19 27	26 31	26 36	21 37	22 27	20 12	15 44	7 56
30	6 48	2♌43	27 43	27 51	22 22	22 29	20 18	15 43	7 57

Pluto 22 Cancer all month

DECEMBER

DAY	☉	☽	☿	♀	♂	♃	♄	♅	♆
1	7♐49	16♌11	28♐53	29♐6	23♐7	22♌31	20♑24	15♈42	7♍57
2	8 50	29 51	0♑0	0♑21	23 52	22 32	20 30	15℞40	7 57
3	9 51	13♍42	1 4	1 35	24 37	22 34	20 36	15 39	7 58
4	10 52	27 47	2 4	2 50	25 22	22 35	20 42	15 38	7 58
5	11 52	12♎4	2 59	4 5	26 7	22 36	20 48	15 37	7 58
6	12 53	26 32	3 50	5 20	26 52	22 37	20 54	15 36	7 58
7	13 54	11♏7	4 35	6 35	27 38	22 38	21 0	15 35	7 58
8	14 55	25 43	5 13	7 49	28 23	22 38	21 6	15 34	7 59
9	15 56	10♐14	5 44	9 4	29 8	22 38	21 12	15 33	7 59
10	16 57	24 32	6 6	10 19	29 54	22℞38	21 18	15 33	7 59
11	17 58	8♑32	6 20	11 34	0♑39	22 38	21 25	15 32	7 59
12	18 59	22 9	6℞24	12 49	1 25	22 38	21 31	15 31	7℞59
13	20 0	5♒22	6 17	14 3	2 11	22 37	21 37	15 30	7 59
14	21 1	18 10	5 59	15 18	2 56	22 36	21 44	15 30	7 59
15	22 2	0♓36	5 30	16 33	3 42	22 35	21 50	15 29	7 59
16	23 3	12 44	4 49	17 47	4 28	22 34	21 57	15 29	7 59
17	24 4	24 40	3 57	19 2	5 14	22 33	22 3	15 28	7 58
18	25 6	6♈29	2 55	20 17	5 59	22 31	22 10	15 28	7 58
19	26 7	18 16	1 44	21 31	6 45	22 30	22 16	15 27	7 58
20	27 8	0♉7	0 26	22 46	7 31	22 28	22 23	15 27	7 57
21	28 9	12 7	29♐5	24 1	8 17	22 26	22 30	15 27	7 57
22	29 10	24 20	27 42	25 15	9 3	22 23	22 36	15 27	7 57
23	0♑11	6♊47	26 21	26 30	9 49	22 21	22 43	15 26	7 56
24	1 12	19 31	25 3	27 45	10 35	22 18	22 50	15 26	7 56
25	2 13	2♋32	23 52	28 59	11 21	22 15	22 57	15 26	7 56
26	3 14	15 48	22 50	0♒14	12 7	22 12	23 4	15 D26	7 55
27	4 15	29 17	21 57	1 28	12 54	22 9	23 11	15 26	7 55
28	5 17	12♌56	21 14	2 42	13 40	22 6	23 18	15 26	7 55
29	6 18	26 43	20 41	3 57	14 26	22 2	23 25	15 27	7 54
30	7 19	10♍37	20 20	5 12	15 12	21 58	23 31	15 27	7 53
31	8 20	24 34	20 8	6 26	15 59	21 54	23 38	15 27	7 53

Pluto 21 Cancer all month

1932

JANUARY

DAY	☉	☽	☿	♀	♂	♃	♄	♅	♆
1	9♑21	8♎36	20♐ 6	7♒40	16♑45	21♌50	23♑45	15♈27	7♍52
2	10 22	22 42	20 D13	8 55	17 31	21 ℞ 46	23 52	15 28	7 ℞ 51
3	11 23	6♏51	20 29	10 9	18 18	21 41	23 59	15 28	7 51
4	12 25	21 0	20 52	11 23	19 4	21 37	24 6	15 29	7 50
5	13 26	5♐ 9	21 22	12 38	19 51	21 32	24 13	15 29	7 49
6	14 27	19 12	21 58	13 52	20 37	21 27	24 20	15 30	7 48
7	15 28	3♑ 6	22 39	15 6	21 24	21 22	24 27	15 30	7 47
8	16 29	16 46	23 26	16 21	22 10	21 17	24 35	15 31	7 46
9	17 31	0♒ 9	24 17	17 35	22 57	21 11	24 42	15 32	7 46
10	18 32	13 12	25 12	18 49	23 44	21 5	24 49	15 33	7 45
11	19 33	25 55	26 11	20 3	24 30	20 59	24 56	15 33	7 44
12	20 34	8♓20	27 12	21 17	25 17	20 53	25 3	15 34	7 43
13	21 35	20 28	28 17	22 31	26 4	20 47	25 10	15 35	7 42
14	22 36	2♈25	29 24	23 45	26 51	20 41	25 17	15 36	7 41
15	23 37	14 14	0♑33	24 59	27 38	20 35	25 24	15 37	7 39
16	24 39	26 2	1 45	26 13	28 25	20 29	25 32	15 38	7 38
17	25 40	7♉54	2 58	27 27	29 12	20 22	25 39	15 39	7 37
18	26 41	19 55	4 13	28 41	29 59	20 15	25 46	15 41	7 36
19	27 42	2♊10	5 29	29 55	0♒46	20 8	25 53	15 42	7 35
20	28 43	14 43	6 47	1♓ 8	1 33	20 1	26 0	15 43	7 34
21	29 44	27 37	8 6	2 22	2 20	19 54	26 7	15 44	7 33
22	0♒45	10♋52	9 26	3 36	3 7	19 47	26 14	15 46	7 31
23	1 46	24 27	10 48	4 49	3 54	19 40	26 21	15 47	7 30
24	2 47	8♌19	12 11	6 3	4 41	19 33	26 29	15 49	7 29
25	3 48	22 26	13 35	7 16	5 28	19 26	26 36	15 50	7 28
26	4 49	6♍40	14 59	8 30	6 15	19 18	26 43	15 52	7 26
27	5 50	20 59	16 24	9 43	7 2	19 10	26 50	15 53	7 25
28	6 51	5♎17	17 51	10 56	7 50	19 2	26 57	15 55	7 24
29	7 52	19 32	19 18	12 10	8 37	18 55	27 4	15 57	7 22
30	8 53	3♏42	20 46	13 23	9 24	18 47	27 11	15 59	7 21
31	9 54	17 45	22 15	14 36	10 11	18 39	27 18	16 0	7 19

Pluto 21 Cancer all month

FEBRUARY

DAY	☉	☽	☿	♀	♂	♃	♄	♅	♆
1	10♒55	1♐40	23♑45	15♓49	10♒59	18♌31	27♑25	16♈ 2	7♍18
2	11 56	15 27	25 15	17 2	11 46	18 ℞ 24	27 32	16 4	7 ℞ 17
3	12 56	29 4	26 46	18 15	12 33	18 16	27 39	16 6	7 15
4	13 57	12♑31	28 18	19 28	13 20	18 8	27 46	16 8	7 13
5	14 58	25 45	29 50	20 41	14 8	18 0	27 53	16 10	7 12
6	15 59	8♒45	1♒23	21 54	14 55	17 52	28 0	16 12	7 10
7	17 0	21 30	2 58	23 7	15 42	17 44	28 7	16 14	7 9
8	18 1	4♓ 1	4 33	24 19	16 29	17 36	28 14	16 16	7 7
9	19 2	16 17	6 9	25 32	17 17	17 28	28 20	16 18	7 6
10	20 2	28 22	7 45	26 44	18 4	17 20	28 27	16 20	7 4
11	21 3	10♈17	9 23	27 57	18 51	17 12	28 34	16 23	7 2
12	22 4	22 6	11 1	29 9	19 39	17 4	28 41	16 25	7 1
13	23 4	3♉54	12 39	0♈22	20 26	16 56	28 47	16 27	6 59
14	24 5	15 45	14 19	1 34	21 14	16 48	28 54	16 30	6 58
15	25 6	27 45	16 0	2 46	22 1	16 40	29 1	16 32	6 56
16	26 6	9♊58	17 42	3 58	22 48	16 32	29 7	16 34	6 54
17	27 7	22 30	19 24	5 10	23 36	16 24	29 14	16 37	6 53
18	28 7	5♋24	21 7	6 21	24 23	16 17	29 21	16 39	6 51
19	29 8	18 42	22 51	7 33	25 10	16 10	29 28	16 42	6 50
20	0♓ 8	2♌25	24 36	8 45	25 58	16 2	29 34	16 44	6 48
21	1 9	16 32	26 22	9 56	26 45	15 55	29 41	16 47	6 46
22	2 9	0♍58	28 9	11 7	27 33	15 47	29 47	16 50	6 45
23	3 10	15 37	29 57	12 19	28 20	15 40	29 53	16 52	6 43
24	4 10	0♎23	1♓46	13 30	29 7	15 33	0♒ 0	16 55	6 41
25	5 10	15 9	3 35	14 41	29 55	15 26	0 6	16 58	6 40
26	6 11	29 48	5 25	15 52	0♓42	15 19	0 12	17 0	6 38
27	7 11	14♏15	7 16	17 3	1 30	15 12	0 18	17 3	6 36
28	8 11	28 27	9 8	18 13	2 17	15 5	0 24	17 6	6 35
29	9 11	12♐23	11 2	19 24	3 5	14 58	0 30	17 9	6 33

Pluto 20 Cancer all month

1932

MARCH

DAY	☉	☽	☿	♀	♂	♃	♄	♅	♆
1	10♓12	26♐ 1	12♓57	20♈35	3♓52	14♌51	0♒36	17♈12	6♍31
2	11 12	9♑22	14 52	21 45	4 39	14R45	0 42	17 15	6R30
3	12 12	22 28	16 47	22 55	5 27	14 39	0 48	17 18	6 28
4	13 12	5♒20	18 43	24 6	6 14	14 32	0 54	17 21	6 26
5	14 12	17 57	20 39	25 16	7 1	14 26	1 0	17 24	6 25
6	15 12	0♓23	22 35	26 25	7 49	14 20	1 6	17 27	6 23
7	16 13	12 38	24 31	27 35	8 36	14 14	1 12	17 30	6 21
8	17 13	24 43	26 27	28 45	9 24	14 8	1 17	17 33	6 20
9	18 13	6♈40	28 23	29 54	10 11	14 3	1 23	17 36	6 18
10	19 12	18 32	0♈18	1♉ 3	10 58	13 58	1 29	17 39	6 16
11	20 12	0♉20	2 11	2 12	11 46	13 53	1 34	17 42	6 15
12	21 12	12 8	4 3	3 21	12 33	13 47	1 40	17 45	6 13
13	22 12	24 0	5 53	4 30	13 20	13 42	1 45	17 48	6 12
14	23 12	6♊ 0	7 40	5 39	14 7	13 38	1 50	17 51	6 10
15	24 12	18 11	9 25	6 48	14 54	13 33	1 56	17 55	6 8
16	25 12	0♋39	11 6	7 56	15 41	13 29	2 1	17 58	6 7
17	26 11	13 27	12 43	9 4	16 28	13 24	2 6	18 1	6 5
18	27 11	26 40	14 16	10 12	17 15	13 20	2 11	18 4	6 4
19	28 11	10♌19	15 45	11 20	18 3	13 16	2 16	18 8	6 2
20	29 10	24 25	17 8	12 27	18 50	13 12	2 21	18 11	6 0
21	0♈10	8♍56	18 25	13 35	19 37	13 9	2 26	18 14	5 59
22	1 9	23 47	19 36	14 42	20 24	13 5	1 31	18 17	5 57
23	2 9	8♎50	20 41	15 49	21 11	13 2	2 36	18 21	5 56
24	3 8	23 58	21 39	16 56	21 58	12 59	2 40	18 24	5 54
25	4 8	9♏ 1	22 30	18 2	22 45	12 56	2 45	18 27	5 53
26	5 7	23 51	23 14	19 9	23 32	12 54	2 49	18 31	5 52
27	6 6	8♐21	23 50	20 15	24 19	12 51	2 54	18 34	5 50
28	7 6	22 27	24 19	21 21	25 5	12 49	2 58	18 37	5 49
29	8 5	6♑ 9	24 41	22 26	25 52	12 47	3 2	18 41	5 47
30	9 4	19 27	24 55	23 32	26 39	12 45	3 6	18 44	5 46
31	10 3	2♒24	25 2	24 37	27 26	12 43	3 11	18 48	5 45

Pluto 20 Cancer all month

APRIL

DAY	☉	☽	☿	♀	♂	♃	♄	♅	♆
1	11♈ 3	15♒ 2	25♈ 2	25♉42	28♓13	12♌42	3♒15	18♈51	5♍44
2	12 2	27 24	24R54	26 47	29 0	12R40	3 19	18 55	5R42
3	13 1	9♓35	24 40	27 52	29 47	12 39	3 23	18 58	5 41
4	14 0	21 36	24 19	28 56	0♈33	12 38	3 27	19 1	5 40
5	14 59	3♈31	23 54	0♊ 0	1 20	12 37	3 30	19 5	5 39
6	15 58	15 22	23 23	1 3	2 6	12 37	3 34	19 8	5 37
7	16 57	27 11	22 46	2 7	2 53	12 36	3 37	19 12	5 36
8	17 56	9♉ 0	22 6	3 10	3 40	12 36	3 41	19 15	5 35
9	18 55	20 51	21 25	4 12	4 26	12D36	3 44	19 18	5 34
10	19 54	2♊46	20 40	5 15	5 13	12 36	3 47	19 22	5 33
11	20 53	14 49	19 55	6 17	5 59	12 37	3 50	19 25	5 32
12	21 52	27 1	19 10	7 18	6 46	12 37	3 54	19 29	5 31
13	22 51	9♋28	18 25	8 19	7 32	12 38	3 57	19 32	5 30
14	23 49	22 13	17 42	9 20	8 18	12 39	4 0	19 36	5 29
15	24 48	5♌18	17 0	10 21	9 4	12 40	4 3	19 39	5 28
16	25 47	18 48	16 21	11 21	9 51	12 41	4 6	19 42	5 27
17	26 46	2♍44	15 46	12 21	10 37	12 43	4 8	19 46	5 26
18	27 44	17 6	15 15	13 20	11 23	12 44	4 11	19 49	5 25
19	28 43	1♎52	14 48	14 19	12 9	12 46	4 13	19 53	5 24
20	29 41	16 57	14 25	15 18	12 56	12 48	4 16	19 56	5 23
21	0♉40	2♏11	14 8	16 16	13 42	12 51	4 18	20 0	5 23
22	1 38	17 27	13 55	17 14	14 28	12 53	4 20	20 3	5 22
23	2 37	2♐31	13 47	18 11	15 14	12 55	4 22	20 6	5 21
24	3 35	17 17	13D44	19 7	16 0	12 58	4 24	20 10	5 20
25	4 34	1♑37	13 47	20 4	16 46	13 1	4 26	20 13	5 19
26	5 32	15 29	13 54	20 59	17 32	13 4	4 28	20 16	5 19
27	6 30	28 52	14 6	21 54	18 18	13 7	4 30	20 20	5 18
28	7 29	11♒49	14 23	22 49	19 4	13 11	4 32	20 23	5 17
29	8 27	24 23	14 44	23 42	19 49	13 14	4 33	20 26	5 17
30	9 25	6♓39	15 10	24 35	20 35	13 18	4 35	20 30	5 16

Pluto 19 Cancer all month

1932

MAY

DAY	☉	☽	☿	♀	♂	♃	♄	♅	♆
1	10 ♉23	18 ♓42	15♈40	25 ♊28	21♈21	13♌22	4♒36	20♈33	5♍16
2	11 22	0♈36	16 14	26 20	22 6	13 26	4 38	20 36	5 ℞ 15
3	12 20	12 26	16 52	27 11	22 52	13 30	4 39	20 40	5 15
4	13 18	24 13	17 34	28 2	23 37	13 35	4 40	20 43	5 14
5	14 16	6 ♉ 2	18 20	28 52	24 23	13 40	4 41	20 46	5 14
6	15 14	17 53	19 9	29 41	25 8	13 44	4 42	20 49	5 14
7	16 12	29 50	20 1	0♋30	25 54	13 49	4 42	20 53	5 13
8	17 10	11 ♊53	20 57	1 17	26 39	13 54	4 43	20 56	5 13
9	18 8	24 4	21 56	2 4	27 24	13 59	4 44	20 59	5 13
10	19 6	6♋25	22 58	2 50	28 9	14 5	4 44	21 2	5 12
11	20 4	18 57	24 2	3 35	28 54	14 11	4 45	21 5	5 12
12	21 2	1♌44	25 9	4 19	29 39	14 16	4 45	21 8	5 12
13	22 0	14 47	26 19	5 2	0 ♉24	14 22	4 45	21 11	5 12
14	22 58	28 10	27 32	5 44	1 9	14 28	4 45	21 14	5 12
15	23 56	11 ♍56	28 47	6 25	1 54	14 34	4 ℞ 45	21 17	5 12
16	24 54	26 5	0 ♉ 4	7 5	2 39	14 40	4 45	21 20	5 12
17	25 52	10♎36	1 25	7 44	3 24	14 47	4 45	21 23	5 D12
18	26 49	25 28	2 48	8 22	4 9	14 53	4 45	21 26	5 12
19	27 47	10 ♏33	4 12	8 58	4 54	15 0	4 45	21 29	5 12
20	28 45	25 43	5 40	9 33	5 39	15 7	4 44	21 32	5 12
21	29 42	10 ♐48	7 9	10 7	6 24	15 14	4 44	21 35	5 12
22	0 ♊40	25 37	8 41	10 39	7 8	15 21	4 43	21 38	5 12
23	1 38	10 ♑ 4	10 16	11 10	7 53	15 29	4 42	21 41	5 12
24	2 35	24 2	11 53	11 40	8 37	15 36	4 41	21 44	5 12
25	3 33	7♒31	13 32	12 8	9 22	15 43	4 40	21 46	5 13
26	4 31	20 32	15 13	12 34	10 6	15 51	4 39	21 49	5 13
27	5 28	3 ♓ 8	16 57	12 59	10 51	15 58	4 38	21 51	5 13
28	6 26	15 25	18 43	13 22	11 35	16 6	4 37	21 54	5 14
29	7 23	27 27	20 31	13 43	12 19	16 14	4 36	21 57	5 14
30	8 21	9♈19	22 22	14 2	13 3	16 22	4 34	21 59	5 14
31	9 18	21 7	24 14	14 20	13 47	16 30	4 33	22 2	5 15

Pluto 20 Cancer all month

JUNE

DAY	☉	☽	☿	♀	♂	♃	♄	♅	♆
	° ′	° ′	° ′	° ′	° ′	° ′	° ′	° ′	° ′
1	10 ♊16	2 ♉55	26 ♉ 9	14♋36	14 ♉31	16♌39	4♒31	22♈ 5	5♍16
2	11 13	14 46	28 7	14 49	15 15	16 48	4 ℞ 29	22 7	5 16
3	12 11	26 43	0 ♊ 6	15 1	15 59	16 56	4 28	22 10	5 17
4	13 8	8 ♊49	2 7	15 10	16 43	17 5	4 26	22 12	5 17
5	14 6	21 3	4 10	15 17	17 27	17 14	4 24	22 15	5 18
6	15 3	3♋27	6 15	15 22	18 11	17 23	4 22	22 17	5 19
7	16 1	16 2	8 21	15 25	18 55	17 32	4 20	22 19	5 19
8	16 58	28 48	10 29	15 ℞ 26	19 38	17 41	4 17	22 22	5 20
9	17 55	11♌45	12 39	15 25	20 22	17 50	4 15	22 24	5 21
10	18 53	24 56	14 49	15 20	21 6	17 59	4 13	22 26	5 21
11	19 50	8 ♍22	17 0	15 13	21 49	18 9	4 10	22 28	5 22
12	20 47	22 3	19 12	15 4	22 33	18 18	4 8	22 30	5 23
13	21 45	6♎ 3	21 24	14 53	23 16	18 28	4 5	22 33	5 24
14	22 42	20 20	23 36	14 39	23 59	18 38	4 2	22 35	5 25
15	23 39	4 ♏53	25 47	14 23	24 43	18 47	4 0	22 37	5 26
16	24 37	19 38	27 58	14 4	25 26	18 57	3 57	22 39	5 27
17	25 34	4 ♐29	0♋ 9	13 43	26 9	19 7	3 54	22 41	5 28
18	26 31	19 18	2 18	13 20	26 52	19 17	3 51	22 43	5 29
19	27 28	3 ♑56	4 26	12 55	27 35	19 27	3 48	22 44	5 30
20	28 26	18 15	6 33	12 28	28 18	19 38	3 44	22 46	5 31
21	29 23	2♒11	8 38	11 58	29 1	19 48	3 41	22 48	5 32
22	0♋20	15 40	10 41	11 28	29 44	19 58	3 38	22 50	5 33
23	1 17	28 42	12 43	10 56	0 ♊27	20 9	3 35	22 52	5 34
24	2 14	11 ♓21	14 42	10 22	1 9	20 19	3 31	22 53	5 35
25	3 12	23 40	16 39	9 47	1 52	20 30	3 28	22 55	5 36
26	4 9	5♈43	18 35	9 11	2 35	20 41	3 24	22 57	5 38
27	5 6	17 37	20 29	8 34	3 17	20 51	3 21	22 58	5 39
28	6 3	29 27	22 21	7 57	4 0	21 2	3 17	23 0	5 40
29	7 1	11 ♉17	24 10	7 20	4 42	21 13	3 13	23 1	5 41
30	7 58	23 12	25 57	6 42	5 24	21 24	3 9	23 3	5 43

Pluto 20 Cancer all month

1932

JULY

DAY	☉	☽	☿	♀	♂	♃	♄	♅	♆
	° ′	° ′	° ′	° ′	° ′	° ′	° ′	° ′	° ′
1	8♋55	5♊15	27♋42	6♋ 5	6♊ 7	21♌35	3♒ 6	23♈ 4	5♍44
2	9 52	17 30	29 25	5℞28	6 49	21 47	3℞ 2	23 5	5 46
3	10 49	29 57	1♌ 6	4 52	7 31	21 58	2 58	23 6	5 47
4	11 47	12♋37	2 45	4 17	8 13	22 9	2 54	23 8	5 49
5	12 44	25 30	4 21	3 42	8 55	22 21	2 50	23 9	5 50
6	13 41	8♌35	5 55	3 9	9 37	22 32	2 46	23 10	5 52
7	14 38	21 52	7 28	2 38	10 19	22 44	2 42	23 11	5 53
8	15 36	5♍19	8 58	2 9	11 1	22 55	2 38	23 12	5 55
9	16 33	18 58	10 26	1 40	11 43	23 7	2 34	23 13	5 56
10	17 30	2♎46	11 52	1 13	12 24	23 18	2 29	23 14	5 58.
11	18 27	16 45	13 15	0 49	13 6	23 30	2 25	23 15	5 59
12	19 24	0♏55	14 36	0 28	13 48	23 42	2 21	23 16	6 1
13	20 22	15 13	15 55	0 8	14 29	23 54	2 17	23 17	6 3
14	21 19	29 37	17 11	29♊50	15 11	24 6	2 12	23 18	6 5
15	22 16	14♐ 4	18 25	29 35	15 52	24 18	2 8	23 18	6 6
16	23 13	28 27	19 36	29 23	16 33	24 30	2 4	23 19	6 8
17	24 10	12♑42	20 45	29 12	17 15	24 42	1 59	23 20	6 10
18	25 8	26 42	21 52	29 4	17 56	24 54	1 55	23 20	6 11
19	26 5	10♒23	22 55	28 59	18 37	25 6	1 50	23 21	6 13
20	27 2	23 42	23 56	28 56	19 18	25 18	1 46	23 21	6 15
21	27 59	6♓40	24 53	28 55	19 59	25 30	1 41	23 22	6 17
22	28 57	19 17	25 47	28 D56	20 40	25 43	1 37	23 22	6 19
23	29 54	1♈35	26 39	29 0	21 21	25 55	1 33	23 22	6 21
24	0♌51	13 40	27 28	29 6	22 2	26 7	1 29	23 23	6 22
25	1 49	25 36	28 13	29 14	22 43	26 20	1 24	23 23	6 24
26	2 46	7♉27	28 54	29 25	23 23	26 32	1 20	23 23	6 26
27	3 43	19 19	29 31	29 37	24 4	26 45	1 15	23 23	6 28
28	4 41	1♊17	0♍ 4	29 52	24 45	26 57	1 11	23 23	6 30
29	5 38	13 25	0 34	0♋ 8	25 25	27 10	1 6	23 23	6 32
30	6 35	25 46	0 59	0 26	26 6	27 22	1 1	23℞23	6 34
31	7 33	8♋23	1 19	0 46	26 46	27 35	0 57	23 23	6 36

Pluto 21 Cancer all month

AUGUST

DAY	☉	☽	☿	♀	♂	♃	♄	♅	♆
	° ′	° ′	° ′	° ′	° ′	° ′	° ′	° ′	° ′
1	8♌30	21♋16	1♍35	1♋ 8	27♊26	27♌48	0♒53	23♈23	6♍38
2	9 28	4♌27	1 47	1 32	28 7	28 0	0℞48	23℞23	6 40
3	10 25	17 54	1 53	1 58	28 47	28 13	0 44	23 23	6 42
4	11 23	1♍35	1℞54	2 24	29 27	28 26	0 40	23 23	6 44
5	12 20	15 27	1 50	2 52	0♋ 7	28 39	0 36	23 22	6 46
6	13 18	29 27	1 41	3 22	0 47	28 51	0 31	23 22	6 48
7	14 15	13♎34	1 26	3 54	1 26	29 4	0 27	23 22	6 50
8	15 13	27 44	1 6	4 26	2 6	29 17	0 23	23 21	6 52
9	16 10	11♏57	0 41	5 0	2 46	29 30	0 19	23 21	6 55
10	17 8	26 8	0 11	5 36	3 26	29 43	0 14	23 20	6 57
11	18 5	10♐18	29♌35	6 12	4 5	29 56	0 10	23 19	6 59
12	19 3	14 23	28 56	6 50	4 45	0♍ 9	0 6	23 19	7 1
13	20 0	8♑20	28 13	7 28	5 25	0 22	0 2	23 18	7 3
14	20 58	22 7	27 27	8 8	6 4	0 35	29♑58	23 17	7 5
15	21 56	5♒41	26 38	8 49	6 44	0 48	29 54	23 17	7 7
16	22 53	19 0	25 48	9 31	7 23	1 1	29 50	23 16	7 10
17	23 51	2♓ 2	24 57	10 14	8 2	1 14	29 46	23 15	7 12
18	24 49	14 47	24 6	10 58	8 41	1 27	29 42	23 14	7 14
19	25 46	27 17	23 16	11 43	9 20	1 40	29 39	23 13	7 16
20	26 44	9♈31	22 28	12 29	9 59	1 53	29 35	23 12	7 18
21	27 42	21 35	21 44	13 16	10 38	2 6	29 31	23 11	7 21
22	28 40	3♉30	21 4	14 3	11 18	2 19	29 28	23 10	7 23
23	29 38	15 22	20 29	14 51	11 56	2 32	29 24	23 9	7 25
24	0♍35	27 14	20 0	15 40	12 34	2 45	29 21	23 8	7 27
25	1 33	9♊12	19 38	16 30	13 13	2 58	29 17	23 7	7 29
26	2 31	21 21	19 23	17 21	13 51	3 11	29 14	23 5	7 31
27	3 29	3♋43	19 16	18 12	14 30	3 24	29 10	23 4	7 34
28	4 27	16 24	19 D17	19 4	15 8	3 37	29 7	23 3	7 36
29	5 25	29 25	19 26	19 56	15 46	3 50	29 4	23 1	7 38
30	6 23	2♌48	19 43	20 49	16 25	4 4	29 1	23 0	7 40
31	7 21	26 32	20 9	21 43	17 3	4 17	28 58	22 58	7 43

Pluto 22 Cancer all month

1932

SEPTEMBER

DAY	☉	☽	☿	♀	♂	♃	♄	♅	♆
	° ′	° ′	° ′	° ′	° ′	° ′	° ′	° ′	° ′
1	8♍19	10♍35	20♌42	22♋37	17♋41	4♍30	28♑55	22♈57	7♍45
2	9 17	24 52	21 24	23 33	18 19	4 43	28℞52	22℞55	7 47
3	10 16	9♎20	22 14	24 28	18 57	4 56	28 49	22 54	7 49
4	11 14	23 53	23 11	25 24	19 35	5 9	28 47	22 52	7 51
5	12 12	8♏24	24 15	26 20	20 13	5 22	28 44	22 51	7 54
6	13 10	22 50	25 25	27 17	20 51	5 35	28 42	22 49	7 56
7	14 8	7♐7	26 42	28 14	21 28	5 48	28 39	22 47	7 58
8	15 7	21 12	28 5	29 12	22 6	6 1	28 37	22 45	8 0
9	16 5	5♑4	29 32	0♌11	22 43	6 14	28 35	22 43	8 3
10	17 3	18 41	1♍5	1 10	23 20	6 27	28 33	22 42	8 5
11	18 2	2♒4	2 42	2 9	23 58	6 40	28 30	22 40	8 7
12	19 0	15 13	4 21	3 8	24 35	6 52	28 28	22 38	8 9
13	19 58	28 8	6 4	4 8	25 12	7 5	28 26	22 36	8 12
14	20 57	10♓49	7 50	5 8	25 49	7 18	28 24	22 34	8 14
15	21 55	23 19	9 37	6 9	26 26	7 31	28 22	22 32	8 16
16	22 54	5♈36	11 26	7 10	27 3	7 44	28 21	22 30	8 18
17	23 52	17 44	13 16	8 12	27 40	7 57	28 19	22 28	8 20
18	24 51	29 43	15 6	9 14	28 17	8 10	28 18	22 26	8 22
19	25 49	11♉37	16 58	10 16	28 54	8 23	28 16	22 24	8 24
20	26 48	23 28	18 50	11 18	29 30	8 35	28 15	22 22	8 26
21	27 47	5♊20	20 41	12 21	0♌7	8 48	28 14	22 20	8 29
22	28 45	17 17	22 33	13 24	0 43	9 1	28 13	22 17	8 31
23	29 44	29 23	24 24	14 28	1 19	9 13	28 12	22 15	8 33
24	0♎43	11♋43	26 15	15 31	1 55	9 26	28 11	22 13	8 35
25	1 42	24 21	28 5	16 35	2 31	9 38	28 10	22 11	8 37
26	2 41	7♌21	29 55	17 40	3 7	9 51	28 9	22 9	8 39
27	3 39	20 45	1♎44	18 44	3 43	10 3	28 9	22 6	8 41
28	4 38	4♍36	3 32	19 49	4 19	10 16	28 8	22 4	8 43
29	5 37	18 51	5 20	20 54	4 55	10 28	28 8	22 2	8 45
30	6 36	3♎27	7 6	22 0	5 30	10 40	28 8	21 59	8 47

Pluto 22 Cancer all month

OCTOBER

DAY	☉	☽	☿	♀	♂	♃	♄	♅	♆
	° ′	° ′	° ′	° ′	° ′	° ′	° ′	° ′	° ′
1	7♎35	18♎19	8♎52	23♌5	6♌5	10♍53	28♑7	8♍49	21♈57
2	8 34	3♏17	10 37	24 11	6 41	11 5	28℞7	8 51	21℞55
3	9 34	18 15	12 20	25 17	7 16	11 17	28D 7	8 53	21 52
4	10 33	3♐2	14 5	26 24	7 51	11 29	28 7	8 55	21 50
5	11 32	17 34	15 47	27 30	8 27	11 42	28 8	8 57	21 48
6	12 31	1♑45	17 28	28 37	9 2	11 54	28 8	8 59	21 45
7	13 30	15 35	19 9	29 44	9 36	12 6	28 8	9 1	21 43
8	14 29	29 3	20 49	0♍51	10 11	12 18	28 8	9 3	21 41
9	15 29	12♒11	22 28	1 59	10 46	12 30	28 9	9 5	21 38
10	16 28	25 1	24 7	3 6	11 20	12 42	28 9	9 7	21 36
11	17 27	7♓37	25 45	4 14	11 55	12 54	28 10	9 9	21 33
12	18 27	20 0	27 21	5 22	12 29	13 6	28 11	9 11	21 31
13	19 26	2♈14	28 57	6 30	13 3	13 17	28 12	9 12	21 28
14	20 26	14 20	0♏33	7 39	13 38	13 29	28 13	9 14	21 26
15	21 25	26 19	2 8	8 47	14 12	13 40	28 14	9 16	21 23
16	22 24	8♉14	3 43	9 56	14 45	13 52	28 15	9 18	21 21
17	23 24	20 6	5 16	11 5	15 19	14 3	28 17	9 19	21 18
18	24 24	1♊57	6 49	12 14	15 52	14 15	28 18	9 21	21 16
19	25 23	13 50	8 22	13 23	16 26	14 26	28 20	9 23	21 14
20	26 23	25 46	9 53	14 33	16 59	14 37	28 22	9 24	21 11
21	27 22	7♋51	11 24	15 42	17 32	14 49	28 23	9 26	21 9
22	28 22	20 7	12 55	16 52	18 5	15 0	28 25	9 28	21 6
23	29 22	2♌40	14 25	18 2	18 38	15 11	28 27	9 29	21 4
24	0♏22	15 33	15 54	19 12	19 11	15 22	28 29	9 31	21 2
25	1 22	28 51	17 23	20 22	19 44	15 33	28 31	9 32	20 59
26	2 21	12♍36	18 52	21 32	20 16	15 43	28 34	9 34	20 57
27	3 21	26 49	20 19	22 43	20 49	15 54	28 36	9 35	20 55
28	4 21	11♎29	21 46	23 53	21 21	16 5	28 38	9 37	20 52
29	5 21	26 31	23 12	25 4	21 53	16 15	28 41	9 39	20 50
30	6 21	11♏45	24 37	26 15	22 25	16 26	28 43	9 40	20 48
31	7 21	27 2	26 2	27 26	22 56	16 36	28 46	9 41	20 45

Pluto 23 Cancer all month

1932

NOVEMBER

DAY	☉	☽	☿	♀	♂	♃	♄	♅	♆
	° ′	° ′	° ′	° ′	° ′	° ′	° ′	° ′	° ′
1	8♏21	12♐11	27♏27	28♍37	23♌28	16♍46	28♑49	20♈43	9♍42
2	9 21	27 1	28 50	29 48	23 59	16 56	28 52	20℞41	9 44
3	10 22	11♑26	0♐13	1♎0	24 31	17 6	28 55	20 38	9 45
4	11 22	25 24	1 34	2 11	25 2	17 16	28 58	20 36	9 46
5	12 22	8♒54	2 54	3 23	25 33	17 26	29 1	20 34	9 47
6	13 22	21 58	4 13	4 34	26 3	17 36	29 5	20 32	9 49
7	14 22	4♓40	5 32	5 46	26 34	17 45	29 8	20 30	9 50
8	15 23	17 5	6 49	6 58	27 5	17 55	29 12	20 27	9 51
9	16 23	29 17	8 4	8 10	27 35	18 4	29 15	20 25	9 52
10	17 23	11♈20	9 17	9 22	28 5	18 14	29 19	20 23	9 53
11	18 23	23 17	10 29	10 34	28 35	18 23	29 22	20 21	9 54
12	19 24	5♉10	11 39	11 46	29 5	18 32	29 26	20 19	9 55
13	20 24	17 2	12 47	12 59	29 34	18 41	29 30	20 17	9 56
14	21 25	28 54	13 52	14 11	0♍3	18 50	29 34	20 15	9 57
15	22 25	10♊48	14 53	15 23	0 32	18 59	29 38	20 13	9 58
16	23 25	22 44	15 51	16 36	1 1	19 8	29 42	20 11	9 59
17	24 26	4♋45	16 46	17 49	1 30	19 17	29 46	20 9	10 0
18	25 26	16 53	17 37	19 2	1 58	19 25	29 51	20 7	10 1
19	26 27	29 11	18 22	20 14	2 27	19 34	29 55	20 5	10 2
20	27 28	11♌41	19 2	21 27	2 55	19 42	0♒0	20 4	10 3
21	28 28	24 29	19 36	22 40	3 23	19 50	0 4	20 2	10 3
22	29 29	7♍39	20 3	23 53	3 51	19 58	0 9	20 0	10 4
23	0♐29	21 13	20 22	25 6	4 17	20 5	0 13	19 58	10 5
24	1 30	5♎14	20 33	26 20	4 44	20 13	0 18	19 57	10 5
25	2 31	19 43	20℞35	27 33	5 11	20 21	0 23	19 55	10 6
26	3 32	4♏36	20 27	28 46	5 38	20 28	0 28	19 54	10 6
27	4 32	19 48	20 8	0♏0	6 5	20 36	0 33	19 52	10 7
28	5 33	5♐8	19 39	1 13	6 31	20 43	0 38	19 51	10 7
29	6 34	20 24	18 58	2 27	6 57	20 50	0 43	19 49	10 8
30	7 35	5♑26	18 7	3 41	7 23	20 57	0 48	19 48	10 8

Pluto 23 Cancer all month

DECEMBER

DAY	☉	☽	☿	♀	♂	♃	♄	♅	♆
	° ′	° ′	° ′	° ′	° ′	° ′	° ′	° ′	° ′
1	8♐36	20♑4	17♐6	4♏54	7♍48	21♍3	0♒53	19♈46	10♍9
2	9 36	4♒12	15℞57	6 8	8 13	21 10	0 58	19℞45	10 9
3	10 37	17 51	14 40	7 22	8 38	21 16	1 3	19 44	10 9
4	11 38	1♓0	13 19	8 36	9 2	21 23	1 9	19 42	10 10
5	12 39	13 45	11 56	9 50	9 26	21 29	1 14	19 41	10 10
6	13 40	26 8	10 34	11 4	9 50	21 35	1 20	19 40	10 10
7	14 41	8♈17	9 16	12 17	10 14	21 41	1 26	19 39	10 10
8	15 42	20 15	8 4	13 31	10 37	21 46	1 31	19 38	10 11
9	16 43	2♉8	7 0	14 45	11 0	21 52	1 37	19 37	10 11
10	17 44	13 58	6 6	15 59	11 22	21 57	1 43	19 36	10 11
11	18 45	25 49	5 23	17 14	11 44	22 2	1 49	19 35	10 11
12	19 46	7♊44	4 51	18 28	12 6	22 7	1 54	19 34	10 11
13	20 47	19 43	4 30	19 42	12 28	22 12	2 0	19 33	10℞11
14	21 48	1♋47	4 20	20 56	12 50	22 17	2 6	19 32	10 11
15	22 49	13 58	4 D20	22 10	13 10	22 21	2 12	19 32	10 11
16	23 50	26 16	4 30	23 25	13 31	22 26	2 18	19 31	10 11
17	24 51	8♌44	4 49	24 39	13 51	22 30	2 25	19 30	10 11
18	25 52	21 22	5 17	25 53	14 10	22 34	2 31	19 30	10 10
19	26 53	4♍14	5 51	27 8	14 30	22 38	2 37	19 29	10 10
20	27 54	17 22	6 32	28 22	14 49	22 41	2 43	19 29	10 10
21	28 55	0♎50	7 18	29 36	15 7	22 45	2 50	19 28	10 10
22	29 56	14 40	8 9	0♐51	15 25	22 48	2 56	19 28	10 10
23	0♑57	28 52	9 5	2 5	15 43	22 51	3 2	19 28	10 10
24	1 59	13♏27	10 6	3 20	16 0	22 54	3 9	19 27	10 9
25	3 0	28 19	11 9	4 34	16 17	22 57	3 15	19 27	10 9
26	4 1	13♐21	12 16	5 49	16 33	22 59	3 22	19 27	10 8
27	5 2	28 26	13 25	7 4	16 49	23 2	3 29	19 27	10 8
28	6 3	13♑21	14 36	8 18	17 4	23 4	3 35	19 27	10 7
29	7 4	27 58	15 50	9 33	17 19	23 6	3 42	19 D27	10 7
30	8 6	12♒11	17 6	10 48	17 34	23 8	3 49	19 27	10 6
31	9 7	25 56	18 23	12 3	17 47	23 9	3 56	19 27	10 6

Pluto 23 Cancer all month

1933

JANUARY

Day	☉	☽	☿	♀	♂	♃	♄	♅	♆
	° ′	° ′	° ′	° ′	° ′	° ′	° ′	° ′	° ′
1	10♑ 8	9♓12	19♐41	13♐18	18♍ 0	23♍11	4♒ 3	19♈27	10♍ 5
2	11 9	22 3	21 1	14 32	18 13	23 12	4 9	19 27	10℞ 4
3	12 10	4♈31	22 23	15 46	18 25	23 13	4 16	19 27	10 4
4	13 11	16 43	23 45	17 1	18 36	23 14	4 23	19 28	10 3
5	14 13	28 42	25 8	18 16	18 47	23 15	4 30	19 28	10 2
6	15 14	10♉35	26 32	19 31	18 57	23 15	4 37	19 29	10 1
7	16 15	22 26	27 57	20 45	19 7	23 16	4 43	19 29	10 1
8	17 16	4♊18	29 23	22 0	19 17	23 16	4 50	19 29	10 0
9	18 17	16 15	0♑49	23 15	19 25	23℞16	4 57	19 30	9 59
10	19 18	28 20	2 17	24 30	19 33	23 16	5 4	19 31	9 58
11	20 19	10♋34	3 45	25 45	19 41	23 15	5 11	19 31	9 57
12	21 21	22 59	5 13	27 0	19 47	23 15	5 18	19 32	9 56
13	22 22	5♌33	6 42	28 14	19 53	23 14	5 25	19 33	9 55
14	23 23	18 19	8 12	29 29	19 59	23 13	5 32	19 33	9 54
15	24 24	1♍15	9 42	0♑44	20 4	23 11	5 39	19 34	9 53
16	25 25	14 23	11 13	1 59	20 8	23 10	5 46	19 35	9 52
17	26 26	27 44	12 44	3 14	20 11	23 8	5 53	19 36	9 51
18	27 27	11♎18	14 16	4 29	20 14	23 6	6 1	19 37	9 50
19	28 28	25 6	15 48	5 44	20 16	23 4	6 8	19 38	9 49
20	29 29	9♏ 9	17 21	6 59	20 17	23 2	6 15	19 39	9 48
21	0♒30	23 26	18 55	8 13	20℞17	23 0	6 22	19 41	9 46
22	1 31	7♐55	20 29	9 28	20 17	22 57	6 29	19 42	9 45
23	2 32	22 30	22 3	10 43	20 16	22 55	6 36	19 43	9 44
24	3 33	7♑ 7	23 39	11 58	20 14	22 52	6 43	19 44	9 43
25	4 35	21 39	25 15	13 13	20 11	22 49	6 50	19 46	9 41
26	5 36	5♒58	26 51	14 28	20 8	22 45	6 58	19 47	9 40
27	6 37	20 0	28 28	15 43	20 4	22 42	7 5	19 49	9 39
28	7 38	3♓39	0♒ 6	16 58	19 59	22 38	7 12	19 50	9 37
29	8 39	16 55	1 44	18 13	19 53	22 34	7 19	19 52	9 36
30	9 39	29 49	3 24	19 28	19 46	22 30	7 27	19 53	9 35
31	10 40	12♈22	5 4	20 43	19 39	22 26	7 34	19 55	9 33

Pluto 22 Cancer all month

FEBRUARY

Day	☉	☽	☿	♀	♂	♃	♄	♅	♆
	° ′	° ′	° ′	° ′	° ′	° ′	° ′	° ′	° ′
1	11♒41	24♈37	6♒44	21♑58	19♍31	22♍21	7♒41	19♈56	9♍32
2	12 42	6♉40	8 25	23 13	19℞22	22℞17	7 48	19 58	9℞30
3	13 43	18 35	10 7	24 28	19 12	22 12	7 55	20 0	9 29
4	14 44	0♊27	11 50	25 43	19 1	22 8	8 2	20 2	9 27
5	15 45	12 21	13 33	26 58	18 50	22 3	8 9	20 4	9 26
6	16 46	24 20	15 17	28 13	18 38	21 58	8 16	20 6	9 24
7	17 46	6♋30	17 2	29 27	18 25	21 52	8 24	20 8	9 23
8	18 47	18 51	18 48	0♒42	18 11	21 47	8 31	20 9	9 21
9	19 48	1♌27	20 34	1 57	17 57	21 41	8 38	20 11	9 20
10	20 48	14 18	22 22	3 12	17 42	21 36	8 45	20 14	9 18
11	21 49	27 24	24 10	4 27	17 26	21 30	8 52	20 16	9 17
12	22 50	10♍44	25 58	5 42	17 10	21 24	8 59	20 18	9 15
13	23 50	24 18	27 47	6 57	16 52	21 18	9 6	20 20	9 14
14	24 51	8♎ 3	29 37	8 12	16 34	21 11	9 13	20 22	9 12
15	25 52	21 58	1♓28	9 27	16 16	21 5	9 20	20 25	9 10
16	26 52	6♏ 0	3 18	10 42	15 57	20 58	9 27	20 27	9 9
17	27 53	20 7	5 9	11 57	15 37	20 51	9 34	20 29	9 7
18	28 53	4♐19	7 1	13 11	15 17	20 45	9 41	20 32	9 5
19	29 54	18 32	8 53	14 26	14 57	20 38	9 48	20 34	9 4
20	0♓54	2♑44	10 44	15 41	14 36	20 31	9 55	20 37	9 2
21	1 55	16 52	12 34	16 56	14 14	20 24	10 2	20 39	9 1
22	2 55	0♒53	14 24	18 11	13 52	20 17	10 9	20 42	8 59
23	3 56	14 44	16 14	19 26	13 30	20 10	10 15	20 44	8 57
24	4 56	28 21	18 2	20 41	13 7	20 3	10 22	20 47	8 56
25	5 56	11♓43	19 48	21 56	12 44	19 55	10 29	20 49	8 54
26	6 57	24 48	21 32	23 11	12 21	19 48	10 36	20 52	8 52
27	7 57	7♈35	23 13	24 25	11 57	19 40	10 42	20 55	8 51
28	8 57	20 6	24 52	25 40	11 33	19 33	10 49	20 57	8 49

Pluto 21 Cancer all month

1933

MARCH

Day	☉ ° ′	☽ ° ′	☿ ° ′	♀ ° ′	♂ ° ′	♃ ° ′	♄ ° ′	♅ ° ′	♆ ° ′
1	9♓57	2♉22	26♓27	26♒55	11♍ 9	19♍25	10♒56	21♈ 0	8♍47
2	10 58	14 27	27 58	28 10	10℞46	19 17	11 2	21 3	8℞46
3	11 58	26 23	29 23	29 25	10 22	19 10	11 9	21 6	8 44
4	12 58	8♊16	0♈44	0♓40	9 58	19 2	11 15	21 9	8 42
5	13 58	20 10	1 58	1 54	9 34	18 54	11 21	21 12	8 41
6	14 58	2♋ 9	3 6	3 9	9 11	18 46	11 28	21 14	8 39
7	15 58	14 18	4 7	4 24	8 47	18 39	11 34	21 17	8 37
8	16 58	26 42	5 0	5 39	8 24	18 31	11 40	21 20	8 36
9	17 58	9♌23	5 46	6 53	8 1	18 23	11 46	21 23	8 34
10	18 58	22 25	6 24	8 8	7 39	18 15	11 53	21 26	8 32
11	19 58	5♍47	6 53	9 23	7 17	18 8	11 59	21 29	8 31
12	20 58	19 29	7 13	10 37	6 55	18 0	12 5	21 32	8 29
13	21 58	3♎30	7 25	11 52	6 33	17 52	12 11	21 36	8 27
14	22 57	17 44	7℞27	13 7	6 12	17 44	12 17	21 39	8 26
15	23 57	2♏ 8	7 21	14 22	5 51	17 36	12 23	21 42	8 24
16	24 57	16 35	7 7	15 36	5 31	17 28	12 29	21 45	8 22
17	25 57	1♐ 1	6 45	16 51	5 11	17 20	12 35	21 48	8 21
18	26 56	15 21	6 16	18 6	4 52	17 13	12 41	21 51	8 19
19	27 56	29 32	5 41	19 20	4 34	17 5	12 46	21 54	8 18
20	28 56	13♑33	5 0	20 35	4 16	16 58	12 52	21 58	8 16
21	29 55	27 21	4 14	21 50	3 59	16 50	12 58	22 1	8 15
22	0♈55	10♒57	3 25	23 4	3 43	16 43	13 4	22 4	8 13
23	1 54	24 20	2 33	24 19	3 27	16 35	13 9	22 7	8 12
24	2 54	7♓31	1 40	25 33	3 12	16 28	13 15	22 11	8 10
25	3 53	20 30	0 47	26 48	2 58	16 21	13 20	22 14	8 9
26	4 53	3♈16	29♓55	28 2	2 44	16 14	13 26	22 17	8 7
27	5 52	15 50	29 5	29 17	2 31	16 7	13 31	22 21	8 6
28	6 52	28 12	28 17	0♈32	2 19	16 0	13 36	22 24	8 5
29	7 51	10♉23	27 33	1 46	2 7	15 53	13 41	22 27	8 3
30	8 50	22 26	26 52	3 1	1 57	15 46	13 46	22 31	8 2
31	9 49	4♊21	26 17	4 15	1 47	15 40	13 51	22 34	8 0

Pluto 21 Cancer all month

APRIL

Day	☉ ° ′	☽ ° ′	☿ ° ′	♀ ° ′	♂ ° ′	♃ ° ′	♄ ° ′	♅ ° ′	♆ ° ′
1	10♈49	16♊13	25♓47	5♈30	1♍38	15♍33	13♒56	22♈37	7♍59
2	11 48	28 6	25℞22	6 44	1℞30	15℞28	14 1	22 41	7℞58
3	12 47	10♋ 3	25 2	7 59	1 23	15 21	14 6	22 44	7 56
4	13 46	22 10	24 49	9 13	1 16	15 15	14 10	22 48	7 55
5	14 45	4♌31	24 40	10 27	1 10	15 8	14 15	22 51	7 54
6	15 44	17 12	24 D38	11 42	1 5	15 2	14 20	22 54	7 53
7	16 43	0♍15	24 41	12 56	1 1	14 56	14 25	22 58	7 52
8	17 42	13 43	24 48	14 11	0 57	14 51	14 29	23 1	7 50
9	18 41	27 38	25 2	15 25	0 55	14 45	14 34	23 5	7 49
10	19 40	11♎57	25 20	16 39	0 53	14 40	14 38	23 8	7 48
11	20 39	26 35	25 43	17 54	0 52	14 35	14 42	23 12	7 47
12	21 38	11♏27	26 11	19 8	0 52	14 30	14 46	23 15	7 46
13	22 36	26 22	26 43	20 22	0 D52	14 25	14 50	23 19	7 45
14	23 35	11♐12	27 18	21 36	0 53	14 20	14 54	23 22	7 44
15	24 34	25 51	27 58	22 51	0 55	14 16	14 58	23 25	7 43
16	25 33	10♑12	28 41	24 5	0 57	14 11	15 2	23 29	7 42
17	26 31	24 14	29 28	25 19	1 0	14 7	15 6	23 32	7 40
18	27 30	7♒55	0♈19	26 34	1 4	14 3	15 10	23 36	7 39
19	28 28	21 18	1 12	27 48	1 9	13 59	15 13	23 39	7 38
20	29 27	4♓23	2 9	29 2	1 14	13 56	15 17	23 42	7 37
21	0♉26	17 14	3 8	0♉15	1 20	13 52	15 20	23 46	7 36
22	1 24	29 53	4 11	1 30	1 26	13 48	15 23	23 49	7 36
23	2 23	12♈20	5 16	2 44	1 33	13 45	15 27	23 53	7 35
24	3 21	24 39	6 24	3 59	1 41	13 42	15 30	23 56	7 34
25	4 20	6♉50	7 34	5 13	1 49	13 39	15 33	24 0	7 33
26	5 18	18 53	8 47	6 27	1 58	13 36	15 36	24 3	7 32
27	6 16	0♊51	10 2	7 41	2 8	13 34	15 39	24 6	7 32
28	7 15	12 44	11 19	8 55	2 18	13 32	15 42	24 10	7 31
29	8 13	24 35	12 38	10 9	2 29	13 29	15 45	24 13	7 30
30	9 11	6♋27	14 0	11 23	2 40	13 27	15 48	24 16	7 30

Pluto 21 Cancer all month

1933

MAY

Day	☉	☽	☿	♀	♂	♃	♄	♅	♆
	° ′	° ′	° ′	° ′	° ′	° ′	° ′	° ′	° ′
1	10 ♉ 10	18 ♋ 23	15 ♈ 23	12 ♉ 36	2 ♍ 52	13 ♍ 26	15 ♒ 50	24 ♈ 20	7 ♍ 29
2	11 8	0 ♌ 27	16 49	13 50	3 5	13 R 24	15 53	24 23	7 R 29
3	12 6	12 45	18 17	15 4	3 17	13 23	15 55	24 26	7 28
4	13 4	25 21	19 47	16 18	3 31	13 21	15 57	24 30	7 28
5	14 2	8 ♍ 20	21 19	17 32	3 45	13 20	15 59	24 33	7 27
6	15 0	21 46	22 52	18 46	4 0	13 19	16 1	24 36	7 27
7	15 58	5 ♎ 42	24 28	20 0	4 15	13 19	16 3	24 40	7 26
8	16 56	20 6	26 6	21 14	4 30	13 18	16 5	24 43	7 26
9	17 54	4 ♏ 55	27 46	22 28	4 46	13 18	16 7	24 46	7 26
10	18 52	20 1	29 28	23 42	5 3	13 17	16 8	24 49	7 25
11	19 50	5 ♐ 16	1 ♉ 11	24 56	5 19	13 D 17	16 10	24 52	7 25
12	20 48	20 27	2 57	26 10	5 37	13 18	16 12	24 56	7 25
13	21 46	5 ♑ 25	4 44	27 24	5 55	13 18	16 13	24 59	7 25
14	22 44	20 2	6 34	28 38	6 13	13 19	16 15	25 2	7 24
15	23 42	4 ♒ 14	8 26	29 52	6 31	13 19	16 16	25 5	7 24
16	24 40	18 0	10 20	1 ♊ 6	6 50	13 20	16 17	25 8	7 24
17	25 37	1 ♓ 20	12 15	2 19	7 10	13 21	16 18	25 11	7 24
18	26 35	14 19	14 12	3 33	7 30	13 23	16 19	25 14	7 24
19	27 33	27 0	16 12	4 47	7 50	13 24	16 20	25 17	7 24
20	28 31	9 ♈ 26	18 13	6 0	8 10	13 26	16 20	25 20	7 D 24
21	29 28	21 41	20 16	7 14	8 31	13 28	16 21	25 23	7 24
22	0 ♊ 26	3 ♉ 48	22 20	8 28	8 52	13 30	16 22	25 26	7 24
23	1 24	15 49	24 26	9 42	9 14	13 32	16 22	25 29	7 24
24	2 21	27 45	26 34	10 55	9 36	13 34	16 22	25 32	7 24
25	3 19	9 ♊ 39	28 43	12 9	9 58	13 37	16 23	25 35	7 25
26	4 17	21 30	0 ♊ 53	13 23	10 20	13 39	16 23	25 38	7 25
27	5 14	3 ♋ 22	3 3	14 37	10 43	13 42	16 23	25 41	7 25
28	6 12	15 15	5 15	15 50	11 7	13 45	16 R 23	25 44	7 25
29	7 9	27 13	7 27	17 4	11 31	13 48	16 23	25 46	7 26
30	8 7	9 ♌ 19	9 39	18 18	11 54	13 52	16 22	25 49	7 26
31	9 5	21 36	11 51	19 31	12 19	13 55	16 22	25 52	7 26

Pluto 21 Cancer all month

JUNE

Day	☉	☽	☿	♀	♂	♃	♄	♅	♆
	° ′	° ′	° ′	° ′	° ′	° ′	° ′	° ′	° ′
1	10 ♊ 2	4 ♍ 10	14 ♊ 2	20 ♊ 45	12 ♍ 44	13 ♍ 59	16 ♒ 21	25 ♈ 54	7 ♍ 27
2	11 0	17 5	16 13	21 59	13 8	14 3	16 R 21	25 57	7 27
3	11 57	0 ♎ 26	18 23	23 12	13 33	14 7	16 20	26 0	7 28
4	12 54	14 14	20 31	24 26	13 58	14 11	16 20	26 2	7 28
5	13 52	28 32	22 39	25 39	14 24	14 15	16 19	26 5	7 29
6	14 49	13 ♏ 17	24 45	26 53	14 49	14 20	16 18	26 7	7 29
7	15 47	28 23	26 48	28 7	15 15	14 24	16 17	26 10	7 30
8	16 44	13 ♐ 42	28 49	29 20	15 41	14 29	16 16	26 12	7 30
9	17 41	29 1	0 ♋ 49	0 ♋ 34	16 8	14 34	16 14	26 15	7 31
10	18 39	14 ♑ 10	2 47	1 47	16 35	14 39	16 13	26 17	7 32
11	19 36	28 59	4 42	3 1	17 2	14 45	16 11	26 19	7 32
12	20 33	13 ♒ 21	6 35	4 14	17 29	14 50	16 10	26 22	7 33
13	21 31	27 16	8 26	5 28	17 57	14 56	16 8	26 24	7 34
14	22 28	10 ♓ 42	10 15	6 41	18 24	15 1	16 7	26 26	7 35
15	23 25	23 43	12 1	7 55	18 52	15 7	16 5	26 29	7 36
16	24 23	6 ♈ 22	13 44	9 8	19 20	15 13	16 4	26 31	7 36
17	25 20	18 45	15 25	10 22	19 49	15 19	16 2	26 33	7 37
18	26 17	0 ♉ 54	17 4	11 35	20 18	15 25	16 0	26 35	7 38
19	27 14	12 55	18 40	12 48	20 47	15 32	15 58	26 37	7 39
20	28 12	24 50	20 13	14 2	21 16	15 38	15 55	26 39	7 40
21	29 9	6 ♊ 43	21 44	15 15	21 46	15 45	15 53	26 41	7 41
22	0 ♋ 6	18 34	23 13	16 29	22 15	15 51	15 51	26 43	7 42
23	1 3	0 ♋ 26	24 39	17 42	22 45	15 58	15 49	26 45	7 43
24	2 1	12 21	26 2	18 55	23 15	16 5	15 46	26 47	7 44
25	2 58	24 20	27 23	20 8	23 45	16 12	15 43	26 49	7 46
26	3 55	6 ♌ 25	28 41	21 22	24 16	16 20	15 40	26 50	7 47
27	4 52	18 38	29 56	22 36	24 46	16 27	15 38	26 52	7 48
28	5 50	1 ♍ 2	1 ♌ 9	23 49	25 17	16 35	15 35	26 54	7 49
29	6 47	13 40	2 19	25 2	25 48	16 43	15 32	26 56	7 51
30	7 44	26 37	3 26	26 16	26 19	16 51	15 29	26 57	7 52

Pluto 21 Cancer all month

1933

JULY

Day	☉	☽	☿	♀	♂	♃	♄	♅	♆
	° ′	° ′	° ′	° ′	° ′	° ′	° ′	° ′	° ′
1	8♋41	9♎55	4♌30	27♋29	26♍51	16♍59	15♒26	26♈59	7♍53
2	9 38	23 37	5 31	28 43	27 22	17 7	15℞23	27 0	7 55
3	10 36	7♏44	6 29	29 56	27 54	17 15	15 20	27 2	7 56
4	11 33	22 16	7 23	1♌ 9	28 26	17 23	15 17	27 3	7 57
5	12 30	7♐ 9	8 14	2 22	28 58	17 32	15 14	27 5	7 59
6	13 27	22 15	9 2	3 35	29 30	17 40	15 10	27 6	8 0
7	14 24	7♑25	9 46	4 49	0♎ 2	17 49	15 6	27 7	8 2
8	15 22	22 30	10 26	6 2	0 35	17 58	15 2	27 8	8 3
9	16 19	7♒19	11 3	7 15	1 7	18 7	14 59	27 10	8 5
10	17 16	21 46	11 35	8 28	1 40	18 16	14 55	27 11	8 6
11	18 13	5♓46	12 4	9 41	2 13	18 25	14 51	27 12	8 8
12	19 10	19 19	12 28	10 54	2 46	18 34	14 47	27 13	8 9
13	20 8	2♈25	12 48	12 7	3 20	18 43	14 44	27 14	8 11
14	21 5	15 8	13 3	13 21	3 53	18 52	14 40	27 15	8 12
15	22 2	27 33	13 14	14 34	4 27	19 2	14 36	27 16	8 14
16	22 59	9♉42	13 19	15 47	5 0	19 11	14 32	27 17	8 16
17	23 56	21 42	13℞20	17 0	5 34	19 21	14 28	27 18	8 18
18	24 54	3♊36	13 16	18 13	6 8	19 31	14 24	27 19	8 19
19	25 51	15 27	13 7	19 26	6 42	19 41	14 20	27 19	8 21
20	26 48	27 19	12 53	20 39	7 16	19 51	14 16	27 20	8 23
21	27 46	9♋15	12 35	21 52	7 51	20 1	14 12	27 21	8 24
22	28 43	21 16	12 12	23 5	8 25	20 11	14 8	27 21	8 26
23	29 40	3♌24	11 45	24 18	9 0	20 21	14 3	27 22	8 28
24	0♌37	15 40	11 14	25 31	9 35	20 31	13 59	27 22	8 30
25	1 35	28 7	10 39	26 43	10 10	20 42	13 54	27 23	8 32
26	2 32	10♍46	10 1	27 56	10 45	20 52	13 50	27 23	8 34
27	3 30	23 37	9 20	29 8	11 20	21 2	13 46	27 23	8 36
28	4 27	6♎44	8 38	0♍21	11 55	21 13	13 42	27 24	8 38
29	5 24	20 8	7 54	1 34	12 31	21 23	13 38	27 24	8 39
30	6 22	3♏49	7 9	2 47	13 6	21 34	13 33	27 24	8 41
31	7 19	17 50	6 25	3 59	13 42	21 45	13 29	27 24	8 43

Pluto 22 Cancer all month

AUGUST

Day	☉	☽	☿	♀	♂	♃	♄	♅	♆
	° ′	° ′	° ′	° ′	° ′	° ′	° ′	° ′	° ′
1	8♌16	2♐ 8	5♌42	5♍12	14♎17	21♍56	13♒24	27♈24	8♍45
2	9 14	16 42	5℞ 1	6 25	14 53	22 7	13℞20	27 25	8 47
3	10 11	1♑26	4 23	7 38	15 29	22 18	13 15	27 25	8 49
4	11 9	16 15	3 48	8 50	16 5	22 29	13 11	27℞25	8 51
5	12 6	1♒ 0	3 17	10 3	16 42	22 40	13 6	27 24	8 53
6	13 4	15 35	2 51	11 15	17 18	22 52	13 2	27 24	8 55
7	14 1	29 54	2 30	12 28	17 55	23 3	12 57	27 24	8 57
8	14 58	13♓51	2 15	13 41	18 32	23 14	12 53	27 24	8 59
9	15 56	27 24	2 7	14 53	19 8	23 26	12 48	27 24	9 2
10	16 54	10♈34	2D 5	16 6	19 45	23 37	12 44	27 23	9 4
11	17 51	23 21	2 9	17 18	20 22	23 49	12 39	27 23	9 6
12	18 49	5♉48	2 21	18 31	20 59	24 0	12 35	27 23	9 8
13	19 46	18 0	2 40	19 43	21 36	24 12	12 81	27 22	9 10
14	20 44	0♊ 1	3 6	20 55	22 14	24 23	12 26	27 22	9 12
15	21 42	11 56	3 39	22 8	22 51	24 35	12 22	27 21	9 14
16	22 39	23 47	4 19	23 20	23 28	24 47	12 18	27 21	9 16
17	23 37	5♋41	5 6	24 32	24 6	24 59	12 13	27 20	9 18
18	24 35	17 41	6 0	25 45	24 43	25 11	12 9	27 19	9 21
19	25 32	29 49	7 0	26 58	25 21	25 23	12 4	27 19	9 23
20	26 30	12♌ 7	8 7	28 10	25 59	25 35	12 0	27 18	9 25
21	27 28	24 39	9 20	29 22	26 37	25 47	11 56	27 17	9 27
22	28 26	7♍24	10 39	0♎34	27 16	25 59	11 52	27 16	9 29
23	29 24	20 23	12 4	1 47	27 54	26 11	11 48	27 15	9 31
24	0♍22	3♎37	13 34	2 59	28 32	26 23	11 44	27 14	9 34
25	1 19	17 3	15 8	4 11	29 11	26 36	11 40	27 13	9 36
26	2 17	0♏43	16 46	5 23	29 49	26 48	11 35	27 12	9 38
27	3 15	14 35	18 28	6 35	0♏28	27 1	11 31	27 11	9 40
28	4 13	28 37	20 13	7 47	1 7	27 13	11 27	27 10	9 43
29	5 11	12♐48	22 1	8 59	1 46	27 25	11 23	27 9	9 45
30	6 9	27 6	23 52	10 11	2 25	27 38	11 19	27 8	9 47
31	7 7	11♑27	25 44	11 23	3 4	27 50	11 16	27 6	9 49

Pluto 23 Cancer all month

1933

SEPTEMBER

Day	☉	☽	☿	♀	♂	♃	♄	♅	♆
	° ′	° ′	° ′	° ′	° ′	° ′	° ′	° ′	° ′
1	8♍ 5	25♑49	27♌38	12♎35	3♏43	28♍ 2	11♒13	27♈ 5	9♍52
2	9 3	10♒ 8	29 33	13 46	4 22	28 15	11 R 9	27 R 3	9 54
3	10 1	24 18	1♍29	14 58	5 2	28 27	11 6	27 2	9 56
4	11 0	8♓17	3 26	16 10	5 41	28 40	11 2	27 1	9 58
5	11 58	22 0	5 22	17 21	6 21	28 53	10 59	26 59	10 1
6	12 56	5♈25	7 19	18 33	7 0	29 5	10 55	26 58	10 3
7	13 54	18 30	9 15	19 45	7 40	29 18	10 52	26 56	10 5
8	14 52	1♉16	11 11	20 56	8 20	29 31	10 48	26 55	10 7
9	15 51	13 45	13 6	22 8	9 0	29 44	10 45	26 53	10 9
10	16 49	25 58	15 1	23 19	9 40	29 56	10 42	26 51	10 12
11	17 47	8♊ 0	16 54	24 30	10 20	0♎ 9	10 39	26 49	10 14
12	18 46	19 54	18 47	25 42	11 0	0 22	10 36	26 48	10 16
13	19 44	1♋46	20 39	26 53	11 40	0 35	10 33	26 46	10 18
14	20 42	13 41	22 30	28 4	12 21	0 48	10 30	26 44	10 21
15	21 41	25 42	24 20	29 16	13 1	1 1	10 27	26 42	10 23
16	22 39	7♌54	26 9	0♏27	13 42	1 14	10 24	26 41	10 25
17	23 38	20 21	27 57	1 38	14 23	1 27	10 22	26 39	10 27
18	24 37	3♍ 6	29 44	2 49	15 3	1 40	10 19	26 36	10 29
19	25 35	16 9	1♎30	4 0	15 44	1 52	10 17	26 34	10 31
20	26 34	29 31	3 15	5 11	16 25	2 5	10 14	26 32	10 34
21	27 33	3♎11	4 59	6 22	17 6	2 18	10 12	26 30	10 36
22	28 31	27 5	6 41	7 33	17 47	2 31	10 10	26 28	10 38
23	29 30	11♏10	8 23	8 44	18 29	2 44	10 7	26 26	10 40
24	0♎29	25 22	10 4	9 55	19 10	2 57	10 5	26 24	10 42
25	1 28	9♐37	11 44	11 5	19 51	3 10	10 3	26 22	10 44
26	2 26	23 51	13 23	12 16	20 33	3 24	10 1	26 20	10 46
27	3 25	8♑ 3	15 1	13 27	21 14	3 37	9 59	26 18	10 48
28	4 24	22 9	16 38	14 37	21 56	3 50	9 58	26 15	10 50
29	5 23	6♒ 8	18 14	15 48	22 38	4 3	9 57	26 13	10 52
30	6 22	20 1	19 50	16 58	23 19	4 16	9 55	26 11	10 54

Pluto 24 Cancer all month

OCTOBER

Day	☉	☽	☿	♀	♂	♃	♄	♅	♆
	° ′	° ′	° ′	° ′	° ′	° ′	° ′	° ′	° ′
1	7♎21	3♓44	21♎24	18♏ 8	24♏ 1	4♎29	9♒54	26♈ 8	10♍57
2	8 20	17 17	22 58	19 19	24 43	4 42	9 R 52	26 R 6	10 59
3	9 19	0♈38	24 31	20 29	25 25	4 55	9 51	26 4	11 1
4	10 18	13 46	26 3	21 39	26 7	5 8	9 50	26 1	11 3
5	11 17	26 40	27 34	22 49	26 50	5 21	9 49	25 59	11 5
6	12 16	9♉18	29 4	23 59	27 32	5 34	9 48	25 56	11 7
7	13 16	21 42	0♏34	25 9	28 14	5 47	9 47	25 54	11 9
8	14 15	3♊53	2 3	26 19	28 57	6 0	9 46	25 51	11 11
9	15 14	15 54	3 31	27 28	29 39	6 12	9 45	25 49	11 12
10	16 13	27♋47	4 58	28 38	0♐22	6 25	9 45	25 46	11 14
11	17 13	9 38	6 24	29 48	1 5	6 38	9 45	25 44	11 16
12	18 12	21 30	7 49	0♐57	1 47	6 51	9 44	25 41	11 18
13	19 12	3♌30	9 13	2 6	2 30	7 4	9 44	25 38	11 20
14	20 11	15 42	10 37	3 16	3 13	7 17	9 43	25 36	11 22
15	21 10	28 12	12 0	4 25	3 56	7 30	9 D43	25 34	11 24
16	22 10	11♍ 3	13 22	5 34	4 39	7 43	9 43	25 31	11 26
17	23 10	24 17	14 42	6 42	5 23	7 55	9 44	25 29	11 27
18	24 9	7♎57	16 2	7 51	6 6	8 8	9 44	25 26	11 29
19	25 9	21 59	17 20	9 0	6 49	8 21	9 44	25 24	11 31
20	26 8	6♏20	18 37	10 9	7 33	8 34	9 45	25 21	11 33
21	27 8	20 54	19 53	11 17	8 16	8 46	9 45	25 19	11 34
22	28 8	5♐34	21 7	12 26	9 0	8 59	9 46	25 16	11 36
23	29 8	20 11	22 20	13 34	9 43	9 12	9 47	25 14	11 38
24	0♏ 7	4♑41	23 31	14 42	10 27	9 24	9 48	25 11	11 39
25	1 7	18 58	24 40	15 51	11 10	9 37	9 49	25 9	11 41
26	2 7	3♒ 1	25 47	16 59	11 54	9 49	9 50	25 6	11 42
27	3 7	16 50	26 52	18 6	12 38	10 1	9 51	25 4	11 44
28	4 7	0♓24	27 54	19 14	13 22	10 14	9 52	25 1	11 45
29	5 7	13 45	28 53	20 21	14 6	10 26	9 53	24 59	11 47
30	6 7	26 55	29 50	21 29	14 50	10 38	9 55	24 56	11 48
31	7 7	9♈53	0♐43	22 36	15 34	10 50	9 57	24 54	11 50

Pluto 24 Cancer all month

1933

NOVEMBER

DAY	☉	☽	☿	♀	♂	♃	♄	♅	♆
	° ′	° ′	° ′	° ′	° ′	° ′	° ′	° ′	° ′
1	8♏ 7	22♈41	1♐32	23♐43	16♐18	11♎ 3	9♒58	24♈52	11♍51
2	9 7	5♉18	2 17	24 50	17 3	11 15	10 0	24 R 49	11 53
3	10 7	17 44	2 57	25 57	17 47	11 27	10 2	24 47	11 54
4	11 7	29 59	3 32	27 3	18 32	11 39	10 4	24 44	11 55
5	12 7	12♊ 4	4 1	28 10	19 16	11 51	10 6	24 42	11 56
6	13 7	24 1	4 23	29 16	20 1	12 3	10 9	24 40	11 58
7	14 7	5♋53	4 39	0♑22	20 46	12 15	10 11	24 38	11 59
8	15 8	17 41	4 46	1 28	21 31	12 27	10 13	24 35	12 0
9	16 8	29 31	4 R 44	2 33	22 15	12 39	10 16	24 33	12 1
10	17 8	11♌28	4 34	3 39	23 0	12 51	10 18	24 31	12 2
11	18 9	23 37	4 14	4 44	23 45	13 3	10 21	24 29	12 4
12	19 9	6♍ 3	3 44	5 49	24 30	13 15	10 24	24 27	12 5
13	20 9	18 52	3 4	6 54	25 15	13 26	10 26	24 24	12 6
14	21 10	2♎ 7	2 14	7 58	26 0	13 38	10 29	24 22	12 7
15	22 10	25 52	1 14	9 2	26 45	13 49	10 32	24 20	12 8
16	23 11	0♏ 5	0 6	10 6	27 30	14 0	10 35	24 18	12 9
17	24 11	14 43	28♏52	11 10	28 15	14 12	10 38	24 16	12 10
18	25 12	29 38	27 33	12 13	29 1	14 23	10 42	24 14	12 11
19	26 12	14♐43	26 11	13 16	29 46	14 34	10 45	24 13	12 12
20	27 13	29 45	24 50	14 19	0♑31	14 45	10 49	24 11	12 12
21	28 14	14♑37	23 33	15 22	1 17	14 57	10 53	24 9	12 13
22	29 14	29 11	22 21	16 25	2 2	15 8	10 57	24 7	12 14
23	0♐15	13♒25	21 17	17 26	2 48	15 19	11 0	24 5	12 15
24	1 16	27 15	20 23	18 28	3 34	15 30	11 4	24 4	12 15
25	2 16	10♓45	19 40	19 29	4 19	15 41	11 8	24 2	12 16
26	3 17	23 56	19 8	20 30	5 5	15 51	11 12	24 0	12 17
27	4 18	6♈51	18 47	21 30	5 51	16 2	11 16	23 58	12 17
28	5 18	19 33	18 38	22 31	6 37	16 13	11 20	23 57	12 18
29	6 19	2♈ 3	18 D 40	23 31	7 23	16 24	11 24	23 55	12 19
30	7 20	14 23	18 52	24 30	8 9	16 34	11 28	23 54	12 19

Pluto 24 Cancer all month

DECEMBER

DAY	☉	☽	☿	♀	♂	♃	♄	♅	♆
	° ′	° ′	′	° ′	° ′	° ′	° ′	° ′	° ′
1	8♐21	26♉36	19♏14	25♑28	8♑55	16♎43	11♒33	23♈52	12♍20
2	9 22	8♊40	19 44	26 26	9 41	16 53	11 37	23 R 51	12 20
3	10 22	20 39	20 22	27 24	10 27	17 3	11 42	23 49	12 20
4	11 23	2♋32	21 6	28 21	11 14	17 13	11 46	23 48	12 21
5	12 24	14 21	21 57	29 18	12 0	17 23	11 51	23 47	12 21
6	13 25	26 9	22 53	0♒14	12 46	17 33	11 56	23 46	12 22
7	14 26	7♌59	23 54	1 10	13 32	17 48	12 1	23 44	12 22
8	15 27	19 55	24 59	2 5	14 19	17 52	12 6	23 43	12 22
9	16 28	2♍ 2	26 7	2 59	15 5	18 2	12 11	23 42	12 22
10	17 29	14 25	27 18	3 53	15 51	18 11	12 16	23 41	12 22
11	18 30	27 8	28 32	4 46	16 38	18 20	12 21	23 40	12 23
12	19 31	10♎17	29 48	5 38	17 24	18 29	12 27	23 39	12 23
13	20 32	23 54	1♐ 6	6 30	18 11	18 38	12 32	23 38	12 23
14	21 33	8♏ 3	2 26	7 21	18 57	18 47	12 37	23 37	12 23
15	22 34	22 39	3 48	8 11	19 44	18 56	12 42	23 36	12 23
16	23 35	7♐39	5 11	9 0	20 30	19 4	12 48	23 35	12 23
17	24 36	22 54	6 35	9 49	21 17	19 13	12 53	23 34	12 23
18	25 37	8♑12	7 59	10 37	22 4	19 21	12 59	23 34	12 R 23
19	26 38	23 22	9 25	11 24	22 50	19 30	13 4	23 33	12 23
20	27 40	8♒16	10 51	12 9	23 37	19 38	13 10	23 32	12 23
21	28 41	22 46	12 19	12 54	24 24	19 46	13 16	23 32	12 23
22	29 42	6♓50	13 47	13 38	25 11	19 54	13 22	23 31	12 22
23	0♑43	20 27	15 15	14 20	25 58	20 2	13 28	23 31	12 22
24	1 44	3♈41	16 44	15 2	26 45	20 9	13 34	23 30	12 22
25	2 45	16 32	18 14	15 42	27 32	20 17	13 40	23 30	12 22
26	3 46	29 7	19 43	16 21	28 19	20 24	13 46	23 29	12 21
27	4 47	11♉27	21 13	16 59	29 6	20 32	13 52	23 29	12 21
28	5 49	23 37	22 43	17 35	29 53	20 39	13 58	23 29	12 20
29	6 50	5♊39	24 14	18 10	0♒40	20 46	14 4	23 29	12 20
30	7 51	17 35	25 45	18 44	1 27	20 53	14 10	23 29	12 19
31	8 52	29 27	27 17	19 16	2 14	20 59	14 17	23 28	12 19

Pluto 24 Cancer all month

1934

JANUARY

DAY	☉	☽	☿	♀	♂	♃	♄	♅	♆
	° ′	° ′	° ′	° ′	° ′	° ′	° ′	° ′	° ′
1	9♑53	11♋17	28♐49	19♒47	3♒ 1	21♎ 6	14♒23	23♈28	12♍18
2	10 54	23 7	0♑21	20 16	3 48	21 12	14 30	23 ℞ 28	12 ℞ 18
3	11 55	4♌59	1 53	20 44	4 35	21 18	14 36	23 D28	12 17
4	12 56	16 54	3 26	21 9	5 22	21 24	14 43	23 28	12 17
5	13 58	28 55	5 0	21 33	6 10	21 30	14 49	23 28	12 16
6	14 59	11♍ 6	6 33	21 55	6 57	21 36	14 56	23 29	12 15
7	16 0	23 31	8 7	22 15	7 44	21 42	15 2	23 29	12 14
8	17 1	6♎13	9 41	22 33	8 31	21 47	15 9	23 29	12 14
9	18 2	19 16	11 16	22 49	9 19	21 53	15 15	23 30	12 13
10	19 3	2♏45	12 51	23 3	10 6	21 58	15 22	23 30	12 12
11	20 5	16 40	14 27	23 15	10 53	22 3	15 29	23 30	12 11
12	21 6	1♐ 2	16 4	23 24	11 40	22 8	15 35	23 31	12 10
13	22 7	15 48	17 40	23 31	12 28	22 12	15 42	23 31	12 9
14	23 8	0♑52	19 17	23 36	13 15	22 17	15 49	23 32	12 8
15	24 9	16 6	20 55	23 38	14 2	22 21	15 56	23 32	12 7
16	25 10	1♒18	22 33	23 ℞ 38	14 50	22 25	16 3	23 33	12 6
17	26 11	16 20	24 12	23 36	15 37	22 29	16 10	23 34	12 5
18	27 12	1♓ 2	25 51	23 31	16 25	22 33	16 17	23 34	12 4
19	28 14	15 20	27 31	23 23	17 12	22 37	16 24	23 35	12 3
20	29 15	29 10	29 11	23 13	18 0	22 40	16 31	23 36	12 2
21	0♒16	12♈34	0♒52	23 1	18 47	22 44	16 38	23 37	12 1
22	1 17	25 32	2 33	22 45	19 35	22 47	16 45	23 38	12 0
23	2 18	8♉ 8	4 15	22 28	20 22	22 50	16 52	23 39	11 59
24	3 19	20 27	5 57	22 8	21 9	22 52	16 59	23 40	11 58
25	4 20	2♊33	7 40	21 46	21 57	22 55	17 6	23 41	11 56
26	5 21	14 30	9 24	21 21	22 44	22 57	17 13	23 43	11 55
27	6 22	26 21	11 8	20 54	23 31	23 0	17 20	23 44	11 54
28	7 23	8♋10	12 53	20 25	24 19	23 2	17 27	23 45	11 53
29	8 24	20 0	14 38	19 55	25 6	23 3	17 35	23 46	11 51
30	9 25	1♌53	16 23	19 23	25 54	23 5	17 42	23 48	11 50
31	10 26	13 51	18 9	18 49	26 41	23 7	17 49	23 49	11 49

Pluto 23 Cancer all month

FEBRUARY

DAY	☉	☽	☿	♀	♂	♃	♄	♅	♆
	° ′	° ′	° ′	° ′	° ′	° ′	° ′	° ′	° ′
1	11♒26	25♌56	19♒55	18♒14	27♒29	23♎ 8	17♒56	23♈51	11♍47
2	12 27	8♍10	21 41	17 ℞ 39	28 16	23 9	18 4	23 52	11 ℞ 46
3	13 28	20 34	23 27	17 2	29 4	23 10	18 11	23 54	11 44
4	14 29	3♎11	25 13	16 25	29 52	23 11	18 18	23 56	11 43
5	15 30	16 2	26 59	15 48	0♓39	23 11	18 25	23 57	11 42
6	16 31	29 9	28 44	15 11	1 27	23 12	18 33	23 59	11 40
7	17 31	12♏36	0♓28	14 34	2 14	23 12	18 40	24 1	11 39
8	18 32	26 22	2 11	13 58	3 1	23 ℞ 12	18 47	24 3	11 37
9	19 33	10♐28	3 53	13 22	3 49	23 11	18 54	24 5	11 36
10	20 34	24 54	5 34	12 48	4 36	23 11	19 1	24 6	11 34
11	21 34	9♑35	7 12	12 14	5 23	23 10	19 8	24 8	11 33
12	22 35	24 26	8 46	11 42	6 11	23 10	19 15	24 10	11 31
13	23 36	9♒21	10 18	11 12	6 58	23 9	19 23	24 12	11 29
14	24 36	24 12	11 46	10 43	7 46	23 7	19 30	24 14	11 28
15	25 37	8♓51	13 9	10 17	8 33	23 6	19 37	24 16	11 26
16	26 38	23 11	14 27	9 52	9 20	23 4	19 44	24 19	11 25
17	27 38	7♈ 7	15 39	9 30	10 8	23 3	19 52	24 21	11 23
18	28 39	20 39	16 45	9 10	10 55	23 1	19 59	24 23	11 21
19	29 39	3♉45	17 43	8 52	11 42	22 59	20 6	24 25	11 20
20	0♓40	16 28	18 33	8 36	12 29	22 56	20 13	24 28	11 18
21	1 40	18 51	19 15	8 23	13 17	22 54	20 21	24 30	11 16
22	2 41	10♊58	19 47	8 13	14 4	22 51	20 28	24 32	11 15
23	3 41	22 54	20 10	8 5	14 51	22 48	20 35	24 35	11 13
24	4 41	4♋44	20 23	8 0	15 38	22 45	20 42	24 37	11 12
25	5 42	16 33	20 27	7 57	16 25	22 42	20 49	24 40	11 10
26	6 42	28 24	20 ℞ 20	7 56	17 12	22 38	20 56	24 42	11 8
27	7 42	10♌21	20 4	7 D58	17 59	22 35	21 3	24 45	11 7
28	8 43	22 28	19 39	8 2	18 46	22 31	21 10	24 47	11 5

Pluto 23 Cancer all month

1934

MARCH

DAY	☉	☽	☿	♀	♂	♃	♄	♅	♆
	° ′	° ′	° ′	° ′	° ′	° ′	° ′	° ′	° ′
1	9♓43	4♍45	19♓ 5	8♒ 9	19♓33	22♎27	21♒17	24♈50	11♍ 3
2	10 43	17 15	18℞24	8 18	20 20	22℞23	21 24	24 53	11℞ 2
3	11 43	29 59	17 36	8 29	21 7	22 19	21 31	24 55	11 0
4	12 43	12♎56	16 42	8 42	21 54	22 14	21 38	24 58	10 58
5	13 43	26 7	15 45	8 57	22 41	22 10	21 45	25 1	10 57
6	14 43	9♏31	14 45	9 14	23 28	22 5	21 51	25 4	10 55
7	15 43	23 8	13 44	9 34	24 15	22 0	21 58	25 6	10 53
8	16 43	6♐57	12 44	9 55	25 2	21 55	22 5	25 9	10 52
9	17 43	20 57	11 45	10 18	25 49	21 50	22 12	25 12	10 50
10	18 43	5♑ 7	10 48	10 42	26 35	21 45	22 18	25 15	10 48
11	19 43	19 26	9 55	11 9	27 22	21 40	22 25	25 18	10 46
12	20 43	3♒51	9 8	11 37	28 9	21 34	22 32	25 21	10 45
13	21 43	18 19	8 26	12 7	28 56	21 28	22 39	25 24	10 43
14	22 43	2♓45	7 49	12 38	29 42	21 22	22 45	25 27	10 42
15	23 43	17 4	7 18	13 10	0♈29	21 16	22 52	25 30	10 40
16	24 43	1♈10	6 54	13 44	1 16	21 10	22 59	25 33	10 38
17	25 42	14 59	6 37	14 20	2 2	21 4	23 5	25 36	10 37
18	26 42	28 28	6 25	14 56	2 49	20 57	23 12	25 39	10 35
19	27 42	11♉35	6 20	15 34	3 35	20 51	23 18	25 42	10 33
20	28 41	24 20	6 D21	16 13	4 22	20 44	23 24	25 45	10 32
21	29 41	6♊46	6 27	16 53	5 8	20 38	23 31	25 48	10 30
22	0♈41	18 56	6 39	17 35	5 55	20 31	23 37	25 52	10 29
23	1 40	0♋53	6 57	18 17	6 41	20 24	23 43	25 55	10 27
24	2 40	12 44	7 20	19 0	7 27	20 17	23 49	25 58	10 26
25	3 39	24 33	7 47	19 44	8 14	20 10	23 55	26 1	10 24
26	4 38	6♌25	8 19	20 30	9 0	20 3	24 1	26 5	10 23
27	5 38	18 26	8 55	21 16	9 46	19 56	24 7	26 8	10 21
28	6 37	0♍39	9 35	22 3	10 32	19 49	24 13	26 11	10 20
29	7 36	13 7	10 19	22 51	11 18	19 41	24 19	26 15	10 18
30	8 36	25 53	11 6	23 39	12 4	19 34	24 25	26 18	10 17
31	9 35	8♎57	11 57	24 28	12 50	19 26	24 31	26 21	10 15

Pluto 22 Cancer all month

APRIL

DAY	☉	☽	☿	♀	♂	♃	♄	♅	♆
	° ′	° ′	° ′	° ′	° ′	° ′	° ′	° ′	° ′
1	10♈34	22♎19	12♓51	25♒18	13♈36	19♎19	24♒37	26♈24	10♍14
2	11 33	5♏56	13 47	26 9	14 22	19℞11	24 43	26 28	10℞13
3	12 32	19 45	14 47	27 1	15 8	19 3	24 48	26 31	10 11
4	13 32	3♐44	15 49	27 53	15 54	18 56	24 54	26 35	10 10
5	14 31	17 48	16 54	28 46	16 40	18 48	24 59	26 38	10 9
6	15 30	1♑55	18 2	29 39	17 25	18 41	25 5	26 41	10 7
7	16 29	16 3	19 12	0♓33	18 11	18 33	25 10	26 45	10 6
8	17 28	0♒10	20 23	1 28	18 56	18 25	25 15	26 48	10 5
9	18 27	14 16	21 37	2 23	19 42	18 17	25 20	26 51	10 3
10	19 26	28 19	22 54	3 18	20 28	18 10	25 26	26 55	10 2
11	20 24	12♓18	24 12	4 14	21 13	18 2	25 31	26 58	10 1
12	21 23	26 10	25 33	5 11	21 59	17 55	25 36	27 2	10 0
13	22 22	9♈53	26 55	6 8	22 44	17 47	25 41	27 5	9 59
14	23 21	23 23	28 19	7 5	23 30	17 40	25 46	27 9	9 58
15	24 20	6♉38	29 45	8 3	24 15	17 32	25 51	27 12	9 57
16	25 19	19 35	1♈12	9 2	25 0	17 24	25 56	27 16	9 56
17	26 17	2♊15	2 42	10 0	25 45	17 16	26 1	27 19	9 55
18	27 16	14 38	4 13	11 0	26 31	17 9	26 6	27 23	9 54
19	28 15	26 47	5 46	11 59	27 16	17 1	26 10	27 26	9 53
20	29 13	8♋44	7 20	12 59	28 1	16 54	26 15	27 29	9 52
21	0♉12	20 34	8 57	13 59	28 46	16 46	26 19	27 33	9 51
22	1 10	2♌23	10 35	15 0	29 31	16 39	26 24	27 36	9 50
23	2 9	14 15	12 14	16 0	0♉15	16 31	26 28	27 40	9 49
24	3 7	26 17	13 56	17 1	1 0	16 24	26 32	27 43	9 48
25	4 6	8♍33	15 39	18 3	1 45	16 17	26 36	27 46	9 47
26	5 4	21 7	17 24	19 5	2 30	16 10	26 40	27 50	9 46
27	6 2	4♎ 4	19 10	20 7	3 15	16 4	26 44	27 53	9 45
28	7 1	17 23	20 59	21 9	4 0	15 57	26 48	27 57	9 45
29	7 59	1♏ 5	22 49	22 11	4 45	15 50	26 52	28 0	9 44
30	8 57	15 7	24 41	23 14	5 29	15 43	26 56	28 3	9 43

Pluto 22 Cancer all month

1934

MAY

DAY	☉	☽	☿	♀	♂	♃	♄	♅	♆
1	9♉55	29♏23	26♈35	24♓17	6♉14	15♎37	26♒59	28♈7	9♍42
2	10 54	13♐48	28 30	25 21	6 58	15℞30	27 3	28 10	9℞42
3	11 52	28 16	0♉27	26 24	7 42	15 24	27 6	28 14	9 41
4	12 50	12♑40	2 25	27 28	8 27	15 18	27 10	28 17	9 41
5	13 48	26 59	4 25	28 32	9 11	15 12	27 13	28 20	9 40
6	14 46	11♒8	6 27	29 36	9 55	15 6	27 16	28 24	9 40
7	15 44	25 7	8 30	0♈41	10 39	15 0	27 19	28 27	9 39
8	16 42	8♓57	10 35	1 45	11 24	14 54	27 23	28 30	9 39
9	17 40	22 36	12 41	2 49	12 8	14 48	27 26	28 34	9 38
10	18 38	6♈5	14 49	3 54	12 52	14 43	27 29	28 37	9 38
11	19 36	19 23	16 58	4 59	13 36	14 38	27 32	28 40	9 37
12	20 34	2♉30	19 7	6 5	14 20	14 33	27 34	28 44	9 37
13	21 32	15 25	21 18	7 11	15 4	14 28	27 37	28 47	9 37
14	22 30	28 6	23 29	8 17	15 48	14 23	27 39	28 50	9 36
15	23 28	10♊34	25 40	9 23	16 32	14 19	27 41	28 53	9 36
16	24 26	22 48	27 51	10 29	17 16	14 14	27 44	28 56	9 36
17	25 24	4♋51	0♊2	11 35	17 59	14 10	27 46	28 59	9 36
18	26 22	16 45	2 12	12 41	18 43	14 5	27 48	29 3	9 36
19	27 19	28 34	4 21	13 48	19 27	14 1	27 50	29 6	9 36
20	28 17	10♌22	6 29	14 54	20 10	13 57	27 52	29 9	9 35
21	29 15	22 13	8 36	16 1	20 54	13 53	27 54	29 12	9 D35
22	0♊13	4♍14	10 41	17 8	21 37	13 50	27 56	29 15	9 35
23	1 10	16 30	12 44	18 15	22 20	13 47	27 58	29 18	9 36
24	2 8	29 5	14 45	19 22	23 4	13 44	27 59	29 21	9 36
25	3 5	12♎4	16 44	20 29	23 47	13 41	28 1	29 24	9 36
26	4 3	25 30	18 41	21 37	24 30	13 38	28 2	29 27	9 36
27	5 1	9♏23	20 35	22 44	25 13	13 36	28 3	29 30	9 36
28	5 58	23 40	22 27	23 51	25 56	13 33	28 5	29 33	9 37
29	6 56	8♐16	24 16	24 59	26 39	13 31	28 6	29 36	9 37
30	7 53	23 4	26 2	26 7	27 22	13 29	28 7	29 39	9 37
31	8 51	7♑56	27 45	27 15	28 5	13 27	28 8	29 42	9 37

Pluto 22 Cancer all month

JUNE

DAY	☉	☽	☿	♀	♂	♃	♄	♅	♆
1	9♊48	22♑43	29♊26	28♈23	28♉48	13♎25	28♒9	29♈45	9♍38
2	10 46	7♒20	1♋3	29 31	29 31	13℞23	28 10	29 47	9 38
3	11 43	21 41	2 38	0♉39	0♊14	13 22	28 10	29 50	9 38
4	12 41	5♓46	4 10	1 48	0 57	13 20	28 10	29 53	9 39
5	13 38	19 33	5 39	2 56	1 39	13 19	28 11	29 56	9 39
6	14 36	3♈3	7 5	4 5	2 22	13 18	28 11	29 58	9 40
7	15 33	16 18	8 28	5 13	3 4	13 18	28 11	0♉1	9 40
8	16 30	29 19	9 47	6 22	3 47	13 17	28 11	0 3	9 41
9	17 28	12♉6	11 4	7 31	4 29	13 17	28 11	0 6	9 42
10	18 25	24 42	12 18	8 39	5 12	13 16	28℞11	0 9	9 42
11	19 23	7♊6	13 29	9 49	5 54	13 D16	28 11	0 11	9 43
12	20 20	19 19	14 36	10 58	6 36	13 17	28 10	0 14	9 43
13	21 17	1♋23	15 40	12 7	7 19	13 17	28 10	0 16	9 44
14	22 15	13 19	16 40	13 16	8 1	13 18	28 9	0 18	9 45
15	23 12	25 9	17 37	14 25	8 43	13 19	28 9	0 21	9 45
16	24 9	6♌56	18 31	15 35	9 25	13 19	28 8	0 23	9 46
17	25 7	18 43	19 21	16 44	10 7	13 20	28 7	0 26	9 47
18	26 4	0♍34	20 7	17 54	10 49	13 21	28 7	0 28	9 48
19	27 1	12 35	20 49	19 3	11 31	13 23	28 6	0 30	9 49
20	27 58	24 49	21 28	20 13	12 13	13 24	28 4	0 32	9 50
21	28 56	7♎23	22 2	21 22	12 55	13 26	28 4	0 34	9 51
22	29 53	20 20	22 32	22 32	13 37	13 28	28 3	0 36	9 52
23	0♋50	3♏43	22 52	23 42	14 19	13 30	28 1	0 39	9 53
24	1 47	17 36	23 20	24 52	15 1	13 32	27 59	0 41	9 54
25	2 44	1♐55	23 37	26 2	15 42	13 35	27 58	0 43	9 55
26	3 42	16 38	23 49	27 12	16 24	13 38	27 56	0 45	9 56
27	4 39	1♑38	23 55	28 22	17 5	13 41	27 55	0 47	9 57
28	5 36	16 45	24 0	29 32	17 47	13 43	27 53	0 49	9 58
29	6 33	1♒51	23℞58	0♊42	18 28	13 47	27 51	0 50	10 0
30	7 30	16 47	23 52	1 52	19 10	13 50	27 49	0 52	10 1

Pluto 23 Cancer all month

1934

JULY

DAY	☉	☽	☿	♀	♂	♃	♄	♅	♆
	° ′	° ′	° ′	° ′	° ′	° ′	° ′	° ′	° ′
1	8♋28	1♓26	23♋42	3♊ 3	19♊51	13♎53	27♒47	0♉54	10♍ 2
2	9 25	15 43	23℞28	4 13	20 32	13 57	27℞45	0 56	10 3
3	10 22	29 38	23 9	5 24	21 13	14 1	27 43	0 57	10 5
4	11 19	13♈ 9	22 46	6 34	21 54	14 5	27 41	0 59	10 6
5	12 16	26 20	22 19	7 45	22 35	14 9	27 38	1 1	10 7
6	13 14	9♉11	21 49	8 55	23 16	14 13	27 36	1 2	10 8
7	14 11	21 47	21 17	10 6	23 57	14 18	27 33	1 4	10 10
8	15 8	4♊ 8	20 42	11 17	24 38	14 22	27 31	1 5	10 11
9	16 5	16 19	20 5	12 28	25 19	14 27	27 28	1 7	10 13
10	17 3	28 20	19 27	13 39	26 0	14 32	27 25	1 8	10 14
11	18 0	10♋15	18 49	14 49	26 41	14 37	27 22	1 9	10 16
12	18 57	22 5	18 10	16 0	27 21	14 42	27 19	1 11	10 17
13	19 54	3♌52	17 33	17 11	28 2	14 48	27 16	1 12	10 19
14	20 51	15 39	16 57	18 23	28 43	14 53	27 13	1 13	10 20
15	21 49	27 28	16 23	19 34	29 24	14 59	27 10	1 14	10 22
16	22 46	9♍23	15 51	20 45	0♋ 4	15 5	27 6	1 15	10 23
17	23 43	21 26	15 23	21 56	0 45	15 11	27 3	1 16	10 25
18	24 40	3♎43	14 58	23 8	1 25	15 17	27 0	1 17	10 27
19	25 38	16 16	14 38	24 19	2 6	15 23	26 56	1 18	10 28
20	26 35	29 10	14 23	25 30	2 46	15 29	26 53	1 19	10 30
21	27 32	12♏29	14 13	26 42	3 26	15 36	26 49	1 20	10 32
22	28 30	26 13	14 8	27 54	4 6	15 42	26 45	1 21	10 33
23	29 27	10♐25	14 D 8	29 5	4 47	15 49	26 42	1 22	10 35
24	0♌24	25 1	14 14	0♋17	5 27	15 56	26 38	1 22	10 37
25	1 21	9♑57	14 26	1 29	6 7	16 3	26 34	1 23	10 39
26	2 19	25 6	14 44	2 40	6 47	16 10	26 30	1 24	10 40
27	3 16	10♒19	15 8	3 52	7 27	16 18	26 26	1 24	10 42
28	4 13	25 25	15 38	5 4	8 7	16 25	26 22	1 25	10 44
29	5 11	10♓17	16 14	6 16	8 47	16 33	26 18	1 25	10 46
30	6 8	24 48	16 56	7 28	9 27	16 41	26 14	1 26	10 48
31	7 5	8♈54	17 44	8 40	10 7	16 48	26 10	1 26	10 50

Pluto 23 Cancer all month

AUGUST

DAY	☉	☽	☿	♀	♂	♃	♄	♅	♆
	° ′	° ′	° ′	° ′	° ′	° ′	° ′	° ′	° ′
1	8♌ 3	22♈33	18♋37	9♋52	10♋46	16♎56	26♒ 6	1♉26	10♍52
2	9 0	5♉47	19 37	11 4	11 26	17 4	26℞ 2	1 27	10 54
3	9 58	18 37	20 42	12 16	12 6	17 12	25 58	1 27	10 56
4	10 55	1♊ 8	21 53	13 28	12 46	17 20	25 53	1 27	10 58
5	11 52	13 22	23 9	14 41	13 25	17 29	25 49	1 27	11 0
6	12 50	25 25	24 30	15 53	14 5	17 37	25 44	1 28	11 2
7	13 47	7♋19	25 57	17 5	14 44	17 46	25 40	1℞ 28	11 4
8	14 45	19 8	27 28	18 18	15 24	17 54	25 35	1 27	11 6
9	15 43	0♌55	29 3	19 30	16 3	18 3	25 31	1 27	11 8
10	16 40	12 43	0♌43	20 43	16 42	18 12	25 27	1 27	11 10
11	17 38	24 33	2 26	21 55	17 21	18 21	25 23	1 27	11 12
12	18 35	6♍29	4 13	23 8	18 1	18 30	25 18	1 27	11 14
13	19 33	18 32	6 3	24 21	18 40	18 40	25 14	1 27	11 16
14	20 30	0♎45	7 56	25 34	19 19	18 49	25 9	1 26	11 18
15	21 28	13 9	9 50	26 47	19 58	18 58	25 5	1 26	11 21
16	22 26	25 48	11 47	27 59	20 37	19 8	25 0	1 26	11 23
17	23 24	8♏44	13 46	29 12	21 16	19 17	24 56	1 25	11 25
18	24 21	22 0	15 46	0♌25	21 55	19 27	24 51	1 25	11 27
19	25 19	5♐36	17 46	1 38	22 34	19 37	24 47	1 24	11 29
20	26 17	19 36	19 46	2 51	23 13	19 47	24 42	1 23	11 31
21	27 14	3♑57	21 47	4 4	23 51	20 57	24 38	1 23	11 34
22	28 12	18 38	23 48	5 17	24 30	20 7	24 33	1 22	11 36
23	29 10	3♒34	25 49	6 30	25 9	20 17	24 29	1 21	11 38
24	0♍ 8	18 37	27 49	7 43	25 47	20 28	24 24	1 20	11 40
25	1 6	3♓40	29 48	8 57	26 26	20 38	24 20	1 20	11 42
26	2 4	18 34	1♍47	10 10	27 4	20 48	24 15	1 19	11 44
27	3 1	3♈11	3 45	11 23	27 43	20 59	24 11	1 18	11 47
28	3 59	17 24	5 41	12 37	28 21	21 9	24 6	1 17	11 49
29	4 57	1♉11	7 37	13 50	28 59	21 20	24 2	1 16	11 51
30	5 55	14 30	9 32	15 4	29 38	21 31	23 58	1 15	11 53
31	6 53	27 24	11 25	16 17	0♌16	21 42	23 54	1 14	11 55

Pluto 24 Cancer all month

1934

SEPTEMBER

Day	☉ ° ′	☽ ° ′	☿ ° ′	♀ ° ′	♂ ° ′	♃ ° ′	♄ ° ′	♅ ° ′	♆ ° ′
1	7♍51	9♊56	13♍17	17♌31	0♌55	21♎53	23♒49	1♉12	11♍58
2	8 49	22 9	15 8	18 44	1 33	22 4	23 ℞ 45	1 ℞ 11	12 0
3	9 48	4♋ 8	16 58	19 58	2 11	22 15	23 40	1 10	12 2
4	10 46	16 0	18 46	21 12	2 49	22 26	23 36	1 9	12 4
5	11 44	27 47	20 33	22 26	3 27	22 37	23 32	1 7	12 6
6	12 42	9♌34	22 19	23 40	4 5	22 49	23 28	1 6	12 9
7	13 40	21 25	24 4	24 54	4 43	23 0	23 24	1 5	12 11
8	14 39	3♍22	25 48	26 8	5 21	23 11	23 20	1 3	12 13
9	15 37	15 28	27 30	27 21	5 59	23 23	23 16	1 2	12 15
10	16 35	27 44	29 12	28 35	6 36	23 34	23 12	1 0	12 18
11	17 34	10♎12	0♎52	29 49	7 14	23 46	23 8	0 59	12 20
12	18 32	22 52	2 31	1♍ 3	7 52	23 58	23 4	0 57	12 22
13	19 30	5♏45	4 9	2 17	8 30	24 9	23 0	0 55	12 24
14	20 29	18 52	5 46	3 32	9 7	24 21	22 57	0 54	12 27
15	21 27	2♐13	7 22	4 46	9 45	24 33	22 53	0 52	12 29
16	22 26	15 48	8 57	6 0	10 23	24 45	22 49	0 50	12 31
17	23 24	29 39	10 30	7 14	11 0	24 57	22 46	0 49	12 33
18	24 23	13♑46	12 3	8 28	11 38	25 9	22 42	0 47	12 35
19	25 21	28 7	13 35	9 42	12 15	25 21	22 39	0 45	12 38
20	26 20	12♒42	15 5	10 56	12 52	25 33	22 35	0 43	12 40
21	27 19	27 24	16 35	12 11	13 29	25 45	22 32	0 41	12 42
22	28 17	12♓ 9	18 3	13 25	14 6	25 58	22 28	0 39	12 44
23	29 16	26 50	19 31	14 40	14 43	26 10	22 25	0 37	12 46
24	0♎15	11♈19	20 57	15 54	15 20	26 22	22 22	0 35	12 48
25	1 14	25 29	22 22	17 9	15 57	26 35	22 19	0 33	12 51
26	2 12	9♉16	23 46	18 23	16 34	26 47	22 17	0 31	12 53
27	3 11	22 38	25 10	19 38	17 11	27 0	22 14	0 29	12 55
28	4 10	5♊35	26 31	20 52	17 48	27 12	22 11	0 27	12 57
29	5 9	18 9	27 52	22 7	18 25	27 25	22 8	0 25	12 59
30	6 8	0♋23	29 12	23 21	19 1	27 37	22 6	0 23	13 1

Pluto 25 Cancer all month

OCTOBER

Day	☉ ° ′	☽ ° ′	☿ ° ′	♀ ° ′	♂ ° ′	♃ ° ′	♄ ° ′	♅ ° ′	♆ ° ′
1	7♎ 7	12♋23	0♏30	24♍36	19♌38	27♎50	22♒ 3	0♉21	13♍ 3
2	8 6	24 14	1 47	25 51	20 15	28 3	22 ℞ 0	0 ℞ 18	13 5
3	9 5	6♌ 1	3 2	27 5	20 51	28 15	21 58	0 16	13 7
4	10 4	17 50	4 16	28 20	21 28	28 28	21 56	0 14	13 9
5	11 3	29 45	5 29	29 35	22 4	28 40	21 54	0 12	13 11
6	12 2	11♍49	6 40	0♎50	22 41	28 53	21 52	0 9	13 13
7	13 2	24 7	7 48	2 4	23 17	29 6	21 50	0 7	13 15
8	14 1	6♎38	8 55	3 19	23 54	29 19	21 48	0 5	13 17
9	15 0	19 25	10 0	4 34	24 30	29 32	21 46	0 2	13 19
10	15 59	2♏27	11 3	5 49	25 6	29 45	21 44	0 0	13 21
11	16 59	15 42	12 3	7 4	25 42	29 58	21 43	29♈58	13 23
12	17 58	29 8	13 0	8 19	26 18	0♏10	21 41	29 55	13 25
13	18 58	12♐45	13 55	9 34	26 54	0 23	21 40	29 53	13 27
14	19 57	26 30	14 46	10 49	27 30	0 36	21 39	29 51	13 29
15	20 56	10♑23	15 33	12 4	28 6	0 49	21 37	29 48	13 31
16	21 56	24 24	16 16	13 19	28 41	1 2	21 36	29 46	13 32
17	22 55	8♒32	16 55	14 34	29 17	1 15	21 35	29 43	13 34
18	23 55	22 46	17 30	15 49	29 53	1 28	21 34	29 41	13 36
19	24 55	7♓ 4	17 59	17 4	0♍28	1 41	21 33	29 39	13 38
20	25 54	21 23	18 22	18 19	1 4	1 54	21 33	29 36	13 40
21	26 54	5♈39	18 39	19 34	1 39	2 7	21 32	29 34	13 41
22	27 54	19 47	18 50	20 49	2 14	2 20	21 31	29 31	13 43
23	28 53	3♉42	18 53	22 4	2 50	2 33	21 31	29 29	13 45
24	29 53	17 18	18 ℞ 48	23 20	3 25	2 47	21 30	29 26	13 46
25	0♏53	0♊34	18 34	24 35	4 0	3 0	21 30	29 24	13 48
26	1 53	13 28	18 12	25 50	4 35	3 13	21 30	29 21	13 50
27	2 52	26 0	17 40	27 5	5 10	3 26	21 30	29 19	13 51
28	3 52	8♋15	16 59	28 21	5 45	3 39	21 D30	29 16	13 53
29	4 52	20 16	16 8	29 36	6 20	3 52	21 30	29 14	13 54
30	5 52	2♌ 7	15 9	0♏51	6 55	4 5	21 30	29 11	13 56
31	6 52	13 55	14 4	2 6	7 29	4 18	21 31	29 9	13 58

Pluto 25 Cancer all month

1934

NOVEMBER

Pluto 26 Cancer all month

Day	☉	☽	☿	♀	♂	♃	♄	♅	♆
1	7♏52	25♌44	12♏53	3♏22	8♍4	4♏31	21≈31	29♈6	13♍59
2	8 52	7♍41	11R38	4 37	8 38	4 44	21 32	29R4	14 1
3	9 52	19 50	10 20	5 52	9 13	4 57	21 33	29 2	14 2
4	10 52	2≏15	9 3	7 7	9 47	5 10	21 33	28 59	14 3
5	11 53	14 59	7 48	8 23	10 22	5 24	21 34	28 57	14 5
6	12 53	28 3	6 38	9 38	10 56	5 37	21 35	28 54	14 6
7	13 53	11♏25	5 35	10 53	11 30	5 50	21 36	28 52	14 8
8	14 53	25 5	4 42	12 8	12 4	6 3	21 37	28 50	14 9
9	15 54	8✗57	3 59	13 24	12 38	6 16	21 39	28 47	14 10
10	16 54	12 59	3 27	14 39	13 12	6 29	21 40	28 45	14 11
11	17 54	7♑6	3 7	15 54	13 46	6 42	21 42	28 43	14 13
12	18 55	21 14	2 58	17 10	14 19	6 55	21 43	28 40	14 14
13	19 55	5≈23	3D0	18 25	14 53	7 8	21 45	28 38	14 15
14	20 55	19 29	3 13	19 41	15 26	7 21	21 47	28 36	14 16
15	21 56	3✕33	3 36	20 56	16 0	7 34	21 49	28 33	14 17
16	22 56	17 33	4 9	22 11	16 33	7 47	21 51	28 31	14 18
17	23 57	1♈29	4 50	23 27	17 6	7 59	21 53	28 29	14 19
18	24 57	15 19	5 38	24 42	17 39	8 12	21 55	28 27	14 20
19	25 58	29 0	6 32	25 57	18 13	8 25	21 57	28 25	14 21
20	26 58	12♉29	7 32	27 13	18 46	8 38	22 0	28 23	14 22
21	27 59	25 45	8 37	28 28	19 18	8 50	22 2	28 21	14 23
22	29 0	8♊45	9 47	29 44	19 50	9 3	22 5	28 19	14 24
23	0✗0	21 28	11 0	0✗59	20 23	9 16	22 8	28 17	14 25
24	1 1	3♋54	12 16	2 15	20 55	9 29	22 11	28 15	14 26
25	2 1	16 5	13 35	3 30	21 28	9 41	22 14	28 13	14 26
26	3 2	28 4	14 56	4 46	22 0	9 54	22 17	28 11	14 27
27	4 3	9♌55	16 19	6 1	22 32	10 7	22 20	28 9	14 28
28	5 4	21 42	17 43	7 17	23 4	10 19	22 23	28 7	14 29
29	6 4	3♍31	19 9	8 32	23 36	10 32	22 27	28 5	14 29
30	7 5	15 28	20 37	9 48	24 8	10 44	22 30	28 3	14 30

DECEMBER

Pluto 25 Cancer all month

Day	☉	☽	☿	♀	♂	♃	♄	♅	♆
1	8✗6	27♍37	22♏5	11✗3	24♍39	10♏56	22≈33	28♈2	14♍30
2	9 7	10≏3	23 33	12 18	25 11	11 9	22 37	28R0	14 31
3	10 8	22 51	25 3	13 34	25 43	11 21	22 40	27 58	14 31
4	11 9	6♏3	26 33	14 49	26 14	11 33	22 44	27 57	14 32
5	12 9	19 38	28 4	16 4	26 45	11 45	22 48	27 55	14 32
6	13 10	3✗36	29 35	17 20	27 16	11 58	22 52	27 53	14 33
7	14 11	17 51	1✗6	18 35	27 46	12 10	22 56	27 52	14 33
8	15 12	2♑20	2 37	19 51	28 17	12 22	23 0	27 51	14 34
9	16 13	16 54	4 9	21 6	28 47	12 34	23 4	27 49	14 34
10	17 14	1≈29	5 41	22 22	29 18	12 46	23 8	27 48	14 34
11	18 15	15 58	7 13	23 37	29 48	12 58	23 13	27 46	14 34
12	19 16	0✕17	8 46	24 53	0≏18	13 10	23 17	27 45	14 35
13	20 17	14 26	10 19	26 8	0 48	13 22	23 21	27 44	14 35
14	21 18	28 21	11 51	27 24	1 18	13 33	23 26	27 43	14 35
15	22 19	12♈5	13 24	28 39	1 47	13 45	23 30	27 42	14 35
16	23 20	25 35	14 57	29 55	2 17	13 56	23 35	27 41	14 35
17	24 21	8♉52	16 30	1✗10	2 46	14 8	23 40	27 39	14 35
18	25 23	21 57	18 3	2 26	3 15	14 19	23 45	27 38	14R35
19	26 24	4♊49	19 37	3 41	3 44	14 31	23 50	27 37	14 35
20	27 25	17 28	21 10	4 57	4 13	14 42	23 55	27 37	14 35
21	28 26	29 54	22 44	6 12	4 41	14 53	24 0	27 36	14 35
22	29 27	12♋9	24 18	7 27	5 10	15 4	24 5	27 35	14 35
23	0♑28	24 13	25 52	8 43	5 38	15 15	24 10	27 34	14 35
24	1 29	6♌8	27 26	9 58	6 6	15 26	24 15	27 34	14 34
25	2 30	17 57	29 1	11 13	6 34	15 37	24 20	27 33	14 34
26	3 31	29 44	0✗36	12 29	7 1	15 48	24 26	27 32	14 34
27	4 32	11♍33	2 11	13 44	7 28	15 58	24 32	27 32	14 34
28	5 34	23 28	3 46	15 0	7 56	16 9	24 37	27 31	14 33
29	6 35	5≏35	5 22	16 15	8 23	16 20	24 43	27 31	14 33
30	7 36	17 58	6 58	17 30	8 49	16 30	24 48	27 31	14 32
31	8 37	0♏42	8 34	18 46	9 15	16 41	24 54	27 30	14 32

1935

JANUARY

Day	☉ ° ′	☽ ° ′	☿ ° ′	♀ ° ′	♂ ° ′	♃ ° ′	♄ ° ′	♅ ° ′	♆ ° ′
1	9 ♑ 38	13 ♏ 51	10 ♑ 10	20 ♑ 1	9 ♎ 42	16 ♏ 51	25 ♒ 0	27 ♈ 30	14 ♍ 31
2	10 39	27 26	11 47	21 17	10 8	17 1	25 6	27 R 30	14 R 31
3	11 41	11 ♐ 28	13 24	22 32	10 34	17 11	25 12	27 30	14 30
4	12 42	25 54	15 1	23 48	10 59	17 21	25 18	27 30	14 30
5	13 43	10 ♑ 38	16 39	25 3	11 25	17 31	25 24	27 29	14 29
6	14 44	25 35	18 17	26 18	11 50	17 41	25 30	27 29	14 29
7	15 45	10 ♒ 35	19 56	27 34	12 14	17 51	25 36	27 D 29	14 28
8	16 46	25 30	21 35	28 49	12 39	18 0	25 42	27 29	14 27
9	17 48	10 ♓ 13	23 14	0 ♒ 4	13 3	18 10	25 48	27 30	14 27
10	18 49	24 39	24 54	1 19	13 27	18 19	25 54	27 30	14 26
11	19 50	8 ♈ 44	26 34	2 35	13 51	18 28	26 1	27 30	14 25
12	20 51	22 29	28 14	3 50	14 14	18 37	26 7	27 30	14 24
13	21 52	5 ♉ 52	29 55	5 5	14 37	18 46	26 14	27 31	14 23
14	22 53	18 57	1 ♒ 35	6 20	15 0	18 55	26 20	27 31	14 22
15	23 54	1 ♊ 44	3 16	7 36	15 23	19 4	26 27	27 32	14 22
16	24 56	14 17	4 57	8 51	15 45	19 12	26 33	27 32	14 21
17	25 57	26 38	6 38	10 6	16 7	19 21	26 39	27 33	14 20
18	26 58	8 ♋ 48	8 19	11 21	16 28	19 29	26 46	27 33	14 19
19	27 59	20 50	10 0	12 37	16 49	19 38	26 52	27 34	14 18
20	29 0	2 ♌ 45	11 40	13 52	17 10	19 46	26 59	27 35	14 17
21	0 ♒ 1	14 36	13 20	15 7	17 31	19 54	27 6	27 35	14 16
22	1 2	26 24	14 59	16 22	17 51	20 2	27 13	27 36	14 14
23	2 3	8 ♍ 12	16 38	17 37	18 11	20 10	27 20	27 37	14 13
24	3 4	20 3	18 15	18 52	18 30	20 17	27 27	27 38	14 12
25	4 5	2 ♎ 0	19 50	20 7	18 49	20 25	27 34	27 39	14 11
26	5 6	14 7	21 23	21 22	19 7	20 32	27 41	27 40	14 10
27	6 7	26 28	22 54	22 38	19 26	20 39	27 47	27 41	14 9
28	7 8	9 ♏ 7	24 22	23 53	19 44	20 46	27 54	27 42	14 7
29	8 9	22 7	25 46	25 8	20 1	20 53	28 1	27 43	14 6
30	9 10	5 ♐ 33	27 5	26 23	20 18	21 0	28 8	27 44	14 5
31	10 11	19 25	28 20	27 38	20 35	21 6	28 15	27 46	14 4

Pluto 25 Cancer all month

FEBRUARY

Day	☉ ° ′	☽ ° ′	☿ ° ′	♀ ° ′	♂ ° ′	♃ ° ′	♄ ° ′	♅ ° ′	♆ ° ′
1	11 ♒ 12	3 ♑ 45	29 ♒ 30	28 ♒ 52	20 ♎ 51	21 ♏ 13	28 ♒ 23	27 ♈ 47	14 ♍ 2
2	12 13	18 28	0 ♓ 35	0 ♓ 7	21 6	21 19	28 30	27 48	14 R 1
3	13 13	3 ♒ 31	1 28	1 22	21 21	21 25	28 37	27 50	14 0
4	14 14	18 43	2 16	2 37	21 36	21 31	28 44	27 51	13 58
5	15 15	3 ♓ 56	2 55	3 52	21 50	21 37	28 51	27 53	13 57
6	16 16	19 0	3 24	5 7	22 4	21 43	28 58	27 54	13 55
7	17 17	3 ♈ 46	3 43	6 22	22 17	21 49	29 5	27 56	13 54
8	18 18	18 9	3 52	7 37	22 30	21 54	29 12	27 57	13 53
9	19 18	2 ♉ 5	3 R 50	8 51	22 42	22 0	29 20	27 59	13 51
10	20 19	15 33	3 37	10 6	22 53	22 5	29 27	28 1	13 50
11	21 20	28 37	3 12	11 21	23 4	22 10	29 34	28 2	13 48
12	22 21	11 ♊ 18	2 38	12 36	23 15	22 14	29 41	28 4	13 47
13	23 21	23 42	1 55	13 50	23 25	22 19	29 48	28 6	13 45
14	24 22	5 ♋ 51	1 4	15 5	23 34	22 23	29 56	28 8	13 44
15	25 22	17 50	0 7	16 20	23 42	22 28	0 ♓ 3	28 10	13 42
16	26 23	29 43	29 ♒ 4	17 34	23 51	22 32	0 10	28 12	13 41
17	27 24	11 ♌ 32	27 58	18 49	23 59	22 36	0 18	28 14	13 39
18	28 24	23 20	26 50	20 3	24 6	22 40	0 25	28 16	13 37
19	29 25	5 ♍ 9	25 42	21 18	24 12	22 43	0 32	28 18	13 36
20	0 ♓ 25	17 1	24 36	22 32	24 18	22 47	0 39	28 20	13 34
21	1 25	28 59	23 35	23 47	24 22	22 50	0 47	28 22	13 33
22	2 26	11 ♎ 3	22 36	25 1	24 27	22 53	0 54	28 25	13 31
23	3 26	23 16	21 43	26 15	24 30	22 56	1 1	28 27	13 29
24	4 27	5 ♏ 41	20 55	27 30	24 33	22 59	1 8	28 29	13 28
25	5 27	18 20	20 16	28 44	24 35	23 1	1 16	28 31	13 26
26	6 27	1 ♐ 16	19 44	29 58	24 37	23 4	1 23	28 34	13 24
27	7 28	14 33	19 19	1 ♈ 12	24 37	23 6	1 30	28 36	13 23
28	8 28	28 13	19 1	2 27	24 R 37	23 8	1 37	28 39	13 21

Pluto 24 Cancer all month

1935

MARCH

DAY	☉	☽	☿	♀	♂	♃	♄	♅	♆
	° ′	° ′	° ′	° ′	° ′	° ′	° ′	° ′	° ′
1	9♓28	12♑18	18♒51	3♈41	24♎36	23♏10	1♓45	28♈41	13♍19
2	10 28	26 46	18℞47	4 55	24℞35	23 12	1 52	28 44	13℞17
3	11 29	11♒36	18 D50	6 9	24 33	23 13	1 59	28 46	13 16
4	12 29	26 42	18 59	7 23	24 30	23 14	2 6	28 49	13 14
5	13 29	11♓54	19 14	8 37	24 26	23 15	2 14	28 51	13 12
6	14 29	27 4	19 34	9 51	24 22	23 16	2 21	28 54	13 11
7	15 29	12♈ 1	20 0	11 5	24 16	23 17	2 28	28 57	13 9
8	16 29	26 35	20 30	12 19	24 10	23 17	2 35	28 59	13 7
9	17 29	10♉43	21 5	13 33	24 3	23 18	2 43	29 2	13 6
10	18 29	24 21	21 44	14 47	23 56	23℞18	2 50	29 5	13 4
11	19 29	7♊31	22 27	16 1	23 47	23 18	2 57	29 8	13 2
12	20 29	20 15	23 14	17 14	23 38	23 17	3 4	29 11	13 0
13	21 29	2♋37	24 4	18 28	23 28	23 17	3 11	29 13	12 59
14	22 29	14 44	24 57	19 41	23 17	23 16	3 18	29 16	12 57
15	23 28	26 39	25 54	20 55	23 5	23 16	3 25	29 19	12 55
16	24 28	8♌27	26 53	22 8	22 53	23 14	3 32	29 22	12 54
17	25 28	20 14	27 55	23 22	22 40	23 13	3 39	29 25	12 52
18	26 28	2♍ 3	28 59	24 35	22 27	23 12	3 46	29 28	12 51
19	27 27	13 55	0♓ 6	25 48	22 13	23 10	3 53	29 31	12 49
20	28 27	25 55	1 15	27 2	21 58	23 9	4 0	29 34	12 47
21	29 27	8♎ 2	2 26	28 15	21 42	23 7	4 6	29 37	12 46
22	0♈26	20 18	3 39	29 28	21 25	23 5	4 13	29 40	12 44
23	1 26	2♏44	4 54	0♉41	21 7	23 2	4 20	29 43	12 43
24	2 25	15 21	6 11	1 54	20 49	23 0	4 27	29 47	12 41
25	3 25	28 10	7 30	3 7	20 31	22 57	4 33	29 50	12 39
26	4 24	11♐12	8 51	4 20	20 12	22 54	4 40	29 53	12 38
27	5 23	24 29	10 13	5 33	19 52	22 51	4 47	29 56	12 36
28	6 23	8♑ 3	11 37	6 46	19 32	22 48	4 53	29 59	12 35
29	7 22	21 56	13 2	7 59	19 12	22 45	5 0	0♉ 3	12 33
30	8 21	6♒ 8	14 29	9 12	18 51	22 41	5 6	0 6	12 32
31	9 21	20 39	15 58	10 25	18 30	22 37	5 13	0 9	12 30

Pluto 24 Cancer all month

APRIL

DAY	☉	☽	☿	♀	♂	♃	♄	♅	♆
	° ′	° ′	° ′	° ′	° ′	° ′	° ′	° ′	° ′
1	10♈20	5♓25	17♓28	11♉37	18♎ 8	22♏34	5♓19	0♉12	12♍29
2	11 19	20 20	19 0	12 50	17℞46	22℞29	5 26	0 16	12℞28
3	12 18	5♈16	20 33	14 2	17 24	22 25	5 32	0 19	12 26
4	13 17	20 5	22 8	15 14	17 1	22 21	5 38	0 22	12 25
5	14 17	4♉38	23 44	16 27	16 39	22 16	5 44	0 26	12 23
6	15 16	18 47	25 21	17 39	16 16	22 12	5 51	0 29	12 22
7	16 15	2♊29	27 0	18 51	15 53	22 7	5 57	0 32	12 21
8	17 14	15 43	28 41	20 3	15 30	22 2	6 3	0 36	12 19
9	18 13	28 32	0♈22	21 15	15 7	21 57	6 9	0 39	12 18
10	19 12	10♋57	2 6	22 27	14 44	21 51	6 15	0 43	12 17
11	20 11	23 5	3 51	23 39	14 21	21 46	6 21	0 46	12 16
12	21 9	5♌ 1	5 38	24 51	13 58	21 40	6 27	0 49	12 15
13	22 8	16 50	7 26	26 3	13 35	21 35	6 33	0 52	12 13
14	23 7	28 38	9 15	27 14	13 13	21 29	6 38	0 56	12 12
15	24 6	10♍29	11 6	28 26	12 51	21 23	6 44	1 0	12 11
16	25 4	22 26	12 59	29 37	12 30	21 17	6 50	1 3	12 10
17	26 3	4♎33	14 53	0♊49	12 8	21 11	6 56	1 7	12 9
18	27 2	16 52	16 49	2 0	11 47	21 4	7 1	1 10	12 8
19	28 0	29 23	18 46	3 11	11 25	20 58	7 7	1 14	12 7
20	28 59	12♏ 7	20 45	4 22	11 5	20 51	7 12	1 17	12 6
21	29 57	25 3	22 45	5 33	10 45	20 45	7 18	1 21	12 5
22	0♉56	8♐10	24 47	6 44	10 26	20 38	7 23	1 24	12 4
23	1 54	21 28	26 50	7 55	10 7	20 31	7 28	1 27	12 3
24	2 53	4♑57	28 55	9 6	9 48	20 24	7 33	1 31	12 2
25	3 51	18 37	1♉ 0	10 17	9 30	20 17	7 38	1 34	12 1
26	4 50	2♒29	3 7	11 27	9 13	20 10	7 43	1 38	12 0
27	5 48	16 33	5 15	12 38	8 56	20 3	7 48	1 41	11 59
28	6 46	0♓48	7 23	13 49	8 41	19 56	7 53	1 45	11 58
29	7 45	15 13	9 32	14 59	8 25	19 49	7 58	1 48	11 58
30	8 43	29 44	11 41	16 10	8 11	19 41	8 2	1 51	11 57

Pluto 23 Cancer all month

1935

MAY

DAY	☉	☽	☿	♀	♂	♃	♄	♅	♆
	° ′	° ′	° ′	° ′	° ′	° ′	° ′	° ′	° ′
1	9♉41	14♈16	13♉50	17♊20	7♎57	19♏34	8♓7	1♉55	11♍56
2	10 40	28 43	16 0	18 30	7 R 44	19 R 27	8 12	1 58	11 R 55
3	11 38	12♉57	18 8	19 40	7 31	19 19	8 16	2 2	11 55
4	12 36	26 54	20 16	20 50	7 20	19 12	8 21	2 5	11 54
5	13 34	10♊28	22 23	22 0	7 9	19 4	8 25	2 8	11 53
6	14 32	23 39	24 28	23 10	7 0	18 57	8 29	2 12	11 53
7	15 30	6♋26	26 32	24 19	6 50	18 49	8 34	2 15	11 52
8	16 29	18 53	28 33	25 29	6 42	18 42	8 38	2 19	11 52
9	17 27	1♌3	0♊33	26 38	6 34	18 34	8 42	2 22	11 51
10	18 25	13 1	2 30	27 47	6 28	18 26	8 46	2 25	11 51
11	19 23	24 52	4 25	28 56	6 22	18 19	8 50	2 29	11 50
12	20 21	6♍41	6 17	0♋5	6 17	18 11	8 54	2 32	11 50
13	21 18	18 35	8 6	1 14	6 12	18 3	8 58	2 35	11 50
14	22 16	0♎36	9 51	2 23	6 9	17 55	9 2	2 39	11 49
15	23 14	12 50	11 34	3 32	6 6	17 48	9 5	2 42	11 49
16	24 12	25 18	13 13	4 40	6 4	17 40	9 9	2 45	11 49
17	25 10	8♏3	14 49	5 49	6 3	17 33	9 12	2 48	11 48
18	26 8	21 4	16 21	6 57	6 D 3	17 25	9 15	2 52	11 48
19	27 5	4♐20	17 50	8 5	6 3	17 18	9 19	2 55	11 48
20	28 3	17 50	19 16	9 13	6 5	17 10	9 22	2 58	11 48
21	29 1	1♑32	20 38	10 21	6 7	17 3	9 25	3 1	11 48
22	29 59	15 22	21 57	11 29	6 10	16 56	9 28	3 4	11 48
23	0♊56	29 20	23 12	12 36	6 13	16 48	9 31	3 8	11 48
24	1 54	13♒23	24 23	13 43	6 17	16 41	9 33	3 11	11 48
25	2 51	27 31	25 30	14 51	6 22	16 34	9 36	3 14	11 48
26	3 49	11♓41	26 34	15 48	6 28	16 27	9 39	3 17	11 D 48
27	4 47	25 52	27 34	17 5	6 33	16 20	9 41	3 20	11 48
28	5 44	10♈3	28 29	18 12	6 41	16 13	9 44	3 23	11 48
29	6 42	24 10	29 21	19 18	6 48	16 6	9 46	3 26	11 48
30	7 39	8♉9	0♋9	20 24	6 57	15 59	9 48	3 29	11 48
31	8 37	21 57	0 52	21 30	7 5	15 53	9 51	3 32	11 48

Pluto 23 Cancer all month

JUNE

DAY	☉	☽	☿	♀	♂	♃	♄	♅	♆
	° ′	° ′	° ′	° ′	° ′	° ′	° ′	° ′	° ′
1	9♊35	5♊31	1♋31	22♋36	7♎15	15♏46	9♓53	3♉35	11♍49
2	10 32	18 47	2 6	23 42	7 25	15 R 40	9 55	3 38	11 49
3	11 30	1♋45	2 37	24 48	7 36	15 34	9 57	3 41	11 49
4	12 27	14 24	3 3	25 53	7 48	15 27	9 59	3 44	11 50
5	13 24	26 47	3 25	26 58	8 0	15 21	10 0	3 47	11 50
6	14 22	8♌55	3 42	28 3	8 12	15 15	10 2	3 49	11 50
7	15 19	20 53	3 54	29 8	8 26	15 10	10 3	3 52	11 51
8	16 17	2♍45	4 2	0♌13	8 40	15 4	10 5	3 55	11 51
9	17 14	14 36	4 5	1 17	8 54	14 59	10 6	3 58	11 52
10	18 12	26 30	4 B 4	2 21	9 9	14 53	10 7	4 0	11 52
11	19 9	8♎34	3 58	3 25	9 25	14 48	10 8	4 3	11 53
12	20 6	20 50	3 48	4 29	9 41	14 42	10 9	4 6	11 54
13	21 4	3♏23	3 34	5 32	9 57	14 37	10 10	4 8	11 54
14	22 1	16 15	3 16	6 35	10 14	14 32	10 11	4 11	11 55
15	22 58	29 28	2 54	7 38	10 32	14 27	10 12	4 13	11 56
16	23 55	13♐1	2 29	8 41	10 50	14 23	10 12	4 16	11 56
17	24 53	26 52	2 1	9 43	11 8	14 18	10 13	4 18	11 57
18	25 50	10♑59	1 31	10 45	11 27	14 14	10 13	4 21	11 58
19	26 47	25 15	0 59	11 46	11 47	14 10	10 13	4 24	11 59
20	27 44	9♒38	0 26	12 48	12 7	14 6	10 13	4 26	12 0
21	28 42	24 3	29♊52	13 49	12 27	14 3	10 13	4 28	12 0
22	29 39	8♓25	29 17	14 49	12 48	13 59	10 R 13	4 30	12 1
23	0♋36	22 42	28 42	15 50	13 9	13 56	10 13	4 32	12 2
24	1 33	6♈51	28 9	16 50	13 31	13 53	10 13	4 35	12 3
25	2 31	20 50	27 37	17 49	13 53	13 50	10 13	4 37	12 4
26	3 28	4♉38	27 7	18 49	14 15	13 47	10 13	4 39	12 5
27	4 25	18 14	26 40	19 48	14 38	13 45	10 12	4 41	12 6
28	5 22	1♊36	26 17	20 46	15 1	13 42	10 12	4 43	12 8
29	6 20	14 44	25 56	21 44	15 25	13 40	10 11	4 45	12 9
30	7 17	27 38	25 39	22 42	15 48	13 38	10 10	4 47	12 10

Pluto 24 Cancer all month

1935

JULY

DAY	☉ ° ′	☽ ° ′	☿ ° ′	♀ ° ′	♂ ° ′	♃ ° ′	♄ ° ′	♅ ° ′	♆ ° ′
1	8♋14	10♋18	25♊26	23♌40	16♎13	13♏36	10♓ 9	4♉49	12♍11
2	9 11	22 44	25℞18	24 37	16 37	13℞34	10℞ 8	4 51	12 12
3	10 8	4♌58	25 14	25 33	17 3	13 33	10 7	4 53	12 13
4	11 6	17 1	25 D15	26 29	17 28	13 31	10 6	4 55	12 15
5	12 3	28 56	25 21	27 24	17 54	13 30	10 5	4 57	12 16
6	13 0	10♍48	25 32	28 19	18 19	13 28	10 3	4 58	12 17
7	13 57	22 38	25 48	29 14	18 46	13 27	10 2	5 0	12 18
8	14 55	4♎32	26 9	0♍ 8	19 12	13 27	10 0	5 2	12 20
9	15 52	16 35	26 36	1 1	19 39	13 26	9 58	5 3	12 21
10	16 49	28 50	27 7	1 54	20 6	13 26	9 57	5 5	12 22
11	17 46	11♏23	27 44	2 46	20 34	13 26	9 55	5 6	12 24
12	18 43	24 16	28 25	3 37	21 2	13 D26	9 53	5 8	12 25
13	19 41	7♐32	29 12	4 28	21 30	13 26	9 51	5 9	12 27
14	20 38	21 13	0♋ 3	5 18	21 59	13 26	9 49	5 11	12 28
15	21 35	5♑17	1 0	6 7	22 27	13 27	9 47	5 12	12 30
16	22 32	19 42	2 1	6 56	22 56	13 27	9 44	5 13	12 31
17	23 29	4♒22	3 7	7 44	23 26	13 28	9 42	5 15	12 33
18	24 27	19 10	4 18	8 31	23 55	13 29	9 39	5 16	12 35
19	25 24	4♓ 0	5 33	9 18	24 25	13 31	9 37	5 17	12 36
20	26 21	18 45	6 53	10 3	24 55	13 32	9 34	5 18	12 38
21	27 18	3♈17	8 17	10 48	25 25	13 34	9 31	5 19	12 39
22	28 16	17 34	9 46	11 31	25 55	13 35	9 29	5 20	12 41
23	29 13	1♉32	11 19	12 14	26 26	13 37	9 26	5 21	12 43
24	0♌10	15 11	12 55	12 56	26 57	13 39	9 23	5 22	12 45
25	1 7	28 31	14 36	13 37	27 29	13 41	9 20	5 23	12 46
26	2 5	11♊34	16 20	14 17	28 0	13 44	9 17	5 24	12 48
27	3 2	24 22	18 8	14 55	28 32	13 46	9 14	5 25	12 50
28	3 59	6♋55	20 0	15 33	29 4	13 49	9 11	5 25	12 52
29	4 57	19 17	21 54	16 9	29 36	13 52	9 8	5 26	12 53
30	5 54	1♌29	23 50	16 44	0♏ 8	13 55	9 4	5 27	12 55
31	6 52	13 32	25 49	17 18	0 41	13 59	9 1	5 27	12 57

Pluto 25 Cancer all month

AUGUST

DAY	☉ ° ′	☽ ° ′	☿ ° ′	♀ ° ′	♂ ° ′	♃ ° ′	♄ ° ′	♅ ° ′	♆ ° ′
1	7♌49	25♌29	27♋49	17♍51	1♏14	14♏ 2	8♓57	5♉28	12♍59
2	8 46	7♍21	29 51	18 22	1 47	14 6	8℞54	5 28	13 1
3	9 44	19 11	1♌54	18 52	2 20	14 10	8 50	5 29	13 3
4	10 41	1♎ 2	3 58	19 20	2 54	14 14	8 47	5 29	13 5
5	11 39	12 56	6 2	19 46	3 27	14 18	8 43	5 30	13 7
6	12 36	24 58	8 7	20 11	4 1	14 22	8 39	5 30	13 9
7	13 34	7♏11	10 12	20 35	4 35	14 27	8 35	5 30	13 11
8	14 31	19 40	12 16	20 57	5 9	14 31	8 31	5 30	13 13
9	15 29	2♐29	14 20	21 17	5 44	14 36	8 27	5 30	13 15
10	16 26	15 41	16 23	21 35	6 19	14 41	8 23	5 31	13 17
11	17 24	29 20	18 26	21 51	6 54	14 46	8 19	5 31	13 19
12	18 21	13♑25	20 27	22 6	7 29	14 52	8 15	5℞ 31	13 21
13	19 19	27 56	22 28	22 18	8 4	14 57	8 11	5 31	13 23
14	20 17	12♒48	24 27	22 28	8 40	15 2	8 7	5 31	13 25
15	21 14	27 54	26 25	22 36	9 15	15 8	8 3	5 30	13 27
16	22 12	13♓ 5	28 21	22 42	9 51	15 13	7 58	5 30	13 29
17	23 9	28 11	0♍16	22 45	10 27	15 19	7 54	5 30	13 31
18	24 7	13♈ 2	2 10	22 46	11 3	15 25	7 50	5 30	13 34
19	25 5	27 33	4 2	22℞45	11 40	15 32	7 45	5 29	13 36
20	26 3	11♉39	5 53	22 42	12 16	15 38	7 41	5 29	13 38
21	27 0	25 18	7 43	22 36	12 53	15 45	7 36	5 28	13 40
22	27 58	8♊33	9 31	22 28	13 30	15 52	7 32	5 28	13 42
23	28 56	21 26	11 18	22 18	14 7	15 58	7 27	5 27	13 44
24	29 54	4♋ 1	13 3	22 5	14 44	16 5	7 23	5 27	13 47
25	0♍52	16 21	14 47	21 50	15 21	16 12	7 18	5 26	13 49
26	1 49	28 29	16 29	21 32	15 59	16 19	7 14	5 26	13 51
27	2 47	10♌30	18 11	21 13	16 36	16 27	7 9	5 25	13 53
28	3 45	22 25	19 50	20 51	17 14	16 34	7 5	5 24	13 55
29	4 43	4♍16	21 29	20 27	17 52	16 42	7 0	5 23	13 57
30	5 41	16 7	23 7	20 1	18 30	16 50	6 56	5 22	14 0
31	6 39	27 57	24 43	19 32	19 8	16 58	6 51	5 22	14 2

Pluto 25 Cancer all month

1935

SEPTEMBER

DAY	☉ ° ′	☽ ° ′	☿ ° ′	♀ ° ′	♂ ° ′	♃ ° ′	♄ ° ′	♅ ° ′	♆ ° ′
1	7♍37	9♎50	26♍18	19♍ 2	19♏47	17♏ 6	6♓47	5♉21	14♍ 4
2	8 36	21 47	27 52	18℞31	20 25	17 14	6℞ 42	5℞ 20	14 6
3	9 34	3♏51	29 24	17 58	21 4	17 22	6 37	5 19	14 8
4	10 32	16 5	0♎55	17 24	21 43	17 31	6 33	5 17	14 11
5	11 30	28 32	2 25	16 49	22 22	17 39	6 28	5 16	14 13
6	12 28	11♐16	3 53	16 13	23 1	17 48	6 23	5 15	14 15
7	13 26	24 21	5 20	15 37	23 40	17 57	6 18	5 14	14 17
8	14 25	7♑51	6 46	15 0	24 19	18 5	6 14	5 13	14 20
9	15 23	21 48	8 11	14 23	24 59	18 14	6 9	5 11	14 22
10	16 21	6♒13	9 34	13 46	25 38	18 23	6 5	5 10	14 24
11	17 19	21 2	10 56	13 9	26 18	18 32	6 1	5 9	14 26
12	18 18	6♓11	12 17	12 33	26 58	18 42	5 56	5 7	14 29
13	19 16	21 29	13 36	11 58	27 38	18 51	5 52	5 6	14 31
14	20 14	6♈47	14 53	11 24	28 18	19 1	5 48	5 4	14 33
15	21 13	21 52	16 9	10 51	28 58	19 11	5 44	5 3	14 35
16	22 11	6♉36	17 23	10 19	29 38	19 20	5 39	5 1	14 37
17	23 10	20 52	18 36	9 49	0♐19	19 30	5 35	5 0	14 39
18	24 8	4♊39	19 47	9 20	0 59	19 40	5 31	4 58	14 42
19	25 7	17 57	20 56	8 54	1 40	19 50	5 27	4 56	14 44
20	26 6	0♋49	22 3	8 29	2 20	20 0	5 23	4 55	14 46
21	27 4	13 20	23 8	8 7	3 1	20 11	5 19	4 53	14 48
21	28 3	25 33	24 11	7 47	3 42	20 21	5 15	4 51	14 50
23	29 2	7♌35	25 12	7 29	4 23	20 31	5 11	4 49	14 53
24	0♎ 0	19 29	26 10	7 13	5 5	20 42	5 7	4 47	14 55
25	0 59	1♍20	27 5	7 0	5 46	20 52	5 3	4 45	14 57
26	1 58	13 9	27 57	6 50	6 28	21 3	4 59	4 43	14 59
27	2 57	25 0	28 46	6 42	7 10	21 14	4 55	4 41	15 1
28	3 56	6♎54	29 32	6 36	7 51	21 25	4 51	4 39	15 3
29	4 55	18 53	0♏14	6 33	8 33	21 36	4 48	4 37	15 6
30	5 54	0♏58	0 52	6 D33	9 15	21 47	4 44	4 35	15 8

Pluto 26 Cancer all month

OCTOBER

DAY	☉ ° ′	☽ ° ′	☿ ° ′	♀ ° ′	♂ ° ′	♃ ° ′	♄ ° ′	♅ ° ′	♆ ° ′
1	6♎53	13♏ 9	1♏25	6♍35	9♐57	21♏58	4♓41	4♉33	15♍10
2	7 52	25 30	1 53	6 39	10 39	22 9	4℞ 37	4℞ 31	15 12
3	8 51	8♐ 1	2 16	6 46	11 21	22 20	4 34	4 29	15 14
4	9 50	20 46	2 34	6 55	12 3	22 31	4 31	4 27	15 16
5	10 49	3♑49	2 45	7 6	12 45	22 42	4 28	4 25	15 18
6	11 48	17 12	2 50	7 20	13 28	22 54	4 25	4 22	15 20
7	12 47	0♒58	2℞47	7 35	14 10	23 5	4 22	4 20	15 22
8	13 46	15 9	2 37	7 53	14 53	23 17	4 19	4 18	15 24
9	14 46	29 44	2 19	8 12	15 36	23 29	4 16	4 16	15 26
10	15 45	14♓39	1 53	8 33	16 19	23 41	4 13	4 13	15 28
11	16 44	29 47	1 19	8 55	17 2	23 53	4 10	4 11	15 30
12	17 44	14♈59	0 37	9 20	17 45	24 5	4 7	4 9	15 32
13	18 43	0♉ 4	29♎47	9 46	18 28	24 17	4 5	4 7	15 34
14	19 42	14 52	28 48	10 14	19 11	24 29	4 2	4 4	15 36
15	20 42	29 14	27 44	10 43	19 55	24 41	4 0	4 2	15 38
16	21 41	13♊ 8	26 35	11 14	20 38	24 53	3 58	3 59	15 40
17	22 41	26 32	25 24	11 46	21 22	25 5	3 56	3 57	15 42
18	23 40	9♋28	24 11	12 20	22 5	25 17	3 53	3 55	15 44
19	24 40	22 1	22 58	12 56	22 49	25 30	3 51	3 52	15 45
20	25 39	4♌16	21 48	13 32	23 33	25 42	3 49	3 50	15 47
21	26 39	16 16	20 42	14 10	24 17	25 54	3 47	3 47	15 49
22	27 39	28 9	19 43	14 49	25 1	26 7	3 45	3 45	15 51
23	28 39	9♍59	18 51	15 30	25 45	26 19	3 44	3 42	15 52
24	29 38	21 49	18 11	16 11	26 29	26 32	3 42	3 40	15 54
25	0♏38	3♎43	17 41	16 54	27 13	26 45	3 41	3 38	15 56
26	1 38	15 43	17 22	17 38	27 57	26 57	3 39	3 35	15 57
27	2 38	27 50	17 14	18 23	28 42	27 10	3 38	3 33	15 59
28	3 38	10♏ 7	17 D18	19 8	29 26	27 23	3 37	3 30	16 1
29	4 38	22 32	17 32	19 55	0♑10	27 36	3 36	3 28	16 2
30	5 38	5♐ 7	17 57	20 42	0 55	27 48	3 35	3 25	16 4
31	6 38	17 52	18 31	21 31	1 39	28 1	3 34	3 23	16 6

Pluto 27 Cancer all month

1935

NOVEMBER

DAY	☉	☽	☿	♀	♂	♃	♄	♅	♆
	° ′	° ′	° ′	° ′	° ′	° ′	° ′	° ′	° ′
1	7 ♏ 38	0 ♑ 48	19 ♎ 13	22 ♍ 20	2 ♑ 24	28 ♏ 14	3 ♓ 33	3 ♉ 20	16 ♍ 7
2	8 38	13 58	20 4	23 10	3 9	28 27	3 R 32	3 R 18	16 9
3	9 38	27 23	21 2	24 1	3 54	28 40	3 32	3 15	16 10
4	10 38	11 ♒ 4	22 5	24 53	4 39	28 53	3 31	3 13	16 12
5	11 38	25 4	23 14	25 45	5 24	29 6	3 31	3 10	16 13
6	12 38	9 ♓ 22	24 27	26 38	6 9	29 19	3 31	3 8	16 14
7	13 38	23 56	25 45	27 32	6 54	29 32	3 D 31	3 6	16 16
8	14 39	8 ♈ 41	27 6	28 27	7 39	29 46	3 31	3 3	16 17
9	15 39	23 32	28 29	29 22	8 24	29 59	3 31	3 1	16 19
10	16 39	8 ♉ 19	29 55	0 ♎ 17	9 9	0 ♐ 12	3 31	2 58	16 20
11	17 39	22 54	1 ♏ 23	1 14	9 54	0 25	3 31	2 56	16 21
12	18 40	7 ♊ 10	2 52	2 11	10 40	0 38	3 32	2 54	16 22
13	19 40	21 2	4 23	3 8	11 25	0 51	3 32	2 51	16 24
14	20 41	4 ♋ 28	5 55	4 6	12 11	1 4	3 33	2 49	16 25
15	21 41	17 28	7 27	5 4	12 56	1 18	3 33	2 47	16 26
16	22 41	0 ♌ 5	9 1	6 3	13 42	1 31	3 34	2 44	16 27
17	23 42	12 23	10 35	7 3	14 28	1 45	3 35	2 42	16 28
18	24 42	24 27	12 9	8 3	15 14	1 58	3 36	2 40	16 29
19	25 43	6 ♍ 21	13 44	9 3	15 59	2 12	3 37	2 38	16 30
20	26 43	18 12	15 18	10 4	16 45	2 25	3 39	2 36	16 31
21	27 44	0 ♎ 4	16 53	11 5	17 31	2 38	3 40	2 34	16 32
22	28 45	12 1	18 28	12 7	18 17	2 51	3 41	2 31	16 33
23	29 45	24 6	20 3	13 9	19 3	3 5	3 43	2 29	16 34
24	0 ♐ 46	6 ♏ 22	21 38	14 12	19 49	3 18	3 44	2 27	16 35
25	1 47	18 50	23 13	15 14	20 35	3 32	3 46	2 25	16 36
26	2 47	1 ♐ 31	24 47	16 18	21 21	3 45	3 48	2 23	16 37
27	3 48	14 26	26 22	17 21	22 7	3 59	3 50	2 21	16 38
28	4 49	27 32	27 57	18 25	22 54	4 12	3 52	2 19	16 38
29	5 50	10 ♑ 50	29 31	19 29	23 40	4 25	3 54	2 17	16 39
30	6 51	24 20	1 ♐ 6	20 33	24 26	4 38	3 56	2 15	16 40

Pluto 27 Cancer all month

DECEMBER

DAY	☉	☽	☿	♀	♂	♃	♄	♅	♆
	° ′	° ′	° ′	° ′	° ′	° ′	° ′	° ′	° ′
1	7 ♐ 51	8 ♒ 0	2 ♐ 40	21 ♎ 38	25 ♑ 12	4 ♐ 52	3 ♓ 58	2 ♉ 13	16 ♍ 40
2	8 52	21 50	4 15	22 43	25 59	5 5	4 1	2 R 11	16 41
3	9 53	5 ♓ 49	5 50	23 49	26 45	5 19	4 3	2 9	16 42
4	10 54	19 58	7 24	24 54	27 31	5 32	4 6	2 8	16 42
5	11 55	4 ♈ 15	8 58	26 0	28 18	5 46	4 8	2 6	16 43
6	12 56	18 36	10 33	27 6	29 4	5 59	4 11	2 4	16 43
7	13 57	2 ♉ 57	12 7	28 13	29 51	6 12	4 14	2 3	16 44
8	14 58	17 15	13 41	29 19	0 ♒ 37	6 25	4 17	2 1	16 44
9	15 59	1 ♊ 24	15 15	0 ♏ 26	1 24	6 39	4 20	1 59	16 45
10	16 59	15 19	16 50	1 34	2 10	6 53	4 23	1 58	16 45
11	18 0	28 56	18 24	2 41	2 57	7 6	4 26	1 56	16 45
12	19 1	12 ♋ 14	19 58	3 48	3 44	7 19	4 30	1 55	16 46
13	20 2	25 10	21 32	4 56	4 30	7 33	4 33	1 54	16 46
14	21 3	7 ♌ 48	23 7	6 4	5 17	7 46	4 37	1 52	16 46
15	22 4	20 8	24 41	7 12	6 4	7 59	4 41	1 51	16 46
16	23 5	2 ♍ 14	26 16	8 20	6 51	8 12	4 45	1 50	16 46
17	24 7	14 11	27 51	9 29	7 37	8 25	4 48	1 48	16 47
18	25 8	26 4	29 26	10 38	8 24	8 38	4 52	1 47	16 47
19	26 9	7 ♎ 56	1 ♑ 1	11 47	9 11	8 51	4 56	1 46	16 47
20	27 10	19 54	2 37	12 56	9 58	9 4	5 0	1 45	16 47
21	28 11	2 ♏ 1	4 12	14 5	10 45	9 17	5 4	1 44	16 B 47
22	29 12	14 21	5 48	15 15	11 32	9 30	5 9	1 43	16 47
23	0 ♑ 13	26 57	7 24	16 24	12 19	9 43	5 13	1 42	16 47
24	1 14	9 ♐ 50	9 0	17 34	13 6	9 56	5 18	1 41	16 47
25	2 16	23 2	10 36	18 44	13 53	10 9	5 22	1 40	16 46
26	3 17	6 ♑ 31	12 12	19 54	14 40	10 22	5 27	1 39	16 46
27	4 18	20 16	13 48	21 4	15 27	10 35	5 32	1 39	16 46
28	5 19	4 ♒ 14	15 25	22 14	16 14	10 48	5 37	1 38	16 46
29	6 20	18 20	17 1	23 24	17 0	11 1	5 41	1 37	16 45
30	7 21	2 ♓ 33	18 38	24 35	17 47	11 13	5 46	1 37	16 45
31	8 23	16 48	20 15	25 45	18 34	11 26	5 51	1 36	16 45

Pluto 27 Cancer all month

1936

JANUARY

Day	☉	☽	☿	♀	♂	♃	♄	♅	♆
	° ′	° ′	° ′	° ′	° ′	° ′	° ′	° ′	° ′
1	9♑24	1♈ 2	21♑51	26♏56	19♒21	11♐39	5♓56	1♉35	16♍45
2	10 25	15 13	23 27	28 7	20 8	11 52	6 1	1℞ 35	16℞44
3	11 26	29 18	25 3	29 18	20 55	12 4	6 7	1 34	16 44
4	12 27	13♉17	26 39	0♐29	21 42	12 17	6 12	1 34	16 43
5	13 28	27 6	28 13	1 40	22 29	12 29	6 17	1 34	16 42
6	14 29	10♊45	29 46	2 51	23 17	12 42	6 23	1 34	16 42
7	15 31	24 12	1♒20	4 3	24 4	12 54	6 28	1 33	16 41
8	16 32	7♋25	2 51	5 14	24 51	13 6	6 34	1 33	16 41
9	17 33	20 24	4 21	6 26	25 38	13 18	6 40	1 33	16 40
10	18 34	3♌ 9	5 48	7 37	26 25	13 31	6 45	1 33	16 40
11	19 35	15 39	7 14	8 49	27 12	13 43	6 51	1 D 33	16 39
12	20 36	27 56	8 37	10 1	27 59	13 55	6 57	1 33	16 38
13	21 37	10♍ 2	9 57	11 13	28 46	14 7	7 3	1 33	16 37
14	22 39	21 59	11 13	12 24	29 33	14 19	7 9	1 33	16 36
15	23 40	3♎52	12 25	13 36	0♓20	14 31	7 15	1 33	16 35
16	24 41	15 44	13 31	14 48	1 7	14 43	7 21	1 34	16 34
17	25 42	27 41	14 32	16 0	1 54	14 55	7 27	1 34	16 34
18	26 43	9♏46	15 25	17 12	2 41	15 6	7 33	1 34	16 33
19	27 44	22 4	16 10	18 25	3 27	15 18	7 39	1 35	16 32
20	28 45	4♐40	16 47	19 37	4 14	15 29	7 45	1 35	16 31
21	29 46	17 37	17 14	20 49	5 1	15 40	7 51	1 36	16 30
22	0♒47	0♑57	17 30	22 1	5 48	15 52	7 58	1 36	16 29
23	1 48	14 41	17 36	23 14	6 35	16 3	8 4	1 37	16 28
24	2 49	28 48	17℞30	24 27	7 22	16 14	8 11	1 38	16 26
25	3 50	13♒12	17 14	25 39	8 9	16 25	8 17	1 38	16 25
26	4 52	27 49	16 46	26 52	8 56	16 36	8 24	1 39	16 24
27	5 53	12♓31	16 6	28 4	9 42	16 47	8 30	1 40	16 23
28	6 54	27 12	15 16	29 17	10 29	16 58	8 37	1 41	16 22
29	7 55	11♈45	14 19	0♑30	11 16	17 9	8 44	1 42	16 21
30	8 55	26 5	13 14	1 42	12 3	17 20	8 50	1 43	16 20
31	9 56	10♉10	12 5	2 55	12 49	17 30	8 57	1 44	16 18

Pluto 26 Cancer all month

FEBRUARY

Day	☉	☽	☿	♀	♂	♃	♄	♅	♆
	° ′	° ′	° ′	° ′	° ′	° ′	° ′	° ′	° ′
1	10♒57	23♉58	10♒52	4♑ 8	13♓36	17♐41	9♓ 4	1♉45	16♍17
2	11 58	7♊30	9℞39	5 21	14 23	17 51	9 11	1 46	16℞16
3	12 59	20 46	8 26	6 34	15 10	18 2	9 17	1 47	16 14
4	14 0	3♋48	7 15	7 47	15 56	18 12	9 24	1 48	16 13
5	15 1	16 37	6 9	9 0	16 43	18 22	9 31	1 50	16 12
6	16 2	29 15	5 11	10 13	17 30	18 32	9 38	1 51	16 10
7	17 2	11♌42	4 19	11 26	18 17	18 42	9 45	1 52	16 9
8	18 3	24 0	3 35	12 40	19 3	18 51	9 52	1 54	16 8
9	19 4	6♍10	2 58	13 53	19 50	19 1	9 59	1 55	16 6
10	20 5	18 11	2 29	15 6	20 37	19 11	10 6	1 57	16 5
11	21 5	0♎ 7	2 9	16 19	21 13	19 20	10 13	1 58	16 3
12	22 6	12 0	1 57	17 33	22 0	19 30	10 20	2 0	16 2
13	23 7	23 51	1 D52	18 46	22 56	19 39	10 27	2 2	16 0
14	24 7	5♏46	1 55	19 59	23 42	19 48	10 34	2 3	15 59
15	25 8	17 48	2 5	21 13	24 29	19 57	10 41	2 5	15 57
16	26 9	0♐ 2	2 21	22 26	25 15	20 6	10 49	2 7	15 56
17	27 9	12 33	2 43	23 40	26 1	20 15	10 56	2 9	15 54
18	28 10	25 25	3 11	24 53	26 47	20 24	11 3	2 11	15 53
19	29 10	8♑43	3 44	26 6	27 34	20 32	11 10	2 13	15 51
20	0♓11	22 29	4 21	27 20	28 20	20 41	11 18	2 15	15 50
21	1 11	6♒43	5 2	28 33	29 6	20 49	11 25	2 17	15 48
22	2 12	21 21	5 47	29 47	29 52	20 57	11 32	2 19	15 46
23	3 12	6♓19	6 36	1♒ 0	0♈38	21 5	11 39	2 21	15 45
24	4 13	21 26	7 28	2 14	1 24	21 13	11 47	2 23	15 43
25	5 13	6♈33	8 24	3 28	2 10	21 21	11 54	2 25	15 41
26	6 13	21 30	9 22	4 41	2 56	21 28	12 1	2 27	15 40
27	7 14	6♉ 9	10 24	5 55	3 42	21 36	12 9	2 29	15 38
28	8 14	20 25	11 28	7 8	4 28	21 43	12 16	2 32	15 37
29	9 14	4♊17	12 34	8 22	5 14	21 50	12 24	2 34	15 35

Pluto 25 Cancer all month

1936

MARCH

DAY	☉	☽	☿	♀	♂	♃	♄	♅	♆
	° ′	° ′	° ′	° ′	° ′	° ′	° ′	° ′	° ′
1	10♓14	17♊45	13♒42	9♒35	6♈ 0	21♐57	12♓31	2♉36	15♍33
2	11 15	0♋51	14 52	10 49	6 46	22 4	12 39	2 39	15℞32
3	12 15	13 39	16 4	12 2	7 31	22 11	12 46	2 41	15 30
4	13 15	26 12	17 18	13 16	8 17	22 18	12 53	2 44	15 28
5	14 15	8♌33	18 34	14 30	9 3	22 24	13 0	2 46	15 27
6	15 15	20 46	19 51	15 43	9 49	22 30	13 8	2 49	15 25
7	16 15	2♍52	21 10	16 57	10 34	22 36	13 15	2 51	15 24
8	17 15	14 52	22 30	18 11	11 20	22 42	13 22	2 54	15 22
9	18 15	26 48	23 52	19 25	12 6	22 48	13 29	2 57	15 20
10	19 15	8♎42	25 16	20 38	12 51	22 54	13 37	2 59	15 19
11	20 15	20 34	26 41	21 52	13 37	22 59	13 44	3 2	15 17
12	21 15	2♏27	28 7	23 6	14 22	23 5	13 52	3 5	15 15
13	22 14	14 23	29 35	24 20	15 7	23 10	13 59	3 8	15 14
14	23 14	26 25	1♓ 4	25 33	15 53	23 15	14 7	3 10	15 12
15	24 14	8♐37	2 34	26 47	16 38	23 20	14 14	3 13	15 10
16	25 14	21 4	4 6	28 1	17 23	23 25	14 21	3 16	15 9
17	26 13	3♑50	5 39	29 15	18 8	23 29	14 28	3 19	15 7
18	27 13	17 1	7 14	0♓28	18 53	23 34	14 35	3 22	15 5
19	28 13	0♒39	8 49	1 42	19 38	23 38	14 43	3 25	15 4
20	29 12	14 47	10 26	2 56	20 23	23 42	14 50	3 28	15 2
21	0♈12	29 24	12 4	4 10	21 8	23 46	14 57	3 31	15 1
22	1 12	14♓24	13 43	5 23	21 53	23 49	15 4	3 34	14 59
23	2 11	29 40	15 23	6 37	22 38	23 53	15 12	3 37	14 57
24	3 11	15♈ 1	17 5	7 51	23 23	23 56	15 19	3 40	14 56
25	4 10	0♉14	18 48	9 5	24 8	23 59	15 26	3 43	14 54
26	5 9	15 10	20 33	10 18	24 53	24 2	15 33	3 46	14 52
27	6 9	29 41	22 19	11 32	25 37	24 5	15 40	3 49	14 51
28	7 8	13♊44	24 6	12 46	26 22	24 8	15 47	3 52	14 49
29	8 8	27 18	25 55	14 0	27 7	24 10	15 54	3 56	14 48
30	9 7	10♋26	27 45	15 13	27 51	24 13	16 1	3 59	14 46
31	10 6	23 11	29 36	16 27	28 36	24 15	16 8	4 2	14 45

Pluto 25 Cancer all month

APRIL

DAY	☉	☽	☿	♀	♂	♃	♄	♅	♆
	° ′	° ′	° ′	° ′	° ′	° ′	° ′	° ′	° ′
1	11♈ 5	5♌39	1♈28	17♓41	29♈20	24♐17	16♓15	4♉ 5	14♍43
2	12 4	17 52	3 22	18 55	0♉ 5	24 19	16 22	4 8	14℞42
3	13 4	29 56	5 18	20 8	0 49	24 20	16 29	4 12	14 40
4	14 3	11♍54	7 14	21 22	1 34	24 22	16 35	4 15	14 39
5	15 2	23 48	9 12	22 36	2 18	24 23	16 42	4 18	14 37
6	16 1	5♎41	11 11	23 50	3 2	24 24	16 49	4 22	14 36
7	17 0	17 34	13 12	25 3	3 46	24 24	16 56	4 25	14 35
8	17 59	29 28	15 14	26 17	4 30	24 25	17 2	4 28	14 33
9	18 58	11♏24	17 17	27 31	5 14	24 26	17 9	4 32	14 32
10	19 56	23 25	19 21	28 45	5 58	24 26	17 16	4 35	14 31
11	20 55	5♐33	21 26	29 58	6 42	24℞26	17 22	4 38	14 29
12	21 54	17 50	23 32	1♈12	7 26	24 26	17 29	4 42	14 28
13	22 53	0♑19	25 38	2 26	8 10	24 25	17 35	4 45	14 27
14	23 52	13 6	27 44	3 39	8 54	24 25	17 41	4 48	14 26
15	24 50	26 12	29 51	4 53	9 38	24 24	17 48	4 52	14 24
16	25 49	9♒43	1♉58	6 6	10 21	24 23	17 54	4 55	14 23
17	26 48	23 40	4 4	7 20	11 5	24 22	18 0	4 59	14 22
18	27 46	8♓ 5	6 9	8 34	11 49	24 21	18 6	5 2	14 21
19	28 45	22 53	8 13	9 47	12 32	24 20	18 13	5 5	14 20
20	29 44	8♈ 0	10 16	11 1	13 16	24 18	18 19	5 9	14 19
21	0♉42	23 15	12 17	12 15	13 59	24 16	18 25	5 12	14 18
22	1 41	8♉28	14 16	13 29	14 43	24 14	18 31	5 16	14 17
23	2 39	23 28	16 13	14 42	15 26	24 12	18 37	5 19	14 16
24	3 38	8♊ 6	18 7	15 56	16 10	24 10	18 43	5 23	14 15
25	4 36	22 18	19 58	17 10	16 53	24 7	18 49	5 26	14 14
26	5 34	6♋ 0	21 46	18 24	17 36	24 4	18 55	5 29	14 13
27	6 33	19 15	23 31	19 37	18 20	24 1	19 1	5 33	14 12
28	7 31	2♌ 5	25 13	20 51	19 3	23 58	19 6	5 36	14 11
29	8 29	14 34	26 51	22 5	19 46	23 55	19 12	5 40	14 10
30	9 28	26 47	28 25	23 19	20 29	23 52	19 18	5 43	14 10

Pluto 25 Cancer all month

1936

MAY

Day	☉	☽	☿	♀	♂	♃	♄	♅	♆
	° ′	° ′	° ′	° ′	° ′	° ′	° ′	° ′	° ′
1	10 ♉ 26	8 ♍ 49	29 ♉ 55	24 ♈ 32	21 ♉ 12	23 ♐ 48	19 ♓ 23	5 ♉ 47	14 ♍ 9
2	11 24	20 45	1 ♊ 21	25 46	21 55	23 ℞ 44	19 29	5 50	14 ℞ 8
3	12 22	2 ♎ 37	2 42	26 59	22 38	23 40	19 34	5 54	14 7
4	13 20	14 28	3 59	28 13	23 21	23 36	19 39	5 57	14 7
5	14 19	26 23	5 12	29 26	24 4	23 32	19 45	6 1	14 6
6	15 17	8 ♏ 21	6 20	0 ♉ 40	24 46	23 27	19 50	6 4	14 6
7	16 15	20 25	7 24	1 54	25 29	23 23	19 55	6 7	14 5
8	17 13	2 ♐ 36	8 24	3 7	26 12	23 18	20 0	6 11	14 4
9	18 11	14 55	9 19	4 21	26 54	23 13	20 5	6 14	14 4
10	19 9	27 24	10 9	5 34	27 37	23 8	20 10	6 18	14 3
11	20 7	10 ♑ 5	10 54	6 48	28 19	23 3	20 15	6 21	14 3
12	21 4	23 0	11 35	8 2	29 1	22 57	20 20	6 25	14 2
13	22 2	6 ♒ 12	12 10	9 15	29 44	22 52	20 25	6 28	14 2
14	23 0	19 43	12 41	10 29	0 ♊ 26	22 46	20 29	6 31	14 2
15	23 58	3 ♓ 34	13 7	11 43	1 8	22 41	20 34	6 35	14 1
16	24 56	17 46	13 28	12 56	1 50	22 35	20 38	6 38	14 1
17	25 54	2 ♈ 18	13 44	14 10	2 33	22 29	20 43	6 41	14 1
18	26 52	17 4	13 55	15 23	3 15	22 23	20 47	6 45	14 0
19	27 49	2 ♉ 0	14 2	16 37	3 57	22 16	20 51	6 48	14 0
20	28 47	16 55	14 ℞ 3	17 51	4 39	22 10	20 55	6 51	14 0
21	29 45	1 ♊ 43	14 0	19 4	5 21	22 4	21 0	6 55	14 0
22	0 ♊ 42	16 14	13 52	20 18	6 3	21 57	21 4	6 58	14 0
23	1 40	0 ♋ 24	13 40	21 32	6 45	21 51	21 8	7 1	14 0
24	2 38	14 8	13 24	22 45	7 27	21 44	21 12	7 4	14 0
25	3 35	27 27	13 4	23 59	8 9	21 37	21 16	7 7	14 D 0
26	4 33	10 ♌ 21	12 41	25 12	8 50	21 30	21 19	7 11	14 0
27	5 31	22 55	12 15	26 26	9 32	21 23	21 23	7 14	14 0
28	6 28	5 ♍ 11	11 46	27 40	10 14	21 16	21 26	7 17	14 0
29	7 26	17 15	11 15	28 53	10 56	21 9	21 30	7 20	14 0
30	8 23	29 11	10 43	0 ♊ 7	11 37	21 2	21 33	7 23	14 0
31	9 21	11 ♎ 4	10 10	1 21	12 19	20 54	21 36	7 26	14 0

Pluto 25 Cancer all month

JUNE

Day	☉	☽	☿	♀	♂	♃	♄	♅	♆
	° ′	° ′	° ′	° ′	° ′	° ′	° ′	° ′	° ′
1	10 ♊ 18	22 ♎ 57	9 ♊ 36	2 ♊ 34	13 ♊ 0	20 ♐ 47	21 ♓ 39	7 ♉ 29	14 ♍ 0
2	11 16	4 ♏ 54	9 ℞ 2	3 48	13 42	20 ℞ 40	21 42	7 32	14 1
3	12 13	16 57	8 29	5 1	14 23	20 32	21 45	7 35	14 1
4	13 11	29 10	7 58	6 15	15 4	20 25	21 48	7 38	14 1
5	14 8	11 ♐ 33	7 29	7 28	15 45	20 17	21 51	7 41	14 2
6	15 5	24 8	7 2	8 42	16 27	20 9	21 54	7 44	14 2
7	16 3	6 ♑ 56	6 37	9 55	17 8	20 2	21 56	7 47	14 2
8	17 0	19 56	6 16	11 9	17 49	19 54	21 59	7 50	14 3
9	17 58	3 ♒ 10	5 59	12 23	18 30	19 47	22 2	7 53	14 3
10	18 55	16 37	5 46	13 36	19 12	19 39	22 4	7 55	14 4
11	19 52	0 ♓ 19	5 36	14 50	19 53	19 31	22 7	7 58	14 4
12	20 50	14 14	5 31	16 4	20 34	19 24	22 9	8 1	14 5
13	21 47	28 21	5 D 30	17 18	21 15	19 16	22 11	8 4	14 5
14	22 44	12 ♈ 39	5 34	18 31	21 56	19 8	22 13	8 6	14 6
15	23 42	27 6	5 42	19 45	22 37	19 1	22 14	8 9	14 7
16	24 39	11 ♉ 36	5 55	20 59	23 18	18 53	22 16	8 12	14 7
17	25 36	26 6	6 12	22 12	23 59	18 45	22 18	8 14	14 8
18	26 33	10 ♊ 29	6 34	23 26	24 40	18 38	22 19	8 17	14 9
19	27 31	24 40	7 0	24 39	25 20	18 30	22 21	8 19	14 10
20	28 28	8 ♋ 35	7 31	25 53	26 1	18 23	22 22	8 22	14 10
21	29 25	22 10	8 6	27 7	26 42	18 16	22 23	8 24	14 11
22	0 ♋ 22	5 ♌ 25	8 46	28 20	27 22	18 8	22 25	8 26	14 12
23	1 20	18 19	9 30	29 34	28 3	18 1	22 26	8 29	14 13
24	2 17	0 ♍ 54	10 19	0 ♋ 48	28 43	17 54	22 27	8 31	14 14
25	3 14	13 13	11 12	2 2	29 23	17 47	22 28	8 34	14 15
26	4 11	25 18	12 8	3 15	0 ♋ 4	17 39	22 29	8 36	14 16
27	5 9	7 ♎ 16	13 9	4 29	0 44	17 32	22 29	8 38	14 17
28	6 6	19 9	14 14	5 43	1 24	17 25	22 30	8 40	14 18
29	7 3	1 ♏ 3	15 22	6 57	2 4	17 18	22 31	8 43	14 19
30	8 0	13 2	16 34	8 10	2 45	17 11	22 31	8 45	14 20

Pluto 25 Cancer all month

1936

JULY

DAY	☉	☽	☿	♀	♂	♃	♄	♅	♆
	° ′	° ′	° ′	° ′	° ′	° ′	° ′	° ′	° ′
1	8♋57	25♏10	17♊51	9♋24	3♋25	17♐ 5	22♓32	8♉47	14♍21
2	9 55	7♐30	19 11	10 38	4 5	16R58	22 32	8 49	14 22
3	10 52	20 5	20 35	11 52	4 45	16 51	22 32	8 51	14 23
4	11 49	2♑56	22 3	13 5	5 26	16 45	22R32	8 53	14 26
5	12 46	16 4	23 34	14 19	6 6	16 38	22 32	8 55	14 27
6	13 43	29 28	25 9	15 33	6 46	16 32	22 31	8 57	14 27
7	14 40	13♒ 7	26 47	16 47	7 26	16 26	22 31	8 59	14 28
8	15 38	26 59	28 29	18 0	8 6	16 20	22 31	9 0	14 30
9	16 35	11♓ 1	0♋14	19 14	8 45	16 15	22 30	9 2	14 31
10	17 32	25 10	2 2	20 28	9 25	16 9	22 30	9 4	14 32
11	18 29	9♈23	3 53	21 42	10 5	16 4	22 29	9 5	14 34
12	19 26	23 37	5 48	22 56	10 45	15 58	22 28	9 7	14 35
13	20 24	7♉50	7 45	24 10	11 24	15 53	22 27	9 9	14 37
14	21 21	21 59	9 44	25 24	12 4	15 48	22 26	9 10	14 38
15	22 18	6♊ 3	11 45	26 38	12 44	15 43	22 25	9 12	14 40
16	23 15	19 58	13 48	27 51	13 24	15 38	22 24	9 13	14 41
17	24 13	3♋43	15 53	29 5	14 3	15 34	22 23	9 15	14 43
18	25 10	17 16	17 59	0♌19	14 43	15 29	22 22	9 16	14 44
19	26 7	0♌34	20 6	1 33	15 23	15 25	22 20	9 17	14 46
20	27 5	13 36	22 13	2 47	16 2	15 20	22 19	9 19	14 47
21	28 2	26 23	24 21	4 1	16 42	15 16	22 17	9 20	14 49
22	28 59	8♍53	26 29	5 15	17 21	15 12	22 15	9 21	14 50
23	29 56	21 10	28 37	6 29	18 1	15 9	22 13	9 22	14 52
24	0♌54	3♎15	0♌44	7 42	18 40	15 5	22 11	9 23	14 54
25	1 51	15 12	2 51	8 56	19 20	15 2	22 9	9 24	14 56
26	2 48	27 5	4 56	10 10	19 59	14 59	22 7	9 26	14 57
27	3 46	8♏58	7 1	11 24	20 38	14 56	22 5	9 26	14 59
28	4 43	20 57	9 5	12 38	21 18	14 53	22 3	9 27	15 1
29	5 40	3♐ 5	11 7	13 52	21 57	14 51	22 0	9 28	15 3
30	6 38	15 29	13 8	15 6	22 36	14 48	21 58	9 29	15 4
31	7 35	28 10	15 7	16 20	23 15	14 46	21 55	9 30	15 6

Pluto 26 Cancer all month

AUGUST

DAY	☉	☽	☿	♀	♂	♃	♄	♅	♆
	° ′	° ′	° ′	° ′	° ′	° ′	° ′	° ′	° ′
1	8♌32	11♑13	17♌ 4	17♌34	23♋54	14♐44	21♓53	9♉30	15♍ 8
2	9 30	24 38	19 0	18 48	24 33	14R43	21R50	9 31	15 10
3	10 27	8♒24	20 55	20 2	25 12	14 41	21 47	9 32	15 12
4	11 25	22 30	22 48	21 16	25 51	14 40	21 44	9 32	15 13
5	12 22	6♓50	24 39	22 29	26 30	14 38	21 41	9 33	15 15
6	13 20	21 19	26 29	23 43	27 9	14 37	21 38	9 33	15 17
7	14 17	5♈50	28 17	24 57	27 48	14 36	21 35	9 34	15 19
8	15 15	20 18	0♍ 4	26 11	28 27	14 35	21 32	9 34	15 21
9	16 12	4♉39	1 49	27 25	29 6	14 35	21 28	9 34	15 23
10	17 10	18 49	3 33	28 39	29 44	14 34	21 25	9 35	15 25
11	18 7	2♊47	5 15	29 53	0♌23	14 D34	21 21	9 35	15 27
12	19 5	16 32	6 56	1♍ 7	1 2	14 34	21 18	9 35	15 29
13	20 2	0♋ 4	8 35	2 21	1 41	14 35	21 14	9 35	15 31
14	21 0	13 25	10 13	3 35	2 19	14 35	21 11	9 35	15 33
15	21 58	26 34	11 49	4 49	2 58	14 35	21 7	9R36	15 35
16	22 55	9♌31	13 24	6 3	3 37	14 36	21 3	9 35	15 38
17	23 53	22 16	14 57	7 17	4 16	14 37	21 0	9 35	15 40
18	24 51	4♍49	16 29	8 31	4 54	14 38	20 56	9 35	15 42
19	25 49	17 11	17 59	9 45	5 33	14 40	20 52	9 35	15 44
20	26 46	29 21	19 28	10 59	6 11	14 42	20 48	9 35	15 46
21	27 44	11♎23	20 55	12 13	6 50	14 43	20 44	9 34	15 48
22	28 42	23 17	22 20	13 27	7 28	14 45	20 39	9 34	15 50
23	29 40	5♏ 8	23 44	14 41	8 6	14 47	20 35	9 34	15 52
24	0♍38	16 59	25 7	15 55	8 45	14 49	20 31	9 34	15 55
25	1 36	28 55	26 28	17 9	9 23	14 52	20 27	9 33	15 56
26	2 33	11♐ 2	27 47	18 23	10 2	14 54	20 22	9 33	15 59
27	3 31	23 23	29 4	19 37	10 40	14 57	20 18	9 32	16 1
28	4 29	6♑ 5	0♎20	20 51	11 18	15 0	20 14	9 31	16 3
29	5 27	19 12	1 34	22 5	11 56	15 3	20 10	9 31	16 6
30	6 25	2♒45	2 46	23 19	12 34	15 7	20 5	9 30	16 8
31	7 23	16 45	3 56	24 33	13 12	15 10	20 1	9 29	16 10

Pluto 27 Cancer all month

1936

SEPTEMBER

DAY	☉	☽	☿	♀	♂	♃	♄	♅	♆
	° ′	° ′	° ′	° ′	° ′	° ′	° ′	° ′	° ′
1	8♍21	1♓ 9	5♎ 3	25♍47	13♌51	15♐14	19♓57	9♉28	16♍12
2	9 19	15 53	6 8	27 1	14 29	15 17	19℞52	9℞ 28	16 14
3	10 17	0♈48	7 12	28 15	15 8	15 21	19 48	9 27	16 16
4	11 16	15 44	8 14	29 29	15 46	15 25	19 43	9 26	16 19
5	12 14	0♉34	9 12	0♎43	16 24	15 29	19 39	9 25	16 21
6	13 12	15 10	10 8	1 57	17 2	15 34	19 34	9 24	16 23
7	14 10	29 28	11 1	3 11	17 40	15 38	19 30	9 23	16 25
8	15 8	13♊25	11 51	4 25	18 18	15 43	19 25	9 22	16 28
9	16 7	27 3	12 38	5 39	18 56	15 48	19 21	9 20	16 30
10	17 5	10♋23	13 22	6 53	19 34	15 53	19 16	9 19	16 32
11	18 3	23 26	14 1	8 7	20 11	15 59	19 12	9 18	16 34
12	19 2	6♌16	14 37	9 21	20 49	16 4	19 7	9 17	16 37
13	20 0	18 55	15 8	10 35	21 27	16 10	19 3	9 15	16 39
14	20 59	1♍23	15 35	11 49	22 5	16 16	18 58	9 14	16 41
15	21 57	13 42	15 56	13 2	22 43	16 22	18 54	9 12	16 43
16	22 56	25 52	16 12	14 16	23 21	16 28	18 49	9 11	16 45
17	23 54	7♎55	16 23	15 30	23 59	16 34	18 44	9 10	16 48
18	24 53	19 51	16 28	16 44	24 36	16 40	18 40	9 8	16 50
19	25 51	1♏42	16℞26	17 58	25 14	16 47	18 35	9 7	16 52
20	26 50	13 31	16 18	19 12	25 51	16 53	18 30	9 5	16 54
21	27 49	25 21	16 2	20 26	26 29	17 0	18 25	9 3	16 57
22	28 47	7♐15	15 40	21 40	27 7	17 7	18 21	9 2	16 59
23	29 46	19 19	15 10	22 53	27 44	17 14	18 16	9 0	17 1
24	0♎45	1♑37	14 33	24 7	28 22	17 21	18 12	8 58	17 3
25	1 44	14 15	13 47	25 21	29 0	17 29	18 8	8 56	17 5
26	2 43	27 17	12 58	26 35	29 37	17 36	18 3	8 55	17 8
27	3 41	10♒48	12 2	27 48	0♍15	17 44	17 59	8 53	17 10
28	4 40	24 49	11 0	29 2	0 52	17 52	17 55	8 51	17 12
29	5 39	9♓20	9 55	0♏16	1 29	18 0	17 51	8 49	17 14
30	6 38	24 14	8 47	1 30	2 7	18 8	17 46	8 47	17 16

Pluto 27 Cancer all month

OCTOBER

DAY	☉	☽	☿	♀	♂	♃	♄	♅	♆
	°	° ′	° ′	° ′	° ′	° ′	° ′	° ′	° ′
1	7♎37	9♈24	7♎39	2♏44	2♍44	18♐16	17♓42	8♉45	17♍18
2	8 36	24 39	6℞32	3 58	3 21	18 24	17℞38	8℞ 43	17 20
3	9 35	9♉49	5 28	5 12	3 58	18 33	17 34	8 41	17 22
4	10 34	24 44	4 29	6 26	4 36	18 41	17 30	8 39	17 25
5	11 33	9♊16	3 35	7 39	5 13	18 50	17 26	8 37	17 27
6	12 33	23 24	2 49	8 53	5 50	18 59	17 22	8 34	17 29
7	13 32	7♋ 5	2 11	10 7	6 27	19 8	17 18	8 32	17 31
8	14 31	20 23	1 45	11 20	7 5	19 17	17 14	8 30	17 33
9	15 30	3♌21	1 29	12 34	7 42	19 26	17 11	8 28	17 35
10	16 30	16 1	1 D23	13 47	8 19	19 35	17 7	8 26	17 37
11	17 29	28 27	1 28	15 1	8 56	19 44	17 3	8 23	17 39
12	18 28	10♍42	1 44	16 15	9 33	19 54	17 0	8 21	17 41
13	19 28	22 49	2 10	17 28	10 10	20 3	16 56	8 19	17 43
14	20 27	4♎50	2 45	18 42	10 47	20 13	16 53	8 17	17 45
15	21 27	16 46	3 30	19 56	11 24	20 23	16 49	8 14	17 47
16	22 26	28 38	4 22	21 10	12 1	20 33	16 46	8 12	17 48
17	23 26	10♏28	5 22	22 23	12 38	20 44	16 42	8 10	17 50
18	24 25	22 17	6 28	23 37	13 15	20 54	16 39	8 7	17 52
19	25 25	4♐ 9	7 40	24 51	13 52	21 4	16 36	8 5	17 54
20	26 25	16 5	8 57	26 4	14 29	21 15	16 33	8 2	17 56
21	27 24	28 10	10 19	27 18	15 5	21 25	16 31	8 0	17 58
22	28 24	10♑27	11 44	28 31	15 42	21 36	16 28	7 58	18 0
23	29 24	23 2	13 12	29 45	16 19	21 47	16 25	7 55	18 1
24	0♏24	5♒59	14 43	0♐58	16 56	21 57	16 22	7 53	18 3
25	1 23	19 22	16 16	2 12	17 32	22 8	16 20	7 50	18 5
26	2 23	3♓14	17 50	3 25	18 9	22 19	16 17	7 48	18 7
27	3 23	17 36	19 26	4 39	18 46	22 30	16 15	7 45	18 8
28	4 23	2♈24	21 3	5 52	19 22	22 41	16 12	7 43	18 11
29	5 23	17 31	22 40	7 6	19 59	22 53	16 10	7 40	18 13
30	6 23	2♉50	24 19	8 19	20 35	23 4	16 8	7 38	18 13
31	7 23	18 8	25 57	9 33	21 11	23 15	16 6	7 35	18 15

Pluto 28 Cancer all month

1936

NOVEMBER

DAY	☉	☽	☿	♀	♂	♃	♄	♅	♆
	° ′	° ′	° ′	° ′	° ′	° ′	° ′	° ′	° ′
1	8♏23	3♊14	27♎36	10♐46	21♍48	23♐27	16♓ 4	7♉33	18♍16
2	9 23	18 1	29 15	12 0	22 24	23 38	16℞ 3	7℞ 30	18 18
3	10 23	2♋21	0♏54	13 13	23 0	23 50	16 1	7 28	18 19
4	11 23	16 14	2 33	14 26	23 37	24 2	15 59	7 25	18 21
5	12 23	29 40	4 11	15 40	24 13	24 13	15 58	7 23	18 22
6	13 23	12♌40	5 50	16 53	24 50	24 25	15 56	7 20	18 24
7	14 24	25 20	7 28	18 6	25 26	24 37	15 55	7 18	18 25
8	15 24	7♍42	9 6	19 19	26 2	24 49	15 54	7 16	18 27
9	16 24	19 52	10 44	20 33	26 38	25 1	15 53	7 13	18 28
10	17 25	1♎52	12 22	21 46	27 14	25 13	15 52	7 11	18 29
11	18 25	13 46	13 59	22 59	27 50	25 25	15 51	7 8	18 31
12	19 25	25 38	15 36	24 12	28 26	25 37	15 50	7 6	18 32
13	20 26	7♏28	17 13	25 25	29 2	25 50	15 49	7 4	18 33
14	21 26	19 19	18 49	26 38	29 38	26 2	15 49	7 1	18 34
15	22 27	1♐13	20 25	27 51	0♎14	26 15	15 48	6 59	18 86
16	23 27	13 11	22 1	29 4	0 50	26 27	15 48	6 57	18 37
17	24 28	25 16	23 37	0♑17	1 26	26 40	15 47	6 54	18 38
18	25 28	7♑29	25 12	1 30	2 1	26 52	15 47	6 52	18 39
19	26 29	19 54	26 47	2 43	2 37	27 5	15 D47	6 50	18 40
20	27 29	2♒34	28 22	3 56	3 13	27 18	15 47	6 47	18 41
21	28 30	15 31	29 57	5 9	3 48	27 31	15 47	6 45	18 42
22	29 31	28 50	1♐32	6 21	4 24	27 44	15 48	6 43	18 43
23	0♐31	12♓32	3 6	7 34	4 59	27 57	15 48	6 41	18 44
24	1 32	26 39	4 40	8 47	5 35	28 10	15 48	6 38	18 45
25	2 33	11♈ 8	6 14	10 0	6 10	28 23	15 49	6 36	18 46
26	3 33	25 57	7 48	11 12	6 46	28 36	15 49	6 34	18 47
27	4 34	11♉ 0	9 22	12 25	7 21	28 49	15 50	6 32	18 48
28	5 35	26 6	10 55	13 37	7 56	29 2	15 51	6 30	18 48
29	6 36	11♊ 8	12 29	14 50	8 32	29 15	15 52	6 28	18 49
30	7 36	25 57	14 3	16 2	9 7	29 29	15 53	6 26	18 50

Pluto 28 Cancer all month

DECEMBER

DAY	☉	☽	☿	♀	♂	♃	♄	♅	♆
	° ′	° ′	° ′	° ′	° ′	° ′	° ′	° ′	° ′
1	8♐37	10♋24	15♐36	17♑14	9♎42	29♐42	15♓54	6♉24	18♍51
2	9 38	24 26	17 9	18 27	10 17	29 56	15 55	6℞ 22	18 52
3	10 39	8♌ 2	18 43	19 39	10 52	0♑ 9	15 57	6 20	18 52
4	11 40	21 11	20 16	20 51	11 27	0 23	15 58	6 18	18 53
5	12 41	3♍56	21 49	22 4	12 2	0 37	16 0	6 16	18 54
6	13 42	16 22	23 22	23 16	12 37	0 50	16 2	6 14	18 54
7	14 42	28 32	24 55	24 28	13 12	1 4	16 3	6 13	18 55
8	15 43	10♎31	26 28	25 40	13 46	1 17	16 5	6 11	18 55
9	16 44	22 23	28 1	26 52	14 21	1 30	16 7	6 9	18 56
10	17 45	4♏12	29 34	28 4	14 56	1 43	16 9	6 8	18 56
11	18 46	16 3	1♑ 7	29 16	15 30	1 57	16 11	6 6	18 56
12	19 47	27 57	2 40	0♒27	16 5	2 10	16 14	6 4	18 57
13	20 48	9♐57	4 12	1 39	16 39	2 24	16 16	6 3	18 57
14	21 50	22 6	5 45	2 51	17 13	2 38	16 19	6 1	18 57
15	22 51	4♑25	7 17	4 2	17 48	2 51	16 21	6 0	18 57
16	23 52	16 55	8 48	5 14	18 22	3 5	16 24	5 58	18 58
17	24 53	29 37	10 19	6 25	18 56	3 19	16 27	5 57	18 58
18	25 54	12♒33	11 49	7 36	19 30	3 33	16 30	5 56	18 58
19	26 55	25 42	13 19	8 48	20 5	3 46	16 33	5 54	18 58
20	27 56	9♓ 7	14 47	9 59	20 39	4 0	16 36	5 53	18 58
21	28 57	22 48	16 15	11 10	21 13	4 14	16 39	5 52	18 58
22	29 58	6♈45	17 41	12 21	21 47	4 28	16 42	5 51	18 58
23	0♑59	20 57	19 6	13 32	22 20	4 41	16 46	5 50	18℞58
24	2 1	5♉22	20 29	14 42	22 54	4 55	16 49	5 49	18 58
25	3 2	19 58	21 50	15 53	23 27	5 9	16 53	5 48	18 58
26	4 3	4♊39	23 8	17 4	24 1	5 23	16 57	5 47	18 58
27	5 4	19 19	24 23	18 14	24 34	5 36	17 1	5 46	18 58
28	6 5	3♋51	25 34	19 24	25 8	5 50	17 5	5 45	18 58
29	7 6	18 10	26 41	20 34	25 41	6 4	17 9	5 44	18 57
30	8 7	2♌10	27 43	21 44	26 14	6 18	17 13	5 43	18 57
31	9 9	15 48	28 39	22 54	26 47	6 32	17 17	5 42	18 57

Pluto 28 Cancer all month

1937

JANUARY

DAY	☉	☽	☿	♀	♂	♃	♄	♅	♆
	° ′	° ′	° ′	° ′	° ′	° ′	° ′	° ′	° ′
1	10♑10	29♌ 3	29♑29	24♒ 4	27♎20	6♑46	17♓21	5♉42	18♍57
2	11 11	11♍54	0♒12	25 14	27 53	7 0	17 25	5℞41	18℞56
3	12 12	24 24	0 46	26 23	28 26	7 14	17 29	5 41	18 56
4	13 13	6♎38	1 12	27 32	28 59	7 28	17 34	5 40	18 55
5	14 14	18 38	1 28	28 41	29 31	7 41	17 38	5 39	18 55
6	15 15	0♏31	1 32	29 51	0♏ 4	7 55	17 43	5 39	18 54
7	16 17	12 20	1℞25	0♓59	0 37	8 9	17 48	5 38	18 54
8	17 18	24 11	1 7	2 8	1 9	8 23	17 53	5 38	18 53
9	18 19	6♐ 8	0 36	3 17	1 42	8 36	17 58	5 38	18 52
10	19 20	18 15	29♑55	4 25	2 14	8 50	18 3	5 38	18 52
11	20 21	0♑34	29 2	5 33	2 46	9 4	18 8	5 37	18 51
12	21 22	13 9	28 0	6 41	3 18	9 17	18 13	5 37	18 50
13	22 24	25 59	26 50	7 49	3 50	9 31	18 18	5 37	18 49
14	23 25	9♒ 4	25 36	8 56	4 21	9 44	18 23	5 D 37	18 49
15	24 26	22 25	24 18	10 4	4 53	9 58	18 28	5 37	18 48
16	25 27	5♓58	22 59	11 11	5 24	10 11	18 34	5 37	18 47
17	26 28	19 42	21 43	12 18	5 56	10 25	18 39	5 37	18 46
18	27 29	3♈36	20 30	13 24	6 27	10 39	18 45	5 38	18 45
19	28 30	17 36	19 23	14 31	6 58	10 53	18 50	5 38	18 44
20	29 31	1♉42	18 22	15 37	7 29	11 6	18 56	5 38	18 43
21	0♒33	15 52	17 31	16 43	8 0	11 20	19 1	5 39	18 42
22	1 34	0♊ 4	16 48	17 49	8 31	11 33	19 7	5 39	18 41
23	2 35	14 16	16 14	18 54	9 1	11 46	19 13	5 39	18 40
24	3 36	28 27	15 50	20 0	9 32	12 0	19 19	5 40	18 39
25	4 37	12♋32	15 34	21 4	10 2	12 13	19 25	5 41	18 38
26	5 38	26 28	15 28	22 9	10 33	12 26	19 31	5 41	18 37
27	6 39	10♌12	15 D30	23 13	11 2	12 39	19 37	5 42	18 36
28	7 39	23 39	15 39	24 18	11 32	12 53	19 43	5 43	18 35
29	8 40	6♍48	15 54	25 21	12 2	13 6	19 50	5 43	18 34
30	9 41	19 38	16 15	26 25	12 32	13 19	19 56	5 44	18 33
31	10 42	2♎10	16 43	27 27	13 1	13 32	20 2	5 45	18 31

Pluto 27 Cancer all month

FEBRUARY

DAY	☉	☽	☿	♀	♂	♃	♄	♅	♆
	° ′	° ′	° ′	° ′	° ′	° ′	° ′	° ′	° ′
1	11♒43	14♎24	17♑17	28♓30	13♏30	13♑45	20♓ 8	5♉46	18♍30
2	12 44	26 26	17 55	29 32	13 59	13 58	20 15	5 47	18℞29
3	13 45	8♏19	18 39	0♈34	14 29	14 11	20 21	5 48	18 28
4	14 46	20 9	19 26	1 35	14 58	14 24	20 27	5 49	18 26
5	15 47	1♐59	20 17	2 36	15 26	14 37	20 34	5 50	18 25
6	16 47	13 57	21 11	3 36	15 54	14 50	20 40	5 51	18 24
7	17 48	26 7	22 8	4 37	16 22	15 3	20 47	5 52	18 23
8	18 49	8♑33	23 8	5 37	16 50	15 16	20 54	5 54	18 21
9	19 50	21 18	24 11	6 36	17 18	15 28	21 0	5 55	18 20
10	20 50	4♒24	25 17	7 35	17 46	15 41	21 7	5 56	18 18
11	21 51	17 52	26 25	8 34	18 13	15 53	21 14	5 58	18 17
12	22 52	1♓38	27 35	9 31	18 40	16 6	21 21	5 59	18 15
13	23 53	15 40	28 46	10 29	19 8	16 18	21 28	6 1	18 14
14	24 53	29 53	0♒ 0	11 25	19 34	16 31	21 35	6 2	18 12
15	25 54	14♈10	1 15	12 22	20 1	16 43	21 42	6 4	18 11
16	26 54	28 28	2 31	13 17	20 27	16 55	21 49	6 6	18 9
17	27 55	12♉42	3 49	14 13	20 54	17 7	21 56	6 8	18 8
18	28 56	26 51	5 8	15 7	21 19	17 19	22 3	6 9	18 6
19	29 56	10♊53	6 29	16 1	21 45	17 31	22 10	6 11	18 5
20	0♓57	24 47	7 51	16 54	22 11	17 43	22 17	6 13	18 3
21	1 57	8♋33	9 15	17 46	22 36	17 55	22 24	6 14	18 1
22	2 57	22 12	10 39	18 38	23 1	18 6	22 31	6 16	18 0
23	3 58	5♌41	12 5	19 29	23 26	18 18	22 38	6 18	17 58
24	4 58	19 0	13 32	20 19	23 50	18 30	22 45	6 20	17 57
25	5 58	2♍ 8	15 0	21 8	24 14	18 41	22 52	6 22	17 55
26	6 59	15 2	16 29	21 56	24 38	18 53	23 0	6 24	17 53
27	7 59	27 41	17 59	22 44	25 1	19 4	23 7	6 26	17 52
28	8 59	10♎ 6	19 31	23 30	25 25	19 15	23 14	6 29	17 50

Pluto 27 Cancer all month

1937

MARCH

DAY	☉	☽	☿	♀	♂	♃	♄	♅	♆
	° ′	° ′	° ′	° ′	° ′	° ′	° ′	° ′	° ′
1	9 ♓ 59	22 ♎ 17	21 ♒ 3	24 ♈ 16	25 ♏ 48	19 ♑ 27	23 ♓ 21	6 ♉ 31	17 ♍ 48
2	11 0	4 ♏ 17	22 37	25 0	26 10	19 38	23 29	6 33	17 ℞ 47
3	12 0	16 10	24 11	25 44	26 33	19 49	23 36	6 35	17 45
4	13 0	27 58	25 47	26 26	26 55	20 0	23 43	6 38	17 43
5	14 0	9 ♐ 48	27 24	27 7	27 17	20 11	23 50	6 40	17 42
6	15 0	21 44	29 2	27 47	27 38	20 21	23 58	6 42	17 40
7	16 0	3 ♑ 53	0 ♓ 41	28 26	27 59	20 32	24 5	6 45	17 38
8	17 0	16 19	2 21	29 4	28 19	20 42	24 12	6 47	17 37
9	18 0	29 8	4 2	29 40	28 40	20 53	24 20	6 50	17 35
10	19 0	12 ♒ 22	5 44	0 ♉ 15	29 0	21 3	24 27	6 52	17 33
11	20 0	26 2	7 28	0 49	29 20	21 13	24 35	6 55	17 32
12	21 0	10 ♓ 6	9 13	1 21	29 39	21 23	24 42	6 58	17 30
13	22 0	24 32	10 58	1 52	29 58	21 33	24 50	7 0	17 28
14	23 0	9 ♈ 10	12 45	2 21	0 ♐ 16	21 43	24 57	7 3	17 27
15	24 0	23 55	14 34	2 49	0 34	21 53	25 5	7 6	17 25
16	24 59	8 ♉ 38	16 23	3 15	0 51	22 3	25 12	7 8	17 23
17	25 59	23 12	18 14	3 39	1 9	22 12	25 20	7 11	17 22
18	26 59	7 ♊ 33	20 5	4 1	1 25	22 22	25 27	7 14	17 20
19	27 58	21 39	21 58	4 22	1 42	22 31	25 34	7 17	17 18
20	28 58	5 ♋ 29	23 53	4 40	1 57	22 40	25 41	7 20	17 17
21	29 58	19 5	25 48	4 56	2 13	22 49	25 49	7 23	17 15
22	0 ♈ 57	2 ♌ 26	27 45	5 11	2 27	22 58	25 56	7 26	17 14
23	1 57	15 35	29 42	5 23	2 42	23 7	26 4	7 28	17 12
24	2 56	28 32	1 ♈ 41	5 33	2 56	23 16	26 11	7 31	17 10
25	3 56	11 ♍ 18	3 40	5 41	3 9	23 24	26 19	7 34	17 9
26	4 55	23 53	5 41	5 46	3 22	23 33	26 26	7 37	17 7
27	5 54	6 ♎ 17	7 42	5 49	3 34	23 41	26 34	7 40	17 6
28	6 54	18 31	9 44	5 50	3 46	23 49	26 41	7 44	17 4
29	7 53	0 ♏ 34	11 47	5 ℞ 48	3 57	23 57	26 49	7 47	17 3
30	8 52	12 30	13 50	5 44	4 8	24 5	26 56	7 50	17 1
31	9 51	24 20	15 53	5 37	4 18	24 13	27 3	7 53	17 0

Pluto 26 Cancer all month

APRIL

DAY	☉	☽	☿	♀	♂	♃	♄	♅	♆
	° ′	° ′	° ′	° ′	° ′	° ′	° ′	° ′	° ′
1	10 ♈ 51	6 ♐ 7	17 ♈ 56	5 ♉ 28	4 ♐ 27	24 ♑ 21	27 ♓ 10	7 ♉ 56	16 ♍ 58
2	11 50	17 56	19 59	5 R 17	4 36	24 28	27 18	7 59	16 R 57
3	12 49	29 52	22 1	5 2	4 44	24 36	27 25	8 2	16 55
4	13 48	11 ♑ 59	24 2	4 46	4 52	24 43	27 32	8 6	16 54
5	14 47	24 23	26 1	4 27	4 59	24 50	27 39	8 9	16 52
6	15 46	7 ♒ 9	27 59	4 6	5 6	24 57	27 47	8 12	16 51
7	16 45	20 22	29 55	3 42	5 11	25 4	27 54	8 15	16 49
8	17 44	4 ♓ 3	1 ♉ 48	3 17	5 17	25 11	28 1	8 19	16 48
9	18 43	18 12	3 38	2 49	5 21	25 17	28 8	8 22	16 45
10	19 42	2 ♈ 46	5 25	2 20	5 25	25 23	28 16	8 25	16 44
11	20 41	17 40	7 8	1 48	5 27	25 29	28 23	8 29	16 43
12	21 40	2 ♉ 44	8 48	1 16	5 30	25 36	28 30	8 32	16 42
13	22 39	17 48	10 24	0 41	5 31	25 42	28 37	8 35	16 41
14	23 37	2 ♊ 44	11 55	0 6	5 32	25 47	28 44	8 39	16 40
15	24 36	17 24	13 22	29 ♈ 29	5 R 32	25 53	28 50	8 42	16 39
16	25 35	1 ♋ 45	14 44	28 52	5 32	25 58	28 57	8 45	16 37
17	26 34	15 43	16 1	28 15	5 30	26 3	29 4	8 49	16 36
18	27 32	29 20	17 43	27 37	5 28	26 8	29 11	8 52	16 35
19	28 31	12 ♌ 37	18 20	27 0	5 25	26 13	29 18	8 56	16 34
20	29 29	25 35	19 21	26 22	5 21	26 18	29 25	8 59	16 33
21	0 ♉ 28	8 ♍ 19	20 17	25 45	5 17	26 22	29 32	9 2	16 32
22	1 26	20 49	21 7	25 9	5 12	26 27	29 39	9 6	16 30
23	2 25	3 ♎ 8	21 52	24 34	5 6	26 31	29 45	9 9	16 29
24	3 23	15 18	22 31	24 0	4 59	26 35	29 52	9 13	16 28
25	4 22	27 20	23 4	23 27	4 51	26 39	29 59	9 16	16 27
26	5 20	9 ♏ 16	23 32	22 56	4 43	26 43	0 ♈ 5	9 20	16 26
27	6 18	21 6	23 54	22 26	4 34	26 46	0 12	9 23	16 25
28	7 17	2 ♐ 55	24 10	21 58	4 25	26 50	0 18	9 26	16 24
29	8 15	14 42	24 21	21 33	4 14	26 53	0 24	9 30	16 24
30	9 13	26 33	24 26	21 10	4 3	26 56	0 31	9 33	16 23

Pluto 26 Cancer all month

1937

MAY

DAY	☉	☽	☿	♀	♂	♃	♄	♅	♆
	° ′	° ′	° ′	° ′	° ′	° ′	° ′	° ′	° ′
1	10 ♉ 12	8 ♑ 31	24 ♉ 25	20 ♈ 48	3 ♐ 51	26 ♑ 58	0 ♈ 37	9 ♉ 37	16 ♍ 22
2	11 10	20 39	24 ℞ 20	20 ℞ 30	3 ℞ 38	27 1	0 43	9 40	16 ℞ 21
3	12 8	3 ♒ 3	24 9	20 14	3 25	27 3	0 49	9 44	16 20
4	13 6	15 47	23 54	20 0	3 11	27 5	0 56	9 47	16 20
5	14 4	28 55	23 34	19 48	2 56	27 7	1 2	9 51	16 19
6	15 2	12 ♓ 29	23 10	19 39	2 41	27 10	1 8	9 54	16 18
7	16 0	26 32	22 43	19 32	2 25	27 12	1 14	9 58	16 17
8	16 58	11 ♈ 2	22 13	19 28	2 9	27 13	1 20	10 1	16 17
9	17 56	25 54	21 41	19 26	1 52	27 15	1 25	10 5	16 16
10	18 54	11 ♉ 1	21 7	19 D 27	1 34	27 16	1 31	10 8	16 16
11	19 52	26 14	20 32	19 30	1 16	27 17	1 37	10 12	16 15
12	20 50	11 ♊ 23	19 55	19 35	0 57	27 17	1 43	10 15	16 14
13	21 48	26 19	19 19	19 42	0 38	27 18	1 48	10 18	16 14
14	22 46	10 ♋ 55	18 44	19 52	0 19	27 ℞ 18	1 54	10 22	16 14
15	23 44	25 6	18 10	20 4	29 ♏ 59	27 18	2 0	10 25	16 13
16	24 42	8 ♌ 52	17 38	20 17	29 39	27 17	2 5	10 29	16 13
17	25 40	22 13	17 8	20 33	29 18	27 17	2 11	10 32	16 13
18	26 38	5 ♍ 12	16 41	20 51	28 58	27 17	2 16	10 35	16 12
19	27 35	17 50	16 17	21 10	28 37	27 16	2 21	10 39	16 12
20	28 33	0 ♎ 13	15 57	21 31	28 16	27 16	2 27	10 42	16 12
21	29 31	12 23	15 41	21 54	27 55	27 15	2 32	10 45	16 11
22	0 ♊ 28	24 23	15 29	22 19	27 34	27 14	2 37	10 48	16 11
23	1 26	6 ♏ 17	15 21	22 45	27 13	27 13	2 42	10 52	16 11
24	2 24	18 7	15 18	23 13	26 52	27 12	2 47	10 55	16 11
25	3 21	29 55	15 D 19	23 42	26 31	27 11	2 52	10 58	16 11
26	4 19	11 ♐ 44	15 24	24 13	26 10	27 9	2 57	11 2	16 11
27	5 17	23 36	15 34	24 45	25 49	27 7	3 2	11 5	16 11
28	6 14	5 ♑ 33	15 49	25 19	25 28	27 4	3 6	11 8	16 D 11
29	7 12	17 38	16 8	25 54	25 8	27 2	3 11	11 11	16 11
30	8 9	29 53	16 31	26 30	24 47	26 59	3 15	11 14	16 11
31	9 7	12 ♒ 23	16 59	27 8	24 28	26 56	3 20	11 18	16 11

Pluto 26 Cancer all month

JUNE

DAY	☉	☽	☿	♀	♂	♃	♄	♅	♆
	° ′	° ′	° ′	° ′	° ′	° ′	° ′	° ′	° ′
1	10 ♊ 4	25 ♒ 9	17 ♉ 31	27 ♈ 46	24 ♏ 8	26 ♑ 53	3 ♈ 24	11 ♉ 21	16 ♍ 11
2	11 2	8 ♓ 15	18 6	28 26	23 ℞ 50	26 ℞ 50	3 29	11 24	16 11
3	11 59	21 44	18 46	29 7	23 31	26 47	3 33	11 27	16 11
4	12 57	5 ♈ 37	19 31	29 48	23 13	26 43	3 37	11 30	16 12
5	13 54	19 54	20 18	0 ♉ 31	22 56	26 40	3 41	11 33	16 12
6	14 51	4 ♉ 33	21 10	1 15	22 39	26 36	3 45	11 36	16 12
7	15 49	19 28	22 5	1 59	22 23	26 32	3 49	11 39	16 12
8	16 46	4 ♊ 33	23 3	2 45	22 8	26 28	3 53	11 42	16 13
9	17 44	19 40	24 5	3 31	21 52	26 24	3 56	11 45	16 13
10	18 41	4 ♋ 39	25 10	4 18	21 38	26 19	4 0	11 48	16 14
11	19 38	19 21	26 19	5 5	21 24	26 14	4 3	11 51	16 14
12	20 36	3 ♌ 42	27 31	5 54	21 11	26 9	4 6	11 54	16 15
13	21 33	17 37	28 46	6 43	20 59	26 4	4 10	11 57	16 15
14	22 30	1 ♍ 6	0 ♊ 5	7 33	20 48	25 59	4 13	11 59	16 16
15	23 28	14 9	1 27	8 24	20 36	25 54	4 16	12 2	16 16
16	24 25	26 49	2 51	9 15	20 27	25 49	4 19	12 5	16 17
17	25 22	9 ♎ 10	4 19	10 7	20 17	25 43	4 22	12 8	16 17
18	26 20	21 16	5 50	10 59	20 9	25 38	4 25	12 11	16 18
19	27 17	3 ♏ 13	7 24	11 52	20 1	25 32	4 28	12 13	16 18
20	28 14	15 3	9 1	12 46	19 55	25 26	4 31	12 16	16 19
21	29 11	26 50	10 41	13 40	19 49	25 20	4 35	12 18	16 20
22	0 ♋ 9	8 ♐ 39	12 24	14 35	19 44	25 13	4 37	12 21	16 21
23	1 6	20 32	14 9	15 30	19 40	25 7	4 39	12 24	16 21
24	2 3	2 ♑ 31	15 58	16 26	19 37	25 0	4 41	12 26	16 22
25	3 0	14 39	17 49	17 22	19 34	24 54	4 44	12 29	16 23
26	3 57	26 57	19 43	18 19	19 32	24 47	4 46	12 31	16 24
27	4 55	9 ♒ 26	21 39	19 16	19 31	24 40	4 48	12 33	16 25
28	5 52	22 9	23 38	20 13	19 D 32	24 33	4 50	12 36	16 26
29	6 49	5 ♓ 6	25 39	21 11	19 32	24 26	4 52	12 38	16 27
30	7 46	18 18	27 42	22 9	19 34	24 19	4 53	12 40	16 28

Pluto 27 Cancer all month

1937

JULY

Pluto 27 Cancer all month

Day	☉ ° ′	☽ ° ′	☿ ° ′	♀ ° ′	♂ ° ′	♃ ° ′	♄ ° ′	♅ ° ′	♆ ° ′
1	8♋43	1♈48	29♊47	23♉8	19♏36	24♑12	4♈55	12♉43	16♍29
2	9 41	15 35	1♋54	24 7	19 40	24 R 5	4 56	12 45	16 30
3	10 38	29 39	4 2	25 6	19 44	23 58	4 58	12 47	16 31
4	11 35	14♉1	6 11	26 6	19 49	23 50	4 59	12 49	16 32
5	12 32	28 37	8 21	27 5	19 54	23 43	5 0	12 52	16 33
6	13 29	13♊23	10 30	28 6	20 1	23 36	5 1	12 54	16 35
7	14 27	28 13	12 41	29 6	20 8	23 28	5 3	12 56	16 36
8	15 24	13♋0	14 50	0♊7	20 17	23 21	5 4	12 58	16 37
9	16 21	27 36	17 0	1 8	20 25	23 13	5 5	13 0	16 38
10	17 18	11♌55	19 9	2 10	20 35	23 5	5 6	13 2	16 40
11	18 16	25 52	21 17	3 12	20 45	22 58	5 6	13 3	16 41
12	19 13	9♍24	23 24	4 14	20 56	22 50	5 7	13 5	16 43
13	20 10	22 30	25 30	5 16	21 7	22 42	5 7	13 7	16 44
14	21 7	5♎13	27 35	6 19	21 20	22 34	5 7	13 9	16 45
15	22 5	17 35	29 38	7 22	21 32	22 27	5 8	13 10	16 47
16	23 2	29 42	1♌40	8 25	21 46	22 19	5 8	13 12	16 48
17	23 59	11♏37	3 40	9 28	22 0	22 12	5 R 8	13 14	16 50
18	24 56	23 27	5 38	10 32	22 15	22 4	5 8	13 15	16 51
19	25 53	5♐15	7 35	11 35	22 31	21 57	5 8	13 17	16 53
20	26 51	17 6	9 30	12 39	22 47	21 49	5 7	13 18	16 54
21	27 48	29 5	11 23	13 44	23 3	21 41	5 7	13 20	16 56
22	28 45	11♑13	13 15	14 48	23 21	21 33	5 7	13 21	16 57
23	29 43	23 34	15 4	15 53	23 39	21 26	5 6	13 23	16 59
24	0♌40	6♒9	16 52	16 58	23 57	21 18	5 6	13 24	17 1
25	1 37	18 57	18 38	18 3	24 16	21 11	5 5	13 25	17 2
26	2 34	2♓0	20 22	19 8	24 36	21 3	5 4	13 26	17 4
27	3 32	15 16	22 4	20 13	24 56	20 56	5 3	13 28	17 6
28	4 29	28 43	23 45	21 19	25 17	20 48	5 2	13 29	17 7
29	5 26	12♈23	25 24	22 25	25 38	20 41	5 1	13 30	17 9
30	6 24	26 13	27 1	23 31	26 0	20 34	5 0	13 31	17 11
31	7 21	10♉12	28 37	24 37	26 22	20 26	4 58	13 32	17 13

AUGUST

Pluto 28 Cancer all month

Day	☉ ° ′	☽ ° ′	☿ ° ′	♀ ° ′	♂ ° ′	♃ ° ′	♄ ° ′	♅ ° ′	♆ ° ′
1	8♌19	24♉22	0♍11	25♊43	26♏45	20♑19	4♈57	13♉33	17♍15
2	9 16	8♊39	1 43	26 50	27 8	20 R 12	4 R 55	13 34	17 16
3	10 13	23 3	3 13	27 57	27 32	20 5	4 53	13 35	17 18
4	11 11	7♋29	4 42	29 3	27 55	19 58	4 52	13 35	17 20
5	12 8	21 53	6 9	0♋10	28 20	19 52	4 50	13 36	17 22
6	13 6	6♌11	7 34	1 17	28 45	19 45	4 48	13 37	17 24
7	14 3	20 15	8 57	2 25	29 11	19 39	4 46	13 38	17 26
8	15 1	4♍3	10 19	3 32	29 36	19 32	4 44	13 38	17 28
9	15 58	17 29	11 39	4 40	0♐3	19 26	4 42	13 39	17 30
10	16 56	0♎33	12 56	5 47	0 29	19 20	4 40	13 39	17 32
11	17 54	13 15	14 12	6 55	0 56	19 14	4 38	13 40	17 34
12	18 51	25 38	15 26	8 3	1 24	19 8	4 35	13 40	17 36
13	19 49	7♏44	16 37	9 12	1 52	19 3	4 33	13 40	17 38
14	20 46	19 40	17 46	10 20	2 20	18 58	4 30	13 41	17 40
15	21 44	1♐29	18 53	11 28	2 49	18 53	4 27	13 41	17 42
16	22 42	13 18	19 58	12 37	3 17	18 47	4 24	13 41	17 44
17	23 39	25 11	21 0	13 46	3 47	18 41	4 21	13 41	17 46
18	24 37	7♑14	21 59	14 55	4 16	18 36	4 18	13 41	17 48
19	25 35	19 31	22 56	16 3	4 47	18 32	4 15	13 42	17 50
20	26 33	2♒4	23 50	17 12	5 17	18 27	4 12	13 R 42	17 52
21	27 30	14 55	24 41	18 22	5 48	18 23	4 9	13 41	17 54
22	28 28	28 4	25 29	19 31	6 18	18 18	4 6	13 41	17 56
23	29 26	11♓30	26 13	20 40	6 50	18 14	4 3	13 41	17 58
24	0♍24	25 11	26 54	21 50	7 21	18 10	3 59	13 41	18 0
25	1 22	9♈2	27 31	23 0	7 53	18 7	3 56	13 41	18 3
26	2 19	23 1	28 4	24 9	8 25	18 3	3 52	13 40	18 5
27	3 17	7♉4	28 32	25 19	8 58	18 0	3 48	13 40	18 7
28	4 15	21 10	28 56	26 29	9 31	17 56	3 45	13 40	18 9
29	5 13	5♊17	29 15	27 39	10 4	17 53	3 41	13 39	18 11
30	6 11	19 23	29 29	28 49	10 37	17 50	3 37	13 39	18 13
31	7 9	3♋29	29 38	0♌0	11 11	17 47	3 33	13 38	18 16

1937

SEPTEMBER

Day	☉	☽	☿	♀	♂	♃	♄	♅	♆
	° ′	° ′	° ′	° ′	° ′	° ′	° ′	° ′	° ′
1	8♍ 7	17♋33	29♍41	1♌10	11♐45	17♑45	3♈29	13♉38	18♍18
2	9 5	1♌32	29℞38	2 21	12 19	17℞42	3℞25	13℞37	18 20
3	10 4	15 25	29 29	3 31	12 53	17 40	3 21	13 36	18 22
4	11 2	29 6	29 15	4 42	13 28	17 38	3 17	13 36	18 25
5	12 0	12♍35	28 53	5 53	14 3	17 37	3 13	13 35	18 27
6	12 58	25 46	28 26	7 4	14 38	17 35	3 9	13 34	18 29
7	13 56	8♎40	27 52	8 15	15 13	17 34	3 5	13 33	18 31
8	14 55	21 16	27 11	9 26	15 49	17 33	3 1	13 32	18 33
9	15 53	3♏34	26 25	10 37	16 25	17 32	2 56	13 31	18 36
10	16 51	15 38	25 34	11 49	17 1	17 31	2 52	13 30	18 38
11	17 50	27 32	24 38	13 0	17 37	17 30	2 47	13 29	18 40
12	18 48	9♐21	23 40	14 11	18 14	17 30	2 43	13 28	18 42
13	19 46	21 10	22 39	15 23	18 50	17 29	2 38	13 27	18 45
14	20 45	3♑3	21 38	16 34	19 28	17 29	2 34	13 26	18 47
15	21 43	15 8	20 36	17 46	20 5	17 D28	2 29	13 24	18 49
16	22 42	27 28	19 36	18 58	20 42	17 29	2 25	13 23	18 51
17	23 40	10♒8	18 40	20 10	21 20	17 29	2 20	13 22	18 54
18	24 39	23 10	17 49	21 22	21 57	17 30	2 16	13 20	18 56
19	25 37	6♓34	17 4	22 34	22 35	17 31	2 11	13 19	18 58
20	26 36	20 21	16 26	23 46	23 14	17 32	2 6	13 18	19 0
21	27 35	4♈25	15 55	24 58	23 52	17 33	2 2	13 16	19 3
22	28 33	18 42	15 34	26 11	24 31	17 34	1 57	13 15	19 5
23	29 32	3♉7	15 22	27 23	25 9	17 36	1 52	13 13	19 7
24	0♎31	17 33	15 D21	28 35	25 48	17 38	1 47	13 11	19 9
25	1 30	1♊56	15 29	29 48	26 27	17 40	1 43	13 10	19 11
26	2 28	16 12	15 47	1♍0	27 6	17 42	1 39	13 8	19 14
27	3 27	0♋21	16 16	2 13	27 46	17 44	1 34	13 6	19 16
28	4 26	14 20	16 53	3 26	28 25	17 47	1 29	13 4	19 18
29	5 25	28 9	17 39	4 38	29 5	17 50	1 25	13 3	19 20
30	6 24	11♌48	18 33	5 51	29 45	17 53	1 20	13 1	19 22

Pluto 29 Cancer all month

OCTOBER

Day	☉	☽	☿	♀	♂	♃	♄	♅	♆
	° ′	° ′	° ′	° ′	° ′	° ′	° ′	° ′	° ′
1	7♎23	25♌17	19♍35	7♍ 4	0♑25	17♑56	1♈15	12♉59	19♍24
2	8 22	8♍34	20 44	8 17	1 5	17 59	1℞10	12℞57	19 27
3	9 21	21 39	21 59	9 30	1 45	18 3	1 6	12 55	19 30
4	10 20	4♎31	23 19	10 44	2 26	18 6	1 1	12 53	19 32
5	11 19	17 8	24 44	11 57	3 7	18 10	0 57	12 51	19 33
6	12 19	29 32	26 12	13 10	3 47	18 14	0 52	12 49	19 35
7	13 18	11♏42	27 44	14 24	4 28	18 18	0 48	12 47	19 37
8	14 17	23 42	29 19	15 37	5 9	18 23	0 43	12 45	19 39
9	15 16	5♐33	0♎56	16 51	5 50	18 28	0 39	12 43	19 41
10	16 16	17 20	2 35	18 4	6 32	18 33	0 34	12 41	19 43
11	17 15	29 7	4 16	19 18	7 13	18 38	0 30	12 39	19 45
12	18 14	11♑0	5 58	20 31	7 54	18 43	0 25	12 37	19 47
13	19 14	23 3	7 41	21 45	8 36	18 48	0 21	12 35	19 49
14	20 13	5♒22	9 25	22 59	9 18	18 54	0 17	12 32	19 51
15	21 13	18 1	11 8	24 13	10 0	18 59	0 13	12 30	19 53
16	22 12	1♓4	12 52	25 27	10 42	19 5	0 9	12 28	19 55
17	23 12	14 34	14 34	26 41	11 24	19 11	0 5	12 25	19 57
18	24 11	28 30	16 18	27 55	12 6	19 17	0 1	12 23	19 59
19	25 11	12♈49	18 1	29 9	12 48	19 23	29♓57	12 21	20 1
20	26 10	27 27	19 45	0♎23	13 31	19 30	29 53	12 19	20 2
21	27 10	12♉15	21 28	1 37	14 13	19 36	29 49	12 16	20 4
22	28 10	27 7	23 10	2 51	14 56	19 43	29 45	12 14	20 6
23	29 9	11♊54	24 52	4 5	15 38	19 50	29 41	12 11	20 8
24	0♏9	26 31	26 33	5 20	16 21	19 57	29 38	12 9	20 10
25	1 9	10♋53	28 15	6 34	17 4	20 4	29 34	12 7	20 12
26	2 9	24 58	29 55	7 48	17 47	20 11	29 30	12 4	20 13
27	3 9	8♌45	1♏35	9 3	18 30	20 19	29 27	12 2	20 15
28	4 9	22 14	3 14	10 17	19 14	20 26	29 23	11 59	20 17
29	5 9	5♍28	4 53	11 32	19 57	20 34	29 20	11 57	20 19
30	6 8	18 26	6 32	12 46	20 40	20 42	29 17	11 54	20 20
31	7 8	1♎10	8 10	14 1	21 24	20 50	29 14	11 52	20 22

Pluto 29 Cancer all month

1937

NOVEMBER

DAY	☉	☽	☿	♀	♂	♃	♄	♅	♆
	° ′	° ′	° ′	° ′	° ′	° ′	° ′	° ′	° ′
1	8♏ 9	13♎42	9♏47	15♎15	22♑ 7	20♑59	29♓11	11♉49	20♍24
2	9 9	26 2	11 24	16 30	22 51	21 7	29℞ 8	11℞47	20 25
3	10 9	8♏11	13 1	17 45	23 34	21 16	29 5	11 44	20 27
4	11 9	20 12	14 37	18 59	24 18	21 24	29 2	11 42	20 28
5	12 9	2♐ 5	16 13	20 14	25 1	21 33	28 59	11 40	20 30
6	13 9	13 54	17 48	21 29	25 45	21 42	28 56	11 37	20 31
7	14 9	25 40	19 23	22 44	26 29	21 51	28 54	11 35	20 33
8	15 10	7♑27	20 58	23 58	27 13	22 0	28 51	11 32	20 34
9	16 10	19 20	22 32	25 13	27 58	22 9	28 49	11 30	20 36
10	17 10	1♒21	24 6	26 28	28 42	22 18	28 47	11 27	20 37
11	18 11	13 37	25 39	27 43	29 26	22 28	28 45	11 25	20 39
12	19 11	26 12	27 12	28 58	0♒10	22 37	28 42	11 22	20 40
13	20 11	9♓ 9	28 45	0♏13	0 55	22 47	28 40	11 20	20 41
14	21 12	22 33	0♐18	1 28	1 39	22 57	28 38	11 17	20 42
15	22 12	6♈25	1 50	2 43	2 23	23 7	28 36	11 15	20 44
16	23 13	20 44	3 22	3 58	3 8	23 17	28 34	11 13	20 45
17	24 13	5♉26	4 54	5 14	3 52	23 28	28 33	11 10	20 46
18	25 14	20 26	6 25	6 29	4 37	23 38	28 31	11 8	20 47
19	26 14	5♊35	7 56	7 44	5 22	23 48	28 30	11 5	20 49
20	27 15	20 44	9 27	8 59	6 6	23 59	28 28	11 3	20 50
21	28 15	5♋44	10 58	10 15	6 51	24 9	28 27	11 1	20 51
22	29 16	20 26	12 29	11 30	7 36	24 20	28 26	10 58	20 52
23	0♐16	4♌47	13 59	12 45	8 21	24 31	28 25	10 56	20 53
24	1 17	18 44	15 29	14 0	9 5	24 42	28 24	10 54	20 54
25	2 18	2♍16	16 59	15 15	9 50	24 54	28 24	10 52	20 55
26	3 19	15 25	18 28	16 30	10 35	25 5	28 23	10 49	20 56
27	4 19	28 14	19 57	17 45	11 20	25 16	28 22	10 47	20 67
28	5 20	10♎45	21 25	19 0	12 5	25 27	28 22	10 45	20 58
29	6 21	23 2	22 53	20 16	12 50	25 39	28 21	10 43	20 59
30	7 22	5♏ 8	24 20	21 31	13 35	25 50	28 21	10 41	21 0

Pluto 0 Leo all month

DECEMBER

DAY	☉	☽	☿	♀	♂	♃	♄	♅	♆
	° ′	° ′	° ′	° ′	° ′	° ′	° ′	° ′	° ′
1	8♐22	17♏ 6	25♐46	22♏46	14♒20	26♑ 2	28♓21	10♉39	21♍0
2	9 23	28 58	27 12	24 2	15 5	26 13	28 D21	10℞36	21 1
3	10 24	10♐47	28 36	25 17	15 50	26 25	28 21	10 34	21 2
4	11 25	22 34	0♑ 0	26 33	16 35	26 37	28 21	10 32	21 2
5	12 26	4♑22	1 23	27 48	17 20	26 49	28 21	10 30	21 3
6	13 27	16 13	2 44	29 3	18 5	27 1	28 22	10 28	21 4
7	14 28	28 10	4 4	0♐19	18 51	27 13	28 22	10 26	21 4
8	15 29	10♒15	5 21	1 34	19 36	27 25	28 23	10 24	21 5
9	16 30	22 32	6 37	2 49	20 21	27 37	28 24	10 23	21 5
10	17 31	5♓ 4	7 50	4 5	21 7	27 50	28 24	10 21	21 6
11	18 32	17 56	9 0	5 20	21 52	28 2	28 25	10 19	21 6
12	19 33	1♈10	10 6	6 36	22 38	28 15	28 26	10 17	21 7
13	20 34	14 49	11 9	7 51	23 23	28 28	28 27	10 16	21 7
14	21 35	28 54	12 6	9 7	24 8	28 40	28 29	10 14	21 8
15	22 36	13♉25	12 58	10 22	24 54	28 53	28 30	10 12	21 8
16	23 37	28 18	13 45	11 38	25 39	29 6	28 32	10 10	21 8
17	24 38	13♊27	14 24	12 53	26 24	29 19	28 34	10 9	21 8
18	25 39	28 42	14 56	14 9	27 10	29 32	28 35	10 7	21 9
19	26 40	13♋54	15 20	15 24	27 55	29 45	28 37	10 6	21 9
20	27 41	28 53	15 33	16 40	28 41	29 58	28 39	10 4	21 9
21	28 42	13♌31	15℞36	17 55	29 26	0♒11	28 41	10 3	21 9
22	29 43	27 43	15 29	19 11	0♓11	0 24	28 43	10 2	21 9
23	0♑44	11♍25	15 10	20 26	0 57	0 37	28 45	10 0	21 9
24	1 46	24 40	14 39	21 42	1 42	0 50	28 47	9 59	21 9
25	2 47	7♎30	13 57	22 58	2 27	1 3	28 49	9 58	21℞9
26	3 48	19 58	13 3	24 13	3 13	1 17	28 52	9 57	21 9
27	4 49	2♏ 9	12 0	25 29	3 58	1 30	28 54	9 56	21 9
28	5 50	14 7	10 48	26 45	4 44	1 44	28 57	9 55	21 9
29	6 51	25 58	9 31	28 0	5 29	1 57	29 0	9 54	21 9
30	7 52	7♐45	8 10	29 16	6 15	2 11	29 3	9 53	21 9
31	8 54	19 32	6 48	0♑31	7 0	2 24	29 6	9 52	21 9

Pluto 29 Cancer all month

1938

JANUARY

DAY	☉	☽	☿	♀	♂	♃	♄	♅	♆
	° ′	° ′	° ′	° ′	° ′	° ′	° ′	° ′	° ′
1	9 ♑ 55	1 ♑ 20	5 ♑ 28	1 ♑ 47	7 ♓ 46	2 ♒ 38	29 ♓ 9	9 ♉ 51	21 ♍ 8
2	10 56	13 13	4 R 13	3 2	8 31	2 52	29 12	9 R 50	21 R 8
3	11 57	25 13	3 3	4 18	9 17	3 5	29 16	9 49	21 8
4	12 58	7 ♒ 19	2 2	5 33	10 2	3 19	29 19	9 48	21 7
5	14 0	19 35	1 11	6 49	10 47	3 33	29 23	9 47	21 7
6	15 1	2 ♓ 2	0 28	8 4	11 33	3 47	29 26	9 47	21 6
7	16 2	14 40	29 ♐ 55	9 20	12 18	4 1	29 30	9 46	21 6
8	17 3	27 34	29 33	10 35	13 4	4 15	29 33	9 46	21 5
9	18 4	10 ♈ 44	29 22	11 50	13 49	4 29	29 37	9 45	21 5
10	19 5	24 13	29 D 21	13 6	14 34	4 43	29 41	9 45	21 4
11	20 6	8 ♉ 3	29 27	14 21	15 20	4 57	29 45	9 45	21 4
12	21 8	22 15	29 41	15 37	16 5	5 11	29 50	9 44	21 3
13	22 9	6 ♊ 48	0 ♑ 2	16 52	16 50	5 25	29 54	9 44	21 2
14	23 10	21 39	0 29	18 8	17 35	5 39	29 58	9 44	21 2
15	24 11	6 ♋ 41	1 3	19 23	18 21	5 53	0 ♈ 2	9 44	21 1
16	25 12	21 46	1 42	20 39	19 6	6 7	0 7	9 44	21 0
17	26 13	6 ♌ 45	2 26	21 54	19 51	6 21	0 11	9 D 44	20 59
18	27 14	21 28	3 14	23 9	20 36	6 35	0 16	9 44	20 59
19	28 15	5 ♍ 48	4 7	24 25	21 21	6 49	0 20	9 44	20 58
20	29 16	19 40	5 3	25 40	22 6	7 3	0 25	9 44	20 57
21	0 ♒ 17	3 ♎ 3	6 2	26 55	22 51	7 17	0 30	9 44	20 56
22	1 18	15 59	7 4	28 11	23 36	7 31	0 35	9 45	20 55
23	2 19	28 30	8 9	29 26	24 21	7 45	0 40	9 45	20 54
24	3 20	10 ♏ 42	9 17	0 ♒ 42	25 6	8 0	0 46	9 45	20 53
25	4 21	22 40	10 26	1 57	25 51	8 14	0 51	9 45	20 52
26	5 22	4 ♐ 30	11 37	3 12	26 36	8 28	0 56	9 46	20 51
27	6 23	16 16	12 50	4 28	27 21	8 42	1 1	9 46	20 50
28	7 24	28 3	14 5	5 43	28 6	8 57	1 7	9 47	20 49
29	8 25	9 ♑ 55	15 22	6 58	28 51	9 11	1 12	9 47	20 48
30	9 26	21 55	16 39	8 13	29 36	9 25	1 17	9 48	20 47
31	10 27	4 ♒ 4	17 58	9 29	0 ♈ 21	9 39	1 23	9 49	20 45

Pluto 29 Cancer all month

FEBRUARY

DAY	☉	☽	☿	♀	♂	♃	♄	♅	♆
	° ′	° ′	° ′	° ′	° ′	° ′	° ′	° ′	° ′
1	11 ♒ 28	16 ♒ 25	19 ♑ 18	10 ♒ 44	1 ♈ 6	9 ♒ 54	1 ♈ 28	9 ♉ 50	20 ♍ 44
2	12 29	28 57	20 40	11 59	1 51	10 8	1 34	9 50	20 R 43
3	13 30	11 ♓ 41	22 3	13 14	2 36	10 22	1 40	9 51	20 42
4	14 31	24 37	23 26	14 30	3 20	10 36	1 46	9 52	20 40
5	15 32	7 ♈ 43	24 51	15 45	4 5	10 51	1 52	9 53	20 39
6	16 33	21 1	26 16	17 0	4 49	11 5	1 58	9 54	20 38
7	17 33	4 ♉ 33	27 43	18 15	5 34	11 19	2 4	9 55	20 37
8	18 34	18 17	29 11	19 31	6 19	11 33	2 10	9 56	20 35
9	19 35	2 ♊ 16	0 ♒ 39	20 46	7 3	11 48	2 16	9 57	20 34
10	20 36	16 30	2 8	22 1	7 48	12 2	2 22	9 58	20 32
11	21 36	0 ♋ 57	3 39	23 16	8 32	12 16	2 28	10 0	20 31
12	22 37	15 34	5 10	24 31	9 17	12 30	2 35	10 1	20 30
13	23 38	0 ♌ 16	6 42	25 46	10 1	12 44	2 41	10 2	20 28
14	24 38	14 56	8 15	27 1	10 45	12 58	2 48	10 4	20 27
15	25 39	29 26	9 49	28 16	11 29	13 12	2 54	10 5	20 25
16	26 39	13 ♍ 38	11 24	29 32	12 14	13 26	3 1	10 6	20 24
17	27 40	27 28	12 59	0 ♓ 47	12 58	13 41	3 7	10 8	20 22
18	28 41	10 ♎ 53	14 36	2 2	13 42	13 55	3 14	10 9	20 21
19	29 41	23 52	16 13	3 17	14 26	14 9	3 21	10 11	20 19
20	0 ♓ 42	6 ♏ 27	17 51	4 32	15 11	14 23	3 27	10 13	20 18
21	1 42	18 42	19 31	5 47	15 55	14 37	3 34	10 14	20 16
22	2 42	0 ♐ 43	21 11	7 2	16 39	14 51	3 41	10 16	20 15
23	3 43	12 34	22 52	8 17	17 23	15 5	3 48	10 18	20 13
24	4 43	24 22	24 34	9 32	18 7	15 19	3 54	10 19	20 12
25	5 44	6 ♑ 11	26 17	10 47	18 51	15 32	4 1	10 21	20 10
26	6 44	18 6	28 1	12 2	19 35	15 46	4 8	10 23	20 8
27	7 44	0 ♒ 12	29 47	13 17	20 19	16 0	4 15	10 25	20 7
28	8 44	12 31	1 ♓ 33	14 32	21 3	16 14	4 22	10 27	20 5

Pluto 28 Cancer all month

1938

MARCH

Day	☉	☽	☿	♀	♂	♃	♄	♅	♆
	° ′	° ′	° ′	° ′	° ′	° ′	° ′	° ′	° ′
1	9 ♓ 45	25 ♒ 6	3 ♓ 20	15 ♓ 47	21 ♈ 46	16 ♒ 27	4 ♈ 29	10 ♉ 29	20 ♍ 4
2	10 45	7 ♓ 56	5 8	17 2	22 30	16 41	4 36	10 31	20 ℞ 2
3	11 45	21 0	6 57	18 17	23 14	16 55	4 43	10 33	20 0
4	12 45	4 ♈ 18	8 48	19 32	23 58	17 8	4 50	10 35	19 59
5	13 45	17 47	10 39	20 47	24 41	17 22	4 58	10 37	19 57
6	14 46	1 ♉ 26	12 31	22 2	25 25	17 35	5 5	10 39	19 55
7	15 46	15 12	14 24	23 17	26 9	17 49	5 12	10 42	19 54
8	16 46	29 6	16 18	24 32	26 52	18 2	5 19	10 44	19 52
9	17 46	13 ♊ 5	18 13	25 46	27 36	18 16	5 27	10 46	19 50
10	18 46	27 11	20 9	27 1	28 19	18 29	5 34	10 48	19 49
11	19 46	11 ♋ 22	22 6	28 16	29 3	18 42	5 41	10 51	19 47
12	20 45	25 37	24 4	29 31	29 46	18 56	5 48	10 53	19 45
13	21 45	9 ♌ 52	26 2	0 ♈ 45	0 ♉ 30	19 9	5 56	10 56	19 44
14	22 45	24 4	28 1	2 0	1 13	19 22	6 3	10 58	19 42
15	23 45	8 ♍ 8	0 ♈ 0	3 15	1 56	19 35	6 10	11 1	19 40
16	24 45	21 58	1 59	4 29	2 39	19 48	6 18	11 3	19 39
17	25 44	5 ♎ 32	3 58	5 44	3 22	20 0	6 25	11 6	19 37
18	26 44	18 46	5 56	6 58	4 5	20 13	6 33	11 8	19 35
19	27 44	1 ♏ 39	7 54	8 13	4 48	20 26	6 40	11 11	19 34
20	28 43	14 12	9 50	9 27	5 31	20 39	6 48	11 14	19 32
21	29 43	26 28	11 45	10 42	6 14	20 51	6 55	11 17	19 31
22	0 ♈ 42	8 ♐ 30	13 39	11 56	6 57	21 4	7 3	11 19	19 29
23	1 42	20 23	15 30	13 11	7 40	21 17	7 10	11 22	19 27
24	2 41	2 ♑ 12	17 18	14 26	8 23	21 29	7 18	11 25	19 26
25	3 41	14 3	19 4	15 40	9 5	21 42	7 25	11 28	19 24
26	4 40	26 0	20 46	16 55	9 48	21 54	7 33	11 31	19 22
27	5 40	8 ♒ 9	22 24	18 9	10 31	22 6	7 40	11 34	19 21
28	6 39	20 34	23 58	19 24	11 14	22 19	7 48	11 37	19 19
29	7 38	3 ♓ 17	25 27	20 38	11 56	22 32	7 55	11 39	19 18
30	8 38	16 19	26 50	21 52	12 39	22 44	8 3	11 42	19 16
31	9 37	29 41	28 9	23 6	13 22	22 55	8 10	11 45	19 15

Pluto 28 Cancer all month

APRIL

Day	☉	☽	☿	♀	♂	♃	♄	♅	♆
	° ′	° ′	° ′	° ′	° ′	° ′	° ′	° ′	° ′
1	10 ♈ 36	13 ♈ 21	29 ♈ 22	24 ♈ 21	14 ♉ 4	23 ♒ 7	8 ♈ 18	11 ♉ 48	19 ♍ 13
2	11 35	27 15	0 ♉ 29	25 35	14 47	23 18	8 25	11 52	19 ℞ 11
3	12 35	11 ♉ 20	1 29	26 49	15 29	23 30	8 33	11 55	19 10
4	13 34	25 31	2 23	28 3	16 11	23 42	8 40	11 58	19 8
5	14 33	9 ♊ 46	3 11	29 18	16 54	23 53	8 48	12 1	19 7
6	15 32	24 0	3 52	0 ♉ 32	17 36	24 5	8 55	12 4	19 5
7	16 31	8 ♋ 12	4 26	1 46	18 18	24 16	9 3	12 7	19 4
8	17 30	22 20	4 54	3 0	19 0	24 27	9 10	12 10	19 3
9	18 29	6 ♌ 23	5 14	4 14	19 43	24 38	9 18	12 13	19 1
10	19 28	20 18	5 28	5 28	20 25	24 49	9 25	12 17	19 0
11	20 27	4 ♍ 5	5 35	6 42	21 7	25 0	9 33	12 20	18 59
12	21 26	17 42	5 ℞ 35	7 56	21 49	25 11	9 40	12 23	18 57
13	22 24	1 ♎ 5	5 30	9 10	22 31	25 22	9 48	12 27	18 56
14	23 23	14 15	5 19	10 23	23 12	25 32	9 55	12 30	18 55
15	24 22	27 9	5 1	11 37	23 54	25 43	10 2	12 33	18 53
16	25 21	9 ♏ 48	4 38	12 51	24 36	25 53	10 9	12 36	18 52
17	26 19	22 12	4 11	14 5	25 18	26 4	10 17	12 39	18 51
18	27 18	4 ♐ 23	3 40	15 18	26 0	26 14	10 24	12 43	18 50
19	28 16	16 23	3 5	16 32	26 42	26 24	10 32	12 47	18 48
20	29 15	28 16	2 27	17 46	27 24	26 34	10 39	12 50	18 47
21	0 ♉ 14	10 ♑ 6	1 47	19 0	28 5	26 44	10 46	12 54	18 46
22	1 12	21 57	1 6	20 13	28 47	26 54	10 53	12 57	18 45
23	2 11	3 ♒ 55	0 24	21 27	29 28	27 4	11 0	13 0	18 44
24	3 9	16 4	29 ♈ 43	22 41	0 ♊ 10	27 13	11 7	13 4	18 43
25	4 7	28 29	29 2	23 54	0 51	27 23	11 15	13 7	18 42
26	5 6	11 ♓ 14	28 23	25 8	1 33	27 32	11 22	13 11	18 41
27	6 4	24 20	27 47	26 21	2 14	27 41	11 29	13 14	18 40
28	7 3	7 ♈ 51	27 14	27 35	2 55	27 50	11 36	13 18	18 39
29	8 1	21 44	26 43	28 48	3 37	27 59	11 43	13 21	18 38
30	8 59	5 ♉ 57	26 17	0 ♊ 2	4 18	28 8	11 50	13 25	18 37

Pluto 27 Cancer all month

1938

MAY

Pluto 27 Cancer all month

DAY	☉	☽	☿	♀	♂	♃	♄	♅	♆
1	9 ♉58	20 ♉ 25	25♈55	1♊15	4♊59	28♒17	11♈57	13 ♉28	18♍36
2	10 56	5 ♊ 2	25 ℞37	2 28	5 40	28 25	12 4	13 31	18℞35
3	11 54	19 43	25 24	3 42	6 22	28 34	12 11	13 35	18 34
4	12 52	4♋21	25 15	4 55	7 3	28 42	12 18	13 38	18 33
5	13 50	18 51	25 11	6 8	7 44	28 50	12 25	13 42	18 32
6	14 48	3♌ 8	25 D12	7 21	8 25	28 58	12 32	13 45	18 31
7	15 46	17 11	25 17	8 34	9 6	29 6	12 38	13 49	18 31
8	16 45	0♍59	25 28	9 47	9 46	29 14	12 45	13 52	18 30
9	17 43	14 30	25 43	11 0	10 27	29 22	12 51	13 56	18 29
10	18 41	27 46	26 2	12 13	11 8	29 29	12 58	13 59	18 28
11	19 38	10♎46	26 26	13 26	11 49	29 37	13 4	14 3	18 28
12	20 36	23 33	26 54	14 39	12 30	29 44	13 11	14 6	18 27
13	21 34	6♏ 7	27 26	15 52	13 11	29 51	13 18	14 10	18 27
14	22 32	18 29	28 2	17 5	13 52	29 58	13 24	14 12	18 26
15	23 30	0♐40	28 42	18 18	14 32	0♓ 5	13 31	14 17	18 26
16	24 28	12 43	29 26	19 31	15 13	0 11	13 37	14 20	18 25
17	25 26	24 38	0♉13	20 44	15 53	0 18	13 43	14 23	18 25
18	26 23	6♑29	1 4	21 56	16 34	0 24	13 49	14 27	18 24
19	27 21	18 19	1 58	23 9	17 14	0 30	13 56	14 30	18 24
20	28 19	0♒11	2 55	24 22	17 55	0 36	14 2	14 34	18 23
21	29 17	12 9	3 56	25 35	18 35	0 42	14 8	14 37	18 23
22	0♊15	24 17	4 59	26 48	19 16	0 47	14 14	14 40	18 23
23	1 12	6♓40	6 6	28 0	19 56	0 53	14 20	14 44	18 23
24	2 10	19 22	7 16	29 13	20 37	0 58	14 25	14 47	18 22
25	3 7	2♈26	8 28	0♋25	21 17	1 3	14 31	14 50	18 22
26	4 5	15 55	9 43	1 37	21 57	1 8	14 37	14 54	18 22
27	5 3	29 50	11 1	2 50	22 38	1 13	14 43	14 57	18 22
28	6 0	14♉10	12 21	4 2	23 18	1 17	14 48	15 0	18 22
29	6 58	28 51	13 44	5 14	23 58	1 22	14 54	15 4	18 22
30	7 55	13♊47	15 10	6 26	24 38	1 26	15 0	15 7	18 22
31	8 53	28 49	16 38	7 39	25 18	1 30	15 5	15 10	18 22

JUNE

Pluto 28 Cancer all month

DAY	☉	☽	☿	♀	♂	♃	♄	♅	♆
1	9 ♊50	13♋50	18 ♉ 9	8♋51	25 ♊58	1♓34	15♈11	15 ♉13	18♍22
2	10 48	28 41	19 43	10 3	26 38	1 38	15 16	15 17	18 D22
3	11 45	13♌15	21 19	11 15	27 18	1 42	15 21	15 20	18 22
4	12 43	27 28	22 58	12 27	27 58	1 45	15 26	15 23	18 22
5	13 40	11♍17	24 39	13 39	28 38	1 49	15 31	15 26	18 22
6	14 38	24 44	26 23	14 51	29 18	1 52	15 36	15 29	18 22
7	15 35	7♎49	28 9	16 3	29 58	1 55	15 41	15 32	18 22
8	16 32	20 35	29 58	17 15	0♋38	1 57	15 46	15 35	18 23
9	17 30	3♏ 6	1♊49	18 26	1 17	2 0	15 51	15 38	18 23
10	18 27	15 23	3 42	19 38	1 57	2 2	15 56	15 42	18 23
11	19 25	27 31	5 38	20 50	2 37	2 4	16 1	15 44	18 24
12	20 22	9♐31	7 36	22 2	3 17	2 6	16 5	15 47	18 24
13	21 19	21 26	9 36	23 13	3 56	2 7	16 9	15 50	18 25
14	22 16	3♑17	11 38	24 25	4 36	2 9	16 14	15 53	18 25
15	23 14	15 7	13 42	25 37	5 16	2 10	16 18	15 56	18 26
16	24 11	26 57	15 48	26 48	5 55	2 12	16 23	15 59	18 26
17	25 8	8♒53	17 55	28 0	6 35	2 13	16 28	16 2	18 27
18	26 6	20 53	20 4	29 11	7 14	2 13	16 31	16 5	18 28
19	27 3	3♓ 2	22 14	0♌22	7 54	2 14	16 35	16 8	18 28
20	28 0	15 24	24 25	1 33	8 33	2 14	16 39	16 11	18 29
21	28 57	28 3	26 36	2 44	9 13	2 15	16 43	16 14	18 29
22	29 55	11♈ 2	28 48	3 55	9 52	2℞15	16 47	16 16	18 30
23	0♋52	24 24	0♋59	5 6	10 32	2 14	16 51	16 19	18 31
24	1 49	8♉12	3 11	6 17	11 11	2 14	16 54	16 22	18 31
25	2 46	22 28	5 22	7 28	11 51	2 13	16 58	16 24	18 32
26	3 44	7♊ 8	7 32	8 39	12 30	2 12	17 1	16 27	18 33
27	4 41	22 8	9 41	9 50	13 9	2 10	17 4	16 29	18 34
28	5 38	7♋20	11 49	11 1	13 49	2 9	17 8	16 32	18 35
29	6 35	22 34	13 55	12 11	14 28	2 9	17 11	16 35	18 36
30	7 33	7♌41	16 0	13 22	15 7	2 8	17 14	16 37	18 37

1938

JULY

DAY	☉	☽	☿	♀	♂	♃	♄	♅	♆
1	8♋30	22♌30	18♋3	14♌33	15♋46	2♓6	17♈17	16♉40	18♍38
2	9 27	6♍55	20 4	15 43	16 25	2 ℞ 4	17 20	16 42	18 39
3	10 24	20 53	22 4	16 54	17 4	2 2	17 23	16 44	18 40
4	11 21	4♎22	24 2	18 4	17 43	1 59	17 26	16 47	18 41
5	12 19	17 25	25 58	19 14	18 22	1 57	17 29	16 49	18 42
6	13 16	0♏6	27 52	20 25	19 2	1 55	17 31	16 51	18 43
7	14 13	12 28	29 45	21 35	19 41	1 52	17 34	16 53	18 44
8	15 10	24 37	1♌35	22 45	20 20	1 49	17 36	16 56	18 45
9	16 7	6♐36	3 23	23 55	20 59	1 46	17 38	16 58	18 47
10	17 5	18 29	5 9	25 5	21 38	1 43	17 40	17 0	18 48
11	18 2	0♑19	6 53	26 14	22 17	1 39	17 42	17 2	18 49
12	18 59	12 9	8 35	27 24	22 56	1 35	17 44	17 4	18 50
13	19 56	24 0	10 15	28 34	23 35	1 31	17 46	17 6	18 52
14	20 53	5♒55	11 53	29 43	24 14	1 27	17 48	17 8	18 53
15	21 51	17 55	13 29	0♍53	24 52	1 22	17 49	17 10	18 55
16	22 48	0♓2	15 3	2 2	25 31	1 18	17 51	17 12	18 56
17	23 45	12 18	16 36	3 11	26 10	1 14	17 53	17 13	18 57
18	24 42	24 44	18 6	4 20	26 49	1 9	17 54	17 15	18 59
19	25 39	7♈24	19 34	5 29	27 27	1 4	17 56	17 17	19 0
20	26 37	20 20	21 0	6 38	28 6	0 59	17 57	17 19	19 2
21	27 34	3♉37	22 24	7 47	28 45	0 54	17 58	17 20	19 3
22	28 31	17 17	23 46	8 56	29 24	0 49	17 59	17 22	19 5
23	29 29	1♊21	25 6	10 5	0♌2	0 43	17 59	17 24	19 7
24	0♌26	15 50	26 24	11 14	0 41	0 38	18 0	17 25	19 8
25	1 23	0♋41	27 39	12 22	1 20	0 32	18 1	17 26	19 9
26	2 21	15 47	28 52	13 30	1 59	0 26	18 1	17 28	19 11
27	3 18	1♌0	0♍3	14 39	2 37	0 20	18 2	17 29	19 13
28	4 15	16 9	1 11	15 47	3 16	0 14	18 2	17 31	19 14
29	5 13	1♍3	2 17	16 55	3 55	0 7	18 2	17 32	19 16
30	6 10	15 36	3 20	18 3	4 33	0 1	18 3	17 33	19 18
31	7 7	29 40	4 21	19 11	5 12	29♒54	18 3	17 34	19 19

AUGUST

DAY	☉	☽	☿	♀	♂	♃	♄	♅	♆
1	8♌5	13♎15	5♍19	20♍18	5♌50	29♒47	18♈3	17♉36	19♍21
2	9 2	26 21	6 13	21 26	6 29	29 ℞ 40	18 ℞ 3	17 37	19 23
3	10 0	9♏3	7 5	22 33	7 7	29 34	18 2	17 38	19 25
4	10 57	21 24	7 53	23 41	7 46	29 27	18 2	17 39	19 27
5	11 55	3♐30	8 38	24 48	8 24	29 20	18 2	17 40	19 28
6	12 52	15 25	9 19	25 54	9 3	29 13	18 1	17 41	19 30
7	13 50	27 16	9 57	27 1	9 41	29 5	18 1	17 42	19 32
8	14 47	9♑5	10 30	28 8	10 20	28 58	18 0	17 42	19 34
9	15 45	20 56	11 0	29 15	10 58	28 50	17 59	17 43	19 36
10	16 42	2♒52	11 25	0♎21	11 37	28 43	17 58	17 44	19 38
11	17 40	14 54	11 46	1 27	12 15	28 35	17 57	17 45	19 40
12	18 37	27 4	12 2	2 33	12 54	28 28	17 55	17 45	19 42
13	19 35	9♓22	12 13	3 39	13 32	28 20	17 54	17 46	19 44
14	20 32	21 50	12 20	4 45	14 10	28 12	17 53	17 46	19 46
15	21 30	4♈27	12 ℞ 19	5 50	14 49	28 5	17 51	17 47	19 48
16	22 28	17 16	12 13	6 56	15 27	27 57	17 50	17 47	19 50
17	23 25	0♉19	12 3	8 1	16 5	27 49	17 48	17 48	19 52
18	24 23	13 37	11 46	9 6	16 44	27 41	17 46	17 48	19 54
19	25 21	27 13	11 24	10 10	17 22	27 34	17 44	17 48	19 56
20	26 18	11♊8	10 56	11 15	18 1	27 26	17 42	17 48	19 58
21	27 16	25 23	10 24	12 20	18 39	27 18	17 40	17 49	20 0
22	28 14	9♋57	9 46	13 24	19 17	27 10	17 38	17 49	20 2
23	29 12	24 45	9 4	14 28	19 56	27 2	17 36	17 49	20 4
24	0♍10	9♌41	8 17	15 31	20 34	26 54	17 33	17 49	20 6
25	1 8	24 37	7 27	16 35	21 12	26 46	17 31	17 ℞ 49	20 8
26	2 6	9♍23	6 34	17 38	21 50	26 38	17 29	17 49	20 11
27	3 3	23 50	5 39	18 41	22 28	26 30	17 26	17 49	20 13
28	4 1	7♎54	4 44	19 44	23 6	26 23	17 23	17 49	20 15
29	4 59	21 30	3 49	20 46	23 44	26 15	17 21	17 48	20 17
30	5 57	4♏39	2 56	21 48	24 22	26 7	17 18	17 48	20 19
31	6 55	17 23	2 6	22 51	25 1	26 0	17 15	17 48	20 21

1938

SEPTEMBER

Day	☉ ° ′	☽ ° ′	☿ ° ′	♀ ° ′	♂ ° ′	♃ ° ′	♄ ° ′	♅ ° ′	♆ ° ′
1	7♍53	29♏46	1♍20	23♎52	25♌39	25♒52	17♈12	17♉47	20♍24
2	8 52	11♐53	0℞39	24 54	26 17	25℞45	17℞ 9	17℞47	20 26
3	9 50	23 49	0 4	25 55	26 55	25 37	17 6	17 46	20 28
4	10 48	5♑40	29♌36	26 55	27 34	25 30	17 3	17 46	20 30
5	11 46	17 31	29 15	27 55	28 12	25 22	16 59	17 45	20 32
6	12 44	29 25	29 3	28 55	28 50	25 15	16 56	17 45	20 34
7	13 42	11♒26	28 D59	29 55	29 28	25 8	16 52	17 44	20 37
8	14 41	23 36	29 4	0♏54	0♍ 6	25 1	16 49	17 43	20 39
9	15 39	5♓57	29 18	1 53	0 44	24 54	16 45	17 42	20 41
10	16 37	18 30	29 40	2 52	1 22	24 47	16 41	17 42	20 43
11	17 35	1♈15	0♍11	3 50	2 0	24 40	16 37	17 41	20 46
12	18 34	14 11	0 52	4 48	2 38	24 34	16 34	17 40	20 48
13	19 32	27 18	1 41	5 46	3 16	24 27	16 30	17 39	20 51
14	20 31	10♉36	2 37	6 43	3 54	24 21	16 26	17 38	20 53
15	21 29	24 6	3 41	7 39	4 32	24 15	16 22	17 37	20 55
16	22 27	7♊48	4 51	8 36	5 11	24 9	16 18	17 36	20 57
17	23 26	21 42	6 8	9 31	5 49	24 3	16 15	17 35	20 59
18	24 25	5♋49	7 30	10 27	6 27	23 57	16 9	17 34	21 1
19	25 23	20 7	8 57	11 21	7 5	23 51	16 5	17 32	21 4
20	26 22	4♌34	10 29	12 16	7 43	23 46	16 1	17 31	21 6
21	27 20	19 6	12 4	13 9	8 21	23 40	15 56	17 30	21 8
22	28 19	3♍37	13 42	14 3	8 59	23 35	15 52	17 28	21 10
23	29 18	18 0	15 23	14 55	9 37	23 30	15 48	17 27	21 12
24	0♎17	2♎ 9	17 6	15 47	10 15	23 25	15 43	17 26	21 14
25	1 15	16 0	18 52	16 38	10 53	23 21	15 39	17 24	21 17
26	2 14	29 29	20 38	17 29	11 31	23 16	15 34	17 23	21 19
27	3 13	12♏34	22 26	18 19	12 9	23 12	15 30	17 21	21 21
28	4 12	25 18	24 14	19 8	12 47	23 8	15 25	17 19	21 23
29	5 11	7♐42	26 3	19 56	13 24	23 4	15 21	17 18	21 25
30	6 10	19 51	27 51	20 43	14 2	23 0	15 16	17 16	21 27

Pluto 0 Leo all month

OCTOBER

Day	☉ ° ′	☽ ° ′	☿ ° ′	♀ ° ′	♂ ° ′	♃ ° ′	♄ ° ′	♅ ° ′	♆ ° ′
1	7♎ 9	1♑49	29♍40	21♏30	14♍40	22♒56	15♈11	17♉15	21♍30
2	8 8	13 41	1♎29	22 16	15 18	22℞53	15℞ 7	17℞13	21 32
3	9 7	25 33	3 17	23 1	15 56	22 49	15 2	17 11	21 34
4	10 6	7♒29	5 5	23 45	16 34	22 46	14 57	17 9	21 36
5	11 5	19 33	6 53	24 28	17 12	22 43	14 52	17 8	21 38
6	12 4	1♓50	8 40	25 10	17 50	22 41	14 48	17 6	21 40
7	13 3	14 20	10 26	25 52	18 28	22 38	14 43	17 4	21 42
8	14 3	27 6	12 12	26 32	19 6	22 36	14 38	17 2	21 44
9	15 2	10♈ 8	13 57	27 11	19 44	22 34	14 33	17 0	21 47
10	16 1	23 26	15 41	27 48	20 22	22 32	14 29	16 58	21 49
11	17 0	6♉57	17 24	28 25	21 0	22 31	14 24	16 56	21 51
12	18 0	20 40	19 7	29 0	21 38	22 29	14 20	16 54	21 53
13	18 59	4♊32	20 49	29 34	22 16	22 28	14 15	16 52	21 55
14	19 59	18 32	22 30	0♐ 7	22 54	22 27	14 10	16 50	21 57
15	20 58	2♋38	24 11	0 38	23 31	22 26	14 5	16 47	21 59
16	21 58	16 48	25 51	1 8	24 9	22 25	14 0	16 45	22 1
17	22 57	0♌59	27 30	1 36	24 47	22 24	13 55	16 43	22 3
18	23 57	15 11	29 8	2 3	25 25	22 24	13 51	16 41	22 5
19	24 56	29 20	0♏46	2 28	26 3	22 24	13 46	16 38	22 7
20	25 56	13♍23	2 23	2 51	26 41	22 D23	13 42	16 36	22 9
21	26 56	27 17	4 0	3 12	27 19	22 24	13 38	16 34	22 11
22	27 55	11♎ 0	5 36	3 32	27 57	22 24	13 33	16 31	22 13
23	28 55	24 28	7 12	3 49	28 34	22 25	13 29	16 29	22 15
24	29 55	7♏40	8 47	4 5	29 12	22 26	13 25	16 27	22 16
25	0♏55	20 34	10 22	4 18	29 50	22 27	13 20	16 24	22 18
26	1 54	3♐11	11 56	4 30	0♎28	22 28	13 16	16 22	22 20
27	2 54	15 32	13 29	4 39	1 6	22 29	13 12	16 20	22 22
28	3 54	27 40	15 2	4 46	1 44	22 31	13 7	16 17	22 24
29	4 54	9♑39	16 34	4 51	2 22	22 33	13 3	16 15	22 26
30	5 54	21 32	18 5	4 53	3 0	22 35	12 59	16 13	22 27
31	6 54	3♒23	19 36	4℞54	3 37	22 38	12 55	16 10	22 29

Pluto 1 Leo all month

1938

NOVEMBER

DAY	☉ ° ′	☽ ° ′	☿ ° ′	♀ ° ′	♂ ° ′	♃ ° ′	♄ ° ′	♅ ° ′	♆ ° ′
1	7♏54	15♒19	21♏ 7	4♐51	4♎15	22♒40	12♈51	16♉ 8	22♍30
2	8 54	27 23	22 37	4℞47	4 53	22 43	12℞47	16℞ 5	22 32
3	9 54	9♓40	24 7	4 41	5 31	22 45	12 43	16 3	22 34
4	10 54	22 13	25 37	4 31	6 8	22 48	12 39	16 0	22 35
5	11 54	5♈ 6	27 6	4 20	6 46	22 51	12 35	15 58	22 37
6	12 55	18 19	28 34	4 6	7 24	22 55	12 31	15 55	22 39
7	13 55	1♉54	0♐ 2	3 50	8 2	22 58	12 27	15 53	22 40
8	14 55	15 48	1 29	3 31	8 39	23 2	12 24	15 50	22 42
9	15 55	29 58	2 56	3 11	9 17	23 6	12 20	15 48	22 43
10	16 55	14♊20	4 22	2 47	9 55	23 10	12 17	15 45	22 45
11	17 56	28 48	5 48	2 22	10 33	23 15	12 13	15 43	22 46
12	18 56	13♋17	7 13	1 55	11 10	23 19	12 10	15 40	22 47
13	19 56	27 43	8 37	1 26	11 48	23 24	12 7	15 38	22 49
14	20 57	12♌ 0	10 0	0 55	12 26	23 29	12 4	15 36	22 50
15	21 57	26 8	11 23	0 22	13 4	23 34	12 1	15 33	22 52
16	22 58	10♍ 3	12 44	29♏49	13 42	23 40	11 58	15 31	22 53
17	23 58	23 46	14 4	29 14	14 20	23 46	11 55	15 28	22 54
18	24 59	7♎15	15 24	28 39	14 58	23 52	11 52	15 26	22 56
19	25 59	20 31	16 41	28 3	15 35	23 57	11 49	15 23	22 57
20	27 0	3♏33	17 58	27 27	16 13	24 3	11 47	15 21	22 58
21	28 0	16 23	19 12	26 50	16 50	24 9	11 44	15 18	22 59
22	20 1	28 59	20 24	26 14	17 28	24 15	11 42	15 16	23 1
23	0♐ 2	11♐24	21 34	25 38	18 6	24 22	11 39	15 14	23 2
24	1 2	23 38	22 42	25 3	18 43	24 28	11 37	15 11	23 3
25	2 3	5♑42	23 46	24 29	19 21	24 35	11 35	15 9	23 4
26	3 4	17 39	24 47	23 56	19 59	24 42	11 33	15 7	23 5
27	4 5	29 31	25 45	23 24	20 37	24 49	11 31	15 4	23 6
28	5 5	11♒22	26 38	22 54	21 14	24 57	11 29	15 2	23 7
29	6 6	23 16	27 26	22 25	21 52	25 4	11 27	15 0	23 8
30	7 7	5♓16	28 8	21 58	22 30	25 12	11 25	14 57	23 9

Pluto 1 Leo all month

DECEMBER

DAY	☉ ° ′	☽ ° ′	☿ ° ′	♀ ° ′	♂ ° ′	♃ ° ′	♄ ° ′	♅ ° ′	♆ ° ′
1	8♐ 8	17♓29	28♐43	21♏33	23♎ 8	25♒19	11♈24	14♉55	23♍10
2	9 9	29 59	29 12	21℞11	23 45	25 27	11℞22	14℞53	23 10
3	10 9	12♈49	29 32	20 50	24 23	25 35	11 21	14 51	23 11
4	11 10	26 3	29 43	20 32	25 1	25 43	11 20	14 49	23 12
5	12 11	9♉43	29℞45	20 16	25 38	25 52	11 19	14 47	23 13
6	13 12	23 49	29 36	20 3	26 16	26 0	11 18	14 44	23 14
7	14 13	8♊18	29 16	19 52	26 53	26 9	11 17	14 42	23 14
8	15 14	23 5	28 45	19 44	27 31	26 18	11 16	14 40	23 15
9	16 15	8♋ 2	28 3	19 38	28 9	26 27	11 16	14 38	23 16
10	17 16	23 0	27 11	19 35	28 46	26 36	11 15	14 36	23 16
11	18 17	7♌50	26 9	19 D34	29 24	26 45	11 15	14 34	23 17
12	19 18	22 27	24 57	19 36	0♏ 2	26 54	11 15	14 32	23 17
13	20 19	6♍44	23 40	19 40	0 39	27 4	11 14	14 31	23 18
14	21 20	20 39	22 19	19 46	1 17	27 13	11 14	14 29	23 18
15	22 21	4♎14	20 56	19 54	1 54	27 23	11 D14	14 27	23 18
16	23 22	17 28	19 35	20 6	2 32	27 33	11 14	14 25	23 19
17	24 23	0♏25	18 18	20 19	3 9	27 42	11 15	14 23	23 19
18	25 24	13 7	17 8	20 34	3 47	27 52	11 15	14 22	23 20
19	26 25	25 37	16 6	20 52	4 24	28 2	11 15	14 20	23 20
20	27 26	7♐56	15 13	21 11	5 2	28 13	11 15	14 18	23 20
21	28 27	20 7	14 30	21 33	5 39	28 23	11 16	14 17	23 20
22	29 28	2♑11	13 59	21 56	6 17	28 34	11 16	14 15	23 21
23	0♑29	14 9	13 39	22 21	6 54	28 45	11 17	14 14	23 21
24	1 31	26 3	13 29	22 48	7 31	28 56	11 18	14 12	23 21
25	2 32	7♒54	13 D29	23 16	8 9	29 7	11 19	14 11	23 21
26	3 33	19 45	13 39	23 46	8 46	29 18	11 21	14 9	23℞21
27	4 34	1♓39	13 57	24 18	9 23	29 29	11 22	14 8	23 21
28	5 35	13 38	14 22	24 51	10 1	29 40	11 23	14 7	23 21
29	6 36	25 47	14 55	25 26	10 38	29 51	11 25	14 5	23 20
30	7 38	8♈10	15 34	26 2	11 16	0♓ 3	11 26	14 4	23 20
31	8 39	20 53	16 18	26 39	11 53	0 14	11 28	14 3	23 20

Pluto 1 Leo all month

1939

JANUARY

DAY	☉	☽	☿	♀	♂	♃	♄	♅	♆
	° ′	° ′	° ′	° ′	° ′	° ′	° ′	° ′	° ′
1	9 ♑ 40	3 ♉ 59	17 ♐ 7	27 ♏ 18	12 ♏ 30	0 ♓ 25	11 ♈ 30	14 ♉ 2	23 ♍ 20
2	10 41	17 33	18 1	27 58	13 8	0 37	11 32	14 R 1	23 R 19
3	11 42	1 ♊ 35	18 59	28 39	13 45	0 49	11 34	14 0	23 19
4	12 43	16 7	20 0	29 21	14 22	1 1	11 36	13 59	23 19
5	13 44	1 ♋ 3	21 4	0 ♐ 4	14 59	1 13	11 38	13 58	23 19
6	14 46	16 15	22 11	0 49	15 36	1 25	11 40	13 57	23 18
7	15 47	1 ♌ 34	23 20	1 34	16 13	1 37	11 43	13 56	23 18
8	16 48	16 48	24 31	2 20	16 50	1 49	11 45	13 55	23 17
9	17 49	1 ♍ 46	25 44	3 7	17 27	2 1	11 48	13 55	23 17
10	18 50	16 21	26 59	3 56	18 5	2 14	11 51	13 54	23 16
11	19 51	0 ♎ 29	28 16	4 45	18 42	2 26	11 54	13 54	23 16
12	20 52	14 8	29 34	5 34	19 19	2 39	11 57	13 53	23 15
13	21 53	27 21	0 ♑ 53	6 25	19 56	2 52	12 0	13 52	23 15
14	22 55	10 ♏ 11	2 14	7 17	20 33	3 4	12 3	13 52	23 14
15	23 56	22 43	3 36	8 9	21 10	3 17	12 6	13 51	23 13
16	24 57	5 ♐ 1	4 59	9 2	21 47	3 30	12 9	13 51	23 13
17	25 58	17 8	6 22	9 55	22 24	3 43	12 13	13 51	23 12
18	26 59	29 8	7 47	10 50	23 1	3 56	12 16	13 51	23 11
19	28 0	11 ♑ 4	9 12	11 44	23 38	4 9	12 20	13 50	23 11
20	29 1	22 57	10 38	12 40	24 15	4 22	12 24	13 50	23 10
21	0 ♒ 2	4 ♒ 49	12 5	13 36	24 52	4 35	12 28	13 50	23 9
22	1 4	16 41	13 33	14 33	25 29	4 49	12 32	13 D 50	23 8
23	2 5	28 35	15 2	15 30	26 5	5 2	12 36	13 50	23 7
24	3 6	10 ♓ 32	16 31	16 28	26 42	5 15	12 40	13 50	23 6
25	4 7	22 34	18 1	17 26	27 19	5 28	12 44	13 50	23 5
26	5 8	4 ♈ 44	19 32	18 24	27 56	5 42	12 48	13 50	23 4
27	6 9	17 6	21 3	19 24	28 32	5 55	12 53	13 51	23 3
28	7 10	29 44	22 34	20 23	29 9	6 9	12 57	13 51	23 2
29	8 11	12 ♉ 43	24 7	21 23	29 46	6 22	13 1	13 51	23 1
30	9 12	26 6	25 40	22 23	0 ♐ 22	6 36	13 6	13 51	23 0
31	10 12	9 ♊ 57	27 14	23 24	0 59	6 49	13 10	13 52	22 59

Pluto 0 Leo all month

FEBRUARY

DAY	☉	☽	☿	♀	♂	♃	♄	♅	♆
	° ′	° ′	° ′	° ′	° ′	° ′	° ′	° ′	° ′
1	11 ♒ 13	24 ♊ 17	28 ♑ 48	24 ♐ 25	1 ♐ 35	7 ♓ 3	13 ♈ 15	13 ♉ 52	22 ♍ 58
2	12 14	9 ♋ 4	0 ♒ 23	25 27	2 12	7 17	13 20	13 53	22 R 57
3	13 15	24 12	1 59	26 28	2 48	7 31	13 25	13 53	22 56
4	14 16	9 ♌ 32	3 36	27 31	3 25	7 45	13 30	13 54	22 54
5	15 17	24 53	5 13	28 33	4 1	7 59	13 35	13 55	22 53
6	16 18	10 ♍ 3	6 52	29 36	4 37	8 13	13 40	13 56	22 52
7	17 18	24 52	8 30	0 ♑ 39	5 14	8 27	13 45	13 56	22 51
8	18 19	9 ♎ 13	10 10	1 42	5 50	8 41	13 51	13 57	22 50
9	19 20	23 4	11 51	2 46	6 26	8 55	13 56	13 58	22 48
10	20 21	6 ♏ 25	13 32	3 50	7 2	9 9	14 1	13 59	22 47
11	21 21	19 19	15 15	4 54	7 38	9 23	14 7	13 59	22 45
12	22 22	1 ♐ 52	16 58	5 59	8 14	9 38	14 12	14 1	22 44
13	23 23	14 7	18 42	7 4	8 50	9 52	14 18	14 2	22 43
14	24 23	26 10	20 27	8 9	9 26	10 6	14 24	14 3	22 41
15	25 24	8 ♑ 6	22 12	9 14	10 2	10 20	14 30	14 4	22 40
16	26 25	19 57	23 59	10 19	10 38	10 35	14 36	14 6	22 38
17	27 25	1 ♒ 48	25 46	11 25	11 14	10 49	14 42	14 7	22 37
18	28 26	13 40	27 34	12 31	11 50	11 3	14 48	14 8	22 35
19	29 26	25 35	29 23	13 37	12 26	11 17	14 54	14 10	22 34
20	0 ♓ 27	7 ♓ 34	1 ♓ 12	14 44	13 1	11 32	15 0	14 11	22 32
21	1 27	19 39	3 3	15 50	13 37	11 46	15 6	14 12	22 30
22	2 28	1 ♈ 50	4 54	16 57	14 13	12 0	15 12	14 14	22 29
23	3 28	14 10	6 46	18 4	14 48	12 15	15 18	14 16	22 27
24	4 29	26 40	8 39	19 11	15 24	12 29	15 25	14 17	22 26
25	5 29	9 ♉ 24	10 32	20 18	15 59	12 44	15 31	14 19	22 24
26	6 29	22 23	12 26	21 26	16 34	12 58	15 37	14 21	22 23
27	7 30	5 ♊ 43	14 20	22 33	17 10	13 13	15 44	14 22	22 21
28	8 30	19 24	16 15	23 41	17 45	13 27	15 50	14 24	22 19

Pluto 0 Leo all month

1939

MARCH

Day	☉ ° ′	☽ ° ′	☿ ° ′	♀ ° ′	♂ ° ′	♃ ° ′	♄ ° ′	♅ ° ′	♆ ° ′
1	9♓30	3♋30	18♓ 9	24♑49	18♐20	13♓42	15♈57	14♉26	22♍18
2	10 30	17 59	20 3	25 57	18 55	13 56	16 4	14 28	22℞16
3	11 31	2♌48	21 57	27 5	19 30	14 11	16 10	14 30	22 15
4	12 31	17 51	23 49	28 13	20 5	14 25	16 17	14 32	22 13
5	13 31	2♍59	25 41	29 22	20 40	14 40	16 24	14 34	22 11
6	14 31	18 1	27 31	0♒30	21 15	14 54	16 31	14 36	22 10
7	15 31	2♎48	29 19	1 39	21 50	15 9	16 37	14 38	22 8
8	16 31	17 12	1♈ 5	2 48	22 25	15 23	16 44	14 40	22 6
9	17 31	1♏ 9	2 48	3 56	23 0	15 38	16 51	14 42	22 5
10	18 31	14 38	4 27	5 5	23 34	15 52	16 58	14 44	22 3
11	19 31	27 40	6 3	6 15	24 9	16 7	17 5	14 47	22 1
12	20 31	10♐18	7 35	7 24	24 43	16 21	17 12	14 49	22 0
13	21 31	22 38	9 1	8 33	25 17	16 36	17 19	14 51	21 58
14	22 30	4♑43	10 22	9 42	25 51	16 50	17 26	14 54	21 57
15	23 30	16 39	11 38	10 52	26 26	17 5	17 33	14 56	21 55
16	24 30	28 31	12 47	12 1	27 0	17 19	17 41	14 59	21 53
17	25 30	10♒22	13 49	13 11	27 34	17 34	17 48	15 1	21 52
18	26 30	22 15	14 45	14 21	28 8	17 48	17 55	15 4	21 50
19	27 29	4♓15	15 33	15 31	28 42	18 3	18 2	15 6	21 49
20	28 29	16 22	16 13	16 41	29 16	18 17	18 10	15 10	21 47
21	29 29	28 37	16 45	17 51	29 50	18 32	18 17	15 11	21 45
22	0♈28	11♈ 3	17 9	19 1	0♑23	18 46	18 24	15 14	21 44
23	1 28	23 39	17 25	20 11	0 57	19 1	18 32	15 17	21 42
24	2 27	6♉26	17 34	21 21	1 30	19 15	18 39	15 19	21 40
25	3 27	19 25	17℞34	22 31	2 3	19 29	18 47	15 22	21 39
26	4 26	2♊38	17 27	23 41	2 36	19 43	18 54	15 25	21 37
27	5 26	16 6	17 12	24 52	3 9	19 58	19 1	15 28	21 35
28	6 25	29 49	16 51	26 2	3 42	20 12	19 9	15 31	21 34
29	7 24	13♋48	16 23	27 13	4 15	20 26	19 16	15 34	21 32
30	8 24	28 3	15 50	28 24	4 48	20 40	19 23	15 37	21 31
31	9 23	12♌32	15 12	29 34	5 20	20 54	19 31	15 40	21 29

Pluto 29 Cancer all month

APRIL

Day	☉ ° ′	☽ ° ′	☿ ° ′	♀ ° ′	♂ ° ′	♃ ° ′	♄ ° ′	♅ ° ′	♆ ° ′
1	10♈22	27♌ 9	14♈30	0♓45	5♑53	21♓ 8	19♈38	15♉42	21♍28
2	11 21	11♍51	13℞44	1 56	6 25	21 22	19 46	15 45	21℞26
3	12 20	26 29	12 57	3 7	6 57	21 36	19 54	15 48	21 24
4	13 20	10♎57	12 9	4 18	7 29	21 50	20 1	15 51	21 23
5	14 19	25 8	11 20	5 29	8 1	22 4	20 9	15 54	21 21
6	15 18	8♏59	10 32	6 40	8 33	22 18	20 17	15 58	21 20
7	16 17	22 27	9 46	7 51	9 5	22 32	20 25	16 1	21 18
8	17 16	5♐31	9 2	9 2	9 36	22 46	20 32	16 4	21 17
9	18 15	18 14	8 20	10 13	10 7	23 0	20 40	16 7	21 15
10	19 14	0♑37	7 43	11 24	10 39	23 14	20 47	16 10	21 14
11	20 12	12 47	7 10	12 35	11 9	23 28	20 55	16 14	21 13
12	21 11	24 46	6 42	13 46	11 40	23 41	21 2	16 17	21 11
13	22 10	6♒39	6 19	14 58	12 11	23 55	21 10	16 20	21 10
14	23 9	18 32	6 1	16 9	12 42	24 8	21 17	16 23	21 8
15	24 8	0♓28	5 48	17 20	13 12	24 22	21 25	16 26	21 7
16	25 6	12 31	5 40	18 31	13 42	24 35	21 32	16 30	21 6
17	26 5	24 44	5 D38	19 43	14 12	24 49	21 40	16 33	21 4
18	27 4	7♈10	5 40	20 55	14 42	25 2	21 48	16 36	21 3
19	28 2	19 50	5 47	22 6	15 11	25 15	21 56	16 40	21 2
20	29 1	2♉44	6 0	23 18	15 41	25 29	22 3	16 43	21 1
21	0♉ 0	15 54	6 17	24 29	16 10	25 42	22 11	16 46	20 59
22	0 58	29 17	6 40	25 41	16 39	25 55	22 18	16 50	20 58
23	1 57	12♊53	7 6	26 53	17 8	26 8	22 26	16 53	20 57
24	2 55	26 41	7 37	28 4	17 37	26 21	22 33	16 57	20 56
25	3 54	10♋39	8 12	29 16	18 5	26 34	22 41	17 0	20 55
26	4 52	24 44	8 51	0♈28	18 33	26 47	22 48	17 3	20 54
27	5 51	8♌56	9 34	1 40	19 1	27 0	22 56	17 7	20 53
28	6 49	23 12	10 20	2 52	19 29	27 13	23 3	17 10	20 52
29	7 47	7♍28	11 9	4 4	19 56	27 26	23 11	17 14	20 51
30	8 45	21 43	12 2	5 16	20 23	27 39	23 18	17 17	20 50

Pluto 29 Cancer all month

1939

MAY

DAY	☉	☽	☿	♀	♂	♃	♄	♅	♆
1	9♉44	5♎52	12♈58	6♈28	20♑50	27♓52	23♈25	17♉21	20♍49
2	10 42	19 52	13 57	7 39	21 17	28 4	23 33	17 24	20 R 48
3	11 40	3♏39	14 59	8 51	21 43	28 17	23 40	17 28	20 47
4	12 38	17 12	16 4	10 3	22 9	28 29	23 47	17 31	20 46
5	13 36	0♐27	17 11	11 15	22 35	28 41	23 54	17 35	20 45
6	14 34	13 24	18 21	12 27	23 1	28 53	24 2	17 38	20 44
7	15 33	26 4	19 34	13 39	23 26	29 5	24 9	17 42	20 43
8	16 31	8♑28	20 49	14 51	23 51	29 17	24 16	17 45	20 43
9	17 29	20 38	22 6	16 3	24 15	29 29	24 23	17 49	20 42
10	18 27	2♒39	23 26	17 15	24 40	29 41	24 31	17 52	20 41
11	19 25	14 34	24 48	18 27	25 4	29 53	24 38	17 55	20 40
12	20 23	26 27	26 12	19 39	25 28	0♈5	24 45	17 59	20 40
13	21 20	8♓24	27 39	20 51	25 51	0 17	24 52	18 2	20 39
14	22 18	20 28	29 8	22 3	26 14	0 28	24 59	18 6	20 39
15	23 16	2♈44	0♉39	23 16	26 36	0 40	25 6	18 10	20 38
16	24 14	15 17	2 12	24 28	26 58	0 51	25 13	18 13	20 37
17	25 12	28 7	3 48	25 40	27 20	1 2	25 20	18 16	20 37
18	26 10	11♉17	5 25	26 52	27 42	1 13	25 27	18 20	20 36
19	27 8	24 48	7 5	28 5	28 3	1 24	25 34	18 23	20 36
20	28 5	8♊36	8 47	29 17	28 23	1 35	25 41	18 27	20 35
21	29 3	22 40	10 31	0♉29	28 43	1 46	25 48	18 30	20 35
22	0♊1	6♋55	12 17	1 41	29 4	1 57	25 55	18 33	20 35
23	0 59	21 17	14 5	2 54	29 23	2 7	26 1	18 37	20 35
24	1 56	5♌40	15 56	4 6	29 42	2 18	26 8	18 40	20 34
25	2 54	20 0	17 48	5 18	0♒0	2 29	26 15	18 44	20 34
26	3 51	4♍14	19 42	6 30	0 18	2 39	26 21	18 47	20 34
27	4 49	18 20	21 39	7 43	0 35	2 50	26 28	18 51	20 33
28	5 47	2♎15	23 38	8 55	0 52	3 0	26 34	18 54	20 33
29	6 44	16 0	25 39	10 7	1 9	3 10	26 40	18 57	20 33
30	7 42	29 34	27 41	11 20	1 25	3 20	26 47	19 1	20 33
31	8 39	12♏55	29 45	12 32	1 40	3 29	26 53	19 4	20 33

Pluto 29 Cancer all month

JUNE

DAY	☉	☽	☿	♀	♂	♃	♄	♅	♆
1	9♊37	26♏4	1♊52	13♉45	1♒55	3♈39	26♈59	19♉7	20♍33
2	10 34	9♐0	3 59	14 57	2 9	3 49	27 5	19 11	20 R 33
3	11 32	21 44	6 8	16 10	2 23	3 58	27 12	19 14	20 33
4	12 29	4♑14	8 18	17 22	2 36	4 8	27 18	19 17	20 D33
5	13 27	16 32	10 29	18 35	2 49	4 17	27 24	19 20	20 33
6	14 24	28 40	12 40	19 48	3 0	4 26	27 30	19 24	20 33
7	15 21	10♒39	14 52	21 0	3 12	4 35	27 36	19 27	20 33
8	16 19	22 33	17 4	22 13	3 23	4 43	27 42	19 30	20 34
9	17 16	4♓25	19 16	23 26	3 33	4 52	27 48	19 33	20 34
10	18 13	16 20	21 28	24 38	3 42	5 1	27 54	19 36	20 34
11	19 11	28 24	23 39	25 51	3 52	5 9	27 59	19 39	20 34
12	20 8	10♈39	25 49	27 3	4 0	5 18	28 5	19 43	20 35
13	21 6	23 13	27 58	28 16	4 8	5 26	28 10	19 46	20 35
14	22 3	6♉7	0♋6	29 29	4 14	5 34	28 16	19 49	20 35
15	23 0	19 26	2 12	0♊41	4 20	5 42	28 21	19 52	20 36
16	23 58	3♊10	4 16	1 54	4 26	5 49	28 27	19 55	20 36
17	24 55	17 18	6 18	3 7	4 31	5 57	28 32	19 58	20 37
18	25 52	1♋46	8 19	4 20	4 34	6 4	28 37	20 1	20 37
19	26 49	16 27	10 17	5 32	4 38	6 12	28 43	20 4	20 38
20	27 47	1♌15	12 12	6 45	4 40	6 19	28 48	20 7	20 38
21	28 44	16 1	14 7	7 58	4 42	6 26	28 53	20 10	20 39
22	29 41	0♍39	15 59	9 11	4 42	6 33	28 58	20 13	20 40
23	0♋38	15 2	17 49	10 24	4 R 43	6 40	29 3	20 15	20 40
24	1 36	29 8	19 36	11 37	4 42	6 46	29 7	20 18	20 .41
25	2 33	12♎55	21 21	12 50	4 41	6 53	29 12	20 21	20 42
26	3 30	26 26	23 4	14 3	4 39	6 59	29 17	20 24	20 42
27	4 27	9♏41	24 45	15 16	4 36	7 5	29 21	20 26	20 43
28	5 25	22 41	26 24	16 29	4 32	7 11	29 26	20 29	20 44
29	6 22	5♐30	28 0	17 42	4 28	7 17	29 30	20 32	20 45
30	7 19	18 7	29 34	18 55	4 22	7 22	29 34	20 34	20 46

Pluto 29 Cancer all month

1939

JULY

DAY	☉	☽	☿	♀	♂	♃	♄	♅	♆
	° ′	° ′	° ′	° ′	° ′	° ′	° ′	° ′	° ′
1	8♋16	0♑34	1♌ 5	20♊ 8	4♒17	7♈28	29♈39	20♉37	20♍47
2	9 13	12 52	2 35	21 21	4℞10	7 33	29 43	20 40	20 48
3	10 10	25 1	4 2	22 34	4 3	7 38	29 47	20 42	20 48
4	11 8	7♒ 3	5 26	23 47	3 54	7 43	29 51	20 45	20 49
5	12 5	18 59	6 48	25 0	3 46	7 48	29 55	20 47	20 51
6	13 2	0♓51	8 8	26 13	3 36	7 52	29 59	20 50	20 52
7	13 59	12 42	9 25	27 26	3 27	7 57	0♉ 3	20 52	20 53
8	14 56	24 36	10 40	28 39	3 16	8 1	0 7	20 54	20 54
9	15 54	6♈37	11 52	29 52	3 5	8 5	0 10	20 57	20 55
10	16 51	18 50	13 1	1♋ 6	2 53	8 9	0 14	20 59	20 56
11	17 48	1♉21	14 8	2 19	2 41	8 13	0 17	21 1	20 57
12	18 45	14 14	15 12	3 32	2 28	8 16	0 20	21 3	20 58
13	19 42	27 32	16 13	4 45	2 15	8 20	0 24	21 6	21 0
14	20 40	11♊20	17 11	5 59	2 0	8 23	0 27	21 8	21 1
15	21 37	25 36	18 6	7 12	1 46	8 26	0 30	21 10	21 2
16	22 34	10♋17	18 58	8 25	1 32	8 29	0 33	21 12	21 4
17	23 31	25 16	19 46	9 39	1 17	8 31	0 36	21 14	21 5
18	24 29	10♌25	20 31	10 52	1 1	8 34	0 38	21 16	21 6
19	25 26	25 32	21 12	12 6	0 46	8 36	0 41	21 18	21 7
20	26 23	10♍29	21 49	13 19	0 30	8 38	0 44	21 20	21 9
21	27 21	25 6	22 23	14 33	0 13	8 39	0 46	21 21	21 10
22	28 18	9♎21	22 52	15 46	29♑57	8 41	0 49	21 23	21 12
23	29 15	23 11	23 17	17 0	29 41	8 42	0 51	21 25	21 13
24	0♌12	6♏38	23 38	18 13	29 24	8 43	0 53	21 27	21 15
25	1 10	19 45	23 54	19 27	29 8	8 44	0 55	21 28	21 16
26	2 7	2♐34	24 6	20 40	28 51	8 45	0 57	21 30	21 18
27	3 4	15 8	24 12	21 54	28 35	8 46	0 59	21 32	21 19
28	4 2	27 31	24℞14	23 8	28 19	8 47	1 1	21 33	21 21
29	4 59	9♑45	24 10	24 21	28 2	8℞47	1 3	21 35	21 23
30	5 56	21 51	24 1	25 35	27 46	8 47	1 4	21 36	21 24
31	6 54	3♒52	23 48	26 49	27 30	8 46	1 6	21 38	21 26

Pluto 0 Leo all month

AUGUST

DAY	☉	☽	☿	♀	♂	♃	♄	♅	♆
	° ′	° ′	° ′	° ′	° ′	° ′	° ′	° ′	° ′
1	7♌51	15♒48	23♌28	28♋ 3	27♑15	8♈46	1♉ 7	21♉39	21♍28
2	8 48	27 41	23℞ 5	29 16	27℞ 0	8℞45	1 9	21 40	21 29
3	9 46	9♓32	22 36	0♌30	26 45	8 45	1 10	21 42	21 31
4	10 43	21 23	22 3	1 44	26 30	8 44	1 11	21 43	21 33
5	11 41	3♈18	21 26	2 58	26 17	8 43	1 12	21 44	21 35
6	12 38	15 19	20 45	4 12	26 3	8 41	1 13	21 45	21 36
7	13 36	27 32	20 1	5 26	25 50	8 40	1 13	21 46	21 38
8	14 33	10♉ 1	19 15	6 40	25 37	8 38	1 14	21 47	21 40
9	15 31	22 50	18 28	7 54	25 26	8 36	1 15	21 48	21 42
10	16 28	6♊ 4	17 40	9 8	25 14	8 34	1 15	21 49	21 44
11	17 26	19 47	16 52	10 22	25 4	8 31	1 16	21 50	21 46
12	18 23	3♋59	16 5	11 36	24 54	8 29	1 16	21 51	21 48
13	19 21	18 39	15 20	12 50	24 46	8 26	1 16	21 52	21 50
14	20 18	3♌41	14 38	14 4	24 37	8 24	1℞16	21 52	21 51
15	21 16	18 57	14 0	15 18	24 30	8 21	1 16	21 53	21 53
16	22 14	4♍15	13 26	16 32	24 23	8 18	1 16	21 54	21 55
17	23 11	19 24	12 58	17 46	24 17	8 14	1 15	21 54	21 57
18	24 9	4♎15	12 35	19 0	24 11	8 11	1 15	21 55	21 59
19	25 7	18 42	12 19	20 14	24 7	8 7	1 14	21 55	22 2
20	26 5	2♏41	12 11	21 28	24 3	8 3	1 14	21 56	22 4
21	27 2	16 13	12D 9	22 42	24 0	7 59	1 13	21 56	22 6
22	28 0	29 20	12 15	23 56	23 58	7 54	1 13	21 57	22 8
23	28 58	12♐ 6	12 29	25 11	23 57	7 49	1 12	21 57	22 10
24	29 56	24 35	12 51	26 25	23D55	7 45	1 11	21 57	22 12
25	0♍54	6♑50	13 21	27 39	23 56	7 40	1 10	21 58	22 14
26	1 52	18 56	13 57	28 53	23 57	7 36	1 9	21 58	22 16
27	2 49	0♒55	14 41	0♍ 8	23 59	7 31	1 7	21 58	22 18
28	3 47	12 50	15 33	1 22	24 2	7 26	1 6	21 58	22 20
29	4 45	24 42	16 32	2 36	24 6	7 20	1 4	21℞58	22 23
30	5 43	6♓34	17 38	3 51	24 10	7 15	1 3	21 58	22 25
31	6 41	18 27	18 50	5 5	24 15	7 9	1 1	21 58	22 27

Pluto 1 Leo all month

1939

SEPTEMBER

Day	☉ ° ′	☽ ° ′	☿ ° ′	♀ ° ′	♂ ° ′	♃ ° ′	♄ ° ′	♅ ° ′	♆ ° ′
1	7♍39	0♈22	20♌ 8	6♍20	24♑21	7♈ 3	0♉59	21♉58	22♍29
2	8 37	12 23	21 32	7 34	24 28	6℞57	0℞57	21℞57	22 31
3	9 35	24 30	23 1	8 49	24 35	6 50	0 55	21 57	22 33
4	10 33	6♉48	24 34	10 3	24 44	6 44	0 53	21 57	22 36
5	11 32	19 19	26 12	11 18	24 53	6 37	0 51	21 57	22 38
6	12 30	2♊ 9	27 54	12 32	25 3	6 30	0 49	21 56	22 41
7	13 28	15 20	29 38	13 47	25 13	6 24	0 46	21 56	22 43
8	14 26	28 55	1♍25	15 1	25 25	6 17	0 44	21 55	22 45
9	15 25	12♋58	3 14	16 16	25 37	6 10	0 41	21 55	22 47
10	16 23	27 26	5 5	17 30	25 50	6 3	0 38	21 54	22 49
11	17 21	12♌16	6 57	18 45	26 4	5 56	0 36	21 53	22 51
12	18 20	27 22	8 50	19 59	26 18	5 48	0 33	21 53	22 53
13	19 18	12♍35	10 43	21 14	26 33	5 41	0 30	21 52	22 56
14	20 16	27 43	12 37	22 29	26 48	5 34	0 27	21 51	22 58
15	21 15	12♎38	14 30	23 43	27 4	5 26	0 24	21 50	23 0
16	22 13	27 11	16 24	24 58	27 22	5 19	0 20	21 49	23 2
17	23 12	11♏19	18 17	26 13	27 39	5 11	0 17	21 49	23 5
18	24 10	24 58	20 10	27 27	27 58	5 3	0 14	21 48	23 7
19	25 9	8♐12	22 2	28 42	28 16	4 55	0 11	21 46	23 9
20	26 8	21 1	23 54	29 56	28 36	4 47	0 7	21 45	23 11
21	27 6	3♑31	25 45	1♎11	28 55	4 39	0 4	21 44	23 13
22	28 5	15 45	27 35	2 26	29 16	4 31	0 0	21 42	23 16
23	29 4	27 48	29 24	3 40	29 37	4 24	29♈57	21 42	23 18
24	0♎ 2	9♒44	1♎13	4 55	29 59	4 16	29 53	21 41	23 20
25	1 1	21 36	3 0	6 10	0♒21	4 8	29 49	21 39	23 22
26	2 0	3♓27	4 46	7 25	0 44	4 0	29 45	21 38	23 25
27	2 59	15 21	6 32	8 39	1 6	3 52	29 41	21 37	23 27
28	3 58	27 19	8 17	9 54	1 30	3 43	29 37	21 35	23 29
29	4 56	9♈22	10 1	11 9	1 54	3 35	29 33	21 34	23 31
30	5 55	21 33	11 44	12 24	2 19	3 27	29 29	21 32	23 33

Pluto 2 Leo all month

OCTOBER

Day	☉ ° ′	☽ ° ′	☿ ° ′	♀ ° ′	♂ ° ′	♃ ° ′	♄ ° ′	♅ ° ′	♆ ° ′
1	6♎54	3♉53	13♎26	13♎38	2♒44	3♈19	29♈25	21♉31	23♍35
2	7 53	16 24	15 7	14 53	3 10	3℞11	29℞20	21℞29	23 38
3	8 52	29 7	16 47	16 8	3 35	3 3	29 16	21 28	23 40
4	9 51	12♊ 6	18 26	17 23	4 2	2 55	29 12	21 26	23 42
5	10 50	25 21	20 5	18 37	4 29	2 48	29 8	21 24	23 44
6	11 50	8♋56	21 42	19 52	4 56	2 40	29 3	21 23	23 46
7	12 49	22 50	23 19	21 7	5 23	2 33	28 59	21 21	23 48
8	13 48	7♌ 3	24 55	22 22	5 51	2 25	28 55	21 19	23 50
9	14 47	21 34	26 30	23 37	6 20	2 18	28 50	21 17	23 52
10	15 47	6♍19	28 5	24 52	6 48	2 10	28 46	21 16	23 55
11	16 46	21 10	29 39	26 7	7 17	2 2	28 41	21 14	23 57
12	17 45	6♎ 1	1♏12	27 22	7 47	1 54	28 36	21 12	23 59
13	18 45	20 44	2 45	28 36	8 17	1 47	28 32	21 10	24 1
14	19 44	5♏12	4 16	29 51	8 47	1 39	28 27	21 8	24 3
15	20 44	19 20	5 48	1♏ 6	9 17	1 32	28 22	21 6	24 5
16	21 43	3♐ 3	7 18	2 21	9 48	1 25	28 18	21 4	24 7
17	22 43	16 22	8 48	3 36	10 19	1 18	28 14	21 2	24 9
18	23 42	29 17	10 17	4 50	10 50	1 12	28 9	20 59	24 11
19	24 42	11♑50	11 45	6 5	11 22	1 5	28 3	20 57	24 13
20	25 41	24 7	13 13	7 20	11 54	0 58	27 58	20 55	24 15
21	26 41	6♒11	14 40	8 35	12 26	0 52	27 54	20 53	24 17
22	27 41	18 6	16 6	9 50	12 59	0 45	27 49	20 51	24 19
23	28 40	29 57	17 31	11 5	13 32	0 39	27 44	20 48	24 21
24	29 40	11♓49	18 56	12 20	14 5	0 33	27 39	20 46	24 23
25	0♏40	23 45	20 19	13 35	14 38	0 27	27 35	20 44	24 25
26	1 40	5♈49	21 42	14 50	15 11	0 22	27 30	20 42	24 26
27	2 40	18 2	23 4	16 5	15 45	0 16	27 25	20 39	24 28
28	3 39	0♉27	24 25	17 20	16 19	0 11	27 20	20 37	24 30
29	4 39	13 4	25 45	18 35	16 54	0 5	27 16	20 35	24 32
30	5 39	25 56	27 4	19 49	17 28	0 0	27 11	20 32	24 34
31	6 39	9♊ 0	28 22	21 4	18 3	29♓55	27 6	20 30	24 35

Pluto 2 Leo all month

1939

NOVEMBER

Pluto 2 Leo all month

DAY	☉ ° ′	☽ ° ′	☿ ° ′	♀ ° ′	♂ ° ′	♃ ° ′	♄ ° ′	♅ ° ′	♆ ° ′
1	7♏39	22♊19	29♏38	22♏19	18♒38	29♓50	27♈ 1	20♉27	24♍37
2	8 39	5♋50	0♐53	23 34	19 13	29℞46	26℞57	20℞25	24 39
3	9 39	19 34	2 6	24 49	19 49	29 41	26 52	20 23	24 40
4	10 39	3♌29	3 18	26 4	20 24	29 37	26 48	20 20	24 42
5	11 39	17 35	4 28	27 19	21 0	29 33	26 43	20 18	24 44
6	12 40	1♍49	5 35	28 34	21 36	29 29	26 38	20 15	24 45
7	13 40	16 10	6 40	29 48	22 12	29 25	26 33	20 13	24 47
8	14 40	0♎34	7 42	1♐ 3	22 49	29 21	26 29	20 10	24 49
9	15 40	14 58	8 41	2 18	23 26	29 18	26 25	20 8	24 50
10	16 41	29 16	9 36	3 33	24 2	29 15	26 20	20 5	24 52
11	17 41	13♏25	10 28	4 48	24 39	29 12	26 16	20 3	24 53
12	18 41	27 19	11 16	6 3	25 16	29 9	26 12	20 0	24 55
13	19 42	10♐55	11 59	7 18	25 53	29 7	26 8	19 58	24 56
14	20 42	24 12	12 36	8 33	26 30	29 4	26 4	19 55	24 58
15	21 43	7♑ 7	13 7	9 47	27 6	29 2	26 0	19 53	24 59
16	22 43	19 43	13 31	11 2	27 42	29 0	25 56	19 51	25 1
17	23 44	2♒ 2	13 48	12 17	28 19	28 59	25 52	19 48	25 2
18	24 44	14 7	13 57	13 32	28 57	28 57	25 48	19 45	25 3
19	25 45	26 3	13℞57	14 47	29 35	28 56	25 44	19 43	25 5
20	26 45	7♓54	13 46	16 2	0♓13	28 55	25 40	19 40	25 6
21	27 46	19 45	13 26	17 17	0 51	28 54	25 36	19 38	25 7
22	28 46	1♈42	12 54	18 32	1 29	28 53	25 33	19 36	25 8
23	29 47	13 49	12 11	19 46	2 7	28 53	25 29	19 33	25 9
24	0♐48	26 9	11 19	21 1	2 45	28 D52	25 26	19 31	25 11
25	1 48	8♉46	10 19	22 16	3 24	28 53	25 23	19 28	25 12
26	2 49	21 41	9 10	23 31	4 2	28 53	25 19	19 26	25 13
27	3 50	4♊55	7 53	24 46	4 41	28 53	25 16	19 23	25 14
28	4 50	18 26	6 32	26 1	5 20	28 54	25 13	19 21	25 15
29	5 51	2♋12	5 11	27 16	5 59	28 54	25 10	19 18	25 16
30	6 52	16 10	3 50	28 31	6 38	28 55	25 7	19 16	25 17

DECEMBER

Pluto 2 Leo all month

DAY	☉ ° ′	☽ ° ′	☿ ° ′	♀ ° ′	♂ ° ′	♃ ° ′	♄ ° ′	♅ ° ′	♆ ° ′
1	7♐53	0♌15	2♐32	29♐45	7♓17	28♓56	25♈ 5	19♉14	25♍18
2	8 53	14 25	1℞22	1♑ 0	7 56	28 57	25℞ 2	19℞12	25 19
3	9 54	28 36	0 20	2 15	8 35	28 58	24 59	19 9	25 20
4	10 55	12♍45	29♏27	3 30	9 14	29 1	24 57	19 7	25 20
5	11 56	26 51	28 44	4 44	9 54	29 3	24 54	19 5	25 21
6	12 57	10♎53	28 12	5 59	10 33	29 5	24 52	19 3	25 22
7	13 58	24 50	27 53	7 14	11 12	29 7	24 50	19 1	25 23
8	14 59	8♏40	27 44	8 29	11 51	29 10	24 47	18 58	25 23
9	16 0	22 21	27 D46	9 43	12 32	29 12	24 45	18 56	25 24
10	17 1	5♐52	27 58	10 58	13 12	29 15	24 43	18 54	25 25
11	18 2	19 10	28 20	12 13	13 52	29 18	24 41	18 52	25 25
12	19 3	2♑14	28 49	13 28	14 31	29 22	24 39	18 50	25 26
13	20 4	15 2	29 26	14 42	15 11	29 25	24 38	18 48	25 27
14	21 5	27 34	0♐ 9	15 57	15 51	29 29	24 36	18 46	25 27
15	22 6	9♒51	0 59	17 12	16 31	29 33	24 35	18 44	25 28
16	23 7	21 56	1 52	18 26	17 11	29 37	24 33	18 42	25 28
17	24 8	3♓50	2 51	19 41	17 51	29 42	24 32	18 40	25 28
18	25 9	15 40	3 53	20 55	18 31	29 47	24 31	18 38	25 29
19	26 10	27 30	4 59	22 10	19 12	29 52	24 30	18 36	25 29
20	27 11	9♈25	6 8	23 24	19 52	29 57	24 29	18 34	25 30
21	28 12	21 31	7 19	24 39	20 33	0♈ 2	24 28	18 33	25 30
22	29 13	3♉53	8 32	25 53	21 13	0 7	24 27	18 31	25 30
23	0♑15	16 34	9 48	27 8	21 53	0 13	24 26	18 29	25 30
24	1 16	29 39	11 6	28 22	22 32	0 18	24 26	18 28	25 31
25	2 17	13♊ 9	12 25	29 37	23 13	0 24	24 25	18 26	25 31
26	3 18	27 2	13 45	0♒51	23 54	0 30	24 25	18 24	25 31
27	4 19	11♋15	15 7	2 6	24 34	0 36	24 25	18 23	25 31
28	5 20	25 42	16 30	3 20	25 15	0 42	24 25	18 21	25 31
29	6 21	10♌17	17 54	4 35	25 55	0 49	24 D25	18 20	25℞31
30	7 22	24 52	19 19	5 49	26 36	0 55	24 25	18 18	25 31
31	8 23	9♍21	20 44	7 4	27 17	1 2	24 25	18 17	25 31

1940

JANUARY

DAY	☉	☽	☿	♀	♂	♃	♄	♅	♆
	° ′	° ′	° ′	° ′	° ′	° ′	° ′	° ′	° ′
1	9♑25	23♍40	22♐10	8♒18	27♓58	1♈ 9	24♈26	18♉16	25♍31
2	10 26	7♎46	23 37	9 33	28 39	1 16	24 26	18R 15	25R 31
3	11 27	21 39	25 4	10 47	29 19	1 23	24 27	18 13	25 31
4	12 28	5♏19	26 32	12 1	0♈ 0	1 31	24 28	18 12	25 30
5	13 29	18 48	28 1	13 16	0 40	1 38	24 28	18 11	25 30
6	14 30	2♐ 5	29 30	14 30	1 21	1 46	24 29	18 10	25 30
7	15 32	15 12	1♑ 0	15 44	2 2	1 54	24 30	18 9	25 29
8	16 33	28 8	2 30	16 58	2 43	2 2	24 31	18 8	25 29
9	17 34	10♑53	4 1	18 12	3 23	2 10	24 33	18 7	25 29
10	18 35	23 26	5 32	19 26	4 4	2 19	24 34	18 6	25 28
11	19 36	5♒48	7 3	20 40	4 45	2 27	24 36	18 5	25 28
12	20 37	17 58	8 35	21 54	5 26	2 36	24 38	18 5	25 27
13	21 39	29 58	10 8	23 8	6 7	2 45	24 39	18 4	25 27
14	22 40	11♓51	11 41	24 22	6 48	2 54	24 41	18 3	25 26
15	23 41	23 39	13 14	25 36	7 29	3 3	24 43	18 3	25 26
16	24 42	5♈27	14 48	26 50	8 10	3 12	24 45	18 2	25 25
17	25 43	17 19	16 22	28 4	8 50	3 22	24 47	18 1	25 24
18	26 44	29 22	17 57	29 17	9 31	3 31	24 49	18 1	25 24
19	27 45	11♉40	19 33	0♓31	10 12	3 41	24 51	18 0	25 23
20	28 46	24 19	21 9	1 45	10 53	3 51	24 54	18 0	25 22
21	29 47	7♊23	22 45	2 58	11 34	4 0	24 56	18 0	25 22
22	0♒48	20 57	24 22	4 12	12 15	4 10	24 59	18 0	25 21
23	1 50	4♋58	26 0	5 25	12 56	4 20	25 2	17 59	25 20
24	2 51	19 26	27 38	6 39	13 37	4 30	25 5	17 59	25 19
25	3 52	4♌14	29 17	7 52	14 18	4 41	25 8	17 59	25 18
26	4 53	19 14	0♒57	9 6	14 58	4 51	25 11	17 59	25 17
27	5 53	4♍15	2 37	10 19	15 39	5 2	25 14	17 D59	25 16
28	6 54	19 9	4 17	11 32	16 20	5 13	25 17	17 59	25 15
29	7 55	3♎48	5 59	12 45	17 1	5 24	25 20	17 59	25 14
30	8 56	18 9	7 41	13 58	17 42	5 35	25 24	17 59	25 13
31	9 57	2♏ 8	9 24	15 11	18 23	5 46	25 27	17 59	25 12

Pluto 2 Leo all month

FEBRUARY

DAY	☉	☽	☿	♀	♂	♃	♄	♅	♆
	° ′	° ′	° ′	° ′	° ′	° ′	° ′	° ′	° ′
1	10♒58	15♏47	11♒ 7	16♓24	19♈ 4	5♈57	25♈31	17♉59	25♍11
2	11 59	29 7	12 52	17 37	19 45	6 8	25 35	17 59	25R 10
3	13 0	12♐11	14 37	18 50	20 25	6 20	25 39	18 0	25 9
4	14 1	25 0	16 22	20 3	21 6	6 31	25 43	18 0	25 8
5	15 2	7♑38	18 8	21 15	21 47	6 43	25 47	18 1	25 7
6	16 3	20 5	19 55	22 28	22 28	6 54	25 51	18 2	25 6
7	17 3	2♒22	21 42	23 41	23 9	7 6	25 55	18 2	25 5
8	18 4	14 31	23 30	24 53	23 50	7 18	25 59	18 3	25 3
9	19 5	26 32	25 18	26 6	24 31	7 30	26 3	18 3	25 2
10	20 6	8♓26	27 7	27 18	25 12	7 42	26 8	18 4	25 1
11	21 6	20 16	28 56	28 30	25 52	7 54	26 12	18 5	25 0
12	22 7	2♈ 3	0♓45	29 42	26 33	8 6	26 17	18 6	24 58
13	23 8	13 51	2 35	0♈54	27 14	8 18	26 22	18 7	24 57
14	24 9	25 43	4 24	2 6	27 55	8 31	26 26	18 8	24 56
15	25 9	7♉44	6 13	3 18	28 35	8 43	26 31	18 9	24 54
16	26 10	19 59	8 1	4 30	29 16	8 55	26 36	18 9	24 53
17	27 10	2♊34	9 48	5 41	29 57	9 8	26 41	18 11	24 51
18	28 11	15 32	11 34	6 53	0♉37	9 20	26 46	18 12	24 50
19	29 11	28 59	13 18	8 5	1 18	9 33	26 52	18 13	24 49
20	0♓12	12♋56	15 0	9 16	1 58	9 46	26 57	18 14	24 47
21	1 12	27 21	16 40	10 27	2 39	9 59	27 2	18 15	24 46
22	2 13	12♌12	18 16	11 39	3 20	10 12	27 7	18 17	24 44
23	3 13	27 20	19 49	12 50	4 0	10 25	27 13	18 18	24 43
24	4 14	12♍36	21 18	14 1	4 41	10 38	27 19	18 19	24 41
25	5 14	27 48	22 42	15 12	5 22	10 51	27 25	18 21	24 39
26	6 14	12♎48	24 1	16 23	6 2	11 4	27 30	18 22	24 38
27	7 15	27 27	25 14	17 33	6 43	11 17	27 36	18 24	24 36
28	8 15	11♏43	26 20	18 44	7 23	11 30	27 42	18 26	24 35
29	9 15	25 32	27 19	19 54	8 4	11 43	27 48	18 28	24 33

Pluto 1 Leo all month

1940

MARCH

DAY	☉	☽	☿	♀	♂	♃	♄	♅	♆
	° ′	° ′	° ′	° ′	° ′	° ′	° ′	° ′	° ′
1	10♓15	8♐57	28♓10	21♈ 5	8♉44	11♈57	27♈54	18♉29	24♍32
2	11 15	21 59	28 53	22 15	9 25	12 10	28 0	18 30	24℞30
3	12 16	4♑43	29 27	23 25	10 5	12 24	28 6	18 32	24 28
4	13 16	17 11	29 52	24 35	10 46	12 38	28 12	18 34	24 27
5	14 16	29 26	0♈ 8	25 44	11 26	12 51	28 18	18 36	24 25
6	15 16	11♒31	0 15	26 54	12 7	13 5	28 25	18 38	24 23
7	16 16	23 30	0℞12	28 4	12 47	13 19	28 31	18 40	24 22
8	17 16	5♓23	0 1	29 13	13 27	13 33	28 37	18 42	24 20
9	18 16	17 12	29♓41	0♉22	14 8	13 46	28 43	18 44	24 18
10	19 16	29 0	29 13	1 31	14 48	14 0	28 50	18 46	24 17
11	20 16	10♈49	28 37	2 40	15 28	14 14	28 56	18 48	24 15
12	21 16	22 40	27 55	3 48	16 8	14 28	29 3	18 51	24 14
13	22 16	4♉37	27 8	4 57	16 49	14 42	29 9	18 53	24 12
14	23 16	16 43	26 17	6 5	17 29	14 56	29 16	18 55	24 10
15	24 15	29 1	25 23	7 13	18 9	15 10	29 23	18 57	24 9
16	25 15	11♊36	24 27	8 21	18 49	15 24	29 30	19 0	24 7
17	26 15	24 32	23 31	9 29	19 30	15 38	29 36	19 2	24 5
18	27 15	7♋51	22 35	10 37	20 10	15 52	29 43	19 5	24 4
19	28 14	21 37	21 41	11 44	20 50	16 6	29 50	19 7	24 2
20	29 14	5♌50	20 49	12 52	21 30	16 20	29 57	19 9	24 0
21	0♈13	20 28	20 2	13 59	22 10	16 34	0♉ 4	19 12	23 59
22	1 13	5♍26	19 18	15 6	22 50	16 49	0 11	19 14	23 57
23	2 12	20 37	18 40	16 12	23 30	17 3	0 18	19 17	23 55
24	3 12	5♎50	18 7	17 18	24 10	17 17	0 25	19 20	23 54
25	4 11	20 57	17 40	18 25	24 50	17 32	0 32	19 22	23 53
26	5 11	5♏48	17 19	19 31	25 30	17 46	0 40	19 25	23 51
27	6 10	20 17	17 4	20 36	26 10	18 1	0 47	19 28	23 49
28	7 9	4♐20	16 54	21 42	26 50	18 15	0 54	19 30	23 47
29	8 9	17 56	16 51	22 47	27 30	18 30	1 1	19 33	23 46
30	9 8	1♑ 5	16 D53	23 52	28 10	18 44	1 9	19 36	23 44
31	10 7	13 51	17 0	24 56	28 50	18 58	1 16	19 39	23 43

Pluto 0 Leo all month

APRIL

DAY	☉	☽	☿	♀	♂	♃	♄	♅	♆
	° ′	° ′	° ′	° ′	° ′	° ′	° ′	° ′	° ′
1	11♈ 6	26♑18	17♓13	26♉ 1	29♉30	19♈12	1♉23	19♉42	23♍41
2	12 6	8♒30	17 31	27 5	0♊10	19 27	1 30	19 45	23℞39
3	13 5	20 30	17 54	28 8	0 49	19 41	1 38	19 48	23 38
4	14 4	2♓23	18 21	29 12	1 29	19 56	1 45	19 50	23 36
5	15 3	14 11	18 53	0♊15	2 9	20 10	1 52	19 53	23 35
6	16 2	25 59	19 29	1 18	2 49	20 25	2 0	19 56	23 33
7	17 1	7♈48	20 9	2 21	3 28	20 39	2 7	20 0	23 32
8	18 0	19 42	20 53	3 23	4 8	20 54	2 15	20 3	23 30
9	18 59	1♉41	21 40	4 25	4 48	21 8	2 22	20 6	23 29
10	19 58	13 48	22 30	5 27	5 27	21 23	2 30	20 9	23 27
11	20 57	26 6	23 24	6 28	6 7	21 37	2 37	20 12	23 26
12	21 56	8♊36	24 21	7 29	6 46	21 52	2 45	20 15	23 24
13	22 55	21 19	25 21	8 29	7 26	22 6	2 53	20 18	23 23
14	23 53	4♋20	26 23	9 30	8 5	22 21	3 0	20 22	23 22
15	24 52	17 39	27 28	10 29	8 45	22 35	3 8	20 25	23 20
16	25 51	1♌18	28 36	11 29	9 24	22 50	3 16	20 28	23 19
17	26 49	15 19	29 45	12 28	10 4	23 4	3 24	20 31	23 17
18	27 48	29 39	0♈58	13 26	10 43	23 19	3 31	20 34	23 16
19	28 47	14♍17	2 12	14 24	11 23	23 33	3 39	20 38	23 15
20	29 45	29 8	3 29	15 22	12 2	23 47	3 46	20 41	23 14
21	0♉44	14♎ 6	4 47	16 19	12 41	24 1	3 54	20 44	23 12
22	1 42	29 3	6 8	17 16	13 21	24 16	4 1	20 48	23 11
23	2 41	13♏50	7 31	18 11	14 0	24 30	4 9	20 51	23 10
24	3 39	28 20	8 56	19 7	14 39	24 45	4 17	20 54	23 9
25	4 38	12♐28	10 23	20 2	15 18	24 59	4 25	20 58	23 8
26	5 36	26 11	11 52	20 56	15 58	25 13	4 32	21 1	23 6
27	6 34	9♑28	13 23	21 50	16 37	25 28	4 40	21 5	23 5
28	7 33	22 20	14 55	22 44	17 16	25 42	4 47	21 8	23 4
29	8 31	4♒50	16 30	23 36	17 55	25 56	4 55	21 12	23 3
30	9 29	17 3	18 7	24 29	18 34	26 10	5 2	21 15	23 2

Pluto 0 Leo all month

1940

MAY

DAY	☉	☽	☿	♀	♂	♃	♄	♅	♆
	° ′	° ′	° ′	° ′	° ′	° ′	° ′	° ′	° ′
1	10 ♉ 27	29 ♒ 3	19 ♈ 45	25 ♊ 19	19 ♊ 13	26 ♈ 25	5 ♉ 10	21 ♉ 18	23 ♍ 1
2	11 26	10 ♓ 54	21 25	26 9	19 52	26 39	5 18	21 22	23 ℞ 0
3	12 24	22 42	23 7	26 59	20 31	26 53	5 26	21 25	22 59
4	13 22	4 ♈ 30	24 51	27 48	21 11	27 8	5 33	21 29	22 58
5	14 20	16 23	26 37	28 36	21 50	27 22	5 41	21 32	22 57
6	15 18	28 23	28 24	29 24	22 29	27 36	5 49	21 36	22 56
7	16 16	10 ♉ 33	0 ♉ 13	0 ♋ 10	23 8	27 50	5 57	21 39	22 55
8	17 14	22 55	2 4	0 56	23 47	28 4	6 4	21 43	22 55
9	18 12	5 ♊ 30	3 57	1 40	24 25	28 18	6 12	21 46	22 54
10	19 10	18 18	5 52	2 24	25 4	28 32	6 19	21 50	22 53
11	20 8	1 ♋ 20	7 48	3 7	25 43	28 46	6 27	21 53	22 52
12	21 6	14 36	9 47	3 49	26 22	29 0	6 34	21 57	22 52
13	22 4	28 5	11 47	4 30	27 1	29 14	6 42	22 0	22 51
14	23 2	11 ♌ 48	13 49	5 9	27 40	29 28	6 49	22 4	22 50
15	24 0	25 43	15 53	5 48	28 19	29 42	6 56	22 7	22 50
16	24 58	9 ♍ 52	17 58	6 25	28 58	29 56	7 4	22 11	22 49
17	25 56	24 11	20 5	7 1	29 36	0 ♉ 9	7 11	22 14	22 48
18	26 53	8 ♎ 39	22 13	7 36	0 ♋ 15	0 23	7 18	22 18	22 48
19	27 51	23 12	24 22	8 9	0 54	0 37	7 25	22 21	22 47
20	28 49	7 ♏ 46	26 32	8 41	1 33	0 50	7 33	22 24	22 47
21	29 47	22 14	28 43	9 12	2 11	1 4	7 40	22 28	22 47
22	0 ♊ 44	6 ♐ 31	0 ♊ 55	9 41	2 50	1 17	7 48	22 31	22 46
23	1 42	20 32	3 6	10 8	3 29	1 31	7 55	22 35	22 46
24	2 40	4 ♑ 11	5 18	10 34	4 8	1 44	8 3	22 38	22 45
25	3 37	17 28	7 29	10 59	4 46	1 58	8 10	22 42	22 45
26	4 35	0 ♒ 22	9 40	11 21	5 25	2 11	8 17	22 45	22 45
27	5 32	12 54	11 50	11 42	6 4	2 24	8 24	22 49	22 44
28	6 30	25 9	13 59	12 1	6 42	2 37	8 31	22 52	22 44
29	7 27	7 ♓ 10	16 7	12 17	7 21	2 50	8 38	22 55	22 44
30	8 25	19 2	18 13	12 33	7 59	3 3	8 45	22 59	22 44
31	9 22	0 ♈ 50	20 17	12 46	8 38	3 16	8 52	23 2	22 44

Pluto 0 Leo all month

JUNE

DAY	☉	☽	☿	♀	♂	♃	♄	♅	♆
	° ′	° ′	° ′	° ′	° ′	° ′	° ′	° ′	° ′
1	10 ♊ 20	12 ♈ 40	22 ♊ 20	12 ♋ 56	9 ♋ 16	3 ♉ 29	8 ♉ 59	23 ♉ 5	22 ♍ 44
2	11 17	24 37	24 20	13 5	9 55	3 42	9 6	23 9	22 ℞ 44
3	12 15	6 ♉ 44	26 18	13 12	10 33	3 55	9 13	23 12	22 44
4	13 12	19 4	28 14	13 16	11 12	4 8	9 20	23 15	22 44
5	14 10	1 ♊ 41	0 ♋ 7	13 18	11 50	4 20	9 27	23 19	22 D 44
6	15 7	14 35	1 58	13 ℞ 18	12 29	4 33	9 33	23 22	22 44
7	16 5	27 46	3 46	13 15	13 7	4 45	9 40	23 25	22 44
8	17 2	11 ♋ 11	5 32	13 10	13 46	4 58	9 47	23 28	22 44
9	18 0	24 50	7 15	13 3	14 24	5 10	9 53	23 32	22 44
10	18 57	8 ♌ 39	8 56	12 53	15 6	5 23	10 0	23 35	22 44
11	19 54	22 36	10 34	12 41	15 41	5 35	10 6	23 38	22 44
12	20 52	6 ♍ 38	12 9	12 27	16 20	5 47	10 13	23 42	22 45
13	21 49	20 44	13 42	12 10	16 58	5 59	10 19	23 45	22 45
14	22 46	4 ♎ 53	15 12	11 50	17 37	6 11	10 26	23 48	22 45
15	23 44	19 3	16 40	11 28	18 15	6 23	10 32	23 51	22 46
16	24 41	3 ♏ 14	18 4	11 5	18 53	6 35	10 38	23 54	22 46
17	25 38	17 22	19 26	10 39	19 32	6 47	10 44	23 57	22 47
18	26 35	1 ♐ 25	20 45	10 11	20 10	6 58	10 50	24 0	22 47
19	27 33	15 19	22 1	9 41	20 48	7 10	10 56	24 3	22 48
20	28 30	29 1	23 15	9 10	21 26	7 22	11 2	24 6	22 48
21	29 27	12 ♑ 27	24 25	8 37	22 5	7 33	11 8	24 9	22 49
22	0 ♋ 24	25 34	25 32	8 3	22 43	7 45	11 14	24 12	22 49
23	1 21	8 ♒ 22	26 36	7 28	23 10	7 56	11 20	24 15	22 50
24	2 19	20 51	27 37	6 52	23 59	8 7	11 26	24 18	22 51
25	3 16	3 ♓ 4	28 35	6 15	24 38	8 18	11 32	24 21	22 51
26	4 13	15 4	29 29	5 37	25 16	8 29	11 37	24 24	22 52
27	5 10	26 56	0 ♌ 20	5 0	25 54	8 40	11 43	24 27	22 53
28	6 8	8 ♈ 45	1 7	4 22	26 32	8 51	11 48	24 30	22 53
29	7 5	20 36	1 51	3 45	27 11	9 2	11 54	24 33	22 54
30	8 2	2 ♉ 34	2 30	3 8	27 49	9 12	11 59	24 35	22 55

Pluto 1 Leo all month

1940

JULY

Pluto 1 Leo all month

DAY	☉	☽	☿	♀	♂	♃	♄	♅	♆
	° ′	° ′	° ′	° ′	° ′	° ′	° ′	° ′	° ′
1	8♋59	14♉46	3♌6	2♋32	28♋27	9♉23	12♉4	24♉38	22♍56
2	9 56	27 14	3 38	1 R 57	29 5	9 33	12 9	24 41	22 57
3	10 54	10♊2	4 6	1 23	29 44	9 43	12 15	24 43	22 58
4	11 51	23 11	4 29	0 51	0♌22	9 53	12 20	24 46	22 59
5	12 48	6♋42	4 48	0 20	1 0	10 3	12 25	24 49	23 0
6	13 45	20 31	5 3	29♊51	1 38	10 13	12 30	24 51	23 1
7	14 42	4♌36	5 13	29 24	2 16	10 23	12 35	24 54	23 2
8	15 40	18 50	5 18	28 58	2 54	10 32	12 40	24 56	23 3
9	16 37	3♍9	5 R 18	28 35	3 32	10 42	12 45	24 59	23 4
10	17 34	17 27	5 14	28 14	4 10	10 51	12 50	25 1	23 5
11	18 31	1♎43	5 5	27 55	4 49	11 1	12 54	25 3	23 6
12	19 29	15 53	4 51	27 38	5 27	11 10	12 59	25 6	23 7
13	20 26	29 56	4 33	27 24	6 5	11 19	13 3	25 8	23 8
15	21 23	13♏52	4 10	27 12	6 43	11 28	13 7	25 10	23 10
14	22 20	27 40	3 44	27 2	7 21	11 37	13 12	25 13	23 11
16	23 17	11♐20	3 14	26 55	7 59	11 46	13 16	25 15	23 12
17	24 15	24 49	2 40	26 50	8 37	11 55	13 20	25 17	23 13
18	25 12	8♑8	2 4	26 47	9 15	12 3	13 24	25 19	23 15
19	26 9	21 13	1 25	26 D47	9 54	12 12	13 28	25 21	23 16
20	27 6	4♒3	0 45	26 49	10 32	12 20	13 31	25 23	23 18
21	28 4	16 39	0 3	26 54	11 10	12 28	13 35	25 25	23 19
22	29 1	29 0	29♋21	27 0	11 48	12 36	13 39	25 27	23 20
23	29 58	11♓7	28 40	27 9	12 26	12 44	13 43	25 29	23 22
24	0♌55	23 4	28 0	27 20	13 4	12 51	13 46	25 31	23 23
25	1 53	4♈54	27 22	27 33	13 42	12 59	13 50	25 33	23 25
26	2 50	16 42	26 46	27 48	14 20	13 6	13 53	25 35	23 26
27	3 47	28 33	26 14	28 5	14 59	13 13	13 56	25 36	23 28
28	4 45	10♉31	25 45	28 24	15 37	13 20	13 59	25 38	23 30
29	5 42	22 43	25 21	28 45	16 15	13 27	14 2	25 40	23 31
30	6 39	5♊13	25 2	29 7	16 53	13 34	14 5	25 41	23 33
31	7 37	18 6	24 49	29 31	17 31	13 40	14 8	25 43	23 34

AUGUST

Pluto 2 Leo all month

DAY	☉	☽	☿	♀	♂	♃	♄	♅	♆
	° ′	° ′	° ′	° ′	° ′	° ′	° ′	° ′	° ′
1	8♌34	1♋23	24♋41	29♊57	18♌9	13♉47	14♉10	25♉45	23♍36
2	9 32	15 6	24 R39	0♋25	18 47	13 53	14 13	25 46	23 38
3	10 29	29 12	24 D43	0 54	19 25	14 0	14 16	25 48	23 40
4	11 27	13♌38	24 54	1 24	20 3	14 5	14 18	25 49	23 41
5	12 24	28 15	25 12	1 56	20 41	14 10	14 21	25 50	23 43
6	13 22	12♍59	25 36	2 29	21 19	14 16	14 23	25 52	23 45
7	14 19	27 40	26 7	3 3	21 57	14 21	14 25	25 53	23 46
8	15 17	12♎13	26 44	3 39	22 36	14 27	14 27	25 54	23 48
9	16 14	26 35	27 28	4 16	23 14	14 32	14 29	25 55	23 50
10	17 12	10♏43	28 19	4 54	23 52	14 37	14 31	25 56	23 52
11	18 9	24 35	29 16	5 33	24 30	14 42	14 33	25 57	23 54
12	19 7	8♐13	0♌19	6 13	25 8	14 46	14 35	25 58	23 56
13	20 4	21 36	1 28	6 54	25 46	14 51	14 36	25 59	23 58
14	21 2	4♑46	2 43	7 37	26 24	14 55	14 38	26 1	24 0
15	22 0	17 43	4 3	8 20	27 2	14 59	14 39	26 1	24 2
16	22 57	0♒28	5 29	9 4	27 41	15 3	14 40	26 2	24 3
17	23 55	13 0	6 59	9 49	28 19	15 6	14 41	26 3	24 5
18	24 53	25 20	8 34	10 35	28 57	15 10	14 42	26 4	24 7
19	25 50	7♓29	10 13	11 22	29 35	15 13	14 43	26 4	24 9
20	26 48	19 29	11 56	12 10	0♍13	15 16	14 44	26 5	24 11
21	27 46	1♈22	13 43	12 58	0 51	15 19	14 45	26 6	24 14
22	28 44	13 10	15 32	13 47	1 29	15 22	14 45	26 6	24 16
23	29 41	24 58	17 24	14 37	2 7	15 24	14 46	26 7	24 18
24	0♍39	6♉46	19 18	15 28	2 46	15 27	14 46	26 7	24 20
25	1 37	18 44	21 13	16 19	3 24	15 29	14 47	26 7	24 22
26	2 35	0♊55	23 10	17 11	4 2	15 31	14 47	26 8	24 24
27	3 33	13 23	25 8	18 4	4 40	15 33	14 R47	26 8	24 26
28	4 31	26 14	27 6	18 57	5 19	15 35	14 47	26 8	24 28
29	5 29	9♋30	29 5	19 51	5 57	15 37	14 47	26 8	24 30
30	6 27	23 15	1♍3	20 45	6 35	15 38	14 46	26 9	24 32
31	7 25	7♌26	3 2	21 40	7 13	15 39	14 46	26 9	24 35

1940

SEPTEMBER

DAY	☉	☽	☿	♀	♂	♃	♄	♅	♆
	° ′	° ′	° ′	° ′	° ′	° ′	° ′	° ′	° ′
1	8♍23	22♌ 0	5♍ 0	22♋35	7♍51	15♉39	14♉45	26♉ 9	24♍37
2	9 21	6♍53	6 57	23 31	8 29	15 40	14℞45	26℞ 9	24 39
3	10 19	21 54	8 54	24 27	9 7	15 41	14 44	26 9	24 41
4	11 18	6♎57	10 50	25 25	9 45	15℞41	14 43	26 9	24 43
5	12 16	21 51	12 44	26 22	10 24	15 41	14 43	26 8	24 45
6	13 14	6♏31	14 38	27 20	11 2	15 40	14 42	26 8	24 48
7	14 12	20 52	16 31	28 19	11 40	15 40	14 41	26 8	24 50
8	15 10	4♐51	18 22	29 18	12 19	15 39	14 40	26 8	24 52
9	16 9	18 29	20 13	0♌17	12 57	15 38	14 38	26 7	24 54
10	17 7	1♑46	22 3	1 17	13 36	15 38	14 37	26 7	24 56
11	18 5	14 45	23 51	2 17	14 14	15 37	14 35	26 6	24 58
12	19 4	27 27	25 38	3 17	14 52	15 35	14 33	26 6	25 1
13	20 2	9♒56	27 25	4 18	15 31	15 34	14 32	26 5	25 3
14	21 1	22 12	29 10	5 20	16 9	15 32	14 30	26 5	25 5
15	21 59	4♓19	0♎54	6 21	16 47	15 30	14 28	26 4	25 7
16	22 58	16 17	2 37	7 23	17 26	15 28	14 26	26 3	25 10
17	23 56	28 10	4 18	8 25	18 4	15 25	14 24	26 2	25 12
18	24 55	9♈59	6 0	9 28	18 43	15 22	14 22	26 2	25 14
19	25 53	21 46	7 39	10 30	19 21	15 19	14 20	26 1	25 16
20	26 52	3♉34	9 18	11 34	19 59	15 16	14 18	26 0	25 18
21	27 50	15 26	10 56	12 37	20 37	15 13	14 15	25 59	25 21
22	28 49	27 26	12 33	13 41	21 16	15 10	14 13	25 58	25 23
23	29 48	9♊37	14 8	14 45	21 54	15 6	14 10	25 57	25 25
24	0♎47	22 5	15 43	15 49	22 32	15 2	14 7	25 56	25 27
25	1 45	4♋52	17 17	16 54	23 11	14 58	14 4	25 55	25 29
26	2 44	18 2	18 50	17 59	23 49	14 54	14 1	25 54	25 32
27	3 43	1♌38	20 22	19 4	24 28	14 50	13 58	25 52	25 33
28	4 42	15 42	21 54	20 9	25 7	14 46	13 55	25 51	25 36
29	5 41	0♍11	23 24	21 15	25 45	14 41	13 52	25 50	25 38
30	6 40	15 2	24 53	22 21	26 24	14 37	13 48	25 48	25 41

Pluto 3 Leo all month

OCTOBER

DAY	☉	☽	☿	♀	♂	♃	♄	♅	♆
	° ′	° ′	° ′	° ′	° ′	° ′	° ′	° ′	° ′
1	7♎39	0♎ 9	26♎22	23♌27	27♍ 3	14♉32	13♉45	25♉47	25♍43
2	8 38	15 21	27 50	24 33	27 41	14℞27	13℞42	25℞46	25 45
3	9 37	0♏30	29 16	25 39	28 20	14 21	13 38	25 44	25 47
4	10 36	15 27	0♏42	26 46	28 58	14 16	13 35	25 42	25 49
5	11 35	0♐ 4	2 6	27 53	29 37	14 10	13 31	25 41	25 51
6	12 35	14 16	3 30	29 0	0♎15	14 4	13 27	25 39	25 53
7	13 34	28 3	4 53	0♍ 8	0 54	13 58	13 24	25 38	25 56
8	14 33	11♑23	6 15	1 15	1 32	13 52	13 20	25 36	25 58
9	15 32	24 19	7 35	2 23	2 11	13 46	13 16	25 34	26 0
10	16 32	6♒55	8 55	3 31	2 50	13 40	13 12	25 33	26 2
11	17 31	19 15	10 13	4 39	3 28	13 33	13 8	25 31	26 4
12	18 30	1♓21	11 30	5 48	4 7	13 27	13 3	25 29	26 6
13	19 30	13 18	12 46	6 56	4 46	13 20	12 59	25 27	26 8
14	20 29	25 10	14 0	8 5	5 25	13 13	12 55	25 25	26 10
15	21 29	6♈58	15 12	9 14	6 4	13 6	12 51	25 23	26 12
16	22 28	18 45	16 23	10 23	6 43	12 58	12 47	25 21	26 14
17	23 28	0♉35	17 32	11 32	7 22	12 51	12 42	25 19	26 16
18	24 27	12 29	18 39	12 42	8 1	12 44	12 37	25 17	26 18
19	25 27	24 28	19 44	13 51	8 39	12 37	12 33	25 15	26 20
20	26 26	6♊36	20 46	15 1	9 18	12 29	12 28	25 13	26 22
21	27 26	18 54	21 46	16 11	9 57	12 22	12 23	25 11	26 24
22	28 26	1♋25	22 43	17 21	10 36	12 14	12 18	25 9	26 26
23	29 25	14 13	23 37	18 31	11 15	12 7	12 14	25 7	26 28
24	0♏25	27 19	24 27	19 41	11 54	11 59	12 9	25 5	26 30
25	1 25	10♌46	25 14	20 52	12 33	11 51	12 5	25 2	26 32
26	2 25	24 37	25 56	22 2	13 12	11 43	12 0	25 0	26 34
27	3 25	8♍51	26 34	23 13	13 51	11 35	11 56	24 58	26 36
28	4 25	23 27	27 6	24 24	14 30	11 27	11 51	24 56	26 38
29	5 25	8♎20	27 32	25 35	15 9	11 19	11 46	24 53	26 40
30	6 25	23 26	27 51	26 46	15 48	11 11	11 41	24 51	26 41
31	7 25	8♏34	28 3	27 57	16 27	11 3	11 37	24 49	26 43

Pluto 4 Leo all month

1940

NOVEMBER

Pluto 4 Leo all month

DAY	☉	☽	☿	♀	♂	♃	♄	♅	♆
	° ′	° ′	° ′	° ′	° ′	° ′	° ′	° ′	° ′
1	8♏25	23♏36	28♏ 8	29♍ 8	17♎ 6	10♉54	11♉32	24♉46	26♍45
2	9 25	8♐22	28℞ 4	0♎20	17 45	10℞46	11℞27	24℞44	26 47
3	10 25	22 45	27 51	1 31	18 24	10 38	11 22	24 42	26 49
4	11 25	6♑42	27 29	2 43	19 3	10 30	11 18	24 39	26 50
5	12 25	20 10	26 57	3 55	19 42	10 22	11 13	24 37	26 52
6	13 26	3♒11	26 14	5 6	20 21	10 14	11 8	24 34	26 54
7	14 26	15 48	25 23	6 18	21 0	10 6	11 3	24 32	26 56
8	15 26	28 6	24 23	7 30	21 39	9 58	10 59	24 29	26 57
9	16 26	10♓ 9	23 16	8 43	22 19	9 49	10 54	24 27	26 59
10	17 27	22 1	22 3	9 55	22 58	9 41	10 49	24 24	27 1
11	18 27	3♈49	20 44	11 7	23 37	9 33	10 44	24 22	27 2
12	19 27	15 36	19 24	12 19	24 17	9 25	10 40	24 19	27 4
13	20 28	27 25	18 5	13 32	24 56	9 17	10 35	24 17	27 5
14	21 28	9♉20	16 49	14 44	25 36	9 9	10 30	24 14	27 7
15	22 28	21 23	15 38	15 57	26 15	9 1	10 25	24 12	27 8
16	23 29	3♊34	14 37	17 9	26 54	8 53	10 21	24 9	27 10
17	24 29	15 56	13 44	18 22	27 34	8 46	10 16	24 7	27 11
18	25 30	28 29	13 2	19 35	28 13	8 38	10 11	24 4	27 12
19	26 30	11♋14	12 30	20 48	28 52	8 31	10 7	24 2	27 14
20	27 31	24 11	12 10	22 1	29 32	8 23	10 2	23 59	27 15
21	28 32	7♌22	12 2	23 15	0♏11	8 16	9 58	23 57	27 16
22	29 32	20 48	12 D 6	24 28	0 51	8 9	9 53	23 54	27 18
23	0♐33	4♍30	12 20	25 41	1 30	8 2	9 49	23 52	27 19
24	1 33	18 29	12 44	26 54	2 10	7 55	9 44	23 49	27 20
25	2 34	2♎45	13 17	28 8	2 49	7 49	9 40	23 47	27 21
26	3 35	17 17	13 57	29 21	3 29	7 42	9 36	23 44	27 22
27	4 36	2♏ 0	14 43	0♏34	4 8	7 36	9 32	23 42	27 24
28	5 36	16 51	15 36	1 48	4 48	7 29	9 28	23 40	27 25
29	6 37	1♐40	16 35	3 1	5 27	7 23	9 24	23 37	27 26
30	7 38	16 19	17 38	4 15	6 7	7 17	9 20	23 35	27 27

DECEMBER

Pluto 4 Leo all month

DAY	☉	☽	☿	♀	♂	♃	♄	♅	♆
	° ′	° ′	° ′	° ′	° ′	° ′	° ′	° ′	° ′
1	8♐39	0♑41	18♏45	5♏29	6♏47	7♉11	9♉16	23♉33	27♍28
2	9 40	14 41	19 55	6 43	7 26	7℞ 6	9℞12	23℞30	27 29
3	10 41	28 13	21 9	7 57	8 6	7 0	9 9	23 28	27 30
4	11 42	11♒19	22 25	9 11	8 46	6 55	9 5	23 25	27 31
5	12 42	24 0	23 43	10 25	9 26	6 50	9 1	23 23	27 31
6	13 43	6♓20	25 3	11 39	10 5	6 45	8 58	23 21	27 32
7	14 44	18 24	26 26	12 53	10 45	6 40	8 54	23 18	27 33
8	15 45	0♈17	27 49	14 7	11 25	6 35	8 51	23 16	27 34
9	16 46	12 4	29 14	15 21	12 5	6 31	8 48	23 14	27 35
10	17 47	23 51	0♐40	16 35	12 44	6 26	8 44	23 12	27 35
11	18 48	5♉43	2 7	17 49	13 24	6 22	8 41	23 10	27 36
12	19 49	17 44	3 34	19 3	14 4	6 18	8 38	23 7	27 37
13	20 50	29 56	5 2	20 17	14 44	6 14	8 35	23 5	27 37
14	21 51	12♊22	6 31	21 32	15 24	6 11	8 32	23 3	27 38
15	22 52	25 1	8 0	22 46	16 4	6 7	8 30	23 1	27 38
16	23 53	7♋54	9 29	24 1	16 44	6 4	8 27	22 59	27 39
17	24 54	21 1	10 59	25 15	17 24	6 1	8 24	22 57	27 39
18	25 55	4♌18	12 30	26 30	18 4	5 58	8 22	22 55	27 39
19	26 56	17 46	14 0	27 44	18 44	5 56	8 19	22 53	27 40
20	27 58	1♍23	15 31	28 59	19 24	5 53	8 17	22 51	27 40
21	28 59	15 9	17 2	0♐13	20 4	5 51	8 15	22 49	27 41
22	0♑ 0	29 3	18 34	1 28	20 44	5 49	8 13	22 47	27 41
23	1 1	13♎ 7	20 6	2 42	21 24	5 48	8 11	22 45	27 41
24	2 2	27 19	21 39	3 57	22 4	5 46	8 9	22 44	27 41
25	3 3	11♏39	23 11	5 12	22 44	5 45	8 7	22 42	27 42
26	4 4	26 2	24 44	6 26	23 24	5 44	8 5	22 40	27 42
27	5 5	10♐25	26 16	7 41	24 5	5 43	8 4	22 38	27 42
28	6 7	24 42	27 49	8 56	24 45	5 42	8 2	22 37	27 42
29	7 8	8♑48	29 22	10 11	25 25	5 41	8 1	22 35	27 42
30	8 9	22 36	0♑56	11 25	26 5	5 40	8 0	22 34	27 42
31	9 10	6♒ 2	2 30	12 40	26 46	5 40	7 59	22 32	27℞42

1941

JANUARY

DAY	☉ ° ′	☽ ° ′	☿ ° ′	♀ ° ′	♂ ° ′	♃ ° ′	♄ ° ′	♅ ° ′	♆ ° ′
1	10♑11	19♒ 6	4♑ 4	13♐55	27♏26	5♉40	7♉58	22♉31	27♍42
2	11 12	1♓47	5 39	15 10	28 6	5D41	7R57	22R29	27R42
3	12 14	14 9	7 14	16 25	28 46	5 41	7 56	22 28	27 42
4	13 15	26 14	8 49	17 39	29 27	5 42	7 55	22 27	27 41
5	14 16	8♈ 8	10 25	18 54	0♐ 7	5 43	7 55	22 25	27 41
6	15 17	19 56	12 1	20 9	0 47	5 44	7 54	22 24	27 41
7	16 18	1♉44	13 37	21 24	1 28	5 45	7 54	22 23	27 41
8	17 19	13 38	15 14	22 38	2 8	5 47	7 54	22 22	27 40
9	18 21	25 42	16 51	23 53	2 49	5 48	7 54	22 21	27 40
10	19 22	8♊ 0	18 29	25 8	3 29	5 50	7D54	22 20	27 40
11	20 23	20 36	20 7	26 23	4 10	5 52	7 54	22 19	27 40
12	21 24	3♋30	21 46	27 38	4 50	5 55	7 54	22 18	27 39
13	22 25	16 42	23 25	28 53	5 31	5 57	7 54	22 17	27 39
14	23 26	0♌12	25 4	0♑ 8	6 11	6 0	7 55	22 16	27 39
15	24 27	13 55	26 44	1 22	6 52	6 3	7 55	22 15	27 38
16	25 28	27 49	28 25	2 37	7 32	6 6	7 56	22 14	27 38
17	26 29	11♍49	0♒ 6	3 52	8 13	6 9	7 57	22 14	27 37
18	27 30	25 53	1 47	5 7	8 53	6 13	7 58	22 13	27 36
19	28 32	9♎59	3 29	6 22	9 34	6 16	7 59	22 12	27 36
20	29 33	24 5	5 11	7 37	10 14	6 20	8 0	22 12	27 35
21	0♒34	8♏11	6 54	8 52	10 55	6 24	8 1	22 11	27 34
22	1 35	22 14	8 37	10 7	11 36	6 28	8 2	22 11	27 33
23	2 36	6♐15	10 21	11 22	12 16	6 33	8 4	22 10	27 33
24	3 37	20 11	12 5	12 37	12 57	6 38	8 5	22 10	27 32
25	4 38	4♑ 0	13 48	13 52	13 38	6 43	8 7	22 10	27 31
26	5 39	17 38	15 33	15 7	14 19	6 48	8 9	22 10	27 30
27	6 40	1♒ 3	17 17	16 22	14 59	6 54	8 11	22 9	27 29
28	7 41	14 12	19 1	17 37	15 40	6 59	8 13	22 9	27 28
29	8 42	27 3	20 44	18 52	16 21	7 5	8 15	22 9	27 27
30	9 43	9♓37	22 27	20 7	17 2	7 11	8 17	22 9	27 26
31	10 44	21 55	24 9	21 22	17 43	7 17	8 19	22D 9	27 25

Pluto 3 Leo all month

FEBRUARY

DAY	☉ ° ′	☽ ° ′	☿ ° ′	♀ ° ′	♂ ° ′	♃ ° ′	♄ ° ′	♅ ° ′	♆ ° ′
1	11♒45	3♈59	25♒50	22♑37	18♐24	7♉23	8♉22	22♉ 9	27♍24
2	12 46	15 53	27 30	23 52	19 5	7 29	8 24	22 9	27R23
3	13 46	27 42	29 7	25 7	19 46	7 36	8 27	22 10	27 22
4	14 47	9♉30	0♓43	26 22	20 27	7 42	8 29	22 10	27 21
5	15 48	21 24	2 16	27 37	21 8	7 49	8 32	22 10	27 19
6	16 49	3♊28	3 45	28 52	21 48	7 56	8 35	22 10	27 18
7	17 50	15 47	5 11	0♒ 7	22 29	8 3	8 38	22 11	27 17
8	18 50	28 25	6 33	1 22	23 10	8 10	8 41	22 11	27 16
9	19 51	11♋25	7 49	2 37	23 51	8 18	8 45	22 12	27 15
10	20 52	24 49	8 59	3 52	24 32	8 25	8 48	22 12	27 14
11	21 53	8♌34	10 2	5 7	25 13	8 33	8 51	22 13	27 13
12	22 53	22 39	10 59	6 22	25 54	8 41	8 55	22 13	27 11
13	23 54	6♍58	11 47	7 37	26 36	8 49	8 58	22 14	27 10
14	24 54	21 27	12 26	8 52	27 17	8 57	9 2	22 15	27 8
15	25 55	5♎58	12 56	10 7	27 58	9 5	9 6	22 16	27 7
16	26 56	20 28	13 16	11 21	28 39	9 13	9 10	22 17	27 5
17	27 56	4♏51	13 26	12 36	29 20	9 22	9 14	22 17	27 4
18	28 57	19 5	13R25	13 51	0♑ 1	9 30	9 18	22 18	27 3
19	29 57	3♐ 8	13 14	15 6	0 42	9 39	9 22	22 19	27 2
20	0♓58	16 59	12 53	16 21	1 23	9 48	9 26	22 20	27 0
21	1 58	0♑38	12 23	17 36	2 4	9 58	9 31	22 21	26 59
22	2 59	14 3	11 44	18 51	2 45	10 7	9 35	22 23	26 57
23	3 59	27 16	10 58	20 6	3 26	10 16	9 40	22 24	26 56
24	4 59	10♒15	10 4	21 20	4 7	10 26	9 44	22 25	26 54
25	6 0	23 1	9 6	22 35	4 49	10 35	9 49	22 27	26 53
26	7 0	5♓34	8 4	23 50	5 30	10 45	9 54	22 28	26 51
27	8 0	17 54	7 1	25 5	6 11	10 55	9 59	22 29	26 50
28	9 1	0♈ 3	5 57	26 20	6 52	11 5	10 4	22 31	26 48

Pluto 2 Leo all month

1941

MARCH

Pluto 2 Leo all month

DAY	☉	☽	☿	♀	♂	♃	♄	♅	♆
	° ′	° ′	° ′	° ′	° ′	° ′	° ′	° ′	° ′
1	10♓ 1	12♈ 2	4♓54	27♒35	7♑34	11♉15	10♉ 9	22♉32	26♍47
2	11 1	23 54	3℞53	28 50	8 15	11 25	10 14	22 34	26℞45
3	12 1	5♉42	2 56	0♓ 5	8 56	11 35	10 19	22 35	26 44
4	13 1	17 31	2 4	1 19	9 38	11 46	10 24	22 37	26 43
5	14 1	29 24	1 17	2 34	10 19	11 56	10 30	22 39	26 41
6	15 2	11♊26	0 37	3 49	11 1	12 7	10 35	22 40	26 39
7	16 2	23 43	0 4	5 4	11 42	12 18	10 41	22 42	26 37
8	17 2	6♋18	29♒37	6 18	12 23	12 28	10 46	22 44	26 36
9	18 2	19 16	29 16	7 33	13 4	12 39	10 52	22 46	26 34
10	19 2	2♌39	29 3	8 48	13 46	12 50	10 58	22 48	26 32
11	20 1	16 28	28 55	10 3	14 27	13 1	11 4	22 50	26 30
12	21 1	0♍41	28D54	11 17	15 9	13 12	11 9	22 51	26 29
13	22 1	15 16	28 59	12 32	15 50	13 24	11 15	22 53	26 27
14	23 1	0♎ 5	29 9	13 47	16 32	13 35	11 21	22 56	26 25
15	24 1	15 2	29 25	15 2	17 13	13 47	11 27	22 58	26 23
16	25 0	29 58	29 47	16 16	17 54	13 58	11 33	23 0	26 22
17	26 0	14♏46	0♓13	17 31	18 36	14 10	11 39	23 2	26 20
18	27 0	29 19	0 44	18 46	19 17	14 22	11 45	23 5	26 19
19	27 59	13♐34	1 20	20 0	19 58	14 34	11 51	23 7	26 17
20	28 59	27 29	2 0	21 15	20 40	14 46	11 58	23 9	26 16
21	29 59	11♑ 2	2 43	22 29	21 21	14 58	12 4	23 12	26 14
22	0♈58	24 16	3 30	23 44	22 3	15 10	12 11	23 14	26 12
23	1 58	7♒12	4 21	24 59	22 44	15 22	12 17	23 16	26 10
24	2 57	19 52	5 14	26 13	23 26	15 34	12 24	23 19	26 9
25	3 57	2♓19	6 11	27 28	24 7	15 47	12 30	23 21	26 7
26	4 56	14 34	7 10	28 43	24 49	15 59	12 37	23 24	26 6
27	5 56	26 40	8 13	29 57	25 30	16 11	12 44	23 26	26 4
28	6 55	8♈39	9 18	1♈12	26 12	16 24	12 50	23 29	26 3
29	7 54	20 31	10 25	2 26	26 53	16 36	12 57	23 32	26 1
30	8 54	2♉21	11 34	3 41	27 35	16 49	13 4	23 34	25 59
31	9 53	14 9	12 45	4 55	28 16	17 2	13 11	23 36	25 57

APRIL

Pluto 2 Leo all month

DAY	☉	☽	☿	♀	♂	♃	♄	♅	♆
	° ′	° ′	° ′	° ′	° ′	° ′	° ′	° ′	° ′
1	10♈52	25♉59	13♓59	6♈10	28♑58	17♉15	13♉18	23♉39	25♍56
2	11 51	7♊54	15 15	7 24	29 39	17 28	13 25	23 43	25℞54
3	12 50	19 57	16 33	8 38	0♒21	17 41	13 32	23 46	25 52
4	13 50	2♋12	17 52	9 53	1 2	17 54	13 39	23 48	25 50
5	14 49	14 43	19 14	11 7	1 44	18 7	13 46	23 50	25 49
6	15 48	27 35	20 37	12 22	2 25	18 20	13 54	23 53	25 47
7	16 47	10♌51	22 2	13 36	3 7	18 33	14 1	23 57	25 46
8	17 46	24 32	23 28	14 50	3 48	18 46	14 8	24 0	25 44
9	18 45	8♍41	24 56	16 5	4 30	18 59	14 15	24 3	25 43
10	19 43	23 15	26 26	17 19	5 11	19 12	14 22	24 6	25 41
11	20 42	8♎11	27 58	18 33	5 53	19 25	14 29	24 9	25 40
12	21 41	23 19	29 31	19 47	6 34	19 38	14 36	24 12	25 39
13	22 40	8♏33	1♈ 6	21 2	7 15	19 52	14 43	24 15	25 37
14	23 39	23 41	2 42	22 16	7 57	20 5	14 51	24 18	25 36
15	24 37	8♐34	4 20	23 31	8 38	20 19	14 58	24 21	25 35
16	25 36	23 6	6 0	24 45	9 19	20 32	15 5	24 25	25 34
17	26 35	7♑12	7 41	26 0	10 1	20 46	15 13	24 28	25 32
18	27 33	20 51	9 24	27 14	10 42	20 59	15 20	24 31	25 31
19	28 32	4♒ 5	11 9	28 28	11 24	21 13	15 28	24 34	25 29
20	29 31	16 55	12 55	29 42	12 5	21 27	15 35	24 38	25 28
21	0♉29	29 26	14 43	0♉56	12 46	21 40	15 43	24 41	25 26
22	1 28	11♓41	16 32	2 10	13 28	21 54	15 50	24 44	25 25
23	2 26	23 44	18 23	3 24	14 9	22 8	15 58	24 47	25 24
24	3 25	5♈40	20 16	4 38	14 50	22 22	16 5	24 51	25 23
25	4 23	17 31	22 10	5 53	15 32	22 36	16 13	24 54	25 21
26	5 22	29 19	24 6	7 7	16 13	22 50	16 20	24 57	25 20
27	6 20	11♉ 8	26 4	8 21	16 54	23 4	16 28	25 1	25 19
28	7 18	22 57	28 3	9 35	17 35	23 18	16 36	25 4	25 18
29	8 17	4♊53	0♉ 4	10 49	18 17	23 32	16 43	25 7	25 17
30	9 15	16 53	2 6	12 3	18 58	23 45	16 51	25 11	25 16

1941

MAY

DAY	☉ ° ′	☽ ° ′	☿ ° ′	♀ ° ′	♂ ° ′	♃ ° ′	♄ ° ′	♅ ° ′	♆ ° ′
1	10 ♉ 13	29 ♊ 1	4 ♉ 10	13 ♉ 17	19 ♒ 39	23 ♉ 59	16 ♉ 59	25 ♉ 14	25 ♍ 15
2	11 11	11 ♋ 20	6 15	14 31	20 20	24 13	17 7	25 17	25 ℞ 14
3	12 10	23 52	8 22	15 45	21 1	24 27	17 14	25 21	25 13
4	13 8	6 ♌ 41	10 30	16 59	21 42	24 42	17 22	25 24	25 11
5	14 6	19 50	12 38	18 13	22 23	24 56	17 30	25 28	25 10
6	15 4	3 ♍ 22	14 48	19 27	23 4	25 10	17 38	25 31	25 9
7	16 2	17 19	16 58	20 41	23 45	25 24	17 45	25 35	25 8
8	17 0	1 ♎ 42	19 8	21 55	24 26	25 38	17 53	25 39	25 7
9	17 58	16 28	21 18	23 9	25 7	25 52	18 1	25 42	25 7
10	18 56	1 ♏ 33	23 29	24 23	25 48	26 6	18 9	25 46	25 6
11	19 54	16 47	25 38	25 37	26 29	26 20	18 16	25 49	25 5
12	20 52	2 ♐ 1	27 47	26 50	27 9	26 34	18 24	25 52	25 4
13	21 50	17 4	29 55	28 4	27 50	26 48	18 32	25 55	25 3
14	22 48	1 ♑ 47	2 ♊ 2	29 18	28 31	27 2	18 40	25 59	25 2
15	23 45	16 4	4 7	0 ♊ 32	29 11	27 16	18 47	26 2	25 2
16	24 43	29 52	6 11	1 46	29 52	27 31	18 55	26 6	25 1
17	25 41	13 ♒ 10	8 12	3 0	0 ♓ 32	27 45	19 3	26 9	25 1
18	26 39	26 2	10 11	4 14	1 12	27 59	19 11	26 13	25 0
19	27 37	8 ♓ 31	12 8	5 28	1 53	28 13	19 18	26 16	25 0
20	28 34	20 43	14 2	6 41	2 33	28 28	19 26	26 20	24 59
21	29 32	2 ♈ 42	15 53	7 55	3 13	28 42	19 33	26 23	24 58
22	0 ♊ 30	14 33	17 42	9 9	3 53	28 56	19 41	26 27	24 58
23	1 28	26 21	19 28	10 23	4 33	29 10	19 48	26 30	24 57
24	2 25	8 ♉ 9	21 10	11 36	5 13	29 24	19 56	26 34	24 57
25	3 23	19 59	22 50	12 50	5 53	29 38	20 4	26 37	24 57
26	4 21	1 ♊ 55	24 27	14 4	6 33	29 52	20 12	26 41	24 57
27	5 18	13 57	26 0	15 17	7 13	0 ♊ 6	20 19	26 44	24 56
28	6 16	26 7	27 31	16 31	7 53	0 21	20 27	26 48	24 56
29	7 13	8 ♋ 26	28 58	17 44	8 33	0 35	20 34	26 51	24 55
30	8 11	20 55	0 ♋ 22	18 58	9 12	0 49	20 42	26 55	24 55
31	9 8	3 ♌ 35	1 43	20 12	9 52	1 3	20 49	26 58	24 54

Pluto 2 Leo all month

JUNE

DAY	☉ ° ′	☽ ° ′	☿ ° ′	♀ ° ′	♂ ° ′	♃ ° ′	♄ ° ′	♅ ° ′	♆ ° ′
1	10 ♊ 6	16 ♌ 29	3 ♋ 1	21 ♊ 25	10 ♓ 31	1 ♊ 17	20 ♉ 57	27 ♉ 2	24 ♍ 54
2	11 3	29 39	4 15	22 39	11 10	1 31	21 4	27 5	24 ℞ 54
3	12 1	13 ♍ 7	5 26	23 53	11 50	1 45	21 11	27 8	24 54
4	12 58	26 55	6 33	25 6	12 29	1 59	21 19	27 12	24 54
5	13 56	11 ♎ 4	7 37	26 20	13 8	2 13	21 26	27 15	24 54
6	14 53	25 34	8 37	27 33	13 47	2 27	21 33	27 19	24 D 54
7	15 51	10 ♏ 22	9 34	28 47	14 26	2 41	21 40	27 22	24 54
8	16 48	25 22	10 27	0 ♋ 1	15 5	2 55	21 48	27 25	24 54
9	17 45	10 ♐ 25	11 16	1 14	15 43	3 9	21 55	27 29	24 54
10	18 43	25 22	12 1	2 28	16 22	3 23	22 2	27 32	24 54
11	19 40	10 ♑ 3	12 43	3 42	17 0	3 37	22 9	27 35	24 55
12	20 37	24 21	13 20	4 55	17 38	3 51	22 17	27 39	24 55
13	21 35	8 ♒ 12	13 53	6 9	18 16	4 4	22 24	27 42	24 55
16	22 32	21 35	14 21	7 22	18 54	4 18	22 31	27 45	24 55
15	23 29	4 ♓ 30	14 46	8 35	19 32	4 32	22 38	27 48	24 56
16	24 26	17 2	15 6	9 49	20 10	4 46	22 45	27 52	24 56
17	25 24	29 15	15 21	11 2	20 48	4 59	22 52	27 55	24 56
18	26 21	11 ♈ 14	15 32	12 15	21 25	5 13	22 59	27 58	24 57
19	27 18	23 5	15 38	13 29	22 2	5 27	23 6	28 1	24 57
20	28 16	4 ♉ 54	15 ℞ 40	14 42	22 40	5 40	23 13	28 4	24 58
21	29 13	16 43	15 37	15 56	23 17	5 54	23 19	28 7	24 58
22	0 ♋ 10	28 38	15 30	17 9	23 53	6 7	23 26	28 11	24 59
23	1 7	10 ♊ 40	15 19	18 22	24 30	6 20	23 33	28 14	24 59
24	2 5	22 52	15 3	19 36	25 7	6 34	23 39	28 17	25 0
25	3 2	5 ♋ 15	14 43	20 49	25 43	6 47	23 46	28 20	25 0
26	3 59	17 49	14 20	22 2	26 19	7 0	23 52	28 23	25 1
27	4 56	0 ♌ 35	13 53	23 15	26 55	7 13	23 59	28 26	25 2
28	5 54	13 31	13 24	24 29	27 31	7 27	24 5	28 29	25 2
29	6 51	26 39	12 52	25 42	28 6	7 40	24 12	28 31	25 3
30	7 48	10 ♍ 0	12 18	26 55	28 42	7 53	24 18	28 34	25 4

Pluto 2 Leo all month

1941

JULY

DAY	☉ ° ′	☽ ° ′	☿ ° ′	♀ ° ′	♂ ° ′	♃ ° ′	♄ ° ′	♅ ° ′	♆ ° ′
1	8 ♋ 45	23 ♍ 33	11 ♋ 42	28 ♋ 8	29 ♓ 17	8 ♊ 6	24 ♉ 24	28 ♉ 37	25 ♍ 5
2	9 42	7 ♎ 20	11 ℞ 6	29 22	29 52	8 19	24 31	28 40	25 5
3	10 40	21 22	10 29	0 ♌ 35	0 ♈ 27	8 32	24 37	28 43	25 6
4	11 37	5 ♏ 38	9 53	1 48	1 1	8 45	24 43	28 46	25 7
5	12 34	20 7	9 18	3 1	1 35	8 58	24 49	28 48	25 8
6	13 31	4 ♐ 45	8 44	4 15	2 10	9 11	24 55	28 51	25 9
7	14 28	19 26	8 13	5 28	2 43	9 23	25 1	28 54	25 10
8	15 26	4 ♑ 2	7 45	6 41	3 17	9 36	25 7	28 56	25 11
9	16 23	18 27	7 19	7 54	3 50	9 49	25 13	28 59	25 12
10	17 20	2 ♒ 34	6 58	9 7	4 24	10 1	25 19	29 2	25 13
11	18 17	16 18	6 41	10 20	4 56	10 14	25 24	29 4	25 14
12	19 14	29 37	6 28	11 33	5 29	10 26	25 30	29 7	25 15
13	20 12	12 ♓ 32	6 20	12 46	6 1	10 38	25 35	29 9	25 16
14	21 9	25 5	6 D 17	13 59	6 33	10 51	25 40	29 12	25 17
15	22 6	7 ♈ 20	6 19	15 12	7 5	11 3	25 46	29 14	25 19
16	23 3	19 21	6 27	16 25	7 37	11 15	25 51	29 16	25 20
17	24 0	1 ♉ 14	6 40	17 38	8 8	11 27	25 56	29 19	25 21
18	24 58	13 4	6 59	18 51	8 38	11 39	26 2	29 21	25 22
19	25 55	24 57	7 24	20 4	9 9	11 51	26 7	29 23	25 24
20	26 52	6 ♊ 55	7 54	21 17	9 39	12 3	26 12	29 26	25 25
21	27 50	19 4	8 29	22 30	10 9	12 15	26 17	29 28	25 26
22	28 47	1 ♋ 25	9 10	23 43	10 38	12 27	26 22	29 30	25 28
23	29 44	14 1	9 57	24 56	11 7	12 38	26 27	29 32	25 29
24	0 ♌ 41	26 52	10 49	26 9	11 36	12 50	26 32	29 34	25 31
25	1 39	9 ♌ 56	11 47	27 22	12 4	13 2	26 37	29 36	25 32
26	2 36	23 14	12 50	28 35	12 32	13 13	26 41	29 38	25 34
27	3 33	6 ♍ 44	13 58	29 47	13 0	13 25	26 46	29 40	25 35
28	4 31	20 24	15 11	1 ♍ 0	13 27	13 36	26 50	29 42	25 37
29	5 28	4 ♎ 14	16 29	2 13	13 54	13 47	26 54	29 44	25 38
30	6 26	18 11	17 52	3 26	14 20	13 58	26 59	29 46	25 40
31	7 23	2 ♏ 16	19 20	4 38	14 46	14 9	27 3	29 48	25 41

Pluto 3 Leo all month

AUGUST

DAY	☉ ° ′	☽ ° ′	☿ ° ′	♀ ° ′	♂ ° ′	♃ ° ′	♄ ° ′	♅ ° ′	♆ ° ′
1	8 ♌ 20	16 ♏ 26	20 ♋ 52	5 ♍ 51	15 ♈ 11	14 ♊ 20	27 ♉ 7	29 ♉ 49	25 ♍ 43
2	9 18	0 ♐ 42	22 29	7 4	15 36	14 31	27 11	29 51	25 45
3	10 15	14 59	24 9	8 16	16 1	14 41	27 15	29 53	25 46
4	11 13	29 14	25 54	9 29	16 25	14 52	27 18	29 54	25 48
5	12 10	13 ♑ 24	27 42	10 41	16 48	15 2	27 22	29 56	25 50
6	13 7	27 23	29 32	11 54	17 11	15 12	27 26	29 57	25 52
7	14 5	11 ♒ 7	1 ♌ 26	13 6	17 34	15 23	27 30	29 59	25 53
8	15 2	24 34	3 22	14 19	17 56	15 33	27 33	0 ♊ 0	25 55
9	16 0	7 ♓ 42	5 19	15 31	18 17	15 43	27 37	0 2	25 57
10	16 57	20 30	7 19	16 44	18 38	15 53	27 40	0 3	25 59
11	17 55	2 ♈ 59	9 20	17 56	18 58	16 3	27 43	0 4	26 0
12	18 53	15 13	11 22	19 9	19 18	16 12	27 46	0 6	26 2
13	19 50	27 15	13 24	20 21	19 37	16 22	27 49	0 7	26 4
14	20 48	9 ♉ 9	15 27	21 33	19 55	16 31	27 52	0 8	26 6
15	21 45	21 0	17 29	22 46	20 13	16 41	27 55	0 9	26 8
16	22 43	2 ♊ 54	19 32	23 58	20 30	16 50	27 57	0 10	26 10
17	23 41	14 55	21 34	25 10	20 47	16 59	28 0	0 11	26 12
18	24 38	27 6	23 35	26 22	21 3	17 8	28 3	0 12	26 14
19	25 36	9 ♋ 33	25 36	27 35	21 19	17 17	28 5	0 13	26 16
20	26 34	22 17	27 35	28 47	21 33	17 26	28 8	0 14	26 18
21	27 32	5 ♌ 20	29 34	29 59	21 47	17 35	28 10	0 15	26 20
22	28 30	18 42	1 ♍ 31	1 ♎ 11	22 0	17 43	28 12	0 16	26 22
23	29 27	2 ♍ 22	3 28	2 23	22 13	17 52	28 14	0 16	26 24
24	0 ♍ 25	16 16	5 23	3 35	22 24	18 0	28 16	0 17	26 26
25	1 23	0 ♎ 23	7 17	4 47	22 35	18 8	28 18	0 18	26 28
26	2 21	14 37	9 9	5 59	22 45	18 16	28 20	0 18	26 30
27	3 19	28 55	11 0	7 11	22 55	18 24	28 21	0 19	26 32
28	4 17	13 ♏ 14	12 50	8 22	23 3	18 31	28 23	0 19	26 34
29	5 15	27 30	14 39	9 34	23 11	18 39	28 24	0 20	26 36
30	6 13	11 ♐ 41	16 26	10 46	23 18	18 46	28 25	0 20	26 38
31	7 11	25 45	18 12	11 58	23 24	18 54	28 27	0 20	26 40

Pluto 4 Leo all month

1941

SEPTEMBER

DAY	☉	☽	☿	♀	♂	♃	♄	♅	♆
	° ′	° ′	° ′	° ′	° ′	° ′	° ′	° ′	° ′
1	8♍ 9	9♑40	19♍57	13♎ 9	23♈30	19♊ 1	28♉28	0♊20	26♍43
2	9 7	23 24	21 41	14 21	23 34	19 8	28 29	0 21	26 45
3	10 5	6♒56	23 23	15 33	23 38	19 15	28 30	0 21	26 47
4	11 3	20 15	25 4	16 44	23 40	19 22	28 31	0 21	26 49
5	12 1	3♓19	26 44	17 56	23 42	19 28	28 31	0 21	26 51
6	13 0	16 8	28 23	19 7	23 43	19 35	28 32	0℞21	26 53
7	13 58	28 43	0♎ 0	20 19	23℞43	19 41	28 32	0 21	26 55
8	14 56	11♈ 4	1 36	21 30	23 43	19 47	28 32	0 21	26 57
9	15 54	23 13	3 12	22 42	23 41	19 53	28 33	0 21	27 0
10	16 53	5♉13	4 46	23 53	23 39	19 59	28 33	0 21	27 2
11	17 51	17 7	6 18	25 4	23 35	20 4	28℞33	0 20	27 4
12	18 49	28 58	7 50	26 15	23 31	20 10	28 33	0 20	27 6
13	19 48	10♊51	9 21	27 26	23 26	20 15	28 33	0 20	27 9
14	20 46	22 51	10 50	28 37	23 20	20 20	28 32	0 20	27 11
15	21 45	5♋ 1	12 18	29 48	23 13	20 25	28 32	0 19	27 13
16	22 43	17 28	13 46	0♏59	23 5	20 29	28 31	0 19	27 15
17	23 42	0♌13	15 12	2 10	22 57	20 34	28 31	0 18	27 18
18	24 40	13 20	16 37	3 21	22 48	20 38	28 30	0 18	27 20
19	25 39	26 51	18 0	4 32	22 38	20 42	28 29	0 17	27 22
20	26 38	10♍46	19 23	5 43	22 27	20 46	28 28	0 16	27 24
21	27 36	25 1	20 44	6 53	22 16	20 50	28 27	0 15	27 27
22	28 35	9♎32	22 4	8 4	22 3	20 54	28 26	0 15	27 29
23	29 34	24 14	23 23	9 15	21 51	20 57	28 25	0 14	27 31
24	0♎32	8♏59	24 40	10 25	21 37	21 0	28 23	0 13	27 33
25	1 31	23 40	25 55	11 36	21 23	21 3	28 22	0 12	27 35
26	2 30	8♐12	27 9	12 46	21 8	21 6	28 20	0 11	27 37
27	3 29	22 31	28 22	13 56	20 53	21 9	28 18	0 10	27 39
28	4 28	6♑33	29 33	15 7	20 36	21 11	28 17	0 9	27 41
29	5 27	20 17	0♏42	16 16	20 20	21 14	28 15	0 8	27 44
30	6 26	3♒44	1 49	17 27	20 3	21 16	28 13	0 7	27 46

Pluto 4 Leo all month

OCTOBER

DAY	☉	☽	☿	♀	♂	♃	♄	♅	♆
	° ′	° ′	° ′	° ′	° ′	° ′	° ′	° ′	° ′
1	7♎25	16♒55	2♏54	18♏37	19♈46	21♊18	28♉11	0♊ 5	27♍48
2	8 24	29 50	3 57	19 47	19℞28	21 20	28℞ 9	0℞ 4	27 50
3	9 23	12♓32	4 56	20 57	19 10	21 21	28 6	0 3	27 53
4	10 22	25 2	5 55	22 7	18 51	21 23	28 4	0 1	27 55
5	11 21	7♈22	6 50	23 16	18 33	21 24	28 1	0 0	27 57
6	12 20	19 32	7 41	24 26	18 14	21 25	27 59	29♉59	27 59
7	13 19	1♉34	8 29	25 36	17 56	21 25	27 56	29 57	28 2
8	14 18	13 30	9 14	26 45	17 37	21 26	27 53	29 56	28 4
9	15 18	25 22	9 54	27 55	17 18	21 26	27 50	29 54	28 6
10	16 17	7♊13	10 30	29 4	16 59	21 26	27 47	29 52	28 8
11	17 16	19 6	11 2	0♐13	16 40	21℞26	27 44	29 51	28 11
12	18 16	1♋ 4	11 28	1 22	16 22	21 26	27 41	29 49	28 13
13	19 15	13 12	11 48	2 31	16 3	21 25	27 38	29 47	28 15
14	20 14	25 33	12 2	3 40	15 45	21 25	27 35	29 46	28 17
15	21 14	8♌14	12 9	4 49	15 27	21 24	27 31	29 44	28 19
16	22 13	21 17	12℞ 9	5 58	15 9	21 23	27 28	29 42	28 21
17	23 13	4♍46	12 1	7 7	14 52	21 22	27 24	29 40	28 23
18	24 13	18 42	11 45	8 15	14 35	21 20	27 21	29 38	28 25
19	25 12	3♎ 5	11 20	9 24	14 19	21 19	27 17	29 36	28 27
20	26 12	17 51	10 47	10 32	14 3	21 17	27 13	29 34	28 29
21	27 12	2♏53	10 4	11 40	13 48	21 15	27 9	29 32	28 31
22	28 11	18 2	9 13	12 48	13 33	21 13	27 6	29 30	28 33
23	29 11	3♐ 8	8 14	13 56	13 19	21 10	27 2	29 28	28 35
24	0♏11	18 2	7 9	15 4	13 5	21 8	26 58	29 26	28 37
25	1 11	2♑36	5 58	16 12	12 52	21 5	26 54	29 24	28 39
26	2 10	16 47	4 44	17 20	12 40	21 2	26 50	29 22	28 41
27	3 10	0♒32	3 28	18 27	12 28	20 58	26 45	29 20	28 43
28	4 10	13 54	2 12	19 34	12 17	20 55	26 41	29 18	28 45
29	5 10	26 53	0 59	20 41	12 7	20 51	26 37	29 16	28 47
30	6 10	9♓34	29♎51	21 48	11 57	20 48	26 33	29 14	28 49
31	7 10	22 0	28 50	22 55	11 48	20 44	26 28	29 11	28 50

Pluto 5 Leo all month

1941

NOVEMBER

DAY	☉	☽	☿	♀	♂	♃	♄	♅	♆
	° ′	° ′	° ′	° ′	° ′	° ′	° ′	° ′	° ′
1	8♏10	4♈15	27♎59	24♐ 2	11♈40	20♊40	26♉24	29♉ 9	28♍52
2	9 10	16 21	27℞18	25 8	11℞33	20℞35	26℞19	29℞ 7	28 54
3	10 10	28 21	26 48	26 14	11 26	20 31	26 15	29 4	28 56
4	11 10	10♉16	26 29	27 20	11 21	20 26	26 10	29 2	28 57
5	12 10	22 9	26 D21	28 26	11 16	20 21	26 5	29 0	28 59
6	13 11	4♊ 1	26 25	29 32	11 12	20 16	26 1	28 57	29 1
7	14 11	15 53	26 40	0♑37	11 9	20 11	25 56	28 55	29 3
8	15 11	27 48	27 5	1 42	11 6	20 5	25 51	28 52	29 4
9	16 11	9♋47	27 40	2 48	11 5	20 0	25 46	28 50	29 6
10	17 12	21 55	28 23	3 52	11 4	19 54	25 41	28 48	29 8
11	18 12	4♌14	29 13	4 57	11 D 4	19 48	25 37	28 45	29 9
12	19 12	16 49	0♏ 9	6 1	11 5	19 42	25 32	28 43	29 11
13	20 13	29 44	1 12	7 5	11 6	19 36	25 27	28 40	29 12
14	21 13	13♍ 4	2 19	8 9	11 9	19 30	25 22	28 38	29 14
15	22 13	26 51	3 31	9 13	11 12	19 23	25 18	28 35	29 15
16	23 14	11♎ 7	4 46	10 16	11 16	19 17	25 13	28 33	29 17
17	24 14	25 50	6 4	11 19	11 21	19 10	25 8	28 30	29 18
18	25 15	10♏55	7 25	12 21	11 26	19 3	25 3	28 28	29 20
19	26 16	26 14	8 49	13 24	11 33	18 56	24 58	28 25	29 21
20	27 16	11♐34	10 14	14 26	11 40	18 49	24 53	28 23	29 23
21	28 17	26 45	11 41	15 28	11 48	18 42	24 48	28 20	29 24
22	29 17	11♑37	13 9	16 29	11 56	18 35	24 43	28 18	29 25
23	0♐18	26 2	14 38	17 30	12 5	18 28	24 38	28 15	29 27
24	1 19	9♒57	16 8	18 30	12 15	18 20	24 34	28 13	29 28
25	2 19	23 22	17 39	19 31	12 26	18 13	24 29	28 10	29 29
26	3 20	6♓22	19 10	20 31	12 37	18 5	24 24	28 8	29 30
27	4 21	18 59	20 42	21 30	12 49	17 58	24 19	28 5	29 32
28	5 22	1♈18	22 14	22 29	13 1	17 50	24 15	28 3	29 33
29	6 22	13 25	23 47	23 27	13 14	17 42	24 11	28 0	29 34
30	7 23	25 23	25 20	24 25	13 28	17 34	24 6	27 58	29 35

Pluto 5 Leo all month

DECEMBER

DAY	☉	☽	☿	♀	♂	♃	♄	♅	♆
	° ′	° ′	° ′	° ′	° ′	° ′	° ′	° ′	° ′
1	8♐24	7♉16	26♏53	25♑23	13♈42	17♊26	24♉ 1	27♉55	29♍36
2	9 25	19 8	28 26	26 20	13 57	17℞18	23℞56	27℞53	29 37
3	10 26	0♊59	29 59	27 16	14 12	17 10	23 51	27 50	29 38
4	11 27	12 53	1♐33	28 12	14 28	17 2	23 46	27 48	29 39
5	12 27	24 50	3 6	29 7	14 44	16 54	23 41	27 45	29 40
6	13 28	6♋50	4 39	0♒ 2	15 1	16 45	23 37	27 43	29 41
7	14 29	18 57	6 13	0 56	15 19	16 37	23 33	27 41	29 42
8	15 30	1♌10	7 46	1 49	15 37	16 29	23 29	27 38	29 43
9	16 31	13 34	9 20	2 42	15 55	16 21	23 24	27 36	29 44
10	17 32	26 10	10 54	3 34	16 14	16 13	23 20	27 34	29 44
11	18 33	9♍ 2	12 27	4 26	16 33	16 5	23 16	27 31	29 45
12	19 34	22 15	14 1	5 16	16 53	15 57	23 12	27 29	29 46
13	20 35	5♎51	15 35	6 6	17 13	15 49	23 8	27 27	29 47
14	21 36	19 53	17 9	6 55	17 34	15 40	23 4	27 25	29 47
15	22 37	4♏21	18 43	7 43	17 55	15 32	23 0	27 22	29 48
16	23 38	19 12	20 17	8 30	18 17	15 24	22 56	27 20	29 49
17	24 39	4♐20	21 51	9 16	18 39	15 16	22 52	27 18	29 49
18	25 40	19 35	23 25	10 2	19 1	15 8	22 49	27 16	29 50
19	26 41	4♑46	25 0	10 46	19 24	15 0	22 45	27 14	29 50
20	27 43	19 43	26 35	11 29	19 47	14 52	22 41	27 12	29 50
21	28 44	4♒16	28 9	12 11	20 11	14 44	22 38	27 10	29 51
22	29 45	18 21	29 44	12 53	20 34	14 37	22 34	27 8	29 51
23	0♑46	1♓55	1♑20	13 32	20 59	14 29	22 31	27 6	29 51
24	1 47	15 2	2 55	14 11	21 23	14 21	22 28	27 4	29 52
25	2 48	27 43	4 31	14 48	21 48	14 13	22 25	27 2	29 52
26	3 49	10♈ 4	6 7	15 24	22 13	14 6	22 22	27 0	29 52
27	4 51	22 10	7 43	15 59	22 39	13 59	22 19	26 58	29 52
28	5 52	4♉ 6	9 20	16 32	23 4	13 52	22 16	26 57	29 53
29	6 53	15 58	10 56	17 3	23 30	13 45	22 13	26 55	29 53
30	7 54	27 48	12 33	17 33	23 57	13 39	22 11	26 53	29 53
31	8 55	9♊41	14 10	18 1	24 23	13 32	22 8	26 51	29 53

Pluto 5 Leo all month

1942

JANUARY

Day	☉	☽	☿	♀	♂	♃	♄	♅	♆
	° ′	° ′	° ′	° ′	° ′	° ′	° ′	° ′	° ′
1	9♑56	21♊38	15♑48	18♒28	24♈50	13♊25	22♉ 6	26♉50	29♍53
2	10 57	3♋41	17 26	18 53	25 18	13R 19	22R 3	26R 48	29 53
3	11 59	15 52	19 4	19 16	25 45	13 12	22 1	26 47	29R 53
4	13 0	28 10	20 42	19 37	26 13	13 6	21 59	26 45	29 53
5	14 1	10♌38	22 21	19 56	26 40	13 0	21 57	26 44	29 53
6	15 2	23 15	23 59	20 13	27 9	12 54	21 55	26 42	29 53
7	16 3	6♍ 3	25 38	20 28	27 37	12 49	21 53	26 41	29 52
8	17 4	19 4	27 17	20 41	28 6	12 43	21 51	26 39	29 52
9	18 5	2♎20	28 56	20 52	28 34	12 38	21 49	26 38	29 52
10	19 6	15 53	0♒35	21 0	29 3	12 33	21 48	26 37	29 52
11	20 8	29 46	2 14	21 6	29 32	12 28	21 46	26 36	29 51
12	21 9	13♏58	3 53	21 10	0♉ 2	12 23	21 45	26 34	29 51
13	22 10	28 27	5 31	21 11	0 31	12 18	21 44	26 33	29 51
14	23 11	13♐12	7 9	21R 10	1 2	12 14	21 43	26 32	29 50
15	24 12	28 4	8 45	21 6	1 32	12 9	21 42	26 31	29 50
16	25 13	12♑56	10 21	21 0	2 2	12 5	21 41	26 30	29 49
17	26 14	27 39	11 56	20 52	2 32	12 1	21 40	26 29	29 49
18	27 16	12♒ 5	13 28	20 40	3 3	11 57	21 40	26 28	29 48
19	28 17	26 9	14 59	20 27	3 34	11 54	21 39	26 27	29 48
20	29 18	9♓46	16 28	20 11	4 5	11 50	21 39	26 27	29 47
21	0♒19	22 57	17 53	19 52	4 36	11 47	21 38	26 26	29 46
22	1 20	5♈44	19 15	19 31	5 7	11 44	21 38	26 25	29 46
23	2 21	18 11	20 33	19 8	5 38	11 42	21 38	26 25	29 45
24	3 22	0♉21	21 46	18 43	6 10	11 39	21 D38	26 24	29 44
25	4 23	12 20	22 53	18 15	6 41	11 37	21 38	26 23	29 43
26	5 24	24 12	23 54	17 46	7 13	11 34	21 38	26 23	29 43
27	6 25	6♊ 4	24 48	17 14	7 45	11 32	21 39	26 23	29 42
28	7 26	17 58	25 34	16 42	8 17	11 30	21 39	26 22	29 41
29	8 27	29 58	26 11	16 8	8 49	11 29	21 40	26 22	29 40
30	9 28	12♋ 8	26 38	15 32	9 22	11 27	21 40	26 22	29 39
31	10 29	24 28	26 55	14 56	9 54	11 26	21 41	26 21	29 38

Pluto 5 Leo all month

FEBRUARY

Day	☉	☽	☿	♀	♂	♃	♄	♅	♆
	° ′	° ′	° ′	° ′	° ′	° ′	° ′	° ′	° ′
1	11♒30	7♌ 1	27♒ 1	14♒20	10♉27	11♊25	21♉42	26♉21	29♍37
2	12 30	19 47	26R 56	13R 43	11 0	11R 24	21 43	26R 21	29R 36
3	13 31	2♍44	26 40	13 5	11 32	11 24	21 44	26 21	29 35
4	14 32	15 54	26 12	12 28	12 5	11 23	21 46	26 D21	29 34
5	15 33	29 16	25 34	11 52	12 38	11 23	21 47	26 21	29 33
6	16 34	12♎50	24 47	11 16	13 12	11 D23	21 48	26 21	29 32
7	17 34	26 34	23 52	10 41	13 45	11 23	21 50	26 21	29 31
8	18 35	10♏30	22 50	10 7	14 18	11 24	21 51	26 22	29 30
9	19 36	24 36	21 44	9 34	14 52	11 24	21 53	26 22	29 29
10	20 37	8♐51	20 34	9 3	15 25	11 25	21 55	26 22	29 28
11	21 37	23 13	19 23	8 33	15 59	11 26	21 57	26 23	29 27
12	22 38	7♑37	18 13	8 5	16 32	11 27	22 0	26 23	29 25
13	23 39	21 59	17 5	7 39	17 6	11 28	22 2	26 23	29 24
14	24 39	6♒14	16 2	7 16	17 40	11 30	22 4	26 24	29 23
15	25 40	20 18	15 4	6 55	18 14	11 32	22 7	26 25	29 22
16	26 41	4♓ 5	14 12	6 36	18 48	11 34	22 9	26 25	29 20
17	27 41	17 32	13 28	6 19	19 22	11 36	22 12	26 26	29 19
18	28 42	0♈40	12 50	6 5	19 57	11 39	22 15	26 27	29 18
19	29 42	13 27	12 21	5 53	20 31	11 41	22 17	26 27	29 16
20	0♓43	25 55	11 59	5 44	21 5	11 44	22 20	26 28	29 15
21	1 43	8♉ 9	11 45	5 37	21 40	11 47	22 23	26 29	29 13
22	2 44	20 10	11 38	5 33	22 14	11 50	22 26	26 30	29 12
23	3 44	2♊ 5	11 D38	5 31	22 49	11 54	22 30	26 31	29 10
24	4 45	13 58	11 44	5 D32	23 23	11 57	22 33	26 32	29 9
25	5 45	25 53	11 57	5 35	23 58	12 1	22 37	26 33	29 8
26	6 45	7♋54	12 16	5 40	24 33	12 5	22 41	26 34	29 7
27	7 46	20 7	12 40	5 48	25 8	12 9	22 44	26 35	29 5
28	8 46	2♌34	13 9	5 58	25 42	12 14	22 48	26 37	29 4

Pluto 4 Leo all month

1942

MARCH

DAY	☉ ° ′	☽ ° ′	☿ ° ′	♀ ° ′	♂ ° ′	♃ ° ′	♄ ° ′	♅ ° ′	♆ ° ′
1	9♓46	15♌17	13♒43	6♒ 9	26♉17	12♊18	22♉52	26♉38	29♍ 2
2	10 46	28 18	14 21	6 24	26 52	12 23	22 56	26 39	29℞ 0
3	11 46	11♍36	15 3	6 40	27 28	12 28	23 0	26 41	28 59
4	12 46	25 12	15 49	6 58	28 3	12 33	23 4	26 42	28 57
5	13 47	9♎ 1	16 39	7 18	28 38	12 38	23 8	26 44	28 55
6	14 47	23 2	17 32	7 40	29 13	12 43	23 12	26 45	28 53
7	15 47	7♏11	18 28	8 4	29 48	12 49	23 17	26 47	28 52
8	16 47	21 24	19 27	8 30	0♊24	12 54	23 21	26 48	28 50
9	17 47	5♐39	20 28	8 57	0 59	13 0	23 26	26 50	28 48
10	18 47	19 53	21 32	9 26	1 34	13 6	23 31	26 52	28 46
11	19 47	4♑ 2	22 38	9 56	2 10	13 12	23 35	26 53	28 45
12	20 46	18 6	23 47	10 28	2 45	13 19	23 39	26 55	28 43
13	21 46	2♒ 1	24 58	11 1	3 21	13 25	23 45	26 57	28 42
14	22 46	15 47	26 10	11 36	3 56	13 32	23 50	26 59	28 40
15	23 46	29 21	27 25	12 12	4 32	13 38	23 55	27 1	28 39
16	24 46	12♓43	28 41	12 49	5 7	13 45	24 0	27 3	28 37
17	25 45	25 51	29 59	13 28	5 43	13 52	24 5	27 5	28 35
18	26 45	8♈44	1♓19	14 7	6 19	13 59	24 10	27 7	28 33
19	27 45	21 22	2 41	14 48	6 54	14 7	24 16	27 9	28 32
20	28 45	3♉47	4 4	15 30	7 30	14 14	24 21	27 11	28 30
21	29 44	15 58	5 28	16 13	8 6	14 22	24 27	27 13	28 29
22	0♈44	28 0	6 54	16 56	8 42	14 30	24 33	27 16	28 27
23	1 43	9♊55	8 22	17 41	9 17	14 38	24 38	27 18	28 26
24	2 43	21 48	9 51	18 27	9 53	14 46	24 44	27 20	28 24
25	3 42	3♋42	11 21	19 13	10 29	14 54	24 50	27 23	28 22
26	4 42	15 43	12 53	20 1	11 5	15 2	24 56	27 25	28 20
27	5 41	27 54	14 27	20 49	11 41	15 11	25 1	27 27	28 19
28	6 40	10♌22	16 1	21 38	12 17	15 19	25 7	27 30	28 17
29	7 40	23 8	17 37	22 28	12 53	15 28	25 13	27 32	28 16
30	8 39	6♍17	19 15	23 18	13 29	15 37	25 19	27 35	28 14
31	9 38	19 50	20 53	24 9	14 5	15 46	25 25	27 37	28 13

Pluto 3 Leo all month

APRIL

DAY	☉ ° ′	☽ ° ′	☿ ° ′	♀ ° ′	♂ ° ′	♃ ° ′	♄ ° ′	♅ ° ′	♆ ° ′
1	10♈37	3♎45	22♓33	25♒ 1	14♊42	15♊56	25♉32	27♉40	28♍11
2	11 37	17 59	24 15	25 54	15 18	16 5	25 38	27 43	28℞ 9
3	12 36	2♏29	25 58	26 47	15 54	16 14	25 44	27 45	28 7
4	13 35	17 7	27 42	27 40	16 30	16 24	25 51	27 48	28 6
5	14 34	1♐47	29 28	28 35	17 6	16 33	25 57	27 51	28 4
6	15 33	16 22	1♈15	29 30	17 42	16 43	26 4	27 54	28 3
7	16 32	0♑47	3 4	0♓25	18 18	16 53	26 11	27 56	28 1
8	17 31	14 58	4 54	1 21	18 54	17 3	26 17	27 59	28 0
9	18 30	28 53	6 46	2 17	19 31	17 13	26 24	28 2	27 59
10	19 29	12♒33	8 39	3 14	20 7	17 23	26 30	28 5	27 57
11	20 28	25 57	10 34	4 11	20 43	17 33	26 37	28 8	27 55
12	21 27	9♓ 8	12 30	5 9	21 20	17 43	26 44	28 11	27 54
13	22 25	22 6	14 28	6 7	21 56	17 54	26 51	28 14	27 52
14	23 24	4♈52	16 27	7 6	22 33	18 4	26 58	28 17	27 50
15	24 23	17 27	18 27	8 5	23 9	18 15	27 5	28 20	27 49
16	25 22	29 51	20 29	9 4	23 45	18 25	27 12	28 23	27 47
17	26 20	12♉ 6	22 32	10 4	24 22	18 36	27 19	28 26	27 46
18	27 19	24 12	24 36	11 4	24 58	18 47	27 26	28 29	27 45
19	28 18	6♊10	26 41	12 4	25 34	18 58	27 33	28 32	27 44
20	29 16	18 4	28 47	13 5	26 11	19 9	27 40	28 36	27 42
21	0♉15	29 55	0♉54	14 6	26 47	19 21	27 47	28 39	27 41
22	1 14	11♋48	3 2	15 8	27 24	19 32	27 54	28 42	27 39
23	2 12	23 46	5 10	16 9	28 0	19 43	28 1	28 45	27 38
24	3 10	5♌55	7 19	17 11	28 37	19 54	28 8	28 48	27 36
25	4 9	18 19	9 27	18 13	29 13	20 6	28 16	28 51	27 35
26	5 7	1♍ 3	11 35	19 16	29 50	20 17	28 23	28 55	27 34
27	6 6	14 12	13 42	20 18	0♋27	20 29	28 30	28 58	27 33
28	7 4	27 47	15 48	21 21	1 3	20 40	28 38	29 1	27 31
29	8 2	11♎51	17 53	22 24	1 40	20 52	28 45	29 5	27 30
30	9 1	26 20	19 56	23 28	2 17	21 4	28 53	29 8	27 29

Pluto 3 Leo all month

1942

MAY

DAY	☉	☽	☿	♀	♂	♃	♄	♅	♆
	° ′	° ′	° ′	° ′	° ′	° ′	° ′	° ′	° ′
1	9 ♉ 59	11 ♏ 9	21 ♉ 57	24 ♓ 32	2 ♋ 53	21 ♊ 16	29 ♉ 0	29 ♉ 11	27 ♍ 28
2	10 57	26 12	23 56	25 36	3 30	21 28	29 8	29 14	27 ℞ 27
3	11 55	11 ♐ 17	25 53	26 40	4 6	21 40	29 15	29 17	27 26
4	12 53	26 15	27 48	27 44	4 43	21 52	29 23	29 21	27 25
5	13 51	10 ♑ 58	29 39	28 49	5 20	22 4	29 31	29 25	27 24
6	14 50	25 20	1 ♊ 27	29 53	5 56	22 17	29 38	29 28	27 23
7	15 48	9 ♒ 20	3 12	0 ♈ 58	6 33	22 29	29 46	29 32	27 22
8	16 46	22 56	4 54	2 3	7 10	22 42	29 54	29 35	27 21
9	17 44	6 ♓ 11	6 32	3 9	7 47	22 54	0 ♊ 2	29 39	27 20
10	18 42	19 8	8 7	4 14	8 23	23 7	0 9	29 42	27 19
11	19 40	1 ♈ 50	9 38	5 20	9 0	23 19	0 17	29 46	27 18
12	20 38	14 19	11 5	6 26	9 37	23 32	0 24	29 49	27 17
13	21 36	26 38	12 29	7 32	10 14	23 44	0 32	29 53	27 16
14	22 34	8 ♉ 49	13 48	8 38	10 50	23 57	0 39	29 56	27 15
15	23 31	20 53	15 4	9 44	11 27	24 9	0 47	0 ♊ 0	27 14
16	24 29	2 ♊ 52	16 16	10 51	12 4	24 22	0 55	0 3	27 14
17	25 27	14 46	17 24	11 57	12 41	24 35	1 3	0 7	27 13
18	26 25	26 38	18 28	13 4	13 17	24 48	1 10	0 10	27 13
19	27 23	8 ♋ 29	19 27	14 11	13 54	25 1	1 18	0 14	27 12
20	28 21	20 22	20 23	15 18	14 31	25 14	1 26	0 17	27 12
21	29 18	2 ♌ 19	21 14	16 25	15 8	25 27	1 34	0 21	27 11
22	0 ♊ 16	14 27	22 1	17 32	15 44	25 40	1 41	0 24	27 11
23	1 14	26 48	22 43	18 39	16 21	25 53	1 49	0 28	27 10
24	2 11	9 ♍ 28	23 21	19 47	16 58	26 6	1 57	0 31	27 9
25	3 9	22 32	23 54	20 54	17 35	26 19	2 5	0 35	27 9
26	4 7	6 ♎ 3	24 23	22 2	18 12	26 32	2 12	0 38	27 8
27	5 4	20 4	24 47	23 10	18 49	26 46	2 20	0 42	27 8
28	6 2	4 ♏ 34	25 7	24 18	19 26	26 59	2 28	0 45	27 8
29	6 59	19 29	25 22	25 26	20 3	27 12	2 36	0 49	27 8
30	7 57	4 ♐ 41	25 32	26 34	20 39	27 26	2 43	0 52	27 7
31	8 54	20 0	25 37	27 42	21 16	27 39	2 51	0 56	27 7

Pluto 3 Leo all month

JUNE

DAY	☉	☽	☿	♀	♂	♃	♄	♅	♆
	° ′	° ′	° ′	° ′	° ′	° ′	° ′	° ′	° ′
1	9 ♊ 52	5 ♑ 14	25 ♊ 38	28 ♈ 51	21 ♋ 53	27 ♊ 53	2 ♊ 59	0 ♊ 59	27 ♍ 7
2	10 49	20 13	25 ℞ 34	29 59	22 30	28 6	3 7	1 3	27 7
3	11 47	4 ♒ 50	25 26	1 ♉ 7	23 7	28 19	3 14	1 6	27 6
4	12 44	18 59	25 14	2 16	23 44	28 33	3 22	1 10	27 6
5	13 42	2 ♓ 41	24 58	3 25	24 21	28 46	3 30	1 13	27 6
6	14 39	15 57	24 37	4 33	24 58	28 59	3 38	1 17	27 6
7	15 36	28 51	24 14	5 42	25 35	29 13	3 45	1 20	27 6
8	16 34	11 ♈ 26	23 48	6 51	26 12	29 26	3 53	1 24	27 D 6
9	17 31	23 46	23 19	8 0	26 49	29 40	4 1	1 27	27 6
10	18 29	5 ♉ 56	22 48	9 9	27 26	29 54	4 9	1 30	27 6
11	19 26	17 58	22 16	10 18	28 3	0 ♋ 7	4 16	1 34	27 6
12	20 23	29 54	21 43	11 28	28 40	0 21	4 24	1 37	27 6
13	21 21	11 ♊ 48	21 9	12 37	29 17	0 35	4 31	1 40	27 6
14	22 18	23 40	20 36	13 46	29 54	0 48	4 39	1 43	27 6
15	23 15	5 ♋ 31	20 3	14 56	0 ♌ 31	1 2	4 46	1 47	27 6
16	24 13	17 24	19 31	16 5	1 8	1 15	4 54	1 50	27 7
17	25 10	29 20	19 1	17 15	1 45	1 29	5 1	1 53	27 7
18	26 7	11 ♌ 22	18 34	18 25	2 22	1 43	5 9	1 56	27 7
19	27 5	23 33	18 10	19 35	2 59	1 56	5 16	2 0	27 7
20	28 2	5 ♍ 56	17 49	20 44	3 37	2 10	5 24	2 3	27 8
21	28 59	18 36	17 31	21 54	4 14	2 24	5 31	2 6	27 8
22	29 56	1 ♎ 36	17 17	23 4	4 51	2 38	5 38	2 9	27 8
23	0 ♋ 54	15 2	17 7	24 14	5 28	2 51	5 46	2 13	27 9
24	1 51	28 55	17 2	25 24	6 5	3 5	5 53	2 16	27 9
25	2 48	13 ♏ 16	17 D 1	26 34	6 42	3 19	6 0	2 19	27 10
26	3 45	28 2	17 5	27 44	7 19	3 33	6 7	2 22	27 11
27	4 43	13 ♐ 8	17 14	28 55	7 56	3 46	6 15	2 25	27 11
28	5 40	28 24	17 27	0 ♊ 5	8 34	4 0	6 22	2 28	27 12
20	6 37	13 ♑ 40	17 46	1 15	9 11	4 14	6 29	2 31	27 13
30	7 34	28 45	18 9	2 26	9 48	4 28	6 36	2 34	27 14

Pluto 3 Leo all month

1942

JULY

DAY	☉	☽	☿	♀	♂	♃	♄	♅	♆
	° ′	° ′	° ′	° ′	° ′	° ′	° ′	° ′	° ′
1	8♋31	13♒29	18♊37	3♊36	10♌25	4♋41	6♊43	2♊37	27♍14
2	9 29	27 48	19 10	4 47	11 3	4 55	6 50	2 40	27 15
3	10 26	11♓38	19 47	5 57	11 40	5 8	6 57	2 43	27 15
4	11 23	25 0	20 29	7 8	12 17	5 22	7 4	2 46	27 16
5	12 20	7♈57	21 16	8 19	12 54	5 35	7 10	2 49	27 17
6	13 17	20 33	22 8	9 29	13 32	5 49	7 17	2 52	27 18
7	14 15	2♉52	23 4	10 40	14 9	6 3	7 24	2 55	27 19
8	15 12	14 58	24 4	11 51	14 46	6 17	7 31	2 58	27 20
9	16 9	26 56	25 9	13 2	15 23	6 30	7 37	3 1	27 21
10	17 6	8♊50	26 19	14 13	16 1	6 44	7 44	3 3	27 21
11	18 3	20 41	27 32	15 24	16 38	6 57	7 51	3 6	27 22
12	19 1	2♋33	28 50	16 35	17 15	7 11	7 57	3 9	27 23
13	19 58	14 27	0♋13	17 46	17 53	7 24	8 4	3 11	27 24
14	20 55	26 25	1 39	18 58	18 30	7 38	8 10	3 14	27 26
15	21 52	8♌29	3 9	20 9	19 8	7 51	8 16	3 16	27 27
16	22 50	20 41	4 43	21 20	19 45	8 5	8 22	3 19	27 28
17	23 47	3♍ 2	6 21	22 32	20 23	8 18	8 29	3 21	27 29
18	24 44	15 34	8 3	23 43	21 0	8 32	8 35	3 24	27 30
19	25 41	28 22	9 48	24 55	21 38	8 45	8 41	3 27	27 31
20	26 39	11♎26	11 36	26 7	22 15	8 58	8 47	3 29	27 32
21	27 36	24 51	13 28	27 18	22 53	9 12	8 53	3 32	27 34
22	28 33	8♏38	15 22	28 30	23 30	9 25	8 59	3 34	27 35
23	29 31	22 48	17 19	29 42	24 8	9 38	9 5	3 36	27 37
24	0♌28	7♐19	19 18	0♋54	24 45	9 51	9 11	3 38	27 38
25	1 25	22 7	21 19	2 5	25 23	10 5	9 17	3 41	27 40
26	2 22	7♑ 7	23 22	3 17	26 0	10 18	9 22	3 43	27 41
27	3 20	22 8	25 26	4 29	26 38	10 31	9 28	3 45	27 42
28	4 17	7♒ 3	27 31	5 41	27 16	10 44	9 34	3 47	27 43
29	5 14	21 43	29 37	6 53	27 53	10 57	9 39	3 49	27 45
30	6 12	6♓ 1	1♌43	8 5	28 31	11 10	9 45	3 51	27 46
31	7 9	19 55	3 49	9 17	29 9	11 23	9 50	3 53	27 48

Pluto 4 Leo all month

AUGUST

DAY	☉	☽	☿	♀	♂	♃	♄	♅	♆
	° ′	° ′	° ′	° ′	° ′	° ′	° ′	° ′	° ′
1	8♌ 6	3♈22	5♌55	10♋29	29♌47	11♋36	9♊55	3♊55	27♍49
2	9 4	16 24	8 1	11 41	0♍24	11 49	10 1	3 57	27 51
3	10 1	29 4	10 6	12 54	1 2	12 1	10 6	3 58	27 52
4	10 59	11♉26	12 10	14 6	1 40	12 14	10 11	4 0	27 54
5	11 56	23 33	14 13	15 18	2 18	12 27	10 16	4 2	27 56
6	12 54	5♊31	16 15	16 31	2 55	12 40	10 21	4 4	27 57
7	13 51	17 24	18 16	17 43	3 33	12 52	10 26	4 5	27 59
8	14 49	29 15	20 15	18 56	4 11	13 5	10 31	4 7	28 1
9	15 46	11♋ 9	22 13	20 8	4 49	13 17	10 36	4 9	28 3
10	16 44	23 8	24 10	21 21	5 27	13 30	10 40	4 11	28 5
11	17 41	5♌14	26 5	22 33	6 5	13 42	10 45	4 12	28 7
12	18 39	17 29	27 59	23 46	6 43	13 54	10 49	4 14	28 9
13	19 37	29 55	29 51	24 59	7 21	14 6	10 53	4 15	28 11
14	20 34	12♍33	1♍42	26 12	7 59	14 19	10 58	4 17	28 13
15	21 32	25 23	3 32	27 25	8 37	14 31	11 2	4 18	28 14
16	22 30	8♎27	5 20	28 38	9 15	14 43	11 6	4 19	28 16
17	23 27	21 46	7 6	29 51	9 53	14 55	11 10	4 20	28 18
18	24 25	5♏19	8 51	1♌ 4	10 31	15 7	11 14	4 22	28 20
19	25 23	19 8	10 35	2 17	11 9	15 19	11 18	4 23	28 22
20	26 20	3♐12	12 17	3 30	11 47	15 31	11 22	4 24	28 24
21	27 18	17 29	13 58	4 43	12 25	15 43	11 26	4 25	28 26
22	28 16	1♑57	15 37	5 56	13 3	15 55	11 29	4 26	28 27
23	29 14	16 32	17 15	7 10	13 42	16 6	11 33	4 27	28 29
24	0♍12	1♒ 9	18 52	8 23	14 20	16 18	11 36	4 28	28 31
25	1 9	15 41	20 27	9 36	14 58	16 29	11 39	4 29	28 33
26	2 7	0♓ 3	22 1	10 49	15 36	16 41	11 42	4 30	28 35
27	3 5	14 9	23 33	12 3	16 15	16 52	11 45	4 30	28 38
28	4 3	27 56	25 4	13 16	16 53	17 3	11 48	4 31	28 40
29	5 1	11♈21	26 34	14 30	17 31	17 14	11 51	4 32	28 42
30	5 59	24 25	28 3	15 43	18 9	17 25	11 54	4 32	28 44
31	6 57	7♉ 7	29 30	16 57	18 48	17 36	11 57	4 33	28 46

Pluto 5 Leo all month

1942

SEPTEMBER

DAY	☉	☽	☿	♀	♂	♃	♄	♅	♆
	° ′	° ′	° ′	° ′	° ′	° ′	° ′	° ′	° ′
1	7♍55	19♉31	0♎55	18♌11	19♍26	17♋47	12♊ 0	4 ♊33	28♍48
2	8 53	1♊40	2 19	19 24	20 4	17 58	12 2	4 33	28 50
3	9 51	13 40	3 42	20 38	20 43	18 9	12 5	4 34	28 52
4	10 49	25 33	5 3	21 51	21 21	18 19	12 7	4 34	28 54
5	11 48	7♋25	6 23	23 5	22 0	18 30	12 9	4 34	28 56
6	12 46	19 20	7 42	24 19	22 38	18 40	12 11	4 34	28 58
7	13 44	1♌23	8 58	25 33	23 17	18 51	12 13	4 35	29 0
8	14 42	13 36	10 13	26 47	23 55	19 1	12 15	4 35	29 3
9	15 41	26 3	11 26	28 1	24 34	19 11	12 17	4 35	29 5
10	16 39	8♍45	12 38	29 15	25 13	19 21	12 19	4 35	29 7
11	17 37	21 43	13 47	0♍29	25 51	19 31	12 20	4 ℞ 35	29 9
12	18 36	4♎57	14 55	1 43	26 30	19 41	12 22	4 35	29 12
13	19 34	18 25	16 0	2 57	27 9	19 51	12 23	4 35	29 14
14	20 32	2♏ 7	17 3	4 11	27 48	20 1	12 24	4 35	29 16
15	21 31	16 0	18 4	5 25	28 26	20 10	12 26	4 35	29 18
16	22 29	0♐ 1	19 3	6 40	29 5	20 20	12 27	4 34	29 21
17	23 28	14 9	19 59	7 54	29 44	20 29	12 28	4 34	29 23
18	24 26	28 20	20 51	9 8	0♎23	20 38	12 29	4 34	29 25
19	25 25	12♑34	21 41	10 22	1 1	20 47	12 29	4 33	29 27
20	26 24	26 47	22 27	11 37	1 40	20 56	12 30	4 33	29 30
21	27 22	10♒56	23 10	12 51	2 19	21 5	12 30	4 32	29 32
22	28 21	25 1	23 48	14 5	2 58	21 14	12 30	4 32	29 34
23	29 20	8♓57	24 22	15 20	3 37	21 22	12 31	4 31	29 36
24	0♎18	22 41	24 52	16 34	4 16	21 31	12 31	4 31	29 39
25	1 17	6♈11	25 17	17 49	4 55	21 39	12 31	4 30	29 41
26	2 16	19 25	25 37	19 3	5 34	21 47	12 ℞ 31	4 29	29 43
27	3 15	2♉22	25 51	20 18	6 13	21 55	12 31	4 28	29 45
28	4 14	15 1	25 59	21 32	6 53	22 3	12 30	4 27	29 48
29	5 13	27 25	26 ℞ 0	22 47	7 32	22 11	12 30	4 26	29 50
30	6 11	9♊34	25 54	24 2	8 11	22 19	12 30	4 25	29 52

Pluto 6 Leo all month

OCTOBER

DAY	☉	☽	☿	♀	♂	♃	♄	♅	♆
	° ′	° ′	° ′	° ′	° ′	° ′	° ′	° ′	° ′
1	7♎10	21♊33	25♎41	25♍16	8♎50	22♋26	12♊29	4 ♊24	29♍54
2	8 9	3♋26	25 ℞ 20	26 31	9 29	22 34	12 ℞ 29	4 ℞ 23	29 57
3	9 8	15 18	24 52	27 46	10 8	22 41	12 28	4 22	29 59
4	10 8	27 13	24 16	29 1	10 47	22 48	12 27	4 21	0♎ 1
5	11 7	9♌16	23 32	0♎15	11 27	22 55	12 26	4 20	0 3
6	12 6	21 32	22 41	1 30	12 6	23 1	12 25	4 18	0 5
7	13 5	4♍ 6	21 43	2 45	12 46	23 8	12 24	4 17	0 7
8	14 4	17 0	20 40	4 0	13 25	23 14	12 22	4 16	0 9
9	15 4	0♎15	19 32	5 15	14 5	23 21	12 21	4 15	0 11
10	16 3	13 52	18 22	6 30	14 44	23 27	12 19	4 13	0 14
11	17 2	27 47	17 11	7 45	15 24	23 33	12 17	4 12	0 16
12	18 2	11♏58	16 1	9 0	16 3	23 39	12 15	4 11	0 18
13	19 1	26 18	14 53	10 15	16 43	23 45	12 14	4 9	0 20
14	20 0	10♐42	13 50	11 30	17 22	23 50	12 12	4 8	0 23
15	21 0	25 5	12 53	12 45	18 2	23 56	12 10	4 6	0 25
16	21 59	9♑23	12 5	14 0	18 42	24 1	12 8	4 4	0 27
17	22 59	23 33	11 27	15 15	19 21	24 6	12 6	4 3	0 29
18	23 58	7♒33	10 59	16 30	20 1	24 11	12 3	4 1	0 31
19	24 58	21 24	10 42	17 45	20 41	24 16	12 1	3 59	0 33
20	25 58	5♓ 3	10 D36	19 0	21 21	24 20	11 58	3 57	0 35
21	26 57	18 33	10 41	20 15	22 1	24 25	11 56	3 55	0 37
22	27 57	1♈52	10 57	21 30	22 41	24 29	11 53	3 53	0 39
23	28 57	15 0	11 23	22 45	23 21	24 33	11 50	3 51	0 41
24	29 56	27 56	11 59	24 0	24 1	24 37	11 47	3 49	0 43
25	0♏56	10♉39	12 43	25 15	24 41	24 40	11 44	3 47	0 45
26	1 56	23 10	13 36	26 31	25 21	24 44	11 41	3 45	0 47
27	2 56	5♊27	14 35	27 46	26 1	24 47	11 38	3 43	0 49
28	3 56	17 33	15 41	29 1	26 41	24 50	11 35	3 41	0 51
29	4 56	29 30	16 52	0♏16	27 21	24 53	11 31	3 39	0 53
30	5 55	11♋21	18 8	1 32	28 2	24 56	11 28	3 37	0 55
31	6 55	23 11	19 27	2 47	28 42	24 59	11 24	3 35	0 57

Pluto 6 Leo all month

1942

NOVEMBER

DAY	☉ ° ′	☽ ° ′	☿ ° ′	♀ ° ′	♂ ° ′	♃ ° ′	♄ ° ′	♅ ° ′	♆ ° ′
1	7♏55	5♌ 3	20♎50	4♏ 2	29♎22	25♋ 1	11♊20	3♊33	0♎59
2	8 56	17 4	22 16	5 17	0♏ 2	25 3	11℞17	3℞ 31	1 1
3	9 56	29 19	23 44	6 33	0 43	25 5	11 13	3 28	1 2
4	10 56	11♍53	25 14	7 48	1 23	25 7	11 9	3 26	1 4
5	11 56	24 50	26 46	9 3	2 3	25 8	11 5	3 24	1 6
6	12 56	8♎13	28 19	10 18	2 44	25 10	11 1	3 22	1 8
7	13 56	22 4	29 53	11 34	3 24	25 11	10 57	3 19	1 9
8	14 57	4♏19	1♏28	12 49	4 5	25 12	10 53	3 17	1 11
9	15 57	20 54	3 3	14 4	4 45	25 13	10 49	3 15	1 13
10	16 57	5♐42	4 39	15 20	5 26	25 13	10 45	3 12	1 15
11	17 57	20 34	6 15	16 35	6 6	25 14	10 40	3 10	1 16
12	18 58	5♑21	7 52	17 51	6 47	25 14	10 36	3 7	1 18
13	19 58	19 56	9 28	19 6	7 28	25℞14	10 32	3 5	1 20
14	20 59	4♒16	11 5	20 22	8 8	25 14	10 27	3 2	1 21
15	21 59	18 17	12 41	21 37	8 49	25 13	10 23	3 0	1 23
16	22 59	2♓ 0	14 18	22 52	9 30	25 13	10 18	2 57	1 24
17	24 0	15 27	15 54	24 7	10 11	25 12	10 14	2 55	1 26
18	25 0	28 38	17 30	25 23	10 52	25 11	10 9	2 52	1 27
19	26 1	11♈37	19 6	26 38	11 33	25 10	10 5	2 50	1 29
20	27 2	24 24	20 42	27 54	12 14	25 9	10 0	2 48	1 30
21	28 2	7♉ 0	22 18	29 9	12 55	25 7	9 55	2 46	1 32
22	29 3	19 27	23 54	0♐25	13 36	25 5	9 50	2 43	1 33
23	0♐ 3	1♊45	25 29	1 40	14 17	25 3	9 45	2 41	1 35
24	1 4	13 53	27 4	2 55	14 58	25 1	9 40	2 38	1 36
25	2 5	25 53	28 39	4 10	15 39	24 59	9 35	2 36	1 37
26	3 5	7♋47	0♐14	5 26	16 20	24 56	9 30	2 33	1 39
27	4 6	19 36	1 49	6 41	17 2	24 54	9 26	2 31	1 40
28	5 7	1♌24	3 23	7 57	17 43	24 51	9 21	2 28	1 41
29	6 7	13 15	4 58	9 12	18 24	24 48	9 16	2 26	1 42
30	7 8	25 13	6 32	10 28	19 6	24 44	9 11	2 23	1 44

Pluto 7 Leo all month

DECEMBER

DAY	☉ ° ′	☽ ° ′	☿ ° ′	♀ ° ′	♂ ° ′	♃ ° ′	♄ ° ′	♅ ° ′	♆ ° ′
1	8♐ 9	7♍24	8♐ 7	11♐43	19♏47	24♋41	9♊ 6	2♊21	1♎45
2	9 10	19 53	9 41	12 59	20 29	24℞37	9℞ 1	2℞ 18	1 46
3	10 11	2♎46	11 15	14 14	21 10	24 33	8 56	2 16	1 47
4	11 12	16 6	12 49	15 30	21 52	24 29	8 51	2 13	1 48
5	12 12	29 56	14 24	16 45	22 33	24 25	8 46	2 11	1 49
6	13 13	14♏16	15 58	18 0	23 15	24 21	8 41	2 8	1 50
7	14 14	29 2	17 32	19 15	23 56	24 16	8 36	2 6	1 51
8	15 15	14♐ 5	19 6	20 31	24 38	24 11	8 31	2 3	1 52
9	16 16	29 18	20 40	21 46	25 19	24 6	8 27	2 1	1 52
10	17 17	14♑28	22 14	23 2	26 1	24 1	8 22	1 58	1 53
11	18 18	29 25	23 49	24 17	26 43	23 56	8 17	1 56	1 54
12	19 19	14♒ 3	25 23	25 33	27 25	23 50	8 12	1 53	1 55
13	20 20	28 17	26 57	26 48	28 7	23 45	8 8	1 51	1 55
14	21 21	12♓ 7	28 32	28 4	28 49	23 39	8 3	1 48	1 56
15	22 22	25 34	0♑ 7	29 19	29 31	23 33	7 58	1 46	1 57
16	23 23	8♈39	1 41	0♑35	0♐13	23 27	7 53	1 43	1 58
17	24 24	21 27	3 16	1 50	0 55	23 20	7 49	1 41	1 58
18	25 26	4♉ 1	4 50	3 6	1 37	23 14	7 44	1 39	1 59
19	26 27	16 23	6 25	4 21	2 19	23 8	7 40	1 37	2 0
20	27 28	28 36	8 0	5 37	3 1	23 1	7 35	1 34	2 0
21	28 29	10♊41	9 35	6 52	3 43	22 55	7 31	1 32	2 1
22	29 30	22 40	11 10	8 7	4 25	22 48	7 27	1 30	2 1
23	0♑31	4♋34	12 44	9 22	5 7	22 41	7 23	1 28	2 2
24	1 32	16 25	14 19	10 38	5 49	22 34	7 18	1 26	2 2
25	2 33	28 14	15 53	11 53	6 32	22 26	7 14	1 24	2 3
26	3 34	10♌ 3	17 27	13 9	7 14	22 19	7 10	1 22	2 3
27	4 35	21 56	19 1	14 24	7 56	22 12	7 6	1 20	2 3
28	5 36	3♍56	20 34	15 40	8 39	22 4	7 2	1 18	2 3
29	6 38	16 7	22 6	16 56	9 21	21 57	6 58	1 16	2 4
30	7 39	28 33	23 37	18 11	10 4	21 49	6 54	1 14	2 4
31	8 40	11♎21	25 8	19 26	10 46	21 41	6 50	1 12	2 4

Pluto 7 Leo all month

1943

JANUARY

DAY	☉	☽	☿	♀	♂	♃	♄	♅	♆
	° ′	° ′	° ′	° ′	° ′	° ′	° ′	° ′	° ′
1	9♑41	24♎33	26♑37	20♑42	11♐29	21♋34	6♊46	1♊10	2♎ 4
2	10 42	8♏14	28 5	21 57	12 11	21℞26	6℞ 43	1℞ 9	2 4
3	11 43	22 24	29 30	23 12	12 54	21 18	6 39	1 7	2 4
4	12 45	7♐ 1	0♒54	24 27	13 37	21 10	6 36	1 5	2 4
5	13 46	22 2	2 14	25 43	14 19	21 3	6 32	1 3	2℞ 4
6	14 47	7♑16	3 32	26 58	15 2	20 55	6 29	1 2	2 4
7	15 48	22 34	4 45	28 13	15 45	20 47	6 26	1 0	2 4
8	16 49	7♒45	5 54	29 28	16 28	20 39	6 23	0 58	2 4
9	17 50	22 40	6 58	0♒43	17 11	20 31	6 20	0 57	2 4
10	18 52	7♓11	7 56	1 59	17 54	20 22	6 17	0 55	2 4
11	19 53	21 15	8 48	3 14	18 37	20 14	6 14	0 54	2 3
12	20 54	4♈52	9 31	4 29	19 20	20 6	6 11	0 53	2 3
13	21 55	18 3	10 6	5 44	20 3	19 58	6 8	0 51	2 3
14	22 56	0♉52	10 31	7 0	20 46	19 50	6 6	0 50	2 2
15	23 57	13 22	10 46	8 15	21 29	19 42	6 3	0 49	2 2
16	24 58	25 38	10℞50	9 30	22 12	19 34	6 1	0 48	2 2
17	26 0	7♊42	10 43	10 45	22 55	19 26	5 58	0 46	2 1
18	27 1	19 40	10 24	12 1	23 39	19 18	5 56	0 45	2 1
19	28 2	1♋32	9 53	13 16	24 22	19 10	5 54	0 44	2 0
20	29 3	13 22	9 11	14 31	25 5	19 2	5 52	0 43	2 0
21	0♒ 4	25 12	8 18	15 46	25 48	18 54	5 50	0 42	1 59
22	1 5	7♌ 3	7 17	17 2	26 32	18 46	5 49	0 42	1 59
23	2 6	18 58	6 10	18 17	27 15	18 38	5 47	0 41	1 58
24	3 7	0♍59	4 57	19 32	27 58	18 30	5 45	0 40	1 57
25	4 8	13 7	3 41	20 47	28 42	18 43	5 44	0 39	1 57
26	5 9	25 26	2 25	22 2	29 25	18 15	5 42	0 39	1 56
27	6 10	7♎59	1 11	23 17	0♑ 9	18 8	5 41	0 38	1 55
28	7 11	20 48	0 0	24 32	0 52	18 1	5 40	0 37	1 54
29	8 12	3♏58	28♑54	25 47	1 36	17 54	5 39	0 37	1 54
20	9 13	17 30	27 55	27 2	2 19	17 47	5 39	0 36	1 53
31	10 14	1♐26	27 5	28 17	3 3	17 40	5 38	0 36	1 52

Pluto 6 Leo all month

FEBRUARY

DAY	☉	☽	☿	♀	♂	♃	♄	♅	♆
	° ′	° ′	° ′	° ′	° ′	° ′	° ′	° ′	° ′
1	11♒15	15♐46	26♑22	29♒32	3♑47	17♋33	5♊38	0♊35	1♎51
2	12 15	0♑28	25℞48	0♓47	4 30	17℞26	5℞ 37	0℞ 35	1℞50
3	13 16	15 25	25 23	2 2	5 14	17 20	5 36	0 35	1 49
4	14 17	0♒31	25 6	3 17	5 58	17 13	5 36	0 35	1 48
5	15 18	15 37	24 57	4 32	6 42	17 7	5 35	0 34	1 47
6	16 19	0♓32	24 D56	5 47	7 26	17 0	5 D35	0 34	1 46
7	17 20	15 10	25 2	7 1	8 10	16 54	5 35	0 34	1 45
8	18 21	29 25	25 15	8 16	8 54	16 48	5 36	0 D 34	1 44
9	19 21	13♈13	25 35	9 31	9 38	16 42	5 36	0 34	1 43
10	20 22	26 35	26 0	10 46	10 22	16 37	5 36	0 34	1 42
11	21 23	9♉31	26 31	12 0	11 6	16 31	5 37	0 34	1 40
12	22 23	22 5	27 7	13 15	11 50	16 26	5 37	0 35	1 39
13	23 24	4♊22	27 47	14 30	12 34	16 21	5 38	0 35	1 38
14	24 25	16 25	28 31	15 44	13 18	16 16	5 39	0 35	1 37
15	25 25	28 19	29 19	16 59	14 2	16 11	5 40	0 36	1 35
16	26 26	10♋ 8	0♒11	18 13	14 46	16 6	5 41	0 36	1 34
17	27 27	21 57	1 6	19 28	15 31	16 2	5 42	0 36	1 33
18	28 27	3♌48	2 4	20 42	16 14	15 57	5 43	0 37	1 32
19	29 28	15 45	3 4	21 57	16 59	15 53	5 45	0 37	1 30
20	0♓28	27 48	4 8	23 11	17 43	15 49	5 46	0 38	1 29
21	1 28	10♍ 1	5 13	24 25	18 27	15 46	5 48	0 39	1 28
22	2 29	22 25	6 21	25 40	19 12	15 42	5 49	0 39	1 26
23	3 29	5♎ 1	7 31	26 54	19 56	15 39	5 51	0 40	1 25
24	4 30	17 49	8 43	28 8	20 41	15 36	5 53	0 41	1 23
25	5 30	0♏52	9 56	29 22	21 25	15 33	5 55	0 42	1 22
26	6 30	14 10	11 12	0♈37	22 10	15 30	5 57	0 43	1 20
27	7 31	27 43	12 28	1 51	22 54	15 28	6 0	0 44	1 19
28	8 31	11♐33	13 47	3 5	23 39	15 25	6 2	0 45	1 17

Pluto 5 Leo all month

1943

MARCH

DAY	☉	☽	☿	♀	♂	♃	♄	♅	♆
	° ′	° ′	° ′	° ′	° ′	° ′	° ′	° ′	° ′
1	9 ♓ 31	25 ♐ 39	15 ♒ 7	4 ♈ 19	24 ♑ 23	15 ♋ 23	6 ♊ 4	0 ♊ 46	1 ♎ 16
2	10 31	10 ♑ 0	16 29	5 33	25 8	15 ℞ 21	6 7	0 47	1 ℞ 14
3	11 32	24 33	17 51	6 47	25 52	15 19	6 9	0 48	1 13
4	12 32	9 ♒ 13	19 16	8 1	26 37	15 17	6 12	0 49	1 11
5	13 32	23 56	20 41	9 15	27 22	15 16	6 15	0 50	1 10
6	14 32	8 ♓ 35	22 8	10 29	28 6	15 14	6 18	0 52	1 8
7	15 32	23 3	23 36	11 43	28 51	15 13	6 21	0 53	1 7
8	16 32	7 ♈ 14	25 5	12 57	29 36	15 12	6 24	0 55	1 5
9	17 32	21 4	26 35	14 11	0 ♒ 21	15 11	6 27	0 56	1 4
10	18 32	4 ♉ 30	28 7	15 25	1 5	15 11	6 31	0 58	1 2
11	19 32	17 32	29 40	16 38	1 50	15 10	6 34	0 59	1 1
12	20 32	0 ♊ 11	1 ♓ 14	17 52	2 35	15 10	6 38	1 1	0 59
13	21 32	12 31	2 50	19 6	3 20	15 D 10	6 42	1 3	0 57
14	22 32	24 36	4 26	20 19	4 5	15 11	6 45	1 4	0 56
15	23 32	6 ♋ 31	6 4	21 33	4 50	15 11	6 49	1 6	0 54
16	24 31	18 20	7 43	22 46	5 35	15 11	6 53	1 8	0 52
17	25 31	0 ♌ 9	9 23	23 59	6 20	15 12	6 57	1 10	0 50
18	26 31	12 2	11 4	25 13	7 5	45 13	7 1	1 12	0 49
19	27 30	24 4	12 47	26 26	7 50	15 15	7 6	1 14	0 47
20	28 30	6 ♍ 16	14 30	27 39	8 35	15 16	7 10	1 16	0 45
21	29 30	18 43	16 15	28 52	9 20	15 18	7 14	1 18	0 43
22	0 ♈ 29	1 ♎ 25	18 1	0 ♉ 5	10 5	15 20	7 19	1 20	0 42
23	1 29	14 22	19 49	1 18	10 50	15 22	7 23	1 22	0 40
24	2 28	27 34	21 38	2 31	11 35	15 24	7 28	1 24	0 39
25	3 28	11 ♏ 0	23 28	3 44	12 20	15 26	7 33	1 26	0 37
26	4 27	24 37	25 19	4 57	13 5	15 29	7 37	1 28	0 36
27	5 26	8 ♐ 25	27 12	6 9	13 51	15 31	7 42	1 31	0 34
28	6 26	22 21	29 6	7 22	14 36	15 34	7 47	1 33	0 32
29	7 25	6 ♑ 24	1 ♈ 1	8 35	15 21	15 37	7 52	1 35	0 30
30	8 24	20 33	2 57	9 47	16 6	15 41	7 57	1 38	0 29
31	9 24	4 ♒ 46	4 55	11 0	16 51	15 44	8 2	1 40	0 27

Pluto 5 Leo all month

APRIL

DAY	☉	☽	☿	♀	♂	♃	♄	♅	♆
	° ′	° ′	° ′	° ′	° ′	° ′	° ′	° ′	° ′
1	10 ♈ 23	19 ♒ 2	6 ♈ 54	12 ♉ 12	17 ♒ 36	15 ♋ 48	8 ♊ 7	1 ♊ 43	0 ♎ 25
2	11 22	3 ♓ 18	8 54	13 25	18 21	15 52	8 12	1 45	0 ℞ 23
3	12 21	17 30	10 56	14 37	19 6	15 56	8 18	1 48	0 22
4	13 21	1 ♈ 35	12 58	15 50	19 52	16 0	8 23	1 50	0 20
5	14 20	15 28	15 1	17 2	20 37	16 4	8 29	1 53	0 19
6	15 19	29 6	17 5	18 14	21 22	16 9	8 35	1 56	0 17
7	16 18	12 ♉ 24	19 10	19 26	22 7	16 13	8 41	1 58	0 16
8	17 17	25 23	21 15	20 38	22 53	16 18	8 47	2 1	0 14
9	18 16	8 ♊ 2	23 20	21 50	23 38	16 23	8 53	2 4	0 13
10	19 15	20 23	25 25	23 2	24 23	16 28	8 59	2 7	0 12
11	20 14	2 ♋ 29	27 30	24 13	25 8	16 34	9 5	2 9	0 10
12	21 12	14 24	29 35	25 25	25 54	16 39	9 10	2 12	0 9
13	22 11	26 14	1 ♉ 38	26 37	26 39	16 45	9 16	2 15	0 8
14	23 10	8 ♌ 3	3 40	27 48	27 24	16 51	9 22	2 18	0 7
15	24 9	19 58	5 40	29 0	28 9	16 57	9 28	2 21	0 5
16	25 8	2 ♍ 2	7 39	0 ♊ 11	28 55	17 3	9 35	2 24	0 4
17	26 6	14 21	9 35	1 22	29 40	17 9	9 41	2 27	0 2
18	27 5	26 58	11 28	2 34	0 ♓ 25	17 16	9 47	2 30	0 1
19	28 4	9 ♎ 55	13 19	3 45	1 10	17 22	9 54	2 33	29 ♍ 59
20	29 2	23 12	5 7	4 56	1 56	17 29	10 0	2 36	29 58
21	0 ♉ 1	6 ♏ 48	16 51	6 7	2 41	17 36	10 7	2 39	29 57
22	0 59	20 40	18 31	7 18	3 26	17 43	10 14	2 42	29 56
23	1 58	4 ♐ 45	20 7	8 28	4 12	17 50	10 20	2 45	29 54
24	2 56	18 56	21 40	9 39	4 57	17 57	10 27	2 48	29 53
25	3 55	3 ♑ 10	23 8	10 50	5 43	18 4	10 34	2 51	29 52
26	4 53	17 23	24 31	12 0	6 28	18 12	10 41	2 54	29 51
27	5 51	1 ♒ 34	25 50	13 11	7 14	18 19	10 48	2 57	29 49
28	6 50	15 39	27 5	14 21	7 59	18 27	10 55	3 1	29 48
29	7 48	29 39	28 15	15 31	8 44	18 35	11 2	3 4	29 47
30	8 46	13 ♓ 33	29 20	16 41	9 29	18 43	11 9	3 7	29 46

Pluto 4 Leo all month

1943

MAY

D A Y	☉	☽	☿	♀	♂	♃	♄	♅	♆
	° '	° '	° '	° '	° '	° '	° '	° '	° '
1	9 ♉45	27 ♓21	0 ♊20	17 ♊51	10 ♓14	18 ♋51	11 ♊16	3 ♊10	29 ♍44
2	10 43	10 ♈59	1 15	19 1	10 59	19 0	11 23	3 14	29 R 43
3	11 41	24 28	2 5	20 11	11 44	19 8	11 30	3 17	29 42
4	12 39	7 ♉45	2 50	21 21	12 29	19 17	11 37	3 20	29 41
5	13 37	20 47	3 30	22 30	13 15	19 25	11 44	3 24	29 39
6	14 36	3 ♊34	4 5	23 40	14 0	19 34	11 52	3 27	29 38
7	15 34	16 4	4 34	24 49	14 45	19 43	11 59	3 31	29 37
8	16 32	28 21	4 58	25 59	15 30	19 52	12 6	3 34	29 36
9	17 30	10 ♋24	5 17	27 8	16 15	20 1	12 13	3 38	29 35
10	18 28	22 18	5 31	28 17	17 0	20 11	12 21	3 41	29 34
11	19 26	4 ♌6	5 40	29 26	17 45	20 20	12 28	3 44	29 33
12	20 24	15 55	5 43	0 ♋34	18 30	20 29	12 35	3 47	29 32
13	21 22	27 49	5 R 42	1 43	19 15	20 39	12 43	3 51	29 31
14	22 20	9 ♍54	5 36	2 51	20 0	20 48	12 50	3 54	29 30
15	23 17	22 15	5 25	4 0	20 45	20 58	12 58	3 58	29 29
16	24 15	4 ♎56	5 10	5 8	21 30	21 8	13 5	4 1	29 28
17	25 13	18 1	4 51	6 16	22 15	21 18	13 13	4 5	29 27
18	26 11	1 ♏31	4 28	7 24	23 0	21 28	13 20	4 8	29 26
19	27 9	15 26	4 2	8 32	23 45	21 38	13 28	4 12	29 25
20	28 6	29 40	3 33	9 40	24 30	21 48	13 35	4 15	29 24
21	29 4	14 ♐10	3 2	10 47	25 15	21 59	13 43	4 19	29 23
22	0 ♊2	28 47	2 30	11 55	25 59	22 9	13 50	4 22	29 23
23	0 59	13 ♑25	1 56	13 2	26 44	22 20	13 58	4 26	29 22
24	1 57	27 58	1 21	14 9	27 29	22 30	14 6	4 29	29 21
25	2 55	12 ♒20	0 47	15 16	28 14	22 41	14 13	4 33	29 21
26	3 52	26 31	0 14	16 22	28 58	22 51	14 21	4 36	29 20
27	4 50	10 ♓28	29 ♉42	17 29	29 43	23 2	14 29	4 40	29 20
28	5 48	24 12	29 11	18 35	0 ♈28	23 13	14 37	4 43	29 20
29	6 45	7 ♈42	28 43	19 41	1 12	23 24	14 44	4 47	29 19
30	7 43	21 1	28 17	20 47	1 57	23 35	14 52	4 50	29 19
31	8 40	4 ♉7	27 55	21 53	2 41	23 46	15 0	4 54	29 19

JUNE

D A Y	☉	☽	☿	♀	♂	♃	♄	♅	♆
	° '	° '	° '	° '	° '	° '	° '	° '	° '
1	9 ♊38	17 ♉2	27 ♉36	22 ♋59	3 ♈25	23 ♋57	15 ♊8	4 ♊57	29 ♍19
2	10 35	29 44	27 R 21	24 4	4 10	24 9	15 15	5 1	29 R 18
3	11 33	12 ♊15	27 10	25 9	4 54	24 20	15 23	5 4	29 18
4	12 30	24 33	27 3	26 14	5 38	24 32	15 31	5 8	29 17
5	13 28	6 ♋40	27 D 1	27 19	6 22	24 43	15 39	5 11	29 17
6	14 25	18 37	27 3	28 23	7 7	24 55	15 47	5 15	29 17
7	15 23	0 ♌28	27 9	29 27	7 51	25 6	15 55	5 18	29 17
8	16 20	12 15	27 20	0 ♌31	8 35	25 18	16 3	5 22	29 17
9	17 17	24 3	27 36	1 35	9 19	25 30	16 11	5 25	29 17
10	18 15	5 ♍56	27 56	2 39	10 3	25 41	16 19	5 29	29 17
11	19 12	18 0	28 20	3 42	10 46	25 53	16 26	5 32	29 D 17
12	20 10	0 ♎20	28 49	4 45	11° 30	26 5	16 34	5 36	29 17
13	21 7	13 0	29 22	5 48	12 14	26 17	16 42	5 39	29 17
14	22 4	26 6	29 59	6 50	12 57	26 29	16 50	5 43	29 17
15	23 2	9 ♏39	0 ♊40	7 52	13 41	26 42	16 57	5 46	29 17
16	23 59	23 40	1 25	8 54	14 24	26 54	17 5	5 49	29 17
17	24 56	8 ♐6	2 15	9 56	15 8	27 6	17 13	5 52	29 17
18	25 53	22 51	3 8	10 57	15 51	27 18	17 21	5 56	29 17
19	26 51	7 ♑48	4 5	11 58	16 35	27 31	17 28	5 59	29 17
20	27 48	22 48	5 6	12 59	17 18	27 43	17 36	6 3	29 18
21	28 45	7 ♒42	6 11	13 59	18 1	27 55	17 44	6 6	29 18
22	29 42	22 24	7 20	14 59	18 44	28 8	17 52	6 10	29 19
23	0 ♋40	6 ♓48	8 32	15 59	19 27	28 20	17 59	6 13	29 19
24	1 37	20 53	9 47	16 58	20 10	28 33	18 7	6 16	29 19
25	2 34	4 ♈37	11 6	17 57	20 53	28 45	18 15	6 19	29 20
26	3 31	18 2	12 29	18 55	21 35	28 58	18 22	6 23	29 20
27	4 28	1 ♉9	13 55	19 53	22 18	29 10	18 30	6 26	29 21
28	5 26	14 1	15 24	20 51	23 0	29 23	18 37	6 29	29 21
29	6 23	26 39	16 57	21 48	23 43	29 36	18 45	6 32	29 22
30	7 20	9 ♊4	18 33	22 44	24 25	29 48	18 52	6 35	29 22

1943

JULY

DAY	☉	☽	☿	♀	♂	♃	♄	♅	♆
	° ′	° ′	° ′	° ′	° ′	° ′	° ′	° ′	° ′
1	8♋17	21♊19	20♊13	23♌41	25♈ 7	0♌ 1	19♊ 0	6♊38	29♍23
2	9 15	3♋24	21 55	24 37	25 50	0 14	19 7	6 41	29 24
3	10 12	15 21	23 41	25 32	26 32	0 27	19 15	6 44	29 25
4	11 9	27 13	25 30	26 27	27 14	0 40	19 22	6 47	29 25
5	12 6	9♌ 0	27 22	27 21	27 56	0 53	19 30	6 51	29 26
6	13 4	20 47	29 16	28 14	28 38	1 6	19 37	6 54	29 27
7	14 1	2♍35	1♋13	29 8	29 20	1 19	19 44	6 57	29 28
8	14 58	14 29	3 12	0♍ 0	0♉ 1	1 32	19 52	7 0	29 28
9	15 55	26 34	5 14	0 52	0 43	1 45	19 59	7 2	29 29
10	16 52	8♎53	7 17	1 43	1 24	1 58	20 6	7 5	29 30
11	17 50	21 32	9 22	2 34	2 6	2 11	20 13	7 8	29 31
12	18 47	4♏34	11 28	3 24	2 47	2 24	20 21	7 11	29 32
13	19 44	18 3	13 36	4 13	3 28	2 37	20 28	7 14	29 33
14	20 41	2♐ 0	15 44	5 1	4 9	2 50	20 35	7 17	29 34
15	21 38	16 23	17 53	5 49	4 50	3 3	20 42	7 20	29 35
16	22 36	1♑10	20 2	6 36	5 31	3 16	20 49	7 22	29 36
17	23 33	16 14	22 11	7 22	6 11	3 30	20 56	7 25	29 37
18	24 30	1♒25	24 20	8 7	6 52	3 43	21 3	7 27	29 38
19	25 27	16 34	26 28	8 51	7 32	3 56	21 10	7 30	29 39
20	26 25	1♓33	28 35	9 35	8 13	4 9	21 17	7 32	29 40
21	27 22	16 13	0♌41	10 17	8 53	4 23	21 24	7 35	29 42
22	28 19	0♈31	2 46	10 59	9 33	4 36	21 31	7 38	29 43
23	29 16	14 23	4 50	11 39	10 13	4 49	21 38	7 40	29 44
24	0♌14	27 52	6 52	12 18	10 52	5 2	21 44	7 43	29 45
25	1 11	10♉57	8 53	12 57	11 32	5 16	21 51	7 45	29 47
26	2 8	23 42	10 52	13 34	12 12	5 29	21 57	7 47	29 48
27	3 6	6♊10	12 50	14 10	12 51	5 42	22 4	7 49	29 49
28	4 3	18 25	14 46	14 44	13 30	5 55	22 10	7 52	29 51
29	5 0	0♋28	16 40	15 17	14 9	6 9	22 17	7 54	29 52
30	5 58	12 24	18 33	15 49	14 48	6 22	22 23	7 57	29 54
31	6 55	24 14	20 24	16 20	15 27	6 35	22 29	7 59	29 55

Pluto 5 Leo all month

AUGUST

DAY	☉	☽	☿	♀	♂	♃	♄	♅	♆
	° ′	° ′	° ′	° ′	° ′	° ′	° ′	° ′	° ′
1	7♌53	6♌ 2	22♌14	16♍49	16♉ 5	6♌48	22♊36	8♊ 1	29♍57
2	8 50	17 49	24 2	17 17	16 43	7 2	22 42	8 3	29 58
3	9 47	29 38	25 48	17 43	17 22	7 15	22 48	8 5	0♎ 0
4	10 45	11♍31	27 32	18 7	18 0	7 28	22 54	8 7	0 2
5	11 42	23 30	29 15	18 30	18 38	7 41	23 0	8 9	0 3
6	12 40	5♎40	0♍57	18 51	19 15	7 55	23 6	8 11	0 5
7	13 37	18 3	2 36	19 10	19 53	8 8	23 12	8 13	0 7
8	14 35	0♏43	4 14	19 28	20 30	8 21	23 18	8 15	0 9
9	15 32	13 42	5 51	19 43	21 7	8 34	23 24	8 17	0 10
10	16 30	27 5	7 26	19 57	21 44	8 48	23 29	8 18	0 12
11	17 27	10♐52	8 59	20 8	22 21	9 1	23 35	8 20	0 14
12	18 25	25 5	10 31	20 18	22 58	9 14	23 41	8 22	0 16
13	19 23	9♑40	12 1	20 25	23 34	9 27	23 47	8 24	0 17
14	20 20	24 36	13 29	20 30	24 10	9 41	23 52	8 25	0 19
15	21 18	9♒43	14 56	20 33	24 46	9 54	23 58	8 27	0 21
16	22 15	24 53	15 21	20℞33	25 22	10 7	24 3	8 28	0 23
17	23 13	9♓58	17 45	20 31	25 58	10 20	24 8	8 30	0 24
18	24 11	24 48	19 7	20 27	26 33	10 33	24 13	8 31	0 26
19	25 8	9♈17	20 27	20 21	27 8	10 46	24 18	8 32	0 28
20	26 6	23 20	21 45	20 12	27 43	10 59	24 23	8 33	0 30
21	27 4	6♉56	23 1	20 0	28 17	11 12	24 28	8 35	0 32
22	28 2	20 6	24 16	19 46	28 52	11 25	24 33	8 36	0 34
23	28 59	2♊51	25 29	19 30	29 26	11 38	24 38	8 38	0 36
24	29 57	15 17	26 39	19 12	0♊ 0	11 51	24 42	8 39	0 38
25	0♍55	27 26	27 48	18 51	0 34	12 4	24 47	8 40	0 40
26	1 53	9♋24	28 54	18 29	1 7	12 17	24 51	8 41	0 42
27	2 51	21 15	29 58	18 4	1 40	12 30	24 56	8 42	0 44
28	3 49	3♌ 2	1♎ 0	17 37	2 13	12 43	25 0	8 43	0 46
29	4 47	14 49	1 59	17 8	2 46	12 56	25 5	8 44	0 48
30	5 45	26 39	2 55	16 37	3 18	13 8	25 9	8 44	0 50
31	6 43	8♍33	3 49	16 5	3 50	13 21	25 13	8 45	0 52

Pluto 6 Leo all month

1943

SEPTEMBER

DAY	☉	☽	☿	♀	♂	♃	♄	♅	♆
	° ′	° ′	° ′	° ′	° ′	° ′	° ′	° ′	° ′
1	7♍41	20♍35	4♎40	15♍32	4♊22	13♌34	25♊17	8♊46	0♎54
2	8 39	2♎47	5 27	14℞58	4 54	13 46	25 21	8 47	0 56
3	9 37	15 8	6 11	14 22	5 25	13 59	25 25	8 47	0 59
4	10 35	27 42	6 51	13 46	5 56	14 11	25 29	8 48	1 1
5	11 33	10♏30	7 28	13 9	6 26	14 24	25 33	8 49	1 3
6	12 32	23 34	8 0	12 33	6 56	14 36	25 36	8 49	1 5
7	13 30	6♐55	8 28	11 55	7 26	14 49	25 40	8 50	1 7
8	14 28	20 35	8 51	11 18	7 56	15 1	25 43	8 50	1 9
9	15 26	4♑34	9 9	10 42	8 25	15 13	25 46	8 50	1 11
10	16 25	18 53	9 21	10 6	8 54	15 26	25 50	8 51	1 13
11	17 23	3♒30	9 28	9 31	9 23	15 38	25 53	8 51	1 16
12	18 21	18 19	9℞29	8 58	9 51	15 50	25 56	8 51	1 18
13	19 20	3♓16	9 24	8 25	10 19	16 2	25 59	8 51	1 20
14	20 18	18 12	9 12	7 54	10 46	16 14	26 2	8℞51	1 22
15	21 17	2♈59	8 53	7 24	11 13	16 26	26 4	8 51	1 24
16	22 15	17 29	8 27	6 56	11 40	16 38	26 7	8 51	1 26
17	23 13	1♉36	7 55	6 31	12 6	16 50	26 9	8 51	1 28
18	24 12	15 18	7 16	6 7	12 32	17 2	26 12	8 51	1 30
19	25 11	28 32	6 30	5 46	12 58	17 13	26 14	8 50	1 33
20	26 9	11♊21	6 39	5 27	13 23	17 25	26 16	8 50	1 35
21	27 8	23 48	4 42	5 10	13 48	17 37	26 18	8 50	1 37
22	28 6	5♋58	3 41	4 56	14 12	17 48	26 20	8 50	1 39
23	29 5	17 54	2 37	4 44	14 35	18 0	26 22	8 49	1 42
24	0♎ 4	29 43	1 32	4 34	14 59	18 11	26 24	8 49	1 44
25	1 3	11♌30	0 27	4 27	15 22	18 22	26 26	8 49	1 46
26	2 2	23 19	29♍23	4 23	15 44	18 33	26 27	8 48	1 48
27	3 0	5♍13	28 22	4 21	16 6	18 44	26 29	8 48	1 51
28	3 59	17 17	27 26	4 D21	16 27	18 55	26 30	8 47	1 53
29	4 58	29 31	26 36	4 24	16 48	19 6	26 31	8 46	1 55
30	5 57	11♎58	25 54	4 29	17 8	19 17	26 32	8 45	1 57

Pluto 7 Leo all month

OCTOBER

DAY	☉	☽	☿	♀	♂	♃	♄	♅	♆
	° ′	° ′	° ′	° ′	° ′	° ′	° ′	° ′	° ′
1	6♎56	24♎37	25♍21	4♍36	17♊28	19♌28	26♊33	2♎ 0	8♊44
2	7 55	7♏30	24℞57	4 45	17 47	19 39	26 34	2 2	8℞43
3	8 54	20 35	24 44	4 57	18 6	19 50	26 35	2 4	8 42
4	9 53	3♐52	24 D41	5 10	18 24	20 0	26 36	2 6	8 41
5	10 52	17 21	24 49	5 26	18 41	20 11	26 36	2 9	8 41
6	11 52	1♑ 3	25 7	5 44	18 58	20 21	26 37	2 11	8 40
7	12 51	14 56	25 35	6 4	19 14	20 31	26 37	2 13	8 39
8	13 50	29 1	26 12	6 25	19 29	20 42	26 37	2 15	8 38
9	14 49	13♒18	26 58	6 48	19 44	20 52	26 38	2 18	8 36
10	15 48	27 44	27 53	7 14	19 58	21 2	26℞38	2 20	8 35
11	16 48	12♓17	28 54	7 40	20 11	21 12	26 37	2 22	8 34
12	17 47	26 51	0♎ 1	8 8	20 24	21 22	26 37	2 24	8 33
13	18 46	11♈20	1 15	8 38	20 36	21 31	26 37	2 26	8 31
14	19 46	25 38	2 34	9 10	20 48	21 41	26 37	2 28	8 30
15	20 45	9♉38	3 57	9 43	20 59	21 51	26 36	2 30	8 29
16	21 45	23 16	5 25	10 17	21 9	22 0	26 36	2 32	8 27
17	22 44	6♊30	6 55	10 53	21 19	22 10	26 35	2 35	8 26
18	23 44	19 21	8 28	11 30	21 28	22 19	26 34	2 37	8 24
19	24 43	1♋49	10 2	12 8	21 36	22 28	26 33	2 39	8 22
20	25 43	14 0	11 39	12 48	21 43	22 37	26 32	2 41	8 21
21	26 43	25 57	13 17	13 28	21 50	22 46	26 30	2 43	8 19
22	27 42	7♌46	14 56	14 10	21 56	22 55	26 29	2 45	8 17
23	28 42	19 34	16 36	14 53	22 1	23 3	26 28	2 47	8 15
24	29 42	1♍24	18 16	15 37	22 5	23 12	26 26	2 49	8 14
25	0♏41	13 23	19 57	16 22	22 9	23 20	26 25	2 51	8 12
26	1 41	25 34	21 38	17 8	22 12	23 28	26 23	2 53	8 10
27	2 41	7♎59	23 19	17 55	22 13	23 36	26 21	2 55	8 8
28	3 41	20 43	25 0	18 43	22 14	23 44	26 19	2 57	8 6
29	4 41	3♏41	26 41	19 32	22 14	23 52	26 17	2 59	8 4
30	5 41	16 57	28 22	20 21	22℞13	24 0	26 15	3 1	8 2
31	6 41	0♐26	0♏ 2	21 11	22 11	24 8	26 13	3 3	8 0

Pluto 8 Leo all month

1943

NOVEMBER

DAY	☉ ° ′	☽ ° ′	☿ ° ′	♀ ° ′	♂ ° ′	♃ ° ′	♄ ° ′	♅ ° ′	♆ ° ′
1	7♏41	14♐ 6	1♏42	22♍ 3	22♊ 8	24♌15	26♊10	7♊58	3♎ 5
2	8 41	27 55	3 21	22 55	22℞ 4	24 23	26℞ 7	7℞56	3 7
3	9 41	11♑50	5 1	23 47	21 59	24 30	26 5	7 54	3 9
4	10 41	25 49	6 40	24 40	21 54	24 37	26 2	7 52	3 11
5	11 41	9♒52	8 18	25 34	21 47	24 44	26 0	7 50	3 13
6	12 42	23 58	9 56	26 29	21 40	24 50	25 57	7 47	3 14
7	13 42	8♓ 6	11 34	27 24	21 32	24 57	25 54	7 45	3 16
8	14 42	22 15	13 11	28 20	21 23	25 3	25 51	7 43	3 18
9	15 42	6♈22	14 48	29 16	21 13	25 10	25 48	7 41	3 20
10	16 42	20 24	16 25	0♎13	21 2	25 16	25 45	7 38	3 21
11	17 43	4♉18	18 1	1 11	20 51	25 22	25 42	7 36	3 23
12	18 43	17 58	19 37	2 9	20 38	25 28	25 39	7 34	3 25
13	19 43	1♊22	21 13	3 7	20 25	25 34	25 35	7 31	3 27
14	20 44	14 27	22 48	4 6	20 11	25 39	25 32	7 29	3 28
15	21 44	27 11	24 23	5 6	19 56	25 45	25 28	7 26	3 30
16	22 45	9♋37	25 58	6 6	19 40	25 50	25 24	7 24	3 32
17	23 45	21 47	27 32	7 6	19 23	25 55	25 20	7 21	3 33
18	24 46	3♌44	29 7	8 7	19 6	26 0	25 16	7 19	3 35
19	25 46	15 34	0♐41	9 9	18 48	26 5	25 12	7 17	3 36
20	26 47	27 22	2 14	10 10	18 29	26 9	25 8	7 14	3 38
21	27 47	9♍13	3 48	11 13	18 10	26 14	25 4	7 12	3 39
22	28 48	21 12	5 21	12 15	17 50	26 18	25 0	7 9	3 41
23	29 48	3♎26	7 4	13 18	17 30	26 22	24 56	7 7	3 42
24	0♐49	15 58	8 27	14 21	17 9	26 26	24 52	7 4	3 44
25	1 50	28 50	10 0	15 25	16 48	26 29	24 48	7 2	3 45
26	2 51	12♏ 4	11 33	16 29	16 27	26 33	24 43	6 59	3 47
27	3 51	25 39	13 6	17 33	16 5	26 36	24 39	6 57	3 48
28	4 52	9♐32	14 38	18 38	15 43	26 39	24 35	6 55	3 49
29	5 53	23 39	16 11	19 43	15 20	26 42	24 30	6 52	3 51
30	6 54	7♑55	17 43	20 48	14 58	26 45	24 26	6 50	3 52

Pluto 8 Leo all month

DECEMBER

DAY	☉ ° ′	☽ ° ′	☿ ° ′	♀ ° ′	♂ ° ′	♃ ° ′	♄ ° ′	♅ ° ′	♆ ° ′
1	7♐54	22♑14	21♎53	19♐15	14♊35	26♌48	24♊21	6♊47	3♎53
2	8 55	6♒33	22 59	20 47	14℞12	26 50	24℞16	6℞45	3 54
3	9 56	20 48	24 5	22 18	13 49	26 52	24 12	6 42	3 55
4	10 57	4♓57	25 11	23 50	13 26	26 54	24 7	6 40	3 56
5	11 58	18 59	26 17	25 21	13 3	26 56	24 2	6 37	3 57
6	12 59	2♈53	27 24	26 52	12 40	26 57	23 57	6 35	3 58
7	14 0	16 40	28 31	28 23	12 18	26 59	23 53	6 32	3 59
8	15 1	0♉17	29 38	29 53	11 55	27 0	23 48	6 30	4 0
9	16 2	13 44	0♏46	1♑23	11 33	27 1	23 43	6 27	4 1
10	17 3	26 58	1 53	2 53	11 11	27 2	23 38	6 25	4 2
11	18 3	10♊ 0	3 1	4 22	10 50	27 3	23 33	6 22	4 3
12	19 4	22 47	4 9	5 50	10 28	27 3	23 28	6 20	4 4
13	20 5	5♋19	5 17	7 17	10 7	27 4	23 23	6 17	4 5
14	21 6	17 37	6 26	8 44	9 46	27 4	23 18	6 15	4 6
15	22 7	29 42	7 34	10 9	9 26	27℞ 4	23 13	6 12	4 7
16	23 8	11♌37	8 43	11 33	9 7	27 3	23 8	6 10	4 7
17	24 10	23 26	9 52	12 55	8 48	27 3	23 3	6 7	4 8
18	25 11	5♍13	11 1	14 15	8 29	27 2	22 58	6 5	4 9
19	26 12	17 3	12 10	15 33	8 11	27 1	22 53	6 2	4 9
20	27 13	29 2	13 20	16 49	7 54	27 0	22 49	6 0	4 10
21	28 14	11♎14	14 29	18 1	7 37	26 59	22 44	5 58	4 10
22	29 15	23 44	15 39	19 10	7 21	26 57	22 39	5 56	4 10
23	0♑16	6♏37	16 49	20 15	7 6	26 55	22 34	5 53	4 11
24	1 17	19 54	17 59	21 15	6 51	26 53	22 29	5 51	4 11
25	2 18	3♐37	19 9	22 9	6 38	26 51	22 24	5 49	4 12
26	3 20	17 44	20 19	22 57	6 25	26 49	22 19	5 47	4 12
27	4 21	2♑11	21 30	23 38	6 13	26 46	22 15	5 44	4 13
28	5 22	16 51	22 40	24 11	6 2	26 44	22 10	5 42	4 13
29	6 23	1♒38	23 51	24 34	5 52	26 41	22 5	5 40	4 14
30	7 24	16 24	25 2	24 47	5 43	26 38	22 0	5 38	4 14
31	8 25	1♓ 3	26 12	24℞50	5 34	26 35	21 56	5 36	4 14

Pluto 8 Leo all month

1944

JANUARY

Day	☉	☽	☿	♀	♂	♃	♄	♅	♆
1	9♐27	15✻29	24Ⅱ42	27♏23	5Ⅱ26	26♌31	21Ⅱ52	5Ⅱ34	4♎15
2	10 28	29 40	24B22	28 34	5B20	26B28	21B47	5B32	4 15
3	11 29	13♈35	23 50	29 46	5 14	26 24	21 42	5 30	4 15
4	12 30	27 13	23 6	0♐57	5 8	26 20	21 38	5 28	4 15
5	13 31	10♉34	22 11	2 8	5 3	26 16	21 33	5 27	4 15
6	14 32	23 41	21 7	3 20	4 59	26 12	21 29	5 25	4 15
7	15 33	6Ⅱ33	19 56	4 31	4 57	26 7	21 25	5 23	4B15
8	16 35	19 12	18 39	5 43	4 54	26 3	21 20	5 21	4 15
9	17 36	1♋39	17 20	6 55	4 53	25 58	21 16	5 20	4 15
10	18 37	13 55	16 0	8 6	4 52	25 53	21 12	5 18	4 15
11	19 38	26 1	14 43	9 18	4 D52	25 48	21 8	5 16	4 15
12	20 39	7♌59	13 29	10 30	4 53	25 43	21 4	5 15	4 15
13	21 40	19 51	12 21	11 42	4 55	25 37	21 0	5 13	4 14
14	22 41	1♍39	11 21	12 55	4 57	25 32	20 56	5 12	4 14
15	23 42	13 27	10 30	14 7	5 0	25 26	20 52	5 10	4 14
16	24 44	25 17	9 49	15 19	5 4	25 20	20 49	5 9	4 14
17	25 45	7♎15	9 17	16 32	5 9	25 14	20 45	5 7	4 13
18	26 46	19 25	8 55	17 44	5 14	25 8	20 42	5 6	4 13
19	27 47	1♏51	8 43	18 56	5 20	25 2	20 39	5 5	4 13
20	28 48	14 38	8 D39	20 9	5 26	24 55	20 35	5 4	4 12
21	29 49	27 49	8 43	21 21	5 34	24 49	20 32	5 3	4 12
22	0≈50	11♐27	8 55	22 34	5 42	24 42	20 29	5 2	4 11
23	1 51	25 32	9 14	23 46	5 51	24 35	20 26	5 1	4 10
24	2 52	10♑3	9 39	24 59	6 0	24 28	20 23	5 0	4 10
25	3 53	24 54	10 11	26 11	6 10	24 21	20 20	4 59	4 9
26	4 54	9≈58	10 47	27 24	6 20	24 14	20 17	4 58	4 8
27	5 55	25 6	11 29	28 37	6 31	24 7	20 14	4 57	4 7
28	6 56	10✻9	12 15	29 50	6 43	24 0	20 12	4 56	4 7
29	7 57	24 59	13 5	1♑3	6 56	23 52	20 9	4 55	4 6
30	8 58	9♈29	13 58	2 16	7 9	23 45	20 7	4 54	4 5
31	9 59	23 36	14 55	3 29	7 22	23 38	20 5	4 53	4 4

Pluto 8 Leo all month

FEBRUARY

Day	☉	☽	☿	♀	♂	♃	♄	♅	♆
1	11≈0	7♉19	15♑55	4♑42	7Ⅱ36	23♌30	20Ⅱ2	4Ⅱ53	4♎4
2	12 1	20 38	16 57	5 55	7 51	23B23	20B0	4B52	4B3
3	13 2	3Ⅱ35	18 2	7 8	8 5	23 15	19 58	4 52	4 2
4	14 3	16 14	19 9	8 21	8 21	23 7	19 56	4 51	4 1
5	15 4	28 38	20 19	9 34	8 37	23 0	19 54	4 51	4 1
6	16 4	10♋50	21 30	10 48	8 53	22 52	19 53	4 50	3 59
7	17 5	22 52	22 43	12 1	9 10	22 44	19 51	4 50	3 58
8	18 6	4♌47	23 58	13 14	9 27	22 36	19 50	4 50	3 57
9	19 7	16 39	25 14	14 27	9 45	22 28	19 48	4 50	3 56
10	20 7	28 27	26 32	15 41	10 3	22 20	19 47	4 50	3 55
11	21 8	10♍16	27 51	16 54	10 21	22 12	19 46	4 50	3 54
12	22 9	22 7	29 12	18 7	10 40	22 4	19 45	4 50	3 53
13	23 9	4♎2	0≈33	19 21	11 0	21 56	19 44	4 D50	3 52
14	24 10	16 3	1 56	20 34	11 19	21 48	19 43	4 50	3 50
15	25 11	28 15	3 20	21 48	11 39	21 40	19 42	4 50	3 49
16	26 11	10♏41	4 45	23 1	12 0	21 32	19 42	4 50	3 48
17	27 12	23 23	6 12	24 15	12 21	21 24	19 41	4 51	3 47
18	28 12	6♐26	7 39	25 28	12 42	21 17	19 41	4 51	3 45
19	29 13	19 53	9 8	26 42	13 3	21 9	19 41	4 51	3 44
20	0✻13	3♑46	10 37	27 55	13 25	21 1	19 41	4 51	3 43
21	1 14	18 6	12 7	29 9	13 47	20 54	19 D41	4 51	3 42
22	2 14	2≈49	13 39	0≈22	14 10	20 46	19 41	4 52	3 40
23	3 15	17 52	15 12	1 36	14 33	20 38	19 41	4 52	3 39
24	4 15	3✻5	16 45	2 49	14 56	20 30	19 41	4 53	3 38
25	5 16	18 20	18 19	4 3	15 19	20 23	19 42	4 53	3 37
26	6 16	3♈26	19 55	5 16	15 43	20 15	19 42	4 54	3 35
27	7 16	18 13	21 31	6 30	16 7	20 8	19 43	4 55	3 34
28	8 17	2♉36	23 8	7 44	16 31	20 1	19 44	4 56	3 33
29	9 17	16 31	24 47	8 57	16 55	19 53	19 45	4 57	3 31

Pluto 7 Leo all month

1944

MARCH

DAY	☉	☽	☿	♀	♂	♃	♄	♅	♆
	° ′	° ′	° ′	° ′	° ′	° ′	° ′	° ′	° ′
1	10♓17	29♉57	26♒26	10♒11	17♊20	19♌46	19♊46	4♊58	3♎30
2	11 17	12♊56	28 7	11 25	17 45	19℞39	19 47	4 59	3℞28
3	12 18	25 33	29 48	12 39	18 10	19 32	19 48	5 0	3 27
4	13 18	7♋50	1♓31	13 52	18 36	19 26	19 49	5 1	3 25
5	14 18	19 54	3 14	15 6	19 2	19 19	19 51	5 2	3 24
6	15 18	1♌49	4 59	16 20	19 28	19 13	19 52	5 3	3 22
7	16 18	13 38	6 45	17 34	19 54	19 7	19 54	5 4	3 20
8	17 18	25 25	8 32	18 47	20 20	19 0	19 56	5 5	3 19
9	18 18	7♍14	10 20	20 1	20 47	18 54	19 58	5 7	3 17
10	19 18	19 6	12 9	21 15	21 14	18 48	20 0	5 8	3 15
11	20 18	1♎2	13 59	22 29	21 41	18 42	20 2	5 9	3 13
12	21 17	13 6	15 51	23 42	22 8	18 36	20 4	5 11	3 12
13	22 17	25 17	17 43	24 56	22 36	18 31	20 7	5 12	3 10
14	23 17	7♏38	19 37	26 10	23 3	18 25	20 9	5 14	3 9
15	24 17	20 10	21 32	27 24	23 31	18 20	20 12	5 16	3 7
16	25 17	2♐56	23 28	28 37	23 59	18 15	20 14	5 17	3 6
17	26 16	15 58	25 25	29 51	24 27	18 10	20 17	5 19	3 4
18	27 16	29 19	27 23	1♓5	24 56	18 5	20 20	5 21	3 2
19	28 16	13♑0	29 22	2 19	25 24	18 0	20 23	5 23	3 0
20	29 15	27 4	1♈21	3 32	25 53	17 56	20 26	5 24	2 59
21	0♈15	11♒30	3 21	4 46	26 22	17 51	20 29	5 26	2 57
22	1 14	26 17	5 22	6 0	26 51	17 47	20 32	5 28	2 56
23	2 14	11♓17	7 23	7 14	27 20	17 43	20 35	5 30	2 54
24	3 13	26 25	9 25	8 28	27 49	17 39	20 39	5 32	2 53
25	4 13	11♈29	11 26	9 42	28 18	17 36	20 42	5 34	2 51
26	5 12	26 20	13 27	10 56	28 48	17 32	20 46	5 36	2 49
27	6 12	10♉50	15 28	12 10	29 18	17 29	20 50	5 38	2 47
28	7 11	24 53	17 28	13 24	29 48	17 26	20 53	5 40	2 46
29	8 10	8♊26	19 26	14 37	0♋18	17 23	20 57	5 43	2 44
30	9 10	21 31	21 22	15 51	0 48	17 20	21 1	5 45	2 43
31	10 9	4♋11	23 17	17 5	1 18	17 18	21 5	5 47	2 41

Pluto 6 Leo all month

APRIL

DAY	☉	☽	☿	♀	♂	♃	♄	♅	♆
	° ′	° ′	° ′	° ′	° ′	° ′	° ′	° ′	° ′
1	11♈8	16♋30	25♈9	18♓19	1♋49	17♌16	21♊9	5♊49	2♎40
2	12 7	28 33	26 59	19 32	2 19	17℞14	21 14	5 52	2℞38
3	13 7	10♌26	28 45	20 46	2 50	17 12	21 18	5 54	2 36
4	14 6	22 14	0♉27	22 0	3 20	17 10	21 22	5 56	2 34
5	15 5	4♍1	2 6	23 14	3 51	17 8	21 27	5 59	2 33
6	16 4	15 52	3 40	24 27	4 22	17 7	21 31	6 1	2 31
7	17 3	27 49	5 10	25 41	4 53	17 5	21 36	6 4	2 29
8	18 2	9♎54	6 35	26 55	5 25	17 4	21 41	6 7	2 27
9	19 1	22 9	7 55	28 9	5 56	17 3	21 46	6 9	2 26
10	19 59	4♏35	9 10	29 22	6 27	17 3	21 51	6 12	2 24
11	20 58	17 11	10 19	0♈36	6 59	17 2	21 56	6 15	2 23
12	21 57	29 59	11 22	1 50	7 30	17 2	22 1	6 18	2 21
13	22 56	12♐58	12 19	3 4	8 2	17D 2	22 6	6 20	2 20
14	23 55	26 9	13 11	4 17	8 34	17 2	22 12	6 23	2 18
15	24 53	9♑33	13 56	5 31	9 6	17 2	22 17	6 26	2 17
16	25 52	23 13	14 36	6 45	9 38	17 3	22 22	6 29	2 15
17	26 51	7♒8	15 9	7 59	10 10	17 3	22 28	6 31	2 14
18	27 49	21 19	15 37	9 12	10 42	17 4	22 33	6 34	2 12
19	28 48	5♓46	15 58	10 26	11 14	17 5	22 39	6 37	2 11
20	29 47	20 25	16 13	11 40	11 47	17 6	22 45	6 40	2 9
21	0♉45	5♈11	16 22	12 54	12 19	17 8	22 50	6 43	2 8
22	1 44	19 56	16℞25	14 7	12 52	17 9	22 56	6 46	2 6
23	2 42	4♉34	16 22	15 21	13 24	17 11	23 2	6 49	2 5
24	3 41	18 55	16 14	16 35	13 57	17 13	23 8	6 52	2 4
25	4 39	2♊54	16 0	17 49	14 30	17 15	23 14	6 55	2 2
26	5 37	16 27	15 42	19 2	15 2	17 17	23 20	6 59	2 1
27	6 36	29 34	15 19	20 16	15 35	17 19	23 26	7 2	2 0
28	7 34	12♋16	14 53	21 30	16 8	17 22	23 32	7 5	1 59
29	8 32	24 38	14 22	22 44	16 42	17 25	23 38	7 8	1 57
30	9 31	6♌43	13 49	23 57	17 15	17 28	23 45	7 11	1 56

Pluto 6 Leo all month

1944

MAY

DAY	☉	☽	☿	♀	♂	♃	♄	♅	♆
	° ′	° ′	° ′	° ′	° ′	° ′	° ′	° ′	° ′
1	10 ♉ 29	18 ♌ 38	13 ♉ 14	25 ♈ 11	17 ♋ 48	17 ♌ 31	23 ♊ 51	7 ♊ 14	1 ♎ 55
2	11 27	0 ♍ 27	12 ℞ 37	26 25	18 21	17 34	23 57	7 17	1 ℞ 54
3	12 25	12 17	11 59	27 39	18 54	17 38	24 4	7 21	1 52
4	13 23	24 10	11 20	28 52	19 28	17 41	24 10	7 24	1 51
5	14 22	6 ♎ 12	10 42	0 ♉ 6	20 1	17 45	24 17	7 28	1 50
6	15 20	18 26	10 6	1 20	20 35	17 49	24 24	7 31	1 49
7	16 18	0 ♏ 53	9 31	2 33	21 9	17 54	24 30	7 35	1 48
8	17 16	13 35	8 58	3 47	21 42	17 58	24 37	7 38	1 47
9	18 14	26 30	8 28	5 0	22 16	18 3	24 44	7 41	1 46
10	19 12	9 ♐ 38	8 1	6 14	22 50	18 8	24 51	7 44	1 45
11	20 10	22 57	7 38	7 28	23 24	18 12	24 58	7 48	1 44
12	21 8	6 ♑ 28	7 19	8 41	23 57	18 17	25 5	7 51	1 43
13	22 5	20 8	7 4	9 55	24 31	18 22	25 12	7 55	1 42
14	23 3	3 ♒ 57	6 54	11 9	25 5	18 27	25 19	7 58	1 41
15	24 1	17 55	6 48	12 23	25 39	18 33	25 26	8 1	1 40
16	24 59	2 ♓ 1	6 D 47	13 36	26 14	18 38	25 33	8 5	1 40
17	25 57	16 15	6 50	14 50	26 48	18 44	25 40	8 8	1 39
18	26 55	0 ♈ 34	6 58	16 4	27 22	18 50	25 47	8 11	1 38
19	27 52	14 55	7 10	17 17	27 56	18 56	25 54	8 15	1 37
20	28 50	29 15	7 27	18 31	28 31	19 3	26 2	8 18	1 36
21	29 48	13 ♉ 27	7 48	19 44	29 5	19 9	26 9	8 22	1 36
22	0 ♊ 46	27 27	8 13	20 58	29 39	19 15	26 16	8 25	1 35
23	1 43	11 ♊ 9	8 43	22 12	0 ♌ 14	19 22	26 23	8 29	1 34
24	2 41	24 30	9 17	23 25	0 48	19 28	26 31	8 32	1 33
25	3 39	7 ♋ 30	9 54	24 39	1 23	19 35	26 38	8 36	1 33
26	4 36	20 10	10 36	25 53	1 58	19 42	26 45	8 39	1 32
27	5 34	2 ♌ 31	11 21	27 7	2 32	19 49	26 53	8 43	1 32
28	6 31	14 37	12 10	28 20	3 7	19 57	27 0	8 46	1 31
29	7 29	26 33	13 3	29 38	3 42	20 4	27 8	8 50	1 31
30	8 26	8 ♍ 24	13 59	0 ♊ 47	4 17	20 12	27 15	8 54	1 30
31	9 24	20 15	14 58	2 0	4 52	20 19	27 23	8 57	1 30

Pluto 6 Leo all month

JUNE

DAY	☉	☽	☿	♀	♂	♃	♄	♅	♆
	° ′	° ′	° ′	° ′	° ′	° ′	° ′	° ′	° ′
1	10 ♊ 21	2 ♎ 11	16 ♉ 0	3 ♊ 14	5 ♌ 27	20 ♌ 27	27 ♊ 30	9 ♊ 1	1 ♎ 29
2	11 19	14 17	17 6	4 28	6 2	20 35	27 38	9 5	1 ℞ 29
3	12 16	26 36	18 15	5 42	6 37	20 43	27 46	9 9	1 29
4	13 14	9 ♏ 12	19 27	6 55	7 12	20 51	27 53	9 12	1 29
5	14 11	22 5	20 42	8 9	7 47	21 0	28 1	9 16	1 28
6	15 9	5 ♐ 17	22 0	9 22	8 22	21 8	28 9	9 19	1 28
7	16 6	18 46	23 21	10 36	8 57	21 16	28 17	9 23	1 28
8	17 3	2 ♑ 29	24 45	11 49	9 32	21 25	28 24	9 26	1 28
9	18 1	16 24	26 12	13 3	10 8	21 33	28 32	9 30	1 28
10	18 58	0 ♒ 28	27 41	14 17	10 43	21 42	28 39	9 33	1 28
11	19 55	14 38	29 14	15 31	11 18	21 51	28 47	9 37	1 28
12	20 53	28 40	0 ♊ 49	16 44	11 54	22 0	28 54	9 40	1 28
13	21 50	13 ♓ 3	2 27	17 58	12 29	22 10	29 2	9 44	1 D 28
14	22 47	27 14	4 8	19 12	13 5	22 19	29 10	9 47	1 28
15	23 45	11 ♈ 23	5 51	20 26	13 41	22 28	29 18	9 50	1 28
16	24 42	25 25	7 37	21 39	14 16	22 37	29 26	9 54	1 28
17	25 39	9 ♉ 21	9 26	22 53	14 52	22 47	29 34	9 57	1 28
18	26 37	23 6	11 18	24 6	15 28	22 56	29 42	10 0	1 28
19	27 34	6 ♊ 39	13 12	25 20	16 4	23 6	29 50	10 4	1 28
20	28 31	19 57	15 8	26 33	16 39	23 16	29 57	10 7	1 29
21	29 28	2 ♋ 59	17 7	27 47	17 15	23 26	0 ♋ 5	10 11	1 29
22	0 ♋ 26	15 44	19 8	29 1	17 51	23 36	0 13	10 14	1 30
23	1 23	28 14	21 12	0 ♋ 15	18 27	23 46	0 21	10 17	1 30
24	2 20	10 ♌ 30	23 17	1 28	19 2	23 56	0 28	10 20	1 31
25	3 17	22 33	25 23	2 42	19 38	24 7	0 36	10 23	1 31
26	4 15	4 ♍ 28	27 31	3 56	20 14	24 17	0 44	10 26	1 31
27	5 12	16 19	29 40	5 10	20 50	24 27	0 52	10 29	1 32
28	6 9	28 11	1 ♋ 50	6 23	21 26	24 38	0 59	10 32	1 32
29	7 6	10 ♎ 7	4 1	7 37	22 3	24 48	1 7	10 35	1 33
30	8 3	22 14	6 12	8 51	22 39	24 59	1 15	10 38	1 33

Pluto 6 Leo all month

1944

JULY

DAY	☉	☽	☿	♀	♂	♃	♄	♅	♆
	° ′	° ′	° ′	° ′	° ′	° ′	° ′	° ′	° ′
1	9♋ 1	4♏34	8♋22	10♋ 5	23♌15	25♌10	1♋23	10♊41	1♎34
2	9 58	17 13	10 33	11 18	23 51	25 21	1 30	10 44	1 34
3	10 55	0♐12	12 43	12 32	24 28	25 32	1 38	10 47	1 35
4	11 52	13 33	14 52	13 46	25 4	25 43	1 46	10 50	1 36
5	12 49	27 17	17 1	15 0	25 40	25 54	1 54	10 53	1 37
6	13 47	11♑20	19 8	16 13	26 16	26 5	2 1	10 56	1 37
7	14 44	25 39	21 14	17 27	26 53	26 16	2 9	10 59	1 38
8	15 41	10♒ 9	23 18	18 41	27 29	26 27	2 17	11 2	1 39
9	16 38	24 45	25 21	19 55	28 5	26 38	2 25	11 5	1 40
10	17 35	9♓20	27 22	21 8	28 42	26 50	2 32	11 8	1 40
11	18 33	23 49	29 22	22 22	29 18	27 1	2 40	11 11	1 41
12	19 30	8♈ 9	1♌20	23 36	29 55	27 13	2 48	11 14	1 42
13	20 27	22 17	3 16	24 50	0♍32	27 25	2 56	11 17	1 43
14	21 24	6♉11	5 10	26 4	1 8	27 36	3 3	11 20	1 44
15	22 21	19 50	7 2	27 18	1 45	27 48	3 11	11 23	1 45
16	23 19	3♊13	8 53	28 32	2 22	28 0	3 18	11 26	1 46
17	24 16	16 22	10 41	29 46	2 59	28 12	3 26	11 29	1 47
18	25 13	29 17	12 28	1♌ 0	3 36	28 23	3 33	11 32	1 48
19	26 10	11♋57	14 13	2 13	4 13	28 35	3 41	11 34	1 50
20	27 8	24 26	15 56	3 27	4 50	28 47	3 48	11 37	1 51
21	28 5	6♌42	17 37	4 41	5 27	28 59	3 55	11 40	1 52
22	29 2	18 49	19 17	5 54	6 4	29 11	4 3	11 43	1 53
23	0♌ 0	0♍47	20 54	7 8	6 41	29 23	4 10	11 45	1 55
24	0 57	12 40	22 30	8 22	7 18	29 35	4 17	11 48	1 56
25	1 54	24 30	24 4	9 36	7 55	29 47	4 24	11 51	1 57
26	2 52	6♎21	25 36	10 50	8 32	29 59	4 32	11 54	1 58
27	3 49	18 17	27 6	12 4	9 10	0♍12	4 39	11 56	2 0
28	4 46	0♏22	28 35	13 18	9 47	0 24	4 46	11 59	2 1
29	5 44	12 40	0♍ 1	14 32	10 24	0 36	4 53	12 2	2 2
30	6 41	25 16	1 25	15 46	11 1	0 49	5 0	12 5	2 3
31	7 38	8♐14	2 48	17 0	11 39	1 1	5 7	12 7	2 5

Pluto 7 Leo all month

AUGUST

DAY	☉	☽	☿	♀	♂	♃	♄	♅	♆
	° ′	° ′	° ′	° ′	° ′	° ′	° ′	° ′	° ′
1	8♌36	21♐36	4♍ 9	18♌14	12♍16	1♍14	5♋14	12♊10	2♎ 6
2	9 33	5♑24	5 27	19 28	12 53	1 26	5 21	12 12	2 7
3	10 31	19 36	6 44	20 42	13 31	1 39	5 28	12 15	2 9
4	11 28	4♒11	7 58	21 55	14 8	1 51	5 34	12 17	2 10
5	12 25	19 2	9 10	23 9	14 46	2 4	5 41	12 19	2 12
6	13 23	4♓ 1	10 20	24 23	15 24	2 16	5 48	12 21	2 14
7	14 20	19 1	11 28	25 37	16 1	2 29	5 55	12 23	2 15
8	15 18	3♈52	12 33	26 51	16 39	2 41	6 1	12 25	2 17
9	16 15	18 28	13 35	28 5	17 17	2 54	6 8	12 27	2 19
10	17 13	2♉45	14 35	29 19	17 55	3 7	6 15	12 29	2 21
11	18 11	16 40	15 33	0♍33	18 32	3 19	6 21	12 31	2 22
12	19 8	0♊12	16 27	1 47	19 10	3 32	6 28	12 33	2 24
13	20 6	13 23	17 18	3 1	19 48	3 45	6 34	12 35	2 26
14	21 3	26 16	18 6	4 15	20 26	3 58	6 40	12 37	2 28
15	22 1	8♋53	18 51	5 29	21 4	4 11	6 47	12 39	2 29
16	22 59	21 16	19 33	6 43	21 42	4 24	6 53	12 40	2 31
17	23 56	3♌29	20 10	7 57	22 20	4 37	6 59	12 42	2 33
18	24 54	15 33	20 43	9 11	22 58	4 50	7 5	12 44	2 35
19	25 52	27 31	21 13	10 25	23 36	5 2	7 11	12 45	2 36
20	26 50	9♍24	21 38	11 38	24 14	5 15	7 17	12 47	2 38
21	27 47	21 15	21 58	12 53	24 52	5 28	7 23	12 48	2 40
22	28 45	3♎ 5	22 13	14 7	25 30	5 41	7 29	12 49	2 42
23	29 43	14 57	22 23	15 21	26 8	5 54	7 35	12 51	2 44
24	0♍41	26 53	22 28	16 35	26 47	6 7	7 40	12 52	2 46
25	1 39	8♏57	22℞27	17 49	27 25	6 20	7 46	12 53	2 48
26	2 37	21 14	22 21	19 3	28 3	6 33	7 52	12 54	2 50
27	3 35	3♐45	22 8	20 17	28 42	6 46	7 57	12 56	2 52
28	4 33	16 37	21 49	21 31	29 20	6 59	8 3	12 57	2 54
29	5 31	29 53	21 25	22 45	29 59	7 12	8 8	12 58	2 56
30	6 29	13♑35	20 54	23 59	0♎38	7 25	8 13	12 59	2 58
31	7 27	27 45	20 17	25 13	1 16	7 38	8 18	13 0	3 0

Pluto 8 Leo all month

1944

SEPTEMBER

Pluto ♇ 9 Leo all month

Day	☉	☽	☿	♀	♂	♃	♄	♅	♆
1	8♍25	12≈21	19♍35	26♍26	1≏55	7♍51	8♋23	13Ⅱ 1	3≏ 2
2	9 23	27 20	18 R48	27 40	2 34	8 4	8 28	13 2	3 4
3	10 21	12✕32	17 57	28 54	3 13	8 17	8 33	13 3	3 6
4	11 19	27 49	17 2	0≏ 8	3 51	8 30	8 38	13 4	3 8
5	12 17	12♈59	16 5	1 22	4 30	8 43	8 43	13 4	3 11
6	13 15	27 53	15 6	2 36	5 9	8 56	8 48	13 5	3 13
7	14 14	12♉23	14 7	3 50	5 48	9 9	8 53	13 6	3 15
8	15 12	26 26	13 9	5 4	6 27	9 22	8 57	13 6	3 17
9	16 10	10Ⅱ 1	12 13	6 18	7 6	9 35	9 1	13 7	3 19
10	17 8	23 10	11 21	7 32	7 45	9 48	9 6	13 7	3 21
11	18 7	5♋55	10 35	8 46	8 24	10 1	9 10	13 8	3 23
12	19 5	18 23	9 54	10 0	9 3	10 14	9 15	13 8	3 25
13	20 4	0♌35	9 21	11 13	9 43	10 27	9 19	13 9	3 28
14	21 2	12 38	8 55	12 27	10 22	10 40	9 23	13 9	3 30
15	22 1	24 33	8 39	13 41	11 1	10 53	9 27	13 9	3 32
16	22 59	6♍25	8 31	14 55	11 40	11 6	9 31	13 9	3 34
17	23 58	18 15	8 D33	16 9	12 20	11 19	9 35	13 9	3 37
18	24 56	0≏ 6	8 45	17 23	12 59	11 32	9 39	13 9	3 39
19	25 55	11 58	9 6	18 37	13 38	11 45	9 43	13 R 9	3 41
20	26 53	23 55	9 37	19 51	14 18	11 58	9 46	13 9	3 43
21	27 52	5♏56	10 16	21 4	14 57	12 10	9 50	13 9	3 46
22	28 51	18 4	11 4	22 18	15 37	12 23	9 53	13 9	3 48
23	29 50	0♐22	12 0	23 32	16 17	12 36	9 56	13 9	3 50
24	0≏48	12 54	13 3	24 46	16 56	12 49	9 59	13 8	3 52
25	1 47	25 42	14 13	25 59	17 36	13 1	10 2	13 8	3 55
26	2 46	8♑51	15 29	27 13	18 16	13 14	10 5	13 7	3 57
27	3 45	22 23	16 51	28 27	18 56	13 27	10 8	13 7	3 59
28	4 44	6≈22	18 17	29 41	19 36	13 39	10 11	13 6	4 1
29	5 43	20 48	19 48	0♏54	20 16	13 52	10 13	13 6	4 4
30	6 42	5✕38	21 22	2 8	20 56	14 4	10 16	13 5	4 6

OCTOBER

Pluto ♇ 9 Leo all month

Day	☉	☽	☿	♀	♂	♃	♄	♅	♆
1	7≏41	20✕46	22♍58	3♏22	21≏36	14♍17	10♋18	13Ⅱ 5	4≏ 8
2	8 40	6♈ 4	24 38	4 36	22 16	14 29	10 20	13 R 4	4 10
3	9 39	21 20	26 19	5 49	22 56	14 42	10 23	13 4	4 12
4	10 38	6♉23	28 2	7 3	23 36	14 54	10 25	13 3	4 14
5	11 37	21 4	29 46	8 17	24 16	15 6	10 27	13 2	4 16
6	12 36	5Ⅱ17	1≏31	9 31	24 56	15 19	10 29	13 1	4 18
7	13 35	18 59	3 16	10 44	25 37	15 31	10 31	13 0	4 21
8	14 34	2♋12	5 2	11 58	26 17	15 43	10 33	12 59	4 23
9	15 34	14 59	6 48	13 12	26 57	15 55	10 35	12 58	4 25
10	16 33	27 25	8 33	14 25	27 38	16 7	10 36	12 57	4 27
11	17 32	9♌35	10 19	15 39	28 18	16 19	10 38	12 56	4 30
12	18 32	21 33	12 4	16 52	28 59	16 31	10 39	12 55	4 32
13	19 31	3♍25	13 50	18 6	29 40	16 43	10 40	12 54	4 34
14	20 31	15 14	15 34	19 19	0♏20	16 55	10 41	12 53	4 36
15	21 30	27 4	17 18	20 33	1 1	17 7	10 42	12 51	4 39
16	22 30	8≏58	19 2	21 46	1 42	17 19	10 43	12 50	4 41
17	23 29	20 56	20 45	23 0	2 23	17 31	10 44	12 49	4 43
18	24 29	3♏ 0	22 28	24 13	3 3	17 42	10 44	12 47	4 45
19	25 28	15 11	24 10	25 27	3 44	17 54	10 45	12 46	4 47
20	26 28	27 30	25 51	26 41	4 25	18 5	10 45	12 44	4 49
21	27 28	9♐58	27 32	27 54	5 6	18 17	10 46	12 42	4 51
22	28 28	22 37	29 12	29 8	5 47	18 28	10 46	12 41	4 53
23	29 27	5♑30	0♏51	0♐21	6 28	18 40	10 46	12 39	4 55
24	0♏27	18 38	2 30	1 34	7 9	18 51	10 R46	12 37	4 57
25	1 27	2≈ 5	4 9	2 47	7 50	19 2	10 46	12 35	4 59
26	2 27	15 53	5 47	4 1	8 31	19 13	10 46	12 34	5 1
27	3 27	0✕ 4	7 24	5 15	9 13	19 24	10 45	12 32	5 4
28	4 26	14 36	9 1	6 28	9 54	19 35	10 45	12 30	5 6
29	5 26	29 27	10 37	7 41	10 35	19 46	10 44	12 28	5 8
30	6 26	14♈28	12 13	8 55	11 17	19 57	10 43	12 26	5 10
31	7 26	29 32	13 48	10 8	11 58	20 7	10 42	12 24	5 12

1944

NOVEMBER

Day	☉ ° ′	☽ ° ′	☿ ° ′	♀ ° ′	♂ ° ′	♃ ° ′	♄ ° ′	♅ ° ′	♆ ° ′
1	8♏26	14♉28	15♏23	11♐21	12♏40	20♍18	10♋41	12♊22	5♎14
2	9 26	29 7	16 57	12 34	13 21	20 29	10R40	12R20	5 16
3	10 26	13♊22	18 31	13 48	14 3	20 39	10 39	12 18	5 18
4	11 27	27 9	20 4	15 1	14 44	20 50	10 38	12 16	5 19
5	12 27	10♋28	21 37	16 14	15 26	21 0	10 37	12 14	5 21
6	13 27	23 20	23 10	17 27	16 8	21 10	10 35	12 12	5 23
7	14 27	5♌49	24 43	18 40	16 50	21 20	10 34	12 10	5 25
8	15 27	18 1	26 15	19 53	17 32	21 30	10 32	12 8	5 26
9	16 28	0♍0	27 46	21 6	18 14	21 40	10 30	12 6	5 28
10	17 28	11 53	29 17	22 19	18 56	21 50	10 28	12 4	5 30
11	18 28	23 42	0♐48	23 32	19 38	21 59	10 26	12 2	5 32
12	19 29	5♎34	2 19	24 46	20 20	22 9	10 24	11 59	5 33
13	20 29	17 31	3 49	25 59	21 2	22 18	10 22	11 57	5 35
14	21 29	29 36	5 19	27 12	21 44	22 27	10 20	11 55	5 37
15	22 30	11♏50	6 49	28 25	22 26	22 37	10 17	11 52	5 39
16	23 30	24 14	8 18	29 37	23 9	22 46	10 15	11 50	5 40
17	24 31	6♐49	9 46	0♑50	23 51	22 55	10 12	11 47	5 42
18	25 31	19 35	11 15	2 3	24 33	23 4	10 9	11 45	5 44
19	26 32	2♑32	12 43	3 16	25 16	23 13	10 7	11 42	5 45
20	27 33	15 40	14 10	4 28	25 58	23 21	10 4	11 40	5 47
21	28 33	29 0	15 37	5 41	26 41	23 30	10 1	11 38	5 48
22	29 34	12♒33	17 3	6 54	27 23	23 38	9 58	11 36	5 50
23	0♐35	26 20	18 28	8 6	28 6	23 47	9 55	11 33	5 51
24	1 35	10♓22	19 53	9 19	28 48	23 55	9 51	11 31	5 53
25	2 36	24 38	21 17	10 31	29 31	24 3	9 48	11 28	5 54
26	3 37	9♈5	22 40	11 44	0♐14	24 11	9 45	11 26	5 55
27	4 37	23 41	24 1	12 56	0 57	24 19	9 40	11 23	5 57
28	5 38	8♉18	25 21	14 9	1 40	24 26	9 38	11 21	5 58
29	6 39	22 51	26 40	15 22	2 23	24 34	9 34	11 18	5 59
30	7 40	7♊12	27 58	16 34	3 6	24 41	9 30	11 15	6 0

Pluto 10 Leo all month

DECEMBER

Day	☉ ° ′	☽ ° ′	☿ ° ′	♀ ° ′	♂ ° ′	♃ ° ′	♄ ° ′	♅ ° ′	♆ ° ′
1	8♐40	21♊15	29♐13	17♑46	3♐49	24♍49	9♋26	11♊12	6♎2
2	9 41	4♋56	0♑26	18 59	4 32	24 56	9R22	11R10	6 3
3	10 42	18 13	1 36	20 11	5 15	25 3	9 18	11 7	6 5
4	11 43	1♌7	2 43	21 23	5 58	25 10	9 14	11 4	6 6
5	12 44	13 40	3 47	22 35	6 41	25 17	9 10	11 2	6 7
6	13 45	25 56	4 46	23 47	7 25	25 23	9 6	10 59	6 8
7	14 46	7♍59	5 41	24 59	8 8	25 30	9 2	10 57	6 9
8	15 47	19 53	6 31	26 11	8 51	25 36	8 58	10 55	6 10
9	16 48	1♎44	7 15	27 22	9 34	25 42	8 53	10 52	6 11
10	17 49	13 38	7 53	28 34	10 18	25 48	8 49	10 50	6 12
11	18 50	25 37	8 23	29 46	11 1	25 54	8 44	10 47	6 13
12	19 51	7♏46	8 44	0♒57	11 45	26 0	8 40	10 45	6 14
13	20 52	20 8	8 56	2 9	12 28	26 5	8 35	10 42	6 15
14	21 53	2♐44	8R57	3 20	13 12	26 11	8 31	10 40	6 16
15	22 54	15 35	8 47	4 32	13 56	26 16	8 26	10 37	6 17
16	23 55	28 42	8 26	5 43	14 40	26 21	8 21	10 35	6 18
17	24 56	12♑2	7 54	6 54	15 23	26 26	8 17	10 32	6 18
18	25 57	25 36	7 11	8 5	16 7	26 30	8 12	10 30	6 19
19	26 58	9♒20	6 17	9 16	16 51	26 35	8 7	10 27	6 19
20	27 59	23 13	5 12	10 27	17 35	26 39	8 2	10 25	6 20
21	29 0	7♓13	3 59	11 38	18 19	26 44	7 57	10 23	6 20
22	0♑1	21 19	2 41	12 48	19 3	26 48	7 52	10 21	6 21
23	1 3	5♈30	1 20	13 59	19 47	26 52	7 47	10 18	6 22
24	2 4	19 42	29♐58	15 9	20 31	26 55	7 42	10 16	6 23
25	3 5	3♉54	28 38	16 20	21 15	26 59	7 37	10 13	6 23
26	4 6	18 3	27 23	17 30	22 0	27 2	7 33	10 11	6 24
27	5 7	2♊5	26 14	18 40	22 44	27 5	7 28	10 9	6 24
28	6 8	15 57	25 13	19 50	23 28	27 8	7 23	10 7	6 24
29	7 9	29 35	24 21	21 0	24 12	27 11	7 18	10 4	6 25
30	8 10	12♋58	23 40	22 9	24 57	27 13	7 13	10 2	6 25
31	9 12	26 4	23 10	23 19	25 41	27 16	7 8	10 0	6 25

Pluto 10 Leo all month

1945

JANUARY

Pluto 9 Leo all month

Day	☉	☽	☿	♀	♂	♃	♄	♅	♆
1	10 ♑13	8♌52	22 ♐50	24≈28	26 ♐25	27♍18	7 ♋ 3	9 Ⅱ58	6≏26
2	11 14	21 23	22 ℞40	25 38	27 10	27 20	6 ℞58	9℞56	6 26
3	12 15	3♍39	22 D40	26 47	27 54	27 22	6 53	9 54	6 26
4	13 16	15 43	22 49	27 56	28 39	27 24	6 48	9 52	6 26
5	14 17	27 39	23 5	29 5	29 24	27 25	6 43	9 50	6 26
6	15 18	9≏32	23 29	0)(13	0♑ 8	27 26	6 38	9 48	6 26
7	16 20	21 25	24 0	1 22	0 53	27 27	6 34	9 46	6 ℞26
8	17 21	3♏24	24 37	2 30	1 38	27 28	6 29	9 44	6 26
9	18 22	15 33	25 18	3 38	2 23	27 29	6 24	9 42	6 26
10	19 23	27 57	26 5	4 46	3 7	27 29	6 19	9 40	6 26
11	20 24	10 ♐38	26 57	5 54	3 52	27 30	6 15	9 39	6 26
12	21 25	23 39	27 52	7 1	4 37	27 30	6 10	9 37	6 26
13	22 26	7 ♑ 1	28 50	8 9	5 22	27 ℞30	6 5	9 35	6 26
14	23 28	20 44	29 52	9 16	6 7	27 29	6 0	9 34	6 25
15	24 29	4≈43	0 ♑56	10 23	6 53	27 29	5 56	9 32	6 25
16	25 30	18 57	2 3	11 29	7 38	27 28	5 51	9 31	6 25
17	26 31	3)(20	3 12	12 36	8 23	27 27	5 47	9 30	6 25
18	27 32	17 46	4 24	13 42	9 8	27 26	5 42	9 28	6 25
19	28 33	2♈11	5 37	14 48	9 53	27 25	5 38	9 27	6 24
20	29 34	16 31	6 52	15 54	10 38	27 24	5 34	9 26	6 24
21	0≈35	0♉42	8 8	16 59	11 23	27 22	5 30	9 25	6 24
22	1 36	14 43	9 26	18 4	12 9	27 20	5 25	9 23	6 23
23	2 37	28 32	10 45	19 9	12 54	27 18	5 21	9 22	6 23
24	3 38	12Ⅱ 8	12 5	20 14	13 40	27 16	5 17	9 21	6 22
25	4 39	25 32	13 26	21 18	14 25	27 13	5 13	9 20	6 21
26	5 40	8♋43	14 49	22 22	15 11	27 11	5 9	9 19	6 21
27	6 41	21 42	16 12	23 26	15 56	27 8	5 6	9 18	6 20
28	7 42	4♌28	17 37	24 29	16 42	27 5	5 2	9 17	6 19
29	8 43	17 2	19 2	25 31	17 27	27 2	4 58	9 16	6 19
30	9 44	29 25	20 29	26 34	18 13	26 59	4 54	9 15	6 18
31	10 45	11♍36	21 56	27 36	18 58	26 55	4 51	9 14	6 17

FEBRUARY

Pluto 9 Leo all month

Day	☉	☽	☿	♀	♂	♃	♄	♅	♆
1	11≈46	23♍39	23 ♑24	28)(38	19 ♑44	26♍52	4 ♋47	9 Ⅱ13	6≏16
2	12 47	5≏34	24 53	29 39	20 30	26 ℞48	4 ℞44	9 ℞12	6 ℞15
3	13 48	17 27	26 22	0♈40	21 15	26 44	4 40	9 12	6 15
4	14 49	29 19	27 53	1 41	22 1	26 40	4 37	9 11	6 14
5	15 49	11♏16	29 24	2 41	22 47	26 36	4 34	9 11	6 13
6	16 50	23 22	0≈56	3 41	23 33	26 31	4 31	9 10	6 12
7	17 51	5 ♐42	2 29	4 40	24 19	26 27	4 29	9 10	6 11
8	18 52	18 21	4 3	5 39	25 5	26 22	4 26	9 9	6 10
9	19 52	1 ♑23	5 37	6 37	25 51	26 17	4 23	9 9	6 9
10	20 53	14 49	7 13	7 34	26 37	26 12	4 20	9 9	6 8
11	21 54	28 42	8 49	8 32	27 23	26 7	4 18	9 9	6 7
12	22 55	12≈59	10 25	9 28	28 9	26 1	4 15	9 8	6 6
13	23 55	27 37	12 3	10 24	28 55	25 56	4 13	9 8	6 5
14	24 56	12)(27	13 42	11 20	29 41	25 50	4 11	9 8	6 4
15	25 57	27 23	15 21	12 15	0≈27	25 44	4 8	9 8	6 3
16	26 57	12♈15	17 1	13 9	1 13	25 38	4 6	9 D 8	6 1
17	27 58	26 56	18 43	14 2	1 59	25 33	4 4	9 8	6 0
18	28 58	11♉19	20 25	14 55	2 45	25 26	4 2	9 8	5 59
19	29 59	25 23	22 7	15 47	3 31	25 19	4 1	9 8	5 58
20	0)(59	9Ⅱ 6	23 51	16 39	4 18	25 13	3 59	9 8	5 56
21	2 0	22 29	25 36	17 29	5 4	25 6	3 58	9 9	5 55
22	3 0	5♋35	27 22	18 19	5 50	24 59	3 56	9 9	5 54
23	4 0	18 26	29 9	19 9	6 36	24 53	3 55	9 9	5 52
24	5 1	1♌ 3	0)(56	19 56	7 23	24 46	3 53	9 10	5 51
25	6 1	13 30	2 45	20 43	8 9	24 39	3 52	9 10	5 49
26	7 2	25 49	4 35	21 29	8 55	24 32	3 51	9 10	5 48
27	8 2	7♍59	6 25	22 15	9 42	24 25	3 51	9 11	5 46
28	9 2	20 3	8 17	22 59	10 28	24 17	3 50	9 11	5 45

1945

MARCH

DAY	☉ ° ′	☽ ° ′	☿ ° ′	♀ ° ′	♂ ° ′	♃ ° ′	♄ ° ′	♅ ° ′	♆ ° ′
1	10♓ 2	2♎ 1	10♓ 9	23♈42	11♒15	24♍10	3♋50	9♊12	5♎44
2	11 2	13 55	12 3	24 24	12 1	24℞ 3	3℞ 50	9 13	5℞42
3	12 3	25 47	13 57	25 5	12 48	23 55	3 49	9 13	5 41
4	13 3	7♏39	15 52	25 45	13 34	23 48	3 49	9 14	5 39
5	14 3	19 35	17 47	26 23	14 21	23 40	3 49	9 15	5 38
6	15 3	1♐39	19 43	27 1	15 7	23 33	3 D 49	9 16	5 36
7	16 3	13 55	21 40	27 37	15 54	23 25	3 49	9 17	5 35
8	17 3	26 28	23 37	28 11	16 40	23 18	3 49	9 18	5 33
9	18 3	9♑24	25 34	28 44	17 27	23 10	3 49	9 19	5 32
10	19 3	22 45	27 31	29 16	18 13	23 2	3 50	9 20	5 30
11	20 3	6♒36	29 27	29 46	19 0	22 55	3 50	9 21	5 29
12	21 3	20 55	1♈23	0♉15	19 46	22 47	3 51	9 23	5 27
13	22 3	5♓41	3 18	0 42	20 33	22 39	3 52	9 24	5 25
14	23 2	20 46	5 12	1 7	21 19	22 31	3 53	9 25	5 23
15	24 2	6♈ 1	7 4	1 31	22 6	22 24	3 54	9 26	5 22
16	25 2	21 15	8 54	1 52	22 52	22 16	3 55	9 28	5 20
17	26 2	6♉17	10 41	2 12	23 39	22 8	3 56	9 29	5 19
18	27 2	20 59	12 25	2 30	24 26	22 0	3 57	9 30	5 17
19	28 1	5♊15	14 6	2 46	25 12	21 53	3 59	9 32	5 16
20	29 1	19 5	15 43	3 0	25 59	21 45	4 0	9 33	5 14
21	0♈ 0	2♋28	17 15	3 11	26 46	21 37	4 2	9 35	5 12
22	1 0	15 28	18 42	3 20	27 33	21 29	4 4	9 37	5 10
23	2 0	28 9	20 4	3 27	28 19	21 22	4 6	9 38	5 9
24	2 59	10♌35	21 21	3 32	29 6	21 14	4 8	9 40	5 7
25	3 58	22 50	22 31	3 35	29 53	21 6	4 10	9 42	5 6
26	4 58	4♍56	23 35	3℞35	0♓39	20 59	4 12	9 44	5 4
27	5 57	16 56	24 32	3 32	1 26	20 51	4 15	9 46	5 3
28	6 57	28 53	25 23	3 27	2 12	20 44	4 17	9 48	5 1
29	7 56	10♎47	26 6	3 20	2 59	20 37	4 19	9 50	4 59
30	8 55	22 39	26 43	3 10	3 46	20 30	4 22	9 52	4 57
31	9 54	4♏32	27 12	2 57	4 32	20 23	4 24	9 54	4 56

Pluto 8 Leo all month

APRIL

DAY	☉ ° ′	☽ ° ′	☿ ° ′	♀ ° ′	♂ ° ′	♃ ° ′	♄ ° ′	♅ ° ′	♆ ° ′
1	10♈54	16♏27	27♈33	2♉42	5♓19	20♍16	4♋27	9♊56	4♎54
2	11 53	28 26	27 48	2℞25	6 6	20℞ 9	4 30	9 58	4℞53
3	12 52	10♐32	27 55	2 5	6 53	20 2	4 33	10 0	4 51
4	13 51	22 48	27℞55	1 43	7 39	19 55	4 36	10 2	4 50
5	14 50	5♑19	27 48	1 19	8 26	19 49	4 40	10 5	4 48
6	15 49	18 10	27 35	0 53	9 13	19 42	4 43	10 7	4 46
7	16 48	1♒25	27 15	0 24	10 0	19 36	4 46	10 9	4 44
8	17 47	15 7	26 50	29♈54	10 46	19 30	4 50	10 12	4 43
9	18 46	29 18	26 20	29 22	11 33	19 24	4 53	10 14	4 41
10	19 45	13♓56	25 46	28 49	12 19	19 18	4 57	10 17	4 40
11	20 44	28 58	25 8	28 14	13 6	19 12	5 1	10 19	4 38
12	21 43	14♈14	24 27	27 38	13 53	19 6	5 4	10 22	4 37
13	22 42	29 35	23 44	27 2	14 39	19 1	5 8	10 24	4 35
14	23 40	14♉47	23 0	26 24	15 26	18 55	5 12	10 27	4 34
15	24 39	29 41	22 16	25 47	16 13	18 50	5 16	10 30	4 32
16	25 38	14♊ 9	21 32	25 9	16 59	18 45	5 20	10 32	4 31
17	26 37	28 9	20 49	24 32	17 46	18 40	5 25	10 35	4 29
18	27 35	11♋40	20 8	23 54	18 32	18 35	5 29	10 38	4 28
19	28 34	24 44	19 30	23 17	19 18	18 31	5 33	10 41	4 26
20	29 32	7♌26	18 55	22 42	20 5	18 26	5 38	10 44	4 25
21	0♉31	19 49	18 24	22 7	20 51	18 22	5 42	10 47	4 23
22	1 29	1♍59	17 57	21 33	21 37	18 18	5 47	10 50	4 22
23	2 28	14 0	17 34	21 1	22 24	18 14	5 52	10 53	4 20
24	3 26	25 55	17 16	20 31	23 10	18 10	5 57	10 56	4 19
25	4 25	7♎47	17 3	20 2	23 57	18 7	6 2	10 59	4 17
26	5 23	19 39	16 55	19 35	24 43	18 3	6 7	11 2	4 16
27	6 21	1♏33	16 51	19 10	25 29	18 0	6 12	11 5	4 15
28	7 20	15 29	16 D53	18 47	26 16	17 57	6 17	11 8	4 13
29	8 18	25 30	16 59	18 27	27 2	17 54	6 23	11 11	4 12
30	9 16	7♐37	17 11	18 9	27 48	17 51	6 28	11 14	4 11

Pluto 7 Leo all month

1945

MAY

DAY	☉	☽	☿	♀	♂	♃	♄	♅	♆
	° ′	° ′	° ′	° ′	° ′	° ′	° ′	° ′	° ′
1	10 ♉ 15	19 ♐ 51	17 ♈ 27	17 ♈ 54	28 ♓ 34	17 ♍ 49	6 ♋ 33	11 ♊ 17	4 ♎ 10
2	11 13	2 ♑ 15	17 48	17 ℞ 41	29 21	17 ℞ 46	6 39	11 20	4 ℞ 8
3	12 11	14 52	18 13	17 30	0 ♈ 7	17 44	6 44	11 24	4 7
4	13 9	27 46	18 42	17 22	0 53	17 42	6 50	11 27	4 6
5	14 7	10 ♒ 59	19 16	17 16	1 39	17 40	6 56	11 30	4 5
6	15 5	24 35	19 53	17 13	2 25	17 39	7 1	11 33	4 3
7	16 3	8 ♓ 36	20 34	17 D 12	3 11	17 37	7 7	11 37	4 2
8	17 1	23 1	21 19	17 13	3 57	17 36	7 13	11 40	4 1
9	17 59	7 ♈ 47	22 7	17 17	4 43	17 35	7 19	11 43	4 0
10	18 57	22 49	22 59	17 23	5 29	17 34	7 25	11 46	3 59
11	19 55	7 ♉ 57	23 54	17 31	6 15	17 33	7 31	11 50	3 58
12	20 53	23 2	24 52	17 42	7 1	17 32	7 37	11 53	3 57
13	21 51	7 ♊ 53	25 53	17 54	7 47	17 32	7 43	11 56	3 56
14	22 49	22 24	26 57	18 9	8 33	17 31	7 49	11 59	3 55
15	23 47	6 ♋ 29	28 4	18 25	9 18	17 D 31	7 56	12 3	3 54
16	24 45	20 6	29 14	18 44	10 4	17 31	8 2	12 6	3 53
17	25 43	3 ♌ 17	0 ♉ 26	19 4	10 50	17 32	8 8	12 9	3 52
18	26 41	16 3	1 41	19 26	11 36	17 32	8 15	12 13	3 51
19	27 38	28 30	2 59	19 49	12 21	17 33	8 21	12 16	3 50
20	28 36	10 ♍ 41	4 19	20 16	13 7	17 34	8 28	12 20	3 50
21	29 34	22 41	5 42	20 42	13 53	17 35	8 35	12 23	3 49
22	0 ♊ 32	4 ♎ 36	7 7	21 10	14 38	17 36	8 41	12 27	3 48
23	1 29	16 27	8 34	21 40	15 24	17 38	8 48	12 30	3 48
24	2 27	28 20	10 4	22 11	16 9	17 39	8 55	12 34	3 47
25	3 24	10 ♏ 17	11 37	22 44	16 54	17 41	9 2	12 37	3 46
26	4 22	22 19	13 11	23 18	17 40	17 43	9 9	12 41	3 45
27	5 20	4 ♐ 29	14 48	23 54	18 25	17 45	9 16	12 44	3 45
28	6 17	16 47	16 28	24 30	19 10	17 47	9 23	12 48	3 44
29	7 15	29 16	18 10	25 8	19 55	17 50	9 30	12 51	3 44
30	8 12	11 ♑ 56	19 54	25 47	20 40	17 52	9 37	12 55	3 43
31	9 10	24 48	21 40	26 27	21 25	17 55	9 44	12 58	3 43

Pluto 7 Leo all month

JUNE

DAY	☉	☽	☿	♀	♂	♃	♄	♅	♆
	° ′	° ′	° ′	° ′	° ′	° ′	° ′	° ′	° ′
1	10 ♊ 7	7 ♒ 54	23 ♉ 29	27 ♈ 8	22 ♈ 10	17 ♍ 58	9 ♋ 51	13 ♊ 2	3 ♎ 42
2	11 5	21 16	25 20	27 50	22 55	18 1	9 58	13 5	3 ℞ 42
3	12 2	4 ♓ 55	27 13	28 33	23 40	18 4	10 5	13 9	3 41
4	13 0	18 51	29 9	29 17	24 25	18 8	10 13	13 12	3 41
5	13 57	3 ♈ 5	1 ♊ 6	0 ♉ 2	25 10	18 11	10 20	13 16	3 41
6	14 54	17 33	3 6	0 48	25 55	18 15	10 27	13 20	3 41
7	15 52	2 ♉ 13	5 8	1 34	26 40	18 19	10 35	13 23	3 41
8	16 49	16 58	7 12	2 22	27 24	18 23	10 43	13 27	3 40
9	17 47	1 ♊ 41	9 18	3 10	28 9	18 27	10 49	13 31	3 40
10	18 44	16 15	11 25	3 59	28 54	18 32	10 56	13 35	3 39
11	19 41	0 ♋ 34	13 33	4 48	29 38	18 36	11 4	13 38	3 39
12	20 39	14 33	15 43	5 38	0 ♉ 23	18 41	11 11	13 42	3 39
10	21 36	28 9	17 54	6 29	1 7	18 46	11 19	13 45	3 39
14	22 34	11 ♌ 21	20 5	7 21	1 51	18 51	11 26	13 49	3 39
15	23 31	24 10	22 17	8 13	2 36	18 57	11 34	13 52	3 D 39
16	24 28	6 ♍ 40	24 29	9 6	3 20	19 2	11 41	13 56	3 39
17	25 25	18 54	26 41	9 59	4 4	19 8	11 49	13 59	3 39
18	26 23	0 ♎ 57	28 52	10 53	4 48	19 14	11 57	14 3	3 39
19	27 20	12 52	1 ♋ 3	11 47	5 32	19 19	12 4	14 6	3 39
20	28 17	24 45	3 13	12 42	6 16	19 25	12 12	14 10	3 39
21	29 14	6 ♏ 39	5 21	13 37	7 0	19 31	12 20	14 13	3 40
22	0 ♋ 12	18 39	7 29	14 33	7 44	19 37	12 28	14 16	3 40
23	1 9	0 ♐ 47	9 35	15 30	8 28	19 44	12 35	14 20	3 40
24	2 6	13 6	11 39	16 26	9 11	19 50	12 43	14 23	3 41
25	3 3	25 39	13 41	17 24	9 55	19 57	12 50	14 26	3 41
26	4 1	8 ♑ 25	15 42	18 21	10 38	20 4	12 58	14 29	3 41
27	4 58	21 25	17 41	19 19	11 22	20 10	13 6	14 33	3 41
28	5 55	4 ♒ 39	19 38	20 18	12 5	20 17	13 14	14 36	3 42
29	6 52	18 7	21 33	21 16	12 48	20 24	13 22	14 40	3 42
30	7 49	1 ♓ 48	23 26	22 16	13 31	20 31	13 30	14 43	3 42

Pluto 8 Leo all month

1945

JULY

DAY	☉	☽	☿	♀	♂	♃	♄	♅	♆
	° ′	° ′	° ′	° ′	° ′	° ′	° ′	° ′	° ′
1	8♋47	15♓40	25♋16	23♉15	14♉15	20♍39	13♋38	14♊47	3♎43
2	9 44	29 43	27 5	24 15	14 58	20 46	13 45	14 50	3 43
3	10 41	13♈53	28 52	25 15	15 41	20 54	13 53	14 53	3 44
4	11 38	28 10	0♌36	26 16	16 24	21 2	14 1	14 56	3 45
5	12 35	12♉30	2 19	27 17	17 7	21 10	14 9	15 0	3 45
6	13 33	26 50	3 59	28 18	17 49	21 18	14 16	15 3	3 46
7	14 30	11♊ 5	5 37	29 18	18 32	21 26	14 24	15 6	3 47
8	15 27	25 14	7 13	0♊20	19 15	21 34	14 32	15 9	3 48
9	16 24	9♋10	8 47	1 22	19 57	21 43	14 40	15 13	3 48
10	17 22	22 51	10 19	2 24	20 40	21 51	14 47	15 16	3 49
11	18 19	6♌15	11 48	3 26	21 22	22 0	14 55	15 19	3 50
12	19 16	19 21	13 16	4 29	22 4	22 9	15 3	15 22	2 51
13	20 13	2♍ 8	14 41	5 32	22 47	22 17	15 11	15 25	3 52
14	21 10	14 37	16 5	6 35	23 29	22 26	15 18	15 28	3 53
15	22 8	26 52	17 25	7 38	24 11	22 35	15 26	15 31	3 54
16	23 5	8♎55	18 44	8 42	24 53	22 44	15 34	15 34	3 55
17	24 2	20 51	20 0	9 46	25 35	22 53	15 42	15 37	3 56
18	24 59	2♏44	21 14	10 50	26 16	23 3	15 49	15 40	3 57
19	25 57	14 39	22 25	11 54	26 58	23 12	15 57	15 43	3 58
20	26 54	26 40	23 34	12 59	27 40	23 22	16 5	15 46	3 59
21	27 51	8♐52	24 41	14 4	28 21	23 31	16 13	15 49	4 0
22	28 48	21 18	25 44	15 9	29 2	23 41	16 20	15 51	4 1
23	29 46	4♑ 1	26 45	16 14	29 44	23 51	16 28	15 54	4 2
24	0♌43	17 3	27 43	17 19	0♊25	24 1	16 36	15 57	4 3
25	1 40	0♒25	28 38	18 25	1 7	24 11	16 43	16 0	4 4
26	2 38	14 4	29 30	19 30	1 48	24 21	16 51	16 2	4 6
27	3 35	27 59	0♍18	20 36	2 29	24 31	16 58	16 5	4 7
28	4 32	12♓ 6	1 3	21 42	3 10	24 41	17 6	16 8	4 8
29	5 30	26 21	1 45	22 48	3 51	24 51	17 13	16 10	4 9
30	6 27	10♈40	2 22	23 55	4 31	25 2	17 21	16 13	4 11
31	7 24	24 58	2 56	25 1	5 12	25 13	17 28	16 15	4 12

Pluto 8 Leo all month

AUGUST

DAY	☉	☽	☿	♀	♂	♃	♄	♅	♆
	° ′	° ′	° ′	° ′	° ′	° ′	° ′	° ′	° ′
1	8♌22	9♉12	3♍26	26♊ 8	5♊52	25♍23	17♋36	16♊18	4♎13
2	9 19	23 20	3 51	27 15	6 33	25 34	17 43	16 20	4 14
3	10 17	7♊21	4 12	28 22	7 13	25 44	17 51	16 23	4 16
4	11 14	21 12	4 29	29 29	7 53	25 55	17 58	16 25	4 17
5	12 12	4♋54	4 40	0♋37	8 33	26 6	18 5	16 27	4 18
6	13 9	18 25	4 47	1 44	9 13	26 17	18 13	16 30	4 19
7	14 7	1♌43	4 ℞ 48	2 52	9 53	26 28	18 20	16 32	4 21
8	15 4	14 49	4 44	3 59	10 33	26 39	18 27	16 34	4 22
9	16 2	27 40	4 35	5 7	11 13	26 50	18 34	16 36	4 24
10	16 59	10♍18	4 20	6 15	11 52	27 1	18 42	16 38	4 25
11	17 57	22 41	4 0	7 24	12 32	27 13	18 49	16 40	4 27
12	18 54	4♎53	3 35	8 32	13 11	27 24	18 56	16 42	4 29
13	19 52	16 54	3 4	9 40	13 50	27 35	19 3	16 44	4 31
14	20 50	28 48	2 29	10 49	14 29	27 47	19 10	16 46	4 32
15	21 47	10♏40	1 49	11 58	15 8	27 58	19 17	16 48	4 34
16	22 45	22 33	1 5	13 6	15 47	28 10	19 24	16 50	4 36
17	23 43	4♐33	0 18	14 15	16 26	28 22	19 31	16 52	4 38
18	24 40	16 44	29♌28	15 24	17 4	28 33	19 38	16 54	4 39
19	25 38	29 12	28 37	16 33	17 43	28 45	19 45	16 55	4 41
20	26 36	12♑ 0	27 45	17 43	18 21	28 57	19 52	16 57	4 43
21	27 34	25 12	26 53	18 52	18 59	29 9	19 59	16 59	4 45
22	28 31	8♒49	26 2	20 2	19 37	29 21	20 5	17 1	4 47
23	29 29	22 49	25 14	21 11	20 15	29 33	20 12	17 2	4 49
24	0♍27	7♓ 9	24 20	22 21	20 53	29 45	20 18	17 4	4 51
25	1 25	21 44	23 48	23 31	21 31	29 57	20 25	17 5	4 53
26	2 23	6♈26	23 13	24 41	22 8	0♎ 9	20 31	17 7	4 55
27	3 21	21 8	22 44	25 51	22 46	0 21	20 38	17 8	4 57
28	4 19	5♉43	22 21	27 1	23 23	0 33	20 44	17 9	4 59
29	5 17	20 6	22 6	28 11	24 0	0 45	20 50	17 10	5 1
30	6 15	4♊13	21 59	29 22	24 37	0 58	20 57	17 12	5 3
31	7 13	18 5	22 D 0	0♌32	25 14	1 10	21 3	17 13	5 6

Pluto 9 Leo all month

1945

SEPTEMBER

DAY	☉ ° ′	☽ ° ′	☿ ° ′	♀ ° ′	♂ ° ′	♃ ° ′	♄ ° ′	♅ ° ′	♆ ° ′
1	8♍11	1♋41	22♌ 9	1♌43	25♊51	1♎23	21♋ 9	17♊14	5♎ 8
2	9 9	15 3	22 27	2 54	26 28	1 35	21 15	17 15	5 10
3	10 7	28 12	22 53	4 4	27 4	1 48	21 21	17 17	5 12
4	11 5	11♌ 8	23 28	5 15	27 41	2 0	21 27	17 18	5 15
5	12 3	23 54	24 11	6 26	28 17	2 12	21 33	17 19	5 17
6	13 1	6♍28	25 2	7 37	28 53	2 24	21 39	17 20	5 19
7	14 0	18 52	26 0	8 48	29 29	2 37	21 45	17 21	5 21
8	14 58	1♎ 7	27 5	10 0	0♋ 5	2 49	21 50	17 21	5 23
9	15 56	13 12	28 17	11 11	0 40	3 3	21 56	17 22	5 25
10	16 55	25 9	29 35	12 22	1 15	3 16	22 2	17 23	5 27
11	17 53	7♏ 1	0♍58	13 34	1 51	3 28	22 7	17 23	5 29
12	18 51	18 50	2 27	14 45	2 26	3 41	22 13	17 24	5 32
13	19 50	0♐41	4 0	15 57	3 0	3 54	22 18	17 24	5 34
14	20 48	12 38	5 36	17 9	3 35	4 7	22 23	17 25	5 36
15	21 47	24 46	7 17	18 21	4 9	4 19	22 29	17 25	5 38
16	22 45	7♑11	9 0	19 33	4 44	4 32	22 34	17 26	5 40
17	23 44	19 57	10 45	20 45	5 18	4 45	22 39	17 26	5 42
18	24 42	3♒10	12 32	21 57	5 52	4 58	22 44	17 26	5 44
19	25 41	16 51	14 21	23 9	6 25	5 10	22 49	17 27	5 46
20	26 39	1♓ 1	16 10	24 22	6 59	5 23	22 53	17 27	5 49
21	27 38	15 36	18 1	25 34	7 33	5 36	22 58	17 27	5 51
22	28 37	0♈31	19 52	26 46	8 6	5 49	23 3	17 27	5 52
23	29 35	15 36	21 43	27 59	8 38	6 2	23 8	17 27	5 55
24	0♎34	0♉42	23 34	29 11	9 11	6 15	23 12	17℞27	5 58
25	1 33	15 38	25 24	0♍24	9 44	6 28	23 17	17 27	6 0
26	2 32	0♊17	27 14	1 37	10 16	6 41	23 21	17 27	6 2
27	3 31	14 35	29 4	2 49	10 48	6 54	23 25	17 27	6 4
28	4 29	28 30	0♎54	4 2	11 20	7 7	23 28	17 27	6 7
29	5 28	12♋ 2	2 42	5 15	11 52	7 20	23 33	17 26	6 9
30	6 27	25 14	4 31	6 28	12 23	7 33	23 37	17 26	6 11

Pluto 10 Leo all month

OCTOBER

DAY	☉ ° ′	☽ ° ′	☿ ° ′	♀ ° ′	♂ ° ′	♃ ° ′	♄ ° ′	♅ ° ′	♆ ° ′
1	7♎26	8♌10	6♎18	7♍41	12♋54	7♎46	23♋41	17♊26	6♎13
2	8 25	20 51	8 5	8 55	13 25	7 59	23 45	17℞25	6 16
3	9 24	3♍20	9 51	10 8	13 56	8 12	23 49	17 25	6 18
4	10 24	15 39	11 36	11 21	14 26	8 25	23 53	17 24	6 20
5	11 23	27 51	13 20	12 34	14 57	8 38	23 56	17 24	6 22
6	12 22	9♎55	15 3	13 48	15 27	8 51	24 0	17 23	6 25
7	13 21	21 52	16 46	15 1	15 57	9 4	24 3	17 22	6 27
8	14 20	3♏45	18 28	16 15	16 26	9 17	24 6	17 21	6 29
9	15 20	15 35	20 9	17 28	16 55	9 30	24 9	17 21	6 31
10	16 19	27 24	21 49	18 42	17 24	9 43	24 12	17 20	6 34
11	17 18	9♐14	23 28	19 56	17 53	9 56	24 15	17 19	6 36
12	18 18	21 10	25 7	21 10	18 21	10 9	24 18	17 18	6 38
13	19 17	3♑17	26 45	22 23	18 49	10 22	24 21	17 17	6 40
14	20 17	15 38	28 23	23 37	19 17	10 34	24 23	17 16	6 42
15	21 16	28 20	29 59	24 51	19 44	10 47	24 26	17 15	6 44
16	22 16	11♒26	1♏35	26 5	20 11	11 0	24 28	17 14	6 46
17	23 15	25 2	3 10	27 19	20 38	11 13	24 31	17 13	6 48
18	24 15	9♓ 7	4 45	28 33	21 5	11 26	24 33	17 11	6 51
19	25 14	23 42	6 19	29 47	21 31	11 39	24 35	17 10	6 53
20	26 14	8♈41	7 52	1♎ 1	21 57	11 52	24 37	17 9	6 55
21	27 13	23 56	9 25	2 15	22 22	12 5	24 39	17 8	6 57
22	28 13	9♉15	10 57	3 30	22 48	12 17	24 40	17 6	7 0
23	29 13	24 28	12 29	4 44	23 13	12 30	24 42	17 5	7 2
24	0♏13	9♊24	14 0	5 58	23 37	12 43	24 44	17 4	7 4
25	1 12	23 58	15 30	7 13	24 1	12 55	24 45	17 2	7 6
26	2 12	8♋ 4	17 0	8 27	24 25	13 8	24 47	17 1	7 8
27	3 12	21 43	18 30	9 42	24 48	13 20	24 48	16 59	7 10
28	4 12	4♌58	19 59	10 56	25 11	13 33	24 49	16 57	7 12
29	5 12	17 50	21 27	12 11	25 34	13 45	24 50	16 56	7 14
30	6 12	0♍25	22 55	13 25	25 56	13 58	24 50	16 54	7 16
31	7 12	12 45	24 22	14 40	26 17	14 10	24 51	16 52	7 18

Pluto 11 Leo all month

1945

NOVEMBER

DAY	☉	☽	☿	♀	♂	♃	♄	♅	♆
	° ′	° ′	° ′	° ′	° ′	° ′	° ′	° ′	° ′
1	8♏12	24♍55	25♏48	15≏55	26♋39	14≏23	24♋52	16♊50	7≏20
2	9 12	6≏56	27 14	17 9	27 0	14 35	24 52	16℞49	7 22
3	10 12	18 52	28 39	18 24	27 20	14 48	24 53	16 47	7 24
4	11 12	0♏45	0↗3	19 39	27 40	15 0	24 53	16 45	7 26
5	12 12	12 35	1 26	20 54	27 59	15 12	24 54	16 43	7 28
6	13 13	24 25	2 49	22 8	28 18	15 24	24 54	16 41	7 30
7	14 13	6↗17	4 11	23 23	28 37	15 36	24℞54	16 39	7 31
8	15 13	18 11	5 32	24 38	28 55	15 48	24 54	16 37	7 33
9	16 13	0♑12	6 52	25 53	29 13	16 0	24 54	16 35	7 35
10	17 14	12 23	8 10	27 8	29 30	16 12	24 53	16 33	7 37
11	18 14	24 46	9 27	28 23	29 46	16 24	24 53	16 30	7 39
12	19 14	7≈27	10 43	29 38	0♌2	16 36	24 52	16 28	7 41
13	20 15	20 28	11 57	0♏53	0 17	16 48	24 51	16 26	7 43
14	21 15	3✶55	13 9	2 8	0 32	17 0	24 51	16 24	7 45
15	22 16	17 49	14 19	3 23	0 46	17 12	24 50	16 21	7 46
16	23 16	2♈11	15 26	4 38	1 0	17 24	24 49	16 19	7 48
17	24 17	16 57	16 31	5 53	1 13	17 36	24 48	16 17	7 50
18	25 17	2♉2	17 33	7 8	1 26	17 47	24 47	16 15	7 51
19	26 18	17 16	18 32	8 23	1 38	17 59	24 45	16 12	7 53
20	27 18	2♊30	19 26	9 38	1 49	18 10	24 44	16 10	7 54
21	28 19	17 34	20 16	10 53	1 59	18 21	24 42	16 7	7 56
22	29 19	2♋17	21 1	12 8	2 9	18 33	24 41	16 5	7 57
23	0↗20	16 36	21 41	13 24	2 18	18 44	24 39	16 2	7 59
24	1 21	0♌27	22 14	14 39	2 27	18 55	24 37	16 0	8 0
25	2 21	13 51	22 40	15 54	2 35	19 6	24 35	15 57	8 2
26	3 22	26 49	22 58	17 9	2 42	19 17	24 33	15 55	8 3
27	4 23	9♍26	23 8	18 25	2 49	19 28	24 30	15 52	8 5
28	5 23	21 45	23℞8	19 40	2 55	19 39	24 28	15 50	8 6
29	6 24	3≏52	22 57	20 55	3 0	19 50	24 26	15 48	8 8
30	7 25	15 49	22 36	22 10	3 4	20 0	24 23	15 45	8 9

Pluto 11 Leo all month

DECEMBER

DAY	☉	☽	☿	♀	♂	♃	♄	♅	♆
	° ′	° ′	° ′	° ′	° ′	° ′	° ′	° ′	° ′
1	8↗26	27≏41	22↗4	23♏26	3♌8	20≏11	24♋21	15♊43	8≏11
2	9 27	9♏30	21℞21	24 41	3 11	20 21	24℞18	15♑40	8 12
3	10 28	21 20	20 27	25 56	3 12	20 31	24 15	15 38	8 13
4	11 28	3↗14	19 24	27 12	3 14	20 42	24 12	15 35	8 14
5	12 29	15 12	18 12	28 27	3℞14	20 52	24 9	15 33	8 15
6	13 30	27 16	16 54	29 43	3 13	21 2	24 6	15 30	8 16
7	14 31	9♑29	15 32	0↗58	3 12	21 12	24 3	15 27	8 17
8	15 32	21 52	14 10	2 14	3 10	21 22	24 0	15 25	8 18
9	16 33	4≈27	12 49	3 29	3 7	21 32	23 56	15 22	8 20
10	17 34	17 16	11 33	4 44	3 3	21 42	23 53	15 20	8 21
11	18 35	0✶22	10 23	5 59	2 59	21 52	23 50	15 17	8 22
12	19 36	13 47	9 21	7 15	2 53	22 1	23 46	15 15	8 23
13	20 37	27 32	8 29	8 30	2 47	22 11	23 43	15 12	8 24
14	21 38	11♈37	7 48	9 46	2 40	22 20	23 39	15 10	8 25
15	22 39	26 3	7 18	11 1	2 32	22 29	23 35	15 7	8 26
16	23 40	10♉44	6 59	12 17	2 23	22 38	23 31	15 5	8 27
17	24 41	25 37	6 51	13 32	2 13	22 47	23 27	15 2	8 27
18	25 42	10♊33	6℞54	14 48	2 3	22 56	23 23	15 0	8 28
19	26 43	25 25	7 6	16 3	1 51	23 5	23 19	14 57	8 28
20	27 44	10♋5	7 26	17 19	1 39	23 14	23 15	14 55	8 29
21	28 46	24 25	7 54	18 34	1 26	23 22	23 10	14 52	8 30
22	29 47	8♌23	8 29	19 50	1 12	23 31	23 6	14 50	8 31
23	0♑48	21 54	9 11	21 5	0 58	23 39	23 2	14 47	8 32
24	1 49	5♍1	9 58	22 21	0 43	23 48	22 58	14 45	8 32
25	2 50	17 44	10 50	23 36	0 26	23 56	22 53	14 42	8 33
26	3 51	0≏8	11 46	24 52	0 9	24 4	22 49	14 40	8 33
27	4 52	12 16	12 46	26 7	29♋52	24 12	22 44	14 38	8 34
28	5 53	24 13	13 49	27 23	29 35	24 19	22 40	14 35	8 34
29	6 54	6♏3	14 56	28 38	29 16	24 27	22 35	14 33	8 35
30	7 56	17 53	16 5	29 54	28 57	24 34	22 30	14 31	8 35
31	8 57	29 44	17 16	1↗9	28 37	24 41	22 25	14 29	8 35

Pluto 11 Leo all month

1946

JANUARY

DAY	☉	☽	☿	♀	♂	♃	♄	♅	♆
	° ′	° ′	° ′	° ′	° ′	° ′	° ′	° ′	° ′
1	9♑58	11♐41	18♐30	2♑25	28♋16	24♎48	22♋21	14♊26	8♎36
2	10 59	23 47	19 45	3 40	27R55	24 55	22R16	14R24	8 36
3	12 0	6♑4	21 2	4 56	27 34	25 2	22 11	14 22	8 36
4	13 2	18 33	22 20	6 11	27 12	25 9	22 6	14 20	8 37
5	14 3	1♒16	23 40	7 27	26 50	25 15	22 2	14 18	8 37
6	15 4	14 12	25 1	8 42	26 26	25 22	21 57	14 16	8 37
7	16 5	27 21	26 23	9 58	26 4	25 28	21 52	14 14	8 37
8	17 6	10♓44	27 46	11 13	25 40	25 34	21 47	14 12	8 37
9	18 7	24 19	29 10	12 29	25 17	25 40	21 42	14 10	8 37
10	19 9	8♈7	0♑35	13 44	24 53	25 46	21 37	14 8	8R37
11	20 10	22 6	2 0	15 0	24 29	25 52	21 32	14 6	8 37
12	21 11	6♉16	3 27	16 15	24 5	25 57	21 27	14 4	8 37
13	22 12	20 34	4 54	17 31	23 41	26 3	21 22	14 2	8 37
14	23 13	4♊59	6 22	18 46	23 17	26 8	21 17	14 0	8 37
15	24 14	19 27	7 50	20 1	22 53	26 13	21 12	13 58	8 37
16	25 15	3♋53	9 19	21 16	22 29	26 18	21 7	13 56	8 37
17	26 16	18 11	10 49	22 32	22 6	26 22	21 2	13 55	8 36
18	27 17	2♌18	12 19	23 47	21 42	26 27	20 58	13 53	8 36
19	28 18	16 8	13 49	25 3	21 19	26 32	20 53	13 52	8 36
20	29 19	29 38	15 21	26 18	20 56	26 36	20 48	13 50	8 36
21	0♒20	12♍46	16 53	27 34	20 33	26 40	20 43	13 49	8 35
22	1 22	25 33	18 25	28 49	20 11	26 43	20 39	13 47	8 35
23	2 23	8♎0	19 58	0♒5	19 49	26 47	20 34	13 46	8 34
24	3 24	20 11	21 32	1 20	19 27	26 50	20 29	13 44	8 34
25	4 25	2♏9	23 6	2 36	19 6	26 54	20 24	13 43	8 33
26	5 26	14 1	24 41	3 51	18 46	26 57	20 20	13 41	8 33
27	6 27	25 50	26 17	5 6	18 26	27 0	20 15	13 40	8 32
28	7 28	7♐42	27 53	6 21	18 7	27 3	20 10	13 39	8 32
29	8 28	19 42	29 30	7 37	17 49	27 5	20 5	13 38	8 31
30	9 29	1♑54	1♒8	8 52	17 31	27 8	20 1	13 37	8 31
31	10 30	14 21	2 46	10 8	17 13	27 10	19 56	13 36	8 30

Pluto 11 Leo all month

FEBRUARY

DAY	☉	☽	☿	♀	♂	♃	♄	♅	♆
	° ′	° ′	° ′	° ′	° ′	° ′	° ′	° ′	° ′
1	11♒31	27♑6	4♒25	11♒23	16♋57	27♎12	19♋52	13♊35	8♎29
2	12 32	10♒8	6 4	12 39	16R41	27 14	19R47	13R34	8R29
3	13 33	23 29	7 45	13 54	16 26	27 15	19 43	13 33	8 28
4	14 34	7♓5	9 26	15 9	16 11	27 17	19 39	13 32	8 27
5	15 35	20 55	11 8	16 24	15 58	27 18	19 35	13 31	8 26
6	16 36	4♈53	12 50	17 40	15 44	27 19	19 31	13 30	8 25
7	17 36	18 57	14 33	18 55	15 32	27 20	19 27	13 30	8 24
8	18 37	3♉4	16 18	20 10	15 21	27 21	19 23	13 29	8 23
9	19 38	17 12	18 3	21 25	15 10	27 21	19 19	13 28	8 22
10	20 39	1♊19	19 48	22 41	15 1	27 22	19 15	13 27	8 21
11	21 39	15 24	21 35	23 56	14 52	27 22	19 11	13 27	8 20
12	22 40	29 26	23 22	25 11	14 44	27R22	19 7	13 26	8 20
13	23 41	13♋23	25 10	26 26	14 36	27 22	19 3	13 26	8 19
14	24 41	27 14	26 59	27 42	14 30	27 21	19 0	13 26	8 18
15	25 42	10♌55	28 48	28 57	14 24	27 21	18 56	13 25	8 16
16	26 42	24 25	0♓38	0♓12	14 20	27 20	18 53	13 25	8 15
17	27 43	7♍41	2 29	1 27	14 15	27 19	18 50	13 25	8 14
18	28 44	20 40	4 20	2 42	14 11	27 18	18 47	13 25	8 13
19	29 44	3♎21	6 11	3 57	14 9	27 16	18 44	13 25	8 12
20	0♓44	15 47	8 3	5 12	14 7	27 15	18 41	13 25	8 11
21	1 45	27 57	9 56	6 27	14 6	27 13	18 38	13 D25	8 10
22	2 45	9♏56	11 48	7 42	14 D 6	27 12	18 35	13 25	8 8
23	3 46	21 47	13 39	8 58	14 6	27 10	18 32	13 25	8 7
24	4 46	3♐36	15 31	10 13	14 7	27 8	18 29	13 25	8 5
25	5 46	15 28	17 21	11 28	14 9	27 5	18 27	13 25	8 4
26	6 47	27 28	19 11	12 43	14 12	27 2	18 24	13 25	8 2
27	7 47	9♑41	20 59	13 58	14 15	27 0	18 22	13 26	8 1
28	8 47	22 13	22 46	15 13	14 19	26 57	18 20	13 26	8 0

Pluto 10 Leo all month

1946

MARCH

Pluto 9 Leo all month

DAY	☉	☽	☿	♀	♂	♃	♄	⛢	♆
1	9♓48	5♒6	24♓30	16♓28	14♋24	26♎54	18♋18	13♊26	7♎59
2	10 48	18 23	26 11	17 43	14 30	26 R 50	18 R 16	13 27	7 R 57
3	11 48	2♓4	27 50	18 57	14 36	26 47	18 14	13 27	7 56
4	12 48	16 4	29 24	20 12	14 43	26 43	18 12	13 28	7 54
5	13 48	0♈22	0♈54	21 27	14 50	26 39	18 10	13 29	7 53
6	14 48	14 49	2 19	22 42	14 58	26 35	18 8	13 29	7 51
7	15 49	29 19	3 39	23 57	15 6	26 30	18 7	13 30	7 50
8	16 49	13♉46	4 52	25 12	15 16	26 26	18 5	13 31	7 48
9	17 49	28 6	5 59	26 27	15 25	26 21	18 4	13 32	7 47
10	18 49	12♊16	6 59	27 42	15 36	26 17	18 3	13 33	7 45
11	19 48	26 15	7 51	28 56	15 47	26 12	18 2	13 34	7 44
12	20 48	10♋3	8 36	0♈11	15 58	26 7	18 1	13 35	7 42
13	21 48	23 41	9 12	1 26	16 10	26 2	18 0	13 36	7 41
14	22 48	7♌8	9 40	2 40	16 22	25 57	17 59	13 37	7 39
15	23 48	20 24	10 0	3 55	16 35	25 51	17 59	13 38	7 38
16	24 48	3♍30	10 11	5 9	16 49	25 45	17 58	13 39	7 36
17	25 47	16 25	10 R 13	6 24	17 3	25 40	17 58	13 40	7 34
18	26 47	29 7	10 7	7 38	17 17	25 34	17 57	13 42	7 33
19	27 47	11♎37	9 54	8 53	17 32	25 28	17 57	13 43	7 31
20	28 46	23 54	9 32	10 8	17 48	25 22	17 57	13 45	7 29
21	29 46	5♏59	9 4	11 23	18 4	25 16	17 D 57	13 46	7 27
22	0♈45	17 55	8 29	12 37	18 20	25 9	17 57	13 48	7 26
23	1 45	29 45	7 49	13 52	18 37	25 3	17 57	13 49	7 24
24	2 44	11♐33	7 4	15 6	18 54	24 56	17 58	13 51	7 23
25	3 44	23 23	6 16	16 20	19 12	24 49	17 58	13 53	7 21
26	4 43	5♑22	5 26	17 35	19 30	24 42	17 59	13 54	7 20
27	5 43	17 34	4 34	18 49	19 48	24 35	17 59	13 56	7 18
28	6 42	0♒5	3 42	20 3	20 7	24 28	18 0	13 58	7 16
29	7 41	12 59	2 50	21 17	20 26	24 21	18 1	14 0	7 14
30	8 41	26 20	2 1	22 31	20 46	24 14	18 2	14 1	7 13
31	9 40	10♓9	1 14	23 46	21 5	24 7	18 3	14 3	7 11

APRIL

Pluto 9 Leo all month

DAY	☉	☽	☿	♀	♂	♃	♄	⛢	♆
1	10♈39	24♓24	0♈31	25♈0	21♋26	24♎0	18♋4	14♊5	7♎10
2	11 38	9♈0	29♓51	26 14	21 46	23 R 53	18 5	14 7	7 R 8
3	12 37	23 49	29 R 16	27 28	22 7	23 45	18 7	14 9	7 7
4	13 37	8♉44	28 46	28 42	22 28	23 38	18 8	14 11	7 5
5	14 36	23 36	28 21	29 57	22 50	23 30	18 10	14 13	7 3
6	15 35	8♊17	28 2	1♉11	23 12	23 23	18 12	14 15	7 1
7	16 34	22 42	27 48	2 25	23 34	23 15	18 14	14 17	7 0
8	17 33	6♋49	27 40	3 39	23 56	23 8	18 16	14 20	6 58
9	18 32	20 37	27 D 37	4 53	24 19	23 0	18 18	14 22	6 57
10	19 31	4♌7	27 39	6 7	24 42	22 52	18 20	14 24	6 55
11	20 30	17 22	27 47	7 21	25 5	22 45	18 22	14 27	6 54
12	21 28	0♍21	28 0	8 35	25 29	22 37	18 25	14 29	6 52
13	22 27	13 8	28 19	9 49	25 53	22 29	18 27	14 32	6 51
14	23 26	25 44	28 40	11 3	26 17	22 21	18 30	14 34	6 49
15	24 25	8♎8	29 7	12 17	26 41	22 14	18 32	14 37	6 48
16	25 23	20 23	29 39	13 30	27 6	22 6	18 35	14 39	6 46
17	26 22	2♏29	0♈14	14 44	27 31	21 59	18 38	14 42	6 44
18	27 21	14 27	0 53	15 58	27 56	21 51	18 41	14 45	6 42
19	28 19	26 19	1 36	17 12	28 22	21 44	18 44	14 47	6 41
20	29 18	8♐7	2 23	18 25	28 47	21 36	18 48	14 50	6 39
21	0♉16	19 54	3 13	19 39	29 13	21 28	18 51	14 53	6 38
22	1 15	1♑45	4 6	20 53	29 39	21 20	18 54	14 56	6 37
23	2 13	13 43	5 2	22 6	0♌5	21 13	18 58	14 58	6 35
24	3 12	25 54	6 2	23 20	0 31	21 5	19 1	15 1	6 34
25	4 10	8♒23	7 4	24 33	0 58	20 58	19 5	15 4	6 33
26	5 9	21 15	8 9	25 47	1 25	20 51	19 9	15 7	6 32
27	6 7	4♓32	9 16	27 0	1 52	20 44	19 13	15 10	6 30
28	7 6	18 18	10 26	28 14	2 19	20 37	19 17	15 13	6 29
29	8 4	2♈33	11 39	29 27	2 47	20 30	19 21	15 16	6 27
30	9 2	17 13	12 54	0♊40	3 14	20 23	19 25	15 19	6 26

1946

MAY

DAY	☉	☽	☿	♀	♂	♃	♄	♅	♆
	° ′	° ′	° ′	° ′	° ′	° ′	° ′	° ′	° ′
1	10♉ 0	2♉11	14♈11	1♊54	3♌42	20♎16	19♋29	15♊22	6♎24
2	10 59	17 20	15 30	3 7	4 10	20℞ 9	19 34	15 25	6℞23
3	11 57	2♊29	16 52	4 20	4 38	20 2	19 38	15 28	6 21
4	12 55	17 29	18 15	5 33	5 7	19 55	19 42	15 31	6 20
5	13 53	2♋12	19 41	6 46	5 35	19 49	19 47	15 34	6 18
6	14 51	16 34	21 9	7 59	6 4	19 42	19 51	15 38	6 17
7	15 49	0♌32	22 39	9 12	6 33	19 36	19 56	15 41	6 16
8	16 48	14 7	24 11	10 25	7 2	19 30	20 1	15 44	6 15
9	17 46	27 19	25 46	11 38	7 31	19 23	20 6	15 47	6 14
10	18 44	10♍13	27 22	12 51	8 0	19 17	20 11	15 51	6 13
11	19 41	22 49	29 0	14 4	8 30	19 11	20 16	15 54	6 12
12	20 39	5♎12	0♉40	15 17	8 59	19 5	20 21	15 57	6 11
13	21 37	17 23	2 22	16 30	9 29	19 0	20 26	16 0	6 10
14	22 35	29 26	4 6	17 42	9 59	18 54	20 31	16 4	6 8
15	23 33	11♏22	5 52	18 55	10 29	18 49	20 36	16 7	6 7
16	24 31	23 13	7 41	20 8	10 59	18 44	20 41	16 10	6 6
17	25 29	5♐ 2	9 31	21 21	11 29	18 39	20 47	16 13	6 5
18	26 26	16 50	11 23	22 33	12 0	18 35	20 52	16 17	6 4
19	27 24	28 40	13 17	23 46	12 30	18 30	20 58	16 20	6 3
20	28 22	10♑35	15 13	24 59	13 1	18 26	21 4	16 23	6 2
21	29 20	22 37	17 11	26 11	13 32	18 21	21 10	16 27	6 1
22	0♊17	4♒52	19 11	27 24	14 3	18 17	21 16	16 30	6 1
23	1 15	17 22	21 13	28 36	14 34	18 13	21 22	16 34	6 0
24	2 13	0♓11	23 17	29 49	15 5	18 9	21 28	16 37	5 59
25	3 10	13 24	25 22	1♋ 1	15 37	18 5	21 34	16 41	5 58
26	4 8	27 3	27 29	2 14	16 8	18 2	21 40	16 44	5 58
27	5 6	11♈ 9	29 37	3 26	16 40	17 58	21 46	16 48	5 57
28	6 3	25 39	1♊47	4 38	17 11	17 55	21 52	16 51	5 56
29	7 1	10♉31	3 59	5 51	17 43	17 52	21 58	16 55	5 56
30	7 58	25 38	6 10	7 3	18 15	17 49	22 5	16 58	5 55
31	8 56	10♊49	8 22	8 15	18 47	17 46	22 11	17 2	5 55

Pluto 9 Leo all month

JUNE

DAY	☉	☽	☿	♀	♂	♃	♄	♅	♆
	° ′	° ′	° ′	° ′	° ′	° ′	° ′	° ′	° ′
1	9♊53	25♊57	10♊34	9♋27	19♌19	17♎44	22♋17	17♊ 5	5♎54
2	10 51	10♋52	12 44	10 39	19 51	17℞41	22 23	17 9	5℞54
3	11 48	25 26	14 56	11 51	20 24	17 39	22 30	17 13	5 53
4	12 46	9♌36	17 7	13 3	20 56	17 37	22 36	17 16	5 53
5	13 43	23 20	19 18	14 15	21 29	17 35	22 43	17 19	5 52
6	14 41	6♍38	21 27	15 27	22 1	17 34	22 49	17 23	5 52
7	15 38	19 32	23 35	16 38	22 34	17 32	22 56	17 26	5 51
8	16 36	2♎ 6	25 42	17 50	23 7	17 31	23 3	17 30	5 51
9	17 33	14 23	27 47	19 2	23 40	17 30	23 10	17 33	5 51
10	18 30	26 28	29 50	20 14	24 13	17 29	23 17	17 37	5 51
11	19 28	8♏24	1♋51	21 25	24 46	17 29	23 24	17 40	5 51
12	20 25	20 14	3 50	22 37	25 19	17 28	23 31	17 44	5 51
13	21 22	2♐ 3	5 47	23 48	25 52	17 28	23 38	17 47	5 51
14	22 20	13 51	7 41	25 0	26 26	17 28	23 45	17 51	5 51
15	23 17	25 42	9 34	26 11	26 59	17 27	23 52	17 54	5 50
16	24 14	7♑39	11 24	27 23	27 33	17 27	23 59	17 58	5 50
17	25 11	19 42	13 12	28 34	28 7	17 D27	24 6	18 1	5 D50
18	26 9	1♒55	14 57	29 45	28 40	17 28	24 13	18 5	5 50
19	27 6	14 19	16 40	0♌56	29 14	17 28	24 20	18 8	5 51
20	28 3	26 57	18 20	2 7	29 48	17 29	24 27	18 12	5 51
21	29 0	9♓52	19 58	3 18	0♍22	17 30	24 34	18 15	5 51
22	29 58	23 5	21 34	4 29	0 56	17 31	24 41	18 19	5 51
23	0♋55	6♈38	23 7	5 40	1 30	17 33	24 49	18 22	5 51
24	1 52	20 34	24 38	6 51	2 4	17 34	24 56	18 26	5 51
25	2 49	4♉50	26 6	8 2	2 38	17 36	25 3	18 29	5 51
26	3 47	19 26	27 32	9 13	3 13	17 38	25 11	18 33	5 51
27	4 44	4♊16	28 55	10 23	3 47	17 40	25 18	18 36	5 52
28	5 41	19 16	0♌16	11 34	4 22	17 42	25 26	18 40	5 52
29	6 38	4♋16	1 34	12 44	4 57	17 45	25 33	18 43	5 52
30	7 36	19 8	2 50	13 55	5 31	17 47	25 41	18 47	5 53

Pluto 9 Leo all month

1946

JULY

DAY	☉	☽	☿	♀	♂	♃	♄	♅	♆
	° ′	° ′	° ′	° ′	° ′	° ′	° ′	° ′	° ′
1	8♋33	3♌45	4♌ 2	15♌ 5	6♍ 6	17♎50	25♋48	18♊50	5♎53
2	9 30	18 1	5 12	16 16	6 41	17 53	25 56	18 54	5 54
3	10 27	1♍51	6 19	17 26	7 16	17 56	26 3	18 57	5 54
4	11 25	15 15	7 24	18 36	7 51	17 59	26 11	19 1	5 55
5	12 22	28 13	8 25	19 46	8 27	18 3	26 19	19 4	5 55
6	13 19	10♎49	9 23	20 56	9 2	18 6	26 26	19 7	5 56
7	14 16	23 6	10 18	22 6	9 37	18 10	26 34	19 10	5 57
8	15 13	5♏ 9	11 9	23 16	10 12	18 14	26 41	19 14	5 57
9	16 11	17 2	11 58	24 26	10 48	18 18	26 49	19 17	5 58
10	17 8	28 51	12 42	25 35	11 23	18 22	26 57	19 20	5 59
11	18 5	10♐39	13 23	26 45	11 59	18 27	27 5	19 23	6 0
12	19 2	22 30	14 0	27 54	12 34	18 31	27 12	19 27	6 0
13	19 59	4♑27	14 33	29 4	13 10	18 36	27 20	19 30	6 1
14	20 57	16 33	15 2	0♍13	13 46	18 41	27 28	19 33	6 2
15	21 54	28 49	15 26	1 22	14 22	18 45	27 36	19 36	6 3
16	22 51	11♒18	15 47	2 31	14 57	18 50	27 43	19 39	6 4
17	23 48	23 59	16 2	3 40	15 33	18 56	27 51	19 42	6 5
18	24 45	6♓53	16 13	4 49	16 9	19 2	27 59	19 45	6 6
19	25 43	20 1	16 20	5 58	16 45	19 8	28 7	19 48	6 7
20	26 40	3♈22	16 R 21	7 7	17 21	19 14	28 14	19 52	6 8
21	27 37	16 59	16 18	8 16	17 58	19 20	28 22	19 55	6 9
22	28 34	0♉49	16 9	9 24	18 34	19 26	28 30	19 58	6 10
23	29 32	14 54	15 56	10 33	19 10	19 32	28 38	20 1	6 11
24	0♌29	29 13	15 38	11 41	19 47	19 38	28 45	20 4	6 12
25	1 26	13♊42	15 15	12 49	20 23	19 45	28 53	20 6	6 13
26	2 24	28 20	14 48	13 57	21 0	19 51	29 1	20 9	6 14
27	3 21	13♋ 0	14 17	15 5	21 37	19 58	29 9	20 12	6 15
28	4 18	27 87	13 41	16 13	22 13	20 5	29 16	20 15	6 16
29	5 16	12♌ 3	13 3	17 21	22 50	20 12	29 24	20 18	6 18
30	6 13	26 12	12 22	18 28	23 27	20 19	29 32	20 21	6 19
31	7 11	10♍ 0	11 39	19 36	24 4	20 26	29 40	20 24	6 20

Pluto 10 Leo all month

AUGUST

DAY	☉	☽	☿	♀	♂	♃	♄	♅	♆
	° ′	° ′	° ′	° ′	° ′	° ′	° ′	° ′	° ′
1	8♌ 8	23♍25	10♌54	20♍43	24♍41	20♎34	29♋47	20♊26	6♎21
2	9 5	6♎25	10 R 9	21 50	25 18	20 41	29 55	20 29	6 23
3	10 3	19 2	9 24	22 57	25 55	20 49	0♌ 3	20 31	6 24
4	11 0	1♏20	8 39	24 4	26 32	20 57	0 10	20 34	6 25
5	11 58	13 23	7 57	25 11	27 9	21 5	0 18	20 36	6 27
6	12 55	25 16	7 17	26 17	27 47	21 13	0 25	20 39	6 28
7	13 53	7♐ 5	6 41	27 24	28 24	21 21	0 33	20 41	6 30
8	14 50	18 54	6 9	28 30	29 1	21 29	0 41	20 44	6 31
9	15 48	0♑48	5 42	29 36	29 39	21 38	0 48	20 46	6 33
10	16 45	12 52	5 20	0♎42	0♎16	21 46	0 56	20 49	6 34
11	17 43	25 8	5 5	1 48	0 54	21 55	1 4	20 51	6 36
12	18 40	7♒39	4 55	2 54	1 32	22 4	1 11	20 53	6 38
13	19 38	20 25	4 D 53	3 59	2 9	22 12	1 19	20 55	6 39
14	20 36	3♓27	4 57	5 4	2 47	22 21	1 26	20 57	6 41
15	21 33	16 44	5 9	6 9	3 25	22 30	1 34	20 59	6 43
16	22 31	0♈13	5 28	7 14	4 3	22 39	1 41	21 1	6 45
17	23 28	13 53	5 54	8 19	4 41	22 48	1 49	21 3	6 46
18	24 26	27 42	6 27	9 23	5 20	22 58	1 56	21 5	6 48
19	25 24	11♉38	7 8	10 28	5 58	23 7	2 3	21 7	6 50
20	26 22	25 40	7 56	11 32	6 36	23 17	2 10	21 9	6 52
21	27 19	9♊48	8 50	12 35	7 14	23 26	2 18	21 11	6 53
22	28 17	24 0	9 52	13 39	7 53	23 36	2 25	21 13	6 55
23	29 15	8♋15	11 0	14 42	8 31	23 46	2 33	21 15	6 57
24	0♍13	22 31	12 14	15 46	9 9	23 56	2 40	21 17	6 59
25	1 11	6♌43	13 33	16 48	9 48	24 6	2 47	21 19	7 1
26	2 9	20 47	14 59	17 51	10 26	24 16	2 54	21 20	7 3
27	3 7	4♍39	16 29	18 53	11 5	24 26	3 1	21 22	7 5
28	4 5	18 14	18 4	19 55	11 44	24 36	3 8	21 24	7 7
29	5 3	1♎30	19 42	20 57	12 22	24 47	3 15	21 25	7 9
30	6 1	14 25	21 25	21 59	13 1	24 57	3 22	21 27	7 11
31	6 59	27 0	23 11	23 0	13 40	25 8	3 29	21 28	7 13

Pluto 11 Leo all month

1946

SEPTEMBER

DAY	☉	☽	☿	♀	♂	♃	♄	♅	♆
1	7♍57	9♏17	24♌59	24♎1	14♎19	25♎19	3♌36	21♊29	7♎15
2	8 55	21 19	26 50	25 1	14 58	25 29	3 43	21 31	7 17
3	9 53	3♐12	28 42	26 2	15 37	25 40	3 49	21 32	7 19
4	10 51	15 0	0♍36	27 2	16 16	25 51	3 56	21 33	7 21
5	11 49	26 50	2 30	28 1	16 55	26 2	4 3	21 34	7 23
6	12 47	8♑46	4 26	29 0	17 35	26 13	4 10	21 36	7 25
7	13 46	20 54	6 22	29 59	18 14	26 24	4 16	21 37	7 27
8	14 44	3♒17	8 17	0♏58	18 54	26 35	4 23	21 38	7 29
9	15 42	15 59	10 13	1 56	19 33	26 46	4 30	21 39	7 31
10	16 40	29 2	12 9	2 53	20 13	26 58	4 36	21 40	7 33
11	17 39	12♓24	14 3	3 51	20 52	27 9	4 43	21 40	7 35
12	18 37	26 4	15 58	4 47	21 32	27 21	4 49	21 41	7 37
13	19 35	9♈59	17 52	5 44	22 12	27 32	4 55	21 42	7 39
14	20 34	24 4	19 44	6 40	22 51	27 44	5 2	21 43	7 41
15	21 32	8♉15	21 36	7 35	23 31	27 55	5 8	21 43	7 44
16	22 31	22 27	23 27	8 30	24 11	28 7	5 14	21 44	7 46
17	23 29	6♊38	25 17	9 24	24 51	28 19	5 20	21 45	7 48
18	24 28	20 47	27 7	10 18	25 31	28 30	5 26	21 45	7 50
19	25 26	4♋51	28 55	11 11	26 11	28 42	5 31	21 46	7 53
20	26 25	18 51	0♎42	12 4	26 51	28 54	5 37	21 46	7 55
21	27 24	2♌46	2 28	12 56	27 31	29 6	5 43	21 46	7 57
22	28 22	16 34	4 13	13 47	28 11	29 18	5 49	21 47	7 59
23	29 21	0♍13	5 57	14 38	28 52	29 31	5 54	21 47	8 2
24	0♎20	13 40	7 40	15 28	29 32	29 43	6 0	21 47	8 4
25	1 19	26 55	9 23	16 18	0♏12	29 55	6 6	21 47	8 6
26	2 18	9♎54	11 4	17 7	0 53	0♏7	6 11	21 48	8 8
27	3 16	22 37	12 44	17 55	1 33	0 20	6 17	21 48	8 11
28	4 15	5♏3	14 24	18 42	2 14	0 32	6 22	21℞48	8 13
29	5 14	17 15	16 2	19 28	2 55	0 44	6 27	21 48	8 15
30	6 13	29 14	17 40	20 13	3 35	0 56	6 32	21 47	8 17

Pluto 12 Leo all month

OCTOBER

DAY	☉	☽	☿	♀	♂	♃	♄	♅	♆
1	7♎12	11♐5	19♎16	20♏58	4♏16	1♏9	6♌37	21♊47	8♎20
2	8 11	22 53	20 52	21 41	4 57	1 21	6 42	21℞47	8 22
3	9 10	4♑41	22 27	22 24	5 38	1 34	6 47	21 47	8 24
4	10 9	16 37	24 3	23 6	6 19	1 46	6 52	21 47	8 26
5	11 8	28 45	25 35	23 46	7 1	1 59	6 57	21 46	8 29
6	12 8	11♒10	27 7	24 26	7 42	2 12	7 2	21 46	8 31
7	13 7	23 56	28 39	25 4	8 23	2 25	7 7	21 45	8 33
8	14 6	7♓6	0♏10	25 41	9 4	2 37	7 11	21 45	8 35
9	15 5	20 41	1 40	26 17	9 46	2 50	7 16	21 44	8 37
10	16 4	4♈39	3 9	26 52	10 27	3 3	7 20	21 44	8 39
11	17 4	18 56	4 38	27 25	11 8	3 16	7 24	21 43	8 41
12	18 3	3♉26	6 6	27 57	11 50	3 28	7 28	21 43	8 43
13	19 2	18 3	7 33	28 27	12 31	3 41	7 32	21 42	8 46
14	20 2	2♊40	8 59	28 56	13 13	3 54	7 36	21 41	8 48
15	21 1	17 12	10 25	29 23	13 55	4 7	7 40	21 40	8 50
16	22 1	1♋33	11 49	29 49	14 36	4 20	7 44	21 39	8 52
17	23 0	15 43	13 13	0♐13	15 18	4 33	7 47	21 38	8 55
18	24 0	29 40	14 35	0 35	16 0	4 46	7 51	21 37	8 57
19	24 59	13♌23	15 57	0 56	16 42	4 59	7 55	21 36	8 59
20	25 59	26 53	17 19	1 15	17 24	5 12	7 58	21 35	9 1
21	26 59	10♍10	18 38	1 31	18 6	5 25	8 2	21 34	9 4
22	27 59	23 15	19 56	1 46	18 48	5 38	8 5	21 33	9 6
23	28 58	6♎7	21 13	1 59	19 30	5 51	8 8	21 32	9 8
24	29 58	18 45	22 29	2 9	20 12	6 4	8 11	21 31	9 10
25	0♏58	1♏12	23 44	2 18	20 55	6 17	8 14	21 29	9 12
26	1 58	13 26	24 57	2 24	21 37	6 30	8 17	21 28	9 14
27	2 58	25 30	26 8	2 28	22 19	6 43	8 20	21 27	9 16
28	3 57	7♐24	27 18	2 30	23 2	6 56	8 22	21 25	9 18
29	4 57	19 13	28 25	2℞29	23 44	7 10	8 25	21 24	9 21
30	5 57	0♑59	29 30	2 26	24 27	7 23	8 27	21 22	9 23
31	6 57	12 47	0♐32	2 21	25 10	7 36	8 29	21 20	9 25

Pluto 12 Leo all month

1946

NOVEMBER

DAY	☉	☽	☿	♀	♂	♃	♄	♅	♆
	° ′	° ′	° ′	° ′	° ′	° ′	° ′	° ′	° ′
1	7♏57	24♑41	1♐32	2♐13	25♏52	7♏49	8♌32	21♊19	9♎27
2	8 57	6♒47	2 29	2R 2	26 35	8 3	8 34	21R17	9 29
3	9 58	19 9	3 22	1 49	27 18	8 16	8 36	21 15	9 31
4	10 58	1♓52	4 11	1 34	28 1	8 29	8 38	21 13	9 33
5	11 58	14 59	4 55	1 16	28 44	8 42	8 40	21 12	9 35
6	12 58	28 34	5 35	0 56	29 27	8 55	8 41	21 10	9 36
7	13 58	12♈37	6 10	0 34	0♐10	9 8	8 43	21 8	9 38
8	14 58	27 4	6 38	0 10	0 53	9 21	8 44	21 6	9 40
9	15 59	11♉50	6 59	29♏44	1 36	9 34	8 46	21 4	9 42
10	16 59	26 48	7 14	29 15	2 20	9 47	8 47	21 2	9 44
11	17 59	11♊49	7 20	28 45	3 3	10 0	8 48	21 0	9 46
12	18 59	26 45	7R17	28 13	3 46	10 13	8 49	20 58	9 48
13	20 0	11♋29	7 5	27 40	4 30	10 26	8 50	20 56	9 50
14	21 0	25 55	6 43	27 6	5 13	10 40	8 50	20 54	9 51
15	22 1	10♌ 2	6 10	26 31	5 57	10 53	8 51	20 52	9 53
16	23 1	23 46	5 27	25 55	6 41	11 6	8 51	20 50	9 55
17	24 2	7♍11	4 34	25 19	7 24	11 19	8 52	20 48	9 57
18	25 2	20 16	3 33	24 43	8 8	11 32	8 52	20 45	9 58
19	26 3	3♎ 4	2 24	24 6	8 52	11 45	8 53	20 43	10 0
20	27 3	15 38	1 7	23 30	9 36	11 58	8 53	20 41	10 2
21	28 4	27 59	29♏47	22 54	10 19	12 11	8R 53	20 39	10 3
22	29 4	10♏ 9	28 26	22 20	11 3	12 23	8 53	20 36	10 5
23	0♐ 5	22 11	27 5	21 47	11 47	12 36	8 53	20 34	10 6
24	1 6	4♐ 6	25 49	21 14	12 31	12 49	8 53	20 32	10 8
25	2 6	15 56	24 39	20 43	13 15	13 1	8 52	20 30	10 9
26	3 7	27 43	23 37	20 13	14 0	13 14	8 52	20 27	10 11
27	4 8	9♑30	22 45	19 45	14 44	13 27	8 51	20 25	10 12
28	5 9	21 19	22 4	19 19	15 28	13 40	8 50	20 23	10 14
29	6 10	3♒15	21 34	18 55	16 12	13 52	8 49	20 20	10 15
30	7 10	15 20	21 16	18 34	16 57	14 5	8 48	20 18	10 17

Pluto 13 Leo all month

DECEMBER

DAY	☉	☽	☿	♀	♂	♃	♄	♅	♆
	° ′	° ′	° ′	° ′	° ′	° ′	° ′	° ′	° ′
1	8♐11	27♒40	21♏ 9	18♏15	17♐41	14♏18	8♌47	20♊15	10♎18
2	9 12	10♓17	21 D13	17R58	18 26	14 31	8R 46	20R13	10 20
3	10 13	23 17	21 27	17 43	19 10	14 43	8 44	20 10	10 21
4	11 14	6♈43	21 51	17 31	19 55	14 56	8 43	20 8	10 23
5	12 15	20 36	22 22	17 21	20 40	15 8	8 41	20 5	10 24
6	13 15	4♉56	23 1	17 14	21 25	15 20	8 39	20 3	10 25
7	14 16	19 41	23 47	17 9	22 9	15 33	8 38	20 0	10 26
8	15 17	4♊44	24 38	17 7	22 54	15 45	8 36	19 58	10 27
9	16 18	19 57	25 35	17 D 8	23 39	15 57	8 34	19 55	10 28
10	17 19	5♋16	26 36	17 10	24 24	16 9	8 32	19 52	10 29
11	18 20	20 15	27 41	17 15	25 9	16 22	8 30	19 50	10 31
12	19 21	5♌ 2	28 49	17 23	25 54	16 34	8 28	19 47	10 32
13	20 22	19 25	0♐ 0	17 33	26 39	16 46	8 26	19 44	10 33
14	21 23	3♍22	1 14	17 45	27 24	16 58	8 23	19 41	10 34
15	22 24	16 51	2 29	17 59	28 9	17 10	8 21	19 39	10 35
16	23 25	29 56	3 47	18 15	28 55	17 21	8 18	19 36	10 36
17	24 26	12♎39	5 7	18 33	29 40	17 33	8 15	19 34	10 37
18	25 27	25 3	6 28	18 54	0♑25	17 45	8 12	19 31	10 38
19	26 28	7♏13	7 51	19 16	1 10	17 57	8 9	19 29	10 39
20	27 29	19 12	9 14	19 40	1 56	18 8	8 6	19 26	10 39
21	28 31	1♐ 5	10 39	20 6	2 41	18 20	8 3	19 24	10 40
22	29 32	12 53	12 4	20 33	3 26	18 32	8 0	19 21	10 41
23	0♑33	24 40	13 30	21 3	4 12	18 43	7 56	19 19	10 42
24	1 34	6♑28	14 57	21 34	4 57	18 54	7 53	19 16	10 42
25	2 35	18 19	16 24	22 6	5 43	19 5	7 49	19 14	10 43
26	3 36	0♒15	17 52	22 40	6 29	19 16	7 46	19 11	10 44
27	4 37	12 18	19 21	23 15	7 14	19 27	7 42	19 9	10 44
28	5 39	24 29	20 50	23 51	8 0	19 38	7 39	19 6	10 45
29	6 40	6♓53	22 20	24 29	8 46	19 49	7 35	19 4	10 45
30	7 41	19 31	23 49	25 8	9 32	20 0	7 31	19 2	10 46
31	8 42	2♈26	25 20	25 49	10 18	20 11	7 27	18 59	10 46

Pluto 13 Leo all month

1947

JANUARY

DAY	☉	☽	☿	♀	♂	♃	♄	♅	♆
	° ′	° ′	° ′	° ′	° ′	° ′	° ′	° ′	° ′
1	9♑43	15♈42	26♐51	26♏30	11♑4	20♏21	7♌23	18♊57	10♎47
2	10 44	29 22	28 22	27 13	11 50	20 32	7℞19	18℞55	10 47
3	11 46	13♉26	29 53	27 57	12 36	20 43	7 15	18 53	10 47
4	12 47	27 54	1♑25	28 42	13 22	20 53	7 11	18 50	10 47
5	13 48	12♊43	2 57	29 28	14 8	21 4	7 6	18 48	10 47
6	14 49	27 49	4 30	0♐14	14 54	21 14	7 2	18 46	10 48
7	15 50	13♋1	6 3	1 2	15 40	21 24	6 58	18 44	10 48
8	16 51	28 11	7 36	1 50	16 26	21 34	6 53	18 41	10 48
9	17 52	13♌9	9 10	2 40	17 13	21 43	6 49	18 39	10 48
10	18 54	27 46	10 44	3 30	17 59	21 53	6 44	18 37	10 48
11	19 55	11♍56	12 19	4 21	18 45	22 3	6 40	18 35	10 48
12	20 56	25 36	13 54	5 13	19 32	22 13	6 35	18 33	10℞48
13	21 57	8♎48	15 30	6 5	20 18	22 22	6 31	18 31	10 48
14	22 58	21 34	17 6	6 59	21 5	22 32	6 26	18 29	10 48
15	23 59	3♏58	18 42	7 53	21 51	22 41	6 21	18 27	10 48
16	25 0	16 5	20 19	8 47	22 38	22 50	6 16	18 25	10 48
17	26 1	28 0	21 57	9 42	23 24	22 59	6 11	18 23	10 48
18	27 2	9♐48	23 34	10 38	24 11	23 8	6 6	18 21	10 48
19	28 4	21 34	25 13	11 34	24 57	23 17	6 1	18 19	10 48
20	29 5	3♑21	26 52	12 31	25 44	23 26	5 56	18 18	10 47
21	0♒6	15 13	28 32	13 29	26 30	23 34	5 52	18 16	10 47
22	1 7	27 11	0♒12	14 27	27 17	23 43	5 47	18 15	10 47
23	2 8	9♒17	1 53	15 25	28 4	23 51	5 42	18 13	10 47
24	3 9	21 32	3 34	16 24	28 50	23 59	5 37	18 12	10 46
25	4 10	3♓58	5 16	17 23	29 37	24 7	5 32	18 10	10 46
26	5 11	16 34	6 59	18 23	0♒24	24 15	5 27	18 8	10 45
27	6 12	29 22	8 42	19 23	1 11	24 23	5 22	18 6	10 45
28	7 13	12♈23	10 26	20 24	1 57	24 31	5 17	18 5	10 44
29	8 14	25 39	12 10	21 25	2 44	24 38	5 13	18 3	10 44
30	9 15	9♉12	13 55	22 26	3 31	24 46	5 8	18 2	10 43
31	10 16	23 2	15 41	23 28	4 18	24 53	5 3	18 1	10 43

Pluto 12 Leo all month

FEBRUARY

DAY	☉	☽	☿	♀	♂	♃	♄	♅	♆
	° ′	° ′	° ′	° ′	° ′	° ′	° ′	° ′	° ′
1	11♒17	7♊12	17♒26	24♐30	5♒5	25♏0	4♌58	18♊0	10♎42
2	12 18	21 40	19 13	25 32	5 52	25 7	4℞53	17℞59	10℞41
3	13 18	6♋23	20 59	26 35	6 39	25 14	4 48	17 58	10 41
4	14 19	21 16	22 46	27 38	7 26	25 21	4 43	17 57	10 40
5	15 20	6♌12	24 33	28 41	8 13	25 27	4 38	17 56	10 39
6	16 21	21 2	26 20	29 45	9 0	25 34	4 34	17 54	10 39
7	17 22	5♍37	28 7	0♑49	9 47	25 40	4 29	17 53	10 38
8	18 22	19 50	29 53	1 53	10 34	25 46	4 24	17 52	10 37
9	19 23	3♎36	1♓39	2 57	11 21	25 52	4 19	17 51	10 36
10	20 24	16 54	3 24	4 2	12 8	25 58	4 15	17 51	10 35
11	21 25	29 45	5 8	5 7	12 55	26 4	4 10	17 50	10 34
12	22 25	12♏13	6 50	6 12	13 42	26 9	4 6	17 49	10 33
13	23 26	24 23	8 30	7 18	14 29	26 15	4 1	17 49	10 32
14	24 27	6♐19	10 8	8 23	15 17	26 20	3 57	17 48	10 31
15	25 27	18 8	11 43	9 29	16 4	26 25	3 53	17 47	10 30
16	26 28	29 54	13 14	10 35	16 51	26 30	3 49	17 47	10 29
17	27 28	11♑43	14 41	11 42	17 38	26 34	3 44	17 46	10 28
18	28 29	23 39	16 4	12 48	18 26	26 39	3 40	17 46	10 27
19	29 30	5♒45	17 21	13 55	19 13	26 43	3 36	17 46	10 26
20	0♓30	18 2	18 32	15 2	20 0	26 47	3 32	17 46	10 25
21	1 31	0♓33	19 36	16 9	20 47	26 51	3 28	17 45	10 24
22	2 31	13 16	20 33	17 16	21 35	26 55	3 24	17 45	10 22
23	3 31	26 13	21 21	18 24	22 22	26 59	3 20	17 45	10 21
24	4 32	9♈20	22 1	19 31	23 9	27 2	3 16	17 45	10 20
25	5 32	22 39	22 33	20 39	23 56	27 6	3 12	17 45	10 19
26	6 33	6♉7	22 54	21 47	24 44	27 9	3 9	17 D45	10 17
27	7 33	19 46	23 6	22 55	25 31	27 12	3 5	17 45	10 16
28	8 33	3♊36	23℞9	24 3	26 18	27 15	3 1	17 45	10 15

Pluto 12 Leo all month

1947

MARCH

Day	☉ ° ′	☽ ° ′	☿ ° ′	♀ ° ′	♂ ° ′	♃ ° ′	♄ ° ′	♅ ° ′	♆ ° ′
1	9♓33	17♊36	23♓ 1	25♑11	27♒ 5	27♏17	2♌58	17♊45	10♎14
2	10 34	1♋48	22℞44	26 19	27 53	27 20	2℞54	17 46	10℞12
3	11 34	16 8	22 18	27 28	28 40	27 22	2 51	17 46	10 11
4	12 34	0♌36	21 45	28 36	29 27	27 24	2 48	17 46	10 10
5	13 34	15 6	21 3	29 45	0♓14	27 26	2 45	17 47	10 8
6	14 34	29 32	20 16	0♒54	1 2	27 27	2 42	17 47	10 7
7	15 34	13♍48	19 23	2 3	1 49	27 29	2 39	17 48	10 5
8	16 34	27 47	18 26	3 12	2 36	27 30	2 36	17 48	10 4
9	17 34	11♎26	17 27	4 22	3 23	27 31	2 33	17 49	10 2
10	18 34	24 41	16 28	5 31	4 11	27 32	2 31	17 49	10 1
11	19 34	7♏32	15 28	6 40	4 58	27 33	2 28	17 50	9 59
12	20 34	20 2	14 30	7 50	5 45	27 33	2 25	17 51	9 58
13	21 34	2♐14	13 35	9 0	6 33	27 34	2 23	17 51	9 56
14	22 34	14 13	12 44	10 9	7 20	27 34	2 20	17 52	9 55
15	23 33	26 4	11 57	11 19	8 7	27℞34	2 18	17 53	9 53
16	24 33	7♑52	11 15	12 29	8 54	27 34	2 16	17 54	9 51
17	25 33	19 44	10 39	13 39	9 41	27 33	2 14	17 55	9 50
18	26 33	1♒43	10 9	14 49	10 28	27 33	2 13	17 57	9 48
19	27 32	13 54	9 46	15 59	11 15	27 32	2 11	17 58	9 46
20	28 32	26 20	9 28	17 9	12 2	27 31	2 9	17 59	9 45
21	29 32	9♓ 4	9 17	18 19	12 50	27 30	2 8	18 0	9 43
22	0♈31	22 4	9 12	19 30	13 37	27 28	2 6	18 2	9 41
23	1 31	5♈21	9 D13	20 40	14 24	27 27	2 5	18 3	9 40
24	2 30	18 47	9 20	21 50	15 11	27 25	2 4	18 4	9 38
25	3 30	2♉36	9 32	23 1	15 58	27 24	2 2	18 5	9 37
26	4 29	16 27	9 50	24 11	16 45	27 22	2 1	18 7	9 35
27	5 29	0♊26	10 12	25 22	17 32	27 20	2 0	18 8	9 33
28	6 28	14 28	10 39	26 33	18 19	27 17	1 59	18 10	9 32
29	7 27	28 34	11 10	27 44	19 6	27 15	1 59	18 11	9 30
30	8 27	12♋42	11 46	28 55	19 53	27 12	1 58	18 13	9 28
31	9 26	26 50	12 26	0♓ 6	20 40	27 9	1 58	18 15	9 27

Pluto 11 Leo all month

APRIL

Day	☉ ° ′	☽ ° ′	☿ ° ′	♀ ° ′	♂ ° ′	♃ ° ′	♄ ° ′	♅ ° ′	♆ ° ′
1	10♈25	10♌58	13♓10	1♓17	21♓27	27♏ 6	1♌58	18♊17	9♎25
2	11 24	25 2	13 57	2 28	22 14	27℞ 2	1℞57	18 18	9℞23
3	12 24	9♍ 0	14 47	3 39	23 1	26 59	1 57	18 20	9 22
4	13 23	22 48	15 41	4 50	23 48	26 55	1 D 57	18 22	9 20
5	14 22	6♎23	16 37	6 1	24 35	26 51	1 57	18 24	9 18
6	15 21	19 42	17 37	7 12	25 22	26 47	1 57	18 26	9 17
7	16 20	2♏43	18 39	8 23	26 8	26 43	1 58	18 28	9 15
8	17 19	15 26	19 44	9 34	26 55	26 39	1 58	18 30	9 13
9	18 18	27 51	20 51	10 45	27 42	26 34	1 59	18 32	9 12
10	19 17	10♐ 2	22 1	11 57	28 29	26 30	1 59	18 34	9 10
11	20 16	22 1	23 13	13 8	29 15	26 25	2 0	18 37	9 8
12	21 14	3♑53	24 27	14 20	0♈ 2	26 20	2 1	18 39	9 7
13	22 13	15 42	25 44	15 31	0 49	26 15	2 2	18 41	9 5
14	23 12	27 35	27 2	16 43	1 35	26 10	2 3	18 43	9 4
15	24 11	9♒36	28 22	17 54	2 22	26 4	2 4	18 46	9 2
16	25 10	21 49	29 45	19 6	3 8	25 59	2 5	18 48	9 0
17	26 8	4♓19	1♈ 9	20 17	3 55	25 53	2 6	18 50	8 59
18	27 7	17 8	2 35	21 29	4 41	25 47	2 8	18 53	8 57
19	28 6	0♈19	4 2	22 40	5 28	25 41	2 9	18 55	8 56
20	29 4	13 51	5 32	23 52	6 14	25 35	2 11	18 58	8 54
21	0♉ 3	27 42	7 3	25 4	7 0	25 29	2 13	19 1	8 53
22	1 1	11♉49	8 37	26 15	7 47	25 22	2 15	19 3	8 51
23	2 0	26 8	10 12	27 27	8 33	25 16	2 17	19 6	8 50
24	2 58	10♊32	11 48	28 39	9 19	25 10	2 19	19 9	8 48
25	3 57	24 58	13 27	29 51	10 5	25 3	2 21	19 12	8 47
26	4 55	9♋22	15 7	1♈ 2	10 52	24 57	2 24	19 14	8 45
27	5 54	23 39	16 49	2 13	11 38	24 50	2 26	19 17	8 44
28	6 52	7♌48	18 32	3 26	12 24	24 43	2 29	19 20	8 43
29	7 50	21 47	20 18	4 38	13 10	24 36	2 32	19 23	8 41
30	8 49	5♍35	22 5	5 50	13 56	24 28	2 35	19 25	8 40

Pluto 11 Leo all month

1947

MAY

DAY	☉	☽	☿	♀	♂	♃	♄	♅	♆
	° ′	° ′	° ′	° ′	° ′	° ′	° ′	° ′	° ′
1	9 ♉ 47	19 ♍ 10	23 ♈ 54	7 ♈ 2	14 ♈ 42	24 ♏ 21	2 ♌ 37	19 ♊ 28	8 ♎ 38
2	10 45	2 ♎ 33	25 44	8 14	15 28	24 R 14	2 40	19 31	8 R 37
3	11 43	15 42	27 37	9 26	16 14	24 7	2 43	19 34	8 36
4	12 41	28 37	29 31	10 38	17 0	24 0	2 46	19 37	8 35
5	13 40	11 ♏ 18	1 ♉ 27	11 50	17 46	23 52	2 49	19 40	8 33
6	14 38	23 46	3 25	13 2	18 32	23 45	2 52	19 43	8 32
7	15 36	6 ♐ 1	5 24	14 14	19 18	23 38	2 55	19 46	8 31
8	16 34	18 6	7 25	15 26	20 4	23 30	2 59	19 49	8 30
9	17 32	0 ♑ 3	9 28	16 39	20 49	23 23	3 2	19 53	8 28
10	18 30	11 54	11 32	17 51	21 35	23 15	3 6	19 56	8 27
11	19 28	23 44	13 38	19 3	22 21	23 7	3 10	19 59	8 26
12	20 26	5 ♒ 37	15 45	20 15	23 6	23 0	3 14	20 2	8 25
13	21 24	17 37	17 53	21 28	23 52	22 52	3 18	20 6	8 24
14	22 21	29 49	20 2	22 40	24 37	22 44	3 22	20 9	8 23
15	23 19	12 ♓ 18	22 13	23 52	25 22	22 37	3 26	20 12	8 22
16	24 17	25 7	24 23	25 4	26 8	22 29	3 30	20 15	8 21
17	25 15	8 ♈ 20	26 35	26 17	26 53	22 22	3 35	20 19	8 20
18	26 13	21 57	28 46	27 29	27 38	22 14	3 39	20 22	8 19
19	27 11	5 ♉ 58	0 ♊ 57	28 41	28 23	22 7	3 43	20 25	8 18
20	28 8	20 21	3 8	29 53	29 8	21 59	3 48	20 28	8 17
21	29 6	5 ♊ 0	5 18	1 ♉ 6	29 53	21 52	3 52	20 32	8 16
22	0 ♊ 4	19 49	7 27	2 18	0 ♉ 38	21 44	3 57	20 35	8 15
23	1 2	4 ♋ 41	9 35	3 30	1 23	21 37	4 2	20 38	8 14
24	1 59	19 27	11 41	4 43	2 8	21 29	4 7	20 42	8 13
25	2 57	4 ♌ 3	13 45	5 55	2 53	21 22	4 12	20 45	8 12
26	3 55	18 23	15 48	7 8	3 38	21 14	4 17	20 49	8 12
27	4 52	2 ♍ 25	17 49	8 20	4 23	21 7	4 22	20 52	8 11
28	5 50	16 7	19 47	9 33	5 7	20 59	4 27	20 56	8 10
29	6 47	29 30	21 43	10 45	5 52	20 52	4 32	20 59	8 10
30	7 45	12 ♎ 35	23 36	11 58	6 36	20 45	4 37	21 3	8 9
31	8 42	25 25	25 27	13 10	7 21	20 38	4 42	21 6	8 8

Pluto 10 Leo all month

JUNE

DAY	☉	☽	☿	♀	♂	♃	♄	♅	♆
	° ′	° ′	° ′	° ′	° ′	° ′	° ′	° ′	° ′
1	9 ♊ 40	8 ♏ 0	27 ♊ 15	14 ♉ 23	8 ♉ 5	20 ♏ 31	4 ♌ 48	21 ♊ 10	8 ♎ 8
2	10 37	20 22	29 1	15 35	8 50	20 R 25	4 53	21 13	8 R 7
3	11 35	2 ♐ 35	0 ♋ 44	16 48	9 34	20 18	4 59	21 17	8 6
4	12 32	14 39	2 24	18 0	10 18	20 11	5 5	21 20	8 6
5	13 30	26 36	4 1	19 13	11 3	20 5	5 10	21 24	8 5
6	14 27	8 ♑ 29	5 35	20 25	11 47	19 58	5 16	21 27	8 5
7	15 25	20 19	7 7	21 38	12 31	19 52	5 22	21 31	8 4
8	16 22	2 ♒ 9	8 36	22 51	13 15	19 46	5 28	21 34	8 4
9	17 19	14 3	10 1	24 3	13 59	19 40	5 34	21 38	8 4
10	18 17	26 4	11 24	25 16	14 43	19 34	5 40	21 41	8 3
11	19 14	8 ♓ 16	12 44	26 29	15 27	19 28	5 46	21 45	8 3
12	20 11	20 42	14 1	27 42	16 11	19 22	5 52	21 49	8 3
13	21 9	3 ♈ 27	15 15	28 54	16 55	19 17	5 58	21 52	8 3
14	22 6	16 35	16 25	0 ♊ 7	17 39	19 11	6 5	21 56	8 2
15	23 3	0 ♉ 8	17 33	1 20	18 23	19 6	6 11	22 0	8 2
16	24 1	14 8	18 37	2 33	19 7	19 1	6 17	22 4	8 2
17	24 58	28 34	19 38	3 45	19 50	18 56	6 24	22 7	8 2
18	25 55	13 ♊ 21	20 35	4 58	20 34	18 51	6 30	22 11	8 2
19	26 53	28 24	21 29	6 11	21 17	18 46	6 37	22 14	8 2
20	27 50	13 ♋ 34	22 20	7 24	22 0	18 42	6 43	22 18	8 D 2
21	28 47	28 41	23 7	8 37	22 44	18 37	6 50	22 21	8 2
22	29 44	13 ♌ 36	23 49	9 50	23 27	18 33	6 56	22 25	8 2
23	0 ♋ 42	28 12	24 28	11 3	24 10	18 29	7 3	22 28	8 2
24	1 39	12 ♍ 23	25 3	12 16	24 53	18 25	7 10	22 32	8 2
25	2 36	26 9	25 34	13 29	25 36	18 21	7 17	22 35	8 2
26	3 33	9 ♎ 30	26 1	14 42	26 19	18 18	7 24	22 39	8 2
27	4 31	22 27	26 23	15 55	27 2	18 14	7 31	22 42	8 3
28	5 28	5 ♏ 5	26 41	17 8	27 45	18 11	7 38	22 46	8 3
29	6 25	17 27	26 54	18 21	28 28	18 8	7 45	22 49	8 3
30	7 22	29 37	27 3	19 34	29 11	18 5	7 51	22 53	8 3

Pluto 11 Leo all month

1947

JULY

DAY	☉	☽	☿	♀	♂	♃	♄	♅	♆
	° ′	° ′	° ′	° ′	° ′	° ′	° ′	° ′	° ′
1	8♋19	11♐38	27♋ 8	20♊47	29♉54	18♏ 2	7♌58	22♊56	8♎ 4
2	9 17	23 33	27℞ 7	22 0	0♊37	18℞ 0	8 5	23 0	8 4
3	10 14	5♑25	27 2	23 13	1 19	17 57	8 12	23 3	8 4
4	11 11	17 15	26 52	24 26	2 2	17 55	8 20	23 7	8 5
5	12 8	29 6	26 38	25 39	2 44	17 53	8 27	23 10	8 5
6	13 5	10♒59	26 19	26 52	3 26	17 51	8 34	23 13	8 5
7	14 2	22 57	25 57	28 5	4 9	17 49	8 41	23 17	8 6
8	15 0	5♓ 1	25 30	29 19	4 51	17 48	8 49	23 20	8 6
9	15 57	17 15	25 1	0♋32	5 33	17 46	8 56	23 23	8 7
10	16 54	29 42	24 28	1 45	6 15	17 45	9 3	23 26	8 8
11	17 51	12♈25	23 53	2 58	6 57	17 44	9 10	23 30	8 8
12	18 48	25 27	23 16	4 12	7 39	17 43	9 18	23 33	8 9
13	19 46	8♉53	22 37	5 25	8 21	17 42	9 25	23 37	8 10
14	20 43	22 45	21 58	6 38	9 3	17 42	9 32	23 40	8 11
15	21 40	7♊ 2	21 19	7 52	9 45	17 42	9 40	23 44	8 11
16	22 37	21 44	20 40	9 5	10 26	17 D42	9 47	23 47	8 12
17	23 35	6♋46	20 3	10 19	11 8	17 42	9 55	23 50	8 13
18	24 32	22 0	19 28	11 32	11 50	17 42	10 2	23 53	8 14
19	25 29	7♌16	18 55	12 46	12 31	17 43	10 10	23 56	8 15
20	26 26	22 22	18 25	13 59	13 13	17 43	10 17	23 59	8 16
21	27 24	7♍ 9	18 0	15 13	13 54	17 44	10 25	24 2	8 17
22	28 21	21 31	17 38	16 26	14 35	17 45	10 33	24 5	8 18
23	29 18	5♎24	17 21	17 40	15 17	17 46	10 40	24 9	8 19
24	0♌16	18 49	17 10	18 53	15 58	17 48	10 48	24 12	8 20
25	1 13	1♏46	17 4	20 7	16 39	17 49	10 56	24 15	8 21
26	2 10	14 21	17 D 3	21 21	17 20	17 51	11 4	24 18	8 22
27	3 8	26 38	17 8	22 34	18 1	17 53	11 11	24 21	8 23
28	4 5	8♐41	17 20	23 48	18 41	17 55	11 19	24 24	8 25
29	5 2	20 36	17 37	25 2	19 22	17 57	11 26	24 27	8 26
30	6 0	2♑27	18 0	26 16	20 3	17 59	11 34	24 30	8 27
31	6 57	14 16	18 30	27 29	20 43	18 2	11 41	24 33	8 28

Pluto 11 Leo all month

AUGUST

DAY	☉	☽	☿	♀	♂	♃	♄	♅	♆
	° ′	° ′	° ′	° ′	° ′	° ′	° ′	° ′	° ′
1	7♌54	26♑ 7	19♋ 6	28♋43	21♊24	18♏ 4	11♌49	24♊35	8♎30
2	8 52	8♒ 2	19 48	29 57	22 4	18 7	11 57	24 38	8 31
3	9 49	20 1	20 36	1♌11	22 45	18 10	12 5	24 41	8 32
4	10 46	2♓ 7	21 30	2 24	23 25	18 14	12 12	24 44	8 33
5	11 44	14 20	22 30	3 38	24 6	18 17	12 20	24 46	8 35
6	12 41	26 42	23 36	4 52	24 46	18 21	12 28	24 49	8 36
7	13 39	9♈16	24 47	6 6	25 26	18 25	12 36	24 52	8 37
8	14 36	22 2	26 4	7 20	26 6	18 29	12 43	24 54	8 39
9	15 34	5♉ 4	27 26	8 34	26 46	18 33	12 51	24 57	8 41
10	16 31	18 26	28 53	9 48	27 26	18 37	12 59	24 59	8 42
11	17 29	2♊ 9	0♌25	11 2	28 6	18 42	13 7	25 2	8 43
12	18 26	16 14	2 1	12 16	28 45	18 46	13 14	25 4	8 45
13	19 24	0♋43	3 41	13 30	29 25	18 51	13 22	25 7	8 46
14	20 22	15 32	5 25	14 44	0♋ 4	18 56	13 30	25 9	8 48
15	21 19	0♌34	7 13	15 58	0 44	19 1	13 38	25 12	8 50
16	22 17	15 42	9 3	17 12	1 23	19 6	13 45	25 14	8 51
17	23 15	0♍45	10 56	18 26	2 3	19 12	13 53	25 16	8 53
18	24 12	15 33	12 51	19 40	2 42	19 17	14 0	25 18	8 55
19	25 10	29 58	14 48	20 54	3 21	19 23	14 8	25 20	8 57
20	26 8	13♎55	16 46	22 8	4 0	19 29	14 15	25 23	8 58
21	27 6	27 24	18 45	23 23	4 39	19 35	14 23	25 25	9 0
22	28 3	10♏24	20 45	24 37	5 18	19 41	14 31	25 27	9 2
23	29 1	23 1	22 46	25 51	5 57	19 47	14 39	25 29	9 4
24	29 59	5♐18	24 46	27 5	6 36	19 54	14 46	25 31	9 5
25	0♍57	17 21	26 46	28 20	7 14	20 0	14 54	25 32	9 7
26	1 55	29 15	28 46	29 34	7 53	20 7	15 1	25 34	9 9
27	2 53	11♑ 5	0♍45	0♍48	8 31	20 14	15 9	25 36	9 11
28	3 51	22 55	2 44	2 3	9 10	20 21	15 16	25 38	9 13
29	4 49	4♒49	4 42	3 17	9 48	20 28	15 24	25 39	9 15
30	5 47	16 49	6 38	4 32	10 26	20 35	15 31	25 41	9 17
31	6 45	28 57	8 34	5 46	11 4	20 43	15 38	25 43	9 19

Pluto 12 Leo all month

1947

SEPTEMBER

DAY	☉	☽	☿	♀	♂	♃	♄	♅	♆
	° ′	° ′	° ′	° ′	° ′	° ′	° ′	° ′	° ′
1	7♍43	11♓14	10♍29	7♍ 1	11♋42	20♏50	15♌46	25♊45	9♎21
2	8 41	23 41	12 22	8 15	12 20	20 58	15 53	25 46	9 23
3	9 39	6♈18	14 15	9 29	12 58	21 6	16 0	25 48	9 25
4	10 37	19 6	16 6	10 43	13 36	21 14	16 7	25 50	9 27
5	11 35	2♉ 5	17 56	11 58	14 13	21 22	16 15	25 51	9 29
6	12 33	15 16	19 45	13 12	14 51	21 30	16 22	25 53	9 31
7	13 31	28 42	21 32	14 27	15 28	21 38	16 29	25 54	9 33
8	14 30	12♊23	23 19	15 41	16 5	21 46	16 36	25 55	9 35
9	15 28	26 21	25 4	16 56	16 43	21 55	16 43	25 56	9 37
10	16 26	10♋35	26 48	18 10	17 20	22 3	16 50	25 57	9 39
11	17 24	25 5	28 31	19 25	17 57	22 12	16 57	25 58	9 41
12	18 23	9♌47	0♎13	20 40	18 34	22 21	17 4	25 59	9 43
13	19 21	24 34	1 54	21 54	19 11	22 30	17 11	26 0	9 45
14	20 20	9♍18	3 33	23 9	19 47	22 40	17 18	26 1	9 47
15	21 18	23 51	5 12	24 24	20 24	22 49	17 25	26 2	9 49
16	22 17	8♎ 7	6 49	25 39	21 1	22 58	17 32	26 3	9 51
17	23 15	22 0	8 26	26 53	21 37	23 8	17 39	26 4	9 53
18	24 14	5♏27	10 1	28 8	22 14	23 17	17 45	26 5	9 56
19	25 12	18 29	11 35	29 22	22 50	23 27	17 52	26 6	9 58
20	26 11	1♐ 8	13 9	0♎37	23 26	23 37	17 59	26 7	10 0
21	27 10	13 27	14 41	1 51	24 2	23 46	18 5	26 7	10 2
22	28 8	25 32	16 12	3 6	24 38	23 56	18 12	26 8	10 5
23	29 7	7♑27	17 43	4 21	25 14	24 6	18 18	26 8	10 7
24	0♎ 6	19 19	19 12	5 36	25 50	24 16	18 25	26 9	10 9
25	1 4	1♒10	20 40	6 50	26 25	24 26	18 31	26 9	10 11
26	2 3	13 7	22 7	8 5	27 1	24 37	18 38	26 10	10 14
27	3 2	25 13	23 34	9 20	27 36	24 47	18 44	26 10	10 16
28	4 1	7♓29	24 59	10 35	28 11	24 58	18 50	26 10	10 18
29	5 0	19 58	26 23	11 49	28 46	25 8	18 56	26 11	10 20
30	5 59	2♈41	27 46	13 4	29 21	25 19	19 2	26 11	10 23

Pluto 13 Leo all month

OCTOBER

DAY	☉	☽	☿	♀	♂	♃	♄	♅	♆
	° ′	° ′	° ′	° ′	° ′	° ′	° ′	° ′	° ′
1	6♎58	15♈37	29♎ 8	14♎19	29♋56	25♏30	19♌ 8	26♊11	10♎25
2	7 57	28 45	0♏29	15 34	0♌31	25 41	19 14	26 11	10 27
3	8 56	12♉ 6	1 48	16 48	1 6	25 52	19 20	26 11	10 29
4	9 55	25 37	3 6	18 3	1 40	26 3	19 26	26 ℞ 11	10 32
5	10 54	9♊18	4 23	19 18	2 15	26 14	19 32	26 11	10 34
6	11 53	23 9	5 39	20 33	2 49	26 25	19 38	26 11	10 36
7	12 52	7♋ 9	6 53	21 48	3 23	26 36	19 43	26 11	10 38
8	13 51	21 17	8 6	23 4	3 57	26 48	19 49	26 10	10 41
9	14 51	5♌32	9 16	24 18	4 31	26 59	19 54	26 10	10 43
10	15 50	19 52	10 25	25 33	5 4	27 10	20 0	26 10	10 45
11	16 49	4♍13	11 32	26 48	5 88	27 22	20 5	26 9	10 47
12	17 49	18 29	12 37	28 2	6 11	27 33	20 11	26 9	10 50
13	18 48	2♎37	13 40	29 17	6 45	27 45	20 16	26 8	10 52
14	19 47	16 32	14 40	0♏32	7 18	27 57	20 21	26 7	10 54
15	20 47	0♏ 8	15 38	1 47	7 51	28 9	20 26	26 7	10 56
16	21 46	13 25	16 32	3 1	8 23	28 21	20 31	26 6	10 58
17	22 46	26 21	17 23	4 16	8 56	28 33	20 36	26 5	11 0
18	23 45	8♐58	18 11	5 31	9 29	28 45	20 41	26 4	11 2
19	24 45	21 17	18 54	6 46	10 1	28 57	20 46	26 4	11 4
20	25 45	3♑23	19 33	8 0	10 33	29 9	20 50	26 3	11 7
21	26 44	15 20	20 7	9 15	11 5	29 21	20 55	26 2	11 9
22	27 44	27 12	20 36	10 30	11 37	29 33	20 59	26 1	11 11
23	28 44	9♒ 5	20 59	11 45	12 9	29 46	21 4	26 0	11 13
24	29 43	21 3	21 15	13 0	12 40	29 58	21 8	25 59	11 16
25	0♏43	3♓10	21 25	14 15	13 11	0♐11	21 12	25 58	11 18
26	1 43	15 31	21 ℞ 27	15 30	13 42	0 23	21 16	25 57	11 20
27	2 43	28 8	21 20	16 45	14 13	0 36	21 20	25 56	11 22
28	3 43	11♈ 2	21 6	17 59	14 44	0 48	21 24	25 54	11 24
29	4 43	24 15	20 41	19 14	15 15	1 1	21 28	25 53	11 26
30	5 43	7♉46	20 7	20 29	15 45	1 14	21 32	25 52	11 28
31	6 43	21 31	19 24	21 44	16 15	1 26	21 36	25 50	11 30

Pluto 14 Leo all month

1947

NOVEMBER

DAY	☉	☽	☿	♀	♂	♃	♄	♅	♆
	° ′	° ′	° ′	° ′	° ′	° ′	° ′	° ′	° ′
1	7♏42	5♊30	18♏32	22♏59	16♌45	1♐39	21♌39	25♊49	11♎32
2	8 43	19 37	17 R 32	24 14	17 15	1 52	21 43	25 R 47	11 34
3	9 43	3♋50	16 25	25 29	17 45	2 5	21 46	25 46	11 36
4	10 43	18 6	15 12	26 44	18 14	2 18	21 50	25 44	11 38
5	11 43	2♌20	13 54	27 58	18 43	2 31	21 53	25 43	11 40
6	12 43	16 32	12 36	29 13	19 12	2 41	21 56	25 41	11 42
7	13 43	0♍38	11 18	0♐28	19 41	2 57	21 59	25 39	11 44
8	14 43	14 37	10 3	1 43	20 9	3 10	22 2	25 38	11 46
9	15 44	28 27	8 54	2 58	20 37	3 23	22 4	25 36	11 48
10	16 44	12♎6	7 54	4 13	21 5	3 36	22 7	25 34	11 50
11	17 44	25 33	7 3	5 28	21 33	3 49	22 10	25 32	11 52
12	18 45	8♏46	6 22	6 43	22 1	4 2	22 12	25 30	11 54
13	19 45	21 44	5 52	7 57	22 28	4 16	22 15	25 28	11 56
14	20 45	4♐27	5 34	9 12	22 55	4 29	22 17	25 26	11 58
15	21 46	16 55	5 28	10 27	23 22	4 42	22 19	25 24	12 0
16	22 46	29 11	5 D 33	11 42	23 48	4 55	22 22	25 22	12 2
17	23 47	11♑15	5 49	12 56	24 14	5 9	22 24	25 20	12 3
18	24 47	23 12	6 14	14 11	24 40	5 22	22 26	25 18	12 5
19	25 48	5♒4	6 49	15 26	25 6	5 35	22 28	25 16	12 7
20	26 48	16 55	7 31	16 41	25 31	5 48	22 29	25 14	12 9
21	27 49	28 52	8 20	17 56	25 56	6 2	22 31	25 11	12 10
22	28 50	10♓57	9 15	19 11	26 21	6 15	22 32	25 9	12 12
23	29 50	23 16	10 16	20 26	26 46	6 28	22 33	25 7	12 14
24	0♐51	5♈53	11 21	21 41	27 10	6 42	22 35	25 5	12 15
25	1 52	18 51	12 31	22 55	27 34	6 55	22 36	25 2	12 17
26	2 52	2♉12	13 44	24 10	27 57	7 9	22 37	25 0	12 18
27	3 53	15 57	15 0	25 25	28 20	7 22	22 38	24 58	12 20
28	4 54	0♊3	16 18	26 40	28 43	7 36	22 38	24 56	12 21
29	5 54	14 27	17 39	27 54	29 6	7 49	22 39	24 53	12 23
30	6 55	29 4	19 2	29 9	29 28	8 3	22 39	24 51	12 25

Pluto 14 Leo all month

DECEMBER

DAY	☉	☽	☿	♀	♂	♃	♄	♅	♆
	° ′	° ′	° ′	° ′	° ′	° ′	° ′	° ′	° ′
1	7♐56	13♋47	20♏26	0♑24	29♌49	8♐16	22♌39	24♊49	12♎26
2	8 57	28 29	21 52	1 39	0♍11	8 30	22 40	24 R 46	12 28
3	9 58	13♌2	23 18	2 53	0 32	8 43	22 40	24 44	12 29
4	10 59	27 24	24 46	4 8	0 53	8 57	22 40	24 41	12 30
5	11 59	11♍30	26 14	5 23	1 13	9 10	22 R 40	24 39	12 32
6	13 0	25 20	27 43	6 38	1 33	9 24	22 40	24 36	12 33
7	14 1	8♎52	29 13	7 52	1 52	9 37	22 40	24 34	12 35
8	15 2	22 9	0♐43	9 7	2 11	9 51	22 40	24 31	12 36
9	16 3	5♏11	2 14	10 22	2 30	10 4	22 39	24 29	12 37
10	17 4	18 0	3 45	11 37	2 48	10 17	22 39	24 26	12 38
11	18 5	0♐37	5 16	12 51	3 5	10 31	22 38	24 24	12 39
12	19 6	13 3	6 47	14 6	3 23	10 44	22 37	24 21	12 40
13	20 7	25 19	8 19	15 21	3 39	10 57	22 36	24 19	12 41
14	21 8	7♑27	9 51	16 35	3 56	11 11	22 35	24 16	12 42
15	22 9	19 27	11 23	17 50	4 11	11 24	22 34	24 14	12 44
16	23 10	1♒21	12 56	19 4	4 27	11 38	22 33	24 11	12 45
17	24 11	13 12	14 28	20 19	4 42	11 51	22 32	24 8	12 46
18	25 13	25 3	16 1	21 33	4 56	12 5	22 30	24 6	12 47
19	26 14	6♓58	17 34	22 48	5 10	12 18	22 29	24 3	12 47
20	27 15	18 59	19 7	24 2	5 23	12 31	22 27	24 0	12 48
21	28 16	1♈13	20 40	25 16	5 35	12 44	22 25	23 57	12 49
22	29 17	13 44	22 13	26 31	5 48	12 57	22 23	23 55	12 50
23	0♑18	26 37	23 47	27 45	5 59	13 11	22 21	23 52	12 50
24	1 19	9♉55	25 20	29 0	6 10	13 24	22 19	23 50	12 51
25	2 20	23 40	26 54	0♒14	6 20	13 37	22 17	23 47	12 52
26	3 21	7♊53	28 28	1 29	6 30	13 50	22 15	23 45	12 53
27	4 22	22 31	0♑3	2 43	6 39	14 3	22 12	23 42	12 53
28	5 24	7♋29	1 37	3 58	6 48	14 16	22 10	23 40	12 54
29	6 25	22 37	3 12	5 12	6 56	14 29	22 7	23 37	12 55
30	7 26	7♌46	4 48	6 27	7 3	14 42	22 5	23 35	12 56
31	8 27	22 45	6 23	7 41	7 9	14 55	22 2	23 32	12 56

Pluto 14 Leo all month

1948

JANUARY

DAY	☉	☽	☿	♀	♂	♃	♄	♅	♆
	° ′	° ′	° ′	° ′	° ′	° ′	° ′	° ′	° ′
1	9♑28	7♍26	7♑59	8♒55	7♍15	15♐ 8	21♌59	23♊30	12♎56
2	10 29	21 45	9 35	10 9	7 20	15 21	21℞56	23℞28	12 56
3	11 30	5♎39	11 11	11 24	7 25	15 34	21 53	23 25	12 57
4	12 32	19 8	12 48	12 38	7 29	15 47	21 49	23 23	12 57
5	13 33	2♏15	14 25	13 52	7 32	16 0	21 46	23 21	12 58
6	14 34	15 3	16 3	15 6	7 34	16 13	21 43	23 19	12 58
7	15 35	27 35	17 41	16 20	7 36	16 25	21 39	23 16	12 59
8	16 36	9♐55	19 19	17 34	7 36	16 38	21 36	23 14	12 59
9	17 37	22 6	20 58	18 48	7℞36	16 50	21 32	23 12	12 59
10	18 39	4♑10	22 37	20 2	7 36	17 3	21 29	23 10	12 59
11	19 40	16 9	24 17	21 16	7 34	17 15	21 25	23 7	13 0
12	20 41	28 4	25 57	22 30	7 32	17 28	21 22	23 5	13 0
13	21 42	9♒56	27 37	23 44	7 29	17 40	21 18	23 3	13 0
14	22 43	21 48	29 17	24 58	7 26	17 52	21 14	23 1	13 0
15	23 44	3♓40	0♒58	26 11	7 22	18 4	21 10	22 58	13℞ 0
16	24 46	15 35	2 40	27 25	7 17	18 16	21 5	22 56	13 0
17	25 47	27 37	4 21	28 39	7 11	18 28	21 1	22 54	13 0
18	26 48	9♈48	6 3	29 53	7 4	18 40	20 57	22 52	13 0
19	27 49	22 14	7 45	1♓ 6	6 57	18 52	20 53	22 50	13 0
20	28 50	4♉58	9 27	2 20	6 48	19 4	20 49	22 48	12 59
21	29 51	18 7	11 8	3 34	6 39	19 16	20 45	22 46	12 59
22	0♒52	1♊43	12 50	4 47	6 29	19 28	20 41	22 44	12 59
23	1 53	15 48	14 31	6 1	6 18	19 40	20 36	22 42	12 59
24	2 54	0♋23	16 12	7 14	6 6	19 51	20 32	22 41	12 58
25	3 55	15 22	17 51	8 27	5 53	20 3	20 27	22 39	12 58
26	4 56	0♌39	19 30	9 40	5 40	20 14	20 22	22 37	12 58
27	5 57	16 1	21 7	10 54	5 25	20 26	20 18	22 35	12 58
28	6 58	1♍19	22 43	12 7	5 10	20 37	20 13	22 34	12 57
29	7 59	16 19	24 16	13 20	4 54	20 48	20 8	22 32	12 57
30	9 0	0♎54	25 47	14 33	4 37	20 59	20 3	22 30	12 56
31	10 1	15 1	27 15	15 46	4 20	21 10	19 59	22 29	12 56

Pluto 14 Leo all month

FEBRUARY

DAY	☉	☽	☿	♀	♂	♃	♄	♅	♆
	° ′	° ′	° ′	° ′	° ′	° ′	° ′	° ′	° ′
1	11♒ 2	28♎38	28♒38	16♓59	4♍ 2	21♐21	19♌54	22♊27	12♎55
2	12 3	11♏47	29 57	18 12	3℞43	21 32	19℞49	22℞26	12℞54
3	13 4	24 33	1♓12	19 24	3 23	21 43	19 44	22 25	12 53
4	14 4	7♐ 0	2 20	20 37	3 4	21 53	19 40	22 23	12 53
5	15 5	19 12	3 22	21 50	2 44	22 4	19 35	22 22	12 52
6	16 6	1♑15	4 16	23 2	2 23	22 14	19 30	22 21	12 51
7	17 7	13 11	5 2	24 15	2 2	22 24	19 25	22 20	12 50
8	18 8	25 4	5 39	25 27	1 40	22 35	19 20	22 19	12 50
9	19 9	6♒55	6 7	26 39	1 18	22 45	19 15	22 18	12 49
10	20 9	18 47	6 24	27 51	0 56	22 55	19 10	22 17	12 48
11	21 10	0♓41	6 31	29 4	0 33	23 5	19 5	22 16	12 47
12	22 11	12 38	6℞27	0♈15	0 10	23 15	19 0	22 15	12 46
13	23 11	24 39	6 12	1 27	29♌46	23 25	18 56	22 14	12 45
14	24 12	6♈46	5 47	2 39	29 23	23 35	18 51	22 13	12 44
15	25 13	19 2	5 13	3 51	28 59	23 44	18 46	22 12	12 43
16	26 13	1♉30	4 29	5 3	28 35	23 54	18 41	22 11	12 42
17	27 14	14 13	3 38	6 14	28 12	24 3	18 37	22 11	12 41
18	28 15	27 16	2 40	7 26	27 48	24 12	18 32	22 10	12 40
19	29 15	10♊43	1 37	8 37	27 24	24 21	18 27	22 9	12 39
20	0♓16	24 35	0 31	9 48	27 0	24 30	18 22	22 9	12 38
21	1 16	8♋55	29♒24	10 59	26 36	24 39	18 18	22 8	12 37
22	2 16	23 41	28 17	12 10	26 13	24 48	18 13	22 8	12 36
23	3 17	8♌46	27 12	13 21	25 49	24 57	18 8	22 8	12 35
24	4 17	24 2	26 11	14 32	25 26	25 5	18 4	22 7	12 34
25	5 18	9♍18	25 14	15 43	25 4	25 14	17 59	22 7	12 32
26	6 18	24 23	24 23	16 53	24 41	25 22	17 55	22 7	12 31
27	7 18	9♎ 7	23 37	18 4	24 19	25 30	17 50	22 7	12 30
28	8 18	23 24	22 59	19 14	23 57	25 38	17 46	22 6	12 29
29	9 19	7♏11	22 28	20 24	23 36	25 46	17 41	22 6	12 27

Pluto 13 Leo all month

1948

MARCH

DAY	☉	☽	☿	♀	♂	♃	♄	♅	♆
	° ′	° ′	° ′	° ′	° ′	° ′	° ′	° ′	° ′
1	10♓19	20♏29	22♒ 4	21♈34	23♌15	25♐54	17♌37	22♊ 6	12♎26
2	11 19	3♐21	21℞47	22 44	22℞55	26 1	17℞33	22℞ 6	12℞25
3	12 19	15 51	21 36	23 54	22 35	26 9	17 28	22D 6	12 23
4	13 19	28 4	21D33	25 3	22 16	26 16	17 24	22 6	12 22
5	14 20	10♑ 5	21 36	26 13	21 57	26 23	17 20	22 6	12 20
6	15 20	21 59	21 45	27 22	21 39	26 30	17 16	22 6	12 19
7	16 20	3♒50	22 0	28 31	21 21	26 37	17 12	22 7	12 17
8	17 20	15 41	22 21	29 40	21 5	26 43	17 9	22 7	12 16
9	18 20	27 34	22 47	0♉49	20 48	26 50	17 5	22 8	12 14
10	19 20	9♓32	23 17	1 58	20 33	26 56	17 1	22 9	12 13
11	20 20	21 36	23 52	3 6	20 18	27 3	16 57	22 9	12 11
12	21 19	3♈48	24 31	4 14	20 4	27 9	16 54	22 10	12 10
13	22 19	16 7	25 14	5 22	19 51	27 15	16 50	22 11	12 8
14	23 19	28 36	26 0	6 30	19 38	27 21	16 47	22 12	12 7
15	24 19	11♉16	26 50	7 38	19 27	27 27	16 43	22 12	12 5
16	25 19	24 9	27 44	8 46	19 16	27 32	16 40	22 13	12 4
17	26 18	7♊17	28 40	9 53	19 6	27 38	16 37	22 14	12 2
18	27 18	20 43	29 39	11 0	18 56	27 43	16 34	22 15	12 1
19	28 18	4♋30	0♓41	12 7	18 48	27 48	16 31	22 16	11 59
20	29 17	18 37	1 45	13 14	18 40	27 52	16 28	22 17	11 58
21	0♈17	3♌ 3	2 52	14 21	18 33	27 57	16 25	22 18	11 56
22	1 17	17 47	4 1	15 27	18 27	28 1	16 22	22 19	11 54
23	2 16	2♍40	5 12	16 33	18 22	28 6	16 20	22 20	11 53
24	3 15	17 37	6 25	17 39	18 17	28 10	16 17	22 22	11 51
25	4 15	2♎27	7 40	18 45	18 13	28 14	16 15	22 23	11 49
26	5 14	17 2	8 57	19 50	18 10	28 18	16 13	22 24	11 47
27	6 14	1♏16	10 16	20 55	18 8	28 22	16 10	22 25	11 46
28	7 13	15 6	11 37	22 0	18 7	28 25	16 8	22 27	11 44
29	8 12	28 29	12 59	23 5	18 6	28 29	16 6	22 28	11 43
30	9 12	11♐27	14 23	24 9	18D 6	28 32	16 4	22 29	11 41
31	10 11	24 3	15 49	25 13	18 7	28 35	16 2	22 31	11 40

Pluto 13 Leo all month

APRIL

DAY	☉	☽	☿	♀	♂	♃	♄	♅	♆
	° ′	° ′	° ′	° ′	° ′	° ′	° ′	° ′	° ′
1	11♈10	6♑20	17♓16	26♉17	18♌ 8	28♐37	16♌ 0	22♊32	11♎38
2	12 9	18 25	18 45	27 21	18 11	28 40	15℞58	22 34	11 36
3	13 8	0♒20	20 15	28 24	18 13	28 42	15 57	22 36	11 34
4	14 7	12 12	21 47	29 27	18 17	28 45	15 55	22 37	11 33
5	15 6	24 5	23 21	0♊29	18 21	28 47	15 54	22 39	11 31
6	16 6	6♓ 1	24 56	1 32	18 26	28 49	15 53	22 41	11 30
7	17 5	18 4	26 32	2 33	18 32	28 50	15 52	22 43	11 28
8	18 4	0♈16	28 10	3 35	18 38	28 52	15 50	22 45	11 27
9	19 3	12 39	29 50	4 36	18 45	28 53	15 49	22 47	11 25
10	20 1	25 14	1♈31	5 37	18 52	28 54	15 48	22 49	11 23
11	21 0	8♉ 2	3 13	6 38	19 0	28 55	15 47	22 51	11 21
12	21 59	21 2	4 57	7 38	19 9	28 56	15 47	22 53	11 20
13	22 58	4♊15	6 43	8 37	19 18	28 56	15 47	22 56	11 18
14	23 57	17 40	8 30	9 37	19 28	28 57	15 46	22 58	11 17
15	24 56	1♋18	10 19	10 35	19 39	28 57	15 46	23 0	11 15
16	25 54	15 11	12 10	11 34	19 50	28℞57	15 46	23 2	11 14
17	26 53	29 15	14 2	12 32	20 1	28 56	15D46	23 5	11 12
18	27 52	13♌30	15 55	13 29	20 13	28 56	15 46	23 7	11 11
19	28 50	27 53	17 50	14 26	20 26	28 55	15 46	23 9	11 9
20	29 49	12♍22	19 46	15 23	20 39	28 54	15 46	23 12	11 8
21	0♉47	26 50	21 44	16 19	20 53	28 53	15 46	23 14	11 6
22	1 46	11♎13	23 44	17 14	21 7	28 52	15 47	23 17	11 5
23	2 44	25 25	25 45	18 9	21 22	28 51	15 48	23 19	11 3
24	3 43	9♏23	27 47	19 3	21 37	28 49	15 48	23 22	11 2
25	4 41	23 1	29 51	19 57	21 52	28 48	15 49	23 25	11 0
26	5 39	6♐19	1♉57	20 50	22 8	28 46	15 50	23 27	10 59
27	6 38	19 16	4 3	21 42	22 25	28 44	15 51	23 30	10 57
28	7 36	1♑54	6 10	22 34	22 42	28 42	15 52	23 32	10 56
29	8 34	14 14	8 18	23 25	22 59	28 39	15 53	23 35	10 54
30	9 33	26 22	10 27	24 15	23 17	28 37	15 54	23 38	11 53

Pluto 12 Leo all month

1948

MAY

DAY	☉ ° ′	☽ ° ′	☿ ° ′	♀ ° ′	♂ ° ′	♃ ° ′	♄ ° ′	♅ ° ′	♆ ° ′
1	10 ♉ 31	8 ♒ 20	12 ♉ 37	25 ♊ 5	23 ♌ 35	28 ♐ 34	15 ♌ 55	23 ♊ 41	10 ♎ 51
2	11 29	20 14	14 46	25 53	23 54	28 ℞ 31	15 57	23 43	10 ℞ 50
3	12 27	2 ♓ 7	16 56	26 41	24 13	28 28	15 58	23 46	10 48
4	13 25	14 5	19 5	27 28	24 32	28 25	16 0	23 49	10 47
5	14 23	26 11	21 14	28 15	24 52	28 21	16 2	23 52	10 46
6	15 22	8 ♈ 30	23 22	29 0	25 12	28 18	16 4	23 55	10 45
7	16 20	21 3	25 28	29 45	25 32	28 14	16 6	23 58	10 44
8	17 18	3 ♉ 53	27 33	0 ♋ 28	25 53	28 10	16 8	24 1	10 43
9	18 16	16 59	29 36	1 11	26 14	28 6	16 10	24 4	10 42
10	19 14	0 ♊ 23	1 ♊ 38	1 52	26 36	28 1	16 13	24 7	10 41
11	20 12	14 1	3 37	2 33	26 57	27 57	16 15	24 10	10 39
12	21 10	27 53	5 33	3 12	27 19	27 52	16 18	24 13	10 38
13	22 8	11 ♋ 55	7 27	3 50	27 42	27 47	16 21	24 16	10 37
14	23 6	26 4	9 18	4 27	28 5	27 42	16 23	24 19	10 36
15	24 8	10 ♌ 17	11 6	5 3	28 28	27 37	16 26	24 23	10 35
16	25 1	24 31	12 51	5 37	28 51	27 32	16 29	25 26	10 34
17	25 59	8 ♍ 44	14 33	6 10	29 15	27 27	16 32	24 29	10 33
18	26 57	22 54	16 12	6 42	29 39	27 21	16 35	24 32	10 32
19	27 55	6 ♎ 57	17 47	7 12	0 ♍ 3	27 16	16 39	24 36	10 30
20	28 52	20 52	19 20	7 40	0 28	27 10	16 42	24 39	10 29
21	29 50	4 ♏ 36	20 48	8 7	0 52	27 4	16 45	24 42	10 28
22	0 ♊ 48	18 9	22 14	8 33	1 18	26 58	16 49	24 45	10 27
23	1 45	1 ♐ 27	23 36	8 57	1 43	26 51	16 52	24 49	10 27
24	2 43	14 30	24 55	9 19	2 8	26 45	16 56	24 52	10 26
25	3 41	27 18	26 9	9 39	2 34	26 39	17 0	24 55	10 25
26	4 38	9 ♑ 50	27 21	9 57	3 0	26 32	17 4	24 59	10 24
27	5 36	22 9	28 28	10 13	3 27	26 26	17 8	25 2	10 23
28	6 33	4 ♒ 16	29 32	10 28	3 53	26 19	17 12	25 6	10 22
29	7 31	16 14	0 ♋ 32	10 40	4 20	26 12	17 16	25 9	10 21
30	8 28	28 8	1 29	10 50	4 47	26 5	17 20	25 13	10 20
31	9 26	10 ♓ 2	2 21	10 58	5 14	25 58	17 25	25 16	10 20

Pluto 12 Leo all month

JUNE

DAY	☉ ° ′	☽ ° ′	☿ ° ′	♀ ° ′	♂ ° ′	♃ ° ′	♄ ° ′	♅ ° ′	♆ ° ′
1	10 ♊ 23	21 ♓ 59	3 ♋ 9	11 ♋ 4	5 ♍ 42	25 ♐ 51	17 ♌ 29	25 ♊ 20	10 ♎ 19
2	11 21	4 ♈ 6	3 54	11 8	6 10	25 ℞ 44	17 33	25 23	10 ℞ 18
3	12 18	16 27	4 34	11 9	6 37	25 37	17 38	25 27	10 18
4	13 16	29 4	5 9	11 ℞ 8	7 5	25 29	17 42	25 30	10 17
5	14 13	12 ♉ 3	5 41	11 5	7 34	25 22	17 47	25 34	10 17
6	15 11	25 24	6 8	10 59	8 2	25 15	17 52	25 37	10 16
7	16 8	9 ♊ 8	6 31	10 51	8 31	25 7	17 57	25 41	10 16
8	17 5	23 11	6 49	10 41	9 0	25 0	18 2	25 44	10 15
9	18 3	7 ♋ 30	7 2	10 28	9 29	24 52	18 7	25 48	10 15
10	19 0	22 0	7 11	10 12	9 58	24 44	18 12	25 51	10 15
11	19 58	6 ♌ 34	7 16	9 55	10 28	24 37	18 17	25 55	10 14
12	20 55	21 5	7 ℞ 16	9 35	10 57	24 29	18 22	25 58	10 14
13	21 52	5 ♍ 30	7 11	9 12	11 27	24 21	18 27	26 2	10 14
14	22 50	19 44	7 2	8 48	11 57	24 13	18 32	26 5	10 14
15	23 47	3 ♎ 45	6 49	8 21	12 27	24 6	18 38	26 9	10 13
16	24 44	17 32	6 32	7 53	12 58	23 58	18 43	26 12	10 13
17	25 41	1 ♏ 6	6 11	7 23	13 28	23 51	18 49	26 16	10 13
18	26 39	14 26	5 47	6 51	13 59	23 43	18 55	26 20	10 13
19	27 36	27 34	5 20	6 18	14 30	23 36	19 0	26 23	10 13
20	28 33	10 ♐ 31	4 50	5 43	15 1	23 28	19 6	26 27	10 13
21	29 30	23 15	4 18	5 8	15 32	23 20	19 12	26 31	10 D 13
22	0 ♋ 28	5 ♑ 49	3 44	4 31	16 3	23 12	19 18	26 35	10 13
23	1 25	18 11	3 10	3 54	16 35	23 5	19 24	26 38	10 13
24	2 22	0 ♒ 23	2 34	3 17	17 7	22 57	19 30	26 42	10 13
25	3 19	12 26	1 59	2 39	17 38	22 50	19 36	26 45	10 13
26	4 17	24 22	1 25	2 1	18 10	22 43	19 42	26 49	10 13
27	5 14	6 ♓ 14	0 52	1 24	18 42	22 35	19 48	26 52	10 13
28	6 11	18 6	0 21	0 48	19 5	22 28	19 54	26 56	10 14
29	7 8	0 ♈ 2	29 ♊ 53	0 12	19 47	22 21	20 0	26 59	10 14
30	8 5	12 7	29 28	29 ♊ 37	20 19	22 14	20 6	27 3	10 14

Pluto 12 Leo all month

1948

JULY

Day	☉	☽	☿	♀	♂	♃	♄	♅	♆
	° ′	° ′	° ′	° ′	° ′	° ′	° ′	° ′	° ′
1	9♋ 3	24♈26	29♊ 6	29♊ 4	20♍52	22♐ 7	20♌13	27♊ 6	10♎14
2	10 0	7♉ 4	28℞47	28℞32	21 25	22℞ 0	20 20	27 10	10 15
3	10 57	20 4	28 33	28 1	21 58	21 53	20 26	27 13	10 15
4	11 54	3♊31	28 24	27 33	22 31	21 46	20 32	27 17	10 15
5	12 51	17 25	28 18	27 6	23 4	21 39	20 39	27 20	10 16
6	13 49	1♋45	28 D18	26 41	23 37	21 33	20 45	27 24	10 16
7	14 46	16 25	28 23	26 19	24 11	21 26	20 52	27 27	10 17
8	15 43	1♌19	28 33	25 58	24 44	21 20	20 59	27 31	10 17
9	16 40	16 18	28 48	25 40	25 18	21 13	21 6	27 34	10 18
10	17 38	1♍12	29 8	25 24	25 52	21 7	21 13	27 38	10 18
11	18 35	15 54	29 33	25 10	26 26	21 1	21 20	27 41	10 19
12	19 32	0♎18	0♋ 4	24 59	27 0	20 55	21 27	27 45	10 20
13	20 29	14 21	0 39	24 50	27 34	20 49	21 34	27 48	10 20
14	21 26	28 3	1 20	24 44	28 8	20 44	21 40	27 52	10 21
15	22 24	11♏26	2 7	24 40	28 43	20 38	21 47	27 55	10 22
16	23 21	24 31	2 58	24 38	29 17	20 33	21 54	27 58	10 23
17	24 18	7♐22	3 54	24 D39	29 52	20 28	22 1	28 2	10 23
18	25 15	20 0	4 56	24 42	0♎27	20 23	22 9	28 5	10 24
19	26 13	2♑28	6 2	24 47	1 2	20 18	22 16	28 8	10 25
20	27 10	14 47	7 13	24 54	1 37	20 13	22 23	28 11	10 26
21	28 7	26 57	8 29	25 4	2 12	20 8	22 30	28 15	10 27
22	29 4	9♒ 1	9 49	25 15	2 47	20 4	22 37	28 18	10 28
23	0♌ 2	20 58	11 14	25 29	3 22	19 59	22 44	28 21	10 29
24	0 59	2♓51	12 43	25 45	3 58	19 55	22 51	28 24	10 30
25	1 56	14 42	14 16	26 2	4 33	19 51	22 59	28 27	10 31
26	2 53	26 33	15 54	26 22	5 9	19 47	23 6	28 30	10 32
27	3 51	8♈28	17 35	26 43	5 45	19 43	23 14	28 33	10 33
28	4 48	20 32	19 20	27 6	6 21	19 40	23 21	28 36	10 34
29	5 45	2♉48	21 9	27 31	6 57	19 36	23 29	28 39	10 35
30	6 43	15 23	23 0	27 57	7 33	19 33	23 36	28 42	10 37
31	7 40	28 20	24 55	28 25	8 9	19 30	23 43	28 45	10 38

Pluto 13 Leo all month

AUGUST

Day	☉	☽	☿	♀	♂	♃	♄	♅	♆
	° ′	° ′	° ′	° ′	° ′	° ′	° ′	° ′	° ′
1	8♌38	11♊45	26♋52	28♊54	8♎45	19♐27	23♌50	28♊48	10♎39
2	9 35	25 39	28 50	29 25	9 22	19℞25	23 58	28 51	10 40
3	10 33	10♋ 2	0♌51	29 57	9 58	19 22	24 5	28 54	10 42
4	11 30	24 51	2 53	0♋31	10 35	19 20	24 13	28 57	10 43
5	12 27	9♌58	4 56	1 5	11 11	19 18	24 20	29 0	10 44
6	13 25	25 13	7 0	1 42	11 49	19 16	24 28	29 3	10 45
7	14 22	10♍25	9 4	2 19	12 25	19 14	24 35	29 5	10 47
8	15 20	25 23	11 8	2 57	13 2	19 12	24 43	29 8	10 48
9	16 18	10♎ 1	13 12	3 37	13 39	19 11	24 51	29 11	10 49
10	17 15	24 14	15 16	4 17	14 17	19 10	24 58	29 13	10 51
11	18 13	8♏ 1	17 19	4 59	14 54	19 9	25 6	29 16	10 52
12	19 10	21 23	19 22	5 41	15 31	19 8	25 14	29 18	10 54
13	20 8	4♐24	21 23	6 25	16 9	19 7	25 22	29 21	10 55
14	21 5	17 6	23 23	7 9	16 46	19 7	25 29	29 23	10 57
15	22 3	29 33	25 23	7 55	17 24	19 6	25 37	29 26	10 58
16	23 1	11♑49	27 21	8 41	18 2	19 6	25 44	29 28	11 0
17	23 58	23 57	29 17	9 28	18 39	19 D 6	25 52	29 31	11 2
18	24 56	5♒58	1♍13	10 16	19 18	19 7	25 59	29 33	11 3
19	25 54	17 55	3 7	11 4	19 56	19 7	26 7	29 36	11 5
20	26 52	29 48	5 0	11 54	20 34	19 8	26 15	29 38	11 7
21	27 49	11♓40	6 52	12 44	21 12	19 9	26 23	29 40	11 9
22	28 47	23 31	8 42	13 35	21 50	19 10	26 30	29 43	11 10
23	29 45	5♈24	10 30	14 26	22 29	19 11	26 38	29 45	11 12
24	0♍43	17 22	12 18	15 18	23 7	19 12	26 45	29 47	11 14
25	1 41	29 28	14 4	16 11	23 46	19 14	26 53	29 49	11 16
26	2 39	11♉45	15 48	17 5	24 24	19 15	27 0	29 51	11 17
27	3 36	24 19	17 32	17 59	25 3	19 17	27 8	29 53	11 19
28	4 34	7♊13	19 13	18 53	25 42	19 19	27 16	29 55	11 21
29	5 32	20 32	20 54	19 48	26 21	19 21	27 24	29 57	11 23
30	6 30	4♋19	22 33	20 44	27 0	19 24	27 31	29 59	11 25
31	7 28	18 35	24 12	21 40	27 39	19 26	27 39	0♋ 1	11 27

Pluto 14 Leo all month

1948

SEPTEMBER

DAY	☉ ° ′	☽ ° ′	☿ ° ′	♀ ° ′	♂ ° ′	♃ ° ′	♄ ° ′	♅ ° ′	♆ ° ′
1	8♍27	3♌17	25♍49	22♋37	28♎18	19♐29	27♌46	0♋ 3	11♎29
2	9 25	18 21	27 24	23 34	28 57	19 32	27 54	0 5	11 31
3	10 23	3♍37	28 59	24 31	29 37	19 36	28 1	0 6	11 33
4	11 21	18 54	0♎32	25 29	0♏16	19 39	28 9	0 8	11 35
5	12 19	4♎ 1	2 4	26 28	0 56	19 43	28 16	0 9	11 37
6	13 17	18 49	3 34	27 27	1 36	19 47	28 24	0 11	11 39
7	14 16	3♏13	5 4	28 26	2 15	19 50	28 31	0 12	11 41
8	15 14	17 9	6 32	29 26	2 55	19 54	28 39	0 14	11 43
9	16 12	0♐38	7 59	0♌26	3 35	19 58	28 46	0 15	11 45
10	17 10	13 41	9 25	1 26	4 15	20 3	28 54	0 17	11 47
11	18 9	26 23	10 49	2 27	4 55	20 7	29 1	0 18	11 49
12	19 7	8♑47	12 12	3 28	5 35	20 12	29 9	0 20	11 51
13	20 6	20 59	13 34	4 30	6 15	20 17	29 16	0 21	11 53
14	21 4	3♒ 0	14 54	5 32	6 55	20 22	29 23	0 22	11 55
15	22 2	14 56	16 14	6 34	7 36	20 27	29 31	0 23	11 57
16	23 1	26 49	17 31	7 37	8 16	20 33	29 38	0 24	12 0
17	23 59	8♓40	18 47	8 39	8 57	20 38	29 45	0 25	12 2
18	24 58	20 33	20 1	9 43	9 38	20 44	29 52	0 26	12 4
19	25 57	2♈28	21 14	10 46	10 18	20 50	29 59	0 27	12 6
20	26 55	14 28	22 25	11 50	10 58	20 56	0♍ 6	0 28	12 8
21	27 54	26 34	23 34	12 54	11 40	21 2	0 13	0 29	12 10
22	28 53	8♉48	24 42	13 59	12 21	21 8	0 20	0 30	12 12
23	29 51	21 14	25 47	15 3	13 2	21 15	0 27	0 30	12 14
24	0♎50	3♊54	26 50	16 8	13 43	21 21	0 34	0 31	12 17
25	1 49	16 51	27 50	17 13	14 24	21 28	0 41	0 31	12 19
26	2 48	0♋ 8	28 48	18 19	15 5	21 35	0 48	0 32	12 21
27	3 46	13 48	29 44	19 24	15 47	21 42	0 55	0 32	12 23
28	4 45	27 52	0♏36	20 31	16 28	21 50	1 2	0 33	12 26
29	5 44	12♌19	1 25	21 36	17 10	21 57	1 9	0 33	12 28
30	6 43	27 6	2 11	22 42	17 52	22 5	1 16	0 33	12 30

Pluto 15 Leo all month

OCTOBER

DAY	☉ ° ′	☽ ° ′	☿ ° ′	♀ ° ′	♂ ° ′	♃ ° ′	♄ ° ′	♅ ° ′	♆ ° ′
1	7♎42	12♍ 6	2♏52	23♌49	18♏33	22♐12	1♍22	0♋34	12♎32
2	8 41	27 11	3 30	24 55	19 15	22 20	1 29	0 34	12 35
3	9 40	12♎11	4 3	26 2	19 57	22 28	1 35	0 34	12 37
4	10 40	26 59	4 31	27 10	20 39	22 36	1 42	0 34	12 39
5	11 39	11♏26	4 54	28 17	21 20	22 44	1 48	0 34	12 41
6	12 38	25 28	5 11	29 25	22 2	22 53	1 55	0R 34	12 44
7	13 37	9♐ 4	5 21	0♍32	22 44	23 1	2 1	0 34	12 46
8	14 36	22 14	5 25	1 40	23 26	23 10	2 7	0 34	12 48
9	15 36	5♑ 0	5R 22	2 49	24 9	23 18	2 14	0 34	12 50
10	16 35	17 27	5 11	3 57	24 51	23 27	2 20	0 33	12 53
11	17 34	29 39	4 52	5 5	25 34	23 36	2 26	0 33	12 55
12	18 34	11♒39	4 25	6 14	26 16	23 45	2 32	0 33	12 57
13	19 33	23 33	3 50	7 23	26 59	23 54	2 38	0 33	12 59
14	20 33	5♓24	3 6	8 32	27 41	24 4	2 44	0 32	13 2
15	21 32	17 16	2 14	9 41	28 24	24 13	2 50	0 32	13 4
16	22 31	29 12	1 15	10 51	29 7	24 23	2 56	0 32	13 6
17	23 31	11♈14	0 9	12 0	29 50	24 32	3 2	0 31	13 8
18	24 31	23 24	29♎ 0	13 10	0♐33	24 42	3 7	0 31	13 11
19	25 30	5♉43	27 47	14 20	1 16	24 52	3 13	0 30	13 13
20	26 30	18 14	26 32	15 30	1 59	25 2	3 19	0 29	13 15
21	27 29	0♊56	25 18	16 40	2 42	25 12	3 24	0 29	13 17
22	28 29	13 52	24 8	17 50	3 25	25 22	3 30	0 28	13 20
23	29 29	27 2	23 3	19 1	4 8	25 32	3 35	0 27	13 22
24	0♏29	10♋27	22 4	20 11	4 51	25 42	3 40	0 26	13 24
25	1 28	24 8	21 15	21 22	5 35	25 53	3 46	0 25	13 26
26	2 28	8♌ 4	20 36	22 33	6 18	26 3	3 51	0 24	13 28
27	3 28	22 17	20 8	23 43	7 2	26 14	3 56	0 23	13 30
28	4 28	6♍42	19 51	24 55	7 46	26 25	4 1	0 22	13 32
29	5 28	21 17	19D46	26 6	8 29	26 36	4 6	0 21	13 34
30	6 28	5♎57	19 51	27 17	9 13	26 47	4 10	0 19	13 37
31	7 28	20 36	20 8	28 28	9 57	26 58	4 15	0 18	13 39

Pluto 16 Leo all month

1948

NOVEMBER

Day	☉	☽	☿	♀	♂	♃	♄	♅	♆
	° ′	° ′	° ′	° ′	° ′	° ′	° ′	° ′	° ′
1	8♏28	5♏ 6	20♎35	29♍40	10♐41	27♐ 9	4♍20	0♋17	13♎41
2	9 28	19 23	21 11	0♎51	11 25	27 20	4 25	0℞16	13 43
3	10 28	3♐22	21 56	2 3	12 9	27 32	4 29	0 14	13 45
4	11 28	16 58	22 48	3 15	12 53	27 43	4 34	0 13	13 47
5	12 29	0♑11	23 46	4 27	13 37	27 55	4 38	0 12	13 49
6	13 29	13 2	24 50	5 39	14 21	28 6	4 43	0 10	13 51
7	14 29	25 32	26 0	6 51	15 6	28 18	4 47	0 9	13 53
8	15 29	7♒47	27 14	8 3	15 50	28 30	4 51	0 7	13 55
9	16 30	19 48	28 31	9 16	16 34	28 42	4 55	0 5	13 57
10	17 30	1♓42	29 52	10 28	17 19	28 54	4 59	0 4	13 59
11	18 30	13 33	1♏15	11 41	18 3	29 6	5 2	0 2	14 1
12	19 31	25 25	2 41	12 53	18 48	29 18	5 6	0 0	14 3
13	20 31	7♈24	4 9	14 6	19 33	29 30	5 10	29♊58	14 5
14	21 31	19 32	5 38	15 19	20 17	29 42	5 13	29 57	14 7
15	22 32	1♉52	7 8	16 31	21 2	29 54	5 17	29 55	14 8
16	23 32	14 26	8 39	17 44	21 47	0♑ 6	5 20	29 53	14 10
17	24 33	27 17	10 11	18 57	22 32	0 19	5 23	29 51	14 12
18	25 33	10♊26	11 44	20 10	23 17	0 31	5 27	29 49	14 14
19	26 34	23 42	13 17	21 24	24 2	0 44	5 30	29 47	14 16
20	27 34	7♋16	14 51	22 37	24 47	0 57	5 33	29 45	14 18
21	28 35	21 1	16 25	23 50	25 32	1 10	5 36	29 43	14 20
22	29 36	4♌55	17 59	25 3	26 17	1 22	5 38	29 41	14 21
23	0♐36	18 57	19 33	26 17	27 3	1 35	5 41	29 38	14 23
24	1 37	3♍ 4	21 8	27 30	27 48	1 47	5 43	29 36	14 24
25	2 38	17 15	22 42	28 44	28 33	2 0	5 46	29 34	14 26
26	3 38	1♎27	24 17	29 57	29 19	2 13	5 48	29 32	14 27
27	4 39	15 40	25 51	1♏11	0♑ 4	2 26	5 51	29 30	14 29
28	5 40	29 49	27 26	2 24	0 50	2 39	5 53	29 28	14 31
29	6 41	13♏53	29 0	3 38	1 35	2 52	5 55	29 26	14 33
30	7 41	27 47	0♐35	4 52	2 21	3 5	5 57	29 24	14 34

Pluto 16 Leo all month

DECEMBER

Day	☉	☽	☿	♀	♂	♃	♄	♅	♆
	° ′	° ′	° ′	° ′	° ′	° ′	° ′	° ′	° ′
1	8♐42	11♐28	2♐ 9	6♏ 6	3♑ 6	3♑19	5♍58	29♊21	14♎36
2	9 43	24 54	3 43	7 20	3 52	3 32	6 0	29℞19	14 37
3	10 44	8♑ 1	5 18	8 34	4 38	3 45	6 2	29 17	14 39
4	11 45	20 50	6 52	9 48	5 23	3 58	6 3	29 14	14 40
5	12 46	3♒21	8 26	11 2	6 9	4 12	6 5	29 12	14 42
6	13 47	15 35	10 0	12 16	6 55	4 25	6 6	29 9	14 43
7	14 48	27 38	11 34	13 29	7 41	4 38	6 7	29 7	14 44
8	15 49	9♓31	13 9	14 43	8 27	4 52	6 8	29 4	14 46
9	16 50	21 22	14 43	15 58	9 14	5 5	6 9	29 2	14 47
10	17 51	3♈13	16 17	17 12	10 0	5 19	6 10	28 59	14 48
11	18 52	15 12	17 51	18 26	10 46	5 32	6 11	28 57	14 49
12	19 53	27 21	19 25	19 41	11 32	5 46	6 11	28 54	14 50
13	20 54	9♉48	21 0	20 55	12 19	5 59	6 12	28 52	14 51
14	21 55	22 33	22 34	22 10	13 5	6 13	6 12	28 49	14 52
15	22 56	5♊39	24 9	23 24	13 51	6 27	6 12	28 47	14 53
16	23 57	19 6	25 44	24 39	14 37	6 40	6 12	28 44	14 54
17	24 58	2♋53	27 18	25 53	15 24	6 54	6℞ 12	28 42	14 55
18	25 59	16 56	28 53	27 8	16 10	7 8	6 12	28 39	14 56
19	27 0	1♌10	0♑29	28 22	16 56	7 22	6 12	28 36	14 57
20	28 1	15 29	2 4	29 37	17 43	7 36	6 12	28 34	14 58
21	29 2	29 49	3 39	0♐51	18 29	7 50	6 11	28 31	14 59
22	0♑ 3	14♍ 5	5 15	2 6	19 16	8 4	6 11	28 28	15 0
23	1 4	28 15	6 51	3 20	20 3	8 18	6 10	28 25	15 1
24	2 5	12♎17	8 27	4 35	20 49	8 32	6 9	28 23	15 2
25	3 7	26 11	10 3	5 49	21 36	8 45	6 8	28 20	15 2
26	4 8	9♏56	11 40	7 4	22 23	8 59	6 7	28 18	15 3
27	5 9	23 33	13 16	8 19	23 10	9 13	6 6	28 15	15 4
28	6 10	7♐ 0	14 53	9 33	23 56	9 27	6 5	28 13	15 5
29	7 11	20 17	16 30	10 48	24 43	9 41	6 3	28 10	15 5
30	8 12	3♑22	18 7	12 3	25 30	9 55	6 2	28 8	15 6
31	9 14	16 15	19 44	13 18	26 17	10 9	6 0	28 5	15 6

Pluto 16 Leo all month

1949

JANUARY

DAY	☉ ° '	☽ ° '	☿ ° '	♀ ° '	♂ ° '	♃ ° '	♄ ° '	♅ ° '	♆ ° '
1	10♐15	28♐54	21♐21	14♐33	27♐4	10♐23	5♍59	28Ⅱ3	15♎7
2	11 16	11≈18	22 59	15 48	27 51	10 36	5R57	28R0	15 8
3	12 17	23 29	24 36	17 3	28 38	10 50	5 55	27 58	15 8
4	13 18	5✶30	26 12	18 18	29 25	11 4	5 53	27 55	15 8
5	14 19	17 22	27 49	19 32	0≈12	11 18	5 51	27 53	15 9
6	15 21	29 11	29 25	20 47	0 59	11 32	5 49	27 50	15 9
7	16 22	11♈0	1≈0	22 2	1 46	11 46	5 47	27 48	15 10
8	17 23	22 56	2 34	23 17	2 33	12 0	5 45	27 46	15 10
9	18 24	5♉4	4 8	24 32	3 20	12 14	5 42	27 43	15 10
10	19 25	17 29	5 40	25 47	4 8	12 27	5 40	27 41	15 10
11	20 26	0Ⅱ16	7 11	27 2	4 55	12 41	5 37	27 39	15 11
12	21 28	13 29	8 39	28 17	5 42	12 55	5 34	27 37	15 11
13	22 29	27 8	10 5	29 32	6 29	13 9	5 32	27 34	15 11
14	23 30	11♋13	11 28	0♉47	7 17	13 23	5 29	27 32	15 11
15	24 31	25 40	12 48	2 2	8 4	13 37	5 26	27 29	15 11
16	25 32	10♌21	14 3	3 17	8 51	13 51	5 23	27 27	15 11
17	26 33	25 9	15 14	4 32	9 38	14 5	5 20	27 25	15R11
18	27 34	9♍55	16 19	5 46	10 26	14 18	5 16	27 23	15 11
19	28 35	24 33	17 18	7 1	11 13	14 32	5 13	27 21	15 11
20	29 36	8♎56	18 10	8 16	12 0	14 46	5 10	27 19	15 11
21	0≈37	23 3	18 54	9 31	12 47	14 59	5 6	27 17	15 11
22	1 38	6♏53	19 29	10 45	13 35	15 13	5 3	27 14	15 10
23	2 39	20 27	19 54	12 1	14 22	15 26	4 59	27 12	15 10
24	3 40	3♐47	20 9	13 16	15 9	15 40	4 55	27 10	15 10
25	4 41	16 54	20R13	14 31	15 57	15 53	4 52	27 9	15 9
26	5 42	29 48	20 5	15 47	16 44	16 7	4 48	27 7	15 9
27	6 43	12♐33	19 46	17 2	17 32	16 21	4 44	27 6	15 9
28	7 44	25 6	19 16	18 17	18 19	16 34	4 40	27 4	15 8
29	8 45	7≈30	18 35	19 32	19 7	16 48	4 36	27 3	15 8
30	9 46	19 43	17 44	20 46	19 54	17 1	4 31	27 1	15 7
31	10 47	1✶47	16 45	22 1	20 42	17 14	4 27	26 59	15 7

Pluto 16 Leo all month

FEBRUARY

DAY	☉ ° '	☽ ° '	☿ ° '	♀ ° '	♂ ° '	♃ ° '	♄ ° '	♅ ° '	♆ ° '
1	11≈48	13✶43	15≈40	23♉16	21≈29	17♐27	4♍23	26Ⅱ57	15♎6
2	12 49	25 33	14R30	24 31	22 17	17 41	4R19	26R56	15R6
3	13 50	7♈19	13 18	25 46	23 4	17 54	4 14	26 54	15 5
4	14 51	19 7	12 4	27 1	23 52	18 7	4 10	26 53	15 5
5	15 52	1♉1	10 52	28 16	24 39	18 20	4 6	26 51	15 4
6	16 53	13 6	9 43	29 31	25 27	18 34	4 1	26 50	15 3
7	17 53	25 27	8 39	0≈46	26 14	18 47	3 57	26 48	15 3
8	18 54	8Ⅱ10	7 42	2 1	27 2	19 0	3 52	26 47	15 2
9	19 55	21 19	6 51	3 16	27 49	19 13	3 48	26 46	15 1
10	20 56	4♋58	6 8	4 31	28 37	19 26	3 43	26 44	15 0
11	21 56	19 6	5 33	5 46	29 24	19 38	3 39	26 43	14 59
12	22 57	3♌41	5 7	7 1	0✶12	19 51	3 34	26 42	14 59
13	23 58	18 36	4 48	8 16	0 59	20 4	3 29	26 41	14 58
14	24 58	3♍44	4 37	9 31	1 47	20 17	3 25	26 40	14 57
15	25 59	18 53	4D33	10 46	2 34	20 29	3 20	26 39	14 56
16	26 59	3♎54	4 37	12 1	3 22	20 42	3 15	26 38	14 55
17	28 0	18 39	4 47	13 16	4 9	20 55	3 10	26 37	14 54
18	29 0	3♏2	5 4	14 31	4 56	21 7	3 6	26 36	14 53
19	0✶1	17 2	5 26	15 46	5 44	21 20	3 1	26 36	14 52
20	1 1	0♐40	5 53	17 1	6 31	21 32	2 56	26 35	14 51
21	2 2	13 56	6 26	18 16	7 18	21 44	2 51	26 34	14 50
22	3 2	26 53	7 3	19 31	8 6	21 56	2 46	26 34	14 49
23	4 3	9♐35	7 45	20 45	8 53	22 8	2 41	26 33	14 48
24	5 3	22 4	8 30	22 0	9 41	22 20	2 36	26 33	14 46
25	6 3	4≈22	9 19	23 15	10 28	22 32	2 31	26 32	14 46
26	7 4	16 32	10 11	24 30	11 16	22 44	2 26	26 32	14 44
27	8 4	28 33	11 7	25 45	12 3	22 55	2 22	26 31	14 43
28	9 4	10✶29	12 5	27 0	12 50	23 7	2 17	26 31	14 41

Pluto 15 Leo all month

1949

MARCH

DAY	☉	☽	☿	♀	♂	♃	♄	♅	♆
	° ′	° ′	° ′	° ′	° ′	° ′	° ′	° ′	° ′
1	10♓ 5	22♓20	13♒ 6	28♒15	13♓37	23♑19	2♍12	26♊31	14♎40
2	11 5	4♈ 8	14 10	29 30	14 25	23 31	2R 7	26R31	14R39
3	12 5	15 55	15 16	0♓44	15 12	23 42	2 3	26 31	14 38
4	13 5	27 45	16 24	1 59	15 59	23 54	1 58	26 31	14 36
5	14 5	9♉40	17 34	3 14	16 46	24 5	1 53	26 D31	14 35
6	15 5	21 46	18 46	4 29	17 33	24 16	1 49	26 31	14 34
7	16 5	4♊ 6	20 0	5 44	18 20	24 27	1 44	26 31	14 32
8	17 5	16 45	21 16	6 59	19 7	24 38	1 40	26 31	14 31
9	18 5	29 48	22 33	8 14	19 54	24 49	1 35	26 31	14 30
10	19 5	13♋18	23 53	9 29	20 41	25 0	1 31	26 31	14 28
11	20 5	27 18	25 13	10 43	21 28	25 10	1 26	26 31	14 27
12	21 5	11♌45	26 36	11 58	22 15	25 21	1 22	26 32	14 25
13	22 5	26 37	27 59	13 13	23 2	25 32	1 18	26 32	14 24
14	23 5	11♍46	29 25	14 28	23 49	25 42	1 13	26 33	14 22
15	24 5	27 2	0♓51	15 42	24 36	25 53	1 9	26 33	14 21
16	25 4	12♎15	2 19	16 57	25 23	26 3	1 5	26 34	14 19
17	26 4	27 16	3 48	18 12	26 10	26 13	1 1	26 34	14 18
18	27 4	11♏57	5 19	19 26	26 57	26 23	0 57	26 35	14 16
19	28 3	26 13	6 51	20 41	27 43	26 33	0 53	26 35	14 15
20	29 3	10♐ 2	8 24	21 55	28 30	26 43	0 49	26 36	14 13
21	0♈ 2	23 25	9 59	23 10	29 17	26 53	0 45	26 37	14 11
22	1 2	6♑25	11 35	24 25	0♈ 3	27 2	0 41	26 38	14 10
23	2 2	19 4	13 12	25 39	0 50	27 12	0 38	26 39	14 8
24	3 1	1♒27	14 50	26 54	1 36	27 21	0 34	26 40	14 7
25	4 0	13 37	16 30	28 9	2 23	27 30	0 30	26 41	14 5
26	5 0	25 37	18 11	29 23	3 9	27 39	0 27	26 42	14 4
27	5 59	7♓30	19 54	0♈38	3 56	27 48	0 23	26 44	14 2
28	6 59	19 20	21 37	1 52	4 43	27 57	0 20	26 45	14 0
29	7 58	1♈ 8	23 23	3 7	5 30	28 6	0 17	26 46	13 59
30	8 57	12 58	25 9	4 21	6 16	28 15	0 13	26 47	13 57
31	9 57	24 48	26 57	5 36	7 3	28 23	0 10	26 49	13 55

Pluto 14 Leo all month

APRIL

DAY	☉	☽	☿	♀	♂	♃	♄	♅	♆
	° ′	° ′	° ′	° ′	° ′	° ′	° ′	° ′	° ′
1	10♈56	6♉44	28♓46	6♈50	7♈49	28♑32	0♍ 7	26♊50	13♎54
2	11 55	18 47	0♈37	8 5	8 35	28 40	0R 4	26 51	13R52
3	12 54	1♊ 0	2 29	9 19	9 22	28 48	0 1	26 53	13 50
4	13 53	13 26	4 22	10 34	10 8	28 56	29♌58	26 54	13 49
5	14 52	26 9	6 17	11 48	10 54	29 4	29 55	26 56	13 47
6	15 51	9♋11	8 13	13 2	11 40	29 12	29 52	26 57	13 45
7	16 50	22 35	10 11	14 17	12 27	29 19	29 50	26 59	13 44
8	17 49	6♌23	12 10	15 31	13 13	29 27	29 47	27 0	13 42
9	18 48	20 36	14 10	16 45	13 59	29 34	29 45	27 2	13 40
10	19 47	5♍11	16 12	18 0	14 45	29 41	29 43	27 4	13 39
11	20 46	20 5	18 14	19 14	15 31	29 48	29 40	27 6	13 37
12	21 45	5♎10	20 18	20 29	16 16	29 54	29 38	27 8	13 36
13	22 44	20 18	22 22	21 43	17 2	0♒ 1	29 36	27 10	13 34
14	23 42	5♏20	24 28	22 57	17 48	0 8	29 34	27 12	13 32
15	24 41	20 27	26 34	24 12	18 34	0 14	29 33	27 14	13 31
16	25 40	4♐32	28 41	25 26	19 19	0 21	29 31	27 16	13 29
17	26 39	18 32	0♉48	26 40	20 5	0 27	29 30	27 18	13 27
18	27 37	2♑ 5	2 55	27 54	20 51	0 33	29 28	27 20	13 26
19	28 36	15 12	5 2	29 9	21 37	0 39	29 27	27 22	13 24
20	29 34	27 55	7 8	0♉23	22 22	0 44	29 25	27 25	13 23
21	0♉33	10♒19	9 13	1 37	23 8	0 50	29 24	27 27	13 21
22	1 31	22 27	11 18	2 51	23 53	0 55	29 23	27 29	13 19
23	2 30	4♓24	13 20	4 5	24 39	1 0	29 22	27 31	13 18
24	3 28	16 14	15 21	5 19	25 24	1 5	29 22	27 34	13 16
25	4 27	28 2	17 20	6 33	26 9	1 10	29 21	27 36	13 15
26	5 25	9♈50	19 16	7 47	26 54	1 14	29 20	27 38	13 13
27	6 24	21 42	21 10	9 1	27 40	1 19	29 20	27 41	13 12
28	7 22	3♉40	23 1	10 15	28 25	1 23	29 19	27 43	13 10
29	8 20	15 46	24 48	11 29	29 10	1 27	29 19	27 46	13 9
30	9 19	28 3	26 33	12 43	29 55	1 31	29 19	27 49	13 7

Pluto 14 Leo all month

1949

MAY

Day	☉	☽	☿	♀	♂	♃	♄	♅	♆
	° ′	° ′	° ′	° ′	° ′	° ′	° ′	° ′	° ′
1	10♉17	10♊30	28♉14	13♉57	0♉40	1♒35	29♌19	27♊51	13♎ 6
2	11 15	23 11	29 51	15 11	1 25	1 38	29 D19	27 54	13℞ 4
3	12 13	6♋ 6	1♊24	16 25	2 10	1 42	29 19	27 57	13 3
4	13 11	19 16	2 54	17 39	2 55	1 45	29 19	28 0	13 2
5	14 10	2♌43	4 19	18 53	3 40	1 48	29 19	28 2	13 0
6	15 8	16 27	5 40	20 7	4 24	1 50	29 20	28 5	12 59
7	16 6	0♍29	6 57	21 21	5 9	1 53	29 20	28 8	12 58
8	17 4	14 47	8 10	22 35	5 54	1 55	29 21	28 11	12 56
9	18 2	29 19	9 19	23 49	6 39	1 58	29 22	28 14	12 55
10	19 0	14♎ 2	10 23	25 3	7 23	2 0	29 23	28 17	12 54
11	19 58	28 50	11 22	26 17	8 8	2 2	29 24	28 20	12 53
12	20 56	13♏36	12 18	27 31	8 52	2 4	29 25	28 23	12 51
13	21 53	28 13	13 8	28 45	9 37	2 5	29 26	28 26	12 50
14	22 51	12♐35	13 54	29 58	10 21	2 7	29 28	28 29	12 49
15	23 49	26 35	14 35	1♊12	11 5	2 8	29 29	28 32	12 48
16	24 47	10♑12	15 12	2 26	11 49	2 9	29 30	28 35	12 47
17	25 45	23 23	15 44	3 40	12 34	2 9	29 32	28 38	12 46
18	26 43	6♒11	16 11	4 54	13 18	2 10	29 33	28 42	12 44
19	27 40	18 38	16 34	6 8	14 2	2 10	29 35	28 45	12 43
20	28 38	0♓47	16 51	7 22	14 46	2 10	29 37	28 48	12 42
21	29 36	12 44	17 4	8 36	15 30	2℞10	29 39	28 51	12 41
22	0♊34	24 35	17 10	9 49	16 14	2 10	29 41	28 55	12 40
23	1 31	6♈23	17 13	11 3	16 58	2 10	29 43	28 58	12 39
24	2 29	18 13	17℞11	12 17	17 42	2 9	29 45	29 1	12 38
25	3 27	0♉ 9	17 5	13 30	18 26	2 9	29 48	29 4	12 38
26	4 24	12 15	16 54	14 44	19 9	2 8	29 50	29 8	12 37
27	5 22	24 34	16 39	15 57	19 53	2 7	29 53	29 11	12 36
28	6 19	7♊ 7	16 20	17 11	20 37	2 6	29 56	29 14	12 35
29	7 17	19 54	15 58	18 25	21 20	2 4	29 58	29 18	12 34
30	8 15	2♋56	15 33	19 38	22 4	2 3	0♍ 1	29 21	12 33
31	9 12	16 11	15 5	20 52	22 47	2 1	0 4	29 25	12 33

Pluto 14 Leo all month

JUNE

Day	☉	☽	☿	♀	♂	♃	♄	♅	♆
	° ′	° ′	° ′	° ′	° ′	° ′	° ′	° ′	° ′
1	10♊10	29♋40	14♊35	22♊ 6	23♉30	1♒59	0♍ 7	29♊28	12♎32
2	11 7	13♌19	14℞ 3	23 19	24 14	1℞56	0 10	29 32	12℞31
3	12 5	27 10	13 30	24 33	24 57	1 54	0 14	29 35	12 30
4	13 2	11♍ 9	12 56	25 46	25 40	1 51	0 17	29 38	12 30
5	13 59	25 17	12 23	27 0	26 23	1 48	0 20	29 41	12 29
6	14 57	9♎32	11 50	28 14	27 6	1 45	0 24	29 45	12 29
7	15 54	23 53	11 18	29 27	27 49	1 42	0 27	29 48	12 28
8	16 52	8♏15	10 48	0♋41	28 32	1 39	0 31	29 52	12 27
9	17 49	22 37	10 21	1 55	29 15	1 35	0 35	29 55	12 27
10	18 46	6♐53	9 55	3 8	29 58	1 32	0 39	29 59	12 26
11	19 44	20 57	9 33	4 22	0♊41	1 28	0 43	0♋ 2	12 26
12	20 41	4♑46	9 15	5 35	1 24	1 24	0 47	0 6	12 26
13	21 38	18 15	9 0	6 48	2 7	1 20	0 51	0 10	12 25
14	22 36	1♒23	8 49	8 2	2 49	1 15	0 55	0 13	12 25
15	23 33	14 10	8 42	9 15	3 32	1 11	1 0	0 17	12 25
16	24 30	26 36	8 D40	10 28	4 14	1 6	1 4	0 21	12 24
17	25 27	8♓47	8 42	11 42	4 57	1 1	1 8	0 25	12 24
18	26 25	20 45	8 49	12 55	5 39	0 56	1 13	0 28	12 24
19	27 22	2♈35	9 0	14 9	6 22	0 51	1 17	0 32	12 24
20	28 19	14 24	9 17	15 22	7 4	0 46	1 22	0 35	12 24
21	29 16	26 16	9 37	16 35	7 46	0 41	1 27	0 39	12 23
22	0♋14	8♉16	10 3	17 49	8 29	0 35	1 31	0 42	12 23
23	1 11	20 29	10 33	19 2	9 11	0 30	1 36	0 46	12 23
24	2 8	2♊59	11 7	20 15	9 53	0 24	1 41	0 49	12 D23
25	3 5	15 46	11 46	21 28	10 35	0 18	1 46	0 53	12 23
26	4 3	28 53	12 29	22 42	11 17	0 12	1 51	0 56	12 23
27	5 0	12♋18	13 17	23 55	11 59	0 5	1 57	1 0	12 23
28	5 57	25 58	14 9	25 8	12 41	29♑59	2 2	1 4	12 24
29	6 54	9♌51	15 5	26 21	13 23	29 52	2 7	1 8	12 24
30	7 52	23 52	16 5	27 35	14 5	29 46	2 13	1 11	12 24

Pluto 14 Leo all month

1949

JULY

DAY	☉	☽	☿	♀	♂	♃	♄	♅	♆
	° ′	° ′	° ′	° ′	° ′	° ′	° ′	° ′	° ′
1	8♋49	7♍59	17♊10	28♋48	14♊46	29♑39	2♍18	1♋15	12♎24
2	9 46	22 7	18 19	0♌ 1	15 28	29℞32	2 24	1 18	12 24
3	10 43	6♎16	19 31	1 14	16 10	29 25	2 30	1 22	12 25
4	11 40	20 23	20 47	2 28	16 51	29 18	2 35	1 25	12 25
5	12 38	4♏29	22 8	3 41	17 33	29 11	2 41	1 29	12 26
6	13 35	18 31	23 32	4 54	18 14	29 4	2 47	1 32	12 26
7	14 32	2♐28	25 0	6 7	18 55	28 57	2 53	1 36	12 27
8	15 29	16 18	26 32	7 20	19 37	28 50	2 58	1 39	12 27
9	16 26	29 58	28 7	8 33	20 18	28 42	3 4	1 43	12 28
10	17 24	13♑27	29 46	9 46	20 59	28 35	3 10	1 46	12 28
11	18 21	26 39	1♋28	10 59	21 40	28 27	3 16	1 50	12 29
12	19 18	9♒35	3 14	12 12	22 21	28 20	3 22	1 53	12 29
13	20 15	22 14	5 3	13 25	23 2	28 12	3 29	1 57	12 30
14	21 12	4♓36	6 55	14 38	23 43	28 4	3 35	2 0	12 30
15	22 10	16 43	8 50	15 51	24 24	27 56	3 41	2 4	12 31
16	23 7	28 39	10 47	17 4	25 5	27 49	3 47	2 7	12 32
17	24 4	10♈29	12 47	18 17	25 46	27 41	3 54	2 11	12 33
18	25 1	22 18	14 48	19 30	26 27	27 34	4 0	2 14	12 33
19	25 59	4♉10	16 52	20 43	27 8	27 26	4 6	2 17	12 34
20	26 56	16 12	18 57	21 56	27 49	27 19	4 13	2 21	12 35
21	27 53	28 28	21 8	23 8	28 29	27 11	4 19	2 24	12 36
22	28 50	11♊ 3	23 10	24 21	29 10	27 3	4 26	2 27	12 37
23	29 48	24 0	25 17	25 34	29 50	26 55	4 33	2 30	12 38
24	0♌45	7♋21	27 24	26 47	0♋31	26 48	4 39	2 34	12 39
25	1 42	21 4	29 32	27 59	1 11	26 40	4 46	2 37	12 40
26	2 40	5♌ 7	1♌39	29 12	1 51	26 32	4 53	2 40	12 41
27	3 37	19 25	3 45	0♍25	2 31	26 24	5 0	2 43	12 42
28	4 34	3♍52	5 51	1 38	3 12	26 17	5 7	2 47	12 43
29	5 32	18 21	7 56	2 50	3 52	26 9	5 14	2 50	12 44
30	6 29	2♎48	10 0	4 3	4 32	26 2	5 21	2 53	12 45
31	7 27	17 9	12 2	5 16	5 12	25 54	5 28	2 56	12 46

Pluto 15 Leo all month

AUGUST

DAY	☉	☽	☿	♀	♂	♃	♄	♅	♆
	° ′	° ′	° ′	° ′	° ′	° ′	° ′	° ′	° ′
1	8♌24	1♏20	14♌ 3	6♍28	5♋52	25♑47	5♍35	2♋59	12♎47
2	9 21	15 21	16 3	7 41	6 32	25℞39	5 42	3 2	12 49
3	10 19	29 11	18 1	8 53	7 12	25 32	5 49	3 5	12 50
4	11 16	12♐51	19 58	10 6	7 52	25 25	5 56	3 8	12 52
5	12 14	26 19	21 53	11 18	8 32	25 18	6 3	3 11	12 52
6	13 11	9♑37	23 47	12 31	9 11	25 11	6 11	3 14	12 53
7	14 9	22 42	25 39	13 43	9 51	25 4	6 18	3 17	12 55
8	15 6	5♒34	27 30	14 56	10 31	24 57	6 25	3 20	12 56
9	16 4	18 13	29 19	16 8	11 10	24 50	6 32	3 23	12 58
10	17 1	0♓38	1♍ 7	17 21	11 50	24 44	6 40	3 26	12 59
11	17 59	12 51	2 53	18 33	12 29	24 37	6 47	3 29	13 0
12	18 56	24 52	4 37	19 45	13 8	24 31	6 54	3 32	13 2
13	19 54	6♈45	6 20	20 58	13 48	24 24	7 1	3 35	13 3
14	20 51	18 33	8 2	22 10	14 27	24 18	7 9	3 37	13 4
15	21 49	0♉21	9 42	23 22	15 6	24 12	7 16	3 40	13 6
16	22 47	12 12	11 20	24 34	15 45	24 6	7 23	3 43	13 7
17	23 44	24 13	12 57	25 46	16 25	24 0	7 31	3 45	13 9
18	24 42	6♊29	14 33	26 58	17 4	23 55	7 38	3 48	13 11
19	25 40	19 4	16 7	28 10	17 43	23 49	7 46	3 50	13 12
20	26 38	2♋ 3	17 40	29 22	18 22	23 44	7 53	3 53	13 14
21	27 35	15 29	19 11	0♎34	19 1	23 38	8 1	3 55	13 16
22	28 33	29 20	20 41	1 46	19 39	23 33	8 8	3 58	13 17
23	29 31	13♌36	22 9	2 58	20 18	23 28	8 16	4 0	13 19
24	0♍29	28 12	23 36	4 10	20 57	23 23	8 23	4 2	13 21
25	1 27	13♍ 0	25 1	5 22	21 36	23 19	8 31	4 5	13 23
26	2 25	27 53	26 25	6 33	22 14	23 14	8 38	4 7	13 25
27	3 23	12♎43	27 47	7 45	22 53	23 10	8 46	4 9	13 26
28	4 21	27 23	29 8	8 57	23 31	23 6	8 53	4 11	13 28
29	5 19	11♏48	0♎27	10 9	24 10	23 2	9 1	4 14	13 30
30	6 17	25 56	1 44	11 20	24 48	22 59	9 8	4 16	13 32
31	7 15	9♐46	3 0	12 32	25 26	22 55	9 16	4 18	13 34

Pluto 15 Leo all month

1949

SEPTEMBER

DAY	☉	☽	☿	♀	♂	♃	♄	♅	♆
	° ′	° ′	° ′	° ′	° ′	° ′	° ′	° ′	° ′
1	8♍13	23♐18	4♎14	13♎44	26♋ 4	22♑52	9♍23	4♋20	13♎36
2	9 11	6♑33	5 26	14 55	26 43	22℞48	9 31	4 22	13 37
3	10 9	19 33	6 36	16 7	27 21	22 45	9 38	4 23	13 39
4	11 7	2♒19	7 44	17 18	27 59	22 42	9 46	4 25	13 41
5	12 5	14 52	8 49	18 29	28 37	22 39	9 54	4 27	13 43
6	13 3	27 13	9 53	19 40	29 15	22 37	10 1	4 29	13 45
7	14 1	9♓24	10 54	20 52	29 52	22 34	10 9	4 31	13 47
8	15 0	21 26	11 53	22 3	0♌30	22 32	10 17	4 33	13 49
9	15 58	3♈21	12 49	23 14	1 8	22 30	10 25	4 35	13 51
10	16 56	15 10	13 42	24 25	1 46	22 28	10 32	4 36	13 53
11	17 55	26 57	14 32	25 36	2 23	22 27	10 40	4 38	13 55
12	18 53	8♉45	15 19	26 47	3 1	22 25	10 47	4 39	13 57
13	19 51	20 37	16 2	27 58	3 39	22 24	10 55	4 41	13 59
14	20 50	2♊38	16 42	29 9	4 16	22 23	11 2	4 42	14 2
15	21 48	14 52	17 17	0♏20	4 54	22 22	11 10	4 44	14 4
16	22 47	27 25	17 49	1 31	5 31	22 21	11 17	4 45	14 6
17	23 45	10♋20	18 15	2 42	6 8	22 21	11 24	4 46	14 8
18	24 44	23 41	18 36	3 52	6 45	22 20	11 32	4 48	14 10
19	25 42	7♌30	18 52	5 3	7 22	22 20	11 39	4 49	14 12
20	26 41	21 45	19 3	6 14	7 59	22 D20	11 46	4 50	14 14
21	27 40	6♍25	19 7	7 24	8 36	22 21	11 54	4 51	14 16
22	28 38	21 23	19℞ 5	8 34	9 13	22 21	12 1	4 52	14 18
23	29 37	6♎30	18 56	9 45	9 50	22 22	12 9	4 52	14 21
24	0♎36	21 38	18 40	10 55	10 27	22 23	12 16	4 53	14 23
25	1 35	6♏38	18 16	12 5	11 4	22 24	12 23	4 54	14 25
26	2 34	21 21	17 45	13 16	11 40	22 25	12 31	4 55	14 27
27	3 32	5♐44	17 7	14 26	12 17	22 27	12 38	4 56	14 29
28	4 31	19 43	16 22	15 36	12 53	22 28	12 45	4 57	14 32
29	5 30	3♑17	15 30	16 46	13 30	22 30	12 52	4 58	14 34
30	6 29	16 29	14 32	17 56	14 6	22 32	12 59	4 58	14 36

Pluto 16 Leo all month

OCTOBER

DAY	☉	☽	☿	♀	♂	♃	♄	♅	♆
	° ′	° ′	° ′	° ′	° ′	° ′	° ′	° ′	° ′
1	7♎28	29♑21	13♎29	19♏ 5	14♌43	22♑35	13♍ 7	4♋59	14♎38
2	8 27	11♒55	12℞23	20 15	15 19	22 37	13 14	4 59	14 40
3	9 26	24 15	11 15	21 25	15 55	22 40	13 21	5 0	14 43
4	10 25	6♓23	10 6	22 35	16 31	22 43	13 28	5 0	14 45
5	11 24	18 23	8 58	23 44	17 7	22 46	13 35	5 1	14 47
6	12 24	0♈16	7 53	24 54	17 43	22 49	13 42	5 1	14 50
7	13 23	12 5	6 54	26 3	18 19	22 52	13 49	5 1	14 52
8	14 22	23 53	6 1	27 12	18 55	22 56	13 56	5 1	14 54
9	15 21	5♉41	5 15	28 21	19 30	22 59	14 2	5 1	14 56
10	16 21	17 32	4 40	29 30	20 6	23 3	14 9	5 1	14 58
11	17 20	29 29	4 15	0♐39	20 42	23 7	14 16	5℞ 1	15 1
12	18 19	11♊34	4 1	1 48	21 17	23 12	14 23	5 1	15 3
13	19 19	23 51	3 D57	2 57	21 53	23 16	14 29	5 1	15 5
14	20 18	6♋23	4 4	4 6	22 28	23 21	14 36	5 1	15 7
15	21 17	19 14	4 22	5 14	23 3	23 26	14 43	5 1	15 9
16	22 17	2♌28	4 50	6 22	23 38	23 31	14 50	5 1	15 12
17	23 16	16 6	5 27	7 31	24 13	23 36	14 56	5 0	15 14
18	24 16	0♍10	6 14	8 39	24 48	23 41	15 3	5 0	15 16
19	25 16	14 39	7 8	9 47	25 23	23 47	15 9	5 0	15 18
20	26 15	29 30	8 8	10 55	25 58	23 52	15 16	4 59	15 21
21	27 15	14♎36	9 15	12 3	26 32	23 58	15 22	4 59	15 23
22	28 15	29 48	10 28	13 11	27 7	24 4	15 28	4 58	15 25
23	29 15	14♏58	11 46	14 18	27 41	24 10	15 34	4 57	15 27
24	0♏14	29 55	13 8	15 26	28 16	24 17	15 40	4 57	15 29
25	1 14	14♐32	14 33	16 33	28 50	24 23	15 46	4 56	15 32
26	2 14	28 44	16 0	17 40	29 24	24 30	15 52	4 55	15 34
27	3 14	12♑28	17 31	18 47	29 58	24 37	15 58	4 54	15 36
28	4 14	25 45	19 4	19 54	0♍32	24 44	16 4	4 54	15 38
29	5 14	8♒37	20 39	21 0	1 6	24 52	16 10	4 53	15 40
30	6 14	21 8	22 14	22 7	1 40	24 59	16 16	4 52	15 42
31	7 14	3♓21	23 50	23 13	2 14	25 6	16 22	4 51	15 44

Pluto 17 Leo all month

1949

NOVEMBER

DAY	☉	☽	☿	♀	♂	♃	♄	♅	♆
	° ′	° ′	° ′	° ′	° ′	° ′	° ′	° ′	° ′
1	8♏14	15♓22	25♎27	24♐19	2♍48	25♑14	16♍27	4♋50	15♎46
2	9 14	27 15	27 5	25 25	3 21	25 21	16 33	4℞ 48	15 48
3	10 14	9♈ 3	28 42	26 31	3 55	25 29	16 38	4 47	15 50
4	11 14	20 51	0♏20	27 36	4 28	25 37	16 43	4 46	15 52
5	12 14	2♉39	1 59	28 42	5 1	25 45	16 49	4 45	15 55
6	13 14	14 32	3 37	29 47	5 35	25 54	16 54	4 43	15 57
7	14 14	26 31	5 15	0♑52	6 8	26 2	16 59	4 42	15 59
8	15 15	8♊38	6 54	1 56	6 40	26 11	17 4	4 41	16 1
9	16 15	20 54	8 31	3 0	7 13	26 19	17 10	4 39	16 3
10	17 15	3♋21	10 9	4 5	7 46	26 28	17 15	4 38	16 5
11	18 15	16 0	11 46	5 8	8 18	26 37	17 20	4 36	16 7
12	19 16	28 55	13 24	6 12	8 51	26 46	17 25	4 35	16 9
13	20 16	12♌ 6	15 1	7 15	9 23	26 55	17 30	4 33	16 11
14	21 17	25 36	16 38	8 18	9 55	27 5	17 34	4 32	16 12
15	22 17	9♍26	18 15	9 21	10 27	27 14	17 39	4 30	16 14
16	23 17	23 38	19 51	10 24	10 59	27 24	17 43	4 28	16 16
17	24 18	8♎ 9	21 27	11 26	11 31	27 34	17 48	4 27	16 18
18	25 18	22 57	23 3	12 28	12 3	27 44	17 52	4 25	16 20
19	26 19	7♏56	24 39	13 29	12 34	27 54	17 56	4 23	16 22
20	27 20	22 58	26 14	14 30	13 5	28 4	18 0	4 21	16 24
21	28 20	7♐54	27 49	15 31	13 37	28 14	18 4	4 19	16 25
22	29 21	22 36	29 24	16 21	14 8	28 25	18 8	4 17	16 27
23	0♐22	6♑55	0♐59	17 31	14 39	28 35	18 12	4 15	16 29
24	1 22	20 47	2 33	18 31	15 9	28 45	18 16	4 13	16 31
25	2 23	4♒11	4 7	19 30	15 40	28 56	18 20	4 11	16 32
26	3 24	17 8	5 41	20 29	16 10	29 6	18 23	4 9	16 34
27	4 24	29 42	7 16	21 27	16 41	29 17	18 27	4 7	16 36
28	5 25	11♓55	8 49	22 25	17 11	29 28	18 30	4 5	16 37
29	6 26	23 55	10 23	23 22	17 41	29 39	18 34	4 3	16 39
30	7 27	5♈45	11 57	24 19	18 11	29 51	18 37	4 0	16 40

Pluto 18 Leo all month

DECEMBER

DAY	☉	☽	☿	♀	♂	♃	♄	♅	♆
	° ′	° ′	° ′	° ′	° ′	° ′	° ′	° ′	° ′
1	8♐28	17♈32	13♐31	25♑15	18♍40	0♒ 2	18♍40	3♋58	16♎42
2	9 28	29 20	15 5	26 10	19 10	0 13	18 43	3℞ 56	16 43
3	10 29	11♉12	16 39	27 5	19 39	0 25	18 46	3 54	16 45
4	11 30	23 12	18 12	28 0	20 8	0 36	18 49	3 51	16 46
5	12 31	5♊21	19 46	28 53	20 37	0 48	18 52	3 49	16 48
6	13 32	17 42	21 20	29 46	21 6	1 0	18 55	3 47	16 49
7	14 33	0♋15	22 53	0♒39	21 34	1 11	18 57	3 45	16 51
8	15 34	13 0	24 27	1 30	22 3	1 23	19 0	3 42	16 52
9	16 35	25 56	26 0	2 21	22 31	1 35	19 2	3 40	16 53
10	17 35	9♌ 4	27 34	3 12	22 59	1 47	19 4	3 38	16 55
11	18 36	22 24	29 7	4 1	23 27	1 59	19 6	3 35	16 56
12	19 37	5♍56	0♑41	4 49	23 54	2 12	19 8	3 33	16 57
13	20 38	19 41	2 14	5 37	24 21	2 24	19 10	3 30	16 59
14	21 40	3♎40	3 47	6 24	24 49	2 36	19 12	3 28	17 0
15	22 41	17 52	5 20	7 10	25 15	2 49	19 14	3 25	17 1
16	23 42	2♏17	6 53	7 54	25 42	3 1	19 15	3 23	17 2
17	24 43	16 51	8 26	8 38	26 8	3 14	19 17	3 20	17 3
18	25 44	1♐30	9 58	9 21	26 35	3 27	19 18	3 17	17 4
19	26 45	16 8	11 30	10 3	27 1	3 39	19 20	3 15	17 5
20	27 46	0♑36	13 1	10 43	27 26	3 52	19 21	3 12	17 6
21	28 47	14 48	14 32	11 22	27 52	4 5	19 22	3 9	17 7
22	29 48	28 38	16 2	12 0	28 17	4 18	19 23	3 6	17 8
23	0♑49	12♒ 3	17 32	12 37	28 42	4 31	19 24	3 4	17 9
24	1 51	25 3	19 0	13 12	29 6	4 44	19 24	3 1	17 10
25	2 52	7♓40	20 27	13 46	29 30	4 57	19 25	2 59	17 11
26	3 53	19 56	21 52	14 19	29 55	5 10	19 26	2 56	17 12
27	4 54	1♈57	23 16	14 50	0♎18	5 23	19 26	2 54	17 13
28	5 55	13 48	24 37	15 19	0 42	5 37	19 26	2 51	17 13
29	6 56	25 36	25 55	15 46	1 5	5 50	19 26	2 49	17 14
30	7 57	7♉24	27 9	16 12	1 28	6 3	19℞ 26	2 46	17 15
31	8 59	19 19	28 20	16 36	1 50	6 17	19 26	2 44	17 15

Pluto 18 Leo all month

1950

JANUARY

Day	☉	☽	☿	♀	♂	♃	♄	♅	♆
	° ′	° ′	° ′	° ′	° ′	° ′	° ′	° ′	° ′
1	10♑ 0	1♊25	29♑27	16♒59	2♎13	6♒30	19♍26	2♋41	17♎16
2	11 1	13 44	0♒28	17 19	2 35	6 44	19℞26	2℞39	17 17
3	12 2	26 19	1 24	17 37	2 56	6 57	19 25	2 36	17 17
4	13 3	9♋10	2 13	17 54	3 17	7 11	19 25	2 34	17 18
5	14 4	22 16	2 55	18 8	3 38	7 24	19 25	2 31	17 18
6	15 5	5♌36	3 28	18 20	3 59	7 38	19 24	2 28	17 19
7	16 7	19 8	3 51	18 29	4 19	7 52	19 23	2 26	17 19
8	17 8	2♍48	4 5	18 37	4 39	8 6	19 22	2 24	17 20
9	18 9	16 36	4℞ 7	18 42	4 58	8 20	19 21	2 21	17 20
10	19 10	0♎30	3 57	18 44	5 17	8 34	19 20	2 19	17 20
11	20 11	14 29	3 36	18℞44	5 36	8 48	19 19	2 17	17 21
12	21 12	28 33	3 3	18 42	5 54	9 2	19 17	2 14	17 21
13	22 13	12♏41	2 19	18 37	6 12	9 15	19 16	2 12	17 21
14	23 15	26 53	1 24	18 30	6 29	9 29	19 14	2 9	17 21
15	24 16	11♐ 5	0 21	18 20	6 46	9 43	19 12	2 7	17 21
16	25 17	25 14	29♑11	18 8	7 3	9 57	19 11	2 4	17 21
17	26 18	9♑17	27 56	17 53	7 19	10 12	19 9	2 2	17 22
18	27 19	23 7	26 38	17 36	7 34	10 26	19 7	2 0	17 22
19	28 20	6♒41	25 20	17 16	7 49	10 40	19 5	1 58	17℞22
20	29 21	19 55	24 5	16 54	8 4	10 54	19 3	1 55	17 21
21	0♒22	2♓50	22 53	16 30	8 18	11 8	19 0	1 53	17 21
22	1 23	15 24	21 47	16 4	8 32	11 22	18 58	1 51	17 21
23	2 25	27 40	20 49	15 36	8 45	11 36	18 56	1 49	17 21
24	3 26	9♈42	19 59	15 5	8 58	11 50	18 53	1 46	17 21
25	4 27	21 34	19 18	14 33	9 10	12 5	18 51	1 44	17 21
26	5 28	3♉22	18 46	14 0	9 21	12 19	18 48	1 42	17 21
27	6 29	15 12	18 23	13 26	9 32	12 33	18 45	1 40	17 20
28	7 30	27 8	18 9	12 50	9 43	12 47	18 42	1 38	17 20
29	8 30	9♊16	18 3	12 14	9 52	13 2	18 39	1 37	17 20
30	9 31	21 39	18D 5	11 37	10 2	13 16	18 36	1 35	17 19
31	10 32	4♋22	18 15	11 0	10 10	13 30	18 33	1 33	17 19

Pluto 17 Leo all month

FEBRUARY

Day	☉	☽	☿	♀	♂	♃	♄	♅	♆
	° ′	° ′	° ′	° ′	° ′	° ′	° ′	° ′	° ′
1	11♒33	17♋25	18♑32	10♒23	10♎18	13♒45	18♍29	1♋31	17♎18
2	12 34	0♌49	18 55	9℞46	10 26	14 0	18℞26	1℞30	17℞18
3	13 35	14 31	19 23	9 10	10 32	14 14	18 22	1 28	17 18
4	14 36	28 28	19 57	8 34	10 38	14 28	18 19	1 26	17 17
5	15 37	12♍36	20 36	8 0	10 44	14 43	18 15	1 24	17 16
6	16 37	26 50	21 19	7 26	10 49	14 57	18 12	1 23	17 16
7	17 38	11♎ 6	22 6	6 54	10 53	15 11	18 8	1 21	17 15
8	18 39	25 21	22 57	6 23	10 56	15 25	18 4	1 19	17 15
9	19 40	9♏33	23 51	5 54	10 59	15 39	18 0	1 18	17 14
10	20 40	23 39	24 49	5 27	11 1	15 54	17 56	1 16	17 13
11	21 41	7♐39	25 49	5 3	11 2	16 8	17 52	1 15	17 13
12	22 42	21 32	26 52	4 40	11 3	16 22	17 48	1 14	17 12
13	23 43	5♑17	27 57	4 20	11℞ 2	16 36	17 44	1 12	17 11
14	24 43	18 51	29 4	4 2	11 1	16 51	17 39	1 11	17 10
15	25 44	2♒14	0♒14	3 47	11 0	17 5	17 35	1 10	17 9
16	26 44	15 24	1 25	3 34	10 57	17 19	17 31	1 9	17 8
17	27 45	28 18	2 39	3 24	10 54	17 33	17 27	1 8	17 8
18	28 46	10♓58	3 54	3 16	10 50	17 48	17 22	1 7	17 7
19	29 46	23 22	5 10	3 10	10 45	18 2	17 18	1 6	17 6
20	0♓47	5♈33	6 28	3 7	10 39	18 16	17 14	1 5	17 5
21	1 47	17 33	7 48	3 6	10 33	18 30	17 9	1 4	17 4
22	2 48	29 25	9 9	3D 8	10 26	18 45	17 5	1 3	17 3
23	3 48	11♉13	10 31	3 12	10 18	18 59	17 0	1 2	17 2
24	4 48	23 2	11 55	3 19	10 10	19 13	16 55	1 1	17 1
25	5 49	4♊58	13 20	3 27	10 0	19 27	16 51	1 0	16 59
26	6 49	17 4	14 46	3 38	9 50	19 41	16 46	1 0	16 58
27	7 49	29 27	16 13	3 51	9 39	19 55	16 41	0 59	16 57
28	8 50	12♋10	17 41	4 6	9 27	20 9	16 36	0 59	16 56

Pluto 17 Leo all month

1950

MARCH

Pluto 16 Leo all month

Day	☉	☽	☿	♀	♂	♃	♄	♅	♆
	° ′	° ′	° ′	° ′	° ′	° ′	° ′	° ′	° ′
1	9♓50	25♋16	19♒11	4♒23	9♎14	20♒23	16♍32	0♋58	16♎54
2	10 50	8♌46	20 41	4 43	9℞ 1	20 37	16℞27	0℞58	16℞53
3	11 50	22 40	22 13	5 4	8 47	20 51	16 22	0 58	16 52
4	12 50	6♍55	23 46	5 26	8 32	21 5	16 17	0 57	16 51
5	13 50	21 27	25 19	5 51	8 17	21 19	16 13	0 57	16 49
6	14 50	6♎ 8	26 54	6 17	8 0	21 32	16 8	0 57	16 48
7	15 51	20 52	28 30	6 45	7 44	21 46	16 3	0 56	16 47
8	16 51	5♏32	0♓ 8	7 15	7 26	22 0	15 58	0 56	16 45
9	17 51	20 4	1 46	7 46	7 8	22 13	15 54	0 56	16 44
10	18 50	4♐22	3 26	8 18	6 49	22 27	15 49	0D56	16 42
11	19 50	18 26	5 6	8 52	6 30	22 40	15 44	0 56	16 41
12	20 50	2♑13	6 48	9 28	6 10	22 54	15 39	0 56	16 40
13	21 50	15 44	8 31	10 5	5 50	23 7	15 35	0 56	16 38
14	22 50	28 59	10 15	10 42	5 29	23 21	15 30	0 57	16 37
15	28 50	11♒59	12 0	11 22	5 8	23 34	15 25	0 57	16 35
16	24 50	24 45	13 47	12 2	4 46	23 47	15 20	0 57	16 34
17	25 49	7♓18	15 34	12 43	4 24	24 1	15 16	0 57	16 32
18	26 49	19 40	17 23	13 25	4 2	24 14	15 11	0 58	16 31
19	27 49	1♈51	19 13	14 9	3 40	24 27	15 7	0 58	16 29
20	28 48	13 52	21 5	14 53	3 17	24 40	15 2	0 59	16 28
21	29 48	25 47	22 57	15 39	2 54	24 53	14 58	0 59	16 26
22	0♈48	7♉37	24 51	16 25	2 31	25 6	14 53	1 0	16 24
23	1 47	19 25	26 46	17 12	2 8	25 19	14 49	1 1	16 23
24	2 47	1♊15	28 42	18 0	1 44	25 32	14 45	1 2	16 21
25	3 46	13 10	0♈40	18 48	1 21	25 45	14 40	1 2	16 20
26	4 46	25 16	2 38	19 38	0 58	25 57	14 36	1 3	16 18
27	5 45	7♋36	4 38	20 28	0 34	26 10	14 32	1 4	16 16
28	6 44	20 14	6 39	21 19	0 11	26 23	14 28	1 5	16 15
29	7 44	3♌15	8 40	22 10	29♍48	26 35	14 24	1 6	16 13
30	8 43	16 42	10 42	23 2	29 26	26 48	14 20	1 7	16 11
31	9 42	0♍35	12 45	23 55	29 3	27 0	14 16	1 8	16 10

APRIL

Pluto 15 Leo all month

Day	☉	☽	☿	♀	♂	♃	♄	♅	♆
	° ′	° ′	° ′	° ′	° ′	° ′	° ′	° ′	° ′
1	10♈41	14♍54	14♈49	24♒49	28♍41	27♒12	14♍12	1♋ 9	16♎ 8
2	11 41	29 35	16 52	25 43	28℞19	27 25	14℞ 8	1 10	16℞ 6
3	12 40	14♎32	18 56	26 37	27 57	27 37	14 4	1 12	16 5
4	13 39	29 38	20 59	27 32	27 36	27 49	14 0	1 13	16 3
5	14 38	14♏42	23 2	28 28	27 15	28 1	13 56	1 14	16 2
6	15 37	29 37	25 4	29 24	26 54	28 13	13 52	1 16	16 0
7	16 36	14♐16	27 5	0♓21	26 34	28 24	13 49	1 17	15 58
8	17 35	28 33	29 5	1 18	26 15	28 36	13 45	1 19	15 57
9	18 34	12♑26	1♉ 2	2 15	25 56	28 48	13 41	1 20	15 55
10	19 33	25 55	2 58	3 14	25 38	28 59	13 38	1 22	15 53
11	20 32	9♒ 2	4 50	4 12	25 20	29 11	13 34	1 23	15 52
12	21 31	21 49	6 40	5 11	25 3	29 22	13 31	1 25	15 50
13	22 29	4♓20	8 27	6 10	24 47	29 33	13 28	1 27	15 49
14	23 28	16 37	10 10	7 9	24 31	29 45	13 25	1 28	15 47
15	24 27	28 44	11 49	8 9	24 16	29 56	13 22	1 30	15 45
16	25 26	10♈43	13 24	9 9	24 2	0♓ 7	13 19	1 32	15 44
17	26 25	22 36	14 55	10 10	23 49	0 18	13 16	1 34	15 42
18	27 23	4♉26	16 21	11 11	23 36	0 29	13 13	1 36	15 40
19	28 22	16 15	17 42	12 12	23 24	0 39	13 11	1 38	15 39
20	29 20	28 4	18 59	13 14	23 13	0 50	13 8	1 40	15 37
21	0♉19	9♊57	20 11	14 16	23 3	1 1	13 6	1 42	15 36
22	1 18	21 55	21 17	15 18	22 54	1 11	13 3	1 44	15 34
23	2 16	4♋ 3	22 19	16 20	22 45	1 22	13 1	1 47	15 33
24	3 15	16 22	23 15	17 23	22 37	1 32	12 59	1 49	15 31
25	4 13	28 58	24 5	18 26	22 30	1 42	12 57	1 51	15 29
26	5 11	11♌53	24 50	19 29	22 23	1 52	12 55	1 53	15 28
27	6 10	25 11	25 30	20 32	22 18	2 1	12 53	1 56	15 26
28	7 8	8♍55	26 4	21 36	22 13	2 11	12 51	1 58	15 25
29	8 6	23 6	26 32	22 40	22 9	2 21	12 49	2 0	15 23
30	9 5	7♎42	26 55	23 44	22 6	2 30	12 47	2 3	15 22

1950

MAY

Day	☉	☽	☿	♀	♂	♃	♄	♅	♆
	° ′	° ′	° ′	° ′	° ′	° ′	° ′	° ′	° ′
1	10♉ 3	22♎40	27♉12	24♓48	22♍ 3	2♓40	12♍46	2♋ 5	15♎20
2	11 1	7♏51	27 24	25 53	22℞ 2	2 49	12℞44	2 8	15℞19
3	11 59	23 8	27 30	26 58	22 1	2 58	12 43	2 11	15 18
4	12 57	8♐18	27℞31	28 2	22 0	3 7	12 42	2 13	15 16
5	13 56	23 13	27 27	29 7	22D 1	3 16	12 41	2 15	15 15
6	14 54	7♑44	27 14	0♈13	22 2	3 25	12 40	2 19	15 14
7	15 52	21 48	27 4	1 18	22 4	3 34	12 39	2 22	15 12
8	16 50	5♒24	26 45	2 24	22 7	3 42	12 38	2 24	15 11
9	17 48	18 32	26 23	3 30	22 11	3 51	12 38	2 27	15 9
10	18 46	1♓17	25 57	4 36	22 15	3 59	12 37	2 30	15 8
11	19 44	13 41	25 28	5 42	22 20	4 7	12 36	2 33	15 7
12	20 42	25 51	24 57	6 48	22 25	4 15	12 36	2 35	15 5
13	21 40	7♈49	24 24	7 54	22 32	4 22	12 35	2 38	15 4
14	22 38	19 41	23 49	9 1	22 39	4 30	12 35	2 41	15 3
15	23 35	1♉29	23 14	10 8	22 46	4 38	12D35	2 44	15 2
16	24 33	13 17	22 38	11 14	22 54	4 45	12 35	2 47	15 1
17	25 31	25 7	22 3	12 21	23 3	4 53	12 35	2 50	14 59
18	26 29	7♊ 1	21 29	13 28	23 13	5 0	12 35	2 53	14 58
19	27 27	19 0	20 57	14 36	23 23	5 7	12 36	2 56	14 57
20	28 25	1♋ 6	20 27	15 43	23 34	5 14	12 36	2 59	14 56
21	29 22	13 20	20 0	16 50	23 45	5 20	12 37	3 3	14 55
22	0♊20	25 45	19 36	17 58	23 57	5 27	12 37	3 6	14 54
23	1 18	8♌24	19 15	19 5	24 10	5 33	12 38	3 9	14 53
24	2 15	21 18	18 58	20 13	24 23	5 40	12 39	3 12	14 52
25	3 13	4♍32	18 45	21 21	24 36	5 46	12 40	3 16	14 51
26	4 11	18 7	18 36	22 29	24 50	5 52	12 41	3 19	14 50
27	5 8	2♎ 6	18 31	23 37	25 5	5 58	12 42	3 22	14 49
28	6 6	16 29	18D31	24 45	25 20	6 3	12 43	3 25	14 48
29	7 3	1♏14	18 36	25 53	25 36	6 9	12 45	3 29	14 47
30	8 1	16 16	18 45	27 2	25 52	6 14	12 46	3 32	14 46
31	8 58	1♐27	18 58	28 10	26 9	6 19	12 48	3 35	14 45

Pluto 15 Leo all month

JUNE

Day	☉	☽	☿	♀	♂	♃	♄	♅	♆
	° ′	° ′	° ′	° ′	° ′	° ′	° ′	° ′	° ′
1	9♊56	16♐36	19♉16	29♈19	26♍26	6♓24	12♍49	3♋38	14♎45
2	10 53	1♑35	19 38	0♉28	26 43	6 28	12 51	3 42	14℞44
3	11 51	16 13	20 4	1 36	27 1	6 33	12 53	3 45	14 43
4	12 48	0♒25	20 35	2 45	27 20	6 37	12 55	3 48	14 43
5	13 46	14 7	21 10	3 54	27 39	6 41	12 57	3 52	14 43
6	14 43	27 20	21 49	5 3	27 58	6 45	12 59	3 55	14 42
7	15 40	10♓ 7	22 32	6 12	28 18	6 49	13 1	3 59	14 41
8	16 38	22 31	23 19	7 21	28 38	6 53	13 3	4 2	14 40
9	17 35	4♈39	24 10	8 31	28 59	6 56	13 6	4 6	14 40
10	18 33	16 36	25 4	9 40	29 20	7 0	13 8	4 9	14 39
11	19 30	28 26	26 2	10 49	29 41	7 3	13 11	4 13	14 39
12	20 27	10♉13	27 4	11 59	0♎ 3	7 6	13 14	4 17	14 38
13	21 25	22 2	28 9	13 8	0 25	7 9	13 17	4 21	14 38
14	22 22	3♊56	29 17	14 18	0 48	7 11	13 20	4 24	14 37
15	23 19	15 57	0♊29	15 27	1 11	7 14	13 23	4 27	14 37
16	24 17	28 5	1 44	16 37	1 34	7 16	13 26	4 30	14 37
17	25 14	10♋23	3 2	17 47	1 58	7 18	13 29	4 34	14 36
18	26 11	22 51	4 24	18 57	2 22	7 19	13 33	4 37	14 36
19	27 9	5♌29	5 48	20 7	2 46	7 21	13 36	4 41	14 36
20	28 6	18 19	7 16	21 17	3 11	7 22	13 39	4 45	14 35
21	29 3	1♍21	8 47	22 27	3 36	7 24	13 43	4 48	14 35
22	0♋ 0	14 38	10 22	23 37	4 1	7 25	13 46	4 52	14 35
23	0 58	28 12	11 59	24 47	4 27	7 26	13 50	4 56	14 35
24	1 55	12♎ 3	13 39	25 57	4 52	7 26	13 54	5 0	14 35
25	2 52	26 13	15 23	27 8	5 19	7 27	13 58	5 3	14 35
26	3 49	10♏41	17 9	28 18	5 45	7 27	14 2	5 7	14 35
27	4 47	25 24	18 58	29 28	6 12	7 27	14 6	5 10	14D34
28	5 44	10♐17	20 50	0♊39	6 39	7℞27	14 10	5 14	14 34
29	6 41	25 11	22 45	1 49	7 6	7 27	14 14	5 17	14 34
30	7 38	9♑57	24 42	3 0	7 34	7 26	14 19	5 21	14 35

Pluto 16 Leo all month

1950

JULY

DAY	☉	☽	☿	♀	♂	♃	♄	♅	♆
	° ′	° ′	° ′	° ′	° ′	° ′	° ′	° ′	° ′
1	8♋35	24♑28	26♊41	4♊11	8♎ 2	7♓26	14♍23	5♋24	14♎35
2	9 32	8♒36	28 43	5 22	8 30	7℞25	14 27	5 28	14 35
3	10 30	22 18	0♋47	6 32	8 58	7 24	14 32	5 31	14 35
4	11 27	5♓33	2 52	7 43	9 27	7 22	14 36	5 35	14 35
5	12 24	18 22	4 59	8 54	9 56	7 21	14 41	5 39	14 36
6	13 21	0♈49	7 7	10 5	10 25	7 19	14 46	5 43	14 36
7	14 18	12 59	9 16	11 16	10 54	7 18	14 51	5 46	14 36
8	15 16	24 57	11 25	12 27	11 24	7 16	14 56	5 50	14 37
9	16 13	6♉48	13 35	13 38	11 54	7 14	15 1	5 53	14 37
10	17 10	18 37	15 45	14 49	12 24	7 11	15 6	5 57	14 37
11	18 7	0♊29	17 55	16 0	12 54	7 9	15 11	6 0	14 38
12	19 5	12 28	20 4	17 12	13 25	7 6	15 16	6 4	14 38
13	20 2	24 36	22 12	18 23	13 55	7 3	15 21	6 7	14 39
14	20 59	6♋56	24 20	19 34	14 26	7 0	15 26	6 11	14 39
15	21 56	19 28	26 26	20 45	14 57	6 56	15 32	6 14	14 40
16	22 54	2♌12	28 31	21 57	15 29	6 53	15 37	6 18	14 41
17	23 51	15 9	0♌35	23 8	16 0	6 49	15 43	6 21	14 41
18	24 48	28 18	2 37	24 20	16 32	6 45	15 49	6 25	14 42
19	25 45	11♍37	4 38	25 31	17 4	6 41	15 54	6 28	14 43
20	26 43	25 8	6 37	26 43	17 37	6 37	16 0	6 32	14 43
21	27 40	8♎50	8 35	27 55	18 9	6 33	16 6	6 35	14 44
22	28 37	22 43	10 30	29 7	18 42	6 28	16 12	6 39	14 45
23	29 34	6♏48	12 24	0♋18	19 14	6 24	16 17	6 42	14 46
24	0♌32	21 3	14 17	1 30	19 47	6 19	16 23	6 46	14 47
25	1 29	5♐28	16 7	2 42	20 20	6 14	16 29	6 49	14 48
26	2 26	19 57	17 56	3 54	20 54	6 9	16 35	6 52	14 49
27	3 24	4♑26	19 43	5 6	21 27	6 3	16 41	6 56	14 50
28	4 21	18 48	21 28	6 18	22 1	5 58	16 48	6 59	14 51
29	5 18	2♒59	23 12	7 30	22 35	5 52	16 54	7 2	14 52
30	6 16	16 51	24 54	8 42	23 9	5 46	17 0	7 5	14 53
31	7 13	0♓23	26 34	9 54	23 43	5 40	17 7	7 9	14 54

Pluto 16 Leo all month

AUGUST

DAY	☉	☽	☿	♀	♂	♃	♄	♅	♆
	° ′	° ′	° ′	° ′	° ′	° ′	° ′	° ′	° ′
1	8♌10	13♓32	28♌12	11♋ 7	24♎18	5♓34	17♍13	7♋12	14♎55
2	9 8	26 19	29 49	12 19	24 52	5℞28	17 19	7 15	14 56
3	10 5	8♈46	1♍24	13 31	25 27	5 22	17 25	7 18	14 57
4	11 3	20 57	2 57	14 44	26 2	5 15	17 32	7 22	14 58
5	12 0	2♉56	4 29	15 56	26 37	5 9	17 38	7 25	14 59
6	12 57	14 49	5 59	17 9	27 12	5 2	17 45	7 28	15 1
7	13 55	26 40	7 27	18 21	27 48	4 55	17 52	7 31	15 2
8	14 52	8♊35	8 54	19 34	28 23	4 48	17 58	7 34	15 3
9	15 50	20 37	10 19	20 46	28 59	4 41	18 5	7 37	15 5
10	16 48	2♋51	11 42	21 59	29 35	4 34	18 12	7 40	15 6
11	17 45	15 19	13 3	23 12	0♏11	4 27	18 19	7 43	15 7
12	18 43	28 4	14 22	24 25	0 47	4 19	18 25	7 46	15 9
13	19 40	11♌ 5	15 39	25 38	1 24	4 12	18 32	7 48	15 10
14	20 38	24 22	16 55	26 51	2 0	4 4	18 39	7 51	15 11
15	21 36	7♍53	18 8	28 4	2 37	3 57	18 46	7 54	15 13
16	22 33	21 37	19 20	29 16	3 13	3 49	18 53	7 57	15 14
17	23 31	5♎30	20 29	0♌29	3 50	3 42	19 0	8 0	15 16
18	24 29	19 32	21 36	1 42	4 27	3 34	19 7	8 3	15 18
19	25 26	3♏38	22 41	2 55	5 4	3 26	19 14	8 6	15 19
20	26 24	17 49	23 43	4 8	5 41	3 19	19 21	8 8	15 21
21	27 22	2♐ 1	24 42	5 22	6 19	3 11	19 28	8 11	15 22
22	28 20	16 13	25 39	6 35	6 56	3 3	19 35	8 13	15 24
23	29 18	0♑22	26 33	7 48	7 34	2 55	19 42	8 16	15 26
24	0♍15	14 25	27 24	9 2	8 12	2 47	19 49	8 18	15 27
25	1 13	28 20	28 12	10 15	8 50	2 39	19 57	8 21	15 29
26	2 11	12♒ 4	28 57	11 29	9 28	2 31	20 4	8 23	15 31
27	3 9	25 33	29 37	12 42	10 6	2 23	20 11	8 26	15 33
28	4 7	8♓45	0♎14	13 56	10 45	2 15	20 18	8 28	15 34
29	5 5	21 41	0 47	15 9	11 23	2 8	20 26	8 31	15 36
30	6 3	4♈19	1 16	16 23	12 2	2 0	20 33	8 33	15 38
31	7 1	16 41	1 40	17 37	12 41	1 52	20 40	8 35	15 40

Pluto 17 Leo all month

1950

SEPTEMBER

DAY	☉	☽	☿	♀	♂	♃	♄	♅	♆
	° ′	° ′	° ′	° ′	° ′	° ′	° ′	° ′	° ′
1	7♍59	28♈50	2♎ 0	18♌50	13♏19	1♓44	20♍48	8♋38	15♎42
2	8 57	10♉49	2 14	20 4	13 58	1℞ 36	20 55	8 40	15 43
3	9 55	22 42	2 22	21 18	14 37	1 29	21 3	8 42	15 45
4	10 53	4♊34	2℞25	22 32	15 16	1 21	21 10	8 44	15 47
5	11 51	16 29	2 22	23 45	15 56	1 14	21 18	8 46	15 49
6	12 49	28 32	2 13	24 59	16 35	1 6	21 25	8 48	15 51
7	13 48	10♋47	1 58	26 13	17 15	0 58	21 33	8 50	15 53
8	14 46	23 19	1 36	27 27	17 55	0 51	21 40	8 52	15 55
9	15 44	6♌10	1 8	28 41	18 34	0 43	21 48	8 54	15 57
10	16 43	19 21	0 33	29 55	19 14	0 36	21 55	8 55	15 59
11	17 41	2♍54	29♍52	1♍ 9	19 54	0 29	22 3	8 57	16 1
12	18 39	16 46	29 5	2 23	20 34	0 22	22 10	8 59	16 3
13	19 38	0♎55	28 13	3 37	21 14	0 15	22 18	9 1	16 5
14	20 36	15 16	27 17	4 52	21 55	0 8	22 25	9 2	16 7
15	21 35	29 44	26 17	6 6	22 35	0 1	22 33	9 4	16 9
16	22 33	14♏14	25 14	7 20	23 16	29♒54	22 40	9 6	16 11
17	23 32	28 41	24 11	8 34	23 56	29 47	22 48	9 7	16 13
18	24 30	13♐ 1	23 9	9 49	24 37	29 41	22 55	9 9	16 15
19	25 29	27 11	22 9	11 3	25 18	29 34	23 3	9 10	16 17
20	26 27	11♑ 9	21 12	12 17	25 59	29 28	23 10	9 11	16 19
21	27 26	24 54	20 20	13 32	26 40	29 22	23 18	9 13	16 22
22	28 25	8♒26	19 35	14 46	27 22	29 16	23 25	9 14	16 24
23	29 23	21 43	18 57	16 1	28 3	29 10	23 33	9 15	16 26
24	0♎22	4♓47	18 27	17 15	28 44	29 5	23 40	9 16	16 28
25	1 21	17 38	18 7	18 30	29 26	28 59	23 48	9 18	16 30
26	2 20	0♈15	17 57	19 44	0♐ 7	28 54	23 55	9 19	16 32
27	3 19	12 40	17 D57	20 59	0 49	28 49	24 2	9 20	16 35
28	4 17	24 53	18 7	22 14	1 31	28 44	24 9	9 21	16 37
29	5 16	6♉57	18 28	23 28	2 13	28 39	24 17	9 22	16 39
30	6 15	18 54	18 58	24 43	2 55	28 35	24 24	9 22	16 41

Pluto 18 Leo all month

OCTOBER

DAY	☉	☽	☿	♀	♂	♃	♄	♅	♆
	° ′	° ′	° ′	° ′	° ′	° ′	° ′	° ′	° ′
1	7♎14	0♊46	19♍37	25♍58	3♐37	28♒30	24♍32	9♋23	16♎43
2	8 13	12 37	20 25	27 13	4 19	28℞26	24 39	9 24	16 46
3	9 12	24 31	21 21	28 27	5 1	28 21	24 46	9 25	16 48
4	10 11	6♋32	22 24	29 42	5 44	28 17	24 54	9 25	16 50
5	11 10	18 45	23 34	0♎57	6 26	28 13	25 1	9 26	16 52
6	12 10	1♌14	24 49	2 12	7 8	28 10	25 8	9 27	16 54
7	13 9	14 3	26 10	3 26	7 51	28 6	25 16	9 27	16 57
8	14 8	27 15	27 35	4 41	8 33	28 3	25 23	9 28	16 59
9	15 7	10♍53	29 4	5 56	9 16	28 0	25 30	9 28	17 1
10	16 7	24 56	0♎36	7 11	9 59	27 57	25 37	9 28	17 3
11	17 6	9♎22	2 11	8 26	10 42	27 54	25 45	9 29	17 6
12	18 5	24 6	3 48	9 41	11 26	27 52	25 52	9 29	17 8
13	19 5	9♏ 1	5 27	10 56	12 9	27 49	25 59	9 29	17 10
14	20 4	23 58	7 7	12 11	12 52	27 47	26 6	9 29	17 12
15	21 4	8♐49	8 48	13 26	13 35	27 45	26 14	9 30	17 14
16	22 3	23 26	10 30	14 41	14 19	27 43	26 21	9℞30	17 17
17	23 3	7♑46	12 13	15 56	15 2	27 41	26 28	9 30	17 19
18	24 2	21 45	13 56	17 11	15 46	27 40	26 35	9 29	17 21
19	25 2	5♒23	15 39	18 26	16 29	27 39	26 42	9 29	17 23
20	26 1	18 41	17 22	19 41	17 13	27 38	26 48	9 29	17 26
21	27 1	1♓40	19 5	20 56	17 57	27 37	26 55	9 29	17 28
22	28 1	14 24	20 47	22 11	18 41	27 36	27 2	9 29	17 30
23	29 0	26 55	22 30	23 26	19 25	27 36	27 9	9 28	17 32
24	0♏ 0	9♈15	24 12	24 42	20 9	27 35	27 15	9 28	17 34
25	1 0	21 25	25 53	25 57	20 53	27 35	27 22	9 27	17 37
26	2 0	3♉29	27 35	27 12	21 37	27 D35	27 29	9 27	17 39
27	3 0	15 27	29 16	28 27	22 21	27 36	27 35	9 26	17 41
28	3 59	27 21	0♏56	29 43	23 6	27 36	27 42	9 26	17 43
29	4 59	9♊12	2 36	0♏58	23 50	27 37	27 48	9 25	17 45
30	5 59	21 3	4 15	2 13	24 34	27 38	27 55	9 24	17 48
31	6 59	2♋57	5 54	3 28	25 19	27 40	28 1	9 24	17 50

Pluto 19 Leo all month

1950

NOVEMBER

DAY	☉	☽	☿	♀	♂	♃	♄	♅	♆
	° ′	° ′	° ′	° ′	° ′	° ′	° ′	° ′	° ′
1	7♏59	14♋57	7♏32	4♏44	26♐ 3	27♒41	28♍ 8	9♋23	17♎52
2	8 59	27 7	9 10	5 59	26 48	27 43	28 14	9℞22	17 54
3	9 59	9♌31	10 48	7 14	27 33	27 45	28 20	9 21	17 56
4	10 59	22 13	12 25	8 29	28 18	27 47	28 26	9 20	17 58
5	12 0	5♍19	14 1	9 45	29 3	27 49	28 32	9 19	18 0
6	13 0	18 51	15 38	11 0	29 48	27 51	28 38	9 18	18 2
7	14 0	2♎51	17 14	12 15	0♑33	27 54	28 44	9 17	18 4
8	15 0	17 20	18 49	13 30	1 18	27 56	28 50	9 16	18 7
9	16 0	2♏12	20 24	14 46	2 3	27 59	28 56	9 14	18 9
10	17 1	17 22	21 59	16 1	2 48	28 2	29 2	9 13	18 11
11	18 1	2♐39	23 33	17 16	3 33	28 6	29 8	9 12	18 13
12	19 1	17 51	25 7	18 31	4 19	28 9	29 14	9 10	18 15
13	20 2	2♑50	26 41	19 47	5 4	28 13	29 19	9 9	18 17
14	21 2	17 27	28 14	21 2	5 50	28 17	29 25	9 7	18 19
15	22 3	1♒36	29 48	22 17	6 35	28 21	29 30	9 6	18 21
16	23 3	15 18	1♐21	23 33	7 21	28 26	29 36	9 4	18 22
17	24 4	28 34	2 53	24 48	8 6	28 30	29 41	9 3	18 24
18	25 4	11♓26	4 26	26 4	8 52	28 35	29 46	9 1	18 26
19	26 5	24 0	5 58	27 19	9 38	28 40	29 51	8 59	18 28
20	27 5	6♈18	7 30	28 35	10 23	28 45	29 57	8 58	18 30
21	28 6	18 26	9 1	29 50	11 9	28 50	0♎ 2	8 56	18 32
22	29 6	0♉26	10 33	1♐ 6	11 55	28 55	0 7	8 54	18 34
23	0♐ 7	12 22	12 4	2 21	12 41	29 1	0 12	8 52	18 35
24	1 8	24 15	13 35	3 37	13 27	29 7	0 17	8 51	18 37
25	2 8	6♊ 7	15 6	4 52	14 13	29 13	0 21	8 49	18 39
26	3 9	17 59	16 37	6 7	14 59	29 19	0 26	8 47	18 41
27	4 10	29 54	18 7	7 22	15 45	29 25	0 31	8 45	18 42
28	5 10	11♋51	19 37	8 38	16 31	29 32	0 35	8 43	18 44
29	6 11	23 54	21 6	9 53	17 18	29 38	0 40	8 41	18 46
30	7 12	6♌ 6	22 35	11 9	18 4	29 45	0 44	8 39	18 47

Pluto 19 Leo all month

DECEMBER

DAY	☉	☽	☿	♀	♂	♃	♄	♅	♆
	° ′	° ′	° ′	° ′	° ′	° ′	° ′	° ′	° ′
1	8♐13	18♌29	24♐ 4	12♐24	18♑50	29♒52	0♎48	8♋37	18♎49
2	9 13	1♍ 7	25 32	13 40	19 36	29 59	0 53	8℞35	18 50
3	10 14	14 5	27 0	14 55	20 23	0♓ 7	0 57	8 32	18 52
4	11 15	27 27	28 27	16 11	21 9	0 14	1 1	8 30	18 54
5	12 16	11♎16	29 53	17 26	21 55	0 22	1 5	8 28	18 55
6	13 17	25 33	1♑18	18 41	22 42	0 29	1 9	8 26	18 57
7	14 18	10♏17	2 43	19 57	23 28	0 37	1 12	8 23	18 58
8	15 19	25 22	4 5	21 12	24 15	0 45	1 16	8 21	19 0
9	16 20	10♐41	5 27	22 27	25 2	0 53	1 20	8 19	19 1
10	17 21	26 1	6 47	23 43	25 48	1 2	1 23	8 16	19 2
11	18 22	11♑11	8 5	24 58	26 35	1 10	1 27	8 14	19 4
12	19 23	26 1	9 20	26 14	27 22	1 19	1 30	8 11	19 5
13	20 24	10♒24	10 33	27 29	28 9	1 28	1 33	8 9	19 6
14	21 25	24 16	11 43	28 45	28 55	1 37	1 36	8 6	19 8
15	22 26	7♓39	12 49	0♑ 0	29 42	1 46	1 39	8 4	19 9
16	23 27	20 34	13 51	1 16	0♒29	1 55	1 42	8 1	19 10
17	24 28	3♈ 7	14 49	2 31	1 16	2 5	1 45	7 59	19 11
18	25 29	15 23	15 41	3 46	2 3	2 14	1 48	7 56	19 12
19	26 30	27 26	16 26	5 2	2 50	2 24	1 50	7 54	19 13
20	27 31	9♉21	17 5	6 17	3 37	2 34	1 53	7 51	19 15
21	28 32	21 12	17 35	7 32	4 24	2 44	1 55	7 48	19 16
22	29 33	3♊ 3	17 57	8 48	5 11	2 54	1 58	7 46	19 17
23	0♑35	14 55	18 8	10 3	5 58	3 4	2 0	7 43	19 18
24	1 36	26 51	18℞10	11 19	6 45	3 14	2 2	7 40	19 19
25	2 37	8♋52	18 0	12 34	7 32	3 24	2 4	7 37	19 20
26	3 38	20 58	17 38	13 50	8 19	3 35	2 6	7 35	19 20
27	4 39	3♌11	17 4	15 5	9 6	3 45	2 7	7 32	19 21
28	5 40	15 32	16 19	16 21	9 53	3 56	2 9	7 29	19 22
29	6 41	28 3	15 23	17 36	10 40	4 7	2 11	7 26	19 23
30	7 42	10♍47	14 18	18 51	11 27	4 18	2 12	7 24	19 24
31	8 44	23 46	13 5	20 7	12 15	4 29	2 14	7 21	19 24

Pluto 19 Leo all month

1951

JANUARY

DAY	☉	☽	☿	♀	♂	♃	♄	♅	♆
	° ′	° ′	° ′	° ′	° ′	° ′	° ′	° ′	° ′
1	9 ♑ 45	7 ♎ 3	11 ♑ 47	21 ♑ 22	13 ♒ 2	4 ♓ 42	2 ♎ 15	7 ♋ 22	19 ♎ 26
2	10 46	20 42	10 ℞ 23	22 38	13 D 50	4 54	2 16	7 ℞ 19	19 26
3	11 47	4 ♏ 45	9 3	23 53	14 37	5 5	2 17	7 17	19 27
4	12 48	19 10	7 46	25 8	15 24	5 16	2 18	7 14	19 27
5	13 49	3 ♐ 57	6 32	26 23	16 11	5 28	2 19	7 11	19 27
6	14 51	18 58	5 25	27 39	16 58	5 39	2 19	7 9	19 28
7	15 52	4 ♑ 5	4 26	28 54	17 46	5 51	2 20	7 6	19 28
8	16 53	19 7	3 37	0 ♒ 10	18 33	6 2	2 20	7 4	19 29
9	17 54	3 ♒ 55	2 57	1 25	19 20	6 14	2 21	7 1	19 29
10	18 55	18 21	2 27	2 40	20 7	6 26	2 21	6 59	19 29
11	19 56	2 ♓ 20	2 7	3 55	20 54	6 38	2 21	6 56	19 30
12	20 58	15 51	1 57	5 11	21 42	6 50	2 22	6 54	19 30
13	21 59	28 53	1 56	6 26	22 29	7 2	2 ℞ 22	6 51	19 31
14	23 0	11 ♈ 32	2 D 3	7 41	23 16	7 14	2 22	6 49	19 31
15	24 1	23 51	2 18	8 56	24 3	7 27	2 21	6 47	19 31
16	25 2	5 ♉ 56	2 39	10 11	24 50	7 39	2 21	6 44	19 31
17	26 3	17 51	3 7	11 27	25 38	7 52	2 20	6 42	19 32
18	27 4	29 42	3 42	12 42	26 25	8 4	2 20	6 39	19 32
19	28 5	11 ♊ 33	4 22	13 57	27 12	8 17	2 19	6 37	19 32
20	29 6	23 28	5 6	15 12	27 59	8 30	2 18	6 35	19 32
21	0 ♒ 7	5 ♋ 28	5 55	16 27	28 46	8 43	2 17	6 32	19 32
22	1 8	17 36	6 47	17 42	29 34	8 56	2 16	6 30	19 ℞ 32
23	2 9	29 54	7 43	18 57	0 ♓ 21	9 9	2 15	6 27	19 32
24	3 11	12 ♌ 22	8 42	20 12	1 8	9 22	2 14	6 25	19 32
25	4 12	24 59	9 44	21 27	1 55	9 35	2 12	6 23	19 32
26	5 12	7 ♍ 48	10 48	22 42	2 43	9 49	2 11	6 21	19 32
27	6 13	20 48	11 55	23 58	3 30	10 2	2 9	6 18	19 31
28	7 14	4 ♎ 0	13 5	25 13	4 18	10 16	2 8	6 16	19 31
29	8 15	17 26	14 17	26 28	5 5	10 29	2 6	6 14	19 31
30	9 16	1 ♏ 7	15 30	27 43	5 52	10 43	2 4	6 12	19 31
31	10 17	15 3	16 44	28 58	6 39	10 56	2 2	6 10	19 30

Pluto 19 Leo all month

FEBRUARY

DAY	☉	☽	☿	♀	♂	♃	♄	♅	♆
	° ′	° ′	° ′	° ′	° ′	° ′	° ′	° ′	° ′
1	11 ♒ 18	29 ♏ 15	18 ♑ 0	0 ♓ 13	7 ♓ 27	11 ♓ 10	2 ♎ 0	6 ♋ 8	19 ♎ 30
2	12 19	13 ♐ 40	19 18	1 28	8 14	11 23	1 ℞ 58	6 ℞ 6	19 ℞ 29
3	13 20	28 15	20 37	2 43	9 1	11 37	1 56	6 4	19 29
4	14 21	12 ♑ 55	21 57	3 58	9 48	11 51	1 54	6 2	19 28
5	15 22	27 32	23 19	5 13	10 35	12 4	1 51	6 0	19 28
6	16 23	12 ♒ 1	24 42	6 28	11 22	12 18	1 49	5 59	19 27
7	17 23	26 13	26 5	7 42	12 9	12 32	1 46	5 57	19 27
8	18 24	10 ♓ 5	27 30	8 57	12 56	12 46	1 44	5 55	19 26
9	19 25	23 34	28 56	10 12	13 43	13 0	1 41	5 53	19 25
10	20 26	6 ♈ 39	0 ♒ 22	11 26	14 30	13 14	1 38	5 52	19 25
11	21 26	19 22	1 50	12 41	15 17	13 28	1 35	5 50	19 24
12	22 27	1 ♉ 46	3 19	13 55	16 4	13 42	1 32	5 49	19 24
13	23 28	13 55	4 48	15 10	16 51	13 56	1 29	5 47	19 23
14	24 29	25 53	6 19	16 24	17 38	14 10	1 26	5 46	19 22
15	25 29	7 ♊ 46	7 51	17 39	18 25	14 24	1 22	5 44	19 22
16	26 30	19 38	9 23	18 53	19 12	14 39	1 19	5 43	19 21
17	27 30	1 ♋ 34	10 56	20 8	19 58	14 53	1 15	5 41	19 20
18	28 31	13 38	12 30	21 22	20 45	15 7	1 12	5 40	19 19
19	29 31	25 52	14 5	22 36	21 32	15 21	1 8	5 39	19 18
20	0 ♓ 32	8 ♌ 19	15 41	23 51	22 19	15 35	1 5	5 37	19 17
21	1 32	21 1	17 18	25 5	23 6	15 50	1 1	5 36	19 16
22	2 33	3 ♍ 57	18 56	26 20	23 52	16 4	0 57	5 35	19 15
23	3 33	17 9	20 35	27 34	24 39	16 18	0 53	5 34	19 14
24	4 33	0 ♎ 33	22 15	28 48	25 25	16 32	0 49	5 33	19 13
25	5 34	14 10	23 55	0 ♈ 2	26 12	16 47	0 45	5 32	19 12
26	6 34	27 58	25 37	1 17	26 58	17 1	0 41	5 31	19 10
27	7 34	11 ♏ 55	27 20	2 31	27 45	17 16	0 37	5 30	19 9
28	8 35	25 59	29 3	3 45	28 31	17 30	0 33	5 29	19 8

Pluto 18 Leo all month

1951

MARCH

DAY	☉ ° ′	☽ ° ′	☿ ° ′	♀ ° ′	♂ ° ′	♃ ° ′	♄ ° ′	♅ ° ′	♆ ° ′
1	9♓35	10♐ 9	0♓48	4♈59	29♓17	17♓45	0♎29	5♋28	19♎ 7
2	10 35	24 22	2 34	6 13	0♈ 4	17 59	0 ℞25	5 ℞28	19 ℞ 6
3	11 35	8♑37	4 21	7 27	0 50	18 14	0 20	5 27	19 4
4	12 36	22 49	6 8	8 41	1 37	18 28	0 16	5 27	19 3
5	13 36	6♒57	7 57	9 55	2 23	18 43	0 12	5 26	19 2
6	14 36	20 56	9 47	11 9	3 9	18 57	0 7	5 26	19 1
7	15 36	4♓42	11 38	12 23	3 55	19 12	0 3	5 25	19 0
8	16 36	18 15	13 31	13 37	4 42	19 26	29♍58	5 25	18 58
9	17 36	1♈30	15 24	14 50	5 28	19 41	29 54	5 24	18 57
10	18 36	14 27	17 18	16 4	6 14	19 55	29 49	5 24	18 56
11	19 36	27 7	19 13	17 17	7 0	20 10	29 44	5 24	18 55
12	20 36	9♉31	21 9	18 31	7 46	20 24	29 40	5 24	18 53
13	21 36	21 41	23 6	19 44	8 32	20 39	29 35	5 24	18 52
14	22 36	3♊41	25 4	20 58	9 18	20 53	29 31	5 24	18 50
15	23 35	15 36	27 2	22 11	10 4	21 8	29 26	5 D 24	18 49
16	24 35	27 28	29 1	23 24	10 50	21 22	29 21	5 24	18 48
17	25 35	9♋24	1♈ 1	24 37	11 36	21 37	29 17	5 24	18 46
18	26 35	21 28	3 0	25 51	12 22	21 51	29 12	5 25	18 45
19	27 34	3♌44	5 0	27 4	13 7	22 6	29 7	5 25	18 43
20	28 34	16 16	6 59	28 17	13 53	22 20	29 2	5 25	18 42
21	29 34	29 6	8 58	29 30	14 39	22 35	28 57	5 25	18 40
22	0♈33	12♍17	10 56	0♉43	15 24	22 49	28 52	5 26	18 39
23	1 33	25 48	12 53	1 56	16 10	23 4	28 47	5 26	18 37
24	2 32	9♎38	14 49	3 9	16 55	23 18	28 43	5 27	18 36
25	3 32	23 43	16 42	4 22	17 41	23 33	28 38	5 27	18 34
26	4 31	8♏ 0	18 32	5 35	18 26	23 47	28 33	5 28	18 32
27	5 30	22 23	20 20	6 47	19 12	24 2	28 29	5 28	18 31
28	6 30	6♐48	22 5	8 0	19 57	24 16	28 24	5 29	18 29
29	7 29	21 10	23 46	9 12	20 43	24 31	28 20	5 29	18 28
30	8 28	5♑25	25 23	10 25	21 28	24 45	28 15	5 30	18 26
31	9 28	19 31	26 56	11 37	22 13	24 59	28 10	5 31	18 24

Pluto 18 Leo all month

APRIL

DAY	☉ ° ′	☽ ° ′	☿ ° ′	♀ ° ′	♂ ° ′	♃ ° ′	♄ ° ′	♅ ° ′	♆ ° ′
1	10♈27	3♒27	28♈25	12♉49	22♈58	25♓13	28♍ 6	5♋32	18♎23
2	11 26	17 10	29 48	14 2	23 43	25 28	28 ℞ 1	5 33	18 ℞21
3	12 25	0♓42	1♉ 6	15 14	24 28	25 42	27 57	5 34	18 20
4	13 25	14 2	2 18	16 26	25 13	25 56	27 52	5 35	18 18
5	14 24	27 9	3 24	17 38	25 58	26 10	27 48	5 36	18 16
6	15 23	10♈ 4	4 25	18 50	26 43	26 24	27 43	5 37	18 15
7	16 22	22 46	5 20	20 2	27 28	26 38	27 39	5 39	18 13
8	17 21	5♉15	6 7	21 14	28 13	26 52	27 34	5 40	18 12
9	18 20	17 32	6 47	22 26	28 58	27 6	27 30	5 41	18 10
10	19 19	29 40	7 21	23 38	29 43	27 20	27 26	5 43	18 8
11	20 18	11♊39	7 49	24 49	0♉27	27 34	27 22	5 44	18 7
12	21 17	23 32	8 10	26 1	1 12	27 48	27 17	5 46	18 5
13	22 15	5♋24	8 24	27 12	1 56	28 2	27 13	5 47	18 4
14	23 14	17 19	8 31	28 24	2 41	28 16	27 9	5 49	18 2
15	24 13	29 21	8 ℞32	29 35	3 25	28 30	27 5	5 51	18 0
16	25 12	11♌35	8 28	0♊46	4 10	28 44	27 1	5 52	17 59
17	26 10	24 5	8 18	1 58	4 54	28 58	26 57	5 54	17 57
18	27 9	6♍57	8 2	3 9	5 39	29 11	26 54	5 56	17 56
19	28 8	20 13	7 41	4 20	6 23	29 25	26 50	5 58	17 54
20	29 6	3♎55	7 15	5 31	7 7	29 38	26 47	6 0	17 52
21	0♉ 5	18 1	6 45	6 41	7 51	29 52	26 43	6 1	17 51
22	1 3	2♏29	6 11	7 52	8 36	0♈ 5	26 40	6 3	17 49
23	2 2	17 13	5 34	9 2	9 20	0 19	26 36	6 5	17 48
24	3 0	2♐ 4	4 56	10 13	10 4	0 32	26 33	6 7	17 46
25	3 59	16 55	4 16	11 23	10 48	0 45	26 30	6 9	17 45
26	4 57	1♑38	3 35	12 33	11 32	0 58	26 27	6 11	17 43
27	5 56	16 6	2 55	13 44	12 16	1 12	26 24	6 14	17 42
28	6 54	0♒16	2 15	14 54	12 59	1 25	26 21	6 16	17 40
29	7 52	14 7	1 37	16 4	13 43	1 38	26 18	6 18	17 39
30	8 50	27 39	1 1	17 14	14 27	1 51	26 15	6 20	17 37

Pluto 17 Leo all month

1951

MAY

DAY	☉	☽	☿	♀	♂	♃	♄	♅	♆
	° ′	° ′	° ′	° ′	° ′	° ′	° ′	° ′	° ′
1	9 ♉ 49	10 ♓ 54	0 ♉ 27	18 ♊ 23	15 ♉ 10	2 ♈ 4	26 ♍ 12	6 ♋ 22	17 ♎ 36
2	10 47	23 53	29 ℞ 57	19 33	15 54	2 17	26 ℞ 9	6 25	17 ℞ 34
3	11 45	6 ♈ 40	29 ♈ 30	20 42	16 37	2 30	26 7	6 27	17 33
4	12 43	19 15	29 7	21 52	17 21	2 43	26 4	6 29	17 31
5	13 42	1 ♉ 40	28 49	23 1	18 4	2 55	26 2	6 32	17 30
6	14 40	13 56	28 35	24 10	18 48	3 8	26 0	6 34	17 28
7	15 38	26 4	28 25	25 20	19 31	3 20	25 57	6 3[illegible]	17 27
8	16 36	8 ♊ 5	28 21	26 29	20 15	3 33	25 55	6 39	17 26
9	17 34	20 0	28 D 21	27 38	20 58	3 45	25 53	6 42	17 24
10	18 32	1 ♋ 52	28 26	28 46	21 41	3 57	25 51	6 45	17 23
11	19 30	13 43	28 35	29 55	22 24	4 9	25 49	6 47	17 21
12	20 28	25 36	28 49	1 ♋ 3	23 8	4 22	25 47	6 50	17 20
13	21 26	7 ♌ 36	29 8	2 12	23 51	4 34	25 46	6 53	17 18
14	22 24	19 47	29 31	3 20	24 34	4 46	25 44	6 56	17 17
15	23 22	2 ♍ 14	29 ♈ 58	4 28	25 17	4 58	25 43	6 59	17 16
16	24 20	15 2	0 ♉ 29	5 36	26 0	5 10	25 42	7 1	17 15
17	25 17	28 16	1 4	6 44	26 43	5 22	25 40	7 4	17 13
18	26 15	11 ♎ 58	1 43	7 51	27 25	5 33	25 39	7 7	17 12
19	27 13	26 9	2 26	8 59	28 8	5 45	25 38	7 10	17 11
20	28 11	10 ♏ 47	3 13	10 6	28 51	5 57	25 37	7 13	17 10
21	29 8	25 45	4 3	11 13	29 33	6 8	25 36	7 16	17 9
22	0 ♊ 6	10 ♐ 56	4 57	12 20	0 ♊ 16	6 20	25 35	7 19	17 7
23	1 4	26 9	5 54	13 27	0 58	6 31	25 35	7 22	17 6
24	2 1	11 ♑ 12	6 54	14 34	1 41	6 42	25 34	7 25	17 5
25	2 59	25 57	7 57	15 40	2 23	6 53	25 34	7 28	17 4
26	3 57	10 ♒ 19	9 3	16 46	3 6	7 4	25 34	7 31	17 3
27	4 54	24 16	10 12	17 52	3 48	7 15	25 33	7 35	17 2
28	5 52	7 ♓ 48	11 25	18 58	4 31	7 25	25 33	7 38	17 1
29	6 49	20 57	12 41	20 4	5 13	7 36	25 D 33	7 41	17 0
30	7 47	3 ♈ 46	14 0	21 9	5 55	7 46	25 33	7 44	16 59
31	8 45	16 20	15 21	22 14	6 37	7 57	25 33	7 48	16 58

Pluto 17 Leo all month

JUNE

DAY	☉	☽	☿	♀	♂	♃	♄	♅	♆
	° ′	° ′	° ′	° ′	° ′	° ′	° ′	° ′	° ′
1	9 ♊ 42	28 ♈ 42	16 ♉ 41	23 ♋ 20	7 ♊ 19	8 ♈ 7	25 ♍ 34	7 ♋ 51	16 ♎ 58
2	10 40	10 ♉ 54	18 7	24 25	8 1	8 18	25 34	7 55	16 ℞ 57
3	11 37	22 59	10 36	25 30	8 43	8 28	25 34	7 58	16 56
4	12 35	4 ♊ 58	21 7	26 35	9 25	8 38	25 35	8 1	16 55
5	13 32	16 53	22 41	27 39	10 7	8 48	25 35	8 5	16 54
6	14 29	28 45	24 17	28 43	10 49	8 58	25 36	8 8	16 54
7	15 27	10 ♋ 36	25 56	29 47	11 30	9 7	25 36	8 12	16 53
8	16 24	22 28	27 37	0 ♌ 50	12 12	9 17	25 37	8 15	16 52
9	17 22	9 ♌ 23	29 21	1 54	12 54	9 26	25 38	8 18	16 51
10	18 19	16 24	1 ♊ 8	2 57	13 35	9 35	25 39	8 22	16 51
11	19 17	28 35	2 58	4 0	14 17	9 45	25 41	8 25	16 50
12	20 14	11 ♍ 0	4 50	5 2	14 58	9 54	25 42	8 29	16 50
13	21 11	23 45	6 43	6 4	15 40	10 3	25 43	8 32	16 49
14	22 9	6 ♎ 54	8 39	7 6	16 21	10 11	25 45	8 35	16 48
15	23 6	20 30	10 38	8 8	17 3	10 20	25 46	8 39	16 48
16	24 3	4 ♏ 35	12 39	9 9	17 44	10 28	25 48	8 42	16 48
17	25 0	19 9	14 43	10 10	18 26	10 37	25 50	8 46	16 47
18	25 58	4 ♐ 8	16 48	11 10	19 7	10 45	25 52	8 49	16 47
19	26 55	19 22	18 53	12 11	19 48	10 53	25 54	8 53	16 47
20	27 52	4 ♑ 43	21 0	13 11	20 29	11 1	25 57	8 56	16 47
21	28 49	19 57	23 9	14 10	21 10	11 9	25 59	9 0	16 46
22	29 47	4 ♒ 55	25 20	15 9	21 51	11 16	26 2	9 3	16 46
23	0 ♋ 44	19 29	27 31	16 7	22 32	11 24	26 4	9 7	16 46
24	1 41	3 ♓ 35	29 43	17 6	23 13	11 31	26 7	9 11	16 46
25	2 38	17 14	1 ♋ 54	18 4	23 54	11 38	26 9	9 14	16 46
26	3 35	0 ♈ 25	4 5	19 1	24 35	11 46	26 12	9 18	16 46
27	4 33	13 14	6 16	19 58	25 16	11 53	26 15	9 21	16 46
28	5 30	25 45	8 26	20 54	25 57	12 0	26 18	9 25	16 D 46
29	6 27	8 ♉ 0	10 35	21 50	26 38	12 6	26 21	9 29	16 46
30	7 24	20 6	12 43	22 45	27 18	12 13	26 24	9 32	16 46

Pluto 17 Leo all month

1951

JULY

Pluto 18 Leo all month

DAY	☉	☽	☿	♀	♂	♃	♄	♅	♆
	° ′	° ′	° ′	° ′	° ′	° ′	° ′	° ′	° ′
1	8 ♋ 22	2 ♊ 4	14 ♋ 51	23 ♌ 40	27 ♊ 59	12 ♈ 19	26 ♍ 27	9 ♋ 36	16 ♎ 46
2	9 19	13 58	16 57	24 35	28 39	12 26	26 30	9 40	16 46
3	10 16	25 49	19 1	25 29	29 20	12 32	26 33	9 43	16 46
4	11 13	7 ♋ 41	21 4	26 22	0 ♋ 1	12 38	26 37	9 47	16 46
5	12 10	19 34	23 5	27 15	0 41	12 43	26 40	9 50	16 46
6	13 8	1 ♌ 29	25 4	28 7	1 22	12 49	26 44	9 54	16 47
7	14 5	13 30	27 1	28 59	2 2	12 54	26 47	9 58	16 47
8	15 2	25 37	28 56	29 50	2 43	13 0	26 51	10 2	16 47
9	15 59	7 ♍ 54	0 ♌ 49	0 ♍ 41	3 23	13 5	26 55	10 6	16 47
10	16 57	20 24	2 40	1 30	4 3	13 9	26 59	10 9	16 48
11	17 54	3 ♎ 11	4 29	2 19	4 44	13 14	27 3	10 13	16 48
12	18 51	16 18	6 16	3 7	5 24	13 18	27 7	10 16	16 49
13	19 48	29 49	8 2	3 54	6 4	13 23	27 11	10 20	16 49
14	20 45	13 ♏ 46	9 45	4 41	6 44	13 27	27 16	10 24	16 49
15	21 43	28 9	11 27	5 26	7 24	13 31	27 20	10 27	16 50
16	22 40	12 ♐ 54	13 7	6 11	8 4	13 35	27 25	10 31	16 50
17	23 37	27 57	14 44	6 55	8 44	13 38	27 29	10 34	16 51
18	24 34	13 ♑ 9	16 20	7 38	9 24	13 42	27 34	10 38	16 51
19	25 31	28 19	17 54	8 20	10 4	13 45	27 39	10 41	16 52
20	26 29	13 ♒ 17	19 25	9 1	10 44	13 48	27 43	10 45	16 52
21	27 26	27 55	20 55	9 41	11 24	13 51	27 48	10 48	16 53
22	28 23	12 ♓ 8	22 23	10 20	12 3	13 53	27 53	10 52	16 54
23	29 20	25 53	23 49	10 58	12 43	13 56	27 58	10 55	16 55
24	0 ♌ 18	9 ♈ 11	25 13	11 35	13 23	13 58	28 3	10 58	16 56
25	1 15	22 4	26 35	12 11	14 2	14 0	28 8	11 2	16 56
26	2 12	4 ♉ 37	27 54	12 45	14 42	14 2	28 13	11 5	16 57
27	3 10	16 52	29 11	13 17	15 21	14 3	28 18	11 9	16 58
28	4 7	28 56	0 ♍ 27	13 48	16 1	14 5	28 23	11 12	16 59
29	5 4	10 ♊ 52	1 40	14 18	16 41	14 6	28 28	11 15	17 0
30	6 2	22 44	2 50	14 47	17 20	14 7	28 34	11 19	17 1
31	6 59	4 ♋ 36	3 58	15 14	18 0	14 8	28 39	11 22	17 2

AUGUST

Pluto 19 Leo all month

DAY	☉	☽	☿	♀	♂	♃	♄	♅	♆
	° ′	° ′	° ′	° ′	° ′	° ′	° ′	° ′	° ′
1	7 ♌ 57	16 ♋ 29	5 ♍ 4	15 ♍ 39	18 ♋ 39	14 ♈ 9	28 ♍ 45	11 ♋ 26	17 3
2	8 54	28 26	6 7	16 3	19 19	14 10	28 50	11 29	17 4
3	9 51	10 ♌ 30	7 8	16 26	19 58	14 10	28 56	11 32	17 5
4	10 49	22 40	8 6	16 47	20 37	14 R 10	29 1	11 35	17 6
5	11 46	5 ♍ 0	9 0	17 5	21 17	14 10	29 7	11 39	17 8
6	12 44	17 31	9 52	17 21	21 56	14 10	29 13	11 42	17 9
7	13 41	0 ♎ 14	10 41	17 35	22 35	14 10	29 19	11 45	17 10
8	14 39	13 11	11 26	17 47	23 14	14 9	29 25	11 48	17 11
9	15 36	26 25	12 7	17 57	23 53	14 8	29 31	11 51	17 12
10	16 34	9 ♏ 58	12 45	18 6	24 32	14 7	29 37	11 55	17 14
11	17 31	23 49	13 19	18 13	25 11	14 6	29 43	11 58	17 15
12	18 29	8 ♐ 1	13 49	18 18	25 50	14 5	29 49	12 1	17 16
13	19 27	22 29	14 14	18 20	26 29	14 3	29 55	12 4	17 17
14	20 24	7 ♑ 11	14 35	18 ℞ 20	27 8	14 1	0 ♎ 1	12 7	17 19
15	21 22	22 2	14 51	18 17	27 47	13 59	0 8	12 10	17 20
16	22 19	6 ♒ 52	15 2	18 12	28 25	13 57	0 14	12 13	17 22
17	23 17	21 36	15 8	18 4	29 4	13 55	0 20	12 16	17 23
18	24 15	6 ♓ 5	15 ℞ 9	17 54	29 43	13 52	0 26	12 19	17 25
19	25 12	20 14	15 4	17 42	0 ♌ 21	13 49	0 33	12 21	17 26
20	26 10	3 ♈ 59	14 53	17 27	1 0	13 46	0 39	12 24	17 28
21	27 8	17 20	14 36	17 10	1 38	13 43	0 46	12 27	17 29
22	28 6	0 ♉ 18	14 14	16 51	2 17	13 40	0 52	12 30	17 31
23	29 3	12 54	13 46	16 30	2 55	13 36	0 59	12 33	17 33
24	0 ♍ 1	25 13	13 13	16 7	3 34	13 32	1 5	12 35	17 34
25	0 59	7 ♊ 18	12 34	15 41	4 12	13 28	1 12	12 38	17 36
26	1 57	19 15	11 50	15 13	4 51	13 24	1 19	12 40	17 37
27	2 55	1 ♋ 7	11 3	14 43	5 29	13 20	1 26	12 43	17 39
28	3 53	12 59	10 12	14 12	6 7	13 15	1 33	12 46	17 41
29	4 51	24 55	9 19	13 40	6 46	13 10	1 40	12 48	17 43
30	5 49	6 ♌ 58	8 24	13 6	7 24	13 5	1 48	12 51	17 44
31	6 47	19 10	7 26	12 31	8 3	13 1	1 55	12 53	17 46

1951

SEPTEMBER

DAY	☉	☽	☿	♀	♂	♃	♄	♅	♆
	° ′	° ′	° ′	° ′	° ′	° ′	° ′	° ′	° ′
1	7 ♍ 45	1 ♍ 34	6 ♍ 32	11 ♍ 55	8 ♌ 41	12 ♈ 56	2 ♎ 2	12 ♋ 56	17 ♎ 48
2	8 43	14 10	5 ℞ 37	11 ℞ 19	9 19	12 ℞ 50	2 9	12 58	17 50
3	9 41	27 1	4 46	10 43	9 57	12 45	2 16	13 1	17 52
4	10 39	10 ♎ 5	3 58	10 6	10 36	12 39	2 24	13 3	17 54
5	11 37	23 22	3 17	9 29	11 14	12 34	2 31	13 6	17 56
6	12 36	6 ♏ 54	2 42	8 51	11 52	12 28	2 38	13 8	17 58
7	13 34	20 38	2 14	8 14	12 30	12 22	2 45	13 10	18 0
8	14 32	4 ♐ 33	1 53	7 38	13 8	12 15	2 52	13 12	18 2
9	15 30	18 40	1 41	7 4	13 46	12 9	3 0	13 15	18 4
10	16 29	2 ♑ 55	1 D 39	6 31	14 24	12 2	3 7	13 17	18 6
11	17 27	17 17	1 45	5 59	15 2	11 56	3 14	13 19	18 8
12	18 25	1 ♒ 41	2 0	5 29	15 40	11 49	3 21	13 21	18 10
13	19 24	16 5	2 24	5 1	16 18	11 42	3 28	13 23	18 12
14	20 22	0 ♓ 23	2 57	4 34	16 56	11 35	3 36	13 24	18 14
15	21 20	14 31	3 33	4 9	17 33	11 29	3 43	13 26	18 16
16	22 19	28 24	4 28	3 45	18 11	11 22	3 50	13 28	18 18
17	23 17	12 ♈ 0	5 26	3 23	18 49	11 15	3 57	13 30	18 20
18	24 16	25 17	6 31	3 5	19 26	11 7	4 4	13 32	18 22
19	25 14	8 ♉ 13	7 42	2 49	20 4	11 0	4 12	13 33	18 25
20	26 13	20 50	9 0	2 36	20 41	10 52	4 19	13 35	18 27
21	27 12	3 ♊ 11	10 23	2 26	21 19	10 45	4 26	13 37	18 29
22	28 10	15 17	11 51	2 18	21 56	10 37	4 33	13 39	18 31
23	29 9	27 14	13 24	2 12	22 34	10 29	4 41	13 40	18 33
24	0 ♎ 8	9 ♋ 7	14 59	2 8	23 11	10 21	4 48	13 42	18 36
25	1 7	20 59	16 37	2 D 7	23 49	10 14	4 56	13 43	18 38
26	2 5	2 ♌ 56	18 18	2 8	24 26	10 6	5 3	13 45	18 40
27	3 4	15 2	20 1	2 11	25 3	9 58	5 11	13 46	18 42
28	4 3	27 21	21 46	2 16	25 40	9 50	5 18	13 47	18 44
29	5 2	9 ♍ 56	23 32	2 24	26 18	9 42	5 26	13 48	18 47
30	6 1	22 49	25 19	2 34	26 55	9 34	5 33	13 49	18 49

Pluto 20 Leo all month

OCTOBER

DAY	☉	☽	☿	♀	♂	♃	♄	♅	♆
	° ′	° ′	° ′	° ′	° ′	° ′	° ′	° ′	° ′
1	7 ♎ 0	6 ♎ 0	27 ♍ 7	2 ♍ 47	27 ♌ 32	9 ♈ 26	5 ♎ 41	13 ♋ 50	18 ♎ 51
2	7 59	19 29	28 55	3 1	28 9	9 ℞ 18	5 48	13 51	18 53
3	8 58	3 ♏ 14	0 ♎ 43	3 17	28 46	9 10	5 56	13 51	18 55
4	9 57	17 12	2 31	3 35	29 23	9 2	6 3	13 52	18 58
5	10 56	1 ♐ 18	4 19	3 56	0 ♍ 0	8 54	6 11	13 53	19 0
6	11 55	15 29	6 7	4 19	0 37	8 46	6 18	13 54	19 2
7	12 55	29 42	7 54	4 43	1 14	8 38	6 25	13 55	19 4
8	13 54	13 ♑ 54	9 40	5 9	1 51	8 30	6 33	13 55	19 6
9	14 53	28 3	11 26	5 36	2 28	8 22	6 40	13 56	19 9
10	15 52	12 ♒ 7	13 11	6 5	3 4	8 14	6 48	13 56	19 11
11	16 52	26 5	14 56	6 35	3 41	8 6	6 55	13 57	19 13
12	17 51	9 ♓ 55	16 40	7 7	4 18	7 58	7 2	13 57	19 15
13	18 50	23 36	18 24	7 40	4 54	7 50	7 9	13 57	19 17
14	19 50	7 ♈ 6	20 7	8 15	5 31	7 42	7 17	13 58	19 20
15	20 49	20 24	21 49	8 51	6 7	7 35	7 24	13 58	19 22
16	21 49	3 ♉ 27	23 30	9 28	6 44	7 27	7 31	13 58	19 24
17	22 48	16 14	25 11	10 6	7 20	7 20	7 38	13 58	19 26
18	23 48	28 47	26 51	10 45	7 57	7 13	7 45	13 58	19 28
19	24 47	11 ♊ 4	28 30	11 26	8 33	7 5	7 53	13 59	19 31
20	25 47	23 10	0 ♏ 9	12 9	9 10	6 58	8 0	13 59	19 33
21	26 46	5 ♋ 6	1 47	12 53	9 46	6 51	8 7	13 ℞ 59	19 35
22	27 46	16 58	3 24	13 37	10 22	6 44	8 14	13 59	19 37
23	28 46	28 48	5 1	14 22	10 58	6 38	8 21	13 59	19 39
24	29 46	10 ♌ 44	6 37	15 8	11 35	6 31	8 28	13 58	19 41
25	0 ♏ 45	22 49	8 13	15 55	12 11	6 24	8 35	13 58	19 43
26	1 45	5 ♍ 10	9 48	16 44	12 47	6 17	8 42	13 58	19 45
27	2 45	17 50	11 23	17 33	13 23	6 11	8 49	13 58	19 47
28	3 45	0 ♎ 52	12 57	18 23	13 59	6 5	8 56	13 58	19 49
29	4 45	14 19	14 31	19 14	14 35	5 58	9 3	13 57	19 52
30	5 45	28 9	16 4	20 5	15 11	5 52	9 10	13 57	19 54
31	6 45	12 ♏ 20	17 37	20 58	15 47	5 46	9 17	13 57	19 56

Pluto 20 Leo all month

1951

NOVEMBER

Pluto 21 Leo all month

DAY	☉	☽	☿	♀	♂	♃	♄	♅	♆
1	7 ♏ 45	26 ♏ 46	19 ♏ 9	21 ♍ 51	16 ♍ 23	5 ♈ 41	9 ♎ 24	13 ♋ 56	19 ♎ 58
2	8 45	11 ♐ 21	20 41	22 45	16 59	5 ℞ 36	9 31	13 ℞ 56	20 0
3	9 45	25 57	22 12	23 39	17 35	5 30	9 38	13 55	20 3
4	10 45	10 ♑ 29	23 43	24 33	18 10	5 25	9 44	13 55	20 5
5	11 45	24 50	25 13	25 28	18 46	5 20	9 51	13 54	20 7
6	12 45	8 ♒ 59	26 42	26 24	19 21	5 15	9 58	13 53	20 9
7	13 46	22 54	28 12	27 21	19 57	5 11	10 4	13 52	20 11
8	14 46	6 ♓ 36	29 41	28 18	20 32	5 6	10 11	13 51	20 13
9	15 46	20 5	1 ♐ 9	29 15	21 8	5 2	10 17	13 50	20 15
10	16 46	3 ♈ 22	2 38	0 ♎ 13	21 43	4 57	10 24	13 49	20 17
11	17 47	16 29	4 6	1 11	22 18	4 53	10 30	13 48	20 19
12	18 47	29 24	5 33	2 10	22 53	4 50	10 37	13 47	20 21
13	19 47	12 ♉ 8	6 59	3 10	23 29	4 46	10 43	13 45	20 23
14	20 48	24 42	8 25	4 10	24 4	4 43	10 50	13 44	20 25
15	21 48	7 ♊ 4	9 50	5 11	24 39	4 39	10 56	13 43	20 27
16	22 48	19 15	11 15	6 12	25 14	4 36	11 2	13 42	20 29
17	23 49	1 ♋ 16	12 38	7 14	25 49	4 34	11 8	13 40	20 31
18	24 49	13 10	14 1	8 16	26 24	4 31	11 14	13 39	20 33
19	25 50	24 59	15 23	9 18	26 58	4 29	11 20	13 37	20 35
20	26 50	6 ♌ 48	16 44	10 21	27 33	4 26	11 26	13 36	20 37
21	27 51	18 41	18 4	11 23	28 8	4 24	11 32	13 34	20 39
22	28 52	0 ♍ 43	19 22	12 26	28 42	4 23	11 38	13 33	20 41
23	29 52	13 0	20 38	13 30	29 17	4 21	11 44	13 31	20 42
24	0 ♐ 53	25 37	21 53	14 34	29 51	4 20	11 49	13 30	20 44
25	1 54	8 ♎ 40	23 6	15 39	0 ♎ 26	4 19	11 55	13 28	20 46
26	2 54	22 10	24 16	16 43	1 0	4 18	12 0	13 26	20 48
27	3 55	6 ♏ 10	25 23	17 48	1 34	4 18	12 6	13 24	20 49
28	4 56	20 35	26 28	18 53	2 9	4 17	12 11	13 23	20 51
29	5 57	5 ♐ 22	27 29	19 59	2 43	4 16	12 17	13 21	20 52
30	6 57	20 22	28 26	21 5	3 17	4 15	12 22	13 19	20 54

DECEMBER

Pluto 21 Leo all month

DAY	☉	☽	☿	♀	♂	♃	♄	♅	♆
1	7 ♐ 58	5 ♑ 24	29 ♐ 19	22 ♎ 10	3 ♎ 51	4 ♈ 15	12 ♎ 27	13 ♋ 17	20 ♎ 56
2	8 59	20 20	0 ♑ 6	23 16	4 25	4 D 16	12 32	13 ℞ 15	20 57
3	10 0	5 ♒ 1	0 47	24 22	4 59	4 16	12 38	13 14	20 59
4	11 1	19 23	1 22	25 29	5 32	4 17	12 43	13 11	21 0
5	12 2	3 ♓ 24	1 50	26 37	6 6	4 17	12 48	13 9	21 2
6	13 3	17 3	2 9	27 45	6 39	4 19	12 53	13 7	21 4
7	14 4	0 ♈ 23	2 19	28 52	7 13	4 20	12 57	13 5	21 5
8	15 4	13 27	2 ℞ 19	0 ♏ 0	7 46	4 22	13 2	13 2	21 7
9	16 5	26 16	2 8	1 7	8 20	4 23	13 6	13 0	21 8
10	17 6	8 ♉ 53	1 46	2 15	8 53	4 25	13 11	12 58	21 10
11	18 7	21 20	1 12	3 24	9 26	4 28	13 15	12 56	21 11
12	19 8	3 ♊ 37	0 28	4 32	9 59	4 30	13 19	12 53	21 13
13	20 9	15 47	29 ♐ 33	5 41	10 32	4 33	13 24	12 51	21 14
14	21 10	27 49	28 27	6 49	11 5	4 35	13 28	12 48	21 16
15	22 11	9 ♋ 45	27 14	7 58	11 38	4 38	13 32	12 46	21 17
16	23 12	21 36	25 55	9 8	12 11	4 41	13 36	12 44	21 18
17	24 13	3 ♌ 24	24 32	10 17	12 43	4 45	13 40	12 41	21 19
18	25 14	15 13	23 9	11 27	13 16	4 48	13 44	12 39	21 21
19	26 15	27 5	21 49	12 36	13 48	4 52	13 48	12 36	21 22
20	27 17	9 ♍ 5	20 34	13 46	14 21	4 55	13 52	12 34	21 23
21	28 18	21 19	19 25	14 56	14 53	5 0	13 55	12 31	21 24
22	29 19	3 ♎ 52	18 25	16 6	15 25	5 4	13 59	12 29	21 25
23	0 ♑ 20	16 48	17 35	17 17	15 57	5 9	14 2	12 26	21 26
24	1 21	0 ♏ 12	16 56	18 27	16 29	5 13	14 6	12 24	21 27
25	2 22	14 6	16 27	19 37	17 1	5 18	14 9	12 21	21 28
26	3 23	28 30	16 9	20 48	17 32	5 23	14 12	12 18	21 29
27	4 24	13 ♐ 20	16 0	21 58	18 4	5 29	14 15	12 16	21 29
28	5 26	28 29	16 D 4	23 9	18 35	5 34	14 18	12 13	21 30
29	6 27	13 ♑ 45	16 15	24 20	19 7	5 40	14 20	12 11	21 31
30	7 28	29 0	16 34	25 31	19 38	5 45	14 23	12 8	21 32
31	8 29	14 ♒ 1	17 1	26 42	20 9	5 51	14 26	12 5	21 33

1952

JANUARY

Pluto 21 Leo all month

Day	☉	☽	☿	♀	♂	♃	♄	♅	♆
1	9♑30	28♒42	17♐34	27♏53	20♎40	5♈57	14♎28	12♋3	21♎33
2	10 31	12♓57	18 14	29 5	21 11	6 4	14 31	12℞0	21 34
3	11 33	26 47	18 59	0♐16	21 41	6 10	14 33	11 58	21 35
4	12 34	10♈11	19 47	1 27	22 12	6 16	14 36	11 55	21 36
5	13 35	23 14	20 41	2 39	22 42	6 23	14 38	11 52	21 37
6	14 36	5♉57	21 39	3 50	23 12	6 30	14 40	11 50	21 37
7	15 37	18 24	22 40	5 2	23 42	6 38	14 42	11 47	21 38
8	16 38	0♊40	23 44	6 14	24 12	6 45	14 44	11 45	21 38
9	17 40	12 46	24 51	7 26	24 42	6 52	14 46	11 42	21 39
10	18 41	24 45	26 0	8 38	25 11	7 0	14 47	11 39	21 39
11	19 42	6♋39	27 11	9 50	25 41	7 7	14 49	11 37	21 40
12	20 43	18 31	28 24	11 3	26 10	7 15	14 50	11 34	21 40
13	21 44	0♌20	29 39	12 15	26 40	7 23	14 52	11 32	21 41
14	22 45	12 10	0♑56	13 27	27 9	7 31	14 53	11 29	21 41
15	23 46	24 2	2 13	14 39	27 37	7 40	14 54	11 27	21 41
16	24 47	5♍59	3 32	15 52	28 6	7 48	14 55	11 24	21 41
17	25 48	18 4	4 53	17 4	28 34	7 57	14 56	11 22	21 42
18	26 50	0♎21	6 15	18 17	29 3	8 5	14 56	11 19	21 42
19	27 51	12 54	7 37	19 29	29 31	8 14	14 57	11 17	21 42
20	28 52	25 46	9 1	20 42	29 58	8 23	14 57	11 15	21 42
21	29 53	9♏2	10 25	21 54	0♏26	8 33	14 58	11 12	21 42
22	0♒54	22 45	11 50	23 7	0 53	8 42	14 58	11 10	21 42
23	1 55	6♐56	13 16	24 20	1 21	8 52	14 59	11 7	21 42
24	2 56	21 32	14 43	25 33	1 48	9 1	14 59	11 5	21℞42
25	3 57	6♑29	16 11	26 46	2 14	9 11	14℞59	11 3	21 42
26	4 58	21 40	17 40	27 59	2 41	9 21	14 59	11 0	21 42
27	5 59	6♒55	19 9	29 12	3 7	9 31	14 58	10 58	21 42
28	7 0	22 3	20 39	0♑25	3 34	9 41	14 58	10 55	21 42
29	8 1	6♓56	22 10	1 38	4 0	9 51	14 58	10 53	21 42
30	9 2	21 26	23 41	2 51	4 25	10 2	14 57	10 51	21 42
31	10 3	5♈29	25 13	4 4	4 50	10 12	14 57	10 49	21 41

FEBRUARY

Pluto 20 Leo all month

Day	☉	☽	☿	♀	♂	♃	♄	♅	♆
1	11♒4	19♈5	26♑46	5♑18	5♏16	10♈23	14♎56	10♋46	21♎41
2	12 5	2♉15	28 19	6 31	5 41	10 33	14℞55	10℞44	21℞40
3	13 6	15 2	29 53	7 44	6 6	10 44	14 54	10 42	21 40
4	14 7	27 29	1♒28	8 57	6 31	10 55	14 53	10 40	21 40
5	15 7	9♊41	3 4	10 10	6 55	11 6	14 51	10 38	21 39
6	16 8	21 42	4 40	11 24	7 19	11 18	14 50	10 37	21 39
7	17 9	3♋36	6 17	12 37	7 43	11 29	14 48	10 35	21 38
8	18 10	15 25	7 55	13 50	8 6	11 40	14 47	10 33	21 38
9	19 11	27 14	9 34	15 3	8 30	11 52	14 45	10 31	21 37
10	20 11	9♌5	11 13	16 17	8 53	12 3	14 44	10 29	21 37
11	21 12	21 0	12 54	17 30	9 15	12 15	14 42	10 28	21 36
12	22 13	3♍0	14 35	18 44	9 37	12 26	14 41	10 26	21 36
13	23 13	15 8	16 17	19 57	9 58	12 38	14 39	10 24	21 35
14	24 14	27 25	18 0	21 11	10 20	12 50	14 37	10 22	21 34
15	25 14	9♎54	19 44	22 24	10 41	13 2	14 35	10 21	21 34
16	26 15	22 36	21 28	23 38	11 2	13 14	14 32	10 19	21 33
17	27 16	5♏35	23 13	24 51	11 22	13 25	14 30	10 18	21 33
18	28 16	18 51	24 59	26 5	11 42	13 38	14 28	10 16	21 32
19	29 17	2♐28	26 46	27 19	12 2	13 50	14 25	10 15	21 31
20	0♓17	16 25	28 34	28 32	12 21	14 3	14 23	10 13	21 30
21	1 18	0♑43	0♓23	29 46	12 40	14 15	14 20	10 12	21 29
22	2 18	15 18	2 13	0♒59	12 59	14 28	14 18	10 11	21 28
23	3 19	0♒7	4 2	2 13	13 17	14 41	14 15	10 9	21 27
24	4 19	15 4	5 55	3 27	13 35	14 53	14 12	10 8	21 26
25	5 19	29 59	7 47	4 40	13 52	15 5	14 9	10 7	21 25
26	6 20	14♓46	9 40	5 54	14 9	15 18	14 5	10 6	21 24
27	7 20	29 17	11 34	7 8	14 26	15 31	14 2	10 5	21 23
28	8 20	13♈27	13 28	8 22	14 42	15 44	13 59	10 4	21 22
29	9 21	27 11	15 22	9 36	14 58	15 57	13 55	10 3	21 21

1952

MARCH

DAY	☉ ° ′	☽ ° ′	☿ ° ′	♀ ° ′	♂ ° ′	♃ ° ′	♄ ° ′	♅ ° ′	♆ ° ′
1	10 ♓ 21	10 ♉ 29	17 ♓ 17	10 ♒ 49	15 ♏ 13	16 ♈ 10	13 ♎ 52	10 ♋ 2	21 ♎ 20
2	11 21	23 23	19 12	12 3	15 28	16 24	13 ℞ 48	10 ℞ 1	21 ℞ 18
3	12 21	5 ♊ 55	21 7	13 17	15 42	16 37	13 45	10 0	21 17
4	13 22	18 9	23 2	14 31	15 55	16 50	13 41	9 59	21 16
5	14 22	0 ♋ 10	24 56	15 45	16 8	17 3	13 37	9 58	21 15
6	15 22	12 2	26 49	16 58	16 21	17 17	13 34	9 58	21 14
7	16 22	23 51	28 41	18 12	16 33	17 30	13 30	9 57	21 12
8	17 22	5 ♌ 40	0 ♈ 31	19 26	16 45	17 44	13 26	9 57	21 11
9	18 22	17 33	2 19	20 40	16 56	17 57	13 22	9 56	21 10
10	19 22	29 34	4 5	21 54	17 6	18 11	13 18	9 56	21 9
11	20 22	11 ♍ 45	5 48	23 7	17 16	18 24	13 13	9 55	21 7
12	21 21	24 7	7 27	24 21	17 25	18 38	13 9	9 55	21 6
13	22 21	6 ♎ 42	9 2	25 35	17 34	18 52	13 4	9 54	21 4
14	23 21	19 31	10 32	26 49	17 42	19 6	13 0	9 54	21 3
15	24 21	2 ♏ 33	11 58	28 3	17 49	19 20	12 56	9 54	21 2
16	25 20	15 49	13 19	29 16	17 56	19 33	12 51	9 54	21 0
17	26 20	29 17	14 34	0 ♓ 30	18 2	19 47	12 47	9 54	20 59
18	27 20	12 ♐ 59	15 42	1 44	18 8	20 1	12 42	9 D 54	20 58
19	28 20	26 54	16 43	2 58	18 13	20 15	12 38	9 54	20 56
20	29 19	10 ♑ 59	17 37	4 12	18 18	20 29	12 34	9 54	20 55
21	0 ♈ 19	25 16	18 24	5 26	18 21	20 43	12 29	9 54	20 53
22	1 18	9 ♒ 40	19 4	6 40	18 24	20 57	12 25	9 55	20 52
23	2 18	24 10	19 36	7 54	18 26	21 11	12 20	9 55	20 50
24	3 17	8 ♓ 40	19 59	9 8	18 27	21 25	12 16	9 55	20 49
25	4 17	23 6	20 15	10 22	18 R 27	21 39	12 11	9 55	20 47
26	5 16	7 ♈ 22	20 22	11 36	18 27	21 53	12 7	9 56	20 46
27	6 16	21 22	20 23	12 50	18 26	22 8	12 2	9 56	20 44
28	7 15	5 ♉ 2	20 R 17	14 3	18 25	22 22	11 58	9 57	20 43
29	8 14	18 21	20 3	15 17	18 23	22 36	11 53	9 57	20 41
30	9 14	1 ♊ 17	19 42	16 31	18 20	22 50	11 48	9 58	20 39
31	10 13	13 52	19 16	17 45	18 16	23 4	11 44	9 58	20 38

Pluto 19 Leo all month

APRIL

DAY	☉ ° ′	☽ ° ′	☿ ° ′	♀ ° ′	♂ ° ′	♃ ° ′	♄ ° ′	♅ ° ′	♆ ° ′
1	11 ♈ 12	26 ♊ 9	18 ♈ 44	18 ♓ 59	18 ♏ 11	23 ♈ 19	11 ♎ 39	9 ♋ 59	20 ♎ 36
2	12 11	8 ♋ 11	18 ℞ 7	20 12	18 ℞ 6	23 33	11 ℞ 35	9 59	20 ℞ 35
3	13 11	20 4	17 26	21 26	18 0	23 47	11 30	10 0	20 33
4	14 10	1 ♌ 53	16 42	22 40	17 54	24 1	11 25	10 1	20 31
5	15 9	13 43	15 56	23 54	17 46	24 16	11 21	10 2	20 29
6	16 8	25 39	15 9	25 8	17 38	24 30	11 16	10 3	20 28
7	17 7	7 ♍ 45	14 21	26 21	17 29	24 45	11 12	10 4	20 26
8	18 6	20 5	13 34	27 35	17 19	24 59	11 7	10 5	20 24
9	19 5	2 ♎ 41	12 49	28 49	17 9	25 13	11 2	10 6	20 22
10	20 3	15 35	12 5	0 ♈ 3	16 57	25 28	10 58	10 7	20 20
11	21 2	28 46	11 24	1 17	16 45	25 42	10 53	10 9	20 19
12	22 1	12 ♏ 13	10 47	2 30	16 32	25 57	10 49	10 10	20 17
13	23 0	25 54	10 15	3 44	16 18	26 11	10 44	10 11	20 15
14	23 59	9 ♐ 45	9 47	4 58	16 4	26 26	10 40	10 13	20 13
15	24 57	23 45	9 24	6 12	15 49	26 40	10 35	10 14	20 12
16	25 56	7 ♑ 49	9 5	7 26	15 34	26 55	10 31	10 16	20 10
17	26 55	21 55	8 52	8 39	15 18	27 9	10 26	10 17	20 9
18	27 53	6 ♒ 3	8 44	9 53	15 1	27 24	10 22	10 19	20 7
19	28 52	20 12	8 41	11 7	14 44	27 38	10 18	10 21	20 6
20	29 51	4 ♓ 19	8 D 43	12 21	14 26	27 53	10 14	10 22	20 4
21	0 ♉ 49	18 23	8 50	13 35	14 8	28 7	10 9	10 24	20 2
22	1 48	2 ♈ 22	9 2	14 48	13 49	28 22	10 5	10 26	20 1
23	2 46	16 12	9 19	16 2	13 29	28 36	10 1	10 28	19 59
24	3 45	29 52	9 41	17 16	13 9	28 50	9 57	10 30	19 58
25	4 43	13 ♉ 17	10 7	18 30	12 48	29 5	9 53	10 32	19 56
26	5 42	26 24	10 37	19 44	12 27	29 19	9 49	10 34	19 55
27	6 40	9 ♊ 14	11 11	20 57	12 6	29 34	9 45	10 36	19 53
28	7 38	21 45	11 50	22 11	11 44	29 48	9 41	10 38	19 52
29	8 37	4 ♋ 1	12 32	23 25	11 22	0 ♉ 2	9 37	10 40	19 51
30	9 35	16 3	13 17	24 39	11 0	0 17	9 34	10 42	19 49

Pluto 19 Leo all month

1952

MAY

Day	☉	☽	☿	♀	♂	♃	♄	♅	♆
	° ′	° ′	° ′	° ′	° ′	° ′	° ′	° ′	° ′
1	10 ♉ 33	27 ♋ 56	14 ♈ 6	25 ♈ 53	10 ♏ 38	0 ♉ 31	9 ♎ 30	10 ♋ 45	19 ♎ 48
2	11 31	9 ♌ 45	14 59	27 6	10 ℞ 16	0 46	9 ℞ 27	10 47	19 ℞ 46
3	12 30	21 35	15 55	28 20	9 54	1 0	9 23	10 49	19 45
4	13 28	3 ♍ 31	16 53	29 34	9 32	1 14	9 20	10 51	19 43
5	14 26	15 40	17 54	0 ♉ 47	9 10	1 28	9 16	10 54	19 42
6	15 24	28 5	18 58	2 1	8 48	1 43	9 13	10 56	19 40
7	16 22	10 ♎ 50	20 6	3 14	8 26	1 57	9 9	10 59	19 39
8	17 20	23 58	21 16	4 28	8 4	2 11	9 6	11 1	19 37
9	18 18	7 ♏ 28	22 28	5 42	7 42	2 25	9 3	11 4	19 36
10	19 16	21 18	23 43	6 55	7 21	2 39	9 0	11 6	19 34
11	20 14	5 ♐ 25	25 1	8 9	7 0	2 53	8 57	11 9	19 33
12	21 12	19 43	26 21	9 22	6 39	3 7	8 54	11 11	19 31
13	22 10	4 ♑ 7	27 43	10 36	6 19	3 21	8 51	11 14	19 30
14	23 8	18 31	29 8	11 50	5 59	3 35	8 48	11 17	19 29
15	24 5	2 ♒ 50	0 ♉ 35	13 3	5 40	3 49	8 46	11 19	19 28
16	25 3	17 3	2 3	14 17	5 21	4 3	8 43	11 22	19 26
17	26 1	1 ♓ 7	3 34	15 30	5 2	4 17	8 41	11 25	19 25
18	26 59	15 2	5 7	16 44	4 44	4 31	8 38	11 28	19 24
19	27 57	28 48	6 43	17 58	4 27	4 45	8 36	11 31	19 23
20	28 54	12 ♈ 24	8 21	19 11	4 10	4 59	8 34	11 33	19 22
21	29 52	25 51	10 1	20 25	3 54	5 13	8 32	11 36	19 21
22	0 ♊ 50	9 ♉ 6	11 43	21 38	3 38	5 26	8 30	11 39	19 20
23	1 48	22 9	13 27	22 52	3 23	5 40	8 28	11 42	19 19
24	2 45	4 ♊ 59	15 14	24 6	3 8	5 53	8 26	11 45	19 18
25	3 43	17 35	17 3	25 19	2 54	6 7	8 25	11 47	19 17
26	4 41	29 57	18 54	26 33	2 41	6 20	8 23	11 50	19 15
27	5 38	12 ♋ 6	20 47	27 46	2 30	6 34	8 22	11 53	19 14
28	6 36	24 4	22 43	29 0	2 20	6 47	8 20	11 56	19 13
29	7 33	5 ♌ 55	24 41	0 ♊ 14	2 9	7 0	8 19	11 59	19 12
30	8 31	17 43	26 40	1 27	1 59	7 13	8 18	12 3	19 12
31	9 28	29 32	28 41	2 41	1 50	7 27	8 17	12 6	19 11

Pluto 19 Leo all month

JUNE

Day	☉	☽	☿	♀	♂	♃	♄	♅	♆
	° ′	° ′	° ′	° ′	° ′	° ′	° ′	° ′	° ′
1	10 ♊ 26	11 ♍ 28	0 ♊ 44	3 ♊ 55	1 ♏ 43	7 ♉ 40	8 ♎ 16	12 ♋ 10	19 ♎ 10
2	11 23	23 36	2 49	5 9	1 ℞ 37	7 53	8 ℞ 15	12 13	19 ℞ 9
3	12 21	6 ♎ 2	4 56	6 23	1 30	8 6	8 15	12 16	19 8
4	13 18	18 50	7 4	7 36	1 24	8 19	8 14	12 19	19 8
5	14 16	2 ♏ 3	9 14	8 50	1 19	8 32	8 14	12 23	19 7
6	15 13	15 43	11 24	10 4	1 16	8 45	8 13	12 26	19 6
7	16 10	29 48	13 35	11 18	1 14	8 58	8 13	12 29	19 5
8	17 8	14 ♐ 14	15 47	12 32	1 11	9 11	8 13	12 32	19 4
9	18 5	28 55	17 59	13 46	1 9	9 24	8 13	12 36	19 4
10	19 2	13 ♑ 43	20 11	15 0	1 8	9 37	8 12	12 39	19 3
11	20 0	28 30	22 23	16 13	1 D 9	9 49	8 D 12	12 43	19 3
12	20 57	13 ♒ 10	24 36	17 27	1 11	10 2	8 12	12 46	19 2
13	21 54	27 37	26 44	18 41	1 12	10 14	8 12	12 50	19 2
14	22 52	11 ♓ 48	28 53	19 54	1 14	10 27	8 12	12 53	19 2
15	23 49	25 43	1 ♋ 1	21 8	1 17	10 39	8 13	12 57	19 1
16	24 46	9 ♈ 22	3 9	22 21	1 22	10 52	8 13	13 0	19 0
17	25 44	22 45	5 15	23 35	1 28	11 4	8 13	13 4	18 59
18	26 41	5 ♉ 54	7 18	24 49	1 34	11 16	8 14	13 7	18 59
19	27 38	18 50	9 19	26 2	1 41	11 28	8 15	13 11	18 58
20	28 35	1 ♊ 33	11 18	27 16	1 48	11 40	8 16	13 14	18 58
21	29 33	14 4	13 16	28 29	1 56	11 52	8 17	13 18	18 57
22	0 ♋ 30	26 24	15 12	29 43	2 4	12 4	8 18	13 21	18 57
23	1 27	8 ♋ 34	17 5	0 ♋ 57	2 14	12 15	8 19	13 25	18 57
24	2 24	20 34	18 56	2 10	2 24	12 27	8 21	13 28	18 57
25	3 22	2 ♌ 27	20 46	3 24	2 35	12 38	8 22	13 32	18 56
26	4 19	14 15	22 33	4 38	2 46	12 50	8 24	13 35	18 56
27	5 16	26 1	24 17	5 52	2 58	13 1	8 25	13 39	18 56
28	6 13	7 ♍ 50	26 0	7 6	3 11	13 12	8 27	13 43	18 56
29	7 11	19 46	27 40	8 19	3 25	13 23	8 28	13 46	18 56
30	8 8	1 ♎ 53	29 18	9 33	3 39	13 34	8 30	13 50	18 D 56

Pluto 19 Leo all month

1952

JULY

DAY	☉	☽	☿	♀	♂	♃	♄	♅	♆
	° ′	° ′	° ′	° ′	° ′	° ′	° ′	° ′	° ′
1	9 ♋ 5	14 ♎ 18	0 ♌ 54	10 ♋ 47	3 ♏ 53	13 ♉ 45	8 ♎ 32	13 ♋ 53	18 ♎ 56
2	10 2	27 4	2 27	12 1	4 8	13 56	8 34	13 57	18 56
3	10 59	10 ♏ 15	3 58	13 15	4 24	14 7	8 36	14 1	18 56
4	11 57	23 55	5 27	14 28	4 40	14 17	8 39	14 4	18 56
5	12 54	8 ♐ 2	6 54	15 42	4 57	14 28	8 41	14 8	18 57
6	13 51	22 35	8 18	16 56	5 14	14 38	8 44	14 12	18 57
7	14 48	7 ♑ 27	9 40	18 10	5 32	14 49	8 46	14 16	18 57
8	15 45	22 30	11 0	19 24	5 50	14 59	8 49	14 20	18 57
9	16 43	7 ♒ 36	12 17	20 37	6 9	15 9	8 51	14 23	18 58
10	17 40	22 36	13 32	21 51	6 28	15 19	8 54	14 27	18 58
11	18 37	7 ♓ 21	14 44	23 5	6 48	15 29	8 57	14 30	18 59
12	19 34	21 47	15 53	24 19	7 9	15 39	9 0	14 34	18 59
13	20 31	5 ♈ 51	17 0	25 33	7 30	15 49	9 3	14 38	18 59
14	21 29	19 33	18 4	26 46	7 51	15 58	9 7	14 41	19 0
15	22 26	2 ♉ 53	19 5	28 0	8 13	16 8	9 10	14 45	19 0
16	23 23	15 54	20 3	29 14	8 35	16 17	9 14	14 48	19 1
17	24 20	28 37	20 58	0 ♌ 28	8 58	16 27	9 17	14 52	19 1
18	25 18	11 ♊ 6	21 50	1 42	9 21	16 36	9 21	14 56	19 2
19	26 15	23 23	22 39	2 55	9 45	16 45	9 24	14 59	19 2
20	27 12	5 ♋ 30	23 24	4 9	10 9	16 54	9 28	15 3	19 3
21	28 9	17 28	24 5	5 23	10 33	17 3	9 31	15 6	19 3
22	29 7	29 21	24 43	6 37	10 58	17 12	9 35	15 10	19 4
23	0 ♌ 4	11 ♌ 9	25 17	7 51	11 23	17 20	9 39	15 13	19 5
24	1 1	22 56	25 47	9 4	11 49	17 28	9 43	15 17	19 5
25	1 59	4 ♍ 43	26 12	10 18	12 15	17 37	9 48	15 20	19 6
26	2 56	16 34	26 33	11 32	12 41	17 45	9 52	15 24	19 7
27	3 53	28 33	26 49	12 46	13 8	17 53	9 56	15 27	19 8
28	4 51	10 ♎ 42	27 1	14 0	13 35	18 0	10 1	15 30	19 9
29	5 48	23 7	27 8	15 13	14 2	18 8	10 5	15 34	19 9
30	6 45	5 ♏ 51	27 10	16 27	14 30	18 15	10 10	15 37	19 10
31	7 43	18 58	27 R 7	17 41	14 58	18 23	10 14	15 41	19 11

Pluto 19 Leo all month

AUGUST

DAY	☉	☽	☿	♀	♂	♃	♄	♅	♆
	° ′	° ′	° ′	° ′	° ′	° ′	° ′	° ′	° ′
1	8 ♌ 40	2 ♐ 30	26 ♌ 58	18 ♌ 55	15 ♏ 27	18 ♉ 30	10 ♎ 19	15 ♋ 44	19 ♎ 12
2	9 38	16 30	26 44	20 9	15 55	18 37	10 24	15 47	19 13
3	10 35	0 ♑ 57	26 26	21 23	16 24	18 44	10 28	15 51	19 14
4	11 32	15 45	26 2	22 37	16 54	18 51	10 33	15 54	19 15
5	12 30	0 ♒ 50	25 33	23 51	17 24	18 57	10 38	15 58	19 16
6	13 27	16 2	24 59	25 5	17 55	19 4	10 43	16 1	19 17
7	14 25	1 ♓ 13	24 22	26 19	18 25	19 10	10 48	16 4	19 18
8	15 22	16 12	23 41	27 33	18 56	19 16	10 53	16 7	19 19
9	16 20	0 ♈ 52	22 57	28 47	19 27	19 22	10 59	16 11	19 21
10	17 17	15 9	22 10	0 ♍ 1	19 59	19 28	11 4	16 14	19 22
11	18 15	29 0	21 21	1 15	20 31	19 34	11 9	16 17	19 23
12	19 12	12 ♉ 25	20 32	2 29	21 2	19 39	11 14	16 20	19 24
13	20 10	25 26	19 43	3 43	21 34	19 44	11 20	16 23	19 26
14	21 8	8 ♊ 5	18 55	4 57	22 6	19 49	11 25	16 27	19 27
15	22 5	20 27	18 9	6 11	22 39	19 54	11 31	16 30	19 29
16	23 3	2 ♋ 35	17 26	7 25	23 13	19 59	11 36	16 33	19 30
17	24 1	14 33	16 47	8 39	23 46	20 3	11 42	16 36	19 32
18	24 58	26 24	16 12	9 52	24 19	20 7	11 47	16 39	19 33
19	25 56	8 ♌ 12	15 43	11 6	24 53	20 12	11 53	16 42	19 35
20	26 54	19 59	15 20	12 20	25 27	20 16	11 59	16 45	19 36
21	27 52	1 ♍ 47	15 4	13 34	26 2	20 20	12 5	16 48	19 38
22	28 49	13 40	14 55	14 48	26 37	20 24	12 11	16 51	19 40
23	29 47	25 38	14 54	16 1	27 11	20 27	12 17	16 53	19 41
24	0 ♍ 45	7 ♎ 45	15 D 0	17 15	27 46	20 31	12 23	16 56	19 43
25	1 43	20 2	15 14	18 29	28 21	20 34	12 29	16 59	19 44
26	2 41	2 ♏ 32	15 36	19 43	28 56	20 38	12 35	17 2	19 46
27	3 39	15 19	16 6	20 57	29 32	20 40	12 41	17 5	19 48
28	4 37	28 24	16 44	22 11	0 ♐ 8	20 43	12 48	17 7	19 49
29	5 35	11 ♐ 51	17 30	23 25	0 44	20 45	12 54	17 10	19 51
30	6 33	25 40	18 23	24 39	1 20	20 48	13 1	17 12	19 52
31	7 31	9 ♑ 52	19 23	25 53	1 56	20 50	13 7	17 15	19 54

Pluto 20 Leo all month

1952

SEPTEMBER

Pluto 21 Leo all month

Day	☉	☽	☿	♀	♂	♃	♄	♅	♆
	° ′	° ′	° ′	° ′	° ′	° ′	° ′	° ′	° ′
1	8 ♍ 29	24 ♑ 26	20 ♌ 30	27 ♍ 7	2 ♐ 33	20 ♉ 51	13 ♎ 14	17 ♋ 18	19 ♎ 56
2	9 27	9 ♒ 17	21 43	28 21	3 10	20 53	13 20	17 20	19 58
3	10 25	24 20	23 2	29 35	3 47	20 54	13 27	17 23	19 59
4	11 23	9 ♓ 27	24 27	0 ♎ 49	4 24	20 56	13 33	17 25	20 1
5	12 21	24 27	25 57	2 3	5 1	20 57	13 40	17 28	20 3
6	13 20	9 ♈ 14	27 31	3 17	5 39	20 57	13 47	17 30	20 5
7	14 18	23 39	29 9	4 31	6 17	20 58	13 53	17 33	20 7
8	15 16	7 ♉ 39	0 ♍ 51	5 45	6 55	20 58	14 0	17 35	20 8
9	16 14	21 11	2 36	6 59	7 33	20 59	14 6	17 38	20 10
10	17 13	4 ♊ 16	4 23	8 13	8 11	20 59	14 13	17 40	20 12
11	18 11	16 57	6 13	9 27	8 50	20 R 58	14 20	17 42	20 14
12	19 9	29 17	8 3	10 41	9 28	20 58	14 26	17 44	20 16
13	20 8	11 ♋ 23	9 54	11 55	10 7	20 57	14 33	17 46	20 18
14	21 6	23 17	11 46	13 8	10 46	20 57	14 40	17 48	20 20
15	22 5	5 ♌ 5	13 39	14 22	11 25	20 56	14 47	17 50	20 22
16	23 3	16 52	15 32	15 36	12 5	20 54	14 54	17 52	20 24
17	24 2	28 40	17 25	16 50	12 44	20 53	15 1	17 54	20 26
18	25 0	10 ♍ 34	19 17	18 4	13 24	20 51	15 8	17 56	20 28
19	25 59	22 34	21 10	19 17	14 3	20 50	15 15	17 58	20 30
20	26 58	4 ♎ 45	23 2	20 31	14 43	20 48	15 22	18 0	20 32
21	27 56	17 5	24 54	21 45	15 23	20 46	15 29	18 2	20 34
22	28 55	29 37	26 45	22 59	16 3	20 43	15 36	18 3	20 36
23	29 54	12 ♏ 22	28 35	24 13	16 44	20 41	15 44	18 5	20 39
24	0 ♎ 52	25 20	0 ♎ 24	25 26	17 24	20 38	15 51	18 6	20 41
25	1 51	8 ♐ 32	2 12	26 40	18 4	20 36	15 58	18 8	20 43
26	2 50	21 59	3 59	27 54	18 45	20 32	16 5	18 9	20 45
27	3 49	5 ♑ 42	5 46	29 7	19 25	20 29	16 12	18 11	20 47
28	4 48	19 41	7 32	0 ♏ 21	20 6	20 25	16 20	18 12	20 50
29	5 47	3 ♒ 57	9 17	1 34	20 47	20 22	16 27	18 14	20 52
30	6 46	18 27	11 1	2 48	21 28	20 18	16 34	18 15	20 54

OCTOBER

Pluto 22 Leo all month

Day	☉	☽	☿	♀	♂	♃	♄	♅	♆
	° ′	° ′	° ′	° ′	° ′	° ′	° ′	° ′	° ′
1	7 ♎ 45	3 ♓ 9	12 ♎ 44	4 ♏ 2	22 ♐ 10	20 ♉ 14	16 ♎ 41	18 ♋ 16	20 ♎ 56
2	8 44	17 57	14 26	5 15	22 51	20 ℞ 9	16 49	18 17	20 58
3	9 43	2 ♈ 44	16 7	6 29	23 33	20 5	16 56	18 19	21 1
4	10 42	17 22	17 48	7 42	24 14	20 0	17 4	18 20	21 3
5	11 41	1 ♉ 44	19 27	8 56	24 56	19 56	17 11	18 21	21 5
6	12 40	15 44	21 6	10 10	25 38	19 51	17 18	18 22	21 7
7	13 39	29 18	22 44	11 23	26 20	19 45	17 26	18 23	21 9
8	14 38	12 ♊ 27	24 21	12 37	27 3	19 40	17 33	18 24	21 12
9	15 38	25 11	25 58	13 50	27 45	19 34	17 41	18 25	21 14
10	16 37	7 ♋ 34	27 34	15 4	28 27	19 29	17 48	18 26	21 16
11	17 36	19 40	29 9	16 17	29 10	19 23	17 55	18 27	21 18
12	18 36	1 ♌ 34	0 ♏ 43	17 31	29 52	19 17	18 3	18 27	21 21
13	19 35	13 22	2 16	18 44	0 ♑ 35	19 11	18 10	18 28	21 23
14	20 35	25 9	3 49	19 58	1 17	19 5	18 18	18 28	21 26
15	21 34	7 ♍ 0	5 21	21 11	2 0	18 59	18 25	18 29	21 28
16	22 34	18 59	6 53	22 24	2 43	18 52	18 32	18 29	21 30
17	23 33	1 ♎ 9	8 24	23 38	3 26	18 45	18 39	18 30	21 32
18	24 33	13 33	9 54	24 51	4 10	18 38	18 47	18 30	21 35
19	25 32	26 11	11 24	26 5	4 53	18 32	18 54	18 31	21 37
20	26 32	9 ♏ 3	12 53	27 18	5 36	18 25	19 1	18 31	21 39
21	27 32	22 9	14 21	28 31	6 20	18 18	19 8	18 31	21 41
22	28 31	5 ♐ 27	15 49	29 45	7 3	18 11	19 15	18 31	21 43
23	29 31	18 56	17 16	0 ♐ 58	7 47	18 3	19 23	18 32	21 46
24	0 ♏ 31	2 ♑ 35	18 42	2 12	8 30	17 56	19 30	18 32	21 48
25	1 31	16 23	20 7	3 25	9 14	17 49	19 37	18 ℞ 32	21 50
26	2 31	0 ♒ 19	21 32	4 38	9 58	17 41	19 44	18 32	21 52
27	3 31	14 23	22 56	5 51	10 42	17 34	19 51	18 32	21 54
28	4 30	28 35	24 19	7 5	11 27	17 26	19 59	18 31	21 57
29	5 30	12 ♓ 54	25 41	8 18	12 11	17 19	20 6	18 31	21 59
30	6 30	27 16	27 2	9 31	12 55	17 11	20 13	18 31	22 1
31	7 30	11 ♈ 37	28 23	10 44	13 39	17 3	20 20	18 31	22 3

1952

DAY	☉	☽	☿	♀	♂	♃	♄	♅	♆
1	8 ♏ 30	25 ♈ 53	29 ♏ 42	11 ♐ 57	14 ♑ 24	16 ♉ 55	20 ♎ 27	18 ♋ 30	22 ♎ 5
2	9 30	9 ♉ 58	0 ♐ 59	13	11 15	8 16 ℞ 46	20	35 18 ℞ 30	22 7
3	10 30	23 46	2 16	14	24 15	53 16	38 20	42 18	29 22 9
4	11 31	7 ♊ 14	3 31	15	37 16	37 16	30 20	49 18	29 22 11
5	12 31	20 19	4 44	16	50 17	22 16	22 20	56 18	28 22 13
6	13 31	3 ♋ 2	5 56	18	3 18	6 16	14 21	3 18	28 22 15
7	14 31	15 26	7 6	19	16 18	51 16	6 21	10 18	27 22 18
8	15 31	27 32	8 14	20	29 19	36 15	58 21	17 18	26 22 20
9	16 32	9 ♌ 27	9 19	21	42 20	21 15	50 21	24 18	25 22 22
10	17 32	21 16	10 22	22	55 21	6 15	42 21	31 18	24 22 24
11	18 32	3 ♍ 4	11 21	24	8 21	51 15	34 21	38 18	23 22 26
12	19 33	14 56	12 16	25	21 22	36 15	25 21	45 18	22 22 28
13	20 33	26 59	13 8	26	34 23	21 15	17 21	51 18	21 22 30
14	21 33	9 ♎ 15	13 56	27	47 24	6 15	9 21	58 18	20 22 32
15	22 34	21 49	14 38	29	0 24	51 15	1 22	5 18	19 22 34
16	23 34	4 ♏ 42	15 14	0 ♑ 13	25	37 14	54 22	11 18	18 22 36
17	24 35	17 54	15 44	1	26 26	22 14	46 22	18 18	16 22 38
18	25 35	1 ♐ 23	16 8	2	38 27	8 14	38 22	24 18	15 22 40
19	26 36	15 7	16 24	3	51 27	53 14	30 22	31 18	14 22 42
20	27 37	29 2	16 31	5	3 28	38 14	22 22	37 18	13 22 44
21	28 37	13 ♑ 3	16 ℞ 29	6	16 29	24 14	15 22	43 18	11 22 46
22	29 38	27 9	16 17	7	28 0 ♒	9 14	7 22	49 18	10 22 47
23	0 ♐ 38	11 ♒ 15	15 54	8	41 0	55 14	0 22	56 18	9 22 49
24	1 39	25 21	15 21	9	53 1	40 13	52 23	2 18	7 22 51
25	2 40	9 ♓ 26	14 37	11	5 2	26 13	45 23	8 18	5 22 53
26	3 41	23 29	13 43	12	18 3	11 13	38 23	14 18	4 22 55
27	4 41	7 ♈ 29	12 39	13	30 3	57 13	30 23	21 18	2 22 56
28	5 42	21 25	11 27	14	43 4	42 13	23 23	27 18	1 22 58
29	6 43	5 ♉ 13	10 9	15	55 5	28 13	16 23	33 17	59 23 0
30	7 44	18 52	8 48	17	7 6	14 13	9 23	39 17	57 23 2

NOVEMBER

DAY	☉	☽	☿	♀	♂	♃	♄	♅	♆
1	8 ♐ 44	2 ♊ 17	7 ♐ 25	18 ♑ 19	6 ♒ 59	13 ♉ 8	3 ♎ 23	17 ♋ 56	23 ♎ 3
2	9 45	15 27	6 ℞ 5	19	31 7	45 12 ℞ 56 23	51 17 ℞ 54 23	5
3	10 46	28 20	4 49	20	43 8	31 12	50 23	53 17	52 23 6
4	11 47	10 ♋ 56	3 38	21	55 9	17 12	43 24	2 17	50 23 8
5	12 48	23 14	2 38	23	7 10	3 12	37 24	8 17	48 23 10
6	13 49	5 ♌ 19	1 48	24	18 10	49 12	32 24	13 17	46 23 11
7	14 50	17 14	1 7	25	30 11	35 12	26 24	19 17	44 23 13
8	15 50	29 2	0 39	26	41 12	21 12	20 24	24 17	42 23 14
9	16 51	10 ♍ 50	0 22	27	53 13	7 12	14 24	30 17	40 23 16
10	17 52	22 43	0 16	29	4 13	53 12	9 24	35 17	38 23 17
11	18 53	4 ♎ 45	0 D 21	0 ♒ 16	14	39 12	4 24	40 17	36 23 19
12	19 54	17 3	0 35	1	27 15	26 11	59 24	46 17	33 23 20
13	20 55	29 39	0 57	2	39 16	12 11	54 24	51 17	31 23 22
14	21 57	12 ♏ 39	1 27	3	50 16	58 11	49 24	56 17	29 23 23
15	22 58	26 2	2 5	5	1 17	44 11	45 25	1 17	27 23 24
16	23 59	9 ♐ 47	2 49	6	12 18	30 11	41 25	6 17	24 23 25
17	25 0	23 53	3 38	7	23 19	17 11	37 25	11 17	22 23 27
18	26 1	8 ♑ 13	4 33	8	34 20	3 11	33 25	15 17	19 23 28
19	27 2	22 43	5 32	9	45 20	49 11	29 25	20 17	17 23 29
20	28 3	7 ♒ 15	6 35	10	55 21	35 11	26 25	25 17	15 23 30
21	29 4	21 44	7 41	12	6 22	21 11	23 25	29 17	12 23 31
22	0 ♑ 5	6 ♓ 7	8 49	13	16 23	8 11	20 25	34 17	10 23 33
23	1 6	20 20	10 1	14	27 23	54 11	17 25	38 17	7 23 34
24	2 8	4 ♈ 22	11 15	15	37 24	40 11	14 25	43 17	5 23 35
25	3 9	18 12	12 30	16	47 25	26 11	12 25	47 17	2 23 36
26	4 10	1 ♉ 50	13 48	17	57 26	13 11	10 25	51 17	0 23 37
27	5 11	15 15	15 7	19	7 26	59 11	7 25	55 16	57 23 38
28	6 12	28 28	16 26	20	16 27	46 11	5 25	59 16	55 23 39
29	7 13	11 ♊ 29	17 48	21	26 28	32 11	3 26	3 16	52 23 40
30	8 14	24 16	19 10	22	35 29	18 11	2 26	7 16	50 23 41
31	9 16	6 ♋ 51	20 33	23	44 0 ♓ 5 11	1 26	10 16	47 23 42	

DECEMBER

1953

JANUARY

Day	☉	☽	☿	♀	♂	♃	♄	♅	♆
	° ′	° ′	° ′	° ′	° ′	° ′	° ′	° ′	° ′
1	10 ♑ 17	19 ♋ 12	21 ♐ 58	24 ♒ 53	0 ♓ 51	11 ♉ 0	26 ♎ 14	16 ♋ 45	23 ♎ 42
2	11 18	1 ♌ 22	23 23	26 2	1 38	10 ℞ 59	26 17	16 ℞ 42	23 43
3	12 19	13 22	24 49	27 11	2 24	10 58	26 21	16 40	23 44
4	13 20	25 14	26 15	28 19	3 10	10 58	26 24	16 38	23 45
5	14 21	7 ♍ 2	27 42	29 28	3 56	10 58	26 27	16 36	23 45
6	15 22	18 50	29 10	0 ♓ 36	4 43	10 D 58	26 31	16 33	23 46
7	16 23	0 ♎ 42	0 ♑ 39	1 44	5 29	10 58	26 34	16 31	23 46
8	17 25	12 42	2 9	2 52	6 15	10 58	26 37	16 28	23 47
9	18 26	24 57	3 38	3 59	7 1	10 59	26 40	16 25	23 48
10	19 27	7 ♏ 31	5 08	5 7	7 47	11 0	26 42	16 23	23 48
11	20 28	20 27	6 39	6 14	8 34	11 1	26 45	16 20	23 49
12	21 29	3 ♐ 49	8 10	7 22	9 20	11 2	26 47	16 18	23 49
13	22 30	17 37	9 41	8 29	10 6	11 4	26 50	16 15	23 50
14	23 32	1 ♑ 51	11 13	9 36	10 52	11 6	26 52	16 12	23 50
15	24 33	16 26	12 46	10 42	11 38	11 8	26 54	16 10	23 51
16	25 34	1 ♒ 16	14 19	11 48	12 25	11 10	26 57	16 7	23 51
17	26 35	16 14	15 53	12 54	13 11	11 13	26 59	16 5	23 51
18	27 36	1 ♓ 10	17 28	14 0	13 57	11 15	27 1	16 2	23 52
19	28 37	15 58	19 2	15 5	14 43	11 18	27 3	15 59	23 52
20	29 38	0 ♈ 31	20 37	16 10	15 29	11 21	27 4	15 57	23 53
21	0 ♒ 39	14 46	22 13	17 15	16 15	11 25	27 6	15 54	23 53
22	1 40	28 40	23 49	18 20	17 1	11 28	27 7	15 52	23 53
23	2 41	12 ♉ 14	25 26	19 24	17 47	11 31	27 9	15 49	23 53
24	3 42	25 28	27 3	20 27	18 33	11 35	27 10	15 47	23 53
25	4 43	8 ♊ 25	28 41	21 31	19 19	11 39	27 11	15 44	23 53
26	5 44	21 6	0 ♒ 20	22 34	20 5	11 43	27 13	15 42	23 R 53
27	6 45	3 ♋ 33	1 59	23 37	20 51	11 47	27 14	15 39	23 53
28	7 46	15 50	3 39	24 40	21 37	11 51	27 15	15 37	23 53
29	8 47	27 57	5 20	25 42	22 23	11 56	27 16	15 35	23 53
30	9 48	9 ♌ 56	7 1	26 44	23 8	12 1	27 16	15 32	23 53
31	10 49	21 49	8 43	27 45	23 54	12 6	27 17	15 30	23 53

Pluto 22 Leo all month

FEBRUARY

Day	☉	☽	☿	♀	♂	♃	♄	♅	♆
	° ′	° ′	° ′	° ′	° ′	° ′	° ′	° ′	° ′
1	11 ♒ 50	3 ♍ 39	10 ♒ 26	28 ♓ 46	24 ♓ 39	12 ♉ 11	27 ♎ 17	15 ♋ 27	23 ♎ 52
2	12 51	15 27	12 9	29 46	25 25	12 16	27 18	15 ℞ 25	23 ℞ 52
3	13 52	27 16	13 53	0 ♈ 47	26 11	12 21	27 18	15 23	23 52
4	14 52	9 ♎ 10	15 38	1 47	26 56	12 27	27 18	15 21	23 51
5	15 53	21 11	17 24	2 46	27 42	12 33	27 R 18	15 19	23 51
6	16 54	3 ♏ 25	19 10	3 44	28 27	12 39	27 18	15 17	23 50
7	17 55	15 54	20 57	4 41	29 13	12 45	27 18	15 15	23 50
8	18 56	28 44	22 45	5 39	29 58	12 51	27 18	15 13	23 49
9	19 56	11 ♐ 57	24 33	6 36	0 ♈ 44	12 58	27 17	15 11	23 49
10	20 57	25 37	26 22	7 32	1 29	13 5	27 17	15 9	23 48
11	21 58	9 ♑ 44	28 11	8 28	2 15	13 12	27 16	15 7	23 48
12	22 59	24 17	0 ♓ 1	9 23	3 0	13 19	27 16	15 5	23 48
13	23 59	9 ♒ 11	1 50	10 17	3 45	13 26	27 15	15 3	23 47
14	25 0	24 19	3 40	11 11	4 30	13 34	27 14	15 1	23 47
15	26 1	9 ♓ 32	5 30	12 4	5 16	13 41	27 13	15 0	23 46
16	27 1	24 41	7 20	12 57	6 1	13 49	27 12	14 58	23 45
17	28 2	9 ♈ 36	9 9	13 49	6 46	13 56	27 11	14 56	23 44
18	29 2	24 9	10 57	14 40	7 31	14 4	27 9	14 54	23 44
19	0 ♓ 3	8 ♉ 17	12 45	15 30	8 16	14 12	27 8	14 53	23 43
20	1 3	21 58	14 31	16 20	9 2	14 20	27 6	14 51	23 42
21	2 4	5 ♊ 14	16 15	17 9	9 47	14 29	27 5	14 50	23 41
22	3 4	18 5	17 58	17 57	10 32	14 37	27 3	14 48	23 40
23	4 5	0 ♋ 37	19 38	18 44	11 17	14 46	27 1	14 47	23 39
24	5 5	12 54	21 15	19 30	12 1	14 55	26 59	14 45	23 38
25	6 5	24 58	22 47	20 15	12 46	15 4	26 57	14 44	23 37
26	7 6	6 ♌ 54	24 15	20 59	13 31	15 13	26 55	14 42	23 36
27	8 6	18 45	25 38	21 42	14 16	15 22	26 53	14 41	23 35
28	9 6	0 ♍ 34	26 56	22 24	15 1	15 31	26 51	14 40	23 34

Pluto 22 Leo all month

1953

MARCH

DAY	☉	☽	☿	♀	♂	♃	♄	♅	♆
	° ′	° ′	° ′	° ′	° ′	° ′	° ′	° ′	° ′
1	10 ♓ 6	12 ♍ 23	28 ♓ 8	23 ♈ 4	15 ♈ 45	15 ♉ 41	26 ♎ 48	14 ♋ 38	23 ♎ 33
2	11 6	24 13	29 12	23 43	16 30	15 50	26 ℞ 46	14 ℞ 37	23 ℞ 32
3	12 7	6 ♎ 7	0 ♈ 10	24 21	17 15	16 0	26 43	14 36	23 31
4	13 7	18 7	1 0	24 58	18 0	16 10	26 41	14 35	23 30
5	14 7	0 ♏ 15	1 42	25 34	18 44	16 20	26 38	14 34	23 29
6	15 7	12 33	2 15	26 8	19 29	16 30	26 35	14 33	23 27
7	16 7	25 4	2 39	26 41	20 13	16 40	26 32	14 33	23 26
8	17 7	7 ♐ 51	2 54	27 12	20 58	16 50	26 29	14 32	23 25
9	18 7	20 58	3 R 0	27 42	21 42	17 0	26 26	14 31	23 24
10	19 7	4 ♑ 27	2 57	28 11	22 26	17 10	26 23	14 30	23 23
11	20 7	18 20	2 45	28 38	23 11	17 21	26 20	14 30	23 21
12	21 7	2 ♒ 39	2 25	29 2	23 55	17 31	26 16	14 29	23 20
13	22 7	17 20	1 57	29 24	24 40	17 42	26 13	14 29	23 18
14	23 6	2 ♓ 21	1 21	29 44	25 24	17 53	26 10	14 28	23 17
15	24 6	17 32	0 40	0 ♉ 4	26 8	18 4	26 6	14 28	23 16
16	25 6	2 ♈ 45	29 ♓ 55	0 21	26 52	18 15	26 3	14 27	23 14
17	26 6	17 50	29 5	0 36	27 36	18 27	25 59	14 27	23 13
18	27 5	2 ♉ 36	28 11	0 49	28 20	18 38	25 56	14 26	23 11
19	28 5	16 56	27 16	1 0	29 4	18 49	25 52	14 26	23 10
20	29 5	0 ♊ 48	26 21	1 9	29 48	19 0	25 48	14 26	23 9
21	0 ♈ 4	14 11	25 26	1 15	0 ♉ 31	19 12	25 44	14 26	23 7
22	1 4	27 6	24 33	1 19	1 15	19 23	25 40	14 26	23 6
23	2 4	9 ♋ 38	23 43	1 20	1 59	19 35	25 36	14 26	23 4
24	3 3	21 52	22 56	1 ℞ 19	2 43	19 47	25 32	14 26	23 3
25	4 2	3 ♌ 52	22 13	1 16	3 27	19 59	25 28	14 D 26	23 1
26	5 2	15 43	21 35	1 10	4 10	20 11	25 24	14 26	23 0
27	6 1	27 31	21 3	1 2	4 54	20 23	25 19	14 27	22 58
28	7 1	9 ♍ 18	20 36	0 51	5 37	20 35	25 15	14 27	22 57
29	8 0	21 8	20 15	0 38	6 21	20 47	25 11	14 27	22 55
30	8 59	3 ♎ 4	20 0	0 22	7 4	20 59	25 7	14 27	22 53
31	9 58	15 6	19 51	0 4	7 48	21 12	25 3	14 28	22 52

Pluto 21 Leo all month

APRIL

DAY	☉	☽	☿	♀	♂	♃	♄	♅	♆
	° ′	° ′	° ′	° ′	° ′	° ′	° ′	° ′	° ′
1	10 ♈ 58	27 ♎ 17	19 ♓ 47	29 ♈ 44	8 ♉ 31	21 ♉ 24	24 ♎ 58	14 ♋ 28	22 ♎ 50
2	11 57	9 ♏ 37	19 D 50	29 ℞ 21	9 15	21 37	24 ℞ 54	14 29	22 ℞ 49
3	12 56	22 7	19 57	28 56	9 58	21 49	24 50	14 29	22 47
4	13 55	4 ♐ 48	20 9	28 29	10 41	22 2	24 45	14 30	22 45
5	14 54	17 42	20 27	28 0	11 24	22 15	24 41	14 30	22 44
6	15 53	0 ♑ 50	20 49	27 29	12 8	22 27	24 36	14 31	22 42
7	16 52	14 16	21 16	26 57	12 51	22 40	24 32	14 32	22 41
8	17 51	28 0	21 48	26 23	13 34	22 53	24 27	14 33	22 39
9	18 50	12 ♒ 4	22 24	25 47	14 17	23 6	24 22	14 34	22 37
10	19 49	26 28	23 3	25 11	14 59	23 19	24 18	14 35	22 36
11	20 48	11 ♓ 9	23 46	24 34	15 42	23 32	24 13	14 36	22 34
12	21 47	26 3	24 33	23 57	16 25	23 45	24 9	14 37	22 33
13	22 46	11 ♈ 3	25 23	23 19	17 8	23 58	24 4	14 38	22 31
14	23 44	25 59	26 17	22 41	17 51	24 11	23 59	14 39	22 29
15	24 43	10 ♉ 41	27 14	22 4	18 33	24 24	23 55	14 40	22 28
16	25 42	25 3	28 13	21 27	19 16	24 38	23 50	14 42	22 26
17	26 41	8 ♊ 59	29 15	20 50	19 58	24 51	23 46	14 43	22 25
18	27 39	22 26	0 ♈ 20	20 14	20 41	25 4	23 41	14 44	22 23
19	28 38	5 ♋ 26	1 27	19 40	21 23	25 17	23 36	14 46	22 21
20	29 36	18 1	2 37	19 7	22 6	25 31	23 32	14 47	22 19
21	0 ♉ 35	0 ♌ 17	3 49	18 36	22 48	25 44	23 27	14 49	22 18
22	1 34	12 18	5 4	18 6	23 31	25 58	23 23	14 50	22 16
23	2 32	24 10	6 21	17 38	24 13	26 11	23 18	14 52	22 14
24	3 30	5 ♍ 57	7 39	17 12	24 55	26 25	23 14	14 54	22 13
25	4 29	17 46	9 0	16 48	25 37	26 38	23 9	14 55	22 11
26	5 27	29 40	10 24	16 26	26 20	26 52	23 5	14 57	22 10
27	6 26	11 ♎ 42	11 49	16 7	27 2	27 5	23 0	14 58	22 8
28	7 24	23 54	13 16	15 50	27 44	27 19	22 56	15 0	22 7
29	8 22	6 ♏ 18	14 45	15 35	28 26	27 32	22 52	15 2	22 5
30	9 20	18 53	16 16	15 23	29 8	27 46	22 47	15 4	22 4

Pluto 21 Leo all month

1953

MAY

DAY	☉ ° ′	☽ ° ′	☿ ° ′	♀ ° ′	♂ ° ′	♃ ° ′	♄ ° ′	♅ ° ′	♆ ° ′
1	10 ♉ 19	1 ♐ 41	17 ♈ 48	15 ♈ 13	29 ♉ 50	28 ♉ 0	22 ♎ 43	15 ♋ 6	22 ♎ 2
2	11 17	14 40	19 23	15 R 6	0 ♊ 32	28 14	22 ℞ 38	15 8	22 R 1
3	12 15	27 50	20 59	15 1	1 14	28 28	22 34	15 10	21 59
4	13 13	11 ♑ 12	22 38	14 58	1 56	28 42	22 30	15 12	21 58
5	14 11	24 45	24 19	14 D 58	2 37	28 55	22 26	15 14	21 56
6	15 9	8 ♒ 30	26 1	15 0	3 19	29 9	22 22	15 17	21 55
7	16 8	22 29	27 45	15 5	4 0	29 23	22 18	15 19	21 53
8	17 6	6 ♓ 40	29 31	15 11	4 42	29 37	22 14	15 21	21 52
9	18 4	21 3	1 ♉ 19	15 20	5 24	29 51	22 10	15 23	21 51
10	19 2	5 ♈ 34	3 9	15 31	6 5	0 ♊ 5	22 7	15 26	21 49
11	20 0	20 10	5 1	15 44	6 47	0 19	22 3	15 28	21 48
12	20 58	4 ♉ 43	6 55	15 59	7 28	0 33	21 59	15 31	21 46
13	21 56	19 7	8 51	16 17	8 10	0 47	21 55	15 33	21 45
14	22 53	3 ♊ 15	10 49	16 36	8 51	1 1	21 52	15 36	21 44
15	23 51	17 1	12 48	16 57	9 33	1 15	21 48	15 38	21 42
16	24 49	0 ♋ 24	14 49	17 20	10 14	1 29	21 45	15 41	21 41
17	25 47	13 23	16 51	17 44	10 56	1 43	21 41	15 43	21 39
18	26 45	25 59	18 55	18 11	11 37	1 57	21 38	15 46	21 38
19	27 43	8 ♌ 16	21 1	18 39	12 18	2 11	21 35	15 49	21 37
20	28 40	20 19	23 9	19 8	12 59	2 25	21 31	15 51	21 35
21	29 38	2 ♍ 13	25 18	19 39	13 40	2 40	21 28	15 54	21 34
22	0 ♊ 36	14 3	27 28	20 11	14 21	2 54	21 24	15 57	21 32
23	1 33	25 54	29 39	20 44	15 2	3 8	21 21	16 0	21 31
24	2 31	7 ♎ 51	1 ♊ 50	21 19	15 43	3 22	21 18	16 3	21 30
25	3 29	19 58	4 1	21 55	16 23	3 36	21 16	16 6	21 29
26	4 26	2 ♏ 19	6 13	22 32	17 4	3 51	21 13	16 9	21 28
27	5 24	14 54	8 25	23 10	17 45	4 5	21 11	16 12	21 27
28	6 21	27 46	10 36	23 49	18 26	4 19	21 8	16 15	21 26
29	7 19	10 ♐ 52	12 46	24 29	19 7	4 33	21 6	16 18	21 25
30	8 17	24 13	14 56	25 10	19 47	4 47	21 3	16 21	21 23
31	9 14	7 ♑ 46	17 5	25 52	20 28	5 1	21 1	16 24	21 22

Pluto 20 Leo all month

JUNE

DAY	☉ ° ′	☽ ° ′	☿ ° ′	♀ ° ′	♂ ° ′	♃ ° ′	♄ ° ′	♅ ° ′	♆ ° ′
1	10 ♊ 12	21 ♑ 30	19 ♊ 12	26 ♈ 36	21 ♊ 9	5 ♊ 15	20 ♎ 58	16 ♋ 27	21 ♎ 21
2	11 9	5 ♒ 22	21 17	27 21	21 50	5 29	20 ℞ 56	16 30	21 ℞ 20
3	12 7	19 20	23 21	28 6	22 30	5 43	20 54	16 33	21 19
4	13 4	3 ♓ 25	25 23	28 52	23 11	5 57	20 53	16 36	21 18
5	14 1	17 34	27 23	29 39	23 51	6 11	20 51	16 40	21 17
6	14 59	1 ♈ 46	29 20	0 ♉ 26	24 32	6 25	20 49	16 43	21 16
7	15 56	15 59	1 ♋ 15	1 15	25 12	6 39	20 47	16 46	21 16
8	16 54	0 ♉ 11	3 8	2 4	25 52	6 53	20 46	16 49	21 15
9	17 51	14 18	4 58	2 54	26 33	7 6	20 44	16 52	21 15
10	18 48	28 15	6 45	3 45	27 13	7 20	20 43	16 56	21 14
11	19 46	11 ♊ 58	8 30	4 36	27 54	7 34	20 41	16 59	21 14
12	20 43	25 26	10 13	5 28	28 34	7 48	20 40	17 2	21 13
13	21 41	8 ♋ 34	11 53	6 20	29 14	8 2	20 39	17 5	21 12
14	22 38	21 23	13 31	7 13	29 54	8 16	20 38	17 9	21 12
15	23 35	3 ♌ 54	15 6	8 7	0 ♋ 35	8 29	20 37	17 12	21 11
16	24 33	16 10	16 38	9 1	1 15	8 43	20 36	17 16	21 11
17	25 30	28 12	18 8	9 56	1 55	8 57	20 35	17 19	21 10
18	26 27	10 ♍ 7	19 35	10 51	2 35	9 11	20 35	17 23	21 10
19	27 24	21 58	20 59	11 46	3 14	9 25	20 34	17 26	21 9
20	28 22	3 ♎ 50	22 21	12 42	3 54	9 38	20 34	17 30	21 9
21	29 19	15 49	23 40	13 38	4 34	9 52	20 33	17 33	21 8
22	0 ♋ 16	27 58	24 56	14 35	5 14	10 6	20 33	17 37	21 8
23	1 13	10 ♏ 23	26 9	15 32	5 54	10 20	20 33	17 41	21 8
24	2 11	23 6	27 19	16 30	6 33	10 33	20 D 33	17 44	21 7
25	3 8	6 ♐ 08	28 27	17 28	7 13	10 47	20 33	17 48	21 7
26	4 5	19 30	29 32	18 26	7 53	11 0	20 33	17 51	21 7
27	5 2	3 ♑ 10	0 ♌ 33	19 25	8 33	11 14	20 33	17 55	21 7
28	5 59	17 7	1 31	20 24	9 13	11 27	20 34	17 59	21 6
29	6 57	1 ♒ 16	2 25	21 24	9 52	11 40	20 34	18 2	21 6
30	7 54	15 34	3 16	22 24	10 32	11 54	20 35	18 6	21 6

Pluto 20 Leo all month

1953

D A Y	☉	☽	☿	♀	♂	♃	♄	♅	♆
	° ′	° ′	° ′	° ′	° ′	° ′	° ′	° ′	° ′
1	8 ♋ 51	29 ♒ 55	4 ♌ 4	23 ♉ 24	11 ♋ 11	12 ♊ 7	20 ♎ 35	18 ♋ 9	21 ♎ 6
2	9 48	14 ♓ 16	4 48	24 25	11 51	12 20	20 36	18 13	21 R 6
3	10 45	28 35	5 28	25 25	12 30	12 33	20 37	18 17	21 6
4	11 43	12 ♈ 47	6 5	26 26	13 10	12 46	20 38	18 20	21 6
5	12 40	26 52	6 38	27 28	13 49	12 59	20 39	18 24	21 D 6
6	13 37	10 ♉ 47	7 6	28 30	14 29	13 12	20 40	18 27	21 6
7	14 34	24 30	7 30	29 33	15 8	13 25	20 41	18 31	21 6
8	15 31	5 ♊ 2	7 50	0 ♊ 35	15 47	13 38	20 43	18 35	21 6
9	16 29	21 19	8 5	1 37	16 27	13 50	20 44	18 38	21 7
10	17 26	4 ♋ 23	8 16	2 40	17 6	14 3	20 46	18 42	21 7
11	18 23	17 11	8 22	3 43	17 46	14 16	20 47	18 45	21 7
12	19 20	29 46	8 R 23	4 47	18 25	14 29	20 49	18 49	21 7
13	20 18	12 ♌ 6	8 19	5 51	19 4	14 42	20 51	18 53	21 7
14	21 15	24 15	8 10	6 55	19 43	14 54	20 53	18 56	21 8
15	22 12	6 ♍ 15	7 57	7 59	20 23	15 7	20 55	19 0	21 8
16	23 9	18 8	7 39	9 3	21 2	15 19	20 57	19 3	21 8
17	24 7	29 58	7 16	10 7	21 41	15 32	20 59	19 7	21 9
18	25 4	11 ♎ 50	6 50	11 12	22 20	15 44	21 2	19 11	21 10
19	26 1	23 49	6 20	12 17	22 59	15 56	21 4	19 14	21 10
20	26 58	5 ♏ 58	5 46	13 22	23 39	16 9	21 7	19 18	21 11
21	27 56	18 22	5 10	14 27	24 18	16 21	21 9	19 21	21 11
22	28 53	1 ♐ 5	4 31	15 32	24 57	16 33	21 12	19 25	21 12
23	29 50	14 10	3 50	16 38	25 36	16 45	21 15	19 29	21 13
24	0 ♌ 48	27 39	3 8	17 43	26 14	16 56	21 18	19 32	21 14
25	1 45	11 ♑ 32	2 25	18 49	26 53	17 8	21 21	19 36	21 14
26	2 42	25 46	1 43	19 55	27 32	17 20	21 24	19 39	21 15
27	3 39	10 ♒ 17	1 2	21 1	28 11	17 32	21 27	19 43	21 16
28	4 37	25 0	0 21	22 8	28 50	17 43	21 30	19 46	21 17
29	5 34	9 ♓ 48	29 ♋ 43	23 14	29 28	17 55	21 34	19 50	21 17
30	6 31	24 33	29 10	24 21	0 ♌ 7	18 6	21 37	19 53	21 18
31	7 29	9 ♈ 9	28 41	25 28	0 46	18 18	21 41	19 57	21 19

JULY

D A Y	☉	☽	☿	♀	♂	♃	♄	♅	♆
	° ′	° ′	° ′	° ′	° ′	° ′	° ′	° ′	° ′
1	8 ♌ 26	23 ♈ 32	28 ♋ 16	26 ♊ 35	1 ♌ 25	18 ♊ 29	21 ♎ 44	20 ♋ 0	21 ♎ 20
2	9 24	7 ♉ 38	27 R 56	27 42	2 4	18 40	21 48	20 4	21 21
3	10 21	21 26	27 41	28 50	2 42	18 51	21 51	20 7	21 22
4	11 19	4 ♊ 56	27 33	29 57	3 21	19 2	21 55	20 11	21 23
5	12 16	18 8	27 D 31	1 ♋ 5	4 0	19 13	21 58	20 14	21 24
6	13 13	1 ♋ 4	27 35	2 12	4 39	19 24	22 2	20 18	21 25
7	14 11	13 46	27 45	3 20	5 18	19 35	22 6	20 21	21 26
8	15 8	26 16	28 2	4 28	5 56	19 45	22 10	20 25	21 27
9	16 6	8 ♌ 34	28 26	5 37	6 35	19 56	22 15	20 28	21 29
10	17 4	20 42	28 57	6 45	7 13	20 6	22 19	20 32	21 30
11	18 1	2 ♍ 43	29 35	7 53	7 52	20 17	22 23	20 35	21 31
12	18 59	14 38	0 ♌ 19	9 2	8 30	20 27	22 28	20 38	21 32
13	19 56	26 29	1 10	10 10	9 9	20 37	22 32	20 42	21 33
14	20 54	8 ♎ 19	2 8	11 19	9 47	20 47	22 37	20 45	21 35
15	21 52	20 11	3 12	12 28	10 26	20 57	22 41	20 49	21 36
16	22 49	2 ♏ 8	4 22	13 37	11 4	21 7	22 46	20 52	21 37
17	23 47	14 16	5 38	14 46	11 42	21 16	22 51	20 55	21 38
18	24 45	26 37	6 59	15 56	12 21	21 26	22 56	20 58	21 40
19	25 43	9 ♐ 16	8 25	17 5	12 59	21 35	23 1	21 2	21 41
20	26 40	22 17	9 56	18 15	13 38	21 45	23 6	21 5	21 43
21	27 38	5 ♑ 43	11 32	19 24	14 16	21 54	23 11	21 8	21 44
22	28 36	19 36	13 12	20 34	14 54	22 3	23 16	21 11	21 46
23	29 34	3 ♒ 56	14 56	21 43	15 32	22 12	23 22	21 14	21 47
24	0 ♍ 31	18 39	16 43	22 54	16 11	22 20	23 27	21 17	21 49
25	1 29	3 ♓ 39	18 32	24 4	16 50	22 29	23 33	21 20	21 50
26	2 27	18 48	20 24	25 14	17 28	22 38	23 38	21 23	21 52
27	3 25	3 ♈ 55	22 18	26 24	18 6	22 46	23 44	21 26	21 54
28	4 23	18 53	24 14	27 35	18 44	22 54	23 49	21 29	21 56
29	5 21	3 ♉ 32	26 10	28 45	19 23	23 2	23 55	21 32	21 57
30	6 19	17 48	28 7	29 56	20 1	23 11	24 1	21 35	21 59
31	7 17	1 ♊ 39	0 ♍ 5	1 ♌ 6	20 39	23 19	24 6	21 38	22 1

AUGUST

1953

SEPTEMBER

DAY	☉	☽	☿	♀	♂	♃	♄	♅	♆
	° ′	° ′	° ′	° ′	° ′	° ′	° ′	° ′	° ′
1	8 ♍ 15	15 ♊ 5	2 ♍ 3	2 ♌ 17	21 ♌ 17	23 ♊ 27	24 ♎ 12	21 ♋ 41	22 ♎ 3
2	9 13	28 8	4 0	3 28	21 55	23 35	24 17	21 43	22 5
3	10 11	10 ♋ 51	5 58	4 39	22 34	23 42	24 23	21 46	22 6
4	11 9	23 18	7 55	5 50	23 12	23 50	24 29	21 49	22 8
5	12 7	5 ♌ 33	9 51	7 1	23 50	23 58	24 35	21 52	22 10
6	13 6	17 38	11 47	8 13	24 28	24 5	24 41	21 55	22 12
7	14 4	29 37	13 42	9 24	25 6	24 11	24 47	21 57	22 14
8	15 2	11 ♍ 31	15 36	10 36	25 45	24 18	24 53	22 0	22 15
9	16 1	23 22	17 29	11 47	26 23	24 25	24 59	22 3	22 17
10	16 59	5 ♎ 12	19 21	12 59	27 1	24 32	25 5	22 6	22 19
11	17 57	17 3	21 11	14 11	27 39	24 38	25 11	22 8	22 21
12	18 56	28 58	23 1	15 22	28 17	24 44	25 18	22 11	22 23
13	19 54	10 ♏ 57	24 50	16 34	28 55	24 50	25 24	22 13	22 24
14	20 52	23 5	26 37	17 46	29 33	24 56	25 31	22 16	22 26
15	21 51	5 ♐ 24	28 24	18 58	0 ♍ 11	25 2	25 37	22 18	22 28
16	22 49	17 59	0 ♎ 10	20 10	0 49	25 7	25 44	22 20	22 30
17	23 48	0 ♑ 54	1 54	21 22	1 26	25 12	25 50	22 22	22 32
18	24 47	14 13	3 37	22 35	2 4	25 18	25 57	22 25	22 34
19	25 45	27 57	5 20	23 47	2 42	25 23	26 3	22 27	22 36
20	26 44	12 ♒ 10	7 1	24 59	3 20	25 28	26 10	22 29	22 38
21	27 42	26 50	8 41	26 12	3 58	25 32	26 17	22 31	22 40
22	28 41	11 ♓ 51	10 21	27 24	4 35	25 37	26 23	22 33	22 42
23	29 40	27 7	11 59	28 37	5 13	25 41	26 30	22 35	22 44
24	0 ♎ 38	12 ♈ 27	13 36	29 49	5 51	25 46	26 37	22 37	22 46
25	1 37	27 39	15 12	1 ♍ 2	6 29	25 50	26 44	22 39	22 48
26	2 36	12 ♉ 33	16 47	2 15	7 7	25 53	26 51	22 41	22 50
27	3 35	27 2	18 22	3 28	7 44	25 57	26 58	22 42	22 53
28	4 34	11 ♊ 2	19 56	4 41	8 22	26 0	27 5	22 44	22 55
29	5 33	24 33	21 29	5 54	9 0	26 4	27 12	22 45	22 57
30	6 32	7 ♋ 36	23 1	7 7	9 38	26 7	27 19	22 47	22 59

Pluto 23 Leo all month

OCTOBER

DAY	☉	☽	☿	♀	♂	♃	♄	♅	♆
	° ′	° ′	° ′	° ′	° ′	° ′	° ′	° ′	° ′
1	7 ♎ 31	20 ♋ 16	24 ♎ 32	8 ♍ 20	10 ♍ 16	26 ♊ 9	27 ♎ 26	22 ♋ 48	23 ♎ 1
2	8 30	2 ♌ 37	26 2	9 34	10 53	26 11	27 33	22 50	23 3
3	9 29	14 44	27 31	10 47	11 31	26 14	27 41	22 51	23 6
4	10 28	26 42	28 59	12 1	12 9	26 16	27 48	22 53	23 8
5	11 27	8 ♍ 34	0 ♏ 26	13 14	12 47	26 18	27 55	22 54	23 10
6	12 26	20 24	1 53	14 28	13 25	26 20	28 2	22 55	23 12
7	13 25	2 ♎ 14	3 19	15 41	14 2	26 21	28 9	22 56	23 15
8	14 25	14 7	4 43	16 55	14 40	26 23	28 17	22 57	23 17
9	15 24	26 2	6 7	18 8	15 17	26 24	28 24	22 58	23 20
10	16 23	8 ♏ 3	7 30	19 22	15 55	26 26	28 31	22 59	23 22
11	17 22	20 10	8 51	20 36	16 33	26 26	28 38	23 0	23 24
12	18 22	2 ♐ 24	10 12	21 49	17 10	26 26	28 45	23 0	23 26
13	19 21	14 48	11 32	23 3	17 48	26 26	28 52	23 1	23 29
14	20 21	27 25	12 50	24 17	18 25	26 26	28 59	23 2	23 31
15	21 20	10 ♑ 18	14 7	25 31	19 3	26 26	29 6	23 3	23 33
16	22 20	23 30	15 23	26 45	19 40	26 ℞ 26	29 13	23 3	23 35
17	23 19	7 ♒ 5	16 37	27 59	20 18	26 26	29 20	23 4	23 37
18	24 19	21 5	17 50	29 13	20 55	26 26	29 27	23 4	23 40
19	25 18	5 ♓ 30	19 1	0 ♎ 27	21 33	26 25	29 34	23 5	23 42
20	26 18	20 19	20 10	1 41	22 10	26 25	29 41	23 5	23 44
21	27 18	5 ♈ 24	21 17	2 55	22 47	26 24	29 48	23 5	23 46
22	28 17	20 38	22 23	4 10	23 25	26 23	29 55	23 6	23 49
23	29 17	5 ♉ 49	23 26	5 25	24 2	26 21	0 ♏ 3	23 6	23 51
24	0 ♏ 17	20 47	24 26	6 39	24 40	26 20	0 10	23 7	23 54
25	1 16	5 ♊ 23	25 23	7 53	25 17	26 18	0 17	23 7	23 56
26	2 16	19 31	26 17	9 7	25 54	26 16	0 24	23 7	23 58
27	3 16	3 ♋ 8	27 7	10 22	26 32	26 13	0 31	23 7	24 0
28	4 16	16 17	27 53	11 36	27 9	26 11	0 39	23 ℞ 7	24 3
29	5 16	29 0	28 34	12 51	27 47	26 8	0 46	23 7	24 5
30	6 16	11 ♌ 22	29 10	14 5	28 24	26 6	0 53	23 7	24 7
31	7 16	23 29	29 42	15 20	29 1	26 3	1 0	23 7	24 9

Pluto 24 Leo all month

1953

NOVEMBER

DAY	☉	☽	☿	♀	♂	♃	♄	♅	♆
	° ′	° ′	° ′	° ′	° ′	° ′	° ′	° ′	° ′
1	8 ♏ 16	5 ♍ 25	0 ♐ 8	16 ♎ 34	29 ♍ 39	25 ♊ 59	1 ♏ 7	23 ♋ 6	24 ♎ 11
2	9 16	17 16	0 27	17 49	0 ♎ 16	25 ℞ 56	1 15	23 ℞ 6	24 14
3	10 16	29 5	0 38	19 4	0 54	25 52	1 22	23 6	24 16
4	11 16	10 ♎ 57	0 R 41	20 19	1 31	25 29	1 29	23 6	24 18
5	12 16	22 53	0 36	21 34	2 8	25 45	1 36	23 5	24 20
6	13 17	4 ♏ 56	0 22	22 49	2 45	25 41	1 43	23 5	24 22
7	14 17	17 7	29 ♏ 58	24 4	3 23	25 36	1 51	23 4	24 25
8	15 17	29 26	29 24	25 19	4 0	25 32	1 58	23 4	24 27
9	16 17	11 ♐ 54	28 41	26 34	4 37	25 28	2 5	23 3	24 29
10	17 18	24 31	27 48	27 49	5 14	25 23	2 12	23 2	24 31
11	18 18	7 ♑ 20	26 45	29 4	5 51	25 18	2 19	23 2	24 33
12	19 18	20 21	25 35	0 ♏ 19	6 29	25 12	2 27	23 1	24 35
13	20 19	3 ♒ 37	24 20	1 34	7 6	25 7	2 34	23 1	24 37
14	21 19	17 9	23 1	2 49	7 43	25 2	2 41	23 0	24 39
15	22 20	1 ♓ 0	21 40	4 4	8 20	24 56	2 48	22 59	24 41
16	23 20	15 10	20 21	5 19	8 57	24 50	2 55	22 58	24 43
17	24 20	29 39	19 6	6 35	9 34	24 43	3 2	22 57	24 45
18	25 21	14 ♈ 22	17 57	7 50	10 11	24 37	3 9	22 56	24 47
19	26 22	29 14	16 56	9 5	10 48	24 31	3 16	22 55	24 49
20	27 22	14 ♉ 6	16 6	10 20	11 25	24 24	3 23	22 54	24 51
21	28 23	28 50	15 26	11 35	12 1	24 18	3 29	22 52	24 53
22	29 23	13 ♊ 18	14 57	12 51	12 38	24 11	3 36	22 51	24 54
23	0 ♐ 24	27 24	14 40	14 6	13 15	24 4	3 43	22 49	24 56
24	1 24	11 ♋ 3	14 D 35	15 21	13 52	23 57	3 50	22 48	24 58
25	2 25	24 16	14 41	16 36	14 29	23 50	3 57	22 46	25 0
26	3 26	7 ♌ 4	14 57	17 51	15 5	23 43	4 3	22 44	25 2
27	4 27	19 30	15 23	19 7	15 42	23 35	4 10	22 42	25 3
28	5 27	1 ♍ 40	15 56	20 22	16 19	23 28	4 16	22 40	25 5
29	6 28	13 39	16 37	21 37	16 56	23 21	4 23	22 38	25 7
30	7 29	25 31	17 25	22 52	17 33	23 13	4 29	22 37	25 8

Pluto 24 Leo all month

DECEMBER

DAY	☉	☽	☿	♀	♂	♃	♄	♅	♆
	° ′	° ′	° ′	° ′	° ′	° ′	° ′	° ′	° ′
1	8 ♐ 30	7 ♎ 21	18 ♏ 19	24 ♏ 8	18 ♎ 9	23 ♊ 6	4 ♏ 36	22 ♋ 35	25 ♎ 10
2	9 31	19 15	19 18	25 23	18 46	22 ℞ 58	4 42	22 ℞ 34	25 11
3	10 31	1 ♏ 15	20 22	26 39	19 22	22 50	4 49	22 32	25 13
4	11 32	13 25	21 29	27 54	19 59	22 43	4 55	22 31	25 14
5	12 33	25 46	22 40	29 9	20 36	22 35	5 1	22 30	25 16
6	13 34	8 ♐ 19	23 53	0 ♐ 25	21 12	22 27	5 7	22 28	25 18
7	14 35	21 5	25 9	1 40	21 49	22 18	5 14	22 27	25 20
8	15 36	4 ♑ 3	26 27	2 56	22 25	22 10	5 20	22 25	25 22
9	16 37	17 13	27 47	4 11	23 2	22 2	5 26	22 24	25 24
10	17 38	0 ♒ 34	29 9	5 26	23 39	21 54	5 32	22 22	25 25
11	18 39	14 7	0 ♐ 33	6 42	24 15	21 46	5 38	22 20	25 26
12	19 40	27 50	1 57	7 57	24 52	21 38	5 44	22 18	25 28
13	20 41	11 ♓ 44	3 22	9 13	25 28	21 30	5 50	22 16	25 29
14	21 42	25 48	4 48	10 28	26 5	21 22	5 56	22 14	25 30
15	22 43	10 ♈ 2	6 15	11 44	26 41	21 14	6 2	22 12	25 31
16	23 44	24 23	7 42	12 59	27 18	21 6	6 7	22 9	25 33
17	24 45	8 ♉ 47	9 10	14 15	27 54	20 57	6 13	22 7	25 34
18	25 46	23 10	10 39	15 30	28 31	20 49	6 18	22 4	25 36
19	26 47	7 ♊ 27	12 9	16 46	29 7	20 41	6 24	22 2	25 37
20	27 48	21 32	13 39	18 1	29 43	20 33	6 29	22 0	25 38
21	28 49	5 ♋ 20	15 9	19 17	0 ♏ 19	20 26	6 35	21 57	25 39
22	29 51	18 49	16 39	20 32	0 56	20 18	6 40	21 55	25 39
23	0 ♑ 52	1 ♌ 58	18 10	21 48	1 32	20 10	6 46	21 52	25 40
24	1 53	14 45	19 41	23 3	2 8	20 2	6 51	21 50	25 41
25	2 54	27 14	21 12	24 18	2 44	19 54	6 56	21 48	25 42
26	3 55	9 ♍ 27	22 44	25 34	3 20	19 47	7 1	21 45	25 43
27	4 56	21 28	24 16	26 49	3 56	19 39	7 6	21 43	25 44
28	5 57	3 ♎ 23	25 48	28 5	4 32	19 31	7 11	21 40	25 45
29	6 58	15 15	27 21	29 20	5 8	19 23	7 16	21 38	25 46
30	8 0	27 9	28 54	0 ♑ 36	5 44	19 16	7 20	21 36	25 46
31	9 1	9 ♏ 11	0 ♑ 27	1 51	6 19	19 8	7 25	21 33	25 47

Pluto 25 Leo all month

Simplified Ephemerides from July 1970 to December 1971

1970

JULY

Day	☉	☽	☿	♀	♂	♃	♄	♅	♆	♇
1	9♋	14♊	2♋	17♌	19♋	26♎	19♉	4♎	28♏	24♍
2	10	27♊	4	18	19	26	19	4	28	24
3	11	9♋	6	19	20	26	19	4	28	24
4	12	21♋	9	20	21	26	19	4	28	24
5	13	3♌	11	21	21	26	19	4	28	24
6	14	15♌	13	23	22	26	19	4	28	24
7	14	27♌	15	24	23	26	19	4	28	24
8	15	9♍	17	25	23	26	19	4	28	24
9	16	21♍	19	26	24	26	19	4	28	24
10	17	2♎	22	27	25	26	19	4	28	24
11	18	15♎	24	28	25	26	20	4	28	24
12	19	27♎	26	29	26	26	20	4	28	24
13	20	10♏	28	1♍	26	26	20	5	28	24
14	21	23♏	0♌	2	27	26	20	5	28	24
15	22	7♐	2♌	3	28	26	20	5	28	24
16	23	21♐	4♌	4	28	26	20	5	28	24
17	24	5♑	6	5	29	26	20	5	28	25
18	25	20♑	8	6	0♌	26	20	5	28	25
19	26	5♒	10	7	0	27	20	5	28	25
20	27	20♒	11	9	1	27	20	5	28	25
21	28	5♓	13	10	2	27	20	5	28	25
22	29	20♓	15	11	2	27	21	5	28	25
23	0♌	4♈	17	12	3	27	21	5	28	25
24	1	18♈	19	13	4	27	21	5	28	25
25	2	2♉	20	14	4	27	21	5	28	25
26	3	15♉	22	15	5	27	21	5	28	25
27	4	28♉	24	16	5	27	21	5	28	25
28	5	11♊	25	18	6	27	21	5	28	25
29	5	24♊	27	19	7	27	21	5	28	25
30	6	6♋	28	20	7	28	21	5	28	25
31	7	18♋	0♍	21	8	28	21	5	28	25

AUGUST

Day	☉	☽	☿	♀	♂	♃	♄	♅	♆	♇
1	8♌	0♌	1♍	20♍	9♌	28♎	21♉	5♎	28♏	25
2	9	12	3	23	9	28	21	5	28	25
3	10	24	4	24	10	28	21	5	28	25
4	11	6♍	6	25	11	28	21	5	28	25
5	12	17♍	7	26	11	28	21	5	28	25
6	13	29♍	8	27	12	28	21	5	28	25
7	14	11♎	10	29	13	28	21	5	28	25
8	15	23♎	11	0♎	13	28	22	5	28	25
9	16	6♏	12	1	14	29	22	6	28	25
10	17	19♏	14	2	14	29	22	6	28	25
11	18	2♐	15	3	15	29	22	6	28	25
12	19	15♐	16	4	16	29	22	6	28	25
13	20	29♐	17	5	16	29	22	6	28	25
14	21	14♑	18	6	17	29	22	6	28	25
15	22	29♑	19	7	18	29	22	6	28	25
16	23	14♒	20	8	18	0♏	22	6	28	25
17	24	29♒	21	9	19	0	22	6	28	25
18	25	14♓	22	10	20	0	22	6	28	25
19	26	29♓	23	11	20	0	22	6	28	25
20	27	14♈	24	12	21	0	22	6	28	25
21	28	28♈	24	13	21	0	22	6	28	26
22	28	12♉	25	14	22	1	22	6	28	26
23	29	25♉	25	15	23	1	22	6	28	26
24	0♍	8♊	26	16	23	1	22	6	28	26
25	1	21♊	26	17	24	1	22	6	28	26
26	2	3♋	27	18	25	1	22	6	28	26
27	3	15♋	27	19	25	1	22	6	28	26
28	4	27♋	27	20	26	1	22	7	28	26
29	5	9♌	27	21	27	2	22	7	28	26
30	6	21♌	27 ℞	22	27	2	22	7	28	26
31	7	3♍	27	23	28	2	22	7	28	26

1970

SEPTEMBER

Day	☉	☽	☿	♀	♂	♃	♄	♅	♆	♇
1	8♍	14♍	27♍	24♎	28♌	2♏	22♉	7♎	28♏	26♍
2	9	26♍	27	25	29	2	22	7	28	26
3	10	8♎	26	26	0♍	2	22	7	28	26
4	11	20♎	26	27	0	2	22	7	28	26
5	12	3♏	25	28	1	3	22	7	28	26
6	13	15♏	25	29	2	3	22	7	28	26
7	14	28♏	24	0♏	2	3	22	7	28	26
8	15	11♐	23	1	3	3	22	7	28	26
9	16	24♐	22	2	3	3	22	7	28	26
10	17	8♑	21	3	4	4	22	7	28	26
11	18	23♑	20	3	5	4	22	7	28	26
12	19	7♒	19	4	5	4	22	7	28	26
13	20	22♒	18	5	6	4	22	7	28	26
14	21	7♓	17	6	7	4	22	8	28	26
15	22	22♓	16	7	7	4	22	8	28	26
16	23	7♈	16	8	8	5	22	8	28	26
17	24	22♈	15	9	9	5	22	8	28	26
18	25	6♉	14	9	9	5	22	8	28	26
19	26	20♉	14	10	10	5	22	8	28	26
20	27	4♊	13	11	10	5	22	8	28	27
21	28	17♊	13 D	12	11	6	22	8	28	27
22	29	0♋	13	12	12	6	22	8	28	27
23	0♎	12♋	14	13	12	6	22	8	28	27
24	1	24♋	14	14	13	6	22	8	28	27
25	2	6♌	14	15	14	6	22	8	28	27
26	2	18♌	15	15	14	7	22	8	28	27
27	3	0♍	16	16	15	7	22	8	28	27
28	4	11♍	17	17	16	7	22	8	28	27
29	5	23♍	18	17	16	7	22	8	28	27
30	6	5♎	19	18	17	7	22	9	28	27
31										

OCTOBER

Day	☉	☽	☿	♀	♂	♃	♄	♅	♆	♇
1	7♎	17♎	20♍	18♏	17♍	8♏	22♉	9♎	28♏	27♍
2	8	0♏	21	19	18	8	22	9	28	27
3	9	12♏	23	20	19	8	21	9	28	27
4	10	25♏	24	20	19	8	21	9	28	27
5	11	8♐	26	21	20	8	21	9	28	27
6	12	21♐	27	21	21	9	21	9	28	27
7	13	4♑	29	22	21	9	21	9	29	27
8	14	18♑	1♎	22	22	9	21	9	29	27
9	15	2♒	2♎	22	23	9	21	9	29	27
10	16	16♒	4	23	23	9	21	9	29	27
11	17	1♓	6	23	24	10	21	9	29	27
12	18	16♓	7	23	24	10	21	9	29	27
13	19	1♈	9	24	25	10	21	9	29	27
14	20	15♈	11	24	26	10	21	9	29	27
15	21	9♉	13	24	26	10	21	9	29	28
16	22	15♉	15	24	26	11	21	10	29	28
17	23	29♉	16	24	28	11	21	10	29	28
18	24	12♊	18	24	28	11	21	10	29	28
19	25	25♊	20	24	29	11	21	10	29	28
20	26	8♋	21	24	0♎	12	20	10	29	28
21	27	20♋	23	24	0	12	20	10	29	28
22	28	2♌	25	24	1	12	20	10	29	28
23	29	14♌	27	24	1	12	20	10	29	28
24	0♏	26♌	28	24	2	12	20	10	29	28
25	1	8♍	0♏	24	3	13	20	10	29	28
26	2	20♍	2	24	3	13	20	10	29	28
27	3	2♎	3	24	4	13	20	10	29	28
28	4	14♎	5	24	5	13	20	10	29	28
29	5	26♎	6	23	5	13	20	10	29	28
30	6	9♏	8	23	6	14	20	10	29	28
31	7	22♏	10	22	7	14	20	10	29	28

1970

NOVEMBER

Day	☉	☽	☿	♀	♂	♃	♄	♅	♆	♇
1	8♏	5♐	12♏	22♏	7♎	14♏	20♉	10♎	29♏	28♍
2	9	18♐	14	21♏	8	14	19	11	29	28
3	10	1♑	15	21	8	15	19	11	29	28
4	11	15♑	16	20	9	15	19	11	29	28
5	12	29♑	18	20	10	15	19	11	29	28
6	13	13♒	19	19	10	15	19	11	29	28
7	14	27♒	21	19	11	15	19	11	0♐	28
8	15	11♓	22	18	12	16	19	11	0	28
9	16	25♓	24	18	12	16	19	11	0	28
10	17	10♈	26	17	13	16	19	11	0	28
11	18	24♈	27	16	14	16	19	11	0	28
12	19	9♉	29	16	14	17	19	11	0	28
13	20	23♉	0♐	15	15	17	19	11	0	28
14	21	6♊	2	15	15	17	19	11	0	28
15	22	20♊	3	14	16	17	18	11	0	28
16	23	3♋	5	13	17	17	18	11	0	28
17	24	16♋	6	13	17	18	18	11	0	28
18	25	28♋	8	12	18	18	18	11	0	29
19	26	10♌	9	12	19	18	18	11	0	29
20	27	22♌	11	11	19	18	18	12	0	29
21	28	4♍	12	11	20	19	18	12	0	29
22	29	16♍	14	11	20	19	18	12	0	29
23	0♐	28♍	15	10	21	19	18	12	0	29
24	1	10♎	17	10	22	19	18	12	0	29
25	2	22♎	18	10	22	19	18	12	0	29
26	3	5♏	20	10	23	20	18	12	0	29
27	4	17♏	21	10	24	20	17	12	0	29
28	5	1♐	23	9	24	20	17	12	0	29
29	6	14♐	24	9 D	25	20	17	12	0	29
30	7	28♐	25	9	26	21	17	12	0	29
31										

DECEMBER

Day	☉	☽	☿	♀	♂	♃	♄	♅	♆	♇
1	8♐	12♑	27♐	9♏	26♎	21♏	17♉	12♎	0♐	29♍
2	9	26♑	28	9	27	21	17	12	0	29
3	10	10♒	0♑	10	27	21	17	12	0	29
4	11	24♒	1	10	28	21	17	12	1	29
5	12	8♓	2	10	29	22	17	12	1	29
6	13	22♓	4	10	29	22	17	12	1	29
7	14	6♈	5	10	0♏	22	17	12	1	29
8	15	20♈	6	10	1	22	17	12	1	29
9	16	4♉	7	11	2	22	17	12	1	29
10	18	18♉	8	11	2	23	16	12	1	29
11	19	1♊	9	11	3	23	16	12	1	29
12	20	15♊	10	12	3	23	16	12	1	29
13	21	28♊	11	12	4	23	16	12	1	29
14	22	11♋	12	13	4	24	16	12	1	29
15	23	24♋	12	13	5	24	16	13	1	29
16	24	6♌	13	14	6	24	16	13	1	29
17	25	18♌	13	14	6	24	16	13	1	29
18	26	0♍	14	15	7	24	16	13	1	29
19	27	12♍	14	15	8	25	16	13	1	29
20	28	24♍	13	16	8	25	16	13	1	29
21	29	5♎	13	17	9	25	16	13	1	29
22	0♑	17♎	12	17	10	25	16	13	1	29
23	1	0♏	12	18	10	25	16	13	1	29
24	2	12♏	11	19	11	26	16	13	1	29
25	3	25♏	10	19	11	26	16	13	1	29
26	4	9♐	9	20	12	26	16	13	1	29
27	5	22♐	7	21	13	26	16	13	1	29
28	6	7♑	6	22	13	26	16	13	1	29
29	7	21♑	5	22	14	27	16	13	1	29
30	8	5♒	3	23	15	27	16	13	1	29
31	9	20♒	2	24	15	27	16	13	2	29

1971

JANUARY

Day	☉	☽	☿	♀	♂	♃	♄	♅	♆	♇
1	10♑	28♒	2♑	25♏	16♏	27♏	15♉	13♎	2♐	29♍
2	11	11♓	0	25	16	27	15	13	2	29
3	12	26♓	29♐	26	17	27	15	13	2	29
4	13	10♈	29	27	17	27	15	13	2	29
5	14	24♈	28	28	18	28	15	13	2	29
6	15	7♉	28	29	19	28	15	13	2	29
7	16	21♉	27	29	19	28	15	13	2	29
8	17	4♊	27	0♐	20	28	15	13	2	29
9	18	18♊	27	1	21	29	15	13	2	29
10	19	0♋	28	2	21	29	15	13	2	29
11	20	13♋	28	3	22	29	15	13	2	29
12	21	26♋	28	4	23	29	15	13	2	29
13	22	8♌	29	5	23	29	15	13	2	29
14	23	20♌	29	6	24	29	15	13	2	29
15	24	2♍	0♑	7	24	0♐	15	13	2	29
16	25	14♍	1♑	8	25	0	15	13	2	29
17	26	26♍	2♑	9	26	0	15	13	2	29
18	27	7♎	3	10	26	0	15	13	2	29
19	28	19♎	4	11	27	0	15	13	2	29
20	29	1♏	5	12	28	0	15	13	2	29
21	0♒	14♏	6	13	28	1	15	13	2	29
22	1	27♏	7	14	29	1	15	13	2	29
23	2	10♐	8	15	29	1	15	13	2	29
24	3	23♐	9	16	0♐	1	15	13	2	29
25	4	7♑	10	17	1	1	15	13	2	29
26	5	22♑	12	18	1	1	15	13	2	29
27	6	7♒	13	19	2	2	15	13	2	29
28	7	21♒	14	20	3	2	15	13	2	29
29	8	6♓	16	21	3	2	15	13	2	29
30	9	21♓	17	22	4	2	15	13	2	29
31	10	6♈	18	23	4	2	15	13	2	29

FEBRUARY

Day	☉	☽	☿	♀	♂	♃	♄	♅	♆	♇
1	11♒	20♈	20♑	24♐	5♐	2♐	15♉	13♎	2♐	29♍
2	12	4♉	21	26	6	2	15	13	2	29
3	13	18♉	22	27	6	3	15	13	2	29
4	14	1♊	24	28	7	3	15	13	2	29
5	15	14♊	25	29	8	3	16	13	2	29
6	16	27♊	27	0♑	8	3	16	13	2	29
7	17	10♋	28	1	9	3	16	13	2	29
8	18	22♋	0♒	2	10	3	16	13	2	29
9	19	5♌	1	3	10	3	16	13	2	29
10	20	17♌	3	4	11	3	16	13	2	29
11	21	29♌	4	5	11	4	16	13	2	29
12	22	10♍	6	7	12	4	16	13	2	29
13	23	22♍	7	8	13	4	16	13	2	29
14	24	4♎	9	9	13	4	16	13	2	29
15	25	16♎	10	10	14	4	16	13	2	29
16	26	28♎	12	11	14	4	16	13	2	29
17	27	10♏	14	12	15	4	16	13	2	29
18	28	22♏	15	13	16	4	16	13	3	29
19	29	5♐	17	14	16	4	16	13	3	29
20	0♓	18♐	19	16	17	4	16	13	3	29
21	1	1♑	20	17	18	5	16	13	3	29
22	2	15♑	22	18	18	5	16	13	3	29
23	3	0♒	24	19	19	5	16	13	3	29
24	4	14♒	25	20	19	5	16	12	3	28
25	5	29♒	27	21	20	5	17	12	3	28
26	6	15♓	29	22	21	5	17	12	3	28
27	7	0♈	1♓	24	21	5	17	12	3	28
28	8	15♈	2	25	22	5	17	12	3	28
29										
30										
31										

1971

MARCH

Day	☉	☽	☿	♀	♂	♃	♄	♅	♆	♇
1	9♓	0♉	4♓	26♑	23♐	5♐	17♉	12♎	3♐	28♍
2	10	14♉	6	27	23	5	17	12	3	28
3	11	28♉	8	28	24	5	17	12	3	28
4	12	11♊	10	29	24	5	17	12	3	28
5	13	24♊	12	1♒	25	5	17	12	3	28
6	14	7♋	14	2	26	5	17	12	3	28
7	15	19♋	15	3	26	6	17	12	3	28
8	16	2♌	17	4	27	6	17	12	3	28
9	17	14♌	19	5	27	6	17	12	3	28
10	18	25♌	21	6	28	6	18	12	3	28
11	19	7♍	23	8	29	6	18	12	3	28
12	20	19♍	25	9	0♑	6	18	12	3	28
13	21	1♎	27	10	0	6	18	12	3	28
14	22	13♎	29	11	1	6	18	12	3	28
15	23	25♎	1♈	12	2	6	18	12	3	28
16	24	7♏	3♈	13	2	6	18	12	3	28
17	25	19♏	5♈	15	3	6	18	12	3	28
18	26	1♐	7	16	3	6	18	12	3	28
19	27	14♐	9	17	4	6	18	12	3	28
20	28	27♐	11	18	5	6	18	12	3	28
21	29	10♑	13	19	5	6	19	12	3	28
22	0♈	24♑	14	21	6	6	19	12	3	28
23	1	8♒	16	22	6	6	19	12	3	28
24	2	29♒	18	23	7	6	19	11	3	28
25	3	8♓	20	24	8	6	19	11	2	28
26	4	23♓	21	25	8	6	19	11	2	28
27	5	8♈	23	26	9	6	19	11	2	28
28	6	23♈	24	28	9	6	19	11	2	28
29	7	8♉	26	29	10	6	19	11	2	28
30	8	23♉	27	0♓	10	6	20	11	2	28
31	9	7♊	28	1	11	6	20	11	2	28

APRIL

Day	☉	☽	☿	♀	♂	♃	♄	♅	♆	♇
1	10♈	20♊	29♈	2♓	11♑	6♐	20♉	11♎	2♐	28♍
2	11	3♋	0♉	4	12	6	20	11	2	28
3	12	16♋	1	5	12	6	20	11	2	27
4	13	28♋	1	6	13	6	20	11	2	27
5	14	11♌	2	7	14	6	20	11	2	27
6	15	22♌	2	8	14	6	20	11	2	27
7	16	4♍	3	10	15	6	20	11	2	27
8	17	16♍	3	11	15	6	21	11	2	27
9	18	28♍	3 ℞	12	16	6	21	11	2	27
10	19	10♎	3	13	16	5	21	11	2	27
11	20	22♎	3	14	17	5	21	10	2	27
12	21	4♏	3	16	18	5	21	10	2	27
13	22	16♏	3	17	18	5	21	10	2	27
14	23	28♏	2	18	19	5	21	10	2	27
15	24	11♐	2	19	19	5	21	10	2	27
16	25	24♐	1	20	20	5	21	10	2	27
17	26	7♑	1	22	20	5	22	10	2	27
18	27	20♑	0	23	21	5	22	10	2	27
19	28	4♒	29♈	24	21	5	22	10	2	27
20	29	18♒	29	25	22	5	22	10	2	27
21	0♉	2♓	28	26	23	5	22	10	2	27
22	1	16♓	27	28	23	5	22	10	2	27
23	2	1♈	27	29	24	5	22	10	2	27
24	3	16♈	26	0♈	24	4	22	10	2	27
25	4	1♉	25	1	25	4	23	10	2	27
26	5	16♉	25	2	25	4	23	10	2	27
27	6	1♊	24	3	26	4	23	10	2	27
28	7	15♊	24	4	26	4	23	10	2	27
29	8	29♊	23	5	27	4	23	10	2	27
30	9	12♋	23	7	27	4	23	10	2	27
31										

1971

MAY

Day	☉	☽	☿	♀	♂	♃	♄	♅	♆	♇
1	9♉	25♋	23♈	8♈	28♑	4♐	23♉	10♎	2♐	27♍
2	10	7♌	23	10	29	4	23	10	2	27
3	11	19♌	23	11	29	4	24	10	2	27
4	12	1♍	23	12	0♒	3	24	10	2	27
5	13	13♍	23	13	0	3	24	10	2	27
6	14	25♍	23	14	1	3	24	10	2	27
7	15	6♎	23	16	1	3	24	10	2	27
8	16	18♎	23	17	2	3	24	10	2	27
9	17	0♏	24	18	2	3	24	10	2	27
10	18	13♏	24	19	3	3	24	10	2	27
11	19	25♏	25	20	3	3	25	10	2	27
12	20	8♐	25	22	4	3	25	10	2	27
13	21	21♐	26	23	4	2	25	9	1	27
14	22	4♑	27	24	5	2	25	9	1	27
15	23	17♑	28	25	5	2	25	9	1	27
16	24	0♒	28	26	6	2	25	9	1	27
17	25	14♒	29	28	6	2	25	9	1	27
18	26	28♒	0♉	29	7	2	26	9	1	27
19	27	12♓	1	0♉	7	2	26	9	1	27
20	28	26♓	2	1	7	2	26	9	1	27
21	29	11♈	3	2	8	1	26	9	1	27
22	0♊	26♈	5	4	8	1	26	9	1	27
23	1	10♉	6	5	9	1	26	9	1	27
24	2	25♉	7	6	9	1	26	9	1	27
25	3	9♊	8	7	10	1	26	9	1	27
26	4	23♊	10	9	10	1	27	9	1	27
27	5	7♋	11	10	11	1	27	9	1	27
28	6	20♋	13	11	11	1	27	9	1	27
29	6	3♌	14	12	11	0	27	9	1	27
30	7	15♌	15	13	12	0	27	9	1	27
31	8	27♌	17	15	12	0	27	9	1	26

JUNE

Day	☉	☽	☿	♀	♂	♃	♄	♅	♆	♇
1	9♊	4♍	19♉	16♉	13♒	0♐	27♉	9♎	1♐	26♍
2	10	21♍	20	17	13	0	27	9	1	26
3	11	3♎	22	18	13	0	28	9	1	26
4	12	15♎	24	19	14	0	28	9	1	26
5	13	27♎	25	21	14	0	28	9	1	26
6	14	9♏	27	22	14	29♏	28	9	1	26
7	15	21♏	29	23	15	29	28	9	1	26
8	16	4♐	1♊	24	15	29	28	9	1	26
9	17	17♐	3	26	16	29	28	9	1	26
10	18	0♑	5	27	16	29	28	9	1	26
11	19	14♑	7	28	16	29	29	9	1	26
12	20	27♑	9	29	16	29	29	9	1	26
13	21	11♒	11	0♊	17	29	29	9	1	26
14	22	25♒	13	2	17	28	29	9	1	26
15	23	9♓	15	3	17	28	29	9	1	26
16	24	23♓	17	4	18	28	29	9	1	27
17	25	7♈	19	5	18	28	29	9	1	27
18	26	21♈	21	6	18	28	29	9	1	27
19	27	6♉	24	8	18	28	0♊	9	1	27
20	28	20♉	26	9	19	28	0	9	1	27
21	28	4♊	28	10	19	28	0	9	1	27
22	29	18♊	0♋	11	19	28	0	9	0	27
23	0♋	1♋	2	13	19	28	0	9	0	27
24	1	15♋	5	14	20	28	0	9	0	27
25	2	28♋	7	15	20	27	0	9	0	27
26	3	10♌	9	16	20	27	0	9	0	27
27	4	23♌	11	17	20	27	0	9	0	27
28	5	5♍	13	19	20	27	1	9	0	27
29	6	17♍	15	20	21	27	1	9	0	27
30	7	29♍	17	21	21	27	1	9	0	27
31										

1971

JULY

Day	☉	☽	☿	♀	♂	♃	♄	♅	♆	P
1	8 ♋	11 ♎	19 ♋	22 ♊	21 ♒	27 ♏	1 ♊	9 ♎	0 ♐	27 ♍
2	9	23 ♎	21	24	21	27	1	9	0	27
3	10	5 ♏	23	25	21	27	1	9	0	27
4	11	17 ♏	25	26	21	27	1	9	0	27
5	12	0 ♐	27	27	21	27	1	9	0	27
6	13	12 ♐	29	28	21	27	1	9	0	27
7	14	26 ♐	1 ♌	0 ♋	21	27	2	9	0	27
8	15	9 ♑	2	1	21	27	2	9	0	27
9	16	23 ♑	4	2	21	27	2	9	0	27
10	17	7 ♒	6	3	21	26	2	9	0	27
11	18	21 ♒	8	4	21	26	2	9	0	27
12	19	5 ♓	9	6	21	26	2	9	0	27
13	19	20 ♓	11	7	21	26	2	9	0	27
14	20	4 ♈	12	8	21	26	2	9	0	27
15	21	18 ♈	14	9	21	26	2	9	0	27
16	22	2 ♉	16	11	21	26	3	9	0	27
17	23	16 ♉	17	12	21	26	3	9	0	27
18	24	0 ♊	18	13	21	26	3	9	0	27
19	25	14 ♊	20	14	21	26	3	9	0	27
20	26	27 ♊	21	16	21	26	3	9	0	27
21	27	11 ♋	23	17	21	26	3	9	0	27
22	28	29 ♋	24	18	21	26	3	9	0	27
23	29	6 ♌	25	19	21	26	3	9	0	27
24	0 ♌	19 ♌	26	20	20	26	3	10	0	27
25	1	1 ♍	28	22	20	26	3	10	0	27
26	2	13 ♍	29	23	20	26	3	10	0	27
27	3	25 ♍	0 ♍	24	20	26	4	10	0	27
28	4	7 ♎	1	25	20	26	4	10	0	27
29	5	19 ♎	2	27	20	26	4	10	0	27
30	6	1 ♏	3	28	19	26	4	10	0	27
31	7	13 ♏	4	29	19	26	4	10	0	27

AUGUST

Day	☉	☽	☿	♀	♂	♃	♄	♅	♆	P
1	8 ♌	25 ♏	5 ♍	0 ♌	19 ♒	26 ♏	4 ♊	10 ♎	0 ♐	27 ♍
2	9	7 ♐	5	1	19	26	4	10	0	27
3	10	20 ♐	6	3	18	26	4	10	0	27
4	10	4 ♑	7	4	18	26	4	10	0	27
5	11	17 ♑	8	5	18	26	4	10	0	27
6	12	1 ♒	8	6	18	26	4	10	0	27
7	13	16 ♒	9	8	17	26	4	10	0	27
8	14	0 ♓	9	9	17	26	4	10	0	27
9	15	15 ♓	9	10	17	26	5	10	0	27
10	16	0 ♈	10	11	17	27	5	10	0	28
11	17	14 ♈	10	13	16	27	5	10	0	28
12	18	29 ♈	10	14	16	27	5	10	0	28
13	19	13 ♉	10	15	16	27	5	10	0	28
14	20	27 ♉	10	16	16	27	5	10	0	28
15	21	11 ♊	10	18	15	27	5	10	0	28
16	22	24 ♊	10	19	15	27	5	10	0	28
17	23	7 ♋	9	20	15	27	5	10	0	28
18	24	20 ♋	9	21	15	27	5	10	0	28
19	25	3 ♌	8	22	14	27	5	11	0	28
20	26	15 ♌	8	24	14	27	5	11	0	29
21	27	27 ♌	7	25	14	27	5	11	0	28
22	28	9 ♍	6	26	14	27	5	11	0	28
23	29	21 ♍	5	27	13	27	5	11	0	28
24	0 ♍	3 ♎	5	29	13	27	5	11	0	28
25	1	15 ♎	4	0 ♍	13	28	5	11	0	28
26	2	27 ♎	3	1	13	28	6	11	0	28
27	3	9 ♏	2	2	13	28	6	11	0	28
28	4	21 ♏	1	4	12	28	6	11	0	28
29	5	3 ♐	0	5	12	28	6	11	0	28
30	5	16 ♐	29 ♌	6	12	28	6	11	0	28
31	6	28 ♐	29 -	7	12	28	6	11	0	28

1971

SEPTEMBER

Day	☉	☽	☿	♀	♂	♃	♄	♅	♆	P
1	7♍	12♑	28♌	9♍	12♒	28♏	6♊	11♎	0♐	28♍
2	8	25♑	28	10	12	28♏	6	11	0	28
3	9	10♒	27	11	12	28	6	11	0	28
4	10	24♒	27	12	12	29	6	11	0	28
5	11	9♓	27	14	12	29	6	11	0	28
6	12	24♓	27	15	11	29	6	12	0	28
7	13	9♈	27	16	11	29	6	12	0	28
8	14	24♈	27	17	11	29	6	12	0	28
9	15	9♉	28	19	11	29	6	12	0	29
10	16	23♉	29	20	11	29	6	12	0	29
11	17	7♊	29	21	11	29	6	12	0	29
12	18	21♊	0♍	22	11	0♐	6	12	0	29
13	19	4♋	1	23	11	0	6	12	0	29
14	20	17♋	2	25	12	0	6	12	0	29
15	21	0♌	4	26	12	0	6	12	0	29
16	22	12♌	5	27	12	0	6	12	0	29
17	23	24♌	6	28	12	0	6	12	0	29
18	24	6♍	8	0♎	12	0	6	12	0	29
19	25	18♍	9	1	12	1	6	12	0	29
20	26	0♎	11	2	12	1	6	12	0	29
21	27	12♎	13	3	12	1	6	12	0	29
22	28	24♎	14	5	12	1	6	12	0	29
23	29	6♏	16	6	13	1	6	13	0	29
24	0♎	18♏	18	7	13	1	6	13	0	29
25	1	0♐	20	8	13	1	6	13	0	29
26	2	12♐	22	10	13	2	6	13	0	29
27	3	24♐	23	11	13	2	6	13	0	29
28	4	7♑	25	12	14	2	6	13	0	29
29	5	20♑	27	13	14	2	6	13	0	29
30	6	4♒	29	15	14	2	6	13	0	29
31										

OCTOBER

Day	☉	☽	☿	♀	♂	♃	♄	♅	♆	P
1	7♎	18♒	1♎	16♎	14♒	2♐	6♊	13♎	0♐	29♍
2	8	2♓	2	17	15	3	6	13	0	29
3	9	17♓	4	18	15	3	6	13	1	29
4	10	2♈	6	20	15	3	6	13	1	29
5	11	18♈	8	21	16	3	6	13	1	0♎
6	12	3♉	10	22	16	3	6	13	1	0
7	13	18♉	11	23	16	3	6	13	1	0
8	14	3♊	13	25	16	4	6	13	1	0
9	15	17♊	15	26	17	4	6	14	1	0
10	16	1♋	17	27	17	4	6	14	1	0
11	17	14♋	18	28	18	4	6	14	1	0
12	18	27♋	20	0♏	18	4	6	14	1	0
13	18	9♌	22	1	18	5	6	14	1	0
14	19	21♌	23	2	19	5	5	14	1	0
15	20	3♍	25	3	19	5	5	14	1	0
16	21	15♍	27	5	19	5	5	14	1	0
17	22	27♍	28	6	20	5	5	14	1	0
18	23	9♎	0♏	7	20	6	5	14	1	0
19	24	21♎	2	8	21	6	5	14	1	0
20	25	3♏	3	10	21	6	5	14	1	0
21	26	15♏	5	11	22	6	5	14	1	0
22	27	27♏	6	12	22	6	5	14	1	0
23	28	9♐	8	13	22	6	5	14	1	0
24	29	21♐	9	15	23	7	5	14	1	0
25	0♏	4♑	11	16	23	7	5	15	1	0
26	1	16♑	13	17	24	7	5	15	1	0
27	2	29♑	14	18	24	7	5	15	1	0
28	3	13♒	16	20	25	7	5	15	1	0
29	4	27♒	17	21	25	8	5	15	1	0
30	5	11♓	19	22	26	8	5	15	1	0
31	6	25♓	20	23	26	8	5	15	1	0

1971

NOVEMBER

Day	☉	☽	☿	♀	♂	♃	♄	♅	♆	P
1	7♏	11♈	22♏	24♏	27♒	8♐	4♊	15♎	1♐	0♎
2	8	26♈	23	26	27	9	4	15	1	0
3	9	11♉	25	27	28	9	4	15	1	1
4	10	26♉	26	28	28	9	4	15	2	1
5	11	11♊	28	29	29	9	4	15	2	1
6	12	25♊	29	1♐	0♓	9	4	15	2	1
7	13	9♋	0♐	2	0	10	4	15	2	1
8	14	22♋	2	3	1	10	4	15	2	1
9	15	5♌	3	4	1	10	4	15	2	1
10	16	18♌	5	6	2	10	4	15	2	1
11	17	0♍	6	7	2	10	4	16	2	1
12	18	12♍	8	8	3	11	4	16	2	1
13	19	24♍	9	9	4	11	4	16	2	1
14	20	6♎	10	11	4	11	4	16	2	1
15	21	18♎	12	12	5	11	3	16	2	1
16	22	0♏	13	13	5	12	3	16	2	1
17	23	12♏	14	14	6	12	3	16	2	1
18	24	24♏	16	16	6	12	3	16	2	1
19	25	6♐	17	17	7	12	3	16	2	1
20	27	18♐	18	18	8	12	3	16	2	1
21	28	1♑	19	19	8	13	3	16	2	1
22	29	13♑	20	21	9	13	3	16	2	1
23	0♐	26♑	21	22	9	13	3	16	2	1
24	1	9♒	22	23	10	13	3	16	2	1
25	2	23♒	23	24	10	14	3	16	2	1
26	3	6♓	24	26	11	14	3	16	2	1
27	4	21♓	25	27	12	14	2	16	2	1
28	5	5♈	26	28	12	14	2	16	2	1
29	6	20♈	27	29	13	14	2	16	2	1
30	7	4♉	27	1♑	13	15	2	17	2	1
31										

DECEMBER

Day	☉	☽	☿	♀	♂	♃	♄	♅	♆	P
1	8♐	19♉	27♐	2♑	13♓	15♐	2♊	17♎	3♐	1♎
2	9	4♊	28	3	14	15	2	17	3	1
3	10	19♊	28	4	15	15	2	17	3	1
4	11	3♋	28	6	15	16	2	17	3	1
5	12	17♋	27	7	16	16	2	17	3	1
6	13	0♌	27	9	16	16	2	17	3	1
7	14	13♌	26	11	17	16	2	17	3	1
8	15	26♌	26	12	18	16	2	17	3	1
9	16	8♍	25	13	18	17	1	17	3	1
10	17	20♍	23	14	19	17	1	17	3	1
11	18	2♎	22	16	20	17	1	17	3	1
12	19	14♎	21	17	20	17	1	17	3	1
13	20	26♎	20	18	21	18	1	17	3	1
14	21	8♏	18	19	21	18	1	17	3	1
15	22	20♏	17	20	22	18	1	17	3	1
16	23	2♐	16	22	23	18	1	17	3	1
17	24	15♐	14	23	23	18	1	17	3	1
18	25	27♐	14	24	24	19	1	17	3	1
19	26	10♑	13	25	25	19	1	17	3	1
20	27	23♑	12	27	25	19	1	17	3	1
21	28	6♒	12	28	26	19	1	17	3	1
22	29	20♒	12	29	26	20	1	17	3	2
23	0♑	3♓	11	0♒	27	20	0	17	3	2
24	1	17♓	12	2	28	20	0	17	3	2
25	2	1♈	12	3	28	20	0	17	3	2
26	3	15♈	13	4	29	21	0	17	3	2
27	4	0♉	13	5	0♈	21	0	17	3	2
28	5	14♉	13	7	0	21	0	18	3	2
29	6	29♉	14	8	1	21	0	18	4	2
30	7	13♊	15	9	2	21	0	18	4	2
31	8	27♊	16	10	2	22	0	18	4	2

Appendix

How to Erect a Solar Chart

STEP I.
Draw a circle and divide it in half. Label the left-hand side East and the right-hand side West.

STEP II.
Divide the circle in half again from top to bottom. Label the top South and the bottom North.

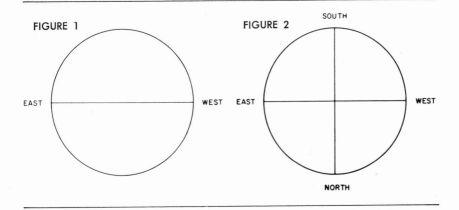

FIGURE 1

EAST ——————— WEST

FIGURE 2

SOUTH

EAST ——————— WEST

NORTH

STEP III.

Divide each quadrant into three equal sections and join them.

STEP IV.

In *counterclockwise* direction, number the segments (houses) from 1 to 12. Always start at the *East* point.

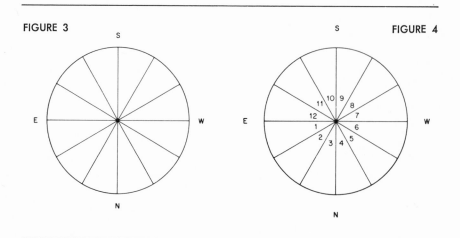

FIGURE 3   **FIGURE 4**

STEP V.

Look at the simplified ephemeris for April, 1942, below. Suppose you choose April 5. Draw a line under this date for easy reading.

D A Y	☉	☽	☿	♀	♂	♃	♄	♅	♆
	° ′	° ′	° ′	° ′	° ′	° ′	° ′	° ′	° ′
1	10♈37	3♎45	22♓33	25♒ 1	14♊42	15♊56	25 ♉32	27 ♉40	28♍11
2	11 37	17 59	24 15	25 54	15 18	16 5	25 38	27 43	28 ℞ 9
3	12 36	2♍29	25 58	26 47	15 54	16 14	25 44	27 45	28 7
4	13 35	17 7	27 42	27 40	16 30	16 24	25 51	27 48	28 6
5	14 34	1♐47	29 28	28 35	17 6	16 33	25 57	27 51	28 4
6	15 33	16 22	1♈15	29 30	17 42	16 43	26 4	27 54	28 3
7	16 32	0♑47	3 4	0♓25	18 18	16 52	26 11	27 56	28 1
8	17 31	14 58	4 54	1 21	18 54	17	17	27 59	28 0
9	18 30	28 53	6 46	2 17	17		24	28 2	27 59
10	19	33	8 39					28 5	27
11			34					28	

Simplified Ephemeris for April 1942

SIGNS		PLANETS	
ARIES	♈	Sun	☉
TAURUS	♉	Moon	☽
GEMINI	♊	Mercury	☿

CANCER	♋	Venus	♀
LEO	♌	Mars	♂
VIRGO	♍	Jupiter	♃
LIBRA	♎	Saturn	♄
SCORPIO	♏	Uranus	♅
SAGITTARIUS	♐	Neptune	♆
CAPRICORN	♑	Pluto	♇
AQUARIUS	♒		
PISCES	♓		

Copy the information onto a piece of paper for handy reference, thus:

Sun	14 ARIES	Jupiter	16 GEMINI
Moon	1 SAGITTARIUS	Saturn	25 TAURUS
Mercury	29 PISCES	Uranus	27 TAURUS
Venus	28 AQUARIUS	Neptune	28 VIRGO
Mars	17 GEMINI	Pluto	3 LEO

STEP VI.
Convert this list into symbolic form (refer to the keys on pages 22 and 24), so that it will take up less space when you are ready to place in your own chart. Place spelled-out words to the left, then arrange them numerically when there is more than one planet to a sign. You will then be certain to allow enough space in your chart.

Sun	☉	14	♈				
Moon	☽	1	♐				
Mercury	☿	29	♓				
Venus	♀	28	♒				
Mars	♂	17	♊	TAURUS	♄	25	♉
Jupiter	♃	16	♊		♅	27	♉
Saturn	♄	25	♉				
Uranus	♅	27	♉	GEMINI	♃	16	♊
Neptune	♆	28	♍		♂	17	♊
Pluto	♇	3	♌				

STEP VII.
Look at the planets you listed on a piece of paper. Learn to use the symbols, because they take up less space on the chart. Note the *number of degrees* and the *sign* in which your Sun is found. Place

the number and the sign at the East point. Then put the symbol of the Sun on the same line, thus:

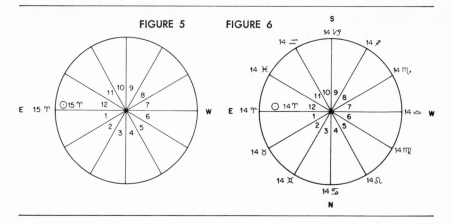

FIGURE 5   FIGURE 6

STEP VIII.

Place the rest of the signs in their logical sequence around the cusps (points of intersection between houses) of the rest of the chart. Repeat the number of your Sun sign degree. Our sample chart has the Sun at 14 Aries, so we repeat 14 all around the chart. Remember always to work in a *counterclockwise* direction.

NOTE:

The natural sequence of the signs is as follows: Aries, Taurus, Gemini, Cancer, Leo, Virgo, Libra, Scorpio, Sagittarius, Capricorn, Aquarius, and Pisces. If, for example, your own Sun sign was Scorpio, Scorpio would be at the East point and you would follow the rest of the signs around in the order in which they are listed here. When you come to Pisces, you would start at the beginning of the signs—with Aries, and so on, until all twelve houses would have one of the signs in them.

STEP IX.

Now you are ready to place the rest of the planets in your own chart. If you remember that the numbers *increase* in a *counterclockwise* direction and *decrease* in a *clockwise* direction, you will have no difficulties in placing the planets in their proper houses.

Now transfer your planets, one by one, onto your chart. Find the house that has the same sign on its cusp as the sign of the planet you are placing on the chart; note the number on the cusp—if your planet contains more degrees, put it after the cusp (or counterclockwise) ; if your planet contains fewer degrees than the number on the cusp, put it before (or clockwise) . If you have many planets in one